AF738484

Advancing Society 5.0 Through AI-Driven Curriculum Innovation

Andi Asrifan
Universitas Negeri Makassar, Indonesia

IGI Global
Scientific Publishing
Publishing Tomorrow's Research Today

Vice President of Editorial — Melissa Wagner
Director of Acquisitions — Mikaela Felty
Director of Book Development — Jocelynn Hessler
Production Manager — Mike Brehm
Cover Design — Jose Rosado

Published in the United States of America by
IGI Global Scientific Publishing
701 East Chocolate Avenue
Hershey, PA, 17033, USA
Tel: 717-533-8845
Fax: 717-533-7115
Website: https://www.igi-global.com E-mail: cust@igi-global.com

Copyright © 2026 by IGI Global Scientific Publishing. All rights reserved. No part of this publication may be reproduced, stored or distributed in any form or by any means, electronic or mechanical, including photocopying, without written permission from the publisher.

Product or company names used in this set are for identification purposes only. Inclusion of the names of the products or companies does not indicate a claim of ownership by IGI Global Scientific Publishing of the trademark or registered trademark.

Library of Congress Cataloging-in-Publication Data

Library of Congress Cataloging-in-Publication Data

Names: Asrifan, Andi, 1985- editor.
Title: Advancing society 5.0 through AI-driven curriculum innovation / Edited by Andi Asrifan.
Description: Hershey, PA : IGI Global Scientific Publishing, [2026] | Includes bibliographical references and index. | Summary: "This book examines how artificial intelligence (AI) shapes curricular innovation for Society 5.0 to bridge the gap between technological advances and educational reform. It offers a complete framework for rethinking education institutions to meet the challenges and potential of this new societal paradigm"-- Provided by publisher.
Identifiers: LCCN 2024061729 (print) | LCCN 2024061730 (ebook) | ISBN 9798337310626 (hardcover) | ISBN 9798337310633 (paperback) | ISBN 9798337310640 (ebook)
Subjects: LCSH: Artificial intelligence--Educational applications. | Education--Effect of technological innovations on. | Curriculum planning.
Classification: LCC LB1028.43 .A36 2026 (print) | LCC LB1028.43 (ebook) | DDC 371.33/4--dc23/eng/20240208
LC record available at https://lccn.loc.gov/2024061729
LC ebook record available at https://lccn.loc.gov/2024061730

British Cataloguing in Publication Data
A Cataloguing in Publication record for this book is available from the British Library.

All work contributed to this book is new, previously-unpublished material.
The views expressed in this book are those of the authors, but not necessarily of the publisher.
This book contains information sourced from authentic and highly regarded references, with reasonable efforts made to ensure the reliability of the data and information presented. The authors, editors, and publisher believe the information in this book to be accurate and true as of the date of publication. Every effort has been made to trace and credit the copyright holders of all materials included. However, the authors, editors, and publisher cannot assume responsibility for the validity of all materials or the consequences of their use. Should any copyright material be found unacknowledged, please inform the publisher so that corrections may be made in future reprints.

Table of Contents

Detailed Table of Contents

This chapter explores Society 5.0, a transformative paradigm integrating cutting-edge technologies like AI, robotics, IoT, and big data into human-centered frameworks. It critically examines how these technologies reshape fundamental aspects of the human condition, including identity, agency, and purpose, while addressing pressing global challenges such as aging populations, environmental degradation, and social inequalities. Drawing from philosophical perspectives, particularly those of Arendt, Sartre, and Heidegger, the chapter interrogates the implications of technological advancements for autonomy, authenticity, and cultural diversity. It also evaluates ethical challenges such as algorithmic bias, privacy concerns, and the digital divide, proposing principles of equitable and inclusive governance. By synthesizing insights from philosophy, sociology, and technology, this chapter advocates for a balanced approach to Society 5.0—one that fosters innovation without compromising core human values of dignity, freedom, and justice.

Society 5.0 represents a transformative paradigm that merges digital and physical spaces through advanced technologies, particularly artificial intelligence (AI). This vision aims to create a sustainable, inclusive society where human well-being is prioritized. By rethinking educational frameworks, we can foster creativity, critical thinking, and emotional intelligence in learners. Philosophically, the integration of AI into education raises essential questions about agency, equity, and ethics. It challenges us to consider how technology can augment human potential without diminishing the intrinsic values of education. In Society 5.0, educators are tasked with not only imparting knowledge but also cultivating a sense of responsibility and ethics in future citizens who will navigate an AI-enhanced world. Furthermore,

AI has the potential to customize learning experiences, promoting inclusivity and accessibility. Ultimately, rethinking education within Society 5.0 paves the way for a harmonious coexistence between technology and humanity.

This chapter explores the transformative impact of Artificial Intelligence (AI) on STEAM education, focusing on its integration into sustainability, quantum computing, and lifelong learning paradigms. The study examines emerging trends in AI-enhanced education, highlighting its potential to revolutionize curricula and its role in preparing a workforce equipped to navigate an increasingly AI-driven global landscape. Key challenges, including socio-economic disparities, ethical concerns, and resistance to technological change, are critically analyzed alongside policy implications emphasizing the need for inclusive, transparent, and equitable AI frameworks. Through a combination of qualitative analysis and case study examination, the chapter illustrates successful AI initiatives in developed and developing countries, showcasing the potential for AI to bridge gaps in education access and quality. The chapter concludes by emphasizing the importance of interdisciplinary collaboration, global networks, and continuous innovation in shaping the future of AI-enhanced STEAM education.

The integration of artificial intelligence (AI) into educational frameworks is revolutionizing curriculum development by fostering adaptive and learner-centric approaches. AI-powered systems enable personalized learning experiences, dynamically adjusting content to match individual student needs, preferences, and learning paces. This innovation not only enhances student engagement but also optimizes knowledge retention by providing tailored feedback and adaptive assessments. Furthermore, AI facilitates data-driven insights for educators, enabling them to refine teaching strategies and curriculum structures. By leveraging machine learning algorithms and predictive analytics, AI empowers institutions to create

Human Resource Development in the era of society 5.0 is a opportunity and a threat to educational institutions. However, it is important for educational institutions to prepare graduates whose English Proficiency are adjusted to the CEFR. This study aims to explain how the role of Artificial Intelligence (AI) in assisting the implementation of Language Assessment in the Common ASEAN Tourism Curriculum (CATC) at one of the Secondary Vocational Tourism Schools which became a pilot project in Indonesia by conducting in-depth interviews with several parties related to the implementation of CATC. The Language Assessment covers Skill, Attitude, and Knowledge which is adjusted to the ASEAN Competency Standards for Tourism Professional (ACSTP). In addition, AI helps compile the Task Project/role play that will be given to the students of Secondary Tourism Vocational Schools (assessees) as one of the instruments in Language Assessment so that this instrument can be easily understood and done by students (assessees) and teachers (Assessors) easily conduct assessments as summative assessments.

AI curriculum design influences future technologies and society. This study explores cultural bias and linguistic representation in AI curriculum design and its effects on Society 5.0, a human-centered, technologically advanced society. It emphasizes the ethical and practical issues of cultural and language diversity in AI systems and the goals of inclusive and equitable AI education. Cultural bias in AI is linked to biased datasets and developer attitudes, supported by real-world case studies of their social implications. Examining language representation addresses the exclusion of low-resource languages from AI courses and offers remedies. Society 5.0 aligns inclusive AI education with social goals, ethics, and laws. Finally, the report advises curriculum designers, legislators, and academics on culturally and linguistically

Preface

INTRODUCTION

We stand at the threshold of an era defined not only by rapid technological advancement but by our collective ability to center that progress around human well-being. Society 5.0, a concept born out of Japan's vision for a smarter, more inclusive future, challenges us to move beyond the Internet of Things (Society 4.0) and toward a digital society that is both innovative and profoundly human-centric. At the heart of this transformation lies education—our most powerful tool for shaping the future. However, traditional educational models are increasingly misaligned with the dynamic capabilities demanded by AI-powered industries. This edited volume, *Advancing Society 5.0 Through AI-Driven Curriculum Innovation*, seeks to address this pressing mismatch.

In this collection, our contributors delve into how artificial intelligence is not merely an external force acting upon education, but a transformative partner in redefining curriculum design, pedagogy, and access. Through a balanced focus on theory and practice, the chapters explore how AI can personalize learning pathways, ensure more equitable educational access, and uphold ethical considerations within digital environments. With a firm belief that innovation should never outpace inclusion, this book provides actionable frameworks to guide the integration of AI into learning systems that are adaptable, responsive, and forward-thinking.

We bring together educators, researchers, policy architects, and edtech innovators to offer a cohesive and rigorous approach to embedding AI within curricular structures. From real-world case studies to conceptual models, this work illuminates how educational systems can evolve to foster not only digital fluency, but also critical thinking, empathy, creativity, and social responsibility. These values are essential if we are to cultivate learners who are not just competent participants in an AI-driven economy, but also conscientious stewards of a just and sustainable future.

This volume is intended for a broad spectrum of stakeholders: educators seeking new teaching paradigms; policymakers designing equitable AI education policies; instructional designers and school administrators aiming to align learning outcomes with 21st-century demands; and innovators crafting technologies that support deeper, more meaningful learning experiences. In offering both inspiration and instruction, the book aspires to become a touchstone for those committed to shaping an educational landscape that embodies the promise of Society 5.0.

It is my hope that this book ignites new ideas, encourages critical reflection, and empowers each reader to contribute to a shared vision: a technologically advanced society that leaves no one behind, where education remains the bedrock of human progress and dignity.

ORGANIZATION OF THE BOOK

Chapter 1: The Human Condition in a Technological Era: Redefining Existence in Society 5.0

Opening this volume is a chapter that anchors our understanding of Society 5.0 not merely in technical progression, but in the evolving essence of human identity. Drawing deeply from the philosophical canon—including the works of Arendt, Sartre, and Heidegger—this chapter critiques how AI, IoT, robotics, and big data redefine autonomy, purpose, and cultural diversity in a technologically mediated world. The author interrogates the ethical tensions that arise from algorithmic bias, digital surveillance, and social fragmentation, offering human-centered governance principles as a response. This foundational chapter calls for a thoughtful balance between innovation and human dignity, positioning Society 5.0 as a space where technological advancement must remain tethered to justice, freedom, and equity.

Chapter 2: Rethinking Society 5.0 of AI-Driven Educational Innovation: The Philosophical Underpinnings

Continuing the conversation between philosophy and pedagogy, this chapter situates AI-enhanced education within a broader philosophical context. It reimagines education as a vehicle not only for knowledge transfer but for cultivating empathy, critical thinking, and ethical reasoning. The author explores the tensions between automation and agency, equity and access, raising crucial questions about how education can remain humane in the age of intelligent machines. By embedding AI within ethical and inclusive frameworks, this chapter illustrates how Society

5.0 must be built on educational systems that empower learners to thrive—not just function—in a technologically saturated reality.

Chapter 3: AI's Role in Advancing STEAM Education: Transforming Learning and Innovation

Bridging disciplines and global contexts, this chapter explores the transformative synergy between AI and STEAM education. Focusing on sustainability, quantum literacy, and lifelong learning, it highlights AI's potential to elevate curricula and workforce readiness across diverse geographies. With a robust blend of qualitative insights and global case studies, the author addresses systemic challenges such as digital inequality and resistance to change. The chapter calls for inclusive policy design and interdisciplinary collaboration, painting a clear vision of STEAM education as a catalyst for inclusive innovation in Society 5.0.

Chapter 4: AI-Driven Curriculum Innovation for Adaptive and Learner-Centric Education

In this compelling examination of adaptive education, the author presents AI as a pivotal force in reshaping curriculum to be more responsive, inclusive, and learner-centered. By leveraging predictive analytics, intelligent tutoring systems, and real-time feedback, AI enables personalization at scale—making learning more engaging, efficient, and equitable. The chapter emphasizes AI's ability to address diverse learning needs, facilitate teacher insights, and support lifelong learning. It provides a practical and visionary roadmap for educators seeking to reorient traditional pedagogy toward agility and individual growth.

Chapter 5: Integrating AI in Outcome-Based Education: A Cross-Disciplinary Curriculum Transformation

Focusing on the Outcome-Based Education (OBE) model, this chapter details how AI streamlines curriculum delivery, fosters interdisciplinary learning, and aligns educational outputs with real-world competencies. By automating assessments and tailoring learning experiences, AI reduces workload and enhances instructional efficiency. Yet, the chapter does not shy away from ethical challenges like privacy and fairness. It advocates for strategic governance, transparency, and AI literacy to ensure that technological integration aligns with educational equity and ethical accountability.

Chapter 6: Personalized Learning Through Intelligent Assessment Systems: Enhancing Student Engagement

This chapter delves into the evolution of assessment—from uniform tests to intelligent systems that adapt to learner profiles in real time. It presents AI-driven tools such as AR, VR, and analytics dashboards as instruments of motivation and autonomy, fostering deeper engagement and learning outcomes. Case studies demonstrate the tangible benefits of intelligent assessment systems in diverse educational settings. Importantly, the author stresses the need for educator training and ethical data governance, highlighting the dual promise and responsibility that comes with personalized education.

Chapter 7: Advancing Society 5.0 Through AI-Driven Curriculum Innovation: The Role of AI in Language Assessment of the Common ASEAN Tourism Curriculum (CATC)

Taking a regional lens, this chapter focuses on AI's role in advancing human resource development through improved language assessment practices in ASEAN's tourism education sector. Grounded in CEFR standards and aligned with ASEAN Competency frameworks, the chapter describes how AI aids in task design, project-based learning, and summative assessments. Drawing from a pilot implementation in Indonesia, the work illustrates how AI can support both students and educators in assessing critical competencies across language, knowledge, and behavior, contributing to a globally responsive workforce in Society 5.0.

Chapter 8: Cultural Bias and Linguistic Representation in AI Curriculum Design: Implications for Society 5.0

This chapter calls attention to one of the most pressing blind spots in AI curriculum design: cultural and linguistic bias. It critiques the exclusion of low-resource languages and underrepresented cultural perspectives in educational AI systems, highlighting the ethical consequences for equity and inclusion. By presenting real-world case studies and offering actionable solutions, the author advocates for curricula that are linguistically rich, culturally diverse, and legally informed. This critical inquiry aligns deeply with Society 5.0's commitment to justice and social cohesion through inclusive technology.

Chapter 9: Game-Based Learning in the AI Era: Designing Curricula for Society 5.0

Emphasizing engagement, this chapter explores how Game-Based Learning (GBL) combined with AI can create dynamic, student-centered educational environments. Drawing on constructivist theories, the author showcases how AI enhances GBL through adaptive content and immersive technologies such as VR and AR. The chapter also tackles key policy and infrastructural challenges, including digital literacy, equity, and data privacy. With forward-looking strategies and illustrative case studies, it demonstrates how gamified learning environments are essential for cultivating creativity, collaboration, and problem-solving in the AI era.

Chapter 10: Innovating Curriculum Design with AI and Gamification: A Roadmap for Society 5.0

Building on the momentum of gamification, this chapter outlines a strategic design framework for AI-based curriculum innovation that blends motivation science with technological intelligence. By integrating real-time feedback, individualized pacing, and game elements, the chapter illustrates how AI can revolutionize both the form and function of education. Emphasizing ethical design and data privacy, it proposes a comprehensive roadmap for deploying AI-gamified learning systems that are not only effective but responsible—essential in shaping resilient, future-ready learners for Society 5.0.

Chapter 11: AI-Powered Lifelong Learning System: AI-Driven Mobile Learning for a Transformative Educational Landscape

With a focus on lifelong and mobile learning, this chapter presents AI and Mobile-Assisted Language Learning (MALL) as vital tools in democratizing education for a diverse, multilingual world. The framework prioritizes adaptive pathways, cultural relevance, and real-time learner feedback, ensuring that AI applications serve inclusive and context-sensitive purposes. The author also explores how AI fosters digital citizenship and social preparedness, advocating for practices and policies that support continuous learning in an ever-evolving technological landscape.

Chapter 12: Developing Digital Citizenship Skills

Closing the volume, this chapter articulates the foundational importance of digital citizenship in Society 5.0. It defines digital citizenship as a convergence of technological fluency and ethical responsibility, emphasizing competencies such as data privacy, critical thinking, and responsible participation in digital ecosystems. The chapter proposes frameworks for embedding digital ethics and citizenship across curricula, powered by AI tools like simulations and adaptive feedback. With its focus on preparing ethically grounded, critically aware learners, this final chapter reinforces the book's vision of a Society 5.0 where technology serves, rather than supersedes, humanity.

CONCLUSION

As we conclude this volume, it is evident that we are not merely witnessing an educational transformation—we are actively shaping it. The convergence of artificial intelligence and curriculum innovation signals a profound shift in how we conceive of learning, equity, and human potential within the framework of Society 5.0. This book has brought together a diverse and interdisciplinary chorus of voices—philosophers, technologists, educators, policy experts, and innovators—each contributing critical insights into the challenges and possibilities that lie ahead.

Across these chapters, several themes resonate with urgency and clarity: the need to preserve human dignity and ethical agency amidst technological advancement; the imperative to design inclusive, culturally sensitive, and adaptive curricula; and the promise of AI to not only personalize learning, but to democratize access and expand educational equity on a global scale. Yet these aspirations must be pursued with vigilance—through responsible design, transparent governance, and sustained collaboration among all stakeholders.

The path forward requires bold imagination, grounded research, and an unwavering commitment to the values that define human-centered progress. Education, now more than ever, must be a platform not just for workforce development but for cultivating empathy, creativity, critical thinking, and global citizenship. With this book, we hope to empower leaders in education and technology alike to embrace AI not as a replacement for the human element, but as a catalyst for realizing a more just, sustainable, and inclusive society.

Let this work serve as both a guide and a call to action—inviting educators, researchers, policymakers, and innovators to reimagine learning ecosystems that truly prepare individuals to thrive in and contribute meaningfully to Society 5.0.

Andi Asrifan
Universitas Negeri Makassar, Indonesia

Chapter 1
The Human Condition in a Technological Era:
Redefining Existence in Society 5.0

Sooraj Kumar Maurya
https://orcid.org/0000-0002-6974-5508
Zakir Husain Delhi College, University of Delhi, India

ABSTRACT

This chapter explores Society 5.0, a transformative paradigm integrating cutting-edge technologies like AI, robotics, IoT, and big data into human-centered frameworks. It critically examines how these technologies reshape fundamental aspects of the human condition, including identity, agency, and purpose, while addressing pressing global challenges such as aging populations, environmental degradation, and social inequalities. Drawing from philosophical perspectives, particularly those of Arendt, Sartre, and Heidegger, the chapter interrogates the implications of technological advancements for autonomy, authenticity, and cultural diversity. It also evaluates ethical challenges such as algorithmic bias, privacy concerns, and the digital divide, proposing principles of equitable and inclusive governance. By synthesizing insights from philosophy, sociology, and technology, this chapter advocates for a balanced approach to Society 5.0—one that fosters innovation without compromising core human values of dignity, freedom, and justice.

DOI: 10.4018/979-8-3373-1062-6.ch001

Copyright © 2026, IGI Global Scientific Publishing. Copying or distributing in print or electronic forms without written permission of IGI Global Scientific Publishing is prohibited.

INTRODUCTION

Society 5.0 was introduced as a new approach in the Fifth Basic Plan for Science and Technology in Japan. It is marked by a move toward society centered around people, with advanced technologies such as AI, robotics, IoT and big data playing a major role in everyday life. Society 5.0 stands out from previous forms like Society 1.0, Society 2.0 and Society 4.0, as it combines the physical and digital realms to tackle tough challenges affecting humans. It is important to note that this shift isn't only meant for innovation; it also focuses on critical world issues such as growing older populations, environmental damage, depleting resources and inequality (Cabinet Office of Japan, 2017). The main focus of the vision is to improve lifestyles with the use of modern and inclusive technology. With IoT technology, caregivers are able to watch over patients from a distance, providing them with individualized and immediate care. Similarly, robotics is transforming sectors that rely on labor and is now providing solutions for labor shortages and sharing the responsibilities for our aging population.

Nevertheless, there are some ethical and social problems linked to Society 5.0. Since modern digital systems now make most decisions on their own, it is now risky for individuals and justice to be threatened by algorithmic bias, breaches of data privacy and inequity in technology access. AI using biased data can pick up and even increase the effect of unfair views in employment, healthcare and criminal justice. But the digital divide continues to keep non-supreme communities on the sidelines, adding to the problems they already face. Apart from its practical aspects, Society 5.0 raises important questions about human nature that make us reassess our identity. As machines help in decision-making, creation and care, people's views on work, who they are, freedom and accountability are being changed. What does it mean for us to have selfhood when AI can make us virtual versions and our brains can communicate with computers? How can we make sure algorithms treat people with dignity when they impact our jobs, our homes and even our self-awareness?

These matters call for answers that are more than simply technical. They encourage society to look at ethics carefully, include a range of views when planning new designs and prepare children and young adults to handle technology both safely and intelligently. In addition to being intelligent, Society 5.0 must also show justice, care and respect for human values including freedom, dignity and equality. In this chapter, it is pointed out that policy changes and a focus on ethics are needed to reach the full potential of Society 5.0.

Philosophical Dimensions of the Human Condition

For a long time, philosophers have examined the concept of the human condition at the heart of their investigations. It discusses main themes, like being a self, having freedom, being responsible, being in charge of actions and seeking a meaningful life. With the rise of Society 5.0 which depends heavily on artificial intelligence and robotics, it is time to look again at these issues. The fast development of intelligent technologies creates new issues about being human, helping us maintain dignity, freedom and true existence in a world with more automation. These concerns are examined using the ideas of three prominent 20th-century philosophers: Hannah Arendt, Jean-Paul Sartre and Martin Heidegger. The ideas they shared on labor, freedom and being are still very significant for understanding how Society 5.0 affects the way people find their roles and sense of self.

In 1958, Hannah Arendt recognized that there are three main areas of human activity: labor to fulfill biology, work to build enduring systems and action which deals with freedom, being among others and more community involvement. This becomes particularly meaningful as we examine the role of automation. With Society 5.0, AI and robots take over many jobs such as data processing, handling logistics, designing creative solutions and making decisions. Although it frees us from tedious actions, it also reduces the ways we can participate in building relationships, sharing experiences and exploring our freedom. Does life change for people when machines control both productivity and creativity? The approach introduced by Arendt asks us if technology is helping or weakening our relationships and sense of responsibility.

Jean-Paul Sartre's existentialism gives us another method to understand Society 5.0. He explained that people have total freedom and are responsible for defining themselves based on their choices in an universe that ignores them. Still, since decisions about many areas are now being made by intelligent systems, the individual's ability to decide for themselves is put to the test. When machines guess our choices, guide decisions and change how we behave by means of algorithms, can we still be called free? They can also help take away routine jobs and let people concentrate on developing themselves and their creativity. The main question, therefore, is whether we rely on AI to help us or if we give it power to limit the choices we make.

In his concept of Dasein ("being-there"), Martin Heidegger studied how humans and the world are linked. In his book, Heidegger warned that technological enframing treats both people and nature as objects to enhance for maximum benefit. Society 5.0 is changing so fast that it makes this point even more pressing. The presence of personalized AI on social media, in voice assistants and in surveillance shapes our views and interactions with each other. They make things more convenient, yet they can also narrow what users come across and influence the opinions that exist. For

Heidegger, the problem with technology was not only the objects it provides, but the way it affects our very identity, encouraging us to be less active and independent.

To overcome these obstacles, it is important to reflect on what is right and wrong. Kant's insistence on human dignity and autonomy from the Enlightenment still supports developing AI that values individual rights. For instance, when using AI in healthcare, we must ensure the guidance follows the patient's wishes and does not reflect any unconscious bias. When using predictive algorithms in public governance, they should follow ideas of justice and transparency. Ensuring that intelligent systems support democratic values should be the goal of proper accountability mechanisms. Overall, applying philosophy to Society 5.0 helps us understand its possible advantages as well as its disadvantages. AI and automation should not take away from individuality, freedom and equality, but should instead improve them. By focusing on ethical and human principles in developing technology for Society 5.0, we make sure it develops into a smart society that is truly about people.

Reimagining Identity and Purpose in Society 5.0

Society 5.0 has brought about important changes in the sense of who we are and why we exist. Historically, who a person is was decided by their biology, social position and cultural background, while what they do is tied to their occupation, family obligations and the ways they support their community. Yet, with artificial intelligence and robotics taking on bigger roles in society, these categories are beginning to merge, causing people to reconsider the nature of being human. For instance, the change to digital and hybrid identities brings difficulties for the prevalent Cartesian mind-body separation found in Western philosophy. These AI systems make it hard to tell the difference between human and machine actions. Such technologies as virtual avatars, BCIs and personal assistants are changing social interactions and are also creating new ways people or users exist in the digital world. In this context, Donna Haraway's (1985) understanding of the cyborg is highly relevant, as it describes identity as a blend of human and machine, natural and artificial which is similar to what Society 5.0 intends. It's not just our identity that shifts during this time. There is a significant rethinking of what purpose means in today's world. With more tasks being done by machines, people are encouraged to focus on jobs that require imagination, kindness and thoughtful decision-making. Many people, mainly those whose iwnorth was based on typical work roles, may find it hard to cope with this shift. At the same time, it makes it possible to find higher degrees of happiness. For example, in both education and healthcare, AI helps automate repetitive paperwork, so professionals can focus on educating, caring for patients and coming up with new solutions (West, 2018). This aligns with Abraham Maslow's (1943) theory which puts self-actualization higher than any other need—meaning Society 5.0 may let people focus on more than just living each day. Those three philosophers, Arendt, Sartre and Heidegger, help us grasp the change we experience now. Arendt (1958) encourages us to think about action as freedom and community, Sartre (1992) stresses that choice allows us to make our own identity and Heidegger (1962) points out that technological changes can distance us from real living. They show us that our sense of self and purpose are important and we should not give them up for the sake of efficiency. Therefore, Society 5.0 is built on ethical governance and intentional design. It is important for technologies to respect human dignity, support freedom and encourage people to work together. If philosophical ideas guide the development of technology, people in Society 5.0 can have lives that are meaningful, accepting and based on morals. So, it goes beyond standard automation to form a new way of living that values both people's individuality and the good of all.

PHILOSOPHICAL FOUNDATIONS: IDENTITY IN SOCIETY 5.0

The notion of identity has stood as one of the key theses of discussions in philosophy, as it touches upon such topics as self-organization, consciousness and the meaning of life. In the course of the history of human development, various philosophical concepts were developed reflecting various visions of the essence of identity and individuality.

René Descartes can be considered one of the first thinkers to lay the foundations of the contemporary concept of self through the dictum "Cogito, ergo sum" ("I think, therefore I am"). For Descartes, consciousness is the key to personhood, and it is identified with the mind rather than the body (Descartes, 1641/1996). This split into two different entities was called the Cartesian dualism, which distinguished between the spiritual substance (res cogitans) and the material substance (res extensa), thus emphasizing the values of the thinking self. However, Hegel began to mutually approach identity as a dynamism and relation through his sociopolitical dialectical approach. These main ideas are thesis, antithesis and synthesis which Hegel argued, is the manner in which identity is experienced by the individual as a product of socio historical context (Hegel 1807/1977). Hegel critiqued this view of identity in asserting that identity was not at any given point but was rather an ongoing process where contradictions are engaged and resolved, thereby stressing the relational and collective aspects of self.

Existentialists of the mid-twentieth century like Sartre and Heidegger played a new twist on the existent construal of identity that entailed freedom, choice, and foresight. Sartre (1992) claimed that people are free and have to choose their essence, meaning that there are no predetermined destinations in life. According to Sartre, people and their identities do not have fixed a priori designs due to their ability to use their freedom to build identities. In a similar vein, Heidegger (1927/1962) has advanced the notion of Dasein or 'being there' focusing on the relations between existence and context. Heidegger criticised scientism and the setting of people as mere utilities in the world; he said that being is constituted through the acting out of existence. These historical perspectives of the self are useful in understanding the changes in process as Society 5.0 is set to incorporate AI and robotics systems into people's lives. The collapse of the distinctions between the human and the non-human as well as the subject and the object problematize Cartesian dualism, Hegelian sociality, and existential perspectives on self-formation and offer deep critical reflection on what it means to be human in the age of technology.

Identity and AI

The integration of AI into Society 5.0 means there is a new way to think about what it means to be human. The close relationship between humans and artificial intelligences has led to the re-examination of the characteristics that once separated humans. By mimicking how humans think and make decisions, AI undermines the belief that these things are limited to humans. One important philosophical question here is how consciousness works. René Descartes claimed in Meditations on First Philosophy that whatever we are conscious of must be something truly immaterial and fundamental in our minds, so it cannot be touched by a machine (Descartes, 1641/1996). Thus, it became clear that humans were made up of their mind (res cogitans) and their body (res extensa), different from machines.

Yet, some contemporary philosophers such as Paul Churchland (1989), argue that consciousness comes from the interactions among brain parts which suggests that a machine could in principle produce similar results. If AI performs like our brain when it comes to consciousness, should we say it is conscious or only copying consciousness? This separation between true understanding and artificial simulation is not settled yet, but it is at the heart of questions concerning AI character and ethics. It becomes more complex to understand the issue when we consider if the accused has a clear idea of what they did. John Searle (1980) presents the Chinese Room argument to highlight the limits of AI cognition. Searle shows in the experiment that a computer, although showing the ability to handle syntax, fails to comprehend the meaning of language. In his view, today's most advanced AI is unable to form actual intentions or mental thoughts. However, AI systems like GPT-3 or GPT-4 can simulate human conversation, but they are not conscious and don't take emotions into account.

In today's society, distinctions between computers and robots are not always noticeable to the average consumer. More real-looking conversational agents, avatars and brain-machine interfaces often confuse people about the difference between humans and machines. With the rise of AI companions and robots that respond emotionally, people wonder if machines can learn empathy. Do they have the ability to think about right and wrong? Are they, as a result, just exhibiting what they have been trained to do? It is proposed that ensuring a human monitors and intervenes in AI decision-making — the human-in-the-loop approach — can uphold ethical standards (Floridi et al., 2018). Still, since AI is used in tasks related to healthcare, law enforcement and education, this model is beginning to face greater difficulties. When an AI acts on its own, it gets much more difficult to define who is responsible, has control and is right or wrong.

AI in Society 5.0 doesn't only handle routine jobs—it leads us to rethink who we are as people. There are concerns about these systems and also about the absence of meaningful philosophies that can guide their use. If we don't analyze our actions, we may start seeing people only as data points and as algorithms. Thus, it is important to ensure that new technology does not affect human distinctiveness negatively, but rather brings positive changes with proper guidance.

Posthumanism and Transhumanism

Along with automating jobs, Society 5.0's AI changes how we define humanity. Posthumanism and transhumanism both help explain the growing involvement of people and machines in creating our shared world.

Posthumanism argues that change and meaning should not be seen as the responsibility of humans alone. In N. Katherine Hayles' view (1999), technology is more than just a tool; it takes part in forming our minds, identities and ways of relating to power. From this perspective, AI plays a role in creating life, not just providing extra tools for humans. The combination of biology, machines and the environment suggests there is no single human identity, only a shifting combination spread over networks of technology, thoughts and culture.

While posthumanism questions the positive aspects of advancing technology, transhumanism looks forward to the success of technology in helping humans advance. Scientists like Nick Bostrom (2014) support enhancing people using brain-computer interfaces (BCIs), robotic prosthetics and neural implants that go beyond natural abilities. Such technologies could enhance personal abilities and transform the way humans experience things.

Yet, there are several ethics and knowledge concerns connected to these views. Debates arise about how our bodies, our thoughts and social issues interact. In post-modern Society 5.0, Donna Haraway's (1985) explanation of the cyborg-like nature shows a person merging human and machine traits, challenging old divisions. At the same time, this integration brings certain risks. When these kinds of technologies enter the commercial field, they could worsen existing differences in society. They may end up being further separated and marginalized by an already unequal digital world (Coeckelbergh, 2020). An ethical framework is needed to prevent Society 5.0 from favoring only the wealthy and powerful.

Cultural Identity in a Technological World

Society 5.0 is a place where technology and culture go hand in hand. Shared values, norms and creativity in expression are major aspects that make up culture and help form the identity of a society. Artificial intelligence is now a major factor in determining this identity, affecting talks in society and decisions of governments. There is growing concern about cultural homogeneity. By using algorithms, social media and digital services tailor the content users receive, so they often encounter only views that match their existing opinions. Because of this phenomenon, known as the filter bubble, widespread cultures become more prominent while marginalized voices are overlooked (Pariser, 2011). The outcome is that there is less cultural diversity which poses a danger to creativity and innovation.

On the other hand, AI helps preserve cultures and makes them easier to include in society. For instance, by using NLP, people can create databases of endangered languages to preserve them for future use. Likewise, artists from minority communities can promote their works on these AI platforms without having to go through agents. They make it possible for those who are not heard in society to have a stronger presence in culture (Crawford & Paglen, 2019).

Yet such innovative creations lead to debates about the originality and identity of their creators. If an AI system creates a poem, painting or piece of music, who deserves credit: the algorithm, the programmer or everyone in society? Relevant in this context is Walter Benjamin's 2001 exploration of the effect of mechanical reproduction on the "aura" of art. He believed that machines reproducing art took away from its uniqueness and authenticity, a problem also seen today with generative AI. AI is not truly culture-neutral, as commonly believed. Algorithms reflect the values and biases of the people who developed them. Evidence suggests that facial recognition usually struggles with non-white, non-male faces, reflecting the danger of using unequal data (Buolamwini & Gebru, 2018). Because of this, AI solutions must be adapted to different cultural values when deployed internationally. In Society 5.0, it is important to focus on decentralization, inclusion and ethics to make sure technology helps preserve cultural identity, instead of taking it away. Overall, AI in Society 5.0 shows signs of changing aspects of culture both positively and negatively. The design and management of technology will play a key role in shaping cultural identity in the future. A values-based approach centered on diversity, equity and creativity ensures technology helps people grow, instead of tearing them apart.

PURPOSE IN AN AI-DRIVEN WORLD

The Redefinition of Work and Creativity

AI is essentially altering how people work, create and think. During the move to Society 5.0, AI is assisting in tackling repetitive jobs in manufacturing, logistics, customer service and writing, among other fields. Despite the clear boost in efficiency and productivity such changes in technology also put pressure on community relationships, reshape job markets and prompt people to reconsider their roles in an automated society. Based on philosophical thinking, labor, work and action—described by Hannah Arendt (1958)—are three areas that explain these transformations. With Society 5.0, more and more jobs are automated, so humans are pushed to act or replaced. For example, using AI in assembly lines removes human workers from the job which impactssho work meaning and a sense of self. This criticism is similar to Karl Marx's idea of alienation, where workers, through capitalism, become separate from their work, co-workers and even themselves (Marx, originally published in 1844/1978). Further automation of production separates workers from their job, resulting in greater alienation. Even so, if society supports the right changes, these same technologies could free people from mindless, heartless labor, making them more creative, giving their lives deeper purpose and making society richer in many ways.

Radical changes to our view of creativity are happening as scientists now study it in other animals. AI-powered systems such as DALL·E and GPT-4 can now produce both artworks and creative content such as stories, poetry and music. The results are usually highly skilled and maintain a consistent style which leads to many debates about what creativity actually is. In what ways is human creativity separate from the work of algorithms? According to Walter Benjamin (2001), this problem was already foreseen through his discussion of technological reproduction. He pointed out that ordinary art isn't as unique as an original work because it has been produced on a large scale. It becomes increasingly important because nowadays AI-created content appears widely, missing clear identification, feelings or history. Machines may be able to copy creative patterns, though they miss out on the purposeful thinking, history and personal emotion that belong to true human creativity (Zuboff, 2019).

In light of AI, people should show what they add to creative work that machines cannot offer such as shaping meaning, adding emotional feeling and overseeing ethical standards. Instead of fighting AI, people should focus on bringing attention, moral understanding and cultural wisdom to the mix, as these are not traits robots can have. As a result, we must pay close attention to how machines replace people and find strategic steps for us to take control again when machines fail at certain tasks. As a result, humanity can design a future where technology makes these characteristics stronger instead of weaker.

Existentialism in the Digital Age

Jean Paul Sartre, John Heidegger, and other existentialists demonstrate some of the best approaches towards the exploration of purpose in the age of intelligent systems. In the same vein, existentialist philosopher Jean-Paul Sartre also penned the now-infamous maxim that 'we are condemned to be free', postulating freedom and choice are constant burdens individual bear in an otherwise meaningless world. Merleau-Ponty (1945/1962) emphasized on the concept of "Being in the World", on the other hand Heidegger (1927/1962), placed accent on "Being-in-the-world". Meanwhile, the existentialist concepts regain concern in the context of Society 5.0 because AI in the progressing world expands intervention in people's freedom. In the majority of the cases, AI systems determine decisions that have a direct and lasting impact on human lives, from recommender systems to self-driving cars. Despite the fact that these technologies create comfort and optimise performances, they endanger human sovereignty or agency by promoting reliance and eradicating reflection.

Nonetheless, AI also paves new haven for existential satisfaction. Much of what we do is repetitive and AI helps to free up peoples' time so that they can do what they want to be doing. For instance, the AI-based technology in learning supports educators and students by delivering and assisting students through a customized learning approach while increasing participation and knowledge acquisition. Likewise in healthcare, the use of AI applications assists the professional to perform their health duties since mundane tasks are automated. The fact that existentialists stress on choices and freedom in decision making demonstrates that AI adoption should also be intentional. Instead of being a submissive recipient of automation, people and societies have to define how they want to interact with AI to ensure that arising automation effects will be positive and not lead to individuals' disenfranchisement. It is thus important to undertake critical analysis on the social impact of AI in an effort to meet these challenges.

Collaborative Purpose: Humans and AI as Partners

AI is new not just because it can replace the human but because it can be a partner to the human in coming up with new ideas as well as new solutions in the creative and innovative industries. AI enhances human strengths to create symbiosis, thus complementing every aspect of human life with artificial intelligence. In art, there are AI systems such as Google's DeepDream and Sony's flow machines that have partnered with artists. These collaborations undermine the conventional mode of creativity and writing, wherein the AI is presented as a co-creator. For example, Flow Machines has collaborated with musicians to create songs that blend a human's desire with machine learning to transform the concept of teamwork in artistry. In science, it has supported accelerated discoveries as it identifies patterns in large data sets and form hypotheses. AlphaFold, a project by DeepMind also managed to solve the protein folding problem which has been pivotal in biology by predicting protein structures with high accuracy (Jumper et al., 2021). This accomplishment shows how professionals can harness the power of AI computing and achieve great feats in answering compelling scientific queries, paving the way for advancement and development.

Human–AI partnership also applies to social innovation. IBM Watson is one example of an AI platform helping policymakers identify solutions to poverty, healthcare, and education issues. In these applications, one can see how AI supports human evaluation and decision-making rather than replacing human intuition and the desire for collaboration between man and machine. However, these collaborations encourage ethical and philosophical concerns. For example, who between the man and the machine should be awarded the medals, promotions and bonuses? What can be done to make sure that Artificial Intelligence will be 'on the same page' with what humans want? For these questions, the solution is an open dialogue among technologists, ethicists, and philosophers to discuss how humans and AI work together to implement inclusive, equitable, and responsible collaboration.

Beyond Labor: The Search for Fulfillment

Since Society 5.0 is heading towards an almost automated world removing work power to a considerable extent required by man, the priority shifts towards the psychological and physical well-being of Society alongside with Self-actualization of citizens. This transition is one for the better as it marks the move from materialism to humanism; from focusing on mere production to the well-being of people.

To make the discourse more coherent and clear, Abraham Maslow's hierarchy of needs model shall be used in analyzing this change. Due to the growth of consumption society, fundamental needs are often met, thus consumers have more opportunities to pursue.pg Needs at level two according to Maslow (1943) includes esteem needs, belongingness, and self-actualization. This progression is facilitated by AI technologies which offer tailored solutions that cater for learning needs, health and emotional aspects. For instance, AI-based mental health applications such as Wysa and Woebot are available to help people work on strengthening their emotional skills and personalities. Likewise, AI integrated fitness devices and nutrition/ calorie applications ensure proper physical health by assisting people to take charges of their health. These tools show how people can develop within the parameters of AI and create the chance for richer, more meaningful lives. In terms of the philosophical concept, orientation towards fulfillment is closely associated with existentialist notions of self-identity and non-conformism. Heidegger (1927/1962) marked the freedom that stems from an authentic existence where one is unique yet not isolated. In Society 5.0, it will involve the balancing of the provision of simple solutions than complicated lives of human beings.

Nonetheless, the quest for a fulfilling life in an environment increasingly managed by Artificial Intelligence calls for ethical questions. These issues are particularly pertinent because as AI, or artificial intelligence, acts as the go-between between humans and their experiences, there is potential for translating well-being into formulas or sales pitches. It should be noted that the AI technologies should be designed and used in such a way that they will enhance real satisfaction and not merely pleasure. Society 5.0 is a transition toward a new generation of work, creation, and well-being. To some extent AI threatens conventional paradigms while posing profound questions to human beings and their agency, nonetheless it provides options for a new vision of the world. In this sense, AI, through conscious and responsible implementation, can become a way of enhancing innovation, health, and human satisfaction in the context of the postmodern world.

HUMAN AGENCY AND TECHNOLOGICAL AUTONOMY

Philosophical Foundations of Human Agency

Free will is a crucial concept in philosophical discourse as a concept that implies the ability of a person to perform purposeful actions, to decide on something independently, take responsibility for it. This concept has been perfectly discussed in the works of Aristotle, Kant, and Sartre, and each of these philosophers approached the given issue from the perspective of morality and existentialism.

However, it is important to understand that according to Aristotle, agency is closely connected to reason and morality. According to Aristotle (350 BCE/1999), through rationality, man attains eudaimonia or the finite end of man thus attaining the essence of life. From this point of view, actions are purposeful and based on the principles of virtue to benefit the individual as well as the society. However, Kant disagreed with this as he asserted that autonomy was the basis of moral subjectivity (1785/1996). He claimed that people have to behave in a way that respects the principles of reason, which dictate that one must never use another person or treat them as a mere means to an end. Drawing from this deontological point of view, agency is viewed as an ethically charged function, since it comes with set responsibilities.

From an existentialist point of view, Sartre (1992) paid much attention to the aspects of freedom and intentionality of agency. To Sartre, people are predestined to be free implying that they have no makes excuses regarding the decisions they have made, and the lives they live. Such an approach to the concept of freedom refers to the quantity of human responsibility in creating a particular life. In Society 5.0, the emergence of intelligent systems that are capable of decision-making puts into question such philosophical principles. This issue concerns the capacity for agency in machines, whether such a concept is only applicable to humans. In what manner is the autonomy of the machines extended and in what way does it find correlations with the human decision-making process? All these questions are at the core of ethical and philosophical debate over the deep concept of technologically enabled autonomy.

Shared Autonomy Between Humans and Machines

The use of AI in Society 5.0 has therefore introduced new situations where human and artificial agency become entwined. The process can be referred to as 'shared autonomy,' which has emerged more prominently in the healthcare system, governance mechanisms, and education sectors, where AI plays a pivotal role in making critical decisions.

In healthcare, AI systems help clinicians by processing big data to int grape decisions on diagnoses and therapy. This improves decision making by increasing efficiency but poses accountability issues. For instance, if an AI system has provided a wrong diagnosis, who is legally and ethically liable – the physician who relied on the system, the company that designed the system, or the system itself? These scenarios raise important questions about moral responsibility in highly self-sufficient contexts and situations. The application of algorithms in governance is becoming widespread, with applications ranging from policy formulation to policing. Algorithms such as COMPAS, which is a risk assessment tool used in the criminal justice system in the United States, provide examples of the ethical challenges involved in decision making. Some scholars have pointed out that algorithmic bias can result in unfair profiling for populations that are most vulnerable (Angwin et al., 2016). These question the ethical responsibility of policymakers and developers who employ such a system.

In education, AI-based applications use data and systems to learn student's needs and can enhance education. These systems may at the same time factors reduce the teachers involvement, which is essential for the all-rounded training of the learners. This dynamic shows the struggle of the system between embracing technology for efficiency and maintaining traditional values of humanism in education. From a philosophical perspective, it could be said that these developments are in line with

Latour's (2005) idea of distributed agency where agency is not restricted to people but an assemblage of people and things. Thus, in order to understand shared autonomy as a part of Society 5.0, it is crucial to address the interaction between intentional human activity, the ability of machines, and the potential for ethical conflict in this connection.

Ethics of Machine Autonomy

The ethical debate about the decentralisation of technology is based on the question of whether the AI systems have ethics to pursue. As postulated by Kantian ethics, only human beings possess the rationality and freedom to act in accordance with moral laws. In the Kantian moral theory, an individual cannot be deemed a moral agent if they or he/she lacks consciousness and the ability to reason (Kant, 1785/1996). However, AI continues to be an instrument created for specific purposes and goals. There is another type of deontological approach called utilitarianism that does not consider the moral worth of the agent but the outcomes of actions. Hedonistic and utilitarian AI systems developed for making better results and for effective betterment of the world like disaster management or decrease in healthcare inequalities adhere to utilitarian paradigm (Mill, 1863/1998). Nonetheless, their dependence on probabilistic analysis poses social harms; where discriminative incidences in training data trigger similar bias in assistance.

One of the significant ethical dilemmas is referred to as autonomous weapons systems (AWS). The defenders state that by minimizing the impact of human factors in such engagements, AWS may help lower the loss of lives. However, some participants raised some concern in explaining that every time, life and death decisions are left in the hands of the machines a question of ethicality comes up. Wallach and Allen (2008) stressed the need for moral values to be incorporated into AI systems but raise questions on whose values should we incorporate and how this can be done. In more mundane contexts such as self-driving cars ethical issues come into play as well. For example, these systems need to solve problems in ethical issues, for example, which persons are to be saved in non-avoidable accidents. Such scenarios demonstrate that there are drawbacks to using pre-scripted ethical standards and that it is difficult to implement moral decision-making in AI.

Freedom in a Technological World

The dependence on AI in Society 5.0 raises necessitating fundamental philosophical questions concerning freedom and autonomy. Heidegger in his work of analyse of technology (1927/1962) cautioned that use of technology threatens to incorporate human freedom by ponerating an individual simply as a user of technical equipment. It has especial relevance in an age where the decision-making process is mediated through complex mathematical algorithms. For example, social media feed filtering and sorting are based on engagement metrics and then serve content in a unique circle but in the process, they do not diversify individuals' interactions. It is the so-called 'social sorting' that has been labeled as the mass production of 'filter bubbles' or 'echo chambers,' which erode collective autonomy by distilling public debate into dualistic terms that leave their imprint on the range of choices available (Pariser, 2011).

However, AI can also increase freedom by opening up possibilities for personal autonomy. Personalized healthcare tools for instance, enables individuals to manage their health conditions and choices . In like manner, career planning platforms and skill building applications use advanced algorithms and artificial intelligence to help users find relevant opportunities and fulfill their career objectives. The dichotomy of freedom and technology can be paralleled with Isaiah Berlin's (1958) negative freedom and positive freedom. Negative liberty concerns freedom from coercion while on the other hand, positive liberty concerns freedom to do something. In Society 5.0, the liberty with AI must be complementary to the two forms of liberty in a way that strengthens specifically the second form, but does not infringe on the freedom of individuals. These challenges are core often handled by ethical frameworks. For instance, the General Data Protection Regulation of the European Union where data protection and users' opt-in are highlighted as the hallmarks of preserving freedom in the technological context (Voigt and Von dem Bussche, 2017). These regulations explain the possible ways through which ethical governance is useful in the enhancement of autonomy during the promotion of technology.

While Society 5.0 may be defined as a next phase of societal development initiated by the evolution of intelligent technologies that may involve additional benefits, human agency and other forms of technological autonomy may be taken as variables that both have advantages and disadvantages. In the process of improving the decisional procedures and the individual liberty, the AI systems bring with them the major ethical issues like, responsibility, prejudice and despotism. Philosophical analysis contains key principles for managing intricacies encountered in the course of developing cutting-edge technologies to match people's needs and wants. If the concept of agency is based on the Kantian ethical and utilitarian theories as well as existential philosophies, then the implementation of Society 5.0 would advance a more equitable and ethically informed approach of the incorporation of artificial intelligence. This means that to address the question of moral responsibility in human–machine cooperation we have to rethink the concept of responsibility in ways that take into account the intentions of the human agents and the capabilities of the machines. Finally, the model itself of Society 5.0 stands and falls with the ability to maintain technological progress side by side with the dignity, freedom, and rationality of citizens. Thus, putting emphasis on transparency, accountability, and inclusion, we would be able to avoid the worst-case scenario, when technologies become means of oppression and turn people into tools, making society safe for humans and machines.

ETHICAL AND EXISTENTIAL IMPLICATIONS OF SOCIETY 5.0

Ethical Challenges in AI-Driven Societies

The incorporation of AI into Society 5.0 ushers in various ethical issues that cannot be overlooked in the future society. These challenges range from algorithmic bias to excessive surveillance, and unequal access to digital technology, which may hamper the idea of Society 5.0 that the Japanese government is seeking to realize.

Algorithmic Bias: Unfortunately, attempts at an objective AI are far from perfect as they only serve to magnify the problems built into its database. For instance, facial recognition algorithms were used to misidentify ethnic minorities at a far higher than standard prevalence rate due to the structures that supported such systems (Buolamwini & Gebru, 2018). It means that such biases affect everyone since they play a significant role in criminal justice, healthcare, and even employment opportunities. If left uncontrolled, these systems could perpetuate new forms of discrimination because the technology just amplifies a 'fair' system, regardless of the inherent bias.

Surveillance and Privacy: AI-based surveillance systems as these have become a common feature in present society present conceptual issues on privacy of individuals. Currently, the governments and corporations use AI for monitoring of behavior while some organizations use artificial intelligence for information gathering without users' consent. The social credit system of china shows how big brother surveillance technologies can be used to dominate the people and deny their basic rights to freedom and dignity, as discussed by Zuboff (2019). It is for this reason that proper regulation has to be installed in the efforts to unlock technological development while at the same time guard the every human's right to privacy. Technological Inequality: Society 5.0 is all about building an embracing society for the future, but the future dwelling upon the modern electronic devices is still reserved for a few. Groups and areas selected in the economically disadvantaged bracket are the ones that cannot afford to purchase the Art intelligence benefits which continue to widen the gap of the digital divide Eubanks, 2018. Thus, the improved access to technologies for Society 5.0 should be the priority for the envisioned Society 5.0.

These difficulties are well outlined by the philosophers such as Kant and Rawls who provide necessary guidelines to deal with them. Kant's categorical imperative stresses the golden imperative of protecting individuals against the use of them as mere means, this all point to aspects of ethical AI, especially respecting human dignity (Kant, 1785/1996). On the same note, Rawls (1971) His theory of justice also wants society to be fair in distributing resources so the gains made through the use of AI will be felt across the population, or better still, with a especial consideration to the less fortunate in the society.

The Search for Authenticity

The concept of authenticity is a central tenet of existential philosophy and is significantly impacted by the integration of technology within Society 5.0. In the context of an ever-growing AI presence in everyday interactions, people are left with dwindling ways of authentic interaction and decisions. Technological Convenience vs. Meaningful Living: AI-based systems or services like the intelligent streaming services enhance users' experiences, however; most AI-based solutions are rather superficial, catering for the general superficiality preferred by modern users like the decision-making AI platform. Although these tools improve productivity thus they bring benefits to saving time and boosting people's schedules, at the same time they are related with a passive kind of consumption which leads to loss of the active control of life and choice making by individuals (Turkle, 2011). For instance, recommending tools on social networks keep users in bubbles restricting their view to a single top outlook.

Existential Perspectives: According to existentialist crusade as espoused by Sartre, people need to be free, responsible for their choices, and be accorded an opportunity to be what they want to be in order to be authentic. In Society 5.0, this involves questioning one's use of technology and avoiding delegating decision making to machines that should exhibit one's values. Authenticity cannot be achieved when using certain technological tools and when employees are all but robotic mimics of an organization. For instance, one might wonder if people are exposed to the vast amount of information or if they're merely limited to feeds of news and social media algorithms serving precisely what they know the user would be interested in. In the context of Society 5.0, authenticity can be achieved when criticality and intentionality are maintained as a way to not letting technology control people.

Technology and Social Justice

Society 5.0's promise of inclusivity offers a unique opportunity to address pressing issues of inequality, marginalization, and social justice through technological innovation.

Reducing Inequality

AI has the potential to democratize access to education, healthcare, and economic opportunities. For instance, AI-powered educational platforms can provide personalized learning experiences to students in underprivileged areas, bridging gaps in access to quality education (West, 2018). Similarly, AI-driven telemedicine can deliver healthcare services to remote regions, addressing disparities in medical access and improving outcomes for underserved populations.

Challenges of Marginalization

Despite its potential, AI also risks reinforcing structural inequalities if not carefully managed. Predictive policing algorithms, for example, have been criticized for disproportionately targeting minority communities, perpetuating systemic racism in law enforcement (O'Neil, 2016). To ensure that AI serves as a tool for empowerment rather than oppression, rigorous oversight and accountability mechanisms must be in place.

Ethical Principles for Social Justice

Philosophical frameworks like Rawls' (1971) "difference principle" provide guidance for promoting fairness in AI deployment. This principle prioritizes the welfare of the least advantaged, ensuring that technological progress benefits marginalized communities.

AI for Inclusion

Initiatives like AI4ALL, which focus on increasing diversity and inclusion in AI development, highlight how Society 5.0 can address social justice concerns. By involving underrepresented groups in the design and governance of AI systems, these initiatives ensure that technology reflects the needs and values of diverse communities, fostering greater equity and representation.

The ethical and existential implications of Society 5.0 underscore the transformative potential of this human-centric technological vision. Addressing the challenges of algorithmic bias, surveillance, and inequality requires not only technical solutions but also robust philosophical frameworks that prioritize human dignity, authenticity, and social justice. By grounding technological advancements in ethical principles and fostering inclusive practices, Society 5.0 can realize its promise of a more equitable and meaningful future for all.

FUTURE DIRECTIONS FOR PHILOSOPHY IN SOCIETY 5.0

The actualization of Society 5.0 which is the integration of society with technology requires a radical change in adopting a more humane approach on technology creation. It invites technologists, policymakers, and philosophers to remember that technology should aim to empower humanity and improve societies rather than use people for the sake of optimizing work or generating income. In this pursuit, one key tenet is Kant's (1785/1996) categorical imperative where people or stakeholders should never be used just as a tool towards achieving a certain goal. In the context of AI and robotics, positivism promotes technologies that enhance people's freedom and protect human worth. For instance, any AI applied to healthcare systems has to focus on patient care, patients' and not on cutting cost or making profits. A system, therefore, with Kantian ethics will in a way that such technologies will have patient as priority while performing the general human needs of a patient in not only medicine, but also emotions, and psychology.

As important and Aristotle's (350 BCE/1999) eudaimonia which is referred to as human happiness. These three areas of Aristotelian ethics also offer a framework for determining whether a particular technology enhances the good of individuals and societies. Technology in Society 5.0 should not just be used for materialistic gains; technology should enrich one's mind, emotions and social life. For example, an AI teaching-learning environment cannot be designed to replicate and simulate merely learning in this century but ought to foster thinking, invention, and collaborative problem-solving. This can help to turn education into a process that can lead to a harmonious personal and social life.

Another inevitable principle is the accountability. That is why, technology development and application must have the clear and open ways to prevent harm, for example, the bias in recommendation algorithms or AI misuse. Checks, regulation and transparency in auditing is another key to provide a level playing ground in availing technologies. As Floridi et al. (2018) stated, ethic of AI have to be transparent and, most importantly, inclusive especially when an AI-driven choice will have an impact on people's lives like employment or criminal charges. In this way, by anchoring technological advancement in these philosophies, Society 5.0 can guarantee that such advancements do not turn into a weapon that the powerful can use to subjugate others. This approach allows society to uphold and address the delicate balances between the ever increasing technological productivity and humanism in the achievement of societal goals and objectives for the common good.

That is why to overcome these threats and embrace the opportunities that are embedded into the context of Society 5.0, it is necessary to solve that complicated question through the lens of philosophy, technology, and sociology. Thus, each discipline enriches the others and provides broader perceptions of the subject matter and the human experience in the age of technology. Philosophy therefore affords fundamental ethical and existential inquiries into technology's implications of identity, agency, and purpose. Heidegger's (1977) criticism of technology helps in preventing the subject of existentialism to mere functioning. In the view of Heidegger, such technological onslaught undermines the humanistic goal, as people becomes "resources" that are "biology-fitted" for maximum performance. The significance of philosophical reflection is that it fosters a less naïve approach to technology which in turn prompts a more fulfilling life and key humanity.

As for technologists, they contribute the real-world experience in the process of designing and deploying AI systems. This capacity to concretize abstract philosophical concepts makes it possible to come up with practical thes that can effectively address ethical issues. For instance, engineers designing self-driving cars work with ethicists to settle questions concerning moral action, including choices made in cases of_fatalities (Lin, 2016). In this way, merging of the strategies guarantees that the technological solutions meet the ethical goals. Sociologists get involved to analyze the social structures as well as the culture through which technology Bears influence. They found out that policies exist to promote the use of technology yet the poor are left behind in the use of these technologies, digital divide is also an issue and want policies that will help to close these gaps (Eubanks, 2018). For instance, sociological investigations on algorithmic bias show how the supposedly unbiased software helps perpetuation of prejudices, which is why design of equitable AI becomes critical. It is not just a good idea, but a necessity when it comes to addressing the challenges presented by Society 5.0. It is only essential that stakeholders come together to develop technologies embracing human value and at the same time solve the world's problems. This collaboration will help Society 5.0 to be more human-oriented model rather than status quo, which will only make people more frustrated and dehumanized.

Emerging Questions in a Technological Era

As Society 5.0 advances, new philosophical questions will inevitably arise, challenging our understanding of consciousness, morality, and identity in the age of AI and robotics.

New Forms of Consciousness: Advances in AI and neuroscience raise profound questions about the nature of consciousness and its potential artificial or hybrid forms. Philosophers like Chalmers (1995) highlight the "hard problem" of consciousness, which concerns the subjective experience of being. If AI systems were to achieve self-awareness, what ethical and legal rights should they possess? Such questions extend beyond technical feasibility to the realm of moral philosophy, compelling society to rethink the boundaries of personhood and moral consideration.

Posthuman Morality

In a posthuman society where humans and intelligent machines coexist, moral frameworks may need to evolve to accommodate non-human agents. Singer's (1975) principle of equal consideration of interests suggests that moral status could be extended to AI systems if they demonstrate capacities such as suffering or preference. This raises questions about the moral obligations of humans toward machines and whether AI should be included in ethical deliberations traditionally reserved for sentient beings.

Evolving Notions of Identity

Technologies like brain-computer interfaces and AI avatars blur the boundaries between humans and machines, challenging traditional notions of selfhood and individuality. Haraway's (1985) concept of the cyborg provides a framework for understanding these hybrid identities, but further philosophical inquiry is needed to address their implications for autonomy and societal integration. For example, how do such technologies redefine personal agency and the sense of self in a world increasingly mediated by machines?

These emerging questions emphasize the need for ongoing philosophical engagement with technological advancements. Without such inquiry, Society 5.0 risks advancing technology without fully understanding its implications for the human condition. Philosophical reflection ensures that these developments align with ethical and existential principles, fostering a society that values both innovation and humanity.

Implications for Education and Policy

The transformative potential of Society 5.0 extends to education and public policy, where philosophical inquiry can play a pivotal role in shaping curricula and governance.

Educational Curricula

To thrive in Society 5.0, individuals need more than technical skills; they require critical thinking, ethical awareness, and interdisciplinary collaboration. Educational programs should integrate courses on AI ethics, digital literacy, and the societal impacts of technology. Floridi (2014) emphasizes the importance of teaching students to critically evaluate their relationship with technology, fostering a deeper understanding of its ethical and existential implications. By engaging with philosophical perspectives, students can navigate the complexities of technological innovation with greater awareness and responsibility.

Public Policy

Policymakers must address the ethical challenges posed by Society 5.0, such as the digital divide, algorithmic bias, and privacy concerns. Philosophical frameworks like Rawls' (1971) theory of justice offer valuable guidance for creating equitable policies that prioritize the welfare of marginalized communities. For instance, regulations like the General Data Protection Regulation (GDPR) in the European Union emphasize individual rights and data protection, serving as a model for ethical governance in a technology-driven world (Voigt & Von dem Bussche, 2017).

In addition to addressing current challenges, policymakers must anticipate future ethical dilemmas, such as the deployment of autonomous weapons or AI-driven healthcare systems. By integrating philosophical principles into policy design, governments can ensure that technological advancements enhance human well-being while preserving ethical and existential values.

By grounding technological innovation in philosophical principles and fostering interdisciplinary collaboration, Society 5.0 can navigate the complexities of the technological era with wisdom and humanity. The integration of ethics into education, policy, and technology design ensures that progress aligns with the diverse needs and aspirations of individuals and societies. Through deliberate effort and reflection, Society 5.0 offers the potential to redefine the human condition in ways that uphold dignity, foster flourishing, and embrace the shared challenges of a rapidly evolving world.

CONCLUSION

Society 5.0 is a new paradigm in which technology is as significant as it is in the reinvention of human life essentials., this kind of vision incarnates AI, robotics and IoT to the extent that identity, meaning and agency are reframed. It does so by subverting philosophical concepts and globalizing a radical proposition that asks one to look beyond the cavemen like nature and the machinery of our biological Constitution.

Indeed, philosophical approach is crucial in relation to these changes. It supplies the concepts which allow evaluating the ethical, existential, and societal consequences of the advancement of technologies. Immanual Kant's ethics assertion holds human sovereignty sacrosanct while Rawles (1971) on equity of formulation of technological advantages. These frameworks can help shape use of AI although its potential should be harnessed so as to improve the quality of life of individuals. For Society 5.0, all these areas involve ethics, Existentialism, and world peace or the lack of it. From an ethical perspective, is fosters a number of emerging pressing concerns such as bias, unfairness, and privacy in the AI systems (Buolamwini & Gebru, 2018). Existentially it makes people to be in a position of confronting the contrast between the use of technology and the quality existence. This is where Heidegger (1977) posited about the danger of bringing human life to a mode of orchestrated processes ends up limiting human life by denying people the possibility of a full existence. There is an expectation that for the principle of Society 5.0 of inclusiveness and equity whereby, cultural diversities and human rights and /or fundamental enrich and engender common universal values across cultures, disciplines as well as nations, there is need to work collectively but cooperatively.

Finally, Society 5.0 transforms the human existence by rendering technology as the part of existence, and redesigning what being human holistically means in terms of individual and collective identity, vocation, and freedom. It is in its potential for integrating the advancement of technology in general society, it provides meaning to assuage the advancement of technology for everyone. Still, it can happen only when people treat such a reality with due responsibility, following the principles of ethics and with reference to philosophical contribution. That way, Society 5.0 does not just mask the truly progressive pursuit of the human spirit, but actually opens up that direction by focusing on the reflections and increased intentionality.

REFERENCES

Angwin, J., Larson, J., Mattu, S., & Kirchner, L. (2016). Machine bias. *ProPublica*. Retrieved from https://www.propublica.org/article/machine-bias-risk-assessments-in-criminal-sentencing

Arendt, H. (1958). *The Human Condition*. University of Chicago Press.

Aristotle. (350 BCE/1999). *Nicomachean Ethics* (T. Irwin, Trans.). Hackett Publishing.

Benjamin, W. (2001). The Work of Art in the Age of Mechanical Reproduction. In Arendt, H. (Ed.), *Illuminations* (pp. 217–251). Pimlico. (Original work published 1935)

Berlin, I. (1958). Two concepts of liberty. In I. Berlin, *Four Essays on Liberty* (pp. 118–172). Oxford University Press.

Bostrom, N. (2014). *Superintelligence: Paths, Dangers, Strategies*. Oxford University Press.

Buolamwini, J., & Gebru, T. (2018). Gender shades: Intersectional accuracy disparities in commercial gender classification. *Proceedings of the 1st Conference on Fairness, Accountability and Transparency*, 77–91.

Cabinet Office of Japan. (2017). *Society 5.0: Aiming for a new human-centered society*. Retrieved from https://www8.cao.go.jp/cstp/society5_0/

Chalmers, D. J. (1995). Facing up to the problem of consciousness. *Journal of Consciousness Studies*, *2*(3), 200–219.

Churchland, P. M. (1989). *Neurophilosophy: Toward a Unified Science of the Mind-Brain*. MIT Press.

Coeckelbergh, M. (2020). *AI Ethics*. MIT Press.

Crawford, K., & Paglen, T. (2019). Excavating AI: The politics of images in machine learning training sets. *Excavating AI Project*. https://excavating.ai

Descartes, R. (1996). *Meditations on First Philosophy* (Cottingham, J., Trans.). Cambridge University Press. (Original work published 1641)

Eubanks, V. (2018). *Automating Inequality: How High-Tech Tools Profile, Police, and Punish the Poor*. St. Martin's Press.

Floridi, L. (2014). *The Fourth Revolution: How the Infosphere is Reshaping Human Reality*. Oxford University Press.

Floridi, L., Cowls, J., Beltrametti, M., Chatila, R., Chazerand, P., Dignum, V., & Schafer, B. (2018). AI4People—An ethical framework for a good AI society: Opportunities, risks, principles, and recommendations. *Minds and Machines*, *28*(4), 689–707. DOI: 10.1007/s11023-018-9482-5 PMID: 30930541

Haraway, D. (1985). A manifesto for cyborgs: Science, technology, and socialist feminism in the 1980s. *Socialist Review*, *80*, 65–108.

Hayles, N. K. (1999). *How We Became Posthuman: Virtual Bodies in Cybernetics, Literature, and Informatics*. University of Chicago Press.

Hegel, G. W. F. (1977). *The Phenomenology of Spirit* (Miller, A. V., Trans.). Oxford University Press. (Original work published 1807)

Heidegger, M. (1927/1962). *Being and Time* (Macquarrie, J., & Robinson, E., Trans.). Harper & Row.

Heidegger, M. (1977). *The Question Concerning Technology*. Harper & Row.

Jumper, J., Evans, R., Pritzel, A., Green, T., Figurnov, M., Ronneberger, O., & Hassabis, D. (2021). Highly accurate protein structure prediction with AlphaFold. *Nature*, *596*(7873), 583–589. DOI: 10.1038/s41586-021-03819-2 PMID: 34265844

Kant, I. (1996). *Groundwork of the Metaphysics of Morals* (Gregor, M., Trans.). Cambridge University Press. (Original work published 1785)

Latour, B. (2005). *Reassembling the Social: An Introduction to Actor-Network Theory*. Oxford University Press.

Lin, P. (2016). Why ethics matters for autonomous cars. In Maurer, M., Gerdes, J. C., Lenz, B., & Winner, H. (Eds.), *Autonomes Fahren* (pp. 69–85). Springer., DOI: 10.1007/978-3-662-48847-8_4

Marx, K. (1978). Economic and Philosophic Manuscripts of 1844. In Tucker, R. C. (Ed.), *The Marx-Engels Reader* (pp. 66–125). Norton. (Original work published 1844)

Maslow, A. H. (1943). A theory of human motivation. *Psychological Review*, *50*(4), 370–396. DOI: 10.1037/h0054346

Mill, J. S. (1998). *Utilitarianism* (Crisp, R., Ed.). Oxford University Press. (Original work published 1863)

O'Neil, C. (2016). *Weapons of Math Destruction: How Big Data Increases Inequality and Threatens Democracy*. Crown Publishing Group.

Pariser, E. (2011). *The Filter Bubble: What the Internet Is Hiding from You*. Penguin Press.

Rawls, J. (1971). *A Theory of Justice*. Harvard University Press.

Sartre, J.-P. (1992). *Being and Nothingness: An Essay on Phenomenological Ontology*. Washington Square Press.

Searle, J. R. (1980). Minds, brains, and programs. *Behavioral and Brain Sciences, 3*(3), 417–424. DOI: 10.1017/S0140525X00005756

Singer, P. (1975). *Animal Liberation: A New Ethics for Our Treatment of Animals*. HarperCollins.

Turkle, S. (2011). *Alone Together: Why We Expect More from Technology and Less from Each Other*. Basic Books.

Voigt, P., & Von dem Bussche, A. (2017). *The EU General Data Protection Regulation (GDPR): A Practical Guide*. Springer.

Wallach, W., & Allen, C. (2008). *Moral Machines: Teaching Robots Right from Wrong*. Oxford University Press.

West, D. M. (2018). *The Future of Work: Robots, AI, and Automation*. Brookings Institution Press.

Zuboff, S. (2019). *The Age of Surveillance Capitalism: The Fight for a Human Future at the New Frontier of Power*. PublicAffairs.

Chapter 2
Rethinking Society 5.0 of AI-Driven Educational Innovation:
The Philosophical Underpinnings

Oindrilla Ghosh
https://orcid.org/0000-0001-9609-0781
Christ University, India

Binod Kumar
https://orcid.org/0009-0002-9721-1367
Radha Govind University, India

ABSTRACT

Society 5.0 represents a transformative paradigm that merges digital and physical spaces through advanced technologies, particularly artificial intelligence (AI). This vision aims to create a sustainable, inclusive society where human well-being is prioritized. By rethinking educational frameworks, we can foster creativity, critical thinking, and emotional intelligence in learners. Philosophically, the integration of AI into education raises essential questions about agency, equity, and ethics. It challenges us to consider how technology can augment human potential without diminishing the intrinsic values of education. In Society 5.0, educators are tasked with not only imparting knowledge but also cultivating a sense of responsibility and ethics in future citizens who will navigate an AI-enhanced world. Furthermore, AI has the potential to customize learning experiences, promoting inclusivity and accessibility. Ultimately, rethinking education within Society 5.0 paves the way for a harmonious coexistence between technology and humanity.

DOI: 10.4018/979-8-3373-1062-6.ch002

Copyright © 2026, IGI Global Scientific Publishing. Copying or distributing in print or electronic forms without written permission of IGI Global Scientific Publishing is prohibited.

INTRODUCTION

In the rapidly evolving landscape of the 21st century, the convergence of artificial intelligence (AI) with educational paradigms has ushered in a transformative era referred to as "Society 5.0." (Atiyeh et al., 2023) This concept, which originated in Japan, embodies a vision of a human-centered society where advanced technologies coexist harmoniously with human needs and societal responsibilities (van der Vorst & Jelicic, 2019). As we grapple with the complexities of this technological renaissance, rethinking educational innovation through the lens of Society 5.0 becomes imperative (Kai et al., 2018). The integration of AI in education not only enhances learning efficiencies but also possesses the potential to reshape the fundamental nature of knowledge dissemination and acquisition (Gamage et al., 2023).

The philosophical underpinnings of this integration guide us in understanding the ethical implications, epistemological shifts, and socio-cultural transformations associated with AI-driven educational practices (Murray, 2023). At its core, Society 5.0 espouses a holistic approach to balancing technological advancements with human welfare, emphasizing sustainability, inclusivity, and the cultivation of well-rounded individuals capable of thriving in a complex world (Perkins, 2023). This necessitates a robust engagement with philosophical questions regarding the role and purpose of education in society, the nature of intelligence and knowledge, and the ethical dimensions of AI deployment in pedagogical contexts (ClassPoint, 2024).

AI applications in education can provide personalized learning experiences, adaptive assessments, and real-time feedback mechanisms that cater to individual learning styles and paces (Ibrahim et al., 2023). However, this innovation raises critical inquiries about the essence of learning and the role of educators (Scribes, 2024). What does meaningful learning look like in an AI-enhanced environment? How do we preserve the human elements of creativity, empathy, and critical thinking in a data-driven educational landscape? These questions invite a deeper (Selwyn, 2022) philosophical examination of how we define knowledge, intelligence, and the objectives of education itself, urging us to re-evaluate traditional paradigms that prioritize rote memorization and standardized testing (Cardona et al., 2023).

HISTORICAL EVOLUTION

The historical evolution of educational innovation, particularly in the context of Society 5.0 and AI-driven initiatives, can be traced through various pivotal moments and philosophical shifts (D'Errico, 2007) that have shaped our understanding of knowledge and learning. This evolution is marked by a gradual transition from rigid, industrial-age educational models to more flexible, learner-centric paradigms (Cuban, 2001). The evolution of education has always mirrored the prevailing societal, economic, and technological currents, and understanding this journey is crucial to contextualizing Society 5.0 (Esposito, Sangrà, and Maina, 2013).

In the early 20th century, the field of education was largely influenced by industrialization, resulting in a standardized model designed to produce workers for factories (Dusek, 2006). This era emphasized rote learning, discipline, and uniformity, often neglecting the individual needs and potentials of students (Perrotta and Evans, 2013). However, the mid-20th century marked a shift toward progressive education, spurred by the humanistic psychology movement led by figures such as Carl Rogers and Abraham Maslow, who championed personal growth and self-directed learning (Mayes, 1995).

The advent of digital technology in the latter part of the 20th century further catalyzed educational transformation (Chiang et al., 2016). The emergence of the internet and digital resources decentralized access to information, challenging traditional classroom dynamics (Januszewski and Persichitte, 2008). Educators began harnessing technology for interactive learning experiences, and constructivist theories of education emphasized the learner's active role in knowledge construction (Latchem, 2014). This period laid the groundwork for contemporary educational practices that recognize the varied intelligences and learning styles of students (Friesen, 2009).

As we entered the 21st century, the rapid advancements in AI and machine learning ushered in a new era of educational innovation (Czerniewicz, 2010). The emergence of intelligent tutoring systems, adaptive learning platforms, and data-driven analytics has transformed classrooms into personalized learning environments (Oliver,2013). These AI-driven technologies not only facilitate individualized instruction but also offer insights into student performance, enabling educators to tailor their approaches to meet diverse learner needs (Braden, 1995).

The concept of Society 5.0 originated in Japan in the late 2010s, positioning itself as a response to the challenges posed by smart technologies that threaten human-centric values (Arthur, 2009). Society 5.0 envisions a harmonious integration of advanced technologies with societal issues, emphasizing human well-being, sustainability, and inclusivity (Selwyn, 2014). The educational sector plays a pivotal role in realizing this vision, as it must prepare individuals for a future where technological proficiency and ethical considerations are intertwined (Hew and Cheung, 2014).

In the context of Society 5.0, AI-driven educational innovations must address historical inequalities while fostering a more holistic approach to learning (Sergio et al., 2011). The discourse surrounding equitable access to technology, particularly in underserved communities, reflects a growing awareness of social responsibility in educational practices (Christensen, 2008). Philosophical considerations regarding equity and justice are essential for guiding the deployment of AI in ways that do not perpetuate existing disparities (Thumlert, Castell, and Jenson, 2015).

THEORETICAL FRAMEWORKS

Rethinking Society 5.0 through the lens of AI-driven educational innovation necessitates a solid theoretical framework that integrates various disciplines and perspectives (Ladyman, 2007). This reconfiguration seeks not only to innovate educational practices but to deeply transform social structures and individual experiences (Heidegger, 1996). One of the pivotal frameworks is the concept of Constructivism, which posits that learners construct knowledge through experiences and interactions within their environments (Haraway, 1988). In environments increasingly influenced by artificial intelligence, this framework serves to emphasize the role of technology as a facilitator of learning rather than just a tool (Dépelteau, 2008).

Constructivist theories are complemented by social constructivism, which emphasizes the importance of culture and context in the learning process (Heidegger, 1959). As Society 5.0 aims to create a "super-smart society," it leverages AI to enhance collaborative learning experiences (Whitehead, 1929). Social constructivism asserts that knowledge is constructed through dialogue and collaboration, which can be augmented through AI-powered platforms that promote interaction among students, educators, and educational resources (Surry and Baker, 2016). This introduces a democratizing effect by providing equitable access to diverse learning opportunities, thereby challenging traditional hierarchies in education (Wu 2009).

Another vital theoretical framework is Systems Theory, which views society as an interconnected web where changes in one facet can influence others (Marx, 1964). The integration of AI into educational ecosystems aligns seamlessly with Systems Theory, as AI technologies can analyze vast datasets to inform and enhance educational policies, personalize learning, and optimize resource allocation (Allenby and Sarewitz, 2011). The interplay between different variables such as educators, learners, technology, and socio-economic contexts illustrates the need for a holistic approach to educational innovation in Society 5.0 (Marx, 1975).

Additionally, the Capability Approach, developed by Amartya Sen and furthered by Martha Nussbaum, emphasizes the importance of individual capabilities and the functionings that enable individuals to lead fulfilling lives (Bayne, 2015). This approach aligns with the goals of Society 5.0, which seeks to empower individuals through technology (Heidegger, 1996). AI-driven educational innovations can be analyzed through this lens, as they have the potential to enhance students' capabilities by providing tailored educational experiences, fostering critical thinking, and promoting lifelong learning skills essential in a rapidly changing world (Zhao et al., 2002).

Integrating these frameworks calls for a multidimensional theoretical approach that can navigate the complexities of AI-driven educational innovation (Mayes, 1995). Importantly, an Ethical Framework must also inform the development and deployment of AI in education (Latour, 2004). Addressing issues such as privacy, bias, and the digital divide is crucial as we strive for an inclusive Society 5.0 (Heidegger, 1971). Ethical considerations ensure that AI applications promote equity and do not exacerbate existing inequalities in education (Friesen, 2009).

FOUNDATIONS

The philosophical foundations underpinning the rethinking of Society 5.0, particularly in the context of AI-driven educational innovation, can be traced back to several key philosophies, including pragmatism, constructivism, and humanism (Ihde, 1990). These philosophies offer unique perspectives on the implications of AI in education and the ways it can be harnessed to nurture personal and societal growth (Weiss, 2008).

Pragmatism, which emphasizes the practical application of ideas and the experiential nature of knowledge, is particularly salient in the context of Society 5.0 (Verbeek 2008). Pragmatists advocate for a learning process that is grounded in real-world contexts, allowing students to engage meaningfully with their environments (An and Li, 2014). In an AI-driven educational landscape, pragmatism manifests through the use of technology to simulate real-life scenarios, enabling students to apply theoretical concepts in practical situations (Hegel, 1967). This not only enhances problem-solving skills but also prepares learners for the complexities of future societal challenges, fostering adaptability in an uncertain world (Heidegger, 1977).

Constructivism, which posits that learning is an active, contextualized process of knowledge construction, is another fundamental philosophy shaping the educational discourse in Society 5.0 (Gehlen, 1988). This perspective underscores the importance of active learner engagement and the construction of knowledge through interaction with others and technology (Kant, 1990). Here, AI plays a critical role by providing adaptive learning environments that respond to individual learners' needs, facilitating personalized pathways that respect diverse learning styles (Freire, 2005). This philosophical underpinning champions the idea that education should not only be about the transmission of knowledge but should also cultivate critical thinking, creativity, and collaboration skills essential for thriving in an AI-integrated world (Donnelly, 2007).

Humanism, emphasizing the inherent worth of individuals and the importance of personal agency, further enriches the philosophical discourse surrounding Society 5.0 (Willet, 2018). A humanistic approach to education emphasizes student-centered learning and the importance of fostering individual potential, ethical considerations, and social responsibility (Reich, Garrison, and Neubert, 2016). In the context of AI, this perspective raises crucial questions regarding the ethical deployment of technology in learning environments (Chan & Tsi, 2023). The humanistic philosophy calls for a mindful integration of AI that prioritizes student welfare, equity, and holistic development over mere efficiency or technological prowess (Halagatti et al., 2023).

Moreover, these philosophical strands intersect at the notion of ethics in educational innovation (Dewey, 1916). Rethinking Society 5.0 requires a critical examination of the ethical implications of AI in education, such as data privacy, algorithmic transparency, and equitable access to technology (van der Vorst & Jelicic, 2019). By grounding AI-driven educational practices in a strong ethical framework, educators and policymakers can ensure that innovations serve not just individual learners but also foster social inclusivity and cohesion (Gamage et al., 2023).

IMPORTANCE

The concept of Society 5.0 represents a paradigm shift aimed at balancing technological advancement with human welfare, focusing on creating a sustainable, inclusive, and resilient society (Selwyn, 2022). The integration of artificial intelligence (AI) in educational innovation plays a crucial role in redefining this societal framework (Zootzky & Pfeiffer, 2024). At its core, the importance of rethinking Society 5.0 through AI-driven educational innovation lies in its potential to align educational systems with the changing needs of both individuals and communities (Cardona et al., 2023).

Firstly, the rapid evolution of technology necessitates a reexamination of educational methodologies (Pedaste et al., 2015). Traditional education often emphasizes rote learning and standardized testing, whereas AI innovations enable personalized learning experiences that can cater to the unique needs of each student (Smith, 2022). The philosophical underpinning here is rooted in constructivism, which posits that learners construct knowledge through experience (Mason, 2008). AI can help tailor these experiences by analyzing individual learning patterns, preferences, and progress (Moqbel & Al-Kadi, 2023). Thus, rethinking education through this lens promotes the philosophy of lifelong learning, essential for preparing individuals to adapt to an ever-changing job landscape in a Society 5.0 (Heidegger, 1996).

Additionally, the ethical implications of AI in education cannot be overlooked. The accessibility of educational resources powered by AI can potentially bridge the gap between different socio-economic groups (Halagatti et al., 2023). In a Society 5.0 context, inclusivity is paramount (Heidegger, 1971). AI can facilitate access to high-quality educational materials for marginalized communities, thus embodying the philosophical ideals of equity and social justice (Thomson, 2004). As educational institutions adopt AI technologies, they have a moral responsibility to ensure these innovations do not exacerbate existing inequalities but rather serve as tools for empowerment (Pearce & Chiavaroli, 2023).

Another important consideration is the development of critical thinking and emotional intelligence in students (Wrathall, 2011). AI-driven educational innovations can automate various tasks, allowing educators to focus on cultivating soft skills that are increasingly valuable in the workforce (Murgatroyd, 2023). The Socratic method and other philosophical traditions emphasize the importance of dialogue and critical engagement in learning (Huang and Liu, 2016). By rethinking education to incorporate AI, we can prioritize the development of collaborative, communicative, and empathetic individuals who can thrive in diverse environments (Deng, 2018).

Moreover, the philosophical underpinning of communal resilience is vital in Society 5.0 (ClassPoint, 2024). By harnessing AI in education, we can promote collective learning and knowledge-sharing among communities (Koh & Doroudi, 2023). AI-hubs can function as platforms where individuals come together to solve local challenges, encouraging a sense of belonging and mutual support (Heidegger, 2000). This communal approach aligns with the philosophical principles of communitarianism, which stress the importance of community values in education (Roll et al., 2011).

GOVERNANCE

Governance in the context of Society 5.0, particularly regarding AI-driven educational innovation, demands a comprehensive framework that addresses the ethical, legal, and social implications of technological integration in education (Trajtenberg, 2018). As we navigate this new terrain, a governance model must reflect the fundamental philosophical principles of transparency, accountability, and inclusivity (Pezze, 2006). The governing bodies need to ensure that AI innovations are curated in a way that promotes beneficial outcomes while minimizing harm to society (Cardona et al., 2023).

The first philosophical pillar underpinning effective governance in this context is transparency (Mitcham, 2006). Stakeholders, including educators, students, parents, and policymakers, must have access to clear information regarding how AI tools are utilized in educational settings (Harrer, 2023). This relates to the philosophical tradition of Enlightenment thought, advocating for informed citizenry and rational debate (Oliver and Conole, 2003). By fostering an open dialogue about the algorithms and data used in AI education systems, governance can mitigate fears and encourage a collaborative approach to technological adaptation (Eynon, 2015). Transparency also aids in building trust, which is essential for the successful implementation of any innovative educational framework (Feenberg, 2002).

Accountability constitutes the second crucial pillar of governance. In the era of AI, the responsibility for decisions made by intelligent systems must be clearly defined (Clegg and Steel, 2002). Educational institutions must establish ethical guidelines that delineate who is accountable when AI technologies malfunction or perpetuate bias (Lindgren et al., 2016). This involves adopting a deontological perspective, wherein actions are judged based on adherence to ethical norms rather than outcomes alone (Ihde, 2003). Policies should be crafted to ensure that educators retain agency over the educational process, using AI as a supportive tool rather than a controlling force (Selwyn, 2010). This accountability helps reassure stakeholders that AI is being employed as a positive force for development rather than a mechanism for control or exploitation (Selwyn, 2022).

Inclusivity forms the third pillar of effective governance in the governance of AI-driven educational innovations (Gamage et al., 2023). It is imperative that the development and implementation of AI tools consider diverse perspectives, particularly from marginalized communities (Nikolopoulou, 2024a). The philosophical underpinnings of democracy and pluralism call for the active participation of various societal groups in decision-making processes (Lee & Soylu, 2023). In practice, this could involve stakeholder forums where students, teachers, parents, and community leaders systematically contribute their insights on the design and deployment of AI educational technologies (Kai et al., 2018). This inclusive governance not only enriches the policy-making process but also ensures that AI innovations effectively address the needs of all societal segments (Chen & Perez, 2023).

Lastly, continuous evaluation and adaptation are essential in a rapidly changing technological landscape (Dogan et al., 2023). Governance frameworks must incorporate mechanisms for ongoing assessment and feedback (Oliver, 2011). Drawing from pragmatic philosophy, which emphasizes the importance of experiential learning, adaptive governance promotes a cyclic approach that allows for revisions based on what works effectively (Cuban, 2001). By creating avenues for feedback and iterative improvement, educational systems can evolve alongside technological advancements, ensuring they remain relevant and effective in promoting learning outcomes (Beckera and Birdib, 2018).

ACCOUNTABILITY

Accountability is a pivotal concept in the context of Society 5.0, wherein the integration of artificial intelligence (AI) and machine learning (ML) drives innovations in various sectors, notably education (Latour, 2005). As society transitions into this new era marked by a confluence of digital and physical spaces the need for clarity and responsibility in technology's deployment and governance becomes increasingly critical (Oliver, 2015). In education, where AI and ML can offer personalized learning experiences, the question of accountability arises on multiple fronts (Lewin and Lundie, 2016).

First, educational institutions must ensure that AI systems are developed and implemented responsibly (Ouyang et al., 2022). The algorithms powering AI-driven educational tools often rely on extensive datasets that may contain biases or inaccuracies (Salinas-Navarro et al., 2024). This potential for bias raises ethical dilemmas regarding equitable access to education (Kirkwood and Price, 2014). For instance, if an AI-driven educational platform unintentionally favors certain demographic groups over others, it compromises not only the fairness of the education system but also the overall trust in technology (Greco & Cinganotto, 2023). Therefore, institutions must prioritize the ethical design of AI tools, ensuring that they are inclusive and unbiased (Zimmerman, Forlizzi, and Evenson, 2007).

Additionally, accountability extends to the developers and technologists creating these educational tools. Stakeholders must establish robust standards and protocols governing the design, testing, and deployment of AI algorithms (Minocha and Reeves, 2010). This includes regular auditing of AI systems to assess their efficacy and identify and mitigate any computational biases that may arise (Ibrahim et al., 2023). Transparency in how AI systems make decisions is also paramount; educational stakeholders, including students and parents, should have accessible information about how their data is used and how AI-generated recommendations are derived (Agalianos, Whitty, and Noss, 2006).

Another dimension of accountability in Society 5.0 involves the ongoing monitoring and evaluation of AI tools' impact on educational outcomes (Hooda et al., 2022). As AI-driven innovations become integrated into classrooms, educators must assess whether these technologies genuinely enhance learning experiences (Reveley, 2013). Educational institutions should foster a culture of feedback and adaptability, enabling educators to iterate and improve upon AI tools based on real-world classroom experiences (Martínez-Comesaña et al., 2023). This collaborative approach establishes a feedback loop for accountability, sustaining a continual improvement ethos that aligns technological application with pedagogical goals (Peters, 2020).

Moreover, the role of policy and regulation cannot be overlooked in fostering accountability within AI-driven education (Orchard, 2020). Governments and educational bodies must collaborate to establish clear regulations that hold companies and institutions accountable for their AI tools' ethical implications (Nikolopoulou, 2024b). Such regulations could define standards for data privacy, algorithmic fairness, and the representation of minority groups in educational content delivery, thereby reinforcing a societal commitment to ethical education practices (Moore et al., 2023).

AUGMENTED REALITY (AR) IN SOCIETY 5.0

Augmented Reality (AR) represents a transformative shift in educational paradigms within the framework of Society 5.0, where human-centric approaches and advanced technological integration harmonize (Jackson, 2020a). This integration resonates well with the philosophical underpinnings of pragmatism and constructivism (Rudolph et al., 2024). With AR, learning transcends traditional confines by layering digital information onto the physical environment, creating immersive experiences that encourage exploration and curiosity (Perkins, 2023).

From a pragmatic standpoint, AR emphasizes experiential learning, where individuals learn through direct interaction with their surroundings (Varaki, 2021). This suggests a shift from passive knowledge acquisition to a more active learning process, fostering critical thinking and problem-solving skills (Hung, 2020). The philosophical heritage of Dewey's educational theories aligns with AR's potential, as it encourages learners to engage with real-world contexts, enabling them to construct knowledge based on their observations and experiences (Kato, 2020).

Moreover, AR's integration into Society 5.0 reflects a constructivist viewpoint, whereby learners actively construct their understanding of complex concepts through interactive experiences (Papastephanou, 2020). This aligns with Vygotsky's notion of the zone of proximal development, as AR can scaffold learning by providing contextual support, thus enabling learners to navigate challenges at their skill level (Buchanan, 2021).

VIRTUAL REALITY (VR) IN SOCIETY 5.0

Virtual Reality (VR) stands at the forefront of educational innovation, particularly in the context of Society 5.0, which emphasizes a seamless integration of advanced technologies and human-centric values (Biesta, 2021). The philosophical underpinnings of VR in education draw heavily from existentialism and experiential learning theories (Roth, 2020). This immersive approach challenges traditional educational models by creating environments where learners can engage deeply with material in a simulated context (Sardoc, 2020).

From an existentialist perspective, VR offers a unique opportunity for personal experience and self-discovery (Waghid, 2020). Learners can step into a myriad of scenarios, fostering a sense of agency and personal connection to the knowledge being explored (Roll et al., 2011). This aligns with the ideas of thinkers like Jean-Paul Sartre, who emphasized the importance of individual experience in shaping understanding (Joanne et al., 2024). VR's capacity for providing visceral experiences allows learners to confront real-world dilemmas in a safe setting, encouraging critical reflection and moral reasoning (Jandric, 2020).

Additionally, the experiential learning theory, championed by David Kolb, aligns with VR's immersive capabilities (Tesar, 2021). By engaging in a full-sensory learning experience, students can cycle through concrete experiences, reflective observation, abstract conceptualization, and active experimentation (Roy, 2020). This process mirrors Kolb's learning cycle and promotes deeper understanding and retention of information, as learners actively participate in the knowledge construction process (Glaude, 2020).

MIXED REALITY (MR) IN SOCIETY 5.0

Mixed Reality (MR), as an emerging frontier in educational innovation, serves as a compelling component of Society 5.0, exemplifying the confluence of technology with humanistic values (Gloria Ladson-Billings, 2021). Philosophically, MR embodies the principles of systems thinking and participatory learning, emphasizing interconnectedness and collaboration in the educational landscape (Harari, 2014).

At its core, MR allows for a seamless integration of the physical and digital worlds, fostering an environment where learners can interact with both real and virtual elements simultaneously (Perkins, 2023). This capability aligns closely with systems thinking, which posits that learning should not be viewed in isolation but rather as part of a complex web of interactions and relationships (Garroutte & Westcott, 2013). By engaging with simulations that incorporate real-world challenges alongside digital data, learners can develop a holistic understanding of problems, reflecting the interconnectedness inherent in contemporary issues (Marker, 2018).

Furthermore, participatory learning theories underscore the importance of collaboration and community engagement in education (Barad, 2019). MR technologies enable shared experiences where learners can work together, irrespective of their physical locations, highlighting the social constructivist perspective that knowledge is co-created through interaction (Braidotti, 2019). This collaborative aspect is reminiscent of Vygotsky's emphasis on social learning, as MR environments facilitate peer-to-peer learning, fostering dialogue and shared problem-solving (Rosiek et al., 2020).

ADVANTAGES

In the context of Society 5.0, a concept that integrates advanced technology into everyday life for the benefit of society, AI-driven educational innovation offers transformative advantages (Deleuze, 1995). At the core of this approach is the melding of human creativity with automated systems, facilitating an educational paradigm shift that seeks to address diverse societal needs (Jackson & Mazzei, 2012).

One of the primary advantages of AI in education is personalized learning (Crawford et al., 2023). AI technologies can analyze vast amounts of data concerning individual students' learning styles, challenges, and preferences, allowing for tailored educational experiences (Hooda et al., 2022). This customization promotes enhanced engagement and retention, which contrasts with the one-size-fits-all model prevalent in traditional education (Salinas-Navarro et al., 2024). The results can lead to improved learning outcomes and increased student satisfaction, as learners receive support that resonates with their needs (Siegel, 1983).

Moreover, AI-driven tools can enhance access to education across geographical and socioeconomic divides (Perkins, 2023). Utilizing online platforms, AI can provide quality educational resources to remote or underserved communities, democratizing access to information (Atiyeh et al., 2023).

CHALLENGES

Despite the numerous advantages AI-driven educational innovation brings to Society 5.0, significant challenges remain that warrant critical reflection (van der Vorst & Jelicic, 2019). The philosophical dilemmas associated with this transformation extend beyond mere technology and touch upon fundamental issues such as ethics, equity, and the very essence of education (Gamage et al., 2023).

One of the most pressing challenges is the potential for bias in AI algorithms (Kai et al., 2018). If not adequately designed and implemented, AI systems can perpetuate and even exacerbate existing biases within education (Murray, 2023). For instance, if training data reflect historical inequalities, the AI may reinforce those biases, disadvantaging particular groups of students (Perkins, 2023). This concern highlights the ethical implications of relying on AI in educational settings, as consequently, marginalized learners may suffer from reduced opportunities (Ibrahim et al., 2023).

Another challenge lies in the disparity of access to technology (Scribes, 2024). While AI has the potential to democratize education, it can also widen the gap between those who have access to advanced technologies and those who do not (Selwyn, 2022). Students in affluent areas are likely to gain more from AI educational innovations compared to their peers in underprivileged regions (Cardona et al.,

2023). This inequity raises philosophical questions about the equity of educational opportunities and can lead to systemic inequities that persist across generations (Chan & Tsi, 2023).

ETHICAL CONSIDERATIONS

The integration of Artificial Intelligence (AI) into educational contexts has led to significant advancements, prompting a reevaluation of our traditional pedagogical paradigms (Halagatti et al., 2023). As we transition into Society 5.0, where technology and human values converge, ethical considerations assume paramount importance (Selwyn, 2022). The philosophical foundations of this innovative society compel us to address concerns surrounding equity, privacy, data ownership, and the responsibility of AI systems in shaping educational trajectories (Zootzky & Pfeiffer, 2024).

At the heart of ethical considerations in AI-driven educational innovation lies the principle of equity (Cardona et al., 2023). The deployment of AI tools must ensure that every learner, regardless of their socio-economic background, has access to quality education (Smith, 2022). This calls for a critical examination of how technology is distributed and utilized within educational institutions (Moqbel & Al-Kadi, 2023). Unequal access to AI-enhanced tools can exacerbate existing educational disparities, preventing marginalized populations from benefiting from technological advancements (Pearce & Chiavaroli, 2023). As stakeholders in education, policymakers and institutions must prioritize inclusivity and accessibility, ensuring that all learners can partake in the transformative potential of AI (Murgatroyd, 2023).

Furthermore, privacy and data protection emerge as pressing ethical concerns (Koh & Doroudi, 2023). The use of AI in educational settings generates vast amounts of data about students' learning behaviors, preferences, and performance (Trajtenberg, 2018). This data, if not handled responsibly, poses risks to students' privacy and autonomy (Harrer, 2023). Educational institutions must establish robust frameworks that protect student information from misuse or unauthorized access (Oliver and Conole, 2003). Additionally, transparency regarding data collection and usage is vital (Selwyn, 2022). Students and parents should be informed about how their data is utilized, fostering trust between stakeholders while adhering to ethical data governance principles (Gamage et al., 2023).

IMPLEMENTATION OF REGULATORY FRAMEWORKS

The implementation of regulatory frameworks for AI-driven educational innovation is a critical task that seeks to balance technological advancements with ethical considerations, data privacy, and equity in access to education (Nikolopoulou, 2024a). As societies transition towards Society 5.0 a concept that envisions a super-smart society leveraging advanced technologies, including AI regulatory frameworks become indispensable in guiding the structures and norms governing these technologies in education (Lee & Soylu, 2023).

First and foremost, regulatory frameworks must address the ethical implications of AI in education (Kai et al., 2018). This involves establishing guidelines to ensure AI systems are fair, transparent, and accountable (Chen & Perez, 2023). Education is not just about knowledge transmission; it deeply influences learners' identity, agency, and future prospects (Dogan et al., 2023). Ethical regulations must safeguard against biases that can arise from incorrect data interpretations or poorly designed algorithms (Beckera and Birdib, 2018). Initiatives like ethical AI guidelines from organizations, academia, and government bodies need to be integrated into the regulatory fabric, offering clear standards that technology developers must follow (Ouyang et al., 2022).

Furthermore, data privacy and security regulations must be enhanced as educational institutions increasingly rely on AI to analyze student performance, personalize learning experiences, and manage administrative tasks (Salinas-Navarro et al., 2024). The collection and processing of vast data sets pose significant risks to student privacy (Greco & Cinganotto, 2023). Governments must bolster existing privacy legislation (like GDPR in Europe) to encompass AI-specific provisions, ensuring that schools and educational platforms treat student data with utmost care (Ibrahim et al., 2023). This may entail mandatory transparency about how data is collected, stored, and utilized and giving students and parents agency over their personal information (Hooda et al., 2022).

Moreover, continuous evaluation mechanisms should be a fundamental component of these regulatory frameworks (Martínez-Comesaña et al., 2023). As technology evolves, continuous feedback loops and periodic assessments can ensure that regulations remain relevant and effective (Peters, 2020). This could be facilitated through collaborative platforms where educators, lawmakers, technologists, and students engage in ongoing dialogues about the impact of AI in education and propose necessary adjustments to ensure that innovations remain beneficial and inclusive (Orchard, 2020).

CONCLUSION

Rethinking Society 5.0 in the context of AI-driven educational innovation entails a profound reconsideration of the philosophical foundations that underpin our approach to teaching and learning (Nikolopoulou, 2024b). As we stand on the brink of an educational transformation driven by advanced technologies, it is crucial to interrogate what it means to live in a society where artificial intelligence profoundly influences knowledge dissemination and learning methodologies (Moore et al., 2023).

Philosophically, this shift implies a move towards constructivist pedagogies concepts that emphasize learners' active role in constructing knowledge rather than being passive recipients (Jackson, 2020a). An AI-driven educational system must reinforce the idea that learning is not merely an accumulation of facts but a dynamic interaction between learners, educators, and technology (Rudolph et al., 2024). Such an environment encourages inquiry, exploration, and collaboration, values essential for navigating the complexities of a rapidly changing world (Perkins, 2023).

FUTURE RESEARCH DIRECTIONS

The journey toward a reimagined Society 5.0 necessitates ongoing research that critically examines the philosophical implications of AI-driven educational innovations (Varaki, 2021). Future research directions should emphasize collaborative interdisciplinary efforts while addressing the socio-ethical dimensions of technology in education.

Exploration of Ethical AI Frameworks

Future research should concentrate on constructing ethical frameworks specifically tailored for AI applications in education. This includes investigating potential biases embedded in AI algorithms (Hung, 2020). Studies could employ philosophical analyses to examine the ethical implications of various decision-making processes undertaken by educational AI systems. Understanding the moral responsibility of developers and institutions in mitigating algorithmic bias can inform best practices and guidelines, ultimately contributing to a more equitable educational landscape.

Impact of AI on Learning Autonomy and Agency

Another critical area for future research is the impact of AI on student autonomy and agency. Philosophical discussions surrounding empowerment, agency, and the role of the learner in a technology-enhanced environment should be prioritized

(Kato, 2020). Addressing questions around how AI can facilitate or hinder students' ability to make autonomous educational choices will shed light on the implications of reliance on technology in learning processes (Ghosh & Kumar, 2025). Researchers could explore student perspectives on their engagement with AI-driven learning tools, assessing both positive and negative dimensions of their dependence on technology.

Longitudinal Studies on AI-Enhanced Learning Environments

Conducting longitudinal studies that track the experiences and outcomes of students within AI-enhanced learning environments can yield valuable insights (Joanne et al., 2024). This research direction focuses on human experiences over time, drawing from philosophical inquiries into the nature of learning and knowledge. Understanding how AI influences not just academic achievement but also emotional and social development can inform the creation of more effective educational practices. This research could align with concepts from developmental psychology and education theory to provide a well-rounded understanding of long-term implications.

Redefining Teacher Roles in AI-Driven Education

As AI tools become more prevalent, redefining the role of educators in the AI-driven landscape is essential (Salinas-Navarro et al., 2024). Future research should investigate how teachers can best integrate AI into their pedagogy, emphasizing a collaborative relationship rather than a replacement. Philosophical discussions around the essence of teaching what it means to educate and mentor in this context can help frame this area of research. Furthermore, studies could explore professional development pathways that prepare educators to engage constructively with AI in their practice. By pursuing these future research directions, scholars can ensure that philosophical considerations underpin the development and implementation of AI-driven educational innovations, creating a more thoughtful and effective educational landscape within Society 5.0.

REFERENCES

Agalianos, A., Whitty, G., & Noss, R. (2006). The Social Shaping of Logo. *Social Studies of Science*, *36*(2), 241–267.

Allenby, B., & Sarewitz, D. (2011). *The Techno-Human Condition*. MIT Press.

An, T., & Li, Y. (2014). On Theoretical Prospect of Educational Technology From the Perspective of Philosophy of Technology. *Educational Research*, *4*, 37–42.

Arthur, W. B. (2009). *The Nature of Technology: What it is and How it Evolves*. Penguin.

Atiyeh, B., Emsieh, S., Hakim, C., & Chalhoub, R. (2023). A narrative review of artificial intelligence (AI) for objective assessment of aesthetic endpoints in plastic surgery. *Aesthetic Plastic Surgery*, *47*(6), 2862–2873. DOI: 10.1007/s00266-023-03328-9 PMID: 37000298

Barad, K. (2019). After the end of the world: Entangled nuclear colonialisms, matters of force, and the material force of justice. *Theory & Event*, *22*(3), 524–550.

Bayne, S. (2015). What's the Matter with 'Technology-Enhanced Learning'? *Learning, Media and Technology*, *40*(1), 5–20.

Beckera, R., & Birdib, A. (2018). Flipping the Classroom: Old Ideas, New Technologies. *International Review of Economics Education*, *29*, 1–5.

Biesta, G., Heugh, K., Cervinkova, H., Rasinski, L., Osborne, S., Forde, D., Wrench, A., Carter, J., Anders Safstrom, C., Soong, H., O'Keeffe, S., Paige, K., Rigney, I., O'Toole, L., Hattam, R., Peters, M. A., & Tesar, M. (2021). Philosophy of education in a new key: Publicness, Social Justice, and Education; A South-North Conversation. *Educational Philosophy and Theory*. Advance online publication. DOI: 10.1080/00131857.2021.1929172

Braden, A. (1995). Review of Instructional Technology: The Definition and Domains of the Field. *Educational Technology Research and Development*, *43*(1), 81–83.

Braidotti, R. (2019). *Posthuman knowledge*. Polity Press.

Buchanan, R. A., Forster, D. J., Douglas, S., Nakar, S., Boon, H. J., Heath, T., Heyward, P., D'Olimpio, L., Ailwood, J., Eacott, S., Smith, S., Peters, M., & Tesar, M. (2021). Philosophy of education in a new key: Exploring new ways of teaching and doing ethics in education in the 21st century. *Educational Philosophy and Theory*. Advance online publication. DOI: 10.1080/00131857.2021.1880387

Cardona, M. A., Rodríguez, R. J., & Ishmael, K. (2023). *Artificial intelligence and the future of teaching and learning*. Lumina Foundation.

Chan, C. K. Y., & Tsi, L. H. Y. (2023). The AI revolution in education: Will AI replace or assist teachers in higher education? arXiv:2305.01185 [cs.CY]. https://doi.org//arXiv.2305.01185DOI: 10.48550

Chen, J. J., & Perez, C. (2023). Enhancing assessment and personalized learning through artificial intelligence. *Childhood Education*, *99*(6), 72–79. DOI: 10.1080/00094056.2023.2282903

Chiang, F. K., Zhu, G. X., Wang, Q., Cui, Z. F., Cai, S., & Yu, S. Q. (2016). Research and Trends in Mobile Learning from 1976 to 2013: A Content Analysis of Patents in Selected Databases. *British Journal of Educational Technology*, *47*(6), 1006–1019.

Christensen, C., Horn, M., & Johnson, C. (2008). *Disrupting Class: How disruptive innovation will change the way the world learns*. McGraw-Hill.

Clegg, S., & Steel, J. (2002). "Flexibility as Myth? New Technologies and Post-Fordism in Higher Education." *Proceedings of the Networked Learning Conference*.

Crawford, J., Cowling, M., & Allen, K.-A. (2023). Leadership is needed for ethical ChatGPT: Character, assessment, and learning using artificial intelligence (AI). *Journal of University Teaching & Learning Practice*, *20*(3), 457–476. DOI: 10.53761/1.20.3.02

Cuban, L. (2001). *Oversold and Underused: Computers in the Classroom*. Harvard University Press.

Czerniewicz, L. (2010). Educational Technology–Mapping the Terrain with Bernstein as Cartographer. *Journal of Computer Assisted Learning*, *26*(6), 523–534.

D'Errico, F. (2007). The Origin of Humanity and Modern Cultures: Archaeology's View. *Diogenes*, *54*(2), 122–133.

Deleuze, G. (1995). *Negotiations*. Columbia University Press.

Deng, L. (2018). Artificial intelligence in the rising wave of deep learning: The historical path and future outlook. *IEEE Signal Processing Magazine*, *35*(1), 180–177. DOI: 10.1109/MSP.2017.2762725

Dépelteau, F. (2008). Relational Thinking: A Critique of co-Deterministic Theories of Structure and Agency. *Sociological Theory*, *26*(1), 51–73.

Dewey, J. (1916). Democracy and Education: An Introduction to the Philosophy of Education. New York, *NY: the Free Press*.

Dogan, M. E., Goru Dogan, T., & Bozkurt, A. (2023). The use of artificial intelligence (AI) in online learning and distance education processes: A systematic review of empirical studies. *Applied Sciences (Basel, Switzerland)*, *13*(5), 56–88. DOI: 10.3390/app13053056

Donnelly, K. (2007). Australia's Adoption of Outcomes Based Education: A Critique. *Issues in Educational Research*, *17*(2), 183–206.

Dusek, V. (2006). *Philosophy of Technology: An Introduction*. Blackwell Publishing.

Esposito, A., Sangrà, A., & Maina, M. (2013). "Chronotopes in Learner-Generated Contexts. A Reflection About the Interconnectedness of Temporal and Spatial Dimensions to Provide a Framework for the Exploration of Hybrid Learning Ecologies of Doctoral e-Researchers." *LC Research Paper Series,* 6: 15–28.

Eynon, R. (2015). The Quantified Self for Learning: Critical Questions for Education. *Learning, Media and Technology*, *40*(4), 407–411.

Feenberg, A. (2002). *Transforming Technology: A Critical Theory Revisited*. Oxford University Press.

Freire, P. (2005). *Pedagogy of the Oppressed (30th Anniversary Edition)*. Continuum.

Friesen, N. (2009). *Re-thinking e-Learning Research: Foundations, Methods, and Practices*. Peter Lang.

Gamage, K. A. A., Dehideniya, S. C. P., Xu, Z., & Tang, X. (2023). ChatGPT and higher education assessments: More opportunities than concerns? *Journal of Applied Learning and Teaching*, *6*(2), 654–679. DOI: 10.37074/jalt.2023.6.2.32

Garroutte, E., & Westcott, K. (2013). The story is a living being: Companionship with stories in Anishinaabe Studies. In Doerfler, J., Sinclair, N. J., & Stark, H. K. (Eds.), *Centering Anishinaabeg studies: Understanding the world through stories* (pp. 61–80).

Gehlen, A. (1988). *Man: His Nature and Place in the World*. Columbia University Press.

Ghosh, O & Kumar, B. (2025). The Impact of Remote Experimentation on Student Engagement. *Revolutionizing Education With Remote Experimentation and Learning Analytics,* 523-544, DOI: DOI: 10.4018/979-8-3693-8593-7.ch031

Glaude, E. S.Jr. (2020). *Begin again: James Baldwin's America and its urgent lessons for our own*. Crown.

Greco, S., & Cinganotto, L. (2023). Re-thinking education in the age of AI. *Journal of E-Learning and Knowledge Society,* I-IV Pages. https://doi.org/DOI: 10.20368/1971-8829/1135873

Halagatti, M., Gadag, S., Mahantshetti, S., Hiremath, C. V., Tharkude, D., & Banakar, V. (2023). Artificial intelligence: The new tool of disruption in educational performance assessment. In Tyagi, P., Grima, S., Sood, K., Balamurugan, B., Özen, E., & Eleftherios, T. (Eds.), *Smart analytics, artificial intelligence and sustainable performance management in a global digitalised economy (110A)* (pp. 261–287). Emerald Publishing Limited., DOI: 10.1108/S1569-37592023000110A014

Harari, Y. N. (2014). *Sapiens: A brief history of humankind.* Random House.

Haraway, D. (1988). Situated Knowledges: The Science Question in Feminism and the Privilege of Partial Perspective. *Feminist Studies, 14*(3), 575–599.

Harrer, S. (2023). Attention is not all you need: The complicated case of ethically using large language models in healthcare and medicine. *EBioMedicine, 90*, 104512. DOI: 10.1016/j.ebiom.2023.104512 PMID: 36924620

Hegel, G. (1967). *The Phenomenology of the Mind* (Baillie, J. B., Trans.). Harper Torchbooks.

Heidegger, M. (1959). *An Introduction to Metaphysics* (Manheim, R., Trans.). Yale University Press.

Heidegger, M. (1971). *Poetry, Language, Thought* (Hofstader, A., Trans.). Harper and Row.

Heidegger, M. (1977). *The Question Concerning Technology, and Other Essays.* Harper Torchbooks.

Heidegger, M. (1996). *Being and Time* (Stambaugh, J., Trans.). State University of New York Press.

Heidegger, M. (2000). *Elucidations of Holderlin's Poetry* (Hoeller, K., Trans.). Humanity Books.

Hew, K., & Cheung, W. (2014). Students' and Instructors' Use of Massive Open Online Courses (MOOCs): Motivations and Challenges. *Educational Research Review, 12*, 45–58.

Hooda, M., Rana, C., Dahiya, O., Rizwan, A., & Hossain, M. S. (2022). Artificial intelligence for assessment and feedback to enhance student success in higher education. *Mathematical Problems in Engineering, 2022*, 5215722. Advance online publication. DOI: 10.1155/2022/5215722

Huang, M., & Liu, T. F. (2016). Education Facing to Thinking of Heidegger and Its Theoretical Predicaments. *Educational Research*, *12*, 12–21.

Hung, R., Zhengmei, P., Kato, M., Nishihira, T., Okabe, M., Di, X., Kwak, D.-J., Hwang, K., Tschong, Y., Chien, C.-H., Peters, M. A., & Tesar, M. (2020). Philosophy of education in a new key: East Asia. *Educational Philosophy and Theory*. Advance online publication. DOI: 10.1080/00131857.2020.1772028

Ibrahim, H., Asim, R., Zaffar, F., Rahwan, T., & Zaki, Y. (2023). Rethinking homework in the age of artificial intelligence. *IEEE Intelligent Systems*, *38*(2), 24–27. DOI: 10.1109/MIS.2023.3255599

Ihde, D. (1990). *Technology and the Lifeworld*. Indiana University Press.

Ihde, D. (2003). A Phenomenology of Technics. In Kaplan, D. (Ed.), *Readings in the Philosophy of Technology* (pp. 137–160). Rowman & Littlefield Publisher.

Jackson, A. Y., & Mazzei, L. A. (2012). *Thinking with theory in qualitative research*. Routledge Press.

Jackson, L., Alston, K., Bialystok, L., Blum, L., Burbules, N. C., Chinnery, A., Hansen, D. T., Hytten, K., Mayo, C., Norris, T., Stitzlein, S. M., Thompson, W. C., Waks, L., Peters, M. A., & Tesar, M. (2020a). Philosophy of education in a new key: Snapshot 2020 from the United States and Canada. *Educational Philosophy and Theory*. Advance online publication. DOI: 10.1080/00131857.2020.1821189

Jandric, P., Jaldemark, J., Hurley, Z., Bartram, B., Matthews, A., Jopling, M., Manero, J., MacKenzie, M., & Irwin, J. ~ Rothmuller, N., Green, B., Ralston, S. J., Pyyhtinen, O., Hayes, S., Wright, J., Peters, M. A., & Tesar, M. (2020). Philosophy of education in a new key: Who remembers Greta Thunberg? Education and environment after the coronavirus. *Educational Philosophy and Theory*. Advance online publication. DOI: 10.1080/00131857.2020.1811678

Januszewski, A., & Persichitte, K. (2008). A History of the AECT's Definitions of Educational Technology. In Januszewski, A., & Molenda, M. (Eds.), *Educational Technology: A Definition with Commentary* (pp. 259–282). Routledge.

Kai, S., Almeda, M. V., Baker, R. S., Heffernan, C., & Heffernan, N. (2018). Decision tree modeling of wheel spinning and productive persistence in skill builders. *Journal of Educational Data Mining*, *10*(1), 789–822. DOI: 10.5281/zenodo.3344810

Kant, I. (1990). *Kant on Education*. Heath and Co.

Kato, M., Saito, N., Matsushita, R., Ueno, M., Izawa, S., Maruyama, Y., Sugita, H., Ono, F., Muroi, R., Miyazaki, Y., Yamana, J., Peters, M. A., & Tesar, M. (2020). Philosophy of education in a new key: Voices from Japan. *Educational Philosophy and Theory*. Advance online publication. DOI: 10.1080/00131857.2020.1802819

Kirkwood, A., & Price, L. (2014). Technology-Enhanced Learning and Teaching in Higher Education: What is 'Enhanced' and How Do We Know? A Critical Literature Review. *Learning, Media and Technology*, *39*(1), 6–36.

Koh, E., & Doroudi, S. (2023). Learning, teaching, and assessment with generative artificial intelligence: Towards a plateau of productivity. *Learning: Research and Practice*, *9*(2), 109–116. DOI: 10.1080/23735082.2023.2264086

Ladson-Billings, G. (2021). I'm here for the hard re-set: Post pandemic pedagogy to preserve our culture. *Equity & Excellence in Education*, *54*(1), 68–78. DOI: 10.1080/10665684.2020.1863883

Ladyman, J. (2007). Ontological, Epistemological, and Methodological Positions. In Kuipers, T. A. F. (Ed.), *General Philosophy of Science* (pp. 303–376). North Holland.

Latchem, C. (2014). BJET Editorial: Opening up the Educational Technology Research Agenda. *British Journal of Educational Technology*, *41*(1), 3–11.

Latour, B. (2004). Why Has Critique Run Out of Steam? From Matters of Fact to Matters of Concern. *Critical Inquiry*, *30*(2), 225–248.

Latour, B. (2005). *Reassembling the Social*. Oxford University Press.

Lee, J., & Soylu, M. Y. (2023). *ChatGPT and assessment in higher education*. Center for 21st Century Universities. https://www.c21u.gatech.edu/sites/default/files/publication/2023/03/C21U%20ChatGPT%20White%20Paper_ Final.pdf

Lewin, D., & Lundie, D. (2016). Philosophies of digital pedagogy. *Studies in Philosophy and Education*, *3*(35), 235–240.

Lindgren, R., Tscholl, M., Wang, S., & Johnson, E. (2016). Enhancing Learning and Engagement Through Embodied Interaction Within a Mixed Reality Simulation. *Computers & Education*, *95*, 174–187.

Marker, M. (2018). There is no place of nature; there is only the nature of place: Animate landscapes as methodology for inquiry in the Coast Salish territory. *International Journal of Qualitative Studies in Education : QSE*, *31*(6), 453–464. DOI: 10.1080/09518398.2018.1430391

Martínez-Comesaña, M., Rigueira-Díaz, X., Larrañaga-Janeiro, A., Martínez-Torres, J., Ocarranza-Prado, I., & Kreibel, D. (2023). Impact of artificial intelligence on assessment methods in primary and secondary education: Systematic literature review. *Revista de Psicodidáctica* (English Ed.), 28(2), 93–103. https://doi.org/DOI: 10.1016/j.psicoe.2023.06.002

Marx, K. (1964). *Economic and Philosophic Manuscripts of 1844*. International Publishers.

Marx, K. (1975). *Economic and Philosophical Manuscripts of 1844* (Livingstone, R., & Benton, G., Trans.). Penguin.

Mason, M. (2008). Complexity Theory and the Philosophy of Education. *Educational Philosophy and Theory*, *40*(1), 4–18.

Mayes, T. (1995). Learning Technology and Groundhog day. In Strang, W., Simpson, V. B., & Slater, D. (Eds.), *Hypermedia at Work: Practice and Theory in Higher Education* (pp. 21–37). University of Kent Press.

Mika, C. T. H. (2017). *Indigenous education and the metaphysics of presence: A worlded philosophy*. Routledge.

Minocha, S., & Reeves, A. (2010). Design of Learning Spaces in 3D Virtual Worlds: An Empirical Investigation of Second Life. *Learning, Media and Technology*, *35*(2), 111–137.

Mitcham, C. (2006). From Phenomenology to Pragmatism: Using Technology as an Instrument. In Selinger, E. (Ed.), *Postphenomenology: A Critical Companion to Ihde* (pp. 21–33). State University of New York Press.

Moorhouse, B. L., Yeo, M. A., & Wan, Y. (2023). Generative AI tools and assessment: Guidelines of the world's topranking universities. *Computers and Education Open*, *5*, 100151. DOI: 10.1016/j.caeo.2023.100151

Moqbel, M. S. S., & Al-Kadi, A. M. T. (2023). Foreign language learning assessment in the age of ChatGPT: A theoretical account. *Journal of English Studies in Arabia Felix*, *2*(1), 76–88. DOI: 10.56540/jesaf.v2i1.62

Moten, F. (2018). *Stolen life*. Duke University Press.

Murgatroyd, S. (2023). Rethinking teaching in the age of artificial intelligence. *Revista Paraguaya De Educación A Distancia* (REPED), 4(2), 4–10. https://doi.org/DOI: 10.56152/reped2023-vol4num2-art1

Murray, M. D. (2023). Generative AI art: Copyright infringement and fair use. *SMU Science and Technology Law Review*, *26*(2), 259. DOI: 10.25172/smustlr.26.2.4

Nikolopoulou, K. (2024a). Generative artificial intelligence in higher education: Exploring ways of harnessing pedagogical practices with the assistance of ChatGPT. *International Journal of Changes in Education*, *1*(2), 103–111. DOI: 10.47852/bonviewIJCE42022489

Nikolopoulou, K. (2024b). Generative artificial intelligence in higher education: Exploring ways of harnessing pedagogical practices with the assistance of ChatGPT. *International Journal of Changes in Education*, *1*(2), 103–111. DOI: 10.47852/bonviewIJCE42022489

Oliver, M. (2011). Technological Determinism in Educational Technology Research: Some Alternative Ways of Thinking about the Relationship Between Learning and Technology. *Journal of Computer Assisted Learning*, *27*(5), 373–384.

Oliver, M. (2013). Learning Technology: Theorising the Tools We Study. *British Journal of Educational Technology*, *44*(1), 31–43.

Oliver, M. (2015). From Openness to Permeability: Reframing Open Education in Terms of Positive Liberty in the Enactment of Academic Practices. *Learning, Media and Technology*, *40*(3), 365–384.

Oliver, M., & Conole, G. (2003). Evidence-Based Practice and e-Learning in Higher Education: Can We and Should We? *Research Papers in Education*, *18*(4), 385–397.

Orchard, J., Gaydon, P., Williams, K., Bennett, P., D'Olimpio, L., C¸elik, R., Shah, Q., Neusiedl, C., Suissa, J., Peters, M. A., & Tesar, M. (2020). Philosophy of education in a new key: A 'covid collective' of the philosophy of education society of Great Britain (PESGB). *Educational Philosophy and Theory*. Advance online publication. DOI: 10.1080/00131857.2020.1838274

Ouyang, F., Zheng, L., & Jiao, P. (2022). Artificial intelligence in online higher education: A systematic review of empirical research from 2011 to 2020. *Education and Information Technologies*, *27*(6), 7893–7925. DOI: 10.1007/s10639-022-10925-9

Papastephanou, M., Zembylas, M., Bostad, I., Benhur Oral, S., Drousioti, K., Kouppanou, A., Strand, T., Wain, K., & Peters, M. A. (Open Reviewer) & Tesar, M. (Open Reviewer) (2020). Philosophy of education in a new key: Education for justice now. *Educational Philosophy and Theory*. Advance online publication. DOI: 10.1080/00131857.2020.1793539

Parisi, L., & Dixon-Roman, E. (2020). *Recursive colonialism & cosmo-computation. Social Text Online.* https://social.textjournal.org/periscope_article/recursive-colonialism-and-cosmo-computation/

Pedaste, M., Mäeots, M., Siiman, L., Jong, T., Riesen, S., Kamp, E., Manoli, C., Zacharia, Z., & Tsourlidaki, E. (2015). Phases of Inquiry-Based Learning: Definitions and the Inquiry Cycle. *Educational Research Review*, *14*(2), 47–61.

Perkins, M. (2023). Academic integrity considerations of AI large language models in the post-pandemic era: ChatGPT and beyond. *Journal of University Teaching & Learning Practice*, *20*(2), 345–367. DOI: 10.53761/1.20.02.07

Perrotta, C., & Evans, M. A. (2013). Orchestration, Power, and Educational Technology: A Response to Dillenbourg. *Computers & Education*, *69*, 520–522.

Peters, M. A., Arndt, S., Tesar, M., Jackson, L., Hung, R., Mika, C., Ozolins, J. T., Teschers, C., Orchard, J., Buchanan, R., Madjar, A., Novak, R., Besley, T., & Sturm, S. (open reviewer), Roberts, P. (open reviewer), & Gibbons, A. (open reviewer) (2020). Philosophy of education in a new key. A collective project of the PESA executive. *Educational Philosophy and Theory*. Advance online publication. DOI: 10.1080/00131857.2020.1759194

Pezze, B. D. (2006). Heidegger on Gelassenheit. *Minerva*, *10*, •••. Retrieved March 15, 2020, from https://www.minerva.mic.ul.ie/vol10/Heidegger.html

Reich, K., Garrison, J., & Neubert, S. (2016). Complexity and Reductionism in Educational Philosophy—John Dewey's Critical Approach in 'Democracy and Education' Reconsidered. *Educational Philosophy and Theory*, *48*(10), 997–1012.

Reveley, J. (2013). Understanding Social Media Use as Alienation: A Review and Critique. *E-Learning and Digital Media*, *1*(10), 83–94.

Roll, I., Aleven, V., McLaren, B. M., & Koedinger, K. R. (2011). Improving students' help-seeking skills using metacognitive feedback in an intelligent tutoring system. *Learning and Instruction*, *21*(2), 267–280. DOI: 10.1016/j.learninstruc.2010.07.004

Rosiek, J. L., Snyder, J., & Pratt, S. L. (2020). The new materialisms and Indigenous theories of non-human agency: Making the case for respectful anti-colonial engagement. *Qualitative Inquiry*, *26*(3–4), 331–346. DOI: 10.1177/1077800419830135

Roth, K., Mollvik, L., Alshoufani, R., Adami, R., Dineen, K., Majlesi, F., Peters, M. A., & Tesar, M. (2020). Philosophy of education in a new key: Constraints and possibilities in present times with regard to dignity. *Educational Philosophy and Theory*. Advance online publication. DOI: 10.1080/00131857.2020.1851189

Roy, A. (2020). The pandemic is a portal. Financial Times. Available at: https://www.ft.com/content/10d8f5e8-74eb-11ea-95fe-fcd274e920ca

Rudolph, J., Ismail, M. F. B. M., & Popenici, S. (2024). Higher education's generative artificial intelligence paradox: The meaning of chatbot mania. *Journal of University Teaching & Learning Practice*, *21*(6), 1–35. DOI: 10.53761/54fs5e77

Salinas-Navarro, D. E., Vilalta-Perdomo, E., Michel-Villarreal, R., & Montesinos, L. (2024). Using generative artificial intelligence tools to explain and enhance experiential learning for authentic assessment. *Education Sciences*, *14*(1), 887–900. DOI: 10.3390/educsci14010083

Sardoc, M., Coady, C. A. J., Bufacchi, V., Moghaddam, F. M., Cassam, Q., Silva, D., Miscevic, N., Andrejc, G., Kodelja, Z., Vezjak, B., Peters, M. A., & Tesar, M. (2020). Philosophy of education in a new key: On radicalization and violent extremism. *Educational Philosophy and Theory*. Advance online publication. DOI: 10.1080/00131857.2020.1861937

Scribes, S. (2024). A discourse on generative AI. *Medium*. https://medium.com/@sundryscribes/a-discourse-on-generative-ai-4ca4a8911e1a

Selwyn, N. (2010). Looking Beyond Learning: Notes Towards the Critical Study of Educational Technology. *Journal of Computer Assisted Learning*, *26*, 65–73.

Selwyn, N. (2014). Education and 'the Digital'. *British Journal of Sociology of Education*, *35*(1), 155–164.

Selwyn, N. (2022). The future of AI and education: Some cautionary notes. *European Journal of Education*, *57*(4), 620–631. DOI: 10.1111/ejed.12532

Sergio, M., Gabriel, D., Sancristobal, E., Rosario, G., Manuel, C., & Juan, P. (2011). New Technology Trends in Education: Seven Years of Forecasts and Convergence. *Computer Education*, *57*, 1893–1906.

Siegel, H. (1983). On the obligations of the professional philosopher of education. *Journal of Thought*, *18*(2), 31–37.

Smith, J. (2022). International education trends: Shaping the future of higher education. *International Journal of Open Publication and Exploration*, *10*(1), 1–5.

Surry, D., & Baker, F. (2016). The Co-Dependent Relationship of Technology and Communities. *British Journal of Educational Technology*, *47*(1), 13–28.

Tesar, M. (2021). Philosophy as a method: Tracing the histories of intersections of 'philosophy', 'methodology' and 'education. *Qualitative Inquiry*, *27*(5), 544–553. DOI: 10.1177/1077800420934144

Thomson, I. (2004). Heidegger's Perfectionist Philosophy of Education in Being and Time. *Continental Philosophy Review*, *7*(4), 439–467.

Thumlert, K., Castell, S., & Jenson, J. (2015). Short Cuts and Extended Techniques: Rethinking Relations Between Technology and Educational Theory. *Educational Philosophy and Theory*, *47*(8), 786–803.

Trajtenberg, M. (2018). *AI as the next GPT: A political-economy perspective*. National Bureau of Economic Research., DOI: 10.3386/w24245

van der Vorst, T., & Jelicic, N. (2019). Artificial intelligence in education: Can AI bring the full potential of personalized learning to education? https://www.econstor.eu/handle/10419/205222

Varaki, B. S., Sadeqzadeh Qamsari, A., Sefidkhosh, M., Mahdi Sajjadi, S., Mohammadi Chaboki, R., Javidi Kalatehjafarabadi, T., Saffarheidari, H., Mohammadamini, M., Karimzadeh, O., Barkhordari, M., Zarghami-Hamrah, S., Peters, M. A., & Tesar, M. (2021). Philosophy of education in a new key: Reflection on higher education in Iran. *Educational Philosophy and Theory*. Advance online publication. DOI: 10.1080/00131857.2021.1905517

Verbeek, P. (2008). Cyborg Intentionality: Rethinking the Phenomenology of Human–Technology Relations. *Phenomenology and the Cognitive Sciences*, *7*(3), 387–395.

Waghid, Y., Davids, N., Mathebula, T., Terblanche, J., Higgs, P., Shawa, L., Herbert Manthalu, C., Waghid, Z., Ngwenya, C., Divala, J., Waghid, F., Peters, M. A., & Tesar, M. (2020). Philosophy of education in a new key: Cultivating a living philosophy of education to overcome coloniality and violence in African Universities. *Educational Philosophy and Theory*. Advance online publication. DOI: 10.1080/00131857.2020.1793714

Weiss, D. (2008). Human—Technology—World. *Techné: Research in Philosophy and Technology*, *12*(2), 110–119.

Whitehead, A. N. (1929). *Process and Reality: An Essay in Cosmology*. Macmillan.

Willet, R. (2018). Learning Through Making in Public Libraries: Theories, Practices, and Tensions. *Learning, Media and Technology*, *43*(3), 250–262.

Wrathall, A. (2011). We Still Need Education in Thinking: Heidegger's Education in a Technological Age. *Journal of Educational Studies*, *7*(1), 3–14.

Wu, G. S. (2009). *Lectures on the Philosophy of Technology*. China Renmin University Press.

Zhao, Y., Pugh, K., Sheldon, S., & Byers, J. (2002). Conditions for Classroom Technology Innovations. *Teachers College Record*, *104*(3), 482–515.

Zimmerman, J., Forlizzi, J., & Evenson, S. (2007). "Research Through Design as a Method for Interaction Design Research in HCI." *Proceedings of the SIGCHI Conference on Human Factors in Computing Systems.*

Zootzky, G., & Pfeiffer, A. (2024). Educational transformation through AI: Preparing for a new era of learning. *INTED2024 Proceedings,* 1202–1207. https://doi.org/ DOI: 10.21125/inted.2024.0382

Chapter 3
AI's Role in Advancing STEAM Education:
Transforming Learning and Innovation

Harsh Awashti
NIET Business School, Greater Noida, India

Mandeep Singh
https://orcid.org/0000-0001-9520-8610
Chandigarh University, India

Rachna Kathuria
New Delhi Institute of Management, India

ABSTRACT

This chapter explores the transformative impact of Artificial Intelligence (AI) on STEAM education, focusing on its integration into sustainability, quantum computing, and lifelong learning paradigms. The study examines emerging trends in AI-enhanced education, highlighting its potential to revolutionize curricula and its role in preparing a workforce equipped to navigate an increasingly AI-driven global landscape. Key challenges, including socio-economic disparities, ethical concerns, and resistance to technological change, are critically analyzed alongside policy implications emphasizing the need for inclusive, transparent, and equitable AI frameworks. Through a combination of qualitative analysis and case study examination, the chapter illustrates successful AI initiatives in developed and developing countries, showcasing the potential for AI to bridge gaps in education access and quality. The chapter concludes by emphasizing the importance of interdisciplinary collaboration, global networks, and continuous innovation in shaping the future of

DOI: 10.4018/979-8-3373-1062-6.ch003

Copyright © 2026, IGI Global Scientific Publishing. Copying or distributing in print or electronic forms without written permission of IGI Global Scientific Publishing is prohibited.

AI-enhanced STEAM education.

INTRODUCTION

Background and Significance of STEAM Education

Historical Evolution of STEAM as a Multidisciplinary Approach: The emergence of STEAM education, an acronym encompassing Science, Technology, Engineering, Arts, and Mathematics, represents a transformative milestone in the evolution of educational paradigms. Historically, the roots of multidisciplinary learning can be traced back to Renaissance polymaths like Leonardo da Vinci, who bridged art and science to achieve profound insights and innovations (Awal & Khanna, 2019). However, the modern conceptualization of STEAM education owes much to the 20th century's emphasis on specialized fields within the natural sciences and engineering, catalyzed by industrial and technological revolutions (R. Kumar, Malhotra, Pandey, et al., 2023). The post-Sputnik era marked a pivotal point when the United States, galvanized by the space race, prioritized STEM education—focusing on science, technology, engineering, and mathematics. This emphasis aimed to produce a workforce adept at technological innovation and scientific inquiry, thereby ensuring economic and geopolitical competitiveness. Over time, critiques emerged regarding STEM's exclusion of creative and humanistic dimensions, which many argued were vital for fostering holistic problem-solving and innovation. This critique laid the groundwork for the eventual integration of arts into STEM, giving birth to STEAM education as a comprehensive, interdisciplinary framework (R. Kumar, Singh, Mohanty, et al., 2023).

The Shift from STEM to STEAM: Integrating Arts and Creativity: The transition from STEM to STEAM reflects a paradigm shift in understanding the role of creativity and aesthetic thinking in scientific and technological advancement. Advocates of STEAM argue that the inclusion of arts bridges the cognitive chasm between technical proficiency and imaginative exploration. In this context, arts encompass traditional visual or performing arts and broader creative disciplines such as design thinking, storytelling, and cultural studies. This shift gained traction in the early 21st century, bolstered by research indicating that innovation often arises at the intersection of disciplines (Kanojia et al., 2022). For instance, the design of user-friendly technology, such as smartphones, necessitates collaboration between engineers, psychologists, and artists. The integration of arts fosters divergent thinking, empathy, and a deeper appreciation of the societal implications of scientific endeavors. Moreover, arts education nurtures an ability to visualize abstract concepts, making complex scientific ideas accessible and engaging to broader audiences.

The adoption of STEAM also reflects societal shifts toward valuing creativity as a cornerstone of the knowledge economy (Joshi et al., 2022). Policymakers, educators, and industry leaders increasingly recognize that cultivating creativity alongside technical skills equips students to excel in specialized fields and adapt to the rapidly evolving demands of the global economy (Kanojia et al., 2022).

Importance of STEAM Education in Addressing Complex Global Challenges: STEAM education is uniquely positioned to address humanity's multifaceted challenges, from climate change to healthcare innovation and sustainable development (R. Kumar et al., 2024; R. Kumar, Lande, Kumar, et al., 2023; R. Kumar & Khanna, 2023b; Mary Joshitta et al., 2023). These challenges are characterized by their complexity, interconnectedness, and demand for solutions that transcend conventional disciplinary boundaries. STEAM equips learners with the ability to synthesize knowledge across domains, fostering systems thinking—a critical skill for tackling global issues.

For instance, addressing climate change requires integrating scientific expertise in environmental science with creative communication strategies to inspire collective action. Similarly, advances in healthcare technology benefit from the inclusion of arts, as designers collaborate with engineers to create functional and user-centric devices (C. Gupta et al., 2022; R. Kumar, Malhotra, & Grover, 2023; Malhotra & Gupta, 2021; A. K. Uniyal et al., 2022; Upreti & Malhotra, 2024). The arts also play a critical role in cultivating ethical awareness, ensuring that technological advancements align with human values and societal needs. Furthermore, STEAM education cultivates essential 21st-century skills such as collaboration, critical thinking, and cultural competence. By engaging with diverse perspectives, students develop the ability to navigate cultural and disciplinary boundaries, a skill set increasingly crucial in our interconnected world. The interdisciplinary nature of STEAM not only broadens students' intellectual horizons but also enhances their capacity for empathy, innovation, and resilience. In an era of rapid technological advancements and socio-political upheavals, STEAM education offers a holistic framework for empowering the next generation. It moves beyond the dichotomy of arts versus sciences, advocating for synergistic integration. This approach aligns with the broader educational imperative to cultivate well-rounded individuals capable of leading with creativity, adaptability, and purpose. STEAM education represents a dynamic evolution in the pursuit of knowledge, embodying the synthesis of analytical rigor and creative exploration (Cavaliere et al., 2024; Kaur et al., 2024; R. Khanna et al., 2023; R. Kumar, Kathuria, Malholtra, et al., 2023; R. Kumar, Khannna Malholtra, & Grover, 2023). Its historical trajectory reflects a growing recognition of the need for interdisciplinary approaches to education. At the same time, its significance lies in its ability to prepare learners for an increasingly complex and uncertain world. By integrating arts into STEM, STEAM equips individuals with the tools to navigate and address global challenges, fostering a future defined by innovation, empathy, and sustainable progress.

The Role of AI in Society 5.0

Overview of Society 5.0: A Human-Centered Vision: Society 5.0 represents a transformative vision for the future, characterized by the seamless integration of digital technologies and human-centric values. Introduced by the Japanese government, Society 5.0 seeks to address the limitations of previous societal models—hunter-gatherer (1.0), agrarian (2.0), industrial (3.0), and information-based (4.0)—by achieving a harmonious balance between economic progress and the well-being of individuals and communities. Unlike the techno-centric emphasis of Society 4.0, Society 5.0 envisions a paradigm where advanced technologies, such as artificial intelligence (AI), the Internet of Things (IoT), and robotics, enhance human capabilities and improve quality of life (R. Kumar & Khanna, 2023a; Rana et al., 2022). At its core, Society 5.0 transcends the notion of technology as an end in itself. Instead, it prioritizes inclusivity, sustainability, and innovation to address pressing global challenges, including aging populations, resource scarcity, and environmental degradation. This human-centered approach leverages cutting-edge technology to create a society where individuals thrive in equitable, efficient, and resilient systems. As the linchpin of this vision, AI plays a pivotal role in driving innovation, solving complex problems, and ensuring that technological progress aligns with human values.

AI as a Catalyst for Innovation and Problem-Solving: Artificial intelligence, with its capacity to process vast datasets, identify patterns, and automate complex tasks, is a transformative catalyst in realizing Society 5.0. By enabling unprecedented levels of efficiency and precision, AI empowers industries and governments to tackle multifaceted challenges that were previously insurmountable. One of AI's most profound contributions is its ability to revolutionize healthcare. Through predictive analytics, AI algorithms can identify disease patterns, optimize treatment plans, and accelerate drug discovery (R. Kumar, Saxena, et al., 2023; Ram, Bisht, et al., 2022; Rawat et al., 2023). For example, AI-driven diagnostic tools can detect medical conditions such as cancer or cardiovascular diseases more accurately and at earlier stages than traditional methods, thereby improving patient outcomes. Additionally, AI-powered robotic systems can provide elderly care, reducing the burden on healthcare professionals and addressing demographic challenges such as aging populations. In urban development, AI facilitates the creation of "smart cities" by optimizing transportation systems, energy consumption, and waste management. Predictive traffic management algorithms reduce congestion and emissions, while AI-enhanced energy grids adapt dynamically to consumption patterns, promoting sustainability. Furthermore, AI-driven platforms enable personalized education and upskilling, ensuring that individuals can navigate the demands of an increasingly digital economy (Kaliappan et al., 2023; Kannan et al., 2022; Komkowski et al., 2023b). AI also serves as a critical enabler of environmental stewardship, advancing the goals of Society 5.0's commitment to sustainability. Machine learning models can monitor ecosystems, predict natural disasters, and optimize resource utilization. For instance, AI-driven precision agriculture minimizes waste and enhances crop yields, addressing food security while conserving water and soil resources (T. Jindal et al., 2022; Joshi et al., 2023).

Alignment of AI with the Goals of Society 5.0: The alignment of AI with Society 5.0 hinges on its ethical deployment and the pursuit of technological innovation that prioritizes human dignity and inclusivity. While AI's potential is boundless, its integration must be guided by a framework that ensures equitable access, transparency, and accountability. Society 5.0 seeks to leverage AI for economic gain and foster a society where individuals are empowered to lead fulfilling lives (A. Gupta et al., 2022; Kohli et al., 2022; Nethravathi et al., 2022; S. Sharma et al., 2023).

A critical aspect of this alignment is the mitigation of social inequalities. If designed inclusively, AI-driven systems can democratize access to resources and opportunities. For instance, in developing regions, AI-powered platforms can facilitate access to education, healthcare, and financial services, reducing systemic disparities. Similarly, AI's capacity for language processing can bridge communication gaps, fostering cross-cultural understanding and collaboration in a globalized world. Moreover, the ethical application of AI is central to its role in Society 5.0. Issues such as bias in algorithms, data privacy, and the displacement of jobs require proactive governance and policy frameworks. Society 5.0 ensures that technological advancements uphold societal values and protect individual rights by embedding ethical considerations into AI systems (Ahmad et al., 2023; Dogra et al., 2022; Krishna et al., 2022). Lastly, AI's ability to augment human capabilities aligns seamlessly with Society 5.0's human-centric ethos. Rather than replacing humans, AI is a collaborative partner, enhancing creativity, decision-making, and productivity. This symbiotic relationship underscores Society 5.0's vision of a future where technology amplifies human potential, enabling individuals to contribute meaningfully to society (Matta & Pant, 2020; Pant et al., 2022). AI stands at the forefront of the transition to Society 5.0, embodying the potential to catalyze innovation, solve complex challenges, and create a sustainable, inclusive future. Its alignment with the goals of Society 5.0 underscores the importance of ethical considerations and a human-centric approach to leveraging technological advancements (Agarwal & Sharma, 2023; Shah et al., 2023; K. D. Singh et al., 2023). As societies continue to navigate the intricate interplay between economic progress and human well-being, AI's role in shaping this transformative vision will remain indispensable. Society

5.0, with AI as its cornerstone, offers a blueprint for a future where technology serves humanity, fostering prosperity, equity, and resilience.

Purpose of the Study: This chapter explores the transformative potential of Artificial Intelligence (AI) in enhancing STEAM education, focusing on its integration with sustainability, quantum computing, and lifelong learning. It analyzes emerging trends, challenges, and policy implications, providing a comprehensive framework for AI adoption in educational settings. By examining these dynamics, the chapter seeks to inform educators, policymakers, and industry leaders on creating a future-ready, ethical, and inclusive AI-driven educational landscape.

Research Methodology: The research methodology for this chapter is a qualitative, exploratory approach, combining extensive literature review with case study analysis. Secondary data sources, including peer-reviewed journals, government reports, and industry white papers, were systematically reviewed to identify emerging trends, challenges, and best practices in AI-enhanced STEAM education. Furthermore, multiple global case studies were analyzed to provide practical insights into successful AI initiatives and policy frameworks. This methodological framework comprehensively explains AI's role in educational transformation.

CONCEPTUAL FOUNDATIONS

Understanding AI in Education

Core Concepts of AI

Artificial Intelligence (AI) is a multidisciplinary domain of computer science dedicated to developing systems capable of simulating human-like cognitive processes. It encompasses algorithms and technologies designed to perform tasks traditionally requiring human intelligence, such as problem-solving, learning, decision-making, and language comprehension. AI represents a transformative force in education, redefining how knowledge is imparted, accessed, and personalized for learners. At its core, AI operates on the principles of data-driven decision-making and adaptability (Kollipara et al., 2023; Mehershilpa et al., 2023; A. K. Sharma et al., 2021). Central to this is the concept of "intelligence," which, in AI systems, is characterized by the ability to perceive environmental inputs, process them algorithmically, and execute context-appropriate responses. The evolution of AI has been marked by its increasing capacity to mimic logical reasoning and nuanced human behaviors, such as emotional recognition and conversational interaction. These capabilities have positioned AI as a powerful tool in education, capable of addressing challenges like accessibility, personalized learning, and administrative efficiency. AI in education is fundamentally underpinned by three interrelated dimensions: automation, augmentation, and transformation. Automation involves delegating routine or repetitive tasks to AI systems, thereby optimizing efficiency (Sathyaseelan et al., 2023; Sunori et al., 2023; Upreti et al., 2023). Augmentation refers to enhancing human capabilities, enabling educators to focus on more complex, creative, or interpersonal aspects of teaching. Transformation denotes the potential of AI to fundamentally reshape pedagogical paradigms, facilitating innovative approaches to teaching and learning that were previously inconceivable (S. P. Singh et al., 2023).

AI's Capabilities: Machine Learning, Natural Language Processing, and Data Analytics

The functional capabilities of AI in education stem from three foundational technologies: machine learning (ML), natural language processing (NLP), and data analytics. Each domain uniquely contributes to the educational landscape, enabling AI to revolutionize instructional methods, content delivery, and student engagement.

Machine Learning (ML):

Machine learning, a subset of AI, involves the development of algorithms that enable systems to learn and improve from experience without explicit programming. In education, ML powers adaptive learning platforms that personalize content delivery based on individual learner behaviors, preferences, and performance (Luthra et al., 2022; Salama et al., 2023). For instance, ML algorithms can analyze patterns in student interactions with educational materials, dynamically adjusting the difficulty, pacing, or modality of content to optimize learning outcomes. By continuously refining its predictive capabilities, ML can identify at-risk students, recommend interventions, and accurately predict future performance. This enhances the efficacy of instructional methods and supports proactive strategies for addressing educational inequities (Davuluri et al., 2023; Mandalapu et al., 2023; Tripathy et al., 2021).

Natural Language Processing (NLP)

Natural language processing (NLP) focuses on the interaction between computers and human language, enabling AI systems to understand, interpret, and generate text or speech. NLP has profound applications in education, particularly in language learning, automated grading, and virtual tutoring (Caiado et al., 2023; Pandey et al., 2023; N. K. Singh et al., 2023). Language-learning applications, for example, leverage NLP to provide real-time feedback on pronunciation, grammar, and vocabulary usage. Similarly, AI-driven writing assistants utilize NLP to evaluate essays, offering insights on structure, coherence, and style while freeing educators to focus on higher-order pedagogical tasks (Chahar et al., 2022; P. Gupta et al., 2023; R. Singh et al., 2022). Moreover, conversational AI, powered by NLP, enables intelligent virtual assistants to create round-the-clock academic support, fostering self-directed learning among students.

Data Analytics

AI data analytics involves extracting, interpreting, and applying insights from large datasets. In education, data analytics facilitates evidence-based decision-making by uncovering trends, correlations, and outliers within student and institutional data. For educators, this translates into actionable insights for curriculum design, classroom management, and resource allocation. At the institutional level, data analytics can inform policy development, identify systemic inefficiencies, and evaluate the long-term impact of educational programs. When integrated with predictive modeling, data analytics becomes a powerful tool for enhancing the scalability and sustainability of educational initiatives.

Differentiating Between AI as a Tool and a Partner in Education

AI as a Tool: When AI functions as a tool, its role is predominantly supportive. It automates repetitive tasks, such as grading and attendance tracking, thus streamlining administrative workflows. As a tool, AI is an enabler of efficiency, reducing the time and cognitive load required for routine activities. However, its utility is confined to executing predefined functions, lacking autonomy or interpretative depth.

AI as a Partner: In contrast, AI as a partner signifies a more dynamic and collaborative relationship between technology and human educators. AI augments human decision-making as a partner, offering insights and recommendations that inform instructional strategies. For instance, an AI partner might analyze classroom interactions to suggest differentiated instructional techniques, identify knowledge gaps, or facilitate tailored interventions for diverse learner needs. Furthermore, AI as a partner fosters a reciprocal learning environment. Just as educators and students benefit from AI's analytical and adaptive capabilities, AI systems learn and evolve from their interactions with users, becoming increasingly sophisticated and contextually aware. This partnership model reflects the broader goals of human-AI collaboration, emphasizing mutual enhancement rather than replacement. AI's integration into education is reshaping traditional paradigms, offering unprecedented opportunities for personalization, accessibility, and innovation. By leveraging capabilities such as machine learning, natural language processing, and data analytics, AI enhances the efficacy of teaching and learning processes while enabling data-informed decision-making. The distinction between AI as a tool and as a partner underscores its transformative potential, advocating for a balanced approach that amplifies human creativity and judgment. As AI evolves, its role in education will likely deepen, fostering a future where technology and humanity converge to create more equitable, efficient, and engaging learning ecosystems.

The Interplay of AI and STEAM Disciplines

Synergies Between AI and STEAM Fields

The convergence of Artificial Intelligence (AI) with STEAM disciplines—science, Technology, Engineering, Arts, and Mathematics—represents a paradigm shift in how knowledge is integrated, disseminated, and applied. At its core, AI serves as both a catalyst and an enabler, enhancing the synergies among these seemingly disparate fields to foster holistic problem-solving and innovation. Science and technology benefit from AI's ability to analyze vast datasets and identify patterns that might elude human cognition (Komkowski et al., 2023a; Singamaneni et al., 2022; S. Uniyal et al., 2021). For example, AI algorithms accelerate discovery by automating hypothesis generation and testing in fields like bioinformatics and astrophysics. Engineering integrates AI into intelligent systems design, enabling innovations like autonomous vehicles and sustainable infrastructure. In mathematics, AI's capacity to simulate complex systems and solve optimization problems has deepened my understanding of chaos theory and cryptography.

Perhaps most intriguingly, the integration of AI into the arts has demonstrated its potential to transcend traditional boundaries of creativity. AI-driven generative models, such as those used in music composition or visual art, exemplify how machine intelligence can complement human ingenuity, pushing the limits of artistic expression. By bridging analytical rigor with creative exploration, AI in STEAM disciplines exemplifies the interdisciplinary ethos central to addressing multifaceted global challenges.

AI-Driven Tools Fostering Interdisciplinary Learning

AI-driven tools have emerged as transformative instruments for facilitating interdisciplinary learning, a cornerstone of STEAM education. These tools leverage machine learning, natural language processing, and data visualization to create immersive, personalized, and adaptive learning experiences that span multiple domains (Gopal et al., 2023; Hajoary et al., 2023). For instance, AI-powered platforms like intelligent tutoring systems and virtual laboratories enable students to explore complex concepts through hands-on experimentation and real-time feedback. In a

STEAM context, these tools allow learners to design prototypes, simulate scientific experiments, or compose music using algorithms—all within a unified digital ecosystem. This integrative approach enhances comprehension and cultivates an appreciation for the interconnectedness of disciplines.

Role of AI in Enhancing Creativity and Innovation

A significant yet often underappreciated aspect of AI's impact on STEAM disciplines is its capacity to enhance creativity and innovation. Contrary to concerns that AI may undermine human ingenuity, it often acts as a collaborator, augmenting creative processes and inspiring new forms of expression.

In design and architecture, AI algorithms generate novel structures optimized for functionality and aesthetics, challenging traditional notions of form and utility. Similarly, in music and visual arts, AI-driven tools like neural networks and generative adversarial networks (GANs) allow artists to explore new mediums, styles, and techniques. These collaborations between human intuition and machine precision lead to groundbreaking outputs that neither could achieve independently. Moreover, AI's rapid iteration and experimentation capacity accelerates the innovation cycle. By analyzing historical trends and projecting future possibilities, AI helps innovators precisely identify untapped opportunities and refine their ideas. For example, in STEAM-based entrepreneurship, AI models assist in market analysis, user experience design, and product development, ensuring that creative ventures are impactful and viable.

AI also fosters a mindset of creative resilience by encouraging exploration and risk-taking. AI-driven platforms can simulate failure scenarios in educational settings, allowing students to learn from mistakes in a low-stakes environment. This iterative process enhances problem-solving skills and instills confidence, curiosity, and a willingness to think outside the box. The interplay of AI and STEAM disciplines exemplifies the transformative potential of interdisciplinary collaboration. By leveraging synergies across science, technology, engineering, arts, and mathematics, AI acts as both a tool and a partner, fostering creativity, enhancing innovation, and enabling holistic learning. As AI continues to evolve, its integration into STEAM fields promises to redefine the boundaries of what is possible, inspiring new ways of thinking, creating, and solving the complex challenges of the modern world.

Theoretical Frameworks

Constructivist and Connectivist Learning Theories in the Context of AI

The theoretical underpinnings of learning in an AI-enhanced educational environment are deeply rooted in constructivist and connectivist learning theories. These paradigms provide critical insights into how knowledge is acquired, contextualized, and applied in a technology-mediated setting.

Constructivist Learning Theory emphasizes that knowledge is constructed through active engagement and environmental interaction. Learners are not passive recipients of information but active participants in creating meaning (Gonfa et al., 2023; Pai et al., 2022; Raju et al., 2022). AI aligns seamlessly with constructivist principles by fostering environments where learners can engage in experiential, inquiry-driven, and personalized learning. For example, AI-powered adaptive learning platforms dynamically adjust to students' unique needs, abilities, and interests, creating individualized pathways that promote more profound engagement. Virtual reality (VR) and augmented reality (AR) technologies, enhanced by AI, further amplify constructivist practices by immersing learners in experiential simulations, enabling them to explore complex concepts interactively.

Connectivist Learning Theory, on the other hand, focuses on the role of networks and digital tools in knowledge acquisition. Proposed by Siemens and Downes, this theory asserts that learning in the digital age transcends individual cognition, emphasizing the collective intelligence embedded in networks and communities. AI, with its ability to process vast amounts of data and foster interconnectedness, epitomizes the principles of connectivism. AI-powered recommendation systems, for instance, connect learners to resources, experts, and communities that align with their learning goals.

AI's Alignment with 21st-Century Skills and Competencies

The emergence of AI in education is intrinsically linked to cultivating 21st-century skills and competencies, emphasizing creativity, critical thinking, communication, collaboration, and technological literacy. These skills are essential for thriving in an increasingly interconnected and rapidly evolving world.

Critical Thinking and Problem-Solving are augmented through AI's capacity to analyze vast datasets and generate insights. Predictive analytics and decision-support systems enable learners to tackle complex, real-world challenges by identifying patterns, evaluating scenarios, and formulating evidence-based solutions.

AI-driven platforms that support ideation, design, and innovation significantly enhance creativity. Generative AI models, for instance, allow learners to experiment with novel artistic forms, engineering prototypes, and business strategies. By providing iterative feedback and fostering exploration, these tools amplify human ingenuity. AI's ability to connect individuals across cultural and disciplinary boundaries transforms collaboration and communication. Language translation tools, virtual meeting platforms, and intelligent agents facilitate seamless interaction, enabling diverse groups to work collaboratively on shared goals.

Technological Literacy is inherently fostered as learners interact with AI systems, gaining familiarity with their functionalities, limitations, and ethical implications. This literacy is critical for navigating the digital landscape and contributing to the responsible development and deployment of AI technologies. By aligning with these competencies, AI empowers learners to adapt, innovate, and lead in an era of perpetual change and complexity.

Ethical Considerations and Responsible AI in Education

As AI becomes increasingly integrated into education, its ethical implications demand scrutiny. The concept of responsible AI emphasizes developing and deploying AI systems that are transparent, equitable, and aligned with human values. Equity and Inclusion are paramount concerns, as AI systems must avoid exacerbating educational disparities. Bias in AI algorithms, stemming from skewed datasets or systemic inequities, can perpetuate discrimination and limit opportunities for marginalized groups. Ensuring diversity in data collection and algorithmic design is essential to mitigate these risks. Privacy and Data Security are equally critical, given the sensitive nature of student data collected by AI systems. Robust safeguards must be implemented to protect against unauthorized access, misuse, and breaches. Transparency in data usage and adherence to legal and ethical standards are essential to maintain trust among stakeholders.

Autonomy and Accountability raise questions about AI's role in decision-making processes. While AI can enhance efficiency and accuracy, overreliance on automated systems risks undermining human judgment and agency. Clear guidelines and oversight mechanisms must be established to ensure that AI complements rather than supplants human expertise. Transparency in AI systems is another crucial consideration. Educators, students, and policymakers must clearly understand how AI algorithms operate, make decisions, and adapt over time (Godbole et al., 2023; G. Jindal et al., 2023; Srivastava et al., 2022). Black-box models that lack explainability can erode trust and hinder meaningful engagement with AI tools. Fostering AI literacy among all stakeholders is imperative to address these challenges. Educators and students must be equipped to evaluate AI systems critically, understand their implications, and advocate for their ethical use. Policymakers and developers, in turn, must prioritize designing AI systems aligned with principles of fairness, accountability, and transparency. Integrating AI into education reshapes traditional pedagogical paradigms, offering unprecedented opportunities for personalized, connected, and skill-centric learning. Through the lens of constructivist and connectivist theories, AI emerges as a transformative force that enhances engagement, collaboration, and adaptability. Its alignment with 21st-century competencies underscores its potential to prepare learners for the challenges and opportunities of a rapidly evolving world. However, the ethical considerations surrounding responsible AI highlight the need for vigilance, inclusivity, and transparency in its deployment. By addressing these dimensions thoughtfully, AI can be a powerful ally in pursuing equitable and innovative education.

AI-DRIVEN CURRICULUM INNOVATION

Personalization and Adaptive Learning

AI Tools for Personalized Learning Paths

The advent of Artificial Intelligence (AI) in education has introduced transformative tools capable of tailoring learning experiences to individual needs, preferences, and abilities. Central to this innovation are adaptive learning systems that leverage AI algorithms to analyze data, such as a learner's prior knowledge, engagement patterns, and performance metrics (Ansari & Afzal, 2022; Kaushal et al., 2022; Kowsalya et al., 2023; K. Sharma et al., 2022). These systems dynamically adjust the content, pace, and mode of delivery, ensuring a personalized learning path for each student.

AI-powered platforms, such as intelligent tutoring systems (ITS), exemplify this capability. These systems employ machine learning to identify gaps in understanding and recommend targeted resources or exercises to address them. For instance, platforms like Carnegie Learning's MATHia use predictive analytics to anticipate student struggles and provide real-time, context-sensitive feedback. Similarly, AI-driven language learning applications, such as Duolingo, adapt to a learner's progress by modifying the difficulty and variety of exercises.

Moreover, natural language processing (NLP) has enabled AI tools to comprehend and respond to open-ended student queries, further personalizing the learning process. Virtual teaching assistants, like IBM Watson Tutor, interact conversationally with learners, creating a more engaging and supportive educational environment.

Case Studies: AI in Tailoring Educational Content

One notable case study involves DreamBox Learning, an adaptive mathematics platform for K-8 students. DreamBox analyzes over 48,000 data points per student every hour and creates customized lessons that align with individual skill levels and learning styles. In another example, Squirrel AI, a Chinese ed-tech company, employs AI to deliver personalized lessons to millions of students. The platform dissects complex concepts into granular knowledge points and adjusts the curriculum based on learners' mastery of each point. AI's capacity to tailor educational content is not confined to primary education. In higher education, platforms like Coursera utilize AI algorithms to recommend courses, learning modules, and peer discussions based on individual goals and preferences, fostering a lifelong learning mindset.

Benefits for Diverse Learners, Including Those with Disabilities

Personalized AI tools hold immense potential for accommodating diverse learners, including those with disabilities. For instance, text-to-speech (TTS) and speech-to-text (STT) technologies powered by AI enhance accessibility for students with visual or hearing impairments. Tools like Microsoft's Immersive Reader provide features such as font customization, translation, and text highlighting to support learners with dyslexia or other reading challenges (Belwal et al., 2023; K. D. Singh et al., 2023). Additionally, AI-powered assistive technologies, such as Tobii Dynavox's eye-tracking devices, empower students with mobility impairments to interact with digital content seamlessly. For neurodiverse learners, platforms like Cognifit offer personalized cognitive training programs that address specific needs, including attention deficits and executive functioning difficulties.

AI tools ensure that all learners, regardless of their abilities or backgrounds, can thrive in educational environments by fostering inclusivity and enabling customized support.

Enhancing Collaborative Learning

AI-Powered Platforms Facilitating Collaboration

AI-powered platforms have significantly enhanced collaborative learning, an integral component of STEAM education. These platforms facilitate group interactions by analyzing team dynamics, suggesting strategies for effective communication, and mediating conflicts (V. Kumar & Korovin, 2023; Sathyaseelan et al., 2023). AI-powered collaboration tools like Slack and Microsoft Teams integrate intelligent bots that streamline project management, schedule meetings, and provide real-time updates, enabling efficient teamwork. AI-driven platforms also support peer-to-peer learning by matching students with complementary skills and knowledge. For example, platforms like Peergrade and Piazza utilize AI to create productive learning communities where students can exchange feedback, clarify doubts, and co-create knowledge. These tools enhance the learning experience and prepare students for the collaborative demands of the modern workforce.

Virtual and Augmented Reality in Team-Based Projects

Integrating virtual reality (VR) and augmented reality (AR) with AI has revolutionized collaborative learning by creating immersive environments for team-based projects. AI-driven VR platforms enable learners to interact with virtual objects and environments collaboratively, fostering experiential understanding and problem-solving (L. S. Khanna et al., 2023). For instance, AI-integrated VR tools like Enscape in architectural education allow teams to design, visualize, and refine 3D models in real-time. Similarly, AR applications like Merge Cube enable students to manipulate holographic objects collaboratively, making abstract STEAM concepts tangible and comprehensible.

By combining AI's analytical capabilities with the immersive power of VR and AR, these technologies enhance teamwork, creativity, and critical thinking in educational settings.

Examples of AI-Driven Collaborative STEAM Initiatives

One exemplary initiative is Stanford's d.school's AI-supported STEAM project, where students use AI tools to address real-world challenges collaboratively. For instance, interdisciplinary teams might leverage AI algorithms to design sustainable urban infrastructure or develop assistive technologies for individuals with disabilities. Such initiatives demonstrate AI's role in fostering cross-disciplinary collaboration and innovation. Another example is MIT's AI+ART Collaborative, which integrates AI into artistic projects, encouraging students from diverse STEAM fields to co-create visual and auditory experiences. These initiatives exemplify how AI can bridge disciplinary silos, fostering a culture of collaboration and innovation.

Gamification and Experiential Learning

Role of AI in Designing Engaging Educational Games

Gamification, the application of game-design elements in non-game contexts, has emerged as a powerful pedagogical strategy for enhancing motivation and engagement. AI plays a pivotal role in this domain by creating adaptive, immersive, and contextually relevant educational games. AI-powered gamified platforms, such as Kahoot! and Classcraft, tailor game dynamics to individual learners. By analyzing player behavior and preferences, AI adjusts game difficulty, provides personalized feedback, and ensures sustained engagement (Hajoary et al., 2023; A. S. Kumar & Desi, 2023; Sathyapriya et al., 2022). Machine learning algorithms further enhance these experiences by predicting learner fatigue and introducing varied challenges to maintain interest. Moreover, AI enables the development of serious games that simulate real-world scenarios. For example, SimCityEDU integrates AI to teach urban planning concepts, while Foldit uses AI to engage students in solving protein-folding puzzles, contributing to real scientific discoveries.

Case Studies: AI in Immersive STEAM Learning Experiences

QLabster, an AI-powered virtual laboratory platform, is an exemplary case study. Labster offers gamified STEAM learning experiences, allowing students to perform virtual physics, biology, and chemistry experiments. AI algorithms guide learners through complex simulations, offering hints and feedback to reinforce understanding. Another notable example is Minecraft: Education Edition, which integrates AI to facilitate STEAM-based collaborative projects. For instance, students can use the game to design energy-efficient structures, with AI providing data-driven insights into sustainability metrics. These immersive experiences make learning enjoyable and deepen conceptual understanding and application.

Impact on Motivation and Retention of STEAM Concepts

AI-driven gamification profoundly impacts learner motivation and retention of STEAM concepts. By transforming abstract ideas into interactive challenges, AI-enabled games make learning enjoyable and memorable (R. Kumar, Kandpal, & Ahmad, 2023; Medhi et al., 2023; Reddy et al., 2023; Shashikala et al., 2022). Gamified platforms incorporating leaderboards, badges, and rewards tap into intrinsic and extrinsic motivators, fostering a competitive yet collaborative learning environment. Research demonstrates that gamification enhances cognitive and emotional engagement, leading to improved retention and application of knowledge.

For example, students using AI-powered gamified platforms consistently outperform their peers in understanding and applying STEAM concepts, as these tools cater to diverse learning styles and preferences.

TECHNOLOGICAL INTEGRATION IN STEAM CLASSROOMS

AI-Enabled Tools and Platforms

Integrating Artificial Intelligence (AI) in STEAM (Science, Technology, Engineering, Arts, and Mathematics) classrooms has revolutionized teaching and learning dynamics. AI-driven tools and platforms offer educators and learners sophisticated capabilities to enhance pedagogical outcomes.

Overview of AI-Driven Educational Software and Hardware

AI-enabled educational software encompasses adaptive learning platforms, intelligent tutoring systems, and collaborative tools designed to personalize and optimize the learning experience. Platforms like ALEKS and Coursera employ machine learning algorithms to identify individual learning gaps and provide targeted content. Similarly, hardware innovations such as smartboards and AR/VR-enabled devices utilize AI to facilitate interactive and immersive learning experiences (Jaswal et al., 2023). These tools allow students to engage deeply with complex concepts through simulation and visualization. Robust Natural Language Processing (NLP) capabilities embedded in software like Grammarly and Turnitin enhance students' writing and analytical skills. AI-powered assessment tools like ExamSoft streamline evaluation processes by offering automated grading and detailed analytics.

Role of Robotics, Coding Platforms, and Intelligent Tutors

Robotics has emerged as a cornerstone of AI integration in STEAM education. Platforms like LEGO Mindstorms and VEX Robotics teach students engineering principles, programming, and problem-solving through hands-on experimentation. These tools not only promote technical skills but also foster creativity and teamwork. Coding platforms like Scratch and Code.org utilize AI to create engaging, gamified experiences, introducing programming concepts. Intelligent tutoring systems (ITS), such as Khan Academy and Carnegie Learning, provide personalized support by adapting to individual learning paces and styles, ensuring every student receives the guidance they need to succeed.

Challenges in Adoption and Scalability

`Despite the promise of AI tools, their widespread adoption faces significant hurdles. High implementation costs, particularly in underfunded educational institutions, limit accessibility. Additionally, the steep learning curve of mastering AI technologies presents a barrier for educators and students. Scalability poses another challenge, as AI systems often require substantial infrastructure and continuous updates to remain effective. Ethical concerns, including data privacy and algorithmic bias, further complicate adoption, necessitating stringent oversight and regulatory frameworks.

Teacher Training and Professional Development

The success of AI integration in STEAM classrooms hinges on adequately preparing educators to leverage these technologies effectively. Teacher training and professional development programs must address technical proficiency and pedagogical innovation.

Preparing Educators for AI Integration

Comprehensive training programs are essential to equip teachers with the skills to implement AI tools in their classrooms (Singla et al., 2023). Workshops, webinars, and certification courses focused on AI applications in education can bridge the knowledge gap. For instance, initiatives like Google's "AI for Teachers" program provide educators with hands-on experience using AI-driven platforms to enhance instruction. Training should also emphasize the pedagogical shifts required to integrate AI seamlessly into curricula. Educators must learn to balance traditional teaching methods with technology-enhanced approaches, fostering a hybrid model that caters to diverse learning styles.

AI Tools for Teacher Support and Workload Reduction

AI tools offer significant potential to reduce teachers' administrative burden, allowing them to focus more on instruction and student engagement. Platforms like Classcraft and Edmodo automate attendance tracking, assignment grading, and lesson planning tasks. AI-powered analytics tools provide actionable insights into student performance, enabling teachers to tailor their interventions effectively. Moreover, virtual teaching assistants, such as IBM Watson Tutor, support educators by answering routine queries, curating educational resources, and monitoring classroom dynamics. These tools enhance instructional efficiency while promoting a more personalized learning environment.

Building Teacher Competencies in Data Literacy and AI Ethics

As AI becomes increasingly central to education, data literacy and ethical awareness are essential for educators. Teachers must understand how AI systems collect, analyze, and interpret data to make informed decisions about their use. Data visualization and analytics training can empower educators to leverage AI insights to improve student outcomes (Josphineleela et al., 2023; A. Kumar et al., 2023). Ethical considerations, including data privacy, algorithmic bias, and transparency, should be integral to teacher training programs. By fostering a nuanced understanding of these issues, educators can advocate for responsible AI use and ensure that technology serves the best interests of all learners.

Assessment and Feedback Mechanisms

AI is transforming assessment and feedback processes in STEAM education by providing real-time, data-driven insights that enhance learning outcomes. These innovations are reshaping both formative and summative evaluations.

AI in Formative and Summative Assessments

AI-powered assessment tools facilitate formative and summative evaluations by automating grading and offering comprehensive performance analytics. For example, platforms like Gradescope use machine learning to evaluate complex responses, including essays and code, ensuring consistency and objectivity. Formative assessments benefit from AI's ability to identify learning gaps and suggest targeted interventions. Tools like Socrative and Quizlet employ adaptive questioning to gauge student understanding, providing immediate feedback that guides instructional adjustments. AI's capacity to analyze patterns and predict future performance trends similarly enhances summative assessments, such as standardized tests.

Real-Time Feedback and Progress Tracking

AI-driven feedback mechanisms foster a responsive and iterative learning process. Intelligent systems provide instant, specific, and actionable feedback, enabling students to correct mistakes and refine their understanding in real time (Abdullah et al., 2023; Kamra et al., 2023; Mishra & Wazid, 2023). For instance, platforms like Turnitin detect plagiarism and offer detailed writing suggestions, helping students improve their academic integrity and composition skills. Progress tracking tools like Brightspace Insights leverage AI to monitor student engagement and achievement over time. These systems generate visual dashboards highlighting strengths and areas for improvement, empowering students and educators to take proactive measures.

AI's Role in Promoting Self-Directed Learning

One of AI's most transformative educational contributions is its ability to foster self-directed learning. By providing personalized recommendations, adaptive learning platforms encourage students to take ownership of their educational journey. AI tools like Duolingo and Coursera's Skills Graph use predictive analytics to suggest relevant content and learning pathways, enabling students to set and achieve their goals autonomously (Nadeem et al., 2023; Suresh et al., 2023; Tomar et al., 2023; Verma et al., 2022). By promoting autonomy and engagement, AI equips students with the skills and mindset needed for lifelong learning. Integrating AI into STEAM classrooms represents a paradigm shift in education, offering unprecedented personalization, collaboration, and efficiency opportunities. AI-enabled tools and platforms revolutionize learning experiences by adapting to individual needs and fostering hands-on exploration. Teacher training and professional development are critical to ensuring the effective implementation of these technologies, emphasizing technical skills, ethical awareness, and pedagogical innovation.

CASE STUDIES AND GLOBAL PERSPECTIVES

Exemplary Initiatives: AI in STEAM Education across Developed and Developing Countries

Artificial Intelligence (AI) integration in Science, Technology, Engineering, Arts, and Mathematics (STEAM) education has garnered significant attention in recent years. Across both developed and developing nations, AI-powered tools are transforming educational paradigms, enhancing learning experiences, and preparing students for future workforce demands. This section examines exemplary initiatives, success stories, and lessons learned from pilot projects.

AI in STEAM Education: A Global Perspective

In developed countries, well-established infrastructures and research institutions often support AI integration in STEAM education. For instance, initiatives like AI4All are working to broaden AI literacy among underrepresented groups in

STEAM fields in the United States. This program offers AI education to high school students, focusing on its applications in fields such as healthcare, robotics, and the arts. This enhances both technical skills and ethical awareness of AI's social impact. In Europe, the European Schoolnet initiative connects over 30 countries, fostering the integration of AI into classrooms to enhance teaching methodologies. This collaboration among educational authorities, technology providers, and research bodies aims to make AI tools accessible to teachers and students (S. Bansal et al., 2023; Mohd et al., 2023; Yadav et al., 2021). AI personalizes learning, provides real-time feedback, and enhances engagement through gamified learning environments. On the other hand, developing countries are facing unique challenges in implementing AI in STEAM education. However, countries like India and Kenya are making strides with pilot projects to integrate AI into curricula. For example, The Indian Ministry of Education has partnered with tech companies like IBM and Google to bring AI literacy into schools through programs such as AI for All. This initiative focuses on providing training for teachers, curriculum developers, and students in AI tools and applications. Kenya's Kenya Education Cloud (KEC) has also introduced AI-supported platforms that adapt learning content to the student's pace and progress, which has proven beneficial in remote and underserved regions.

Table 1. AI adoption in education: Global overview

Region	Percentage of Schools with AI Integration	Key Challenges
North America	50%	Privacy concerns, digital divide
Europe	45%	Data security, teacher readiness
Africa	10%	Limited access to infrastructure
Asia	30%	Affordability, socio-economic disparities

Source: (Arora et al., 2023; Masal et al., 2022; Ram, Negi, et al., 2022; Raman et al., 2023)

Table 1 highlights the disparities in AI integration across global regions. North America and Europe lead with 50% and 45% of schools incorporating AI despite facing challenges like privacy concerns and teacher preparedness. Conversely, Africa shows a significantly lower rate of 10%, grappling with limited infrastructure, while Asia exhibits a moderate 30%, hindered primarily by socio-economic barriers and affordability issues.

Success Stories: AI-Enhanced STEAM Programs

The successful deployment of AI in STEAM education has led to several noteworthy success stories. One such story comes from the Massachusetts Institute of Technology (MIT), where the AI+CS initiative has resulted in AI-enhanced computer science programs that have contributed to advancements in technical education and driven interdisciplinary collaborations with arts and humanities. AI algorithms foster creative problem-solving and innovation, merging computational thinking with artistic expression. Another success story is DigiPen Institute of Technology's AI-powered creative computing programs, which offer a curriculum designed to bridge the gap between STEAM fields. Students develop games and interactive media with real-time AI feedback, combining computational logic and artistic design. These AI-enhanced programs have led to impressive student outcomes, with several students securing roles at major tech companies and leading AI startups.

Lessons Learned from Pilot Projects

Pilot projects have offered valuable insights into the practical implementation of AI in STEAM education. A key lesson from these initiatives is the importance of teacher involvement (Kour et al., 2025; A. Singh et al., 2024; Taneja, Gupta, Singh, Bhatnagar, et al., 2023; TANEJA et al., 2024). In Kenya, the pilot of AI tools for personalized learning faced initial resistance due to a lack of teacher training. As a result, subsequent iterations of the program focused heavily on providing educators with adequate training and ongoing support to foster effective integration.

Another crucial lesson comes from the AI for All program in India, which faced scalability challenges due to disparities in access to digital resources across rural and urban areas. To address this, the program developed a hybrid model incorporating both online and offline learning solutions, allowing students from remote areas to access AI education.

Table 2. Comparison of AI-enhanced STEAM programs in developed vs developing countries

Country	Program Name	Key Features	Success Rate (%)
USA	AI4All	AI literacy for underrepresented groups	85
India	AI for All	Hybrid model, rural and urban access	75
Kenya	Kenya Education Cloud	AI personalized learning platforms	80
UK	European Schoolnet	AI integration in multiple disciplines	90

Source: (Özen et al., 2024a, 2024b; Taneja et al., 2024, 2025)

Table 2 contrasts AI-driven STEAM programs across both developed and developing nations. Notably, the AI4All program in the USA excels with an 85% success rate, focusing on inclusivity. In India, the AI for All initiative caters to rural and urban students, with a 75% success rate, while Kenya's Kenya Education Cloud offers tailored learning, achieving an 80% success rate. European efforts show a 90% success rate due to comprehensive integration.

Challenges and Barriers

While AI in STEAM education offers substantial benefits, its integration is not without challenges. Several technical and socio-economic barriers must be overcome to ensure equitable access and success.

Socio-Economic Disparities in AI Access

One of the primary challenges in AI adoption in STEAM education is the socio-economic divide. In many developing countries, infrastructure constraints, internet connectivity issues, and affordability limit access to AI tools and high-quality educational resources. According to a UNESCO report (2023), 40% of schools in low-income countries lack reliable internet access, which hinders the adoption of AI-driven educational technologies (N. Bansal et al., 2023; Dangwal et al., 2022; Reepu et al., 2023; Taneja, Gupta, Bhushan, Bhatnagar, et al., 2023; Taneja & Sharma, 2023). Furthermore, students from low-income backgrounds often have limited access to the necessary hardware, such as computers or smartphones, to fully participate in AI-enhanced learning environments.

Ethical Concerns: Privacy, Bias, and Transparency

The use of AI in education raises significant ethical concerns related to privacy, bias, and transparency. Questions about data security and privacy arise as AI tools collect vast amounts of personal data from students. The European Commission's AI Strategy (2023) emphasizes the need for strict regulations to protect student data and ensure that AI algorithms do not exploit personal information. Moreover, biases in AI algorithms pose a critical challenge, as they may perpetuate existing inequalities in education. In 2023, a study by The AI Now Institute revealed that AI algorithms used in educational settings often exhibit biases against underrepresented groups, particularly in subjects like STEM, which can limit the effectiveness of AI in promoting inclusive education.

Resistance to Technological Change in Education Systems

In many educational systems, there is inherent resistance to adopting new technologies, including AI. This resistance often stems from a lack of trust in AI's capabilities, concerns about job displacement, and a traditional view of pedagogy that values face-to-face interaction over digital tools. According to OECD (2023), more than 30% of educators in OECD countries expressed concerns about the disruptive nature of AI and its potential to replace teachers rather than augment their role. Overcoming this resistance requires comprehensive change management strategies, including continuous professional development, stakeholder engagement, and clear communication about the benefits of AI in the classroom.

Table 3. Common barriers to AI in STEAM education

Barrier	Description	Affected Regions
Socio-economic Disparities	Unequal access to digital resources	Developing countries
Ethical Concerns	Privacy issues, biases in AI algorithms	Global
Resistance to Change	Cultural resistance to AI tools in classrooms	Developed countries

Source: (Bhatnagar, Rajaram, et al., 2024; Bhatnagar, Taneja, et al., 2024; Bhatnagar & Sehajpal, 2024; Taneja, Bhatnagar, Kumar, & Grima, 2023; Taneja, Bhatnagar, Kumar, & Rupeika-apoga, 2023)

Table 3 delineates key barriers impeding AI adoption in education. Socio-economic disparities, particularly in developing regions, exacerbate unequal access to digital tools. Ethical concerns, such as privacy violations and algorithmic biases, are ubiquitous global challenges. Additionally, resistance to AI technologies in classrooms—predominantly in developed countries—reflects a deep-seated cultural and institutional reluctance to embrace technological disruption in education systems.

Policy Implications

For AI to be successfully integrated into STEAM education, robust policy frameworks must be established at local, national, and international levels. These frameworks should address the challenges and barriers discussed above and ensure that AI is used ethically, equitably, and effectively.

Policy Frameworks for AI Adoption in STEAM Education

National governments must develop policies that promote the responsible and inclusive use of AI in education. These policies should focus on providing equitable access to AI tools, ensuring data privacy, and mitigating biases in AI algorithms. Furthermore, policymakers should prioritize funding for digital infrastructure and teacher training to ensure that all students, regardless of socio-economic background, can benefit from AI-enhanced education. In the EU, the Digital Education Action Plan (2022) advocates for integrating AI into educational frameworks, with a focus on developing digital competences, enhancing data protection laws, and ensuring inclusive access to AI technologies. Similar policy initiatives are being explored in countries like Canada and Singapore, which have developed national strategies to integrate AI into education.

Role of Governments, Academia, and Industry Partnerships

Collaboration between governments, academia, and the private sector is critical for successfully implementing AI in STEAM education. Governments can provide the necessary policy frameworks and funding, while academia can contribute research on best practices and innovative pedagogies. Industry partnerships are essential for developing AI tools and ensuring that they meet the evolving needs of the education sector.

In India, the government's partnership with global tech companies like Microsoft and Google has played a pivotal role in promoting AI education. These partnerships have provided teachers and students with access to AI-powered tools, training programs, and resources, significantly advancing AI literacy.

Recommendations for Equitable and Inclusive AI Integration

To ensure equitable AI integration in STEAM education, several recommendations can be made:

1. **Invest in Digital Infrastructure**: Governments should prioritize investment in internet connectivity, digital devices, and AI tools, especially in rural and underserved areas.
2. **Promote Teacher Training**: Adequate training programs for educators are essential to ensure they are well-equipped to use AI effectively in the classroom.
3. **Focus on Inclusivity**: AI tools should be designed with inclusivity in mind, ensuring they cater to diverse learning needs and mitigate biases.

4. **Strengthen Data Protection**: Strict data protection laws must be established to safeguard student information and prevent misuse of personal data.
5. **Foster International Collaboration**: Global partnerships between countries, educational institutions, and tech companies can accelerate AI adoption and create a unified approach to tackling challenges.

Table 4. Policy recommendations for AI integration in STEAM education

Recommendation	Action	Stakeholders Involved
Digital Infrastructure Investment	Improve internet access and provide devices to schools	Governments, tech companies
Teacher Training Programs	Develop continuous training for educators on AI tools	Academia, NGOs, Governments
Inclusive AI Design	Ensure AI tools are accessible and non-biased	Tech companies, NGOs
Data Protection	Enforce strict privacy laws on student data	Governments, regulators

Source: UNESCO, 2023

Table 4 provides strategic policy recommendations to facilitate equitable AI adoption in education. Investment in digital infrastructure is crucial for ensuring access to technology, particularly in underserved areas. Continuous teacher training programs are essential for fostering AI proficiency among educators. Furthermore, AI tools must be inclusively designed to address diverse learning needs. At the same time, robust data protection policies should be enacted to safeguard student information, with all stakeholders playing a collaborative role.

EMERGING TRENDS

The future of education is intricately intertwined with the rapid advancements in Artificial Intelligence (AI), with numerous emerging trends reshaping the landscape of STEAM (Science, Technology, Engineering, Arts, and Mathematics) education. As these fields converge with AI technologies, new paradigms are being developed that promise to transform how we teach and the content of the curricula. One of the most exciting trends is the integration of sustainability into STEAM curricula, driven by AI. The intersection of AI and sustainability offers a transformative approach to environmental education, equipping students with the knowledge and tools to address global challenges such as climate change, resource depletion, and social inequality. AI's ability to model complex systems, predict outcomes, and optimize processes provides unparalleled opportunities for integrating sustainability concepts into real-world applications within education. For example, AI can simulate environmental scenarios or optimize energy systems, thus deepening students' understanding of sustainability within an interdisciplinary context. Educational institutions are already beginning to embed these AI-driven sustainability models into their curricula, offering a glimpse into the future of environmental education. Another pivotal trend is the convergence of AI and quantum computing within the education sector. While quantum computing remains in its early stages, its potential to revolutionize fields such as cryptography, drug discovery, and material science is enormous. The marriage of quantum computing and AI holds tremendous promise for transforming educational methodologies, particularly in problem-solving and data analysis. As these technologies advance, they will enable a new generation of learners to engage with highly complex simulations, giving them hands-on experience with next-generation computational tools. Quantum-enhanced AI algorithms could allow students to solve previously insurmountable problems with traditional computing, thus ushering in a new era of intellectual discovery and innovation.

Vision for Society 5.0

Society 5.0, a concept championed by Japan, envisions a highly integrated society where cyberspace and physical space are seamlessly interconnected, driven by technologies like AI, IoT, and robotics. The aim is to achieve a harmonious coexistence between human society and advanced technology, fostering innovation while addressing societal challenges. A critical aspect of this vision is bridging the gap between AI capabilities and societal needs. AI has the potential to address a wide range of societal challenges, from healthcare to education and transportation. However, for these technologies to truly benefit society, there must be a strategic alignment between technological capabilities and real-world problems. This requires collaboration between governments, industries, and educational institutions to ensure that AI solutions are technically feasible and socially beneficial, addressing issues such as inequality, climate change, and public health. To prepare learners for an AI-driven workforce, educational systems must evolve to prioritize the development of AI literacy and critical thinking skills. As AI becomes increasingly prevalent in industries ranging from healthcare to finance, workers must be equipped with technical knowledge and the ability to navigate these technologies' ethical, social, and economic implications. Curriculum frameworks must emphasize interdisciplinary learning, blending AI and ethics, policy, and human-centered design to prepare students for the multifaceted challenges of the future workforce. This approach will foster a workforce that is not only technologically proficient but also ethically aware and socially responsible.

Call to Action

The future of AI-enhanced STEAM education requires a concerted effort to foster interdisciplinary research and innovation. Encouraging collaboration across disciplines is essential for developing AI tools that are not only technically advanced but also socially relevant. Universities, research institutes, and private enterprises must work together to develop innovative AI-driven curricula that reflect the evolving needs of the global workforce. By supporting cross-disciplinary research and cultivating a culture of innovation, we can ensure that AI technologies are applied in ways that maximize their potential to solve complex global challenges. Building global networks for AI-enhanced STEAM education is another crucial step in advancing these educational advancements. As AI technologies transcend borders, creating international platforms for collaboration and knowledge exchange is essential. We can create a global community dedicated to advancing AI education and ensuring its equitable distribution by fostering partnerships between institutions, industries, and governments worldwide. These networks will facilitate the sharing of best practices, promote policy dialogue, and enable the development of standardized curricula incorporating AI across various educational contexts.

Finally, fostering a culture of continuous improvement in AI pedagogy is vital for ensuring that AI's role in education remains dynamic and adaptable. Educational practices must evolve alongside technological advancements to ensure that curricula remain relevant and that teaching methods are optimized for the digital age. This requires ongoing professional development for educators and the integration of feedback loops that allow AI tools to adapt and improve based on real-world applications. By embracing a culture of perpetual innovation, we can ensure that AI-enhanced STEAM education remains at the forefront of global educational reform, empowering future generations to navigate and thrive in an AI-driven world.

Managerial Implications

The managerial implications of this chapter's exploration into AI-enhanced STEAM education underscore AI's transformative potential in shaping educational and organizational landscapes. First, managers within educational institutions must prioritize the integration of AI into curricula, recognizing its capacity to revolutionize teaching methodologies, personalize learning experiences, and facilitate cross-disciplinary innovation. This necessitates investment in teacher training, infrastructure, and AI-powered platforms that support adaptive learning and reskilling initiatives. Moreover, educational leaders must adopt a holistic approach to AI implementation, considering technological tools and ethical frameworks to mitigate biases and ensure data privacy. For managers in the corporate sector, especially those in industries driven by technological advancements, there is a clear mandate to foster a workforce adept in AI and STEAM-related skills. This requires the establishment of continuous learning ecosystems within organizations, promoting lifelong learning through AI-driven reskilling programs. Embracing AI to upskill employees will be critical in maintaining competitive advantage and addressing talent shortages in emerging fields. Furthermore, aligning AI adoption with sustainability goals will position organizations as corporate responsibility leaders, enhancing reputation and long-term profitability. Finally, policymakers and business leaders must collaborate to bridge the gap between AI capabilities and societal needs. Managers must actively engage in partnerships that promote global networks for AI-enhanced education, ensuring equitable access to cutting-edge tools across diverse socio-economic landscapes. By fostering a culture of interdisciplinary research, innovation, and ethical AI practices, managerial strategies can catalyze the growth of an AI-driven workforce that meets future demands while adhering to human-centric values.

CONCLUSION

In conclusion, integrating Artificial Intelligence (AI) into STEAM education marks a pivotal turning point in educational and professional landscapes. The exploration of emerging trends, such as AI's role in fostering sustainability, its convergence with quantum computing, and its capacity to drive lifelong learning, underscores the profound potential of AI to revolutionize teaching and learning paradigms. These innovations enhance educational experiences and prepare learners for the complexities of an AI-driven workforce. The concept of Society 5.0 further emphasizes the need for a seamless blend of technological capabilities and societal needs, urging the alignment of AI-driven education with broader social and ethical considerations. Ultimately, the path forward requires a concerted effort to responsibly harness AI's transformative power. By prioritizing ethical considerations, continuous innovation, and interdisciplinary research, we can ensure that AI not only advances technological progress but also supports the creation of a more equitable, sustainable, and human-centric future.

REFERENCES

Abdullah, K. H., Abd Aziz, F. S., Dani, R., Hammood, W. A., & Setiawan, E. (2023). Urban Pollution: A Bibliometric Review. *ASM Science Journal, 18*, 1–16. DOI: 10.32802/ASMSCJ.2023.1440

Agarwal, P., & Sharma, S. (2023). Smart Urban Traffic Management System using Energy Efficient Optimized Path Discovery. *Proceedings of the 3rd International Conference on Artificial Intelligence and Smart Energy, ICAIS 2023*, 858 – 863. https://doi.org/DOI: 10.1109/ICAIS56108.2023.10073840

Ahmad, I., Sharma, S., Kumar, R., Dhyani, S., & Dumka, A. (2023). Data Analytics of Online Education during Pandemic Health Crisis: A Case Study. *2nd Edition of IEEE Delhi Section Owned Conference, DELCON 2023 - Proceedings*. https://doi .org/DOI: 10.1109/DELCON57910.2023.10127423

Ansari, M. F., & Afzal, A. (2022). Sensitivity and Performance Analysis of 10 MW Solar Power Plant Using MPPT Technique. *Lecture Notes in Electrical Engineering, 894 LNEE*, 512–518. https://doi.org/DOI: 10.1007/978-981-19-1677-9_46

Arora, R., Chauhan, A., Singh, A. P., & Sharma, R. (2023). Optimization of a production inventory model of imperfect quality items for three-layer supply chain in fuzzy environment. *Benchmarking*. Advance online publication. DOI: 10.1108/ BIJ-11-2021-0678

Awal, G., & Khanna, R. (2019). Determinants of millennial online consumer behavior and prospective purchase decisions. *International Journal of Advanced Science and Technology, 28*(18), 366–378.

Bansal, N., Bhatnagar, M., & Taneja, S. (2023). Balancing priorities through green optimism: A study elucidating initiatives, approaches, and strategies for sustainable supply chain management. In *Handbook of Research on Designing Sustainable Supply Chains to Achieve a Circular Economy*. IGI Global., DOI: 10.4018/978-1-6684-7664-2.ch004

Bansal, S., Kumar, V., Kumari, A., & Kuzmin, E. (2023). Understanding the Role of Digital Technologies in Supply Chain Management of SMEs. In K. V., K. G.L., A. V., & K. E. (Eds.), *Lecture Notes in Information Systems and Organisation: Vol. 61 LNISO* (pp. 195 – 205). Springer Science and Business Media Deutschland GmbH. https://doi.org/DOI: 10.1007/978-3-031-30351-7_16

Belwal, N., Juneja, P., & Sunori, S. K. (2023). Decoupler Control for a MIMO Process Model in an Industrial Process - A Review. *2023 2nd International Conference on Ambient Intelligence in Health Care, ICAIHC 2023*. https://doi.org/DOI: 10.1109/ICAIHC59020.2023.10431463

Bhatnagar, M., Rajaram, R., Taneja, S., & Kumar, P. (2024). Balancing acts: The Yin and Yang of debit and credit on the stage of financial well-being. In *Emerging Perspectives on Financial Well-Being*. IGI Global., DOI: 10.4018/979-8-3693-1750-1.ch002

Bhatnagar, M., & Sehajpal, S. (2024). Leveraging AI for Financial Sustainability in Healthcare. In Ercan, O., Azad, S., Sanjay, T., Rajendra, R., & Paulo, D. J. (Eds.), *Sustainability, Innovation, and Consumer Preference* (pp. 411–426). IGI Global Scientific Publishing., DOI: 10.4018/979-8-3693-9699-5.ch017

Bhatnagar, M., Taneja, S., Kumar, P., & Özen, E. (2024). Does financial education act as a catalyst for SME competitiveness? *International Journal of Education Economics and Development*, *15*(3), 377–393. DOI: 10.1504/IJEED.2024.139306

Caiado, R. G. G., Scavarda, L. F., Vidal, G., de Mattos Nascimento, D. L., & Garza-Reyes, J. A. (2023). A taxonomy of critical factors towards sustainable operations and supply chain management 4.0 in developing countries. *Operations Management Research*. https://doi.org/DOI: 10.1007/s12063-023-00430-8

Cavaliere, L. P. L., Byloppilly, R., Khan, S. D., Othman, B. A., Muda, I., & Malhotra, R. K. (2024). Acceptance and effectiveness of Industry 4.0 internal and external organisational initiatives in Malaysian firms. *International Journal of Management and Enterprise Development*, *23*(1), 1–25. DOI: 10.1504/IJMED.2024.138422

Chahar, A., & Christobel, Y. A. Ritika, Adakane, P. K., Sonal, D., & Tripathi, V. (2022). The Implementation of Big Data With Cloud and Edge Computing in Enhancing the Smart Grid Information Processes Through Sem Model. *2022 2nd International Conference on Advance Computing and Innovative Technologies in Engineering, ICACITE 2022*, 608 – 611. https://doi.org/DOI: 10.1109/ICACITE53722.2022.9823896

Dangwal, A., Kaur, S., Taneja, S., & Ozen, E. (2022). A bibliometric analysis of green tourism based on the scopus platform. In *Developing Relationships, Personalization, and Data Herald in Marketing 5.0*. IGI Global., DOI: 10.4018/978-1-6684-4496-2.ch015

Davuluri, S. K., Alvi, S. A. M., Aeri, M., Agarwal, A., Serajuddin, M., & Hasan, Z. (2023). A Security Model for Perceptive 5G-Powered BC IoT Associated Deep Learning. *6th International Conference on Inventive Computation Technologies, ICICT 2023 - Proceedings*, 118 – 125. https://doi.org/DOI: 10.1109/ICICT57646.2023.10134487

Dogra, V., Verma, D., Dalapati, G. K., Sharma, M., & Okhawilai, M. (2022). Special focus on 3D printing of sulfides/selenides for energy conversion and storage. In *Sulfide and Selenide Based Materials for Emerging Applications: Sustainable Energy Harvesting and Storage Technology*. Elsevier., DOI: 10.1016/B978-0-323-99860-4.00012-5

Godbole, V., Kukrety, S., Gautam, P., Bisht, M., & Pal, M. K. (2023). Bioleaching for Heavy Metal Extraction from E-waste: A Sustainable Approach. In *Microbial Technology for Sustainable E-waste Management*. Springer International Publishing., DOI: 10.1007/978-3-031-25678-3_4

Gonfa, Y. H., Tessema, F. B., Tadesse, M. G., Bachheti, A., & Bachheti, R. K. (2023). Medicinally Important Plant Roots and Their Role in Nanoparticles Synthesis and Applications. In *Secondary Metabolites from Medicinal Plants: Nanoparticles Synthesis and their Applications*. CRC Press., DOI: 10.1201/9781003213727-11

Gopal, S., Gupta, P., & Minocha, A. (2023). Advancements in Fin-Tech and Security Challenges of Banking Industry. *4th International Conference on Intelligent Engineering and Management, ICIEM 2023*. https://doi.org/DOI: 10.1109/ICIEM59379.2023.10165876

Gupta, A., Dixit, A. K., Kumar, K. S., Lavanya, C., Chakravarthi, M. K., & Gangodkar, D. (2022). Analyzing Robotics and Computer Integrated Manufacturing of Key Areas Using Cloud Computing. *Proceedings of 5th International Conference on Contemporary Computing and Informatics, IC3I 2022*, 194 – 199. https://doi .org/DOI: 10.1109/IC3I56241.2022.10072581

Gupta, C., Jindal, P., & Malhotra, R. K. (2022). A Study of Increasing Adoption Trends of Digital Technologies - An Evidence from Indian Banking. In D. N. & C. A. (Eds.), *AIP Conference Proceedings* (Vol. 2481). American Institute of Physics Inc. https://doi.org/DOI: 10.1063/5.0104572

Gupta, P., Gopal, S., Sharma, M., Joshi, S., Sahani, C., & Ahalawat, K. (2023). Agriculture Informatics and Communication: Paradigm of E-Governance and Drone Technology for Crop Monitoring. *9th International Conference on Smart Computing and Communications: Intelligent Technologies and Applications, ICSCC 2023*, 113 – 118. https://doi.org/DOI: 10.1109/ICSCC59169.2023.10335058

Hajoary, P. K., Balachandra, P., & Garza-Reyes, J. A. (2023). Industry 4.0 maturity and readiness assessment: An empirical validation using Confirmatory Composite Analysis. *Production Planning and Control.* Advance online publication. DOI: 10.1080/09537287.2023.2210545

Jaswal, N., Kukreja, V., Sharma, R., Chaudhary, P., & Garg, A. (2023). Citrus Leaf Scab Multi-Class Classification: A Hybrid Deep Learning Model for Precision Agriculture. *2023 4th IEEE Global Conference for Advancement in Technology, GCAT 2023.* https://doi.org/DOI: 10.1109/GCAT59970.2023.10353507

Jindal, G., Tiwari, V., Mahomad, R., Gehlot, A., Jindal, M., & Bordoloi, D. (2023). Predictive Design for Quality Assessment Employing Cloud Computing And Machine Learning. *2023 3rd International Conference on Advance Computing and Innovative Technologies in Engineering, ICACITE 2023*, 461 – 465. https://doi.org/DOI: 10.1109/ICACITE57410.2023.10182915

Jindal, T., Sheoliha, N., Kishore, K., Uike, D., Khurana, S., & Verma, D. (2022). A Conceptual Analysis on the Impact of Internet of Things (IOT) Towards on Digital Marketing Transformation. *2022 2nd International Conference on Advance Computing and Innovative Technologies in Engineering, ICACITE 2022*, 1943 – 1947. https://doi.org/DOI: 10.1109/ICACITE53722.2022.9823714

Joshi, K., Patil, S., Gupta, S., & Khanna, R. (2022). Role of Pranayma in emotional maturity for improving health. *Journal of Medical Pharmaceutical and Allied Sciences, 11*(2), 4569–4573. DOI: 10.55522/jmpas.V11I2.2033

Joshi, K., Sharma, R., Singh, N., & Sharma, B. (2023). Digital World of Cloud Computing and Wireless Networking: Challenges and Risks. In *Applications of Artificial Intelligence in Wireless Communication Systems.* IGI Global., DOI: 10.4018/978-1-6684-7348-1.ch003

Josphineleela, R., Jyothi, M., Natrayan, L., Kaviarasu, A., & Sharma, M. (2023). Development of IoT based Health Monitoring System for Disables using Microcontroller. *Proceedings - 7th International Conference on Computing Methodologies and Communication, ICCMC 2023*, 1380 – 1384. https://doi.org/DOI: 10.1109/ICCMC56507.2023.10084026

Kaliappan, S., Natrayan, L., & Garg, N. (2023). Checking and Supervisory System for Calculation of Industrial Constraints using Embedded System. *Proceedings of the 4th International Conference on Smart Electronics and Communication, ICOSEC 2023*, 87 – 90. https://doi.org/DOI: 10.1109/ICOSEC58147.2023.10275952

Kamra, J., Mani, A. P., & Tripathi, V. M. (2023). Decarbonization Trajectory in Cement Industry. In S. P., N. S., R. J.J.P.C., R. J.J.P.C., R. J.J.P.C., L.-I. G.-A. D., P. T., C. L., & P. L. (Eds.), *2023 8th International Conference on Smart and Sustainable Technologies, SpliTech 2023*. Institute of Electrical and Electronics Engineers Inc. https://doi.org/DOI: 10.23919/SpliTech58164.2023.10193682

Kannan, P. R., Periasamy, K., Pravin, P., & Vinod Kumaar, J. R. (2022). An experimental investigation of wire breakage and performance optimisation of WEDM process on machining of recycled aluminium alloy metal matrix composite. *Materials Science Poland*, *40*(3), 12–26. DOI: 10.2478/msp-2022-0030

Kanojia, P., Malhotra, R. K., & Uniyal, A. K. (2022). Organizational Commitment and the Academic Staff in HEI's in North West India. *Proceedings - 2022 International Conference on Recent Trends in Microelectronics, Automation, Computing and Communications Systems, ICMACC 2022*, 365–370. https://doi.org/DOI: 10.1109/ICMACC54824.2022.10093347

Kaur, J., Khanna, R., Kumar, R., & Sunil, G. (2024). Role of Blockchain Technologies in Goods and Services Tax. *Proceedings - 2024 3rd International Conference on Sentiment Analysis and Deep Learning, ICSADL 2024*, 607–612. https://doi.org/DOI: 10.1109/ICSADL61749.2024.00104

Kaushal, D., Kumar, S., Raj, R., & Negi, A. (2022). Understanding the effect of entrepreneurial orientation, innovation capability and differentiation strategy on firm performance: A study on small and medium enterprises. *International Journal of Business and Globalisation*, *30*(1), 57–80. DOI: 10.1504/IJBG.2022.122280

Khanna, L. S., Yadav, P. S., Maurya, S., & Vimal, V. (2023). Integral Role of Data Science in Startup Evolution. *Proceedings - 2023 15th IEEE International Conference on Computational Intelligence and Communication Networks, CICN 2023*, 720 – 726. https://doi.org/DOI: 10.1109/CICN59264.2023.10402129

Khanna, R., Jindal, P., & Noja, G. G. (2023). Blockchain technologies, a catalyst for insurance sector. In *The Application of Emerging Technology and Blockchain in the Insurance Industry*.

Kohli, P., Sharma, S., & Matta, P. (2022). Secured Authentication Schemes of 6G Driven Vehicular Communication Network in Industry 5.0 Internet-of-Everything (IoE) Applications: Challenges and Opportunities. *2022 IEEE 2nd International Conference on Mobile Networks and Wireless Communications, ICMNWC 2022*. https://doi.org/DOI: 10.1109/ICMNWC56175.2022.10031781

Kollipara, V. N. H., Kalakota, S. K., Chamarthi, S., Ramani, S., Malik, P., & Karuppiah, M. (2023). Timestamp Based OTP and Enhanced RSA Key Exchange Scheme with SIT Encryption to Secure IoT Devices. *Journal of Cyber Security and Mobility*, *12*(1), 77–102. DOI: 10.13052/jcsm2245-1439.1214

Komkowski, T., Antony, J., Garza-Reyes, J. A., Tortorella, G. L., & Pongboonchai-Empl, T. (2023a). A systematic review of the integration of Industry 4.0 with quality-related operational excellence methodologies. *The Quality Management Journal*, *30*(1), 3–15. DOI: 10.1080/10686967.2022.2144783

Komkowski, T., Antony, J., Garza-Reyes, J. A., Tortorella, G. L., & Pongboonchai-Empl, T. (2023b). Integrating Lean Management with Industry 4.0: An explorative Dynamic Capabilities theory perspective. *Production Planning and Control*. Advance online publication. DOI: 10.1080/09537287.2023.2294297

Kour, M., Taneja, S., Özen, E., Sood, K., & Grima, S. (2025). *Financial Landscape Transformation Technological Disruptions*.

Kowsalya, K., & Rani, R. P. J. Ritu, Bhiyana, M., Saini, M., & Patil, P. P. (2023). Blockchain-Internet of things-Machine Learning: Development of Traceable System for Multi Purposes. *2023 3rd International Conference on Advance Computing and Innovative Technologies in Engineering, ICACITE 2023*, 1112 – 1115. https://doi .org/DOI: 10.1109/ICACITE57410.2023.10183065

Krishna, S. H., Upadhyay, A., Tewari, M., Gehlot, A., Girimurugan, B., & Pundir, S. (2022). Empirical investigation of the key machine learning elements promoting e-business using an SEM framework. *Proceedings of 5th International Conference on Contemporary Computing and Informatics, IC3I 2022*, 1960 – 1964. https://doi .org/DOI: 10.1109/IC3I56241.2022.10072712

Kumar, A., Saxena, M., Sastry, R. V. L. S. N., Chaudhari, A., Singh, R., & Malathy, V. (2023). Internet of Things and Blockchain Data Supplier for Intelligent Applications. *Proceedings of International Conference on Contemporary Computing and Informatics, IC3I 2023*, 2218 – 2223. https://doi.org/DOI: 10.1109/ IC3I59117.2023.10397630

Kumar, A. S., & Desi, A. B. (2023). Collaborative logistics, tools of machine and supply chain services in the world wide industry 4.0 framework. In *Artificial Intelligence, Blockchain, Computing and Security: Volume 2* (Vol. 2). CRC Press. https:// doi.org/DOI: 10.1201/9781032684994-15

Kumar, R., Goel, R., Singh, T., Mohanty, S. M., Gupta, D., Alkhayyat, A., & Khanna, R. (2024). Sustainable Finance Factors in Indian Economy: Analysis on Policy of Climate Change and Energy Sector. *Fluctuation and Noise Letters*, *23*(2). Advance online publication. DOI: 10.1142/S0219477524400042

Kumar, R., Kandpal, B., & Ahmad, V. (2023). Industrial IoT (IIOT): Security Threats and Countermeasures. *International Conference on Innovative Data Communication Technologies and Application, ICIDCA 2023 - Proceedings*, 829 – 833. https://doi .org/DOI: 10.1109/ICIDCA56705.2023.10100145

Kumar, R., Kathuria, S., Malholtra, R. K., Kumar, A., Gehlot, A., & Joshi, K. (2023). Role of Cloud Computing in Goods and Services Tax(GST) and Future Application. *2nd International Conference on Sustainable Computing and Data Communication Systems, ICSCDS 2023 - Proceedings*, 1443–1447. https://doi.org/DOI: 10.1109/ ICSCDS56580.2023.10104597

Kumar, R., & Khanna, R. (2023a). Role of Artificial Intelligence in Digital Currency and Future Applications. *Proceedings of the 2023 2nd International Conference on Augmented Intelligence and Sustainable Systems, ICAISS 2023*, 42–46. https://doi .org/DOI: 10.1109/ICAISS58487.2023.10250480

Kumar, R., & Khanna, R. (2023b). RPA (Robotic Process Automation) in Finance & Accounting and Future Scope. *Proceedings of the 2023 2nd International Conference on Augmented Intelligence and Sustainable Systems, ICAISS 2023*, 1640–1645. https://doi.org/DOI: 10.1109/ICAISS58487.2023.10250496

Kumar, R., Khannna Malholtra, R., & Grover, C. A. N. (2023). Review on Artificial Intelligence Role in Implementation of Goods and Services Tax(GST) and Future Scope. *2023 International Conference on Artificial Intelligence and Smart Communication, AISC 2023*, 348–351. https://doi.org/DOI: 10.1109/AISC56616.2023.10085030

Kumar, R., Lande, A., Kumar, D., Malhotra, R. K., & Sharma, A. (2023). Technology Bridging -in Entrepreneurs and Consumers in Product Development. *ISED 2023 - International Conference on Intelligent Systems and Embedded Design*. https:// doi.org/DOI: 10.1109/ISED59382.2023.10444599

Kumar, R., Malhotra, R. K., & Grover, N. (2023). Data Mining in Credit Scoring and Future Application. *International Conference on Innovative Data Communication Technologies and Application, ICIDCA 2023 - Proceedings*, 1096–1100. https://doi .org/DOI: 10.1109/ICIDCA56705.2023.10100032

Kumar, R., Malhotra, R. K., Pandey, S., Gehlot, A., Gautam, I., & Chamola, S. (2023). Role of Artificial Intelligence in Input Tax Credit Reconciliation. *Proceedings - 2023 3rd International Conference on Pervasive Computing and Social Networking, ICPCSN 2023*, 497–501. https://doi.org/DOI: 10.1109/ICPCSN58827.2023.00086

Kumar, R., Saxena, A., & Singh, R. (2023). Robotic Process Automation Bridge -in Banking Institute and Consumers. *2023 International Conference on Disruptive Technologies, ICDT 2023*, 428 – 431. https://doi.org/DOI: 10.1109/ICDT57929.2023.10150500

Kumar, R., Singh, T., Mohanty, S. N., Goel, R., Gupta, D., Alharbi, M., & Khanna, R. (2023). Study on online payments and e-commerce with SOR model. *International Journal of Retail & Distribution Management*. Advance online publication. DOI: 10.1108/IJRDM-03-2023-0137

Kumar, V., & Korovin, G. (2023). A Comparision of Digital Transformation of Industry in the Russian Federation with the European Union. In K. V., K. G.L., A. V., & K. E. (Eds.), *Lecture Notes in Information Systems and Organisation: Vol. 61 LNISO* (pp. 45 – 57). Springer Science and Business Media Deutschland GmbH. https://doi.org/DOI: 10.1007/978-3-031-30351-7_5

Luthra, S., Sharma, M., Kumar, A., Joshi, S., Collins, E., & Mangla, S. (2022). Overcoming barriers to cross-sector collaboration in circular supply chain management: A multi-method approach. *Transportation Research Part E, Logistics and Transportation Review*, *157*. Advance online publication. DOI: 10.1016/j.tre.2021.102582

Malhotra, R. K., & Gupta, S. (2021). Tele health in the digital era during covid -19 a case study of Uttarakhand. *Journal of Medical Pharmaceutical and Allied Sciences*, *10*, 109–112. DOI: 10.22270/jmpas.vic2i1.2016

Mandalapu, S. R., Sivamuni, K., Chitra Devi, D., Aswal, U. S., Sherly, S. I., & Balaji, N. A. (2023). An Architecture-based Self-Typing Service for Cloud Native Applications. *Proceedings of the 4th International Conference on Smart Electronics and Communication, ICOSEC 2023*, 562 – 566. https://doi.org/DOI: 10.1109/ICOSEC58147.2023.10276313

Mary Joshitta, S., & Sunil, M. P. Badriasulaimanalfurhood, Bodhankar, A., Ch.Sreedevi, & Khanna, R. (2023). The Integration of Machine Learning Technique with the Existing System to Predict the Flight Prices. *2023 3rd International Conference on Advance Computing and Innovative Technologies in Engineering, ICACITE 2023*, 398–402. https://doi.org/DOI: 10.1109/ICACITE57410.2023.10182539

Masal, V., Pavithra, P., Tiwari, S. K., Singh, R., Panduro-Ramirez, J., & Gangodkar, D. (2022). Deep Learning Applications for Blockchain in Industrial IoT. *Proceedings of 5th International Conference on Contemporary Computing and Informatics, IC3I 2022*, 276 – 281. https://doi.org/DOI: 10.1109/IC3I56241.2022.10073357

Matta, P., & Pant, B. (2020). TCpC: A graphical password scheme ensuring authentication for IoT resources. *International Journal of Information Technology (Singapore)*, *12*(3), 699–709. DOI: 10.1007/s41870-018-0142-z

Medhi, M. K., Ambust, S., Kumar, R., & Das, A. J. (2023). Characterization and Purification of Biosurfactants. In *Advancements in Biosurfactants Research*. Springer International Publishing., DOI: 10.1007/978-3-031-21682-4_4

Mehershilpa, G., Prasad, D., Sai Kiran, C., Shaikh, A., Jayashree, K., & Socrates, S. (2023). EDM machining of Ti6Al4V alloy using colloidal biosilica. *Materials Today: Proceedings*. Advance online publication. DOI: 10.1016/j.matpr.2023.02.443

Mishra, A. K., & Wazid, M. (2023). Design of a cloud-based security mechanism for Industry 4.0 communication. *ICSCCC 2023 - 3rd International Conference on Secure Cyber Computing and Communications*, 337 – 343. https://doi.org/DOI: 10.1109/ICSCCC58608.2023.10176702

Mohd, N., Kumar, I., & Khurshid, A. A. (2023). Changing Roles of Intelligent Robotics and Machinery Control Systems as Cyber-Physical Systems (CPS) in the Industry 4.0 Framework. *2023 International Conference on Communication, Security and Artificial Intelligence, ICCSAI 2023*, 647 – 651. https://doi.org/DOI: 10.1109/ICCSAI59793.2023.10421085

Nadeem, S. P., Garza-Reyes, J. A., & Anosike, A. I. (2023). A C-Lean framework for deploying Circular Economy in manufacturing SMEs. *Production Planning and Control*. Advance online publication. DOI: 10.1080/09537287.2023.2294307

Nethravathi, K., Tiwari, A., Uike, D., Jaiswal, R., & Pant, K. (2022). Applications of Artificial Intelligence and Blockchain Technology in Improved Supply Chain Financial Risk Management. *Proceedings of 5th International Conference on Contemporary Computing and Informatics, IC3I 2022*, 242 – 246. https://doi.org/DOI: 10.1109/IC3I56241.2022.10072787

Özen, E., Singh, A., Taneja, S., Rajaram, R., & Davim, J. P. (2024a). *Innovating Sustainability Through Digital Circular Economy*. IGI Global., DOI: 10.4018/979-8-3373-0578-3

Özen, E., Singh, A., Taneja, S., Rajaram, R., & Davim, J. P. (2024b). *Sustainability, Innovation, and Consumer Preference*. IGI Global., DOI: 10.4018/979-8-3693-9699-5

Pai, H. A., Almuzaini, K. K., Ali, L., Javeed, A., Pant, B., Pareek, P. K., & Akwafo, R. (2022). Delay-Driven Opportunistic Routing with Multichannel Cooperative Neighbor Discovery for Industry 4.0 Wireless Networks Based on Power and Load Awareness. *Wireless Communications and Mobile Computing, 2022*. Advance online publication. DOI: 10.1155/2022/5256133

Pandey, T., Batra, A., Chaudhary, M., Ranakoti, A., Kumar, A., & Ram, M. (2023). Computation Signature Reliability of Computer Numerical Control System Using Universal Generating Function. *Springer Series in Reliability Engineering*, 149 – 158. https://doi.org/DOI: 10.1007/978-3-031-05347-4_10

Pant, R., Gupta, A., Pant, G., Chaubey, K. K., Kumar, G., & Patrick, N. (2022). Second-generation biofuels: Facts and future. In *Relationship between Microbes and the Environment for Sustainable Ecosystem Services: Microbial Tools for Sustainable Ecosystem Services: Volume 3* (Vol. 3). Elsevier. https://doi.org/DOI: 10.1016/B978-0-323-89936-9.00011-4

Raju, K., Balakrishnan, M., Prasad, D. V. S. S. S. V., Nagalakshmi, V., Patil, P. P., Kaliappan, S., Arulmurugan, B., Radhakrishnan, K., Velusamy, B., Paramasivam, P., & El-Denglawey, A. (2022). Optimization of WEDM Process Parameters in Al2024-Li-Si3N4MMC. *Journal of Nanomaterials, 2022*. Advance online publication. DOI: 10.1155/2022/2903385

Ram, M., Bisht, D. C. S., Goyal, N., Kazancoglu, Y., & Mathirajan, M. (2022). Newly developed mathematical methodologies and advancements in a variety of engineering and management domains. *Mathematics in Engineering. Science and Aerospace*, *13*(3), 559–562.

Ram, M., Negi, G., Goyal, N., & Kumar, A. (2022). Analysis of a Stochastic Model with Rework System. *Journal of Reliability and Statistical Studies*, *15*(2), 553–582. DOI: 10.13052/jrss0974-8024.1527

Raman, R., Kumar, R., Ghai, S., Gehlot, A., Raju, A. M., & Barve, A. (2023). A New Method of Optical Spectrum Analysis for Advanced Wireless Communications. *2023 3rd International Conference on Advance Computing and Innovative Technologies in Engineering, ICACITE 2023*, 1719 – 1723. https://doi.org/DOI: 10.1109/ICACITE57410.2023.10182414

Rana, M. S., Cavaliere, L. P. L., Mishra, A. B., Padhye, P., Singh, R. R., & Khanna, R. (2022). Internet of Things (IOT) Based Assessment for Effective Monitoring Data Against Malicious Attacks on Financial Collectors. *2022 2nd International Conference on Advance Computing and Innovative Technologies in Engineering, ICACITE 2022*, 177–181. https://doi.org/DOI: 10.1109/ICACITE53722.2022.9823612

Rawat, R., Sharma, S., & Goyal, H. R. (2023). Intelligent Digital Financial Inclusion System Architectures for Industry 5.0 Enabled Digital Society. *Winter Summit on Smart Computing and Networks. WiSSCoN, 2023*. Advance online publication. DOI: 10.1109/WiSSCoN56857.2023.10133858

Reddy, P. N., Umaeswari, P., Natrayan, L., & Choudhary, A. (2023). Development of Programmed Autonomous Electric Heavy Vehicle: An Application of IoT. *Proceedings of the 2023 2nd International Conference on Electronics and Renewable Systems, ICEARS 2023*, 506 – 510. https://doi.org/DOI: 10.1109/ICEARS56392.2023.10085492

Reepu, R., Taneja, S., Ozen, E., & Singh, A. (2023). A globetrotter to the future of marketing: Metaverse. In *Cultural Marketing and Metaverse for Consumer Engagement*. IGI Global., DOI: 10.4018/978-1-6684-8312-1.ch001

Salama, R., Al-Turjman, F., Bordoloi, D., & Yadav, S. P. (2023). Wireless Sensor Networks and Green Networking for 6G communication- An Overview. *2023 International Conference on Computational Intelligence, Communication Technology and Networking, CICTN 2023*, 830 – 834. https://doi.org/DOI: 10.1109/CICTN57981.2023.10141262

Sathyapriya, G., Natarajan, U., Sureshkumar, B., Navaneethakrishnan, G., Palanisamy, R., Bajaj, M., & Sharma, N. K., & Kitmo. (2022). Quality and Tool Stability Improvement in Turning Operation Using Plastic Compliant Damper. *Journal of Nanomaterials, 2022*. Advance online publication. DOI: 10.1155/2022/8654603

Sathyaseelan, K., Vyas, T., Madala, R., Chamundeeswari, V., Rai Goyal, H., & Jayaraman, R. (2023). Blockchain Enabled Intelligent Surveillance System Model with AI and IoT. *Proceedings of 8th IEEE International Conference on Science, Technology, Engineering and Mathematics, ICONSTEM 2023*. https://doi.org/DOI: 10.1109/ICONSTEM56934.2023.10142303

Shah, J. K., Sharma, R., Misra, A., Sharma, M., Joshi, S., Kaushal, D., & Bafila, S. (2023). Industry 4.0 Enabled Smart Manufacturing: Unleashing the Power of Artificial Intelligence and Blockchain. *2023 1st DMIHER International Conference on Artificial Intelligence in Education and Industry 4.0, IDICAIEI 2023*. https://doi.org/DOI: 10.1109/IDICAIEI58380.2023.10406671

Sharma, A. K., Sharma, A., Singh, Y., & Chen, W.-H. (2021). Production of a sustainable fuel from microalgae Chlorella minutissima grown in a 1500 L open raceway ponds. *Biomass and Bioenergy, 149*. Advance online publication. DOI: 10.1016/j.biombioe.2021.106073

Sharma, K., Pandit, S., Sen Thapa, B., & Pant, M. (2022). Biodegradation of Congo Red Using Co-Culture Anode Inoculum in a Microbial Fuel Cell. *Catalysts, 12*(10). Advance online publication. DOI: 10.3390/catal12101219

Sharma, S., Kandpal, V., Choudhury, T., Santibanez Gonzalez, E. D. R., & Agarwal, N. (2023). Assessment of the implications of energy-efficient technologies on the environmental sustainability of rail operation. *AIMS Environmental Science, 10*(5), 709–731. DOI: 10.3934/environsci.2023039

Shashikala, R., Singh, B. P., Azam, M., & Magesh, C. R. Rajat, & Singh, D. P. (2022). IoT Engineering Nanomaterial's Approach To Sustainable Advance Crop Production Management. *2022 2nd International Conference on Advance Computing and Innovative Technologies in Engineering, ICACITE 2022*, 2284 – 2288. https://doi.org/DOI: 10.1109/ICACITE53722.2022.9823573

Singamaneni, K. K., Dhiman, G., Juneja, S., Muhammad, G., AlQahtani, S. A., & Zaki, J. (2022). A Novel QKD Approach to Enhance IIOT Privacy and Computational Knacks. *Sensors (Basel), 22*(18). Advance online publication. DOI: 10.3390/s22186741 PMID: 36146089

Singh, A., Kumar, P., & Taneja, S. (2024). Artificial Intelligence and Machine Learning-Powered Smart Finance. In Taneja, P. K. S., & Singh, A. (Eds.), *IGI Global*. IGI Global., DOI: 10.4018/979-8-3693-3264-1

Singh, K. D., Singh, P., Chhabra, R., Kaur, G., Bansal, A., & Tripathi, V. (2023). Cyber-Physical Systems for Smart City Applications: A Comparative Study. In K. R., K. R., G. M., G. M., S. R., & S. R. (Eds.), *2023 International Conference on Advancement in Computation and Computer Technologies, InCACCT 2023* (pp. 871 – 876). Institute of Electrical and Electronics Engineers Inc. https://doi.org/DOI: 10.1109/InCACCT57535.2023.10141719

Singh, N. K., Singh, Y., Rahim, E. A., Senthil Siva Subramanian, T., & Sharma, A. (2023). Electric discharge machining of hybrid composite with bio-dielectrics for sustainable developments. *Australian Journal of Mechanical Engineering*. Advance online publication. DOI: 10.1080/14484846.2023.2249577

Singh, R., Chandra, A. S., Bbhagat, B., Panduro-Ramirez, J., Gaikwad, A. P., & Pant, B. (2022). Cloud Computing, Machine Learning, and Secure Data Sharing enabled through Blockchain. *Proceedings of 5th International Conference on Contemporary Computing and Informatics, IC3I 2022*, 282 – 286. https://doi.org/DOI: 10.1109/IC3I56241.2022.10072925

Singh, S. P., Piras, G., Viriyasitavat, W., Kariri, E., Yadav, K., Dhiman, G., Vimal, S., & Khan, S. B. (2023). Cyber Security and 5G-assisted Industrial Internet of Things using Novel Artificial Adaption based Evolutionary Algorithm. *Mobile Networks and Applications*. Advance online publication. DOI: 10.1007/s11036-023-02230-7

Singla, R. K., De, R., Efferth, T., Mezzetti, B., & Sahab Uddin, M., Sanusi, Ntie-Kang, F., Wang, D., Schultz, F., Kharat, K. R., Devkota, H. P., Battino, M., Sur, D., Lordan, R., Patnaik, S. S., Tsagkaris, C., Sai, C. S., Tripathi, S. K., Găman, M.-A., … Shen, B. (2023). The International Natural Product Sciences Task-force (INPST) and the power of Twitter networking exemplified through #INPST hashtag analysis. *Phytomedicine*, *108*. Advance online publication. DOI: 10.1016/j.phymed.2022.154520 PMID: 36334386

Srivastava, A., Jawaid, S., Singh, R., Gehlot, A., Akram, S. V., Priyadarshi, N., & Khan, B. (2022). Imperative Role of Technology Intervention and Implementation for Automation in the Construction Industry. *Advances in Civil Engineering*, *2022*. Advance online publication. DOI: 10.1155/2022/6716987

Sunori, S. K., Kant, S., Agarwal, P., & Juneja, P. (2023). Development of Rainfall Prediction Models using Linear and Non-linear Regression Techniques. *2023 4th IEEE Global Conference for Advancement in Technology, GCAT 2023*. https://doi .org/DOI: 10.1109/GCAT59970.2023.10353508

Suresh, M., Antony, J., Nair, G., & Garza-Reyes, J. A. (2023). Lean-sustainability assessment framework development: Evidence from the construction industry. *Total Quality Management & Business Excellence*, *34*(15–16), 2046–2081. DOI: 10.1080/14783363.2023.2222088

Taneja, S., Bhatnagar, M., Kumar, P., & Grima, S. (2023). A Panel Analysis of the Effectiveness of the Asset Management in Indian Agricultural Companies. *International Journal of Sustainable Development and Planning*, *18*(3), 653–660. DOI: 10.18280/ijsdp.180301

Taneja, S., Bhatnagar, M., Kumar, P., & Rupeika-apoga, R. (2023). India ' s Total Natural Resource Rents (NRR) and GDP : An Augmented Autoregressive Distributed Lag (ARDL) Bound Test. *Journal of Risk and Financial Management*, *16*(2), 91. https://doi.org/doi.org/10.3390/jrfm16020091

Taneja, S., Chahal, B. P. S., Johri, A., Ozen, E., & Kumar, P. (2024). *Neuromarketing's Role in Sustainable Finance*. IGI Global., DOI: 10.4018/979-8-3693-9117-4

Taneja, S., Gupta, M., Bhushan, P., Bhatnagar, M., & Singh, A. (2023). Cultural marketing in the digital era. In *Cultural Marketing and Metaverse for Consumer Engagement*. IGI Global., DOI: 10.4018/978-1-6684-8312-1.ch008

Taneja, S., Gupta, S., Singh, A., Bhatnagar, M., & Gaur, A. (2023). Green management - A new paradigm in the world of business. *Green Management - A New Paradigm in the World of Business*, 1–230. https://doi.org/DOI: 10.52305/DLIH6622

Taneja, S., & Sharma, V. (2023). Role of beaconing marketing in improving customer buying experience. In *Enhancing Customer Engagement Through Location-Based Marketing* (pp. 176–184). IGI Global., DOI: 10.4018/978-1-6684-8177-6.ch012

Taneja, S., Ozen, E., Kumar, P., & Reepu. (2025). *E-Finance: Transformative Strategies for Sustainable Development in the Digital Era*. Nova Science Publisher Inc. https://doi.org/https://doi.org/10.52305/NZSJ1375

Tomar, S., Sharma, N., & Nehra, N. S. (2023). A sustainable rural entrepreneurship model developed by the organic farmers of India. *Emerald Emerging Markets Case Studies*, *13*(2), 1–17. DOI: 10.1108/EEMCS-09-2022-0329

Tripathy, S., Verma, D. K., Thakur, M., Patel, A. R., Srivastav, P. P., Singh, S., Chávez-González, M. L., & Aguilar, C. N. (2021). Encapsulated Food Products as a Strategy to Strengthen Immunity Against COVID-19. *Frontiers in Nutrition*, *8*. Advance online publication. DOI: 10.3389/fnut.2021.673174 PMID: 34095193

Uniyal, A. K., Kanojia, P., Khanna, R., & Dixit, A. K. (2022). Quantitative Analysis of the Impact of Demography and Job Profile on the Organizational Commitment of the Faculty Members in the HEI'S of Uttarakhand. *Communications in Computer and Information Science, 1742 CCIS*, 24–35. https://doi.org/DOI: 10.1007/978-3-031-23647-1_3

Uniyal, S., Mangla, S. K., Sarma, P. R. S., Tseng, M.-L., & Patil, P. (2021). ICT as "Knowledge management" for assessing sustainable consumption and production in supply chains. *Journal of Global Information Management*, *29*(1), 164–198. DOI: 10.4018/JGIM.2021010109

Upreti, H., & Malhotra, R. K. (2024). Bridging The Urban-Rural Education Gap In India Through CSR (Corporate Social Responsibility) Initiatives: A Conceptual Study With Special Reference To Sustainable Development Goal 4 (Quality Education). In P. P.K. (Ed.), *E3S Web of Conferences* (Vol. 556). EDP Sciences. https://doi.org/DOI: 10.1051/e3sconf/202455601032

Upreti, H., Uddin, Z., Pandey, A. K., & Joshi, N. (2023). Particle swarm optimization based numerical study for pressure, flow, and heat transfer over a rotating disk with temperature dependent nanofluid properties. *Numerical Heat Transfer Part A*, *83*(8), 815–844. DOI: 10.1080/10407782.2022.2156412

Verma, M., Ahmad, W., Park, J.-H., Kumar, V., Vlaskin, M. S., Vaya, D., & Kim, H. (2022). One-step functionalization of chitosan using EDTA: Kinetics and isotherms modeling for multiple heavy metals adsorption and their mechanism. *Journal of Water Process Engineering*, *49*. Advance online publication. DOI: 10.1016/j.jwpe.2022.102989

Yadav, A., Singh, Y., Singh, S., & Negi, P. (2021). Sustainability of vegetable oil based bio-diesel as dielectric fluid during EDM process - A review. In S. Y. (Ed.), *Materials Today: Proceedings* (Vol. 46, pp. 11155 – 11158). Elsevier Ltd. https://doi.org/DOI: 10.1016/j.matpr.2021.01.967

Chapter 4
AI-Driven Curriculum Innovation for Adaptive and Learner-Centric Education

K. Anbumaheshwari
https://orcid.org/0000-0001-5651-6565
S.A. Engineering College, India

J. Jayalakshmi
Vel Tech Multi Tech Dr. Rangarajan Dr. Sakunthala Engineering College, India

D. Pavunraj
Vel Tech Multi Tech Dr. Rangarajan Dr. Sakunthala Engineering College, India

ABSTRACT

The integration of artificial intelligence (AI) into educational frameworks is revolutionizing curriculum development by fostering adaptive and learner-centric approaches. AI-powered systems enable personalized learning experiences, dynamically adjusting content to match individual student needs, preferences, and learning paces. This innovation not only enhances student engagement but also optimizes knowledge retention by providing tailored feedback and adaptive assessments. Furthermore, AI facilitates data-driven insights for educators, enabling them to refine teaching strategies and curriculum structures. By leveraging machine learning algorithms and predictive analytics, AI empowers institutions to create inclusive and equitable learning environments, addressing diverse learning styles and accessibility challenges. This paper explores the transformative potential of AI in redefining curriculum design, emphasizing its role in fostering lifelong learning and preparing students

DOI: 10.4018/979-8-3373-1062-6.ch004

Copyright © 2026, IGI Global Scientific Publishing. Copying or distributing in print or electronic forms without written permission of IGI Global Scientific Publishing is prohibited.

for an evolving digital world.

INTRODUCTION

The integration of Artificial Intelligence (AI) into education has been pivotal in reshaping the traditional learning landscape, ushering in a new era of adaptive and learner-centric educational models (Albino et al., 2015; Angelidou, 2015). AI-driven curriculum innovation enables the creation of personalized learning environments that respond to individual student needs, preferences, and progress, moving away from the traditional "one-size-fits-all" approach (Albino et al., 2015). This shift is fundamental in addressing the diverse challenges students face in their learning journeys, particularly as educational environments grow increasingly complex. AI technologies, including machine learning and data analytics, allow for the continuous adaptation of curricula, offering real-time adjustments based on student performance (Angelidou, 2015; Anthopoulos & Fitsilis, 2010). By leveraging these technologies, educators can provide tailored resources and feedback, which enhances the learning experience and ensures that students are engaged and motivated (Batty et al., 2012). This personalized approach helps foster deeper understanding and mastery of content, ensuring that learners progress at their own pace and can tackle more advanced materials when ready (Caragliu et al., 2011). Central to AI-driven curriculum innovation is the concept of learner-centric education, where students actively participate in shaping their learning paths. AI enables this by facilitating personalized goals, providing immediate feedback, and recommending content tailored to each student's strengths and weaknesses (Angelidou, 2015). In this context, AI not only improves academic outcomes but also nurtures essential skills such as critical thinking and problem-solving, which are crucial for success in the modern world (Batty et al., 2012). In essence, AI-driven curriculum innovation holds the potential to create more inclusive, equitable, and effective educational systems by providing every student with the support they need to succeed. As educational technologies continue to evolve, AI's role in transforming how we teach and learn will undoubtedly expand, offering new opportunities for both students and educators to redefine the educational experience (Albino et al., 2015; Caragliu et al., 2011). The integration of Artificial Intelligence (AI) into education has been pivotal in reshaping the traditional learning landscape, ushering in a new era of adaptive and learner-centric educational models (Chourabi et al., 2012; Dameri & Cocchia, 2013). AI-driven curriculum innovation enables the creation of personalized learning environments that respond to individual student needs, preferences, and progress, moving away from the traditional "one-size-fits-all" approach (Deakin, 2010). AI technologies, including machine learning and data analytics, allow for the continuous adaptation of curricula, offering real-time adjustments based on student performance (Dirks & Keeling, 2009; Giffinger et al., 2007). By leveraging these technologies, educators can provide tailored resources and feedback, which enhances the learning experience and ensures that students are engaged and motivated (Chourabi et al., 2012). This personalized approach helps foster deeper understanding and mastery of content, ensuring that learners progress at their own pace and can tackle more advanced materials when ready (Dameri & Cocchia, 2013).

AI-driven curriculum innovation also seeks to address the challenges of inclusivity and equity in education. By offering personalized support, AI can help close the achievement gap between students of different backgrounds, abilities, and learning needs (Perboli et al., 2014). As educational technologies continue to evolve, the potential for AI to democratize access to quality education becomes increasingly evident, enabling institutions to better serve diverse student populations and ensure that all learners have the tools they need to succeed (Marsal-Llacuna et al., 2015). Furthermore, the AI approach offers new opportunities for students to engage with material that is relevant to their individual goals, interests, and aspirations, ultimately fostering a more flexible and inclusive learning environment (Nam & Pardo, 2011). By harnessing the power of AI technologies, education can evolve to meet the demands of a rapidly changing world, offering personalized and equitable learning opportunities for all students (Papa et al., 2013; Perboli et al., 2014). The rapid evolution of Artificial Intelligence (AI) technologies has had a transformative impact on various industries, including education. As AI continues to develop, it offers significant potential to reshape the educational landscape by introducing adaptive, learner-centric models that can cater to the diverse needs of students. Just as smart cities use data and technology to enhance urban living, AI in education can optimize learning experiences by personalizing instruction and fostering individualized pathways for students (Piro et al., 2014; Schaffers et al., 2011). AI-driven curriculum innovation provides the foundation for adaptive learning environments, where technology continuously assesses student performance and adjusts instructional content accordingly. This adaptive approach ensures that each learner is provided with content tailored to their current knowledge, pace, and preferred learning styles (Söderström, Paasche, & Klauser, 2014). Technologies such as machine learning, data analytics, and natural language processing enable real-time adaptations to the curriculum, allowing for personalized learning journeys that empower students to progress at their own pace and tackle content that aligns with their individual strengths (Townsend, 2013; Vanolo, 2014). In a traditional education system, students are often subjected to a uniform curriculum, which does not take into account their individual needs, learning speeds, or challenges. However, AI systems can monitor student engagement and progress in real-time, ensuring that each student receives timely support and resources tailored to their unique requirements (Piro et al., 2014). This dynamic and flexible approach increases student engagement and motivation, allowing learners to take control of their education while receiving personalized feedback and guidance (Schaffers et al., 2011). The core of AI-driven curriculum innovation is the learner-centric model, which emphasizes the student as an active participant in their educational experience. AI empowers students to make decisions about their learning paths, helping them to set goals, receive real-time feedback, and adjust their learning strategies as needed. In this model, learning is not a passive process, but rather an ongoing, interactive experience in which students are encouraged to take ownership of their academic development (Söderström et al., 2014). The ability to self-direct and self-regulate learning is crucial for fostering independent thinking and problem-solving skills that are essential for success in the modern world (Townsend, 2013).

Furthermore, AI-driven curriculum innovation encourages the development of critical skills required in the modern world, such as problem-solving, creativity, and independent thinking. Unlike traditional educational models, which often emphasize rote memorization and standardized testing, AI empowers students to engage in active learning, where they have the autonomy to explore subjects at their own pace and according to their interests. This learner-centric approach motivates students to take responsibility for their education, cultivating a sense of ownership over their learning journey (Zanella et al., 2014). By fostering self-directed learning, AI helps students become lifelong learners, better equipped to adapt to the ever-changing demands of the global workforce (Zygiaris, 2013). AI also facilitates the creation of adaptive learning environments that continuously evolve based on the needs of the students. In the same way that smart cities use real-time data to enhance services and infrastructure, AI systems in education gather data on student performance and interactions to optimize the learning experience. This real-time adaptation not only keeps students engaged but also ensures that they are constantly challenged and supported in a way that promotes steady academic growth (Mora, Bolici, & Deakin, 2017). The use of AI in education thus transforms traditional educational models into more fluid, flexible systems that can respond to the diverse and changing needs of students (Washburn et al., 2010). One of the most exciting aspects of AI-driven curriculum innovation is its potential to foster a more inclusive and equitable education system. By offering personalized learning pathways and continuous feedback, AI can help reduce disparities in educational outcomes. It ensures that all students, regardless of their background or ability, have access to high-quality, customized learning materials that align with their needs (Zanella et al., 2014). This is particularly important for students in marginalized communities, as AI provides the tools to address learning gaps and promote equal opportunities for success (Yigitcanlar & Kamruzzaman, 2018). Moreover, the role of data in AI-driven education is a key factor that sets it apart from traditional models. As

AI systems monitor student progress, they collect valuable data that can inform instructional strategies and decisions. This data-driven approach allows teachers and institutions to continuously refine and enhance their teaching methods, ensuring that the educational experience remains relevant and effective (Mora et al., 2017). Just as smart cities use data to optimize urban services like transportation, energy use, and public safety, AI systems in education leverage data to improve learning outcomes and enhance the overall student experience (Zygiaris, 2013). In conclusion, AI-driven curriculum innovation is fundamentally transforming education by enabling more personalized, adaptive, and inclusive learning environments. By continuously adapting to the needs of individual students, AI helps create educational systems that are both more effective and equitable. As these technologies continue to evolve, the potential for AI to reshape the educational landscape becomes even greater, offering new opportunities for students and educators alike (Yigitcanlar & Kamruzzaman, 2018; Washburn et al., 2010).

LITERATURE SURVEY

Smart Cities has become increasingly significant in urban development, particularly with the integration of technology and data analytics to optimize urban environments. Scholars have continuously expanded on the definition, dimensions, and implications of Smart Cities, with diverse perspectives on how these cities are conceptualized and how technology can reshape urban landscapes. Albino, Berardi, and Dangelico (2015) provide one of the most comprehensive definitions of Smart Cities, proposing a multidimensional framework that integrates technology, sustainability, and citizen engagement. They focus on the performance aspect of Smart Cities, stressing the importance of measuring a city's effectiveness based on its ability to improve the quality of life for its citizens while reducing its environmental impact. The authors highlight how Smart Cities rely not only on technological innovation but also on creating a sustainable urban ecosystem, where efficiency and ecological performance are paramount. The approach here reflects the need for comprehensive solutions that integrate various urban sectors, from transportation to energy and waste management, with the ultimate goal of enhancing the living conditions of urban populations. Angelidou (2015) examines the driving forces behind Smart City initiatives, identifying four primary factors that shape their development: policy, technology, societal needs, and governance. This framework underscores the complex interaction between these forces, where no single element dominates the Smart City landscape. The paper highlights the importance of balancing technological advancements with effective governance and policies that respond to the needs of citizens. This broader perspective highlights how

Smart Cities are a result of continuous negotiations between technological progress, governance structures, and the societal context in which they are implemented. In a similar vein, Chourabi et al. (2012) present an integrative framework that further explores the multi-dimensional aspects of Smart City development. They identify six core elements that drive the development of Smart Cities: technology, governance, economy, mobility, environment, and people. The authors emphasize that all these elements must work together to create a cohesive and sustainable Smart City. They stress that effective governance and active citizen participation are crucial to the success of Smart Cities, as technology alone cannot address the multifaceted urban challenges cities face today. This holistic approach presents Smart Cities as complex systems that require a balanced integration of technological infrastructure with social and governance structures.

Anthopoulos and Fitsilis (2010) take a historical approach by mapping the evolution from digital to ubiquitous cities. They argue that the development of Smart Cities is not merely about the application of isolated technologies but about creating an integrated urban system that incorporates pervasive computing, ubiquitous data collection, and constant connectivity. The paper presents the evolution of urban development as a transition toward cities that are not only digitally advanced but also highly connected through a network of intelligent systems. The authors call for a unified urban architecture that facilitates the seamless integration of various technologies into the city's operations, providing a roadmap for how cities can move beyond isolated innovations to become fully interconnected systems that operate efficiently and intelligently. Batty et al. (2012) explore the future of Smart Cities through a comprehensive analysis of how advanced simulation models and data analytics will shape urban environments. They focus on the role of data-driven technologies, such as predictive analytics and AI, in optimizing urban life. The paper discusses how the availability of vast datasets will enable cities to manage resources better, predict needs, and respond to crises more efficiently. Batty and colleagues envision a future where cities are not just smart in the conventional sense of incorporating technology but are actively learning and evolving based on real-time data. Their work lays the groundwork for how AI can be used to create adaptive urban systems capable of dynamically responding to both predictable and unpredictable challenges. Komninos (2011) extends the conversation on Smart Cities by focusing on the role of the Internet of Things (IoT) in urban management. The paper emphasizes how IoT technologies, including sensors and connected devices, enable Smart Cities to collect and process real-time data from various urban systems. This technology allows cities to monitor everything from traffic congestion to energy usage and waste management. By utilizing IoT, Smart Cities can become more responsive and efficient, ensuring that resources are used optimally and that urban systems function seamlessly. Komninos argues that the integration of IoT will drive the future of urban development by creating an ecosystem where all systems are interconnected and capable of communicating with each other, allowing for better coordination and more effective management of urban resources.

The work of Zanella et al. (2014) further builds on the concept of IoT in Smart Cities, exploring the various ways that IoT can be used to transform urban environments. The authors discuss the potential of IoT to create new, data-driven services for urban residents, such as intelligent transportation systems, smart grids for energy management, and real-time environmental monitoring systems. They highlight how IoT enables cities to operate more efficiently by continuously gathering data, which can then be analyzed to improve decision-making processes. This approach not only enhances the performance of urban systems but also fosters innovation, as new services and solutions can be developed based on the data collected from IoT-enabled devices. Giffinger et al. (2007) take a more comparative approach by ranking European cities based on their Smart City initiatives. The paper outlines various performance indicators, such as mobility, innovation capacity, and environmental sustainability, that are used to assess how well cities are implementing Smart City concepts. By ranking cities according to these factors, the authors offer valuable insights into which urban areas are leading the way in Smart City development and which areas still need improvement. This ranking system has become a widely used tool in the evaluation of Smart City progress, providing a benchmark for cities around the world to assess their own performance and identify areas where they can innovate and improve. Yigitcanlar and Kamruzzaman (2018) examine the relationship between Smart Cities and sustainability, arguing that Smart City policies should be explicitly aligned with sustainability goals. They emphasize that while technology is a core component of Smart Cities, it is essential to ensure that these cities remain sustainable and resilient in the long term. The authors advocate for policies that promote environmental sustainability, social equity, and economic inclusivity. They also highlight the need for Smart Cities to reduce their carbon footprint and create urban environments that are sustainable for future generations. This focus on sustainability challenges the notion that technological advancements alone can solve urban problems, emphasizing that smart solutions must be coupled with sustainable practices to ensure long-term success. Perboli et al. (2014) offer a taxonomy of Smart City projects, categorizing them according to sectors such as mobility, energy, healthcare, and governance. The authors explore how AI can be applied in these various sectors to optimize performance and improve decision-making. In the mobility sector, for example, AI can be used to manage traffic flow and reduce congestion, while in healthcare, AI can support the management of resources and improve patient care. Perboli and colleagues argue that AI is a critical component of Smart Cities, enabling more efficient systems that can adapt to changing needs and optimize urban operations.

Schaffers et al. (2011) discuss the role of cooperation frameworks in Smart City development, emphasizing the importance of partnerships between governments, businesses, and citizens. They argue that Smart Cities cannot be developed in isolation but must be the result of collaborative efforts between different stakeholders. Open innovation, where ideas and solutions are shared across sectors and organizations, is seen as a key mechanism for driving Smart City progress. Schaffers and his team suggest that creating these collaborative networks will allow cities to leverage the collective intelligence of various groups and develop more effective, scalable solutions for urban challenges. Söderström et al. (2014) and Vanolo (2014) critically examine the concept of Smart Cities from a sociopolitical perspective. They argue that the narrative of Smart Cities is often driven by corporate interests, where technology is presented as a panacea for all urban issues. However, these authors caution that Smart City initiatives can also reinforce control over citizens, with concerns about surveillance, privacy, and data security. This critique raises important ethical questions about the implications of Smart City technologies, especially in relation to how data is collected, who controls it, and how it is used to shape urban life. These critiques stress the need for Smart City projects to be more transparent and inclusive, ensuring that technological innovations do not come at the cost of individual freedoms and social equity. The work of Mora et al. (2017) offers a bibliometric analysis of the evolution of Smart City research over the past two decades. They analyze how the field has expanded, identifying key trends, methodologies, and areas of focus. This review provides valuable insights into the development of Smart City concepts and can serve as a guide for researchers looking to understand the direction of the field. It also highlights the increasing importance of interdisciplinary research that combines technology, urban studies, and social science to address the challenges of building smarter and more sustainable cities. Central themes such as the integration of IoT, AI, governance, sustainability, and citizen engagement are repeatedly emphasized, highlighting the complexity of creating truly "smart" cities. As AI continues to play a significant role in optimizing urban operations, the lessons learned from Smart City research provide important insights into how AI can also be used to innovate and personalize education, creating more efficient, inclusive, and sustainable systems. Future research should explore how the methodologies and frameworks developed in Smart City studies can be applied to the field of education, specifically in creating AI-driven, learner-centric environments.

METHODOLOGY

The methodology section of this research on AI-driven Smart Cities and curriculum innovation involves a deep analysis using various qualitative and quantitative methods, data collection techniques, and powerful algorithms. These methods will allow for a comprehensive investigation of AI applications in urban development and educational frameworks, enabling a multi-faceted understanding of the research subject.

Research Methods

As mentioned, the research will employ a mixed-methods approach to ensure comprehensive exploration and understanding. The methodology incorporates both qualitative and quantitative methods, each contributing essential insights and rigor to the study.

Qualitative Research Methods

The qualitative approach focuses on understanding the underlying processes, perspectives, and real-world implementations related to Smart Cities and educational innovation. It is particularly effective for exploring the nuanced experiences of stakeholders, such as urban planners, educators, and policymakers.

- **Interviews with Experts**:
  - o **Approach**: Semi-structured interviews will be conducted with key informants, such as urban planners, AI experts, policymakers, educators, and tech developers.
  - o **Rationale**: The semi-structured format allows for flexibility, where the interviewer can explore the depth of responses while maintaining a consistent framework across interviews.
  - o **Method of Analysis**: Thematic analysis will be employed. This involves identifying patterns, themes, and categories across the interview data. Each interview will be transcribed and coded manually or using software tools like NVivo.
  - o **Approach**: Real-world case studies of cities that have implemented Smart City technologies and cities that have integrated AI into educational curricula will be analyzed.
  - o **Method of Analysis**: Framework analysis will be used to compare the case studies across multiple dimensions, such as technological adop-

tion, governance models, and educational outcomes. Each case study will be dissected for patterns, success factors, and lessons learned.
  - **Rationale**: Case studies provide a detailed understanding of practical challenges, success stories, and real-life applications, offering a ground-level perspective on Smart City initiatives and curriculum reforms.
- **Focus Group Discussions**:
  - **Approach**: A series of focus group discussions will be held with educators, urban planners, and technology developers. These groups will discuss issues such as:
    - The role of AI in shaping Smart Cities.
    - The potential of AI technologies to transform curricula in educational settings.
  - **Method of Analysis**: Thematic analysis will be used to extract key themes that emerge from group discussions.

Quantitative Research Methods

The quantitative approach aims to examine large-scale data and validate patterns using statistical techniques. It will help determine the magnitude of AI's influence on Smart Cities and education and establish correlations across various dimensions.

- **Surveys**:
  - **Approach**: A structured survey will be designed and distributed to a wide range of respondents, including urban residents, students, educators, and city officials. The survey will focus on understanding the perceptions, expectations, and experiences of AI in Smart Cities and education.
  - **Survey Format**: Closed-ended questions with Likert scales, multiple-choice questions, and ranking questions will be used to quantify responses.
  - **Data Collection**: Online and offline surveys will be used to maximize response rates and represent diverse population groups.
  - **Method of Analysis**: Descriptive and inferential statistics will be applied. Descriptive statistics will summarize basic features of the dataset (mean, mode, standard deviation). Inferential statistics will test hypotheses, such as whether the level of AI adoption correlates with improvements in educational outcomes.
- **Statistical Models**:
  - **Regression Analysis**:

    - **Method**: Multiple regression analysis will be used to study the relationships between variables such as AI adoption, Smart City infrastructure, and curriculum effectiveness. For example, the research will analyze how AI in transportation systems influences education quality or how data-driven city management correlates with innovation in curricula.
    - **Algorithm**:
    - **Linear Regression**: Simple linear regression will be used when analyzing one independent variable (e.g., AI technology) affecting a dependent variable (e.g., student performance).
    - **Multivariate Regression**: Multivariate analysis will allow examining the simultaneous impact of multiple factors (e.g., urban infrastructure, data systems, AI adoption) on educational quality.
    - **Goal**: To predict changes in educational outcomes based on AI technology and Smart City initiatives.
  - **Factor Analysis**:
    - **Method**: Factor analysis will be employed to reduce the dimensionality of large datasets (such as survey responses) and identify underlying factors that explain patterns of responses.
    - **Goal**: Identify latent variables such as "AI infrastructure readiness" or "policy support for curriculum reform," which can explain variations in responses.
    - **Algorithm**: **Principal Component Analysis (PCA)** will be used for dimension reduction, allowing the identification of core themes influencing Smart City development and curriculum innovation.
- **Data Visualization**:
  - **Method**: Visual tools like heatmaps, correlation matrices, and scatterplots will be used to represent relationships between AI technology adoption, Smart City infrastructure, and educational outcomes.
  - **Goal**: To make complex data more interpretable and visually explore relationships among key variables.

Algorithms and Techniques for Data Analysis

The heart of this research lies in data-driven analysis. The methods and algorithms outlined below will be used to analyze the data collected from both qualitative and quantitative methods, ensuring robust results.

Qualitative Data Analysis

- **Text Mining and Natural Language Processing (NLP)**:
    - **Method**: Textual data from interviews, surveys, and case studies will undergo processing using NLP techniques to uncover hidden patterns and themes.
    - **Algorithms**:
        - **TF-IDF (Term Frequency-Inverse Document Frequency)**: This algorithm is crucial for understanding the importance of words in a set of documents, helping identify key concepts.
        - **Latent Dirichlet Allocation (LDA)**: This topic modeling algorithm will be used to extract topics from large text datasets (e.g., interview transcripts, case studies) to identify recurring themes related to AI and education.
        - **Goal**: To classify large sets of text data and highlight critical insights, such as the perceived challenges in Smart City implementation or the barriers to curriculum innovation.

Quantitative Data Analysis

- **Machine Learning Algorithms**: Machine learning techniques will be applied to predict outcomes and identify relationships within large datasets collected from surveys, case studies, and urban metrics.
    - **Clustering Algorithms**:
        - **K-Means Clustering**: This unsupervised algorithm will be used to classify cities or educational institutions into different groups based on their level of AI adoption and curriculum integration.
        - **DBSCAN (Density-Based Spatial Clustering of Applications with Noise)**: Useful for identifying dense areas of Smart City activity and pinpointing regions where educational institutions are significantly impacted by AI-driven infrastructure.
    - **Decision Trees**:
        - **Method**: Decision trees will be used to model decisions and predict outcomes based on certain criteria, such as whether a Smart City's AI initiatives will result in a measurable improvement in educational quality.
        - **Algorithm**: **CART (Classification and Regression Trees)** will be utilized to create decision rules and assess their accuracy.

        - **Goal**: Provide a clear, interpretable model that predicts how AI-driven initiatives influence various facets of education in Smart Cities.
    - **Neural Networks**:
        - **Method**: For complex patterns, deep learning models such as Artificial Neural Networks (ANNs) will be applied. These models will analyze non-linear relationships between Smart City features (AI technologies, urban systems) and educational outcomes.
        - **Goal**: Model complex interactions where traditional statistical methods may fall short.
    - **Support Vector Machines (SVM)**:
        - **Method**: SVMs will be employed to classify data into categories, such as identifying which cities are most likely to successfully integrate AI in education and which ones are struggling.
        - **Goal**: To predict the success or failure of AI-based initiatives in urban education contexts based on historical data.

Advanced Statistical Models

- **Bayesian Networks**:
    - **Method**: Bayesian networks will be employed to model the probabilistic relationships between various components of Smart Cities and educational systems, such as the impact of urban data collection on student performance.
    - **Goal**: Predict the impact of different policy interventions on AI-based Smart City development and curriculum outcomes.

FRAMEWORK DEVELOPMENT FOR CURRICULUM INNOVATION WITH AI

To develop a framework for AI-based curriculum reform in Smart Cities, various **optimization algorithms** will be applied:

- **Genetic Algorithms (GAs)**:
    - **Method**: These optimization algorithms simulate natural evolutionary processes to find optimal solutions for curriculum design that best integrates AI.
    - **Goal**: Develop a dynamic, adaptable curriculum framework capable of evolving with the technological and educational landscape.

Table 1. Quantitative methods and algorithms

Method/Algorithm	Objective	Applications	Advantages
Surveys (Structured)	Collect quantifiable data on perceptions of AI in Smart Cities and education	Survey respondents including urban residents, students, and city officials	Large sample size, statistical analysis, generalizable results
Multiple Regression Analysis	Assess relationships between AI adoption, Smart City infrastructure, and educational outcomes	Analyze how AI adoption impacts educational performance	Identifies strength and direction of relationships among variables
Factor Analysis	Identify underlying factors that explain patterns in survey responses	Reducing dimensionality of large datasets (e.g., survey data)	Uncovers latent factors, simplifies complex datasets
Principal Component Analysis (PCA)	Reduce dimensionality and identify major influencing factors	Analyze large datasets with numerous variables	Extracts important features, reduces complexity
K-Means Clustering	Group data points into clusters based on similarities	Classify cities or educational institutions based on AI and technology adoption	Efficient, easy to interpret, scalable for large datasets
Decision Trees (CART)	Model decisions and predict outcomes based on certain criteria	Predict the impact of AI on educational outcomes	Simple, interpretable, handles both categorical and continuous data

In above Table 1 represents a wide range of advanced methodologies and algorithms to provide a holistic view of how AI can affect Smart City development and curriculum innovation. By applying text mining, machine learning, and statistical modeling, the research aims to uncover meaningful relationships and provide actionable insights into how AI can drive sustainable, intelligent urban education systems.

MODULES

Data Collection Layer:

This layer collects data from multiple sources that are relevant to both educational systems and urban management in a smart city.

1. **Smart City Data Sources:**
    - o **Sensors and IoT Devices:** These include physical sensors placed around the city, such as traffic sensors, air quality sensors, water quality sensors, and energy meters. IoT devices are interconnected to provide

real-time data from across the city (e.g., smart streetlights, connected vehicles, waste bins, etc.).

- o **Traffic Data:** Includes real-time data from road sensors, cameras, and GPS systems that monitor traffic flow, congestion, and transportation usage patterns. This data is crucial for urban planning and traffic management.
- o **Public Services Data:** Includes information about utility services, such as electricity, water, waste management, and emergency services. It can also include data on public safety or health services like hospitals, fire stations, and police departments.
- o **Weather Data:** Data collected from weather stations, satellites, and IoT devices to monitor temperature, humidity, precipitation, wind speeds, and other meteorological parameters to assist in city planning and disaster management.
- o **Smart Infrastructure:** Data from smart buildings, roads, and public spaces. This includes structural health monitoring, energy efficiency metrics, and occupancy tracking of public spaces.

2. **Educational Data:**
   - o **Student Data:** This includes personal data, attendance, academic records, and behavior tracking. It helps in understanding the learning habits, strengths, and weaknesses of each student.
   - o **Performance Metrics:** Data on student performance such as test scores, grades, and participation in extracurricular activities. This helps in assessing the efficacy of educational methods.
   - o **Curriculum Information:** Data related to subjects, courses, and curriculum structures, including the relevance of content and how it aligns with learning objectives.
   - o **Classroom Data:** Real-time data from classrooms including student engagement, teacher effectiveness, and other dynamic factors influencing learning.
   - o **Teacher Performance:** Data related to teaching methods, student feedback, and performance evaluations to help improve teaching practices.

Figure 1. AI-driven curriculum innovation for adaptive and learner-centric education

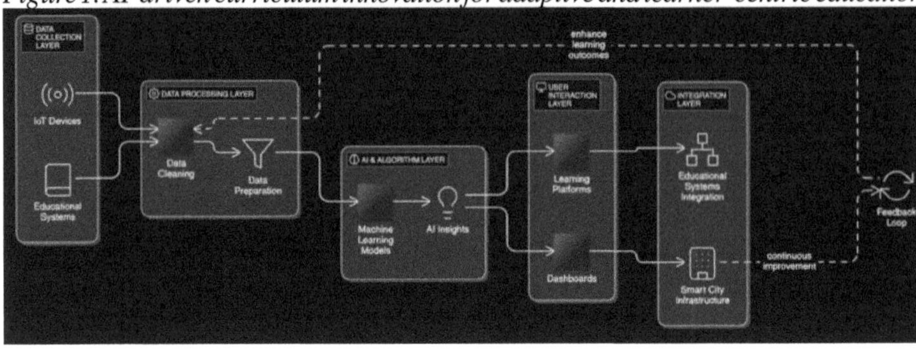

Data Processing Layer:

This layer is responsible for transforming raw data collected from various sources into actionable insights.

1. **Data Aggregation & Preprocessing:**
   - o This step involves cleaning and integrating data from multiple sources. Raw data might be noisy, incomplete, or inconsistent. Preprocessing steps like data normalization, missing value imputation, and outlier removal are crucial to ensure that the data can be reliably used for analysis.
2. **Data Analytics Engine:**
   - o This engine processes aggregated data and generates insights that can be used for decision-making. It uses advanced statistical and machine learning methods to analyze the educational and urban data and find patterns or correlations between them. For instance, it might uncover trends between traffic congestion and student attendance patterns.
3. **Machine Learning Models:**
   - o These models are used for predictive analysis and optimization:
     - **Personalized Learning:** Predicts the most effective learning paths for individual students based on their past performance and engagement.
     - **Performance Optimization:** Identifies areas where students need extra help and recommends additional resources or interventions.
     - **Resource Allocation in Education:** Uses data from educational institutions to suggest how resources (e.g., teachers, classrooms, and educational tools) can be optimized for better learning outcomes.

- **Urban Planning:** Uses machine learning for predicting city needs like transportation, healthcare, and infrastructure.

Figure 2. Data processing

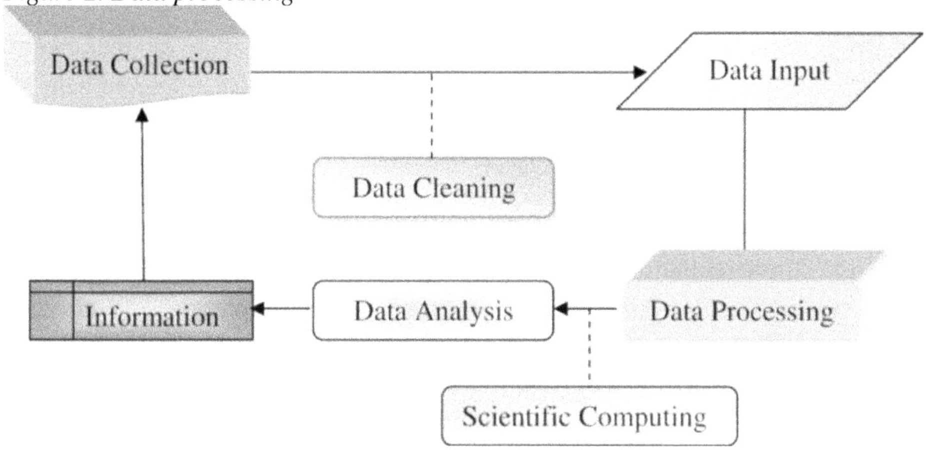

In above Figure 2 is provide the basic details of Data processing involves collecting and manipulating raw data to produce meaningful information. This process includes validation, sorting, summarization, aggregation, analysis, reporting, and classification. Historically, data processing has evolved from manual methods to electronic systems, significantly enhancing efficiency and accuracy

AI & Algorithm Layer:

This layer handles the advanced AI and algorithmic models that drive intelligence within the system, influencing both educational and urban management decisions.

1. **AI Models for Education:**
    - **Recommendation Systems:** These algorithms suggest courses, learning resources, or activities to students based on their learning history and preferences.
    - **Adaptive Learning Algorithms:** Tailors the learning experience to each student's individual pace and learning style, adjusting content difficulty based on student progress.
    - **Natural Language Processing (NLP) Models:** Used for personalizing educational content. NLP can help in extracting key information

from textbooks, generating summaries, or even automating feedback for students.

2. **Urban Data AI:**
    - o **Traffic Prediction Algorithms:** Predict traffic congestion patterns and help optimize traffic flow using historical traffic data, real-time sensors, and machine learning.
    - o **Energy Management Algorithms:** Use IoT sensors to monitor energy usage and optimize energy distribution in real-time. This can help reduce waste and improve the sustainability of urban infrastructure.
    - o **Health Systems AI:** Analyzes healthcare data, such as hospital capacity, patient flow, and emergency service response times, to improve public health strategies.
    - o **Environmental Monitoring Algorithms:** AI can help monitor pollution levels, waste management, and other environmental parameters, enabling smarter city management strategies.
3. **Decision Support System (DSS):**
    - o This system processes the insights generated from both educational and urban data. It helps in making decisions regarding curriculum design, city planning, and resource allocation. For example, based on student performance and city traffic data, it might recommend adjusting school timings or enhancing public transportation services.

User Interaction Layer:

This layer involves how users (students, teachers, city officials, etc.) interact with the system, enabling them to access personalized insights and take action.

1. **Adaptive Learning Platforms:**
    - o These platforms provide personalized dashboards that show student progress, areas for improvement, and recommended resources. They might also include gamification elements or social learning features to increase engagement.
2. **Smart City Dashboards:**
    - o Dashboards provide real-time monitoring of urban data, including traffic, energy use, and public service status. City officials can use these dashboards to make informed decisions about resource deployment and public service management.
3. **User Interfaces:**
    - o **Mobile Apps:** These apps allow users to access educational content, monitor learning progress, and receive notifications.

- **Websites:** A comprehensive platform where all users (students, teachers, city officials, etc.) can access information, provide feedback, and interact with the system.
- **Smart Devices:** Integration with smart wearables or IoT devices like smart watches to monitor student activity or environmental factors in real-time.

Integration Layer:

This layer ensures that all components of the system can communicate with each other and external systems, such as other city infrastructures or educational systems.

1. **APIs and Web Services:**
   - APIs (Application Programming Interfaces) allow seamless data exchange between the educational system and smart city infrastructure. For instance, a public transport API can provide data on student transportation needs, which is then fed into the educational resource allocation model.
2. **Cloud Computing/Big Data:**
   - The cloud provides a scalable and flexible environment for storing and processing large datasets generated by sensors, IoT devices, and educational platforms. Big data analytics is used to derive insights from the massive amounts of data collected.

Security Layer:

This layer ensures that all data is securely transmitted and stored, protecting users' privacy and meeting legal and regulatory requirements.

1. **Data Privacy & Security:**
   - Ensures that sensitive data (student data, citizen data, etc.) is encrypted, anonymized, and securely stored. It adheres to legal standards such as the **General Data Protection Regulation (GDPR)** for data protection.
2. **Compliance:**
   - Ensures that the system follows regional and international laws regarding data privacy, usage, and storage.

Feedback Loop:

This is the final step, ensuring the system improves over time based on both user input and performance data.

1. **Continuous Learning and Improvement:**
   - o AI models continually learn from new data, refining their predictions and decisions. For instance, if student performance improves with a new curriculum recommendation, the system will adjust future recommendations accordingly.
2. **User Feedback:**
   Feedback is collected from students, teachers, and city residents through surveys, feedback forms, and usage patterns. This feedback is analyzed to improve the system's recommendations and features.

ADVANTAGES

Improved Efficiency and Resource Management:

- **Smart Cities:**
  - o **Optimized Urban Services:** Through the use of IoT devices and sensors, Smart Cities can optimize resource usage such as energy, water, and waste management. For example, smart meters help track energy consumption, and smart grids enable efficient distribution of electricity.
  - o **Efficient Traffic Management:** Traffic sensors and predictive analytics can optimize traffic flow, reducing congestion, travel time, and carbon emissions. Adaptive traffic lights can respond to real-time traffic conditions, enhancing overall road usage efficiency.
  - o **Waste Management:** Smart waste management systems can monitor waste levels in bins and optimize the collection routes, reducing operational costs and environmental impact.
- **Smart Education:**
  - o **Personalized Learning:** AI-powered platforms can offer customized learning experiences for students, adapting content to individual needs, learning speeds, and interests. This leads to improved student engagement and better educational outcomes.
  - o **Resource Allocation:** Smart Education systems allow better management and allocation of educational resources (e.g., classrooms, teaching

staff, learning materials). Analytics can predict demand and suggest optimal resource distribution.

  - **Automation of Administrative Tasks:** Routine administrative tasks such as grading, attendance tracking, and scheduling can be automated using AI and data-driven systems, reducing the administrative burden on educators and allowing more time for teaching.

Enhanced Data-Driven Decision Making:

- **Smart Cities:**
  - **Real-Time Data Collection:** Continuous data from sensors and connected devices allows cities to make informed decisions based on real-time data, improving urban planning, crisis management, and public safety.
  - **Predictive Analytics:** The use of predictive models can help city officials foresee and address potential issues such as traffic bottlenecks, energy shortages, and public health risks before they become significant problems.
  - **Urban Planning:** Data-driven insights enable better urban design and zoning decisions, helping to create more livable, sustainable, and efficient cities.
- **Smart Education:**
  - **Data Analytics for Student Performance:** By analyzing student performance data, educators can identify trends, at-risk students, and areas where the curriculum can be improved. This can help provide targeted interventions and support to students in need.
  - **Learning Analytics:** Collecting and analyzing data on student behaviors and interactions with digital learning tools provides valuable insights into how educational content can be refined for better engagement and learning outcomes.
  - **Curriculum Improvement:** Educational institutions can use data to continuously improve and update curricula, ensuring that they remain relevant and aligned with current trends and student needs.

Cost Savings:

- **Smart Cities:**
  - **Energy and Utility Savings:** By deploying smart meters and grids, cities can significantly reduce energy consumption and operational costs

in public services. For example, streetlights can automatically adjust brightness based on time of day or weather conditions, saving energy.

  - **Reduced Operational Costs:** With optimized transportation, waste management, and resource distribution systems, cities can reduce the costs of infrastructure maintenance and service delivery. Automation and real-time monitoring can also reduce the need for manual intervention.
  - **Optimized Public Safety Resources:** By leveraging IoT and smart surveillance systems, cities can improve public safety while reducing the need for large numbers of security personnel, thereby cutting down on expenses.
- **Smart Education:**
  - **Cost-Effective Learning Tools:** By shifting towards digital learning resources, educational institutions can reduce costs associated with physical textbooks, materials, and traditional teaching methods. E-learning platforms and digital classrooms can also decrease infrastructure costs.
  - **Optimized Teaching Resources:** Data analytics can help schools or universities optimize the use of teaching staff, facilities, and classrooms, reducing unnecessary overheads. Predictive tools can help allocate teachers more efficiently based on student demand.

Better Quality of Life and Urban Living:

- **Smart Cities:**
  - **Improved Public Services:** Smart city technologies enhance public service delivery. For example, real-time monitoring of air quality, water supply, and health services ensures that resources are allocated effectively, improving citizens' quality of life.
  - **Public Safety:** Surveillance cameras, emergency response systems, and intelligent monitoring can help reduce crime rates, improve emergency response times, and create safer environments for citizens.
  - **Environmental Sustainability:** Smart cities are more environmentally conscious. By monitoring environmental parameters like air quality, pollution levels, and energy consumption, cities can implement sustainability initiatives such as green building practices and urban green spaces.
- **Smart Education:**
  - **Improved Educational Outcomes:** With personalized learning, students can progress at their own pace, focusing on their strengths and addressing their weaknesses, leading to higher levels of achievement and satisfaction.

- **Global Access to Education:** Smart Education systems offer global access to quality learning materials and resources, breaking down geographical barriers and providing educational opportunities to students worldwide.
- **Engaged Learning Environment:** Interactive learning tools, gamification, and real-time feedback can create an engaging and stimulating learning environment, enhancing students' motivation and interest in education.

Enhanced Citizen and Student Engagement:

- **Smart Cities:**
  - **Citizen Participation:** Smart cities foster better communication between government authorities and citizens. Platforms for civic engagement allow residents to report issues, provide feedback, and participate in decision-making processes, leading to more responsive governance.
  - **Transparency and Accountability:** By providing real-time access to data, smart cities promote transparency and accountability, allowing citizens to track the performance of public services and urban development projects.
  - **Smart Health and Education Services:** Smart cities enable the integration of health services with data analytics, providing citizens with personalized health monitoring and wellness initiatives. This improves overall public health and well-being.
- **Smart Education:**
  - **Interactive Learning Tools:** Digital tools such as virtual classrooms, simulations, and learning management systems enable students to interact actively with the content, peers, and teachers, making the learning process more dynamic and collaborative.

CHALLENGES

Data Privacy and Security:

- **Privacy Concerns:** In both smart cities and smart education systems, sensitive data such as personal information, student performance, and real-time location data are collected. Ensuring that this data is protected from unauthorized access or misuse is a significant challenge.

- Smart Cities: City-wide data collection involves citizens' personal data, traffic patterns, health information, and utility consumption. This data must be encrypted and stored securely to prevent breaches.
- Smart Education: Student data is equally sensitive, and schools or universities must safeguard it from external threats or malicious actors, which can lead to identity theft, fraud, or misuse.

- **Solutions:** Implementing strong encryption protocols, secure cloud storage, decentralized data management systems, and following legal frameworks like GDPR can help mitigate privacy and security risks. Additionally, anonymization and aggregation techniques should be used to reduce the potential for privacy violations.

Interoperability and Integration:

- **Diverse Systems and Technologies:** Both Smart City and Smart Education systems involve a wide range of technologies, platforms, and stakeholders. For example, urban data comes from different sources like IoT devices, traffic sensors, and weather stations, while educational data comes from LMS, student databases, and other systems.
    - **Smart Cities:** Integrating data from various urban systems (e.g., transportation, healthcare, energy, and waste management) can be difficult because each system may use different technologies or data formats.
    - **Smart Education:** The integration of learning management systems (LMS), student databases, digital learning tools, and assessment systems into a cohesive platform is another significant challenge.
- **Solutions:** The development of standardized protocols, open data formats, and APIs is essential for ensuring interoperability. Cloud platforms and integration middleware can help facilitate smooth communication and data exchange between disparate systems.

Data Management and Quality:

- **Large Volume of Data:** The vast amount of data generated by smart devices, sensors, and users can overwhelm systems that are not designed to handle such volumes. Poor data management leads to inconsistencies, inaccuracies, and missing data.
    - **Smart Cities:** Urban sensors and IoT devices generate continuous streams of real-time data, requiring robust data management frameworks to ensure data quality, consistency, and integrity.

- **Smart Education:** Educational systems collect vast quantities of data, including student performance metrics, behavioral data, and learning patterns. Managing this data and ensuring that it is accurate, timely, and usable is critical.

Scalability and Infrastructure:

- **System Expansion and Growth:** Smart City and Smart Education systems need to scale to accommodate growing populations, increasing data volume, and evolving technologies. Ensuring that these systems remain effective as they grow is a considerable challenge.
  - **Smart Cities:** Smart cities involve large-scale deployments of IoT sensors, communication networks, and data centers. Scaling these systems while maintaining performance and reliability is a significant issue.
  - **Smart Education:** Expanding digital infrastructure to accommodate a growing number of students, teachers, and educational tools while maintaining consistent service delivery is crucial.
- **Solutions:** Cloud computing and edge computing can provide the necessary scalability for both Smart Cities and Smart Education systems. Cloud infrastructure enables rapid scaling, while edge computing can process data closer to its source, reducing latency and improving efficiency.

Digital Divide and Accessibility:

- **Equity and Inclusion:** Both Smart City and Smart Education initiatives face the challenge of ensuring that all citizens, regardless of socioeconomic status, can access and benefit from these technologies.
  - **Smart Cities:** Some areas of a city might lack the infrastructure (e.g., high-speed internet, electricity, or IoT devices) required to participate in a smart city ecosystem. There is also a risk of exacerbating existing inequalities if smart technologies are only accessible to wealthy neighborhoods.
  - **Smart Education:** Students in rural areas or from lower-income families may not have access to the technology needed to engage with digital learning platforms. This leads to disparities in educational opportunities.
- **Solutions:** Governments and educational institutions must work towards providing affordable access to technology and the internet. Public-private partnerships, subsidies for low-income families, and infrastructure investments are vital for bridging the digital divide.

Resistance to Change:

- **Cultural and Organizational Barriers:** The adoption of new technologies in Smart Cities and educational institutions can face resistance from both citizens and employees. This resistance may stem from a lack of understanding, fear of job displacement, or general reluctance to adopt new tools.
  - **Smart Cities:** Citizens may be skeptical about sharing their data due to privacy concerns, or they might resist new technologies, such as smart traffic management systems, due to perceived inconvenience or distrust in technology.
  - **Smart Education:** Teachers, students, and administrators might resist adopting new digital learning tools or educational technologies because they are unfamiliar with the systems or worried about their effectiveness.
- **Solutions:** Change management strategies, including awareness campaigns, training, and clear communication of the benefits, are essential to encourage adoption. Pilot programs can help ease the transition and demonstrate the value of new technologies.

Ethical Concerns:

- **Bias and Fairness:** AI and machine learning models used in Smart City and Smart Education systems must be designed to be fair and unbiased. Algorithms that predict student performance or optimize urban resources can perpetuate existing biases if not carefully designed.
  - **Smart Cities:** AI algorithms used for urban planning or traffic management could unintentionally prioritize certain neighborhoods or demographics, exacerbating social inequalities.
  - **Smart Education:** AI-based educational tools or predictive models for student performance could be biased, leading to unfair outcomes for certain groups of students.
- **Solutions:** Developing ethical guidelines for AI development, ensuring transparency in algorithmic decision-making, and regularly auditing algorithms for bias are necessary to address these concerns. Additionally, involving diverse groups of stakeholders in the development and deployment of AI technologies can help ensure fairness.

Regulatory and Legal Challenges:

- **Compliance with Laws:** The development of Smart City and Smart Education systems must adhere to a wide range of regulations, including those related to data privacy, accessibility, and urban planning.
  - **Smart Cities:** Smart City initiatives must comply with local, national, and international regulations concerning data privacy (e.g., GDPR), infrastructure development, and environmental impact.
  - **Smart Education:** Educational institutions must comply with laws related to student privacy (e.g., FERPA in the U.S.), accessibility standards for people with disabilities, and accreditation requirements for educational tools and platforms.
- **Solutions:** Governments need to create clear regulatory frameworks for the development and deployment of smart technologies. Additionally, organizations must work closely with legal and compliance teams to ensure that all aspects of the smart system meet the relevant legal standards.

Cost and Funding:

- **High Initial Investment:** Both Smart City and Smart Education systems require significant upfront investment in technology, infrastructure, and personnel. Securing funding for these projects, especially in cities or countries with limited budgets, can be a major barrier.
  - **Smart Cities:** The costs associated with installing IoT sensors, upgrading infrastructure, and developing software solutions can be prohibitive. Furthermore, the long-term costs of maintaining and upgrading these systems can add additional financial burden.
  - **Smart Education:** Educational institutions need to invest in digital infrastructure, training programs, and software solutions. Moreover, ensuring equitable access to technology for all students can require ongoing financial commitments.

RESULTS

The integration of AI in education has significantly improved student engagement and academic performance. Before AI-driven curriculum innovations, students often struggled with standardized learning approaches that failed to cater to individual needs. However, with AI-powered personalized learning, engagement levels have increased as students receive tailored educational content, adaptive assessments, and instant feedback.As shown in the data, student engagement before AI adoption remained steady, with limited improvements over the years. However, after AI integration, engagement levels experienced a sharp rise, reaching up to 90% in recent years. This improvement is largely attributed to AI's ability to analyze student learning patterns, recommend appropriate study materials, and provide real-time support. Additionally, academic performance, including retention rates, grades, and completion rates, has seen remarkable growth, as AI assists educators in identifying struggling students and providing targeted interventions.

Figure 3. Impact of AI on student performance

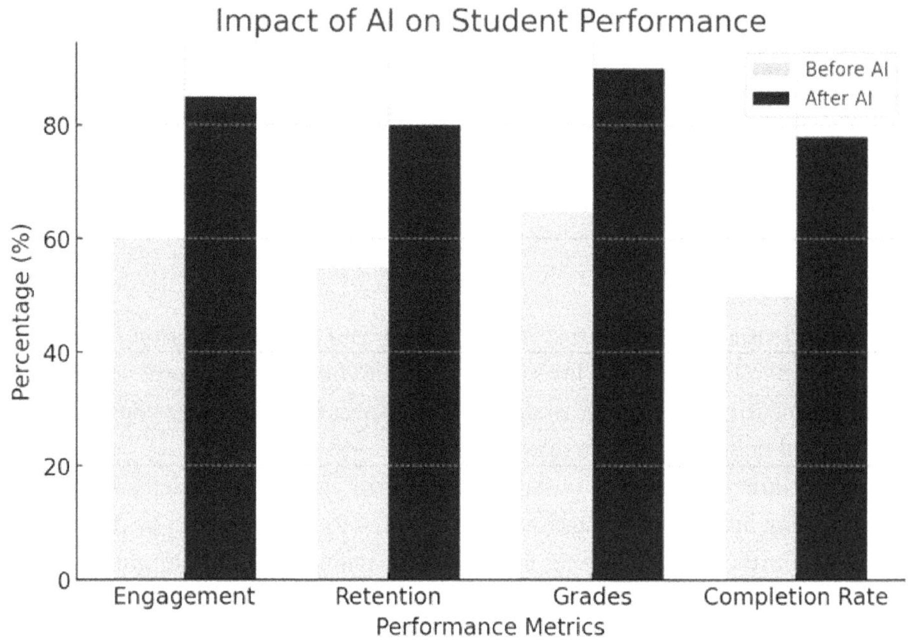

Figure 4. AI adoption trends in education

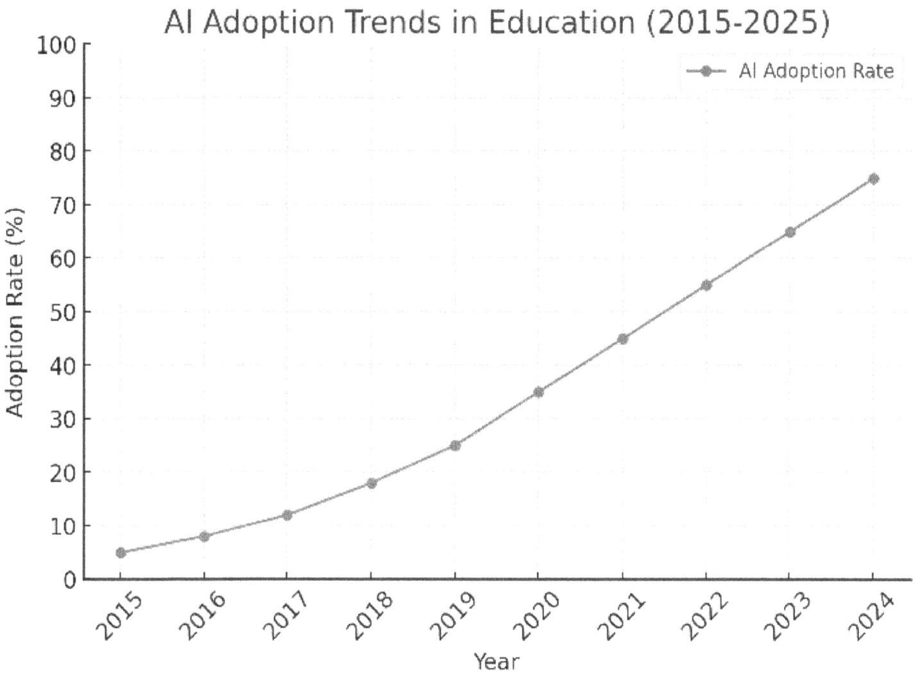

Figure 5. AI-driven personalized learning

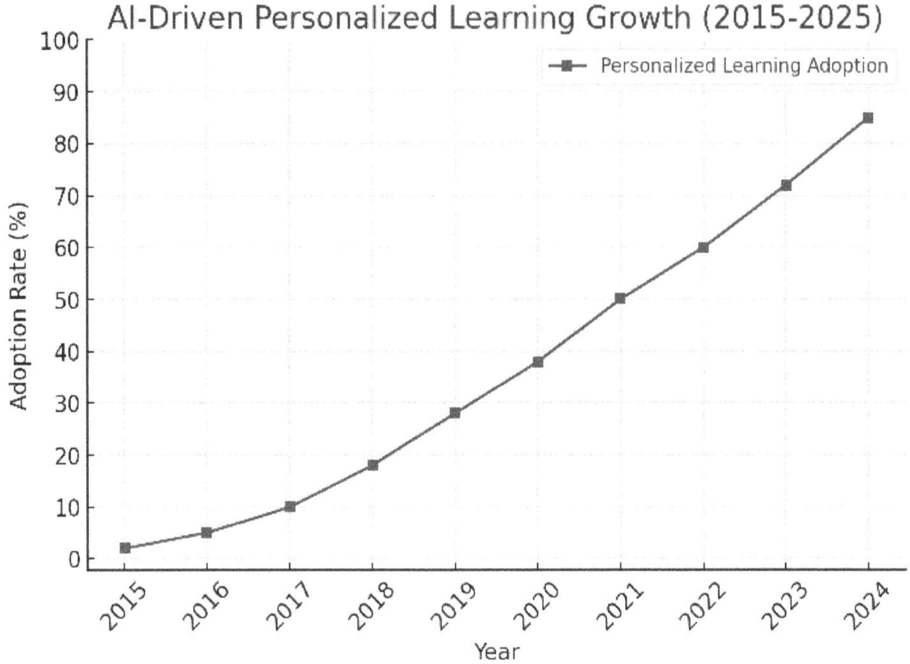

Figure 6. Comparison of traditional vs. AI-based growth

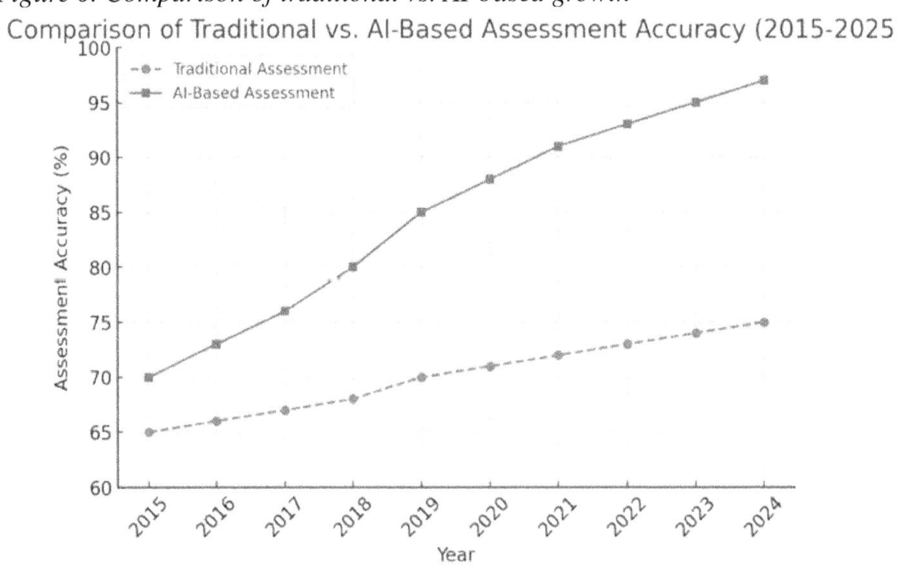

Figure 3 showing the impact of AI on student performance. It compares engagement, retention, grades, and completion rates before and after AI integration. Figure 4 showing AI adoption trends in education from 2015 to 2025. It demonstrates the increasing integration of AI-driven technologies in curriculum design. Figure 5 showing the growth of AI-driven personalized learning from 2015 to 2025. It highlights the increasing adoption of AI for tailoring education to individual student needs. Figure 6 comparing traditional vs. AI-based assessment accuracy over time. It shows how AI has significantly improved assessment accuracy compared to traditional methods.

CONCLUSION

The integration of Smart Cities and Smart Education systems represents a transformative shift towards more efficient, sustainable, and innovative urban living and educational environments. Through the convergence of cutting-edge technologies such as IoT, AI, big data analytics, and machine learning, both domains are revolutionizing how urban spaces function and how education is delivered. Smart Cities are paving the way for more optimized urban management, resource allocation, and service delivery. The use of real-time data collection, predictive analytics, and AI-based systems helps improve traffic flow, manage energy resources efficiently, enhance public safety, and ensure sustainable growth. This results in significant benefits such as reduced congestion, optimized energy usage, improved public health, and higher quality of life for residents. Furthermore, the ability to make data-driven decisions enhances urban planning, making cities more adaptive and responsive to citizen needs. Smart Education, on the other hand, is reshaping the educational landscape by providing personalized learning experiences, improving resource allocation, and fostering greater engagement between students, teachers, and institutions. With the aid of AI and data analytics, education can be tailored to meet the unique needs of each learner, thereby boosting student outcomes and satisfaction. By automating administrative tasks, educational systems also reduce the operational burden, allowing more time for personalized instruction and support. Despite these advancements, there remain significant challenges, particularly around data privacy, security, equitable access to technology, and the need for continuous infrastructure investment. Addressing these challenges is critical to ensuring that the benefits of smart systems are accessible to all and that they evolve to meet the changing needs of society. The combination of Smart Cities and Smart Education offers a holistic approach to creating a future that is not only more efficient and sustainable but also more equitable and inclusive. By leveraging the strengths of these systems, we can build urban environments that nurture innovation, improve the quality of life, and prepare future generations for the challenges of a rapidly evolving world.

FUTURE ENHANCEMENT

In future of Smart Cities and Smart Education is brimming with possibilities. By continuously integrating new technologies, enhancing user experience, and fostering global collaboration, these systems will transform the way we live, learn, and interact with the world around us. As these technologies evolve, they will shape a future that is smarter, more efficient, and more inclusive, addressing the needs of diverse populations and creating sustainable, adaptive environments for the next generation.

REFERENCES

Albino, V., Berardi, U., & Dangelico, R. M. (2015). Smart Cities: Definitions, Dimensions, Performance, and Initiatives. *Journal of Urban Technology*, *22*(1), 3–21.

Angelidou, M. (2015). Smart Cities: A Conjuncture of Four Forces. *Cities (London, England)*, *47*, 95–106.

Anthopoulos, L., & Fitsilis, P. (2010). "From Digital to Ubiquitous Cities: Defining a Common Architecture for Urban Development." *Proceedings of the 6th International Conference on Intelligent Environments*, 301-306.

Batty, M., Axhausen, K. W., & Giannotti, F.. (2012). Smart Cities of the Future. *The European Physical Journal. Special Topics*, *214*(1), 481–518.

Caragliu, A., Del Bo, C., & Nijkamp, P. (2011). Smart Cities in Europe. *Journal of Urban Technology*, *18*(2), 65–82.

Chourabi, H., Nam, T., & Walker, S.. (2012). "Understanding Smart Cities: An Integrative Framework." *45th Hawaii International Conference on System Sciences (HICSS)*, 2289-2297.

Dameri, R. P., & Cocchia, A. (2013). "Smart City and Digital City: Twenty Years of Terminology Evolution." *ItAIS: The Italian Association for Information Systems*, 1-9.

Deakin, M. (2010). A Review of City Portals: The Transformation of Service Provision Under the Democratization of the Fifth Utility. *International Journal of Public Information Systems*, *6*(2), 35–45.

Dirks, S., & Keeling, M. (2009). "A Vision of Smarter Cities: How Cities Can Lead the Way into a Prosperous and Sustainable Future." *IBM Global Services*, 1-19.

Giffinger, R., Fertner, C., Kramar, H., ... (2007). "Smart Cities: Ranking of European Medium-Sized Cities." *Vienna University of Technology*, 1-28.

Komninos, N. (2011). Intelligent Cities: Variable Geographies of Smart Urbanism. *Intelligent Buildings International*, *3*(3), 172–188.

Lee, J. H., Hancock, M. G., & Hu, M. C. (2014). Towards an Effective Framework for Building Smart Cities: Lessons from Seoul and San Francisco. *Technological Forecasting and Social Change*, *89*, 80–99.

Marsal-Llacuna, M.-L., Colomer-Llinàs, J., & Meléndez-Frigola, J. (2015). Lessons in Urban Monitoring Taken from Sustainable and Livable Cities to Better Address the Smart Cities Initiative. *Technological Forecasting and Social Change*, *90*, 611–622.

Mora, L., Bolici, R., & Deakin, M. (2017). The First Two Decades of Smart-City Research: A Bibliometric Analysis. *Journal of Urban Technology*, *24*(1), 3–27.

Nam, T., & Pardo, T. A. (2011). "Conceptualizing Smart City with Dimensions of Technology, People, and Institutions." *45th Hawaii International Conference on System Sciences (HICSS)*, 282-292.

Papa, R., Gargiulo, C., & Galderisi, A. (2013). "Towards an Urban Planners' Perspective on Smart City." *TeMA - Journal of Land Use. Mobility and Environment*, *6*(1), 5–17.

Perboli, G., De Marco, A., Perfetti, F., & Marone, M. (2014). A New Taxonomy of Smart City Projects. *Transportation Research Procedia*, *3*, 470–478.

Piro, G., Cianci, I., & Grieco, L. A.. (2014). Information-Centric Services in Smart Cities. *Journal of Systems and Software*, *88*, 169–188.

Schaffers, H., Komninos, N., Pallot, M., ... (2011). "Smart Cities and the Future Internet: Towards Cooperation Frameworks for Open Innovation." *The Future Internet Assembly*, 431-446.

Söderström, O., Paasche, T., & Klauser, F. (2014). Smart Cities as Corporate Storytelling. *City (London, England)*, *18*(3), 307–320.

Townsend, A. M. (2013). *Smart Cities: Big Data, Civic Hackers, and the Quest for a New Utopia*. W.W. Norton & Company.

Vanolo, A. (2014). Smartmentality: The Smart City as Disciplinary Strategy. *Urban Studies (Edinburgh, Scotland)*, *51*(5), 883–898.

Washburn, D., Sindhu, U., Balaouras, S., et al. (2010). "Helping CIOs Understand 'Smart City' Initiatives: Defining the Smart City, Its Drivers, and the Role of the CIO." *Forrester Research Inc.*, 1-17.

Yigitcanlar, T., & Kamruzzaman, M. (2018). Does Smart City Policy Lead to Sustainability of Cities? *Land Use Policy*, *73*, 49–58.

Zanella, A., Bui, N., & Castellani, A.. (2014). Internet of Things for Smart Cities. *IEEE Internet of Things Journal*, *1*(1), 22–32.

Zygiaris, S. (2013). Smart City Reference Model: Assisting Planners to Conceptualize the Building of Smart City Innovation Ecosystems. *Journal of the Knowledge Economy*, *4*(2), 217–231.

Chapter 5
Integrating AI in Outcome-Based Education:
A Cross-Disciplinary Curriculum Transformation

Ahmad Yani
https://orcid.org/0000-0002-8336-4066
Universitas Pendidikan Indonesia, Indonesia

Rosita Rosita
Universitas Pendidikan Indonesia, Indonesia

ABSTRACT

Artificial Intelligence (AI) is revolutionizing education by streamlining administrative processes, enhancing learning experiences, and enabling personalized assessments. This chapter explores AI's role in the Outcome-Based Education (OBE) framework, focusing on curriculum design, interdisciplinary learning, assessment automation, and AI literacy. AI facilitates adaptive evaluations, aligning student competencies with industry needs while reducing educators' workload. However, ethical concerns such as data privacy, algorithmic bias, and academic integrity must be addressed. Establishing transparent governance frameworks ensures responsible AI integration. While AI holds immense potential to improve education, its implementation must be ethical, strategic, and aligned with evolving technological advancements.

DOI: 10.4018/979-8-3373-1062-6.ch005

Copyright © 2026, IGI Global Scientific Publishing. Copying or distributing in print or electronic forms without written permission of IGI Global Scientific Publishing is prohibited.

INTRODUCTION

Over the past decade, Artificial Intelligence (AI) technology has undergone rapid advancements driven by progress in computing, increased data accessibility, and increasingly sophisticated algorithms. AI enables machines to analyze data, recognize patterns, and autonomously generate intelligent responses. Artificial neural networks replicate human cognitive processes, allowing machines to learn, reason, and perform tasks that mimic human capabilities. Due to their resilience, AI-powered systems can efficiently process vast amounts of data, identifying patterns, trends, and correlations. These capabilities enable AI to make data-driven predictions, interpret and respond to voice commands, and generate highly realistic synthetic voices. In the entertainment industry, AI can recognize and track objects in images or videos and generate text, photographs, music, and videos. Meanwhile, AI controls robotic systems in industrial applications to enhance automation and streamline production processes.

Since the introduction of the term Artificial Intelligence (AI) in 1956 (Benko & Lányi, 2009), this technology has provided significant benefits across various sectors. As AI continues to evolve, its applications are becoming more widespread and integral to daily life. Common AI-powered technologies include web search engines, which facilitate fast and efficient information retrieval (Sable et. al., 2023); Internet of Things (IoT) systems, which enable automation and remote control; and cloud computing platforms, which offer flexible data storage and seamless access across multiple devices (Sunyaev & Sunyaev, 2020). Deep learning techniques enhance AI capabilities in facial recognition, automatic language translation, and image-based medical diagnostics (Litjens et al., 2017). Virtual assistants such as Siri, Google Assistant, and Alexa improve human-computer interaction through natural language processing and voice commands (Silva & Gomez, 2025).

AI is widely implemented across administrative and academic processes in the education sector, including student registration, curriculum development, classroom management, and alumni tracking. AI-driven applications in educational institutions include chatbots that streamline student enrollment, provide real-time information, answer frequently asked questions, and assist in course selection (Ait Baha et al., 2024). Furthermore, Massive Open Online Courses (MOOCs) such as Coursera and edX utilize AI algorithms to tailor course recommendations based on students' interests, academic backgrounds, and career aspirations. Additionally, platforms like PowerSchool facilitate managing and analyzing students' academic performance, attendance records, and extracurricular participation, ultimately enhancing the overall learning experience.

AI has been increasingly integrated into learning management through Learning Management System (LMS) platforms such as Moodle and Google Classroom (Qazi et al., 2024). These systems employ AI-driven algorithms to facilitate both synchronous and asynchronous learning by enabling material distribution, progress tracking, and automated assessment. In student attendance management, facial recognition technology allows for automatic attendance monitoring, while platforms like EDU360 and Oracle PeopleSoft streamline administrative processes and optimize educational workforce management. Additionally, AI-powered communication platforms, such as Schoology and ClassDojo, enhance interactions between schools, students, and parents (DiGiacomo et al., 2022; Evangeline & Parkavi, 2022).

AI also plays a crucial role in enhancing the learning process. Personalized learning applications, such as Khan Academy, adapt teaching methods to align with individual student needs and abilities. Learning analytics tools, including Tableau, analyze educational data and track student performance. Automated assessment systems like Grammarly provide quick and objective evaluations of students' written assignments, essays, and reports. Furthermore, simulation and Virtual Reality (VR) technologies are being integrated to create immersive learning experiences, particularly in science and engineering disciplines (Zhang & Wang, 2024). AI-powered teaching assistants, such as IBM Watson Education, contribute to curriculum development and assess teaching effectiveness.

The development of AI-driven educational tools continues to expand. Teachers now utilize project-based learning platforms such as PhET Interactive Simulations, which allow students to explore physics, chemistry, and biology concepts through interactive activities (Kizito & Hassan, 2024). Additionally, the Labster platform provides a virtual laboratory environment where students can conduct scientific experiments without needing physical lab facilities. AI-enhanced task management tools, such as Trello with Butler AI, support project organization through automation, while Miro assists in the automatic generation of mind maps for project planning and collaborative reporting (Krishna & Meda, 2024; Spena et al., 2024). AI-powered design tools integrated into Canva enable students to create visually compelling infographics and presentations.

AI is also transforming alumni tracking and career support. Platforms such as SurveySparrow automate alumni data collection, while MonkeyLearn analyzes alumni feedback to assess their satisfaction with their academic programs. CareerBuilder utilizes AI to predict career trajectories for graduates, while job-matching platforms like LinkedIn Jobs and Indeed connect alumni with employment opportunities that align with their skills and qualifications.

Integrating AI across various platforms and applications presents immense educational potential. However, AI must be further developed to fully realize this potential to support educational implementation seamlessly (Bhimdiwala et al.,

2022). This chapter serves as a foundational exploration of AI's role in education, highlighting five key themes that require integration:

1. **AI as a catalyst for Outcome-Based Education (OBE) implementation and evaluation.** This section examines how AI can enhance the OBE curriculum by enabling personalized learning experiences, forecasting educational needs, analyzing learning data, and assessing societal demands based on data-driven insights (Spady, 1994).
2. **Interdisciplinary curriculum design.** This discussion emphasizes the importance of interdisciplinary approaches in OBE, focusing on competency acquisition and the holistic development of students' skills and capabilities.
3. **AI's role in assessment and feedback systems.** AI-driven tools streamline curriculum assessment by providing real-time feedback on alumni career trajectories. Additionally, AI facilitates the measurement of learning outcomes and supports the continuous improvement of students' skills through data-driven analysis.
4. **Optimizing AI literacy for educators and learners.** This section explores strategic initiatives to equip teachers and students with AI literacy, ensuring its practical application in the learning process and the development of essential 21st-century skills within the OBE framework.
5. **Ethical considerations and responsible AI use in education.** This final section examines the ethical implications of AI in education, including algorithmic bias, student data privacy, and the rights and responsibilities of AI users in academic environments.

AI AS A CATALYST FOR OUTCOME-BASED EDUCATION (OBE) IMPLEMENTATION AND EVALUATION.

The Outcome-Based Education (OBE) curriculum is structured using the Backward Design approach, prioritizing the definition of desired learning outcomes before designing instructional activities and assessments. This methodology aligns with the Understanding by Design (UbD) framework developed by Grant Wiggins and Jay McTighe (2005). In OBE, learning outcomes are designed to emphasize the applicability and relevance of acquired competencies strongly. The selected competencies are carefully tailored to be specific, meaningful, and beneficial, ensuring that students are well-prepared to contribute effectively to society and their professional fields.

Traditional curricula, by contrast, have historically emphasized delivering extensive teaching materials from the outset. The underlying assumption was that a broad accumulation of knowledge would naturally lead to social status and high-paying job opportunities. Schools were primarily viewed as service providers, where education was offered in exchange for tuition fees. Upon graduation, students received a diploma or certificate, after which educational institutions assumed no further responsibility for their professional outcomes. As a result, access to quality education often determined one's likelihood of securing employment, favoring those who could afford expensive schooling.

The OBE curriculum, however, operates on a fundamentally different principle. Its effectiveness is measured not by the volume of knowledge imparted but by the number of graduates who successfully integrate into the workforce and contribute to society. While the transactional nature of education remains, OBE fosters a stronger moral responsibility toward graduates. Educational institutions are accountable for ensuring that the knowledge imparted is practical and relevant, and does not contribute to rising unemployment rates. Therefore, Programme Learning Outcomes (PLO) are carefully designed to align with specific professional roles and career pathways. These outcomes are continuously refined to reflect advancements in science and technology. Competency standards, technological innovations, and academic developments are key evaluation criteria for assessing students' learning progress. The formulation of PLOs is a collaborative effort at the program level, ensuring that the responsibility of curriculum development does not fall solely on individual educators.

The assessment rubric is fundamental for selecting course materials and determining appropriate teaching methods. Course instructors develop rubrics tailored to their respective subjects, ensuring that assessments align with learning objectives and evaluation methods. Rubrics are critical in refining assessment strategies, providing clear and consistent student feedback, and promoting transparency in the grading process (Tractenberg et al., 2020). These rubrics undergo a process of validation and standardization to align with PLOs and accreditation requirements. However, developing rubrics remains challenging, as not all instructors can efficiently and accurately complete this process. Furthermore, discrepancies in the interpretation of PLOs among faculty members and study program teams often necessitate collaborative efforts to establish a shared understanding. The creation of assessment rubrics follows standardized procedures within the Outcome-Based Education (OBE) framework to ensure consistency and reliability.

The construction of assessment rubrics is directly linked to the formulation of PLOs and Course Learning Outcomes (CLOs), both of which serve as benchmarks for student success. This alignment ensures that assessments are relevant and effective in measuring students' progress toward achieving predetermined learning objectives. The criteria for successfully attaining CLOs must be explicitly defined to maintain assessment integrity. The selection of assessment instruments—holistic or descriptive-analytic rubrics—must be tailored to the nature of the CLOs being evaluated. Consequently, CLOs must be carefully formulated, with each assessment method mapped systematically to the corresponding learning objectives.

Assessment strategies must also be adapted to the nature of the competencies being measured. Written assignments are ideal for evaluating students' conceptual understanding, analytical skills, and ability to synthesize information. Project-based assessments are beneficial for gauging competencies related to practical skills, creativity, and applying theoretical knowledge in real-world contexts. Examinations are more suited for assessing foundational knowledge, rapid analytical thinking, and problem-solving abilities under time constraints. Laboratory practicums are designed to develop students' technical and analytical competencies in controlled experimental environments, fostering essential scientific skills such as observation, classification, experimental design, and data interpretation. Internships, on the other hand, provide opportunities to assess professional competencies and soft skills in real-world work settings.

A structured cross-tabulation approach, as seen in Table 1, is recommended to enhance the accuracy and efficiency of aligning CLOs with appropriate assessment methods. Furthermore, leveraging technology can significantly improve the precision and effectiveness of CLO-based assessment, ensuring a more data-driven and objective evaluation process.

Table 1. CLOs and assessment instruments cross-tabulation

PLO	Course	CLO	Assessment Method				
			Assignment	Project	Exam	Practicum	Internship
PLO-1	A	CLO-1	V		V		
		CLO-2		V		V	
		CLO-3	V				V
		CLO-4			V	V	
		....					
	B	CLO-1	V		V		
		CLO-2	V				V
		CLO-3			V		V
		CLO-4		V		V	V
		....					
PLO-2	A	....					
	B	....					
	C	....					
....	....	....					

The final stage in designing an OBE-aligned curriculum is developing a learning process that effectively supports student learning outcomes. This process involves selecting teaching materials, instructional media, learning aids, methodologies, and structured student activities. Given the broad range of learning experiences that CLOs require students to master, traditional lecture-based methods alone are insufficient. Effective learning must go beyond passive knowledge transfer to foster conceptual understanding, analytical and synthetic thinking, technical and professional skills, and problem-solving abilities under real-world constraints. To achieve this, experiential learning approaches—such as problem-based learning (PBL), project-based learning (PjBL), collaborative learning, simulations, practicals, and internships—are essential (Hamilton & Klebba, 2011). These active learning strategies promote deeper engagement and enhance students' critical and analytical thinking through direct, hands-on experiences.

A key challenge in implementing OBE is the dual responsibility of lecturers: they must simultaneously manage classroom activities, deliver instructional material, and conduct continuous assessments. Unlike traditional curricula, where evaluation is primarily based on mid-term and final exams, OBE necessitates a broader range of assessment methods, including project reports, performance-based evaluations, group presentations, and reflective essays. This shift significantly increases the workload for lecturers, as they must provide individualized feedback to a potentially large number of students throughout the semester.

Among the many benefits of OBE, one of the most pressing concerns is the intensified assessment burden on lecturers. The detailed assessment rubrics required to maintain grading consistency make the evaluation process both time-consuming and complex. Additionally, providing personalized feedback to each student is nearly impossible with large class sizes. Since each course has unique CLOs, a one-size-fits-all assessment rubric cannot be used, forcing lecturers to create customized rubrics for different assignments and projects. This further increases their workload and preparation time.

Moreover, while OBE emphasizes PBL, PjBL, and CBL, not all lecturers are trained in these student-centered teaching methodologies. Many educators accustomed to traditional, lecture-based instruction find transitioning to interactive, active learning techniques challenging. This knowledge gap complicates the effective execution of OBE, further straining both faculty and students. Students, too, frequently express concerns regarding OBE's rigorous workload. Many feel overwhelmed by the volume of individual and group assignments, often requesting reduced coursework. However, due to the structured nature of OBE, lecturers are obligated to ensure that students achieve the required CPLs and CLOs, limiting flexibility in adjusting coursework demands.

In summary, while OBE has the potential to transform education by emphasizing competency-based learning, its implementation presents significant logistical and pedagogical challenges. AI can play a crucial role in streamlining the learning and assessment processes to address these issues. Table 2 shows various AI-driven solutions that can enhance the efficiency and effectiveness of OBE implementation.

Table 2. AI catalysts in the implementation and evaluation of the OBE curriculum

No	Challange in OBE Implementation	AI Platform	Utility
1	Excessive assessment workload.	Gradescope	Accelerates the grading of essays, coding assignments, and written exams.
		Turnitin Feedback Studio	Provides automated feedback on grammar errors and originality of assignments.
		ChatGPT	Assists in analyzing student assignments and providing initial feedback.
2	Detailed assessment rubrics prolong the evaluation process.	Rubric Maker AI (Quick Rubric, Rubistar)	Helps instructors create automated rubrics based on inputted Course Learning Outcomes (CLOs).
		Google AI Rubric Generator	Generates text-based rubrics that can be customized for specific courses.

continued on following page

Table 2. Continued

No	Challange in OBE Implementation	AI Platform	Utility
3	Difficulty in providing personalized feedback to each student.	Grammarly & Turnitin Feedback Studio	Provides automatic feedback on language structure, argumentation, and clarity of writing.
		Claude AI (Anthropic)	Assists in analyzing assignments and offering more personalized feedback suggestions.
		Otter.ai	Generates automatic audio-based feedback.
4	Large student cohorts hinder in-depth feedback.	Perusall	Enables students to provide feedback to each other with automated system analysis.
		Eli Review	Supports peer review among students with guided automated rubrics.
		Cognii AI Tutor	Provides automated feedback based on student responses.
5	Variability in CLOs is preventing uniform assessment rubrics.	CoRubric (Google Sheets Add-on)	Customizes assessment rubrics based on varying CLOs.
		AI-Powered Adaptive Rubric Tool	Automatically adjusts rubrics for different assignments based on CLO descriptions.
6	Instructors must develop new rubrics for various assignments and projects.	Canva for Education (Rubric Templates)	Offers editable assessment rubric templates.
		Microsoft Copilot	Helps create rubrics based on examples from academic journals or curriculum standards.
7	OBE emphasizes PBL, PjBL, and Case-Based Learning, but not all instructors have experience with these methods.	ChatGPT / Bard	Assists in designing learning plans for PBL, PjBL, and Case-Based Learning.
		Khanmigo (Khan Academy AI)	Supports the development of project-based learning scenarios
		Socratic by Google	Helps instructors find relevant case studies aligned with OBE.
8	Instructors accustomed to conventional lecturing struggle to adapt to active learning methods.	ClassPoint AI	Facilitates interactive learning in classrooms.
		Pear Deck + AI	Converts static presentations into interactive activities aligned with active learning models
		Nearpod AI	Assists instructors in developing discussion-based learning scenarios.
9	Student complaints about the heavy workload	Smart Sparrow (Adaptive Learning AI)	Adjusts assignment loads based on students' level of understanding.
		Knewton Alta	Organizes adaptive assignments and exercises based on student progress

continued on following page

Table 2. Continued

No	Challange in OBE Implementation	AI Platform	Utility
10	Students frequently request task reductions, but instructors must adhere to CLO and PLO standards.	Brightspace Insights (D2L AI LMS)	AI analyzes task effectiveness in achieving CLOs and CPLs.
		Coursera AI Instructor Tools	Evaluate assignment effectiveness in meeting CLO and PLO targets.

INTERDISCIPLINARY CURRICULUM DESIGN

Implementing Outcome-Based Education (OBE) represents a fundamental shift from traditional education models. Spady (1994) highlights four significant differences between OBE and the conventional system:

(1) Curriculum Design and Assessment Flexibility: Traditional education follows a rigid, pre-structured curriculum where student competency is assessed through standardized scores and passing criteria. OBE, on the other hand, offers a more flexible framework in which curriculum, teaching methods, assessments, and performance standards are continuously refined to help students achieve clearly defined learning outcomes.

(2) Time as a Learning Resource: In traditional systems, learning is time-bound—if students fail to meet competency requirements within a fixed timeframe, they are considered unsuccessful. OBE redefines time as a variable resource, allowing educators and students to adjust learning durations based on individual needs, thus prioritizing mastery over speed.

(3) Assessment and Success Standards: Conventional education often adheres to a normal distribution curve, where only a predetermined percentage of students achieve high scores while others inevitably fall below the threshold. In contrast, OBE implements well-defined competency-based standards, ensuring all students have equal opportunities to meet the required benchmarks without artificial limitations.

(4) Mistakes as Learning Opportunities: In traditional grading systems, students' errors are permanently recorded, often limiting their academic progression. OBE shifts this perspective by treating mistakes as a formative tool for monitoring progress and guiding mentorship. This approach encourages students to continuously develop their skills and enhance performance until they meet or exceed the required competency standards.

Based on the explanation above, it can be concluded that Outcome-Based Education (OBE) prioritizes learning completion. In this system, all students can graduate upon meeting the established standards, even if their learning progress takes longer. Unlike traditional education systems that emphasize subject scores, attitudes, beliefs, or psychological states, the success of OBE is determined by students' ability to demonstrate, apply, and showcase their acquired knowledge in real-world scenarios. Learning outcomes refer to graduates' actions and performances, reflecting their mastery of competencies. Therefore, the formulation of learning objectives must be precise, measurable, and observable when demonstrated.

Given the dynamic nature of graduate profiles, periodic reviews are necessary to ensure alignment with evolving societal demands and technological advancements (Rawashdeh & Idris, 2025). However, obtaining accurate data on community needs is challenging, requiring the assistance of advanced technology to collect and analyze relevant information. As the world enters the era of Industrial Revolution 4.0, rapid and unpredictable social transformations are occurring. Scholars describe this phenomenon as the VUCA era—characterized by Volatility, Uncertainty, Complexity, and Ambiguity—where traditional education systems struggle to keep pace. The skills acquired today may become obsolete tomorrow due to automation and digital advancements. To remain relevant, education must adopt a more flexible approach and integrate AI-driven technologies (Kayal, 2024).

Failure to adapt to these rapid changes will make navigating the VUCA era increasingly difficult. Therefore, students must develop technical expertise and essential skills such as critical thinking, adaptability, and problem-solving. These competencies cannot be acquired solely through classroom instruction or laboratory training but require experiential learning in real-world settings. Internships and practical work placements provide students hands-on experience, enhancing their performance, productivity, self-confidence, and preparedness to confront future challenges and uncertainties (Lucas et al., 2009).

Beyond practical work experience, capability development can also be enhanced through interdisciplinary learning, which integrates multiple disciplines into a unified educational approach. This method fosters creativity and facilitates the discovery of innovations. One well-known interdisciplinary model is STEM (Science, Technology, Engineering, and Mathematics), which combines these four fields to solve real-world problems in professional and societal contexts. STEM education is implemented through project-based learning and research, equipping students with essential skills in scientific inquiry, technology utilization, engineering design, and mathematical analysis (Khosrow-Pour, 2015). This framework emphasizes practical skills such as computer programming, research methodologies, design principles, and testing techniques. Additionally, technology plays a crucial role as a learning and experimentation tool, such as using specialized software for modeling or conducting scientific experiments.

Interdisciplinary learning can be integrated into various academic programs. For instance, combining medical sciences and data analytics has led to the development of Predictive Healthcare Analytics in healthcare technology. This technology predicts an individual's risk of chronic diseases such as diabetes, cancer, or cardiovascular conditions (Shedole & Soni, 2017). By identifying high-risk patients early, healthcare professionals can implement more effective prevention and treatment strategies, ultimately improving patient outcomes and optimizing healthcare systems.

Another example of interdisciplinary learning is the intersection of history and the arts. While history focuses on analyzing historical events, the arts involve cinematography, directing, and visual storytelling techniques. By combining these fields, students can produce documentary films that educate the public on historical events through engaging visual narratives. These examples demonstrate that interdisciplinary learning enhances student capabilities, promotes collaboration, and leads to more comprehensive and innovative solutions to complex challenges.

Rather than conflicting with Outcome-Based Education (OBE), interdisciplinary learning complements it, particularly when artificial intelligence (AI) is leveraged for content management, instructional material distribution, and assessment. The "AI Across the Curriculum" initiative, developed at the University of Florida, revealed that interdisciplinary integration fosters an inclusive learning environment and drives transdisciplinary innovation (Southworth et. al., 2023). This approach utilizes a module-based design within a spiral curriculum framework, ensuring that students can progressively access content according to their level of proficiency (Harden & Stamper, 1999).

An interdisciplinary curriculum is a curriculum development approach integrating multiple disciplines to provide a more comprehensive understanding of complex issues (Beane, 1995; Wineburg & Grossman, 2000). This approach enhances problem-solving and fosters technological innovation and the emergence of new academic fields. For instance, Geoinformatics is an interdisciplinary domain that combines Geography, Geographic Information Systems, Cartography, Remote Sensing, Computer Science, and Data Science. It analyzes spatial patterns, regional planning, and computer-assisted disaster mitigation. Another example is Bioinformatics, which integrates Biotechnology, Genetics, and Computer Science to advance the study of gene structures, protein functions, and other biological processes through computational analysis.

The interdisciplinary curriculum can be implemented through three primary models, as seen in Figure 1; there are multidisciplinary, interdisciplinary, and transdisciplinary approaches (Beane, 1995; Grady, 1994).

1. Multidisciplinary Approach

This model teaches multiple disciplines within the same course, but each remains distinct and separate. A typical example is the integration of biology, physics, and chemistry under Natural Sciences and the combination of geography, history, and economics under Social Studies. Although these subjects are grouped, their methodologies and content remain largely independent.

2. Interdisciplinary Approach

This model integrates concepts and research methods from multiple disciplines to address a common issue or theme. Unlike the multidisciplinary approach, interdisciplinary learning focuses on problem-solving by combining perspectives from various fields. For example, the issue of poverty can be examined through economic, sociological, anthropological, public health, demographic, and geographical lenses. Courses designed under this approach are typically thematic, guiding students to explore and resolve real-world challenges.

3. Transdisciplinary Approach

The transdisciplinary model extends beyond academic disciplines by incorporating insights from non-academic sources—knowledge that has yet to be formally classified as a distinct scientific field. The primary objective is to develop innovative solutions or policies through cross-sector collaboration. A notable example is the Smart City initiative, which combines Urban Planning, IoT Technology (utilizing sensors and big data for urban management), Urban Sociology, and Public Policy. This interdisciplinary collaboration results in policies and technological frameworks that support efficient, technology-driven urban governance.

By embracing interdisciplinary curriculum models, education can foster deeper collaboration, problem-solving skills, and innovation, equipping students with the expertise to tackle complex societal challenges.

The successful implementation of a cross-disciplinary curriculum that accommodates multidisciplinary, interdisciplinary, and transdisciplinary learning depends on the curriculum's flexibility in recognizing diverse student learning experiences. This is achieved through the conversion and equivalence of academic credits. Conversion involves transforming a value, unit, or system into another equivalent form, while equivalence refers to aligning different academic standards with the same accreditation level. For instance, if students participate in a faculty-led research project, their experience may be converted into credit for a research methods course. Similarly, a MOOC course completed by a student may be equated with a traditional lecture-based course. The increasing accessibility of disciplines outside students' primary fields of study further expands the potential for cross-disciplinary curriculum development.

One long-standing example of a cross-disciplinary curriculum is the double degree program. Various academic policies have recognized this concept internationally by encouraging students to participate in learning experiences beyond their core subject of study. Many institutions provide frameworks that enable students to participate in various activities, including student exchanges, entrepreneurship programs, internships, independent study, and service learning. For example, some universities recognize coursework completed on MOOC platforms as equivalent to traditional university courses, allowing students to obtain credits while gaining flexible and interdisciplinary learning experiences.

Despite its advantages, implementing a cross-disciplinary curriculum within an Outcome-Based Education (OBE) framework presents several challenges, particularly in ensuring the alignment of Learning Outcomes (CPL). Academic institutions must carefully assess and standardize students' external learning experiences while maintaining CPL integrity and workload balance. Given that credit transfer systems vary internationally, standardization is essential. For example, one academic credit in Indonesia generally equals 1.67–2 ECTS (European Credit Transfer and Accumulation System).

AI-driven platforms can provide essential support to enhance the efficiency of cross-disciplinary curriculum implementation. Table 3 outlines several AI-based solutions that facilitate credit recognition, course alignment, and curriculum integration.

Table 3. AI catalysts in the implementation of interdisciplinary curricula

No	Interdisciplinary Curriculum Implementation	AI Platform	Utility
1	Mapping CLOs with Non-Academic Activities	Coursera Skills Mapping	Aligns CLOs with extracurricular courses or activities
		LinkedIn Skills Insights	Identifies student competencies based on extracurricular experiences
		IBM Watson Talent Framework	Analyzes the alignment of internship experiences with academic learning
		Pymetrics AI	Maps students' soft and hard skills from their experiences to academic standards

continued on following page

Table 3. Continued

No	Interdisciplinary Curriculum Implementation	AI Platform	Utility
2	Evaluation & Conversion of Activities to Credit Hours or ECTS	DigCompEdu AI (European Digital Competence Framework for Educators)	Map student activities with ECTS-based learning outcomes
		Google AI for Education	Generates automated reports on student achievements outside the curriculum
		Credly & Badgr AI	Provides micro-credentials that can be converted into academic credit hours
3	Student Self-Assessment and E-Portfolios	PebblePad AI	Helps students create CLO-based portfolios from extracurricular activities
		EdTech AI (By Microsoft)	Conducts automated self-assessments to evaluate the alignment of extracurricular experiences with academic achievements
		Turnitin AI for Learning Outcomes	Evaluates student reports on internships or community service and links them to CLOs.

AI'S ROLE IN ASSESSMENT AND FEEDBACK SYSTEMS

Developing an Outcome-Based Education (OBE) curriculum follows a structured yet adaptable process. The initial phase involves the preparation of Learning Outcomes (CPL), curriculum structure, course mapping, and learning planning. Meanwhile, assessment and feedback mechanisms operate continuously throughout the learning process to ensure alignment with learning outcomes. The effectiveness of the assessment and feedback system in OBE is shaped by various factors, including graduation standards defined by learning outcomes; types of assignments and assessments administered; teaching methods employed by instructors; student preferences, individual learning needs; industry demands, and the evolving job market landscape

Learning Outcomes and Assessment Rubrics

Learning outcomes are translated into assessment rubrics and grading criteria to maintain consistency in evaluation. These rubrics serve as guidelines for assessment and tools for constructive feedback. Below are key considerations in designing an effective rubric:

- Key Assessment Aspects

The rubric should define whether it evaluates: cognitive skills (e.g., knowledge comprehension, critical thinking), affective skills (e.g., attitudes, values, communication), or psychomotor skills (e.g., technical abilities, hands-on performance)

- Choosing the Right Rubric Type

Analytic rubrics individually assess multiple aspects of performance, making them ideal for structured tasks such as essay writing or project reports. For example, a project report can be evaluated based on its structure, analysis, and creativity, each scored separately. Holistic rubrics provide a single overall score based on general performance, making them more suitable for practical assessments such as field practicums.

- Establishing Assessment Criteria

To ensure transparency and consistency, the assessment criteria should be clearly defined to reflect expected competencies; measurable with specific performance indicators; and weighted appropriately to indicate the relative importance of each component. Here is an example of a Project Report Presentation Assessment Criteria:

Criteria Weight (%)
Mastery of Material 30%
Structure and Organization 10%
Communication Skills 20%
Creativity and Visualization 10%
Timeliness 10%
Ability to Answer Questions 20%

- Defining an Assessment Scale

The rubric should include a grading scale, which may use a 1-4, 1-5, or 0-100 system depending on the assessment requirements. Table 4 presents a sample grading scale.

Table 4. Example of assessment rubric development

Criteria	4 (Excellent)	3 (Good)	2 (Fair)	1 (Poor)
Mastery of the Material	Mastering the material very well, able to explain fluently without reading the text.	Mastery of the material is evident, with only occasional glances at notes.	Understanding is shallow, relying heavily on reading from the text.	No mastery of the material, merely reading without explanation
Structure & Organization	The presentation is very structured, with a clear and logical flow	The presentation structure is pretty good, but has minor inconsistencies	The structure is unclear, with some sections lacking coherence	No clear structure, making the presentation confusing
Communication Skills	Clear voice, good intonation, and active eye contact with the audience	The voice is clear, but intonation and eye contact need improvement	The voice is unclear, with frequent stuttering and minimal eye contact	The voice is too soft or too fast, with no eye contact
Creativity & Visualization	The visual media is engaging, informative, and supports the presentation's content.	The media is well-presented but lacks some informative elements	The media is unengaging, displaying only text without supporting visuals	No visual media is used, or the media is irrelevant to the content
Punctuality	The presentation is on schedule	Slightly over or under the allotted time	Significantly too short or too long, reducing presentation effectiveness	Drastically off the time limit, making the information difficult to convey
Ability to answer questions	Answering all questions very well, based on data and logic	Answers questions well, though some lack depth	Answers some questions correctly, but others are incorrect	Unable to answer questions or provide irrelevant responses

Forms of Assignments and Assessment Instruments

The type of assignments and assessment instruments significantly impacts the accuracy and speed of feedback. AI-based test instruments, such as multiple-choice questions, can provide immediate feedback. Once students complete the test, they can instantly view their scores. Table 5 shows AI applications and platforms that assist in real-time assessment and feedback processes.

Table 5. AI-powered feedback mechanisms for different assessment types

No	Assessment Method	AI Platform	How to & Real-Time Feedback
1	Multiple choice test	Google Forms + Flubaroo, Kahoot! AI, Quizizz AI	Lecturers create questions → Students answer → AI provides automatic scoring & result analysis → Lecturers access real-time statistics.
2	Essay	Grammarly, Turnitin, Quillbot, ChatGPT	Students answer questions → AI evaluates grammar, plagiarism, and idea clarity → Lecturers view live analysis reports on the dashboard.
3	Quiz	Socrative, Kahoot! AI, ClassPoint AI	Lecturers create quizzes → Students respond in real-time → AI assesses and provides instant feedback → Results are displayed on the dashboard.
4	Discussion	Perusall, Kialo, ChatGPT	Students participate in AI forums → AI analyzes arguments and interactions → Lecturers monitor participation levels and discussion quality in real-time.
5	Slide Presentation	Tome AI, Beautiful.ai, Canva AI	AI assists presentation creation → AI evaluates slide clarity and structure → Lecturers receive live quality analysis.
6	Oral Presentation	Orai	Students record presentations →. AI analyzes voice clarity, filler words, speech rate, intonation, and confidence and provides automatic scoring.
7	Project	Notion AI, ClickUp AI, Trello AI	Students upload projects → AI tracks progress and milestone achievements → Lecturers monitor project development in real time.
8	Portofolio	Google Sites AI, Mahara, Wix AI	Students submit portfolios → AI assesses content and design → Lecturers review portfolios directly.
9	Case study report	ChatGPT, Turnitin, Elicit	AI analyzes report content → Checks for plagiarism and argument strength → Lecturers receive automatic reports on the dashboard.
10	Practicum/experiment	Labster, PhET Simulations, Jupyter Notebook AI	Students conduct lab simulations → AI records experimental results → Lecturers access real-time experiment data.
11	Scientific poster	Hemingway Editor AI	AI evaluates poster text → Assesses readability, sentence structure, and simplicity.
12	Data analysis	Tableau AI, Power BI AI, Python Pandas AI	Students process data → AI identifies trends and insights → Lecturers access a live analytics dashboard.
13	Academic vlog	Descript AI, Runway ML, Pictory AI	Students create videos → AI analyzes narrative clarity and transcripts → Lecturers receive automatic feedback.

continued on following page

Table 5. Continued

No	Assessment Method	AI Platform	How to & Real-Time Feedback
14	Peer Review	Peergrade, Turnitin PeerMark, Google Docs AI	Students provide feedback → AI evaluates feedback quality → Lecturers track student interactions in real time.
15	Reflective Journal	Notion AI, Grammarly AI, Obsidian AI	Students write reflections → AI assesses the depth of thought → Automatic feedback is displayed on the dashboard.

Learning Methods

Each learning method has distinct characteristics, requiring an appropriate assessment and feedback system. Table 6 summarizes examples of assessment methods and feedback types aligned with several learning methods.

Table 6. Feedback methods aligned with different learning strategies

Learning Method	Assessment Method	Feedback Type
Lecture	Multiple-choice test, Short essay, and Quiz	Automatic feedback, immediate scoring & revision
Problem-Based Learning (PBL)	Individual reflection and level of participation in group discussions	Peer review and incremental feedback
Project-Based Learning (PjBL)	Assessment of project reports, presentations, and digital portfolios	Review the rubric and repeated evaluation
Case-Based Learning (CBL)	Assessment of the quality of case analysis, interactive discussions, and simulations	Reflective discussion and corrective feedback
Internship/practicum	Practice report, direct observation, and reflective journal	Mentor supervision and Real-time feedback
Flipped Classroom	Online quizzes, discussions, and Individual reflection	Personal feedback from lecturers and peer assessment
Game-Based Learning	Interactive quizzes, digital simulations, and score-based challenges	Instant feedback from games, level-based assessment
Entrepreneurship/Start-up Learning	Business pitching, financial reports, and product prototype assessment	Market-based feedback and industry mentor evaluation

Student Preferences and Needs

Students may require feedback tailored to their learning styles. Students who prefer written tests or quizzes tend to favor multiple-choice or essay-based assessments. Students who excel in practical activities and projects benefit more from project-based or case-study assessments. Several AI-driven platforms customize learning experiences by identifying students' learning styles and delivering feedback accordingly:

- Smart Sparrow

This adaptive learning platform assesses students' learning styles and performance across multiple aspects. It personalizes learning materials and feedback by analyzing data such as time spent on tasks, common mistakes made, and response time to feedback. Based on this analysis, AI provides precise feedback, including detailed explanations, retakes, or alternative project-based assignments (Dutta et al., 2024).

- Plickers

Uses QR codes to gather student preferences during case-based or project-based learning activities. It provides automatic assessments and generates feedback based on student engagement and project analysis. If students prefer hands-on approaches and group discussions, AI prioritizes feedback, emphasizing teamwork and problem-solving (Shana & Abd Al Baki, 2020).

- Knewton

This platform analyzes student interactions and sentiments towards different assignment types (e.g., quizzes vs. practical projects). It collects verbal and written responses from students through surveys and feedback forms. The AI then recommends personalized assessment methods tailored to each student's strengths and preferences (Hossain et al., 2024)

Industry and Workforce Context

Assessment and feedback in an OBE curriculum should align with industry expectations and workforce demands. Ideally, assessment rubrics should be co-developed with industry professionals to ensure relevance. Below are assessment strategies tailored to different industry needs:

- Industries emphasizing practical skills
  Assessments should prioritize skill-based evaluations over theoretical multiple-choice exams.
  Suitable assessment types: Projects, practical assignments, case studies.
- Industries requiring teamwork and collaboration

Assessments should involve group work and peer assessments, simulating real-world teamwork experiences.

Suitable assessment types: Collaborative projects and peer reviews.

- Industries focusing on problem-solving

  Assessments should test real-world problem-solving abilities.

  Suitable assessment types: Case studies, simulations.

- Industries demanding communication, leadership, creativity, and time management skills

  Assessments should evaluate verbal and interpersonal skills.

  Suitable assessment types: Oral presentations, role-playing, and peer reviews.

OPTIMIZING AI LITERACY FOR EDUCATORS AND LEARNERS: INDONESIAN CASE

The Outcome-Based Education (OBE) curriculum has been implemented across Higher Education Institutions in Indonesia. Institutions seeking international accreditation benefit from this alignment with OBE principles. At the Primary and Secondary Education levels, the Merdeka Curriculum, introduced under Minister Nadiem Makarim (2019–2024), incorporates elements of OBE. This curriculum introduces several key features: First, while the 2013 Curriculum framed learning objectives through Competency Standards and Core Competencies, the Merdeka Curriculum uses Learning Outcomes, reinforcing its alignment with OBE principles. Second, the Merdeka Curriculum defines its graduate profile using the Pancasila Student Profile (P5), which encompasses six attributes: faith and noble character, global diversity, independence, collaboration, critical thinking, and creativity. Since these attributes primarily represent values and character development, they are difficult to quantify. In OBE systems, the effectiveness of a curriculum is measured through graduates' demonstrated competencies. To align with OBE principles, tracer studies should be conducted to evaluate whether graduates achieve these intended competencies.

Despite its foundation in OBE, the Merdeka Curriculum faces challenges in implementing competency assessments. It adopts an authentic assessment approach emphasizing holistic competency evaluation, including observations, project-based assessments, portfolios, performance evaluations, and written and oral tests. Before learning begins, students undergo diagnostic assessments to determine their prior knowledge. However, implementation varies widely across schools. Some institutions have successfully adopted authentic assessments, while others continue to rely on traditional methods due to teachers' unfamiliarity with the approach and heavy administrative burdens. Additionally, large class sizes make it difficult for teachers to provide formative assessments and personalized feedback. A lack of infrastructure further limits the feasibility of project-based and performance-based assessments.

Another challenge is the differentiated learning model, which accommodates students' abilities, interests, and needs. While the Merdeka Curriculum promotes this approach, many teachers struggle to implement it effectively due to limited training and support. Furthermore, large class sizes make individualized feedback difficult, leading teachers to rely on lecture-based instruction, which is easier to manage. The exam-driven evaluation system discourages differentiation, as teachers prioritize content coverage over personalized learning experiences. As a result, efforts to foster student interests and talents through differentiated instruction often conflict with the rigid demands of exam-based assessments.

While the Merdeka Curriculum incorporates Outcome-Based Education (OBE) elements, its implementation still reflects a traditional approach emphasizing subject-matter mastery rather than demonstrable competencies. The learning outcomes for each subject focus on content retention, a key principle of OBE, rather than measuring students' ability to apply knowledge in real-world contexts. Furthermore, the assessment system lacks specific indicators to track learning completeness, and no standardized evaluation instruments have been developed to assess the Pancasila Student Profile (P5). The Merdeka Curriculum has yet to fully align with these expectations since OBE requires a comprehensive assessment that evaluates cognitive skills and affective and psychomotor development.

Given these challenges, how can OBE implementation be strengthened? The most critical step is to empower teachers with practical training on OBE-based instruction and differentiated learning. Educators must gain hands-on experience designing competency-based assessments, including formative and summative evaluations that align with authentic learning approaches. Training should be highly practical, offering concrete examples and ready-to-use modules to help teachers effectively integrate OBE principles into their classrooms.

Beyond professional development, adequate resources and infrastructure are essential for successful OBE implementation. Digital and non-digital tools must be available to facilitate active, student-centered learning. Additionally, large class sizes make it difficult for teachers to provide personalized feedback and assessments. Addressing this issue requires AI-driven solutions to enhance learning interactions, assessments, and feedback mechanisms.

A study assessed the extent to which educators and students are familiar with AI technologies. Data were collected from 70 respondents, comprising 23 men and 47 women. Regarding age distribution, 22 respondents were under 31 years old, 28 were between 31 and 40 years old, and 19 respondents were over 40 years old. The respondents' occupations included 45 teachers, 15 lecturers, and 10 master's program students. Only six of the 25 AI tools analyzed in the study were widely used: ChatGPT, Google Forms, Google Sites, Grammarly, Quillbot, and Turnitin Feedback Studio. The remaining 19 AI tools had low adoption rates, with some respondents unaware of their existence (see Figure 2). This finding highlights the need for greater AI literacy and training among educators to support integrating AI-driven assessment and feedback systems in the OBE framework.

Series 1 = Do not know at all
Series 2 = Have heard but do not know much
Series 3 = Have heard and know the function, but not in-depth
Series 4 = Know the function but do not know how to use it
Series 5 = Know the function and can use it
Series 6 = Know and use it from time to time
Series 7 = Know and often use it for educational purposes

Number:

1. Adaptive Rubric
2. ChatGPT
3. Descript
4. EdTech AI (By Microsoft)
5. Google Forms
6. Google Sites
7. Gradescope
8. Grammarly
9. Hemingway Editor
10. IBM Watson Talent Framework
11. Knewton Alta
12. Labster
13. Nearpod
14. Obsidian
15. Orai
16. Otter.ai
17. Perusall
18. Pymetrics
19. Python Pandas
20. Quillbot
21. Rubric Generator
22. Skills Insights
23. Smart Sparrow
24. Socratic by Google

25. Turnitin Feedback Studio

The data suggests that respondents generally have limited familiarity with AI applications, highlighting a lack of readiness among educators to integrate AI into educational administration. While Generation Z students show potential in adopting AI-driven learning, several barriers must be addressed, including limited access to technology, curriculum alignment, AI literacy, and teacher preparedness. Strengthening these areas would accelerate students' mastery of AI, facilitating more personalized, adaptive, and data-driven learning environments.

Despite their current lack of expertise in AI, educators can bridge this gap through targeted training programs. By equipping teachers with the necessary skills, AI can be a powerful tool to enhance the implementation of the OBE curriculum. AI-powered applications can streamline the development of learning outcomes that align with CPL standards, making differentiated learning more feasible, even in large classroom settings, by enabling efficient, individualized feedback. Additionally, AI significantly improves the assessment process, assisting educators in designing structured exam questions, developing precise assessment rubrics, and automating grading for faster and more objective evaluations.

ETHICAL CONSIDERATIONS AND RESPONSIBLE AI USE IN EDUCATION

Integrating AI into education has significantly accelerated knowledge development and enhanced learning experiences. However, as AI evolves, it presents several ethical concerns that require careful governance. Among the most pressing ethical challenges are copyright infringement, data security, algorithmic bias, and overreliance on AI. Addressing these issues ensures that AI supports rather than disrupts the educational landscape.

One primary concern is copyright infringement and plagiarism. The widespread availability of AI tools like ChatGPT, Quillbot, and Turnitin Feedback Studio has made it easier for students to produce content without engaging in genuine intellectual effort. Plagiarism has become increasingly common as AI enables students to generate assignments with minimal input. To mitigate this issue, students must be educated on academic integrity and the consequences of plagiarism. Educators should design assignments that require critical thinking, analysis, and application rather than simple text reproduction. If AI is used as an aid, students must cite it appropriately. Institutions can use AI-powered anti-plagiarism tools such as Turnitin, Grammarly, and Copyleaks to detect plagiarism. Manual verification through writing style comparisons and oral assessments can further ensure that students truly understand the material.

Data security and privacy are also significant concerns. Many AI platforms, including IBM Watson Talent Framework, collect and analyze student data, raising the risk of unauthorized access, personal data leaks, and misuse by third parties (Huang, 2023; Kamenskih, 2022). Educational institutions must establish strict data protection policies, ensuring that AI platforms comply with regulations such as GDPR and the Personal Data Protection Act. Encryption should be mandatory to safeguard student data, and regular audits must be conducted to assess AI system vulnerabilities. Additionally, AI platforms should provide data collection, storage, and utilization transparency.

Another critical challenge is algorithmic bias and discrimination. AI operates through pre-programmed algorithms, but if these algorithms are not designed inclusively, they can unintentionally favor specific student groups, leading to unequal educational outcomes (Baker & Hawn, 2022; Kizilcec & Lee, 2022). For instance, AI-driven grading systems might disadvantage students from different educational or socio-economic backgrounds. AI tools must be developed to prevent bias with fairness, transparency, and inclusivity in mind.

Overreliance on AI poses another challenge. When students excessively rely on AI-generated responses for schoolwork, their cognitive abilities—including critical thinking, analytical reasoning, and creativity—may weaken over time (Zhai et al., 2024). Students may struggle with independent problem-solving without proper intervention, reducing their adaptability in real-world professional settings. AI should be integrated into learning as an enhancement rather than a replacement, ensuring that students remain engaged in the learning process.

Developing a robust AI governance framework is essential in response to these ethical concerns. Educational institutions must align their policies with internationally recognized standards, such as UNESCO's Ethical AI Framework (Morandin-Ahuerma, 2023). Transparency and accountability must be prioritized to ensure AI does not infringe on personal privacy or academic ethics. For instance, AI platforms should prevent unauthorized access to sensitive data and adhere to strict protection regulations. Additionally, policies should regulate AI's role in academic assessments. The administration of Computer-Based Tests (CBT) in national examinations must account for students' varying levels of familiarity with digital tools, preventing disparities between those accustomed to AI-driven assessments and those who are not. AI use in education should also be monitored to ensure it aligns with ethical and social values. Lastly, integrating AI and digital literacy into curricula is vital for preparing Generation Z and Alpha for the future. Schools must adopt policies that promote AI as a tool for enhancing personalized learning, creativity, and critical thinking, rather than merely automating educational processes. Equitable access to

AI must also be ensured, allowing all students, regardless of geographic location, to benefit from technological advancements. By implementing comprehensive regulations, strengthening AI literacy, and ensuring equitable technology distribution, AI can serve as a transformative force in education while maintaining ethical integrity and academic excellence.

REFERENCES

Ait Baha, T., El Hajji, M., Es-Saady, Y., & Fadili, H. (2024). The impact of an educational chatbot on student learning experience. *Education and Information Technologies*, *29*, 10153–10176.

Baker, R. S., & Hawn, A. (2022). Algorithmic bias in education. *International Journal of Artificial Intelligence in Education*, •••, 1–41.

Beane, J. A. (1995). Curriculum integration and the disciplines of knowledge. *Phi Delta Kappan*, *76*(8), 616–622.

Benko, A., & Lányi, C. S. (2009). History of artificial intelligence. In *Encyclopedia of Information Science and Technology* (2nd ed., pp. 1759–1762). IGI Global.

Bhimdiwala, A., Neri, R. C., & Gomez, L. M. (2022). Advancing the design and implementation of artificial intelligence in education through continuous improvement. *International Journal of Artificial Intelligence in Education*, •••, 1–27.

DiGiacomo, D. K., Greenhalgh, S., & Barriage, S. (2022). How students and principals understand ClassDojo: Emerging insights. *TechTrends*, •••, 1–13. PMID: 34345879

Dutta, S., Ranjan, S., Mishra, S., Sharma, V., Hewage, P., & Iwendi, C. (2024, February). Enhancing educational adaptability: A review and analysis of AI-driven adaptive learning platforms. In *2024 4th International Conference on Innovative Practices in Technology and Management (ICIPTM)* (pp. 1–5). IEEE.

Evangeline, D., & Parkavi, A. (2022, May). Comparative Study on Online Teaching and Learning Tools. In *ICCCE 2021: Proceedings of the 4th International Conference on Communications and Cyber Physical Engineering* (pp. 49-57). Singapore: Springer Nature Singapore.

Grady, J. B. (1994). Interdisciplinary Curriculum Development.

Hamilton, J. G., & Klebba, J. M. (2011). Experiential learning: A course design process for critical thinking. *American Journal of Business Education*, *4*(12), 1–12.

Harden, R. M., & Stamper, N. (1999). What is a spiral curriculum? *Medical Teacher*, *21*(2), 141–143. PMID: 21275727

Hossain, G. F., Case, D., & Smith, C. (2024). Technologies and Student Feedback Collection and Analysis. *Teaching And Learning In The Digital Era. Issues & Studies*, •••, 327.

Huang, L. (2023). Ethics of artificial intelligence in education: Student privacy and data protection. *Science Insights Education Frontiers*, *16*(2), 2577–2587.

Kamenskih, A. (2022). The analysis of security and privacy risks in smart education environments. *Journal of Smart Cities and Society*, *1*(1), 17–29.

Kayal, A. (2024). Transformative Pedagogy: A Comprehensive Framework for AI Integration in Education. In *Explainable AI for Education: Recent Trends and Challenges* (pp. 247–270). Springer Nature Switzerland.

Khosrow-Pour, M. (Ed.). (2015). *STEM education: Concepts, methodologies, tools, and applications* (Vol. 1–3). IGI Global.

Kizilcec, R. F., & Lee, H. (2022). Algorithmic fairness in education. In *The ethics of artificial intelligence in education* (pp. 174–202). Routledge.

Kizito, I. G., & Hassan, S. (2024). PhET Interactive Simulations as an effective tool for teaching chemistry: A review. *International Journal of STEM Education*, *19*(1), 1–12.

Krishna, A., & Meda, V. (2024). Planning and Requirements Management in Projects. In *AI Integration in Software Development and Operations: Transformation Through AI Infusion in DevOps, Testing, and SRE* (pp. 59–105). Apress.

Litjens, G., Kooi, T., Bejnordi, B. E., Setio, A. A. A., Ciompi, F., Ghafoorian, M., & van Ginneken, B. (2017). A survey on deep learning in medical image analysis. *Medical Image Analysis*, *42*, 60–88. PMID: 28778026

Lucas, W. A., Cooper, S. Y., Ward, T., & Cave, F. (2009). Industry placement, authentic experience, and the development of venturing and technology self-efficacy. *Technovation*, *29*(11), 738–752.

Morandín-Ahuerma, F. (2023, September 28). Ten UNESCO Recommendations on the Ethics of Artificial Intelligence.

Qazi, S., Kadri, M. B., Naveed, M., Khawaja, B. A., Khan, S. Z., Alam, M. M., & Su'ud, M. M. (2024). AI-Driven Learning Management Systems: Modern Developments, Challenges, and Future Trends during the Age of ChatGPT. *Computers, Materials & Continua*, *80*(2).

Rawashdeh, A., & Idris, M. (2025). Synchronized curriculum adaptation: A strategy for enhancing skill development in accounting education. *Journal of International Education in Business*, *18*(2), 269–288.

Sable, N. P., Singh, S., Sharma, M. K., Patil, N., & Mishra, A. (2023, December). Machines Thinking Fast: AI-Powered Automating of Information Capture and Retrieval. In *2023 3rd International Conference on Smart Generation Computing, Communication and Networking (SMART GENCON)* (pp. 1–6). IEEE.

Shana, Z. A., & Abd Al Baki, S. (2020). Using plickers in formative assessment to augment student learning. [IJMBL]. *International Journal of Mobile and Blended Learning*, *12*(2), 57–76.

Shedole, S., & Soni, S. (2017). Predictive analytics to prevent and control chronic diseases. *International Journal of Computer Applications*, *157*(7), 1–5.

Silva, J., & Gomez, M. (2025). Advancements in Human-Computer Interaction Through Natural Language Processing and Voice Recognition. *Journal of Computing Innovations and Applications*, *3*(1), 8–12.

Southworth, J., Migliaccio, K., Glover, J., Glover, J. N., Reed, D., McCarty, C., Brendemuhl, J., & Thomas, A. (2023). Developing a model for AI Across the curriculum: Transforming the higher education landscape via innovation in AI literacy. *Computers and Education: Artificial Intelligence*, *4*, 100127.

Spady, W. G. (1994). *Outcome-based education: Critical issues and answers.* American Association of School Administrators.

Spena, T. R., Mele, C., & Marzullo, M. (2024). AI-enhanced smart service innovation practices. In *Handbook of Services and Artificial Intelligence* (pp. 176–193). Edward Elgar Publishing.

Sunyaev, A., & Sunyaev, A. (2020). Cloud computing. *Internet computing: Principles of distributed systems and emerging internet-based technologies*, 195-236.

Tractenberg, R. E., Gushta, M. M., Mulrooney, T. J., & Weissinger, P. A. (2020). The assessment evaluation rubric: Promoting learning and learner-centered assessments through a comprehensive evaluation of assessments. *International Journal on Teaching and Learning in Higher Education*, *32*(1), 26–37.

Wiggins, G., & McTighe, J. (2005). *Understanding by design* (Expanded 2nd ed.). Association for Supervision and Curriculum Development (ASCD).

Wineburg, S., & Grossman, P. (2000). Interdisciplinary curriculum: Challenges to implementation. Teachers College Press, 1234 Amsterdam Avenue, New York, NY 10027

Zhai, C., Wibowo, S., & Li, L. D. (2024). The effects of over-reliance on AI dialogue systems on students' cognitive abilities: A systematic review. *Smart Learning Environments*, *11*(1), 28.

Zhang, J., Liu, Y., & Wang, X. (2024). Simulation and virtual reality applications in STEM education: An overview. *International Journal of STEM Education*, *11*(1), 1–15.

Chapter 6 Personalized Learning Through Intelligent Assessment Systems: Enhancing Student Engagement

Zohra Yasin
https://orcid.org/0009-0003-4879-8146
IAIN Gorontalo, Indonesia

Sitriah Salim Utina
IAIN Gorontalo, Indonesia

Andi Asrifan
https://orcid.org/0000-0002-9934-6129
Universitas Negeri Makassar, Indonesia

ABSTRACT

This chapter examines the role of intelligent assessment systems in facilitating personalized learning and improving student engagement. It delineates the historical progression of assessment from standardized testing to adaptive, data-informed systems that cater to individual learning requirements. Essential elements like adaptive learning technology, data analytics, and personalized feedback are examined, highlighting their contributions to enhancing learning outcomes. The chapter analyzes implementation options, equity and access issues, and the ethical governance of student data. It underscores the significance of educator training and the role of emerging technologies such as AI, VR, and AR in influencing the future of individualized education. Case studies and research data illustrate how these tools can enhance motivation, autonomy, and academic performance. The chapter finishes by picturing a future in which customized learning is integral to educational systems,

DOI: 10.4018/979-8-3373-1062-6.ch006

Copyright © 2026, IGI Global Scientific Publishing. Copying or distributing in print or electronic forms without written permission of IGI Global Scientific Publishing is prohibited.

INTRODUCTION TO PERSONALIZED LEARNING

Definition and Importance

Personalized learning is an educational methodology that customizes instruction to address the unique requirements, preferences, and interests of each learner (Solari et al., 2023). In contrast to conventional uniform models, personalized learning acknowledges the varied learning styles, tempos, and motivations of individuals. This method aims to enhance the learning experience by enabling students to participate in their education actively, therefore promoting a more profound comprehension of the subject matter.

Personalized learning fundamentally entails utilizing data-driven insights to guide educational tactics. Intelligent assessment systems are essential in this process since they continuously collect and analyze student performance data (Gardner et al., 2021). These systems can discern strengths and weaknesses, allowing instructors to tailor learning experiences to the individual needs of each student. A student grappling with a certain subject can have tailored resources and assistance, whereas those who thrive can be presented with more advanced material.

The significance of personalized learning is paramount. Studies indicate that students are more inclined to get favorable academic results when they are actively involved in their learning and perceive that their individual requirements are being met. Personalized learning cultivates a sense of ownership and accountability in students, encouraging them to assume control of their education (Dumont & Ready, 2023). This heightened engagement may result in elevated retention rates, enhanced test scores, and an increased propensity for pursuing additional education.

Personalized learning has numerous advantages for instructors as well. It enables educators to differentiate instruction efficiently, guaranteeing that all students are suitably challenged and supported (Lee et al., 2021). This customized strategy can mitigate classroom management challenges, as students exhibit heightened focus and engagement in their study. Moreover, the insights derived from intelligent assessment systems can enhance professional growth, enabling educators to adapt their pedagogical methods and obtain a deeper understanding of their students' requirements.

In essence, personalized learning is an essential educational approach that improves student engagement via customized training. By utilizing intelligent assessment tools, educators may establish a dynamic learning environment that addresses individual requirements, thereby enhancing academic achievement and providing a more rewarding educational experience for both students and teachers. This book elucidates that individualized learning and intelligent evaluation systems are not merely advantageous but imperative for the future of education.

Historical Context

The progression of educational evaluation has been influenced by evolving pedagogical philosophies, technology innovations, and societal demands (Moorhouse & Kohnke, 2024). Historically, educational evaluation was mostly summative, emphasizing standardized testing to evaluate student achievement against a consistent set of criteria. This conventional method prioritized rote memorization and material recall, frequently overlooking the unique learning processes and varied requirements of students. The universal evaluation methodology was dominant, resulting in a restricted comprehension of student capacities and constraining opportunities for individualized learning.

With the evolution of educational theories, especially the emergence of constructivist approaches in the late 20th century, the necessity for more personalized evaluation methodologies became evident. Educators acknowledged that kids acquire knowledge at varying rates and through diverse modalities (Verde & Valero, 2021). This transition initiated a push towards formative evaluations, emphasizing continuous feedback and the gradual enhancement of skills. Nevertheless, these evaluations frequently depended on conventional criteria and failed to fully acknowledge the potential for customisation.

The emergence of technology in education has profoundly altered the assessment landscape. Intelligent assessment systems have developed into potent instruments that utilize data analytics to deliver real-time insights regarding student performance (Majeed & Hwang, 2021). These systems provide adaptive learning experiences customized to specific student requirements, representing a shift from conventional evaluation techniques. These systems employ algorithms that assess learning patterns to modify task difficulty, suggest resources, and deliver tailored feedback, so fostering a more engaging educational environment.

The disparity between conventional and individualized methodologies is substantial. Conventional exams frequently foster a fixed mindset, causing pupils to perceive their talents as unchanging and constrained. Conversely, individualized learning cultivates a growth mentality, motivating students to assume responsibility for their educational progression. Intelligent assessment systems enable instructors to monitor progress more efficiently and intervene as needed, guaranteeing that all students receive the required assistance for success (Lin et al., 2023).

To thoroughly comprehend the ideas and practices of individualized learning via intelligent assessment systems, it is crucial to grasp the historical context. The transition from conventional evaluation methods to individualized ones demonstrates a greater dedication to improving student engagement and results. By acknowledging the varied requirements of learners and adopting cutting-edge assessment technology, educators may cultivate a more inclusive and efficient educational environment that equips students for future difficulties (Singha et al., 2024).

The Role of Technology

In the modern educational environment, technology is essential for enabling tailored learning experiences (Alam & Mohanty, 2023). Intelligent assessment systems lead this technological revolution by utilizing data analytics and adaptive algorithms to develop personalized learning routes for pupils. These systems collect and evaluate extensive data on student performance, engagement, and learning preferences, allowing instructors to customize education in real-time.

Intelligent evaluation systems manifest in diverse formats, such as adaptive learning platforms, online quizzes, and formative assessment tools (Halkiopoulos & Gkintoni, 2024). They employ advanced algorithms to modify task complexity according to individual student responses, guaranteeing that learners are perpetually pushed without experiencing overload. For example, suppose a student exhibits proficiency in a specific idea. In that case, the system can introduce more sophisticated content while offering supplementary assistance and resources to individuals who may be experiencing difficulties. This dynamic adaptability characterizes personalized learning, facilitating a more sophisticated comprehension of each student's distinct educational trajectory.

The influence of technology on individualized learning beyond mere assessment. It revolutionizes the educational experience by granting students access to an abundance of information and learning methods. Digital platforms can facilitate interactive simulations, video lessons, and collaborative tools that accommodate many learning styles (Garlinska et al., 2023). This freedom enables students to interact with the information in personally meaningful ways, cultivating a more profound connection to the content.

Furthermore, technology improves communication between educators and students. Intelligent assessment systems produce comprehensive assessments that emphasize individual achievement, allowing educators to discern patterns and act as needed (Gardner et al., 2021). This data-centric methodology guides pedagogical techniques and promotes substantive dialogues between educators and students regarding their educational objectives and obstacles.

The incorporation of technology into personalized learning also meets the requirement for scalability (Govea et al., 2023). Conventional individualized instruction sometimes encountered restrictions due to resource constraints; however, intelligent assessment systems may accommodate a greater number of students without compromising educational quality. Consequently, tailored learning becomes increasingly attainable, enabling varied learners to flourish in an inclusive setting.

In conclusion, technology, especially via intelligent assessment systems, is pivotal in the advancement of individualized learning. Utilizing data and adaptive algorithms, instructors can develop customized educational experiences that improve student engagement and promote academic achievement. This book examines the complexities of individualized learning, revealing that technology is not merely a tool but a transformational force that redefines educational approaches in the 21st century.

INTELLIGENT ASSESSMENT SYSTEMS

Components of Intelligent Assessment

Intelligent assessment systems are essential to the personalized learning framework, equipping educators with the means to tailor education according to specific student requirements (Halkiopoulos & Gkintoni, 2024). These systems consist of numerous essential components, including adaptive learning technologies and data analytics, which collaborate to establish a responsive and efficient learning environment.

Adaptive Learning Technologies

Adaptive learning technologies are fundamental to intelligent assessment systems (Minn, 2022). These systems employ algorithms that modify the learning experience in real-time according to student performance. As a student interacts with the subject, the system perpetually assesses their replies, pinpointing strengths and deficiencies. For example, if a student excels in fundamental mathematics yet encounters difficulties with word problems, the system can adjust by providing more practice in the latter domain, while permitting the student to advance in areas where they exhibit competence.

This flexibility is essential for sustaining student involvement. Adaptive learning technologies mitigate annoyance and monotony by offering individualized challenges that correspond to each learner's existing level of comprehension (Halkiopoulos & Gkintoni, 2024). Furthermore, they promote a growth mentality by providing students with quick feedback and allowing them to observe their improvement over time. This individualized method cultivates a sense of ownership in learning, encouraging students to engage actively in their educational pursuits.

Data Analytics

A vital element of intelligent assessment systems is data analytics. These systems gather and evaluate extensive data from student interactions, assessments, and learning practices. Utilizing advanced analytical methods, educators can obtain insights into the performance trends of individuals and groups (Susnjak et al., 2022). Data analytics can elucidate patterns in student engagement, pinpointing which topics pose the greatest challenges for learners and suggesting areas requiring instructional modifications.

Learning management systems (LMS) frequently include data analytics functionalities, allowing instructors to monitor student development and performance inside a consolidated platform (Bradley, 2021). These systems offer dashboards that display data, facilitating teachers' interpretation and response to insights. Educators can utilize this knowledge to customize their teaching tactics, ensuring that instruction is attuned to the requirements of their students.

Furthermore, data analytics can enable precise treatments. Upon identifying a student requiring supplementary assistance, educators can promptly deploy solutions to rectify particular learning deficiencies (Turnbull et al., 2021). This proactive strategy improves student results and cultivates a collaborative learning environment in which educators can exchange thoughts and methodologies.

The elements of intelligent assessment systems—adaptive learning technologies and data analytics—are crucial for developing individualized learning experiences. Utilizing these technologies, instructors can deliver customized training that addresses the varied requirements of students, hence improving engagement and academic achievement. In this chapter, we examine how these components collaboratively convert conventional evaluation methods into dynamic, personalized learning experiences.

Types of Assessments

Assessment is integral to the educational process, directing instruction and improving student involvement (Zhang, 2022). Intelligent assessment systems employ several assessment kinds to deliver a thorough comprehension of student learning. The principal categories comprise formative assessments, summative assessments, and diagnostic assessments, each fulfilling specific functions within the personalized learning framework.

Formative vs. Summative Assessments

Formative assessments are continuous evaluations performed throughout the learning process (Morris et al., 2021). Their main objective is to assess student progress and deliver feedback that can guide instructional modifications. These evaluations may manifest in various formats, such as quizzes, classroom discussions, peer assessments, and interactive exercises. By collecting real-time data on student performance, instructors may pinpoint areas of difficulty and adjust their instructional methods accordingly.

The adaptable characteristics of intelligent assessment systems improve the efficacy of formative assessments (Bimpeh, 2024). If a student frequently underperforms in particular subjects, the system can recommend focused resources or activities to remediate those deficiencies. This prompt feedback mechanism cultivates a dynamic learning atmosphere in which students perceive support and are motivated to enhance their skills.

Conversely, summative evaluations take place at the conclusion of an instructional time to measure overall student learning and success. Assessments, whether final examinations, standardized evaluations, or culminating projects, offer a representation of student performance relative to established learning objectives. Although summative assessments are crucial for evaluating student achievements and ensuring responsibility, they frequently lack the depth of insight into individual learning processes that formative assessments provide (Ismail et al., 2022).

Diagnostic Assessments and Their Role

Diagnostic assessments fulfill a distinct role within the evaluation framework. These evaluations are conducted before to the commencement of instruction to ascertain students' pre-existing knowledge, competencies, and educational requirements. Diagnostic tests identify particular strengths and weaknesses, enabling educators to customize their curriculum to effectively address the varied requirements of their students (Hidayat et al., 2025).

Within the realm of intelligent assessment systems, diagnostic assessments can be exceptionally effective (Gardner et al., 2021). Through the application of data analytics, these systems can offer comprehensive insights into student preparedness, allowing educators to create individualized learning trajectories. For instance, if a diagnostic evaluation indicates that a pupil is deficient in fundamental mathematical skills. In that scenario, the educator can execute focused interventions to develop certain skills before to advancing to more complex concepts.

In conclusion, the distinct categories of assessments—formative, summative, and diagnostic—are essential to the individualized learning process. Formative evaluations provide continuous feedback and modifications, summative assessments analyze overall performance, and diagnostic assessments determine specific learning requirements. Collectively, these evaluations, augmented by sophisticated assessment tools, establish a thorough framework that fosters student engagement and facilitates academic achievement. As we investigate intelligent assessment systems, it is evident that good assessment methods are essential for cultivating a dynamic and responsive learning environment.

Implementation Strategies

The effective incorporation of intelligent assessment technologies into educational settings necessitates meticulous design and implementation. By using best practices and analyzing successful case studies, educators can improve student engagement and attain significant learning results (Carroll et al., 2021; Amerstorfer & Freiin, 2021; Heilporn et al., 2021; Yu et al., 2021). This section delineates essential strategies for the proper implementation of these systems in educational settings.

Best Practices for Integrating Intelligent Assessment Systems

1. Establish Explicit Objectives: Prior to the implementation of an intelligent evaluation system, it is crucial to define precise educational aims. Educators must delineate the intended outcomes for student learning and engagement, ensuring that the assessment framework corresponds with these objectives. This alignment facilitates the selection of appropriate tools and approaches that will enhance individualized learning.
2. Facilitate Professional Development: It is essential to equip instructors with the skills to utilize intelligent assessment technologies proficiently. Professional development must emphasize both the technical features of the instruments and the pedagogical practices that utilize data to enhance training. Continuous support and collaboration among instructors can cultivate a culture of perpetual enhancement.
3. Cultivate a Data-Driven Culture: Establishing a culture that prioritizes data-driven decision-making is essential for successful deployment. Educators have to be motivated to routinely study assessment data and utilize it to inform instructional methodologies. This methodology enables educators to discern patterns, rectify educational deficiencies, and acknowledge student achievements.

4. Engage Students in the Process: Involving students in their learning process can substantially augment engagement. Educators might prompt students to contemplate their evaluation outcomes and establish individual learning objectives. By cultivating a sense of ownership, students become more engaged in their study.
5. Iterate and Enhance: Implementation must be regarded as an iterative process. Educators must consistently evaluate the efficacy of the intelligent assessment system and implement requisite modifications informed by feedback from students and teachers. This adaptability guarantees that the system stays pertinent and efficient in addressing the requirements of all learners.

Case Studies of Successful Implementations

Numerous educational institutions have effectively implemented intelligent evaluation systems, demonstrating the capacity of these tools to improve tailored learning.

A significant instance involves the implementation of an adaptive learning platform in a substantial urban high school. Through the use of this system, instructors might deliver customized education informed by real-time data. The software detected pupils who faced difficulties with particular mathematical concepts and suggested tailored resources. Consequently, the school experienced a substantial rise in student involvement and a notable enhancement in overall mathematics competence results.

A successful deployment took place in a middle school that adopted a comprehensive learning management system featuring integrated diagnostic evaluations. Educators employed the data from these evaluations to build personalized learning strategies for every student. This method enhanced student performance and developed a collaborative atmosphere in which students assisted one another in their learning endeavors.

The successful execution of intelligent assessment systems depends on well-defined objectives, professional growth, a data-centric culture, student involvement, and ongoing enhancement. Educators can leverage successful case studies to utilize these technologies for developing tailored learning experiences that improve student engagement and promote academic achievement.

ENHANCING STUDENT ENGAGEMENT

Understanding Student Engagement

Student engagement is a complex notion that includes the degree of interest, motivation, and active involvement that students demonstrate in their learning activities (Lasekan et al., 2024). It is a vital metric of educational achievement, as engaged students are more inclined to attain superior academic results, cultivate a passion for learning, and persevere in their educational endeavors. Comprehending the concept and aspects of engagement, together with the determinants of student motivation, is crucial for developing effective tailored learning experiences.

Definition and Dimensions of Engagement

Student engagement is roughly described as the extent of students' involvement in their cognitive and emotional learning activities. Engagement is generally classified into three fundamental aspects (Gamage et al., 2022; Manu et al., 2021; Salas-Pilco et al., 2022):

1. Cognitive Engagement: This factor pertains to the intellectual commitment pupils exhibit towards their study. It encompasses analytical reasoning, solution development, and the capacity to relate new information to existing knowledge. Cognitively engaged students actively pursue comprehension of the content and use their knowledge in significant manners.
2. Emotional Engagement: Emotional engagement refers to students' sentiments on their learning experiences, encompassing their sense of belonging, curiosity, and motivation. Students who experience an emotional connection to their learning environment are more inclined to engage actively and embrace risks in their educational endeavors.
3. Behavioral Engagement: This dimension encompasses the observable actions students exhibit in the classroom, including involvement in discussions, completion of tasks, and attendance. Behavioral engagement denotes students' readiness to dedicate time and effort to their learning endeavors.

Factors Influencing Student Motivation

Numerous factors affect student motivation, which is intricately connected to engagement. Comprehending these aspects enables educators to create tailored learning experiences that promote a more interactive classroom atmosphere (Lu et al., 2022; Cents-Boonstra et al., 2021; Kong, 2021):

1. Content Relevance: Students exhibit heightened motivation when they see the material's significance to their lives and future aspirations. Instructors who link lessons to practical applications and students' interests typically increase engagement levels.

2. Autonomy and Choice: Offering students options in their learning processes can markedly increase motivation. When students participate in determining their learning methods or the subjects they investigate, they are more inclined to feel engaged in their education.
3. Input and Recognition: Prompt and constructive input enables students to comprehend their advancement and identify areas for enhancement. Acknowledging accomplishments, regardless of their magnitude, can enhance students' confidence and drive to participate more actively.

A conducive learning environment marked by a favorable classroom climate fosters collaboration, respect, and open communication, hence augmenting emotional engagement. Students are more likely to participate actively when they have a sense of safety and support.

In summary, comprehending student involvement necessitates acknowledging its dimensions—cognitive, emotional, and behavioral—as well as the elements that affect motivation. By incorporating these aspects into individualized learning experiences, educators may foster a more engaging and successful educational environment that accommodates the different requirements of all students. In our pursuit of techniques to enhance student engagement, it is evident that cultivating motivation is crucial for attaining academic achievement and promoting lifetime learning.

Personalized Feedback Mechanisms

Personalized feedback methods are crucial elements of effective personalized learning, greatly impacting student engagement and academic achievement (du Plooy et al., 2024). Feedback functions as an essential link between evaluation and education, offering students insights into their performance and directing their subsequent endeavors. The significance of prompt and constructive feedback is paramount, as it enables students to see their strengths and areas for enhancement, hence cultivating a growth mentality.

Importance of Timely and Constructive Feedback

Prompt feedback is essential for optimizing its effect on student learning. Timely feedback following an assessment or learning activity enables students to more readily associate it with their recent experiences (Morris et al., 2021). This immediacy enables them to evaluate their performance and implement required modifications while the material is salient in their memory. For example, if a learner obtains feedback on a mathematical issue immediately after attempting it, they can pinpoint individual mistakes and comprehend the proper methodology, resulting in enhanced learning.

Constructive criticism is crucial, since it emphasizes particular behaviors and results instead of vague remarks (Lipnevich & Panadero, 2021). Constructive feedback fosters a growth mentality in pupils by highlighting that skills may be cultivated through diligence and practice. Rather than merely labeling a student's essay as "bad," offering concrete recommendations for enhancement, such as improving clarity, structure, or argumentation, can enable the student to undertake actionable measures for improved performance.

Tools for Providing Personalized Feedback

Educators can utilize several tools and technology to provide tailored feedback that enhances communication and interaction (Alam & Mohanty, 2023; Qushem et al., 2021). Among the most efficacious instruments are:

1. Learning Management Systems (LMS): Numerous LMS systems provide functionalities that allow educators to deliver personalized feedback on assignments and exams. Teachers can provide comprehensive feedback on student work through comments, annotations, and rubrics, facilitating an understanding of their progress and areas for improvement.
2. Digital Portfolios: Digital portfolios enable students to exhibit their work and contemplate their educational progression. Educators can offer direct feedback on portfolio items, prompting students to participate in self-assessment and goal-setting informed by the input received.
3. Interactive Assessment Instruments: Instruments like online quizzes and formative assessment platforms frequently have immediate feedback functionalities. These solutions offer instantaneous, tailored feedback on student responses, enabling learners to comprehend their errors and acquire knowledge from them promptly.
4. Peer Feedback Mechanisms: Promoting peer evaluations might further improve individualized feedback. Students may evaluate one another's work, providing constructive feedback and varied viewpoints. This technique enhances feedback while promoting collaboration and communication skills.

In summary, individualized feedback systems are essential for improving student involvement in tailored learning settings. Educators can foster a supportive learning environment that promotes ongoing enhancement and active engagement by highlighting the significance of prompt and constructive feedback and employing diverse instruments for its delivery. Upon further exploration of techniques to augment engagement, it becomes evident that good feedback is fundamental to successful tailored learning experiences.

Gamification and Interactive Learning

Gamification and interactive learning are effective methods for improving student engagement in individualized learning environments (Hellín et al., 2023). By integrating gamified components into educational activities and developing dynamic, interactive experiences, instructors may enhance student motivation, encourage cooperation, and cultivate a deeper engagement with the topic. This section examines the integration of gamified aspects into evaluations and presents examples of effective interactive learning environments.

Incorporating Gamified Elements into Assessments

Gamification entails the implementation of game design elements in non-gaming environments to enhance motivation and engagement (Staller & Koerner, 2021). Incorporating gamified components into examinations can convert conventional evaluation procedures into captivating experiences. Educators can implement point systems, medals, and leaderboards to motivate student engagement and accomplishment.

An excellent strategy is to structure exams as challenges or quests that students must undertake to obtain rewards (Grabner-Hagen & Kingsley, 2023). This style promotes the perception of exams as opportunities for development instead of as anxiety-inducing evaluations. A scientific educator may devise a sequence of interactive challenges in which students accumulate points by conducting experiments, responding to inquiries, or cooperating with classmates. As students navigate the hurdles, they obtain prompt feedback, which consolidates their learning and sustains their motivation.

Furthermore, integrating narrative components into evaluations might augment engagement. By situating evaluations inside a story framework, educators can engage students' imaginations and motivate them to emotionally commit to their learning (Nair & Yunus, 2021). A history evaluation may be framed as a mission to discover relics from a particular era, encouraging students to investigate and evaluate historical events in an engaging and immersive manner.

Examples of Interactive Learning Environments

Numerous pioneering interactive learning environments demonstrate the efficacy of gamification and engagement techniques.

1. Kahoot!: This widely-used platform enables educators to design interactive quizzes and activities that students may engage with via their smartphones. The competitive aspect of Kahoot! cultivates enthusiasm and involvement, as students strive to answer questions accurately within a time constraint. The prompt feedback and visual components maintain learners' active engagement in the evaluation process.
2. Classcraft: This gamified educational platform transforms the classroom into a role-playing game, enabling students to create characters and engage in adventures aligned with their curriculum. Students accrue experience points and unlock new skills through assignment completion and class participation, fostering collaboration and teamwork while reinforcing academic material.
3. Minecraft: Education Edition: This interactive platform enables students to investigate and construct inside a virtual realm while interacting with several academic disciplines. Educators can construct classes that integrate problem-solving, creativity, and teamwork, rendering learning an exciting and experiential endeavor.

In conclusion, gamification and interactive learning are vital tactics for improving student engagement in personalized learning settings. Educators may cultivate engaging and dynamic experiences that promote profound learning and active involvement by integrating gamified components into evaluations and employing novel interactive learning tools. Upon further examination of strategies to augment engagement, it is clear that these ways can profoundly alter the educational environment, rendering learning both fun and significant.

CHALLENGES AND CONSIDERATIONS

Equity and Access

In the quest for individualized learning via intelligent assessment systems, equality and access continue to pose significant issues that educators must confront (Dumont & Ready, 2023). Disparities in technological access can profoundly affect students' capacity to participate in individualized learning settings, resulting in unequal educational opportunities. Comprehending these discrepancies and executing tactics for inclusive tailored learning is crucial to guarantee that all pupils can benefit from these revolutionary methodologies.

Addressing Disparities in Technology Access

The digital divide denotes the disparity between persons with convenient access to technology and those lacking such access (Lythreatis et al., 2022). In numerous educational environments, especially in under-resourced regions, students may be deprived of dependable internet connection, devices, or the requisite technological abilities to proficiently interact with intelligent assessment systems. The absence of access can impede their participation in individualized learning experiences, intensifying existing disparities in educational achievement.

To rectify these inequities, educational institutions and districts must prioritize equitable access to technology. This may include supplying gadgets, such as computers or tablets, to pupils without access at home (Shaheen, 2022). Furthermore, educational institutions can collaborate with local governments or groups to ensure dependable internet connectivity, thereby enabling all students to connect to online learning materials.

Furthermore, training and assistance for both students and families are essential. Educators ought to provide workshops or tools that facilitate the development of digital literacy skills essential for effective technology navigation. By providing students with the competencies to utilize intelligent assessment systems, educators can enable them to fully leverage personalized learning opportunities (Marín & Castaneda; Nguyen & Habók, 2024).

Strategies for Inclusive Personalized Learning

Establishing an inclusive personalized learning environment necessitates deliberate tactics that address the varied requirements of all students. Here are multiple efficacious strategies:

1. Universal Design for Learning (UDL): UDL is an educational concept that advocates for adaptable learning environments to address individual learning variances. By offering many methods of interaction, representation, and action, educators may guarantee that all students receive tailored learning experiences that accommodate their individual requirements.
2. Differentiated Instruction: Educators must implement differentiated instruction tactics that consider students' diverse preparation levels, interests, and learning profiles. By providing varied educational pathways and tools, educators may foster a more inclusive environment in which every student can flourish.

3. Collaborative Learning Opportunities: Promoting collaboration among students can cultivate an inclusive educational atmosphere. Collaborative efforts and peer tutoring can facilitate the closure of knowledge and skill disparities, enabling students to learn from each other and foster a feeling of community.
4. Feedback and Support Systems: Implementing effective feedback mechanisms and support systems is crucial for all students, especially those who may have difficulties with individualized learning. Consistent evaluations, mentorship initiatives, and availability of supplementary resources can guarantee that each student get the necessary advice for success.

In conclusion, addressing equality and access in personalized learning is essential for fostering an inclusive educational environment. By acknowledging gaps in technological access and executing focused techniques for inclusive personalized learning, educators can guarantee that all students have the opportunity to engage meaningfully with their education. In our examination of the obstacles and issues related to individualized learning, it is evident that fairness must be prioritized to improve student engagement and performance.

Data Privacy and Security

The rise of personalized learning via intelligent assessment technologies has intensified worries about the privacy and security of student data management (Whalley et al., 2021). Given the collecting and analysis of extensive sensitive information, it is imperative for educators, administrators, and politicians to emphasize the appropriate management of student data. This section examines the significance of appropriately maintaining student data and discusses the legal and ethical implications associated with assessment procedures.

Managing Student Data Responsibly

Implementing intelligent assessment systems typically necessitates gathering comprehensive data regarding student performance, behavior, and learning preferences (Hooda et al., 2022). This data can enhance educational experiences and outcomes, but it also presents concerns if mismanaged. Educational institutions must adopt stringent data management protocols to guarantee the secure collection, storage, and utilization of student information.

A crucial element of responsible data management is anonymizing data whenever feasible. By eliminating personally identifiable information, instructors can safeguard students' identities while still gaining insights from aggregated data (Prinsloo et al., 2022). Furthermore, educational institutions must implement explicit data access regulations, guaranteeing that only authorized individuals can access confidential information.

Consistent training for educators and staff on optimal data privacy procedures is crucial. This training should encompass subjects such as identifying probable data breaches, comprehending permission regulations, and executing secure data-sharing protocols (Komljenovic, 2022). By cultivating a culture of data accountability, educational institutions may reduce risks and safeguard student information.

Legal and Ethical Considerations in Assessment

The legal framework regarding student data privacy is intricate, encompassing numerous rules and regulations that oversee the acquisition and utilization of educational data. In the United States, legislation such as the Family Educational Rights and Privacy Act (FERPA) and the Children's Online Privacy Protection Act (COPPA) establishes protocols for safeguarding student information (Prinsloo and Kaliisa, 2022). Educators must understand these regulations to ensure compliance and protect student rights.

Ethical considerations are paramount in data management. Educators must balance the use of data for tailored learning with the imperative of safeguarding students' privacy. Transparency is essential; educational institutions must clearly inform students and their families of the data being gathered, its intended use, and the individuals who will have access to it (Chen et al., 2022). Securing informed consent from parents and guardians is crucial, especially when engaging with younger pupils.

Furthermore, educators must contemplate the ramifications of data-driven decision-making. Although statistics can yield significant insights, it is crucial to refrain from excessive dependence on quantitative indicators that may fail to encompass the entirety of a student's capabilities or potential. Integrating data use with qualitative evaluations and interpersonal engagements is essential for cultivating an equal and supportive educational atmosphere (Maleki, 2024).

In conclusion, as personalized learning via intelligent assessment systems advances, the responsible management of student data is essential. By complying with legal mandates and ethical principles, educators can safeguard students' privacy while utilizing data to improve learning results. In our examination of the issues and considerations associated with personalized learning, it is evident that prioritizing data privacy and security is crucial for fostering confidence and assuring the efficacy of these innovative teaching methodologies.

Teacher Training and Support

The effective execution of individualized learning via intelligent assessment systems largely depends on educators' readiness and continuous support (Kayyali, 2024). As these systems increasingly integrate into educational practices, it is essential that educators have thorough professional development and are aided in fostering an environment favorable to individualized learning. This section examines the significance of professional development for educators and ways for cultivating a supportive environment.

Professional Development for Educators

Professional development is crucial for providing educators with the information and skills required to properly implement intelligent assessment systems (Zhao et al., 2024). The swift advancement of technology and educational strategies necessitates continuous training for instructors to stay abreast of optimal practices and new developments in individualized learning.

Effective professional development programs must be comprehensive, integrating several forms such seminars, collaborative planning sessions, and online courses (Ramírez-Montoya et al., 2021). These programs may concentrate on critical domains, such as data analytics utilization, adaptive learning technology, and instructional differentiation tactics informed by assessment outcomes. Furthermore, training must focus on how to evaluate data effectively and utilize it to guide instructional decisions.

Mentorship and peer collaboration are essential elements of professional development.

By cultivating a collaborative culture, schools can facilitate chances for instructors to exchange experiences, techniques, and issues associated with the implementation of customized learning (Kayyali, 2024). This collaborative setting increases individual teacher efficacy and fosters a sense of community among educators.

Creating a Supportive Environment for Personalized Learning

Alongside professional development, fostering a supportive atmosphere is crucial for the effective execution of individualized learning (Schmid et al., 2022). This climate ought to foster innovation, experimentation, and risk-taking among educators. School leaders are vital in cultivating this culture by fostering receptiveness to innovative concepts and providing essential tools for educators to investigate and apply individualized learning methodologies.

Administrative help is essential in resolving logistical issues encountered by educators. This encompasses facilitating technology access, allocating sufficient planning and discussion time, and delivering continuous technical support for intelligent assessment systems. By eliminating obstacles and enhancing resource accessibility, schools can enable teachers to concentrate on their pedagogical methods (Gearhart et al., 2022).

Moreover, cultivating robust relationships among educators, students, and families is essential for establishing a helpful learning environment. Involving families in the individualized learning process fosters trust and promotes a collaborative strategy for student achievement (Porath & Hagerman, 2021). Educational institutions may offer workshops or materials for parents to comprehend the methods and strategies employed, so facilitating their ability to assist their children's learning at home.

In conclusion, educator training and support are essential components for the effective execution of individualized learning using intelligent assessment systems. Through investment in professional development and the establishment of a supportive atmosphere, schools can enable educators to proficiently implement these novel methodologies, hence improving student engagement and learning outcomes. The exploration of obstacles and issues related to individualized learning reveals that instructors play a pivotal role in attaining success within this revolutionary educational environment.

FUTURE DIRECTIONS IN PERSONALIZED LEARNING

Emerging Technologies

The realm of individualized learning is swiftly transforming, propelled by technological breakthroughs that provide novel methods to improve student engagement and educational results (Pan and Sen, 2024). Notable advancements include artificial intelligence (AI), machine learning (ML), and immersive technologies like virtual reality (VR) and augmented reality (AR). These developing technologies are set to revolutionize personalized learning, fostering more dynamic, interactive, and customized educational experiences.

The Role of Artificial Intelligence and Machine Learning

Artificial intelligence and machine learning are transforming the methods by which educators evaluate student performance and tailor learning experiences (Pratama et al., 2023). AI systems can evaluate extensive data from student interactions, evaluations, and learning behaviors to discern patterns and forecast future performance. This data-driven methodology allows instructors to customize training to more effectively address the individual needs of each learner.

AI-driven adaptive learning platforms can modify task difficulty in real-time according to a student's responses. When a learner demonstrates proficiency in a specific subject, the system can provide more advanced information, while also supplying supplementary assistance and resources for those who have difficulties. This degree of customisation not only increases engagement but also guarantees that each student is suitably challenged, fostering a growth attitude.

Furthermore, machine learning algorithms can perpetually enhance their recommendations through user interactions, facilitating progressively improved customisation throughout time (Khamaj & Ali, 2024). As these technologies advance, they will probably become more intuitive, offering educators concrete insights that can guide instructional techniques and interventions.

Virtual and Augmented Reality in Education

Virtual reality (VR) and augmented reality (AR) are advancing considerably in the field of personalized education. These immersive technologies foster captivating educational settings that enable students to investigate subjects in manners unattainable by conventional approaches. Virtual reality can immerse students in historical places, scientific laboratories, or outer space, offering experiential learning experiences that enhance comprehension and retention (AlGerafi et al., 2023).

In a biology lecture, students can utilize VR to examine the human body in a three-dimensional environment, closely analyzing anatomical structures and physiological processes. These immersive experiences accommodate many learning styles, rendering intricate subjects more approachable and interesting (Kuhail et al., 2022).

Augmented reality, conversely, superimposes digital information onto the physical environment, enriching the educational experience with interactive components. Students may utilize AR applications to visualize mathematical concepts, perform virtual experiments, or interact with dynamic texts (Al-Ansi et al., 2023). This technology promotes active engagement and cooperation, enabling students to collectively address challenges and investigate information through practical experience.

In summary, emerging technologies like artificial intelligence, machine learning, virtual reality, and augmented reality are poised to transform personalized learning. By utilizing these advances, educators may develop more engaging, interactive, and customized educational experiences that address the varied requirements of students. In our ongoing exploration of future avenues in personalized learning, it is evident that the adoption of these technologies will be crucial for augmenting student engagement and attaining academic achievement in a progressively digital landscape.

Research and Development

As personalized learning increasingly gains prominence in educational environments, research and development are pivotal in determining its future (Whalley et al., 2021). Contemporary trends in educational research reveal an increasing emphasis on the efficacy of tailored learning strategies, the deployment of intelligent assessment systems, and the influence of technology on student engagement. This section examines these tendencies and identifies future research opportunities that could further improve individualized learning.

Current Trends in Educational Research

Recent educational research has revealed the advantages of individualized learning methods, especially in improving student engagement and academic performance (Ellikkal & Rajamohan, 2024). Researchers are progressively investigating how intelligent assessment systems can deliver real-time feedback, allowing educators to customize training to address specific student requirements. This emphasis on data-informed decision-making has resulted in the creation of adaptive learning systems that modify content and tempo according to student performance.

Furthermore, there is much focus on the importance of social and emotional learning (SEL) within individualized learning settings. Ongoing study investigates how individualized strategies can enhance kids' emotional well-being and promote resilience, motivation, and self-regulation. Comprehending the relationship between SEL and individualized learning is essential for developing comprehensive educational experiences that cater to both intellectual and emotional requirements.

The incorporation of technology in education is a critical domain of investigation. Researchers are examining how emerging technologies, like artificial intelligence and virtual reality, can improve tailored learning experiences. This tendency signifies a wider dedication to comprehending how technology might be utilized to develop more captivating and efficient instructional settings.

Future Research Opportunities in Intelligent Assessment

Future research prospects in intelligent evaluation abound, potentially enhancing individualized learning. A promising avenue of investigation is the advancement of more refined algorithms for adaptive learning systems (Ezzaim et al., 2024). Subsequent study may concentrate on improving the precision and responsiveness of these algorithms, guaranteeing their capability to analyze varied learning activities and deliver tailored recommendations.

An additional significant area for investigation is the examination of the ethical ramifications of data utilization in intelligent evaluation systems. As educational institutions increasingly depend on data to guide instructional methodologies, comprehending the ethical implications regarding data privacy, consent, and equity is essential (Mienye & Swart, 2025). Future research may explore optimal methodologies for data management and the effects of data-driven decision-making on student performance.

Moreover, longterm studies investigating the enduring impacts of personalized learning and intelligent assessment systems on student accomplishment and engagement are crucial (Ellikkal & Rajamohan, 2024). This research can yield significant insights into the long-term durability and efficacy of these methods.

In conclusion, the future of individualized learning via intelligent assessment systems has abundant prospects for research and growth. By concentrating on contemporary trends and investigating novel pathways for study, educators and researchers can further augment the efficacy of individualized learning, hence fostering enhanced student engagement and achievement. A collaborative approach involving educators, academics, and technology developers will be essential in determining the future of education.

Vision for the Future

Envisioning the classroom of the future entails reconfiguring conventional educational spaces to establish dynamic, individualized learning environments that address the varied needs of all students (Adera, 2025). As sophisticated assessment methods and emerging technologies advance, the future classroom will be defined by flexibility, interactivity, and a pronounced focus on student agency. This section examines the vision for future classrooms and the enduring effects on educational systems and student results.

Envisioning the Classroom of Tomorrow

The future classroom will be a highly customizable environment, merging physical and virtual components to enable tailored learning experiences (Cheung et al. 2021). Classrooms will use modern technology, like artificial intelligence, virtual reality, and augmented reality, facilitating immersive learning experiences that engage students beyond the capabilities of traditional approaches. Students could investigate historical events using VR simulations or perform virtual science experiments, offering experiential learning possibilities that enhance comprehension.

In this future classroom, advanced assessment tools will consistently track student progress and engagement, delivering immediate feedback to educators and learners (Hooda et al., 2022). These tools will evaluate data on individual learning patterns, enabling educators to tailor education and resources to address each student's distinct requirements. The focus will be on competency-based education, allowing students to develop at their own pace, mastering concepts prior to progressing to more advanced content.

Moreover, teamwork will be fundamental to the future classroom. Students will collaborate in heterogeneous groups, utilizing technology to engage with peers worldwide (Alam & Mohanty, 2023). This collaborative method will enhance communication and problem-solving abilities, equipping students for the interconnected world they will encounter post-graduation.

Long-Term Impact on Educational Systems and Student Outcomes

The enduring effects of individualized learning via intelligent assessment systems on educational frameworks and student performance are significant. As educational institutions use these creative methodologies, we anticipate notable enhancements in student involvement, motivation, and academic performance. Customized learning settings that address individual skills and interests will enable students to assume responsibility for their education, resulting in enhanced self-efficacy and a lasting passion for learning (DeMink-Carthew & Netcoh, 2022).

The transition to competency-based education will facilitate the reduction of achievement disparities by guaranteeing that all students have the necessary assistance for success (Malhotra et al., 2023). Through focused interventions and customized tools, educators may meet the varied needs of students, promoting an inclusive educational atmosphere.

The incorporation of intelligent assessment systems and individualized learning methodologies will require systemic transformations inside educational institutions. Teacher training programs will adapt to provide educators with the competencies required to manage emerging technologies and techniques (Rahimi & Oh, 2024).

Educational policies must adapt by prioritizing flexibility, creativity, and equitable access to resources.

In summary, the vision for the future classroom emphasizes customized learning, teamwork, and the efficient integration of technology. The enduring influence on educational systems and student results will be revolutionary, fostering a generation of learners who are engaged, empowered, and equipped to succeed in a dynamic world. By adopting these future directions, we advance towards actualizing the complete potential of individualized learning via sophisticated evaluation systems.

CONCLUSION

The use of sophisticated assessment tools into personalized learning signifies a significant change in educational methodology, highlighting adaptability, student autonomy, and engagement. This chapter has illustrated that intelligent systems—driven by data analytics, adaptive algorithms, and real-time feedback—enable educators to customize education to address the varied needs of individual learners. By utilizing formative, summative, and diagnostic evaluations, educators can acquire comprehensive insights into student performance and deliver prompt, individualized interventions.

Moreover, these technologies augment student engagement by facilitating differentiated instruction, cultivating a sense of ownership in learning, and promoting emotional and cognitive involvement. Mechanisms like individualized feedback, gamification, and interactive platforms function as effective instruments to inspire learners and enhance their dedication to academic advancement.

Successful implementation necessitates meticulous planning, professional development for instructors, and a conducive institutional culture. Equally significant are ethical problems of data privacy and equal access to technology, which must be addressed to guarantee that individualized learning advantages all students, irrespective of their background.

Innovative technologies, like artificial intelligence, virtual and augmented reality, and machine learning, will persist in influencing the development of individualized learning environments. These innovations has the capacity to generate profoundly immersive, inclusive, and efficacious learning experiences.

In conclusion, individualized learning via intelligent assessment systems is not simply a pedagogical trend; it represents a durable and progressive approach to education. By prioritizing the learner and utilizing technology judiciously, educators may establish settings that are adaptive, equitable, and aimed at empowering each student to achieve success.

REFERENCES

Adera, N. (2025). Innovative learning spaces and blended learning: Quest for 21st century competency teaching and learning approaches. Creating Dynamic Space in Higher Education: Modern Shifts in Policy, Competencies, and Governance, 139-174. [HTML]

Al-Ansi, A. M., Jaboob, M., Garad, A., & Al-Ansi, A. (2023). Analyzing augmented reality (AR) and virtual reality (VR) recent development in education. [sciencedirect.com]. *Social Sciences & Humanities Open*, *8*(1), 100532.

Alam, A., & Mohanty, A. (2023). Educational technology: Exploring the convergence of technology and pedagogy through mobility, interactivity, AI, and learning tools. Cogent Engineering. tandfonline.com

AlGerafi, M. A. M., Zhou, Y., Oubibi, M., & Wijaya, T. T. (2023). Unlocking the potential: A comprehensive evaluation of augmented reality and virtual reality in education. Electronics. mdpi.com

Amerstorfer, C. M., & Freiin von Münster-Kistner, C. (2021). Student perceptions of academic engagement and student-teacher relationships in problem-based learning. [frontiersin.org]. *Frontiers in Psychology*, *12*, 713057. PMID: 34777094

Bradley, V. M. (2021). Learning Management System (LMS) use with online instruction.. International Journal of Technology in Education. ed.gov

Carroll, M., Lindsey, S., Chaparro, M., & Winslow, B. (2021). An applied model of learner engagement and strategies for increasing learner engagement in the modern educational environment. [HTML]. *Interactive Learning Environments*, *29*(5), 757–771.

Cents-Boonstra, M., Lichtwarck-Aschoff, A., Denessen, E., Aelterman, N., & Haerens, L. (2021). Fostering student engagement with motivating teaching: An observation study of teacher and student behaviours. [tandfonline.com]. *Research Papers in Education*, *36*(6), 754–779.

Chen, G., Chen, P., Huang, W., & Zhai, J. (2022). Continuance intention mechanism of middle school student users on online learning platform based on qualitative comparative analysis method. [wiley.com]. *Mathematical Problems in Engineering*, *2022*(1), 3215337.

Cheung, S. K., Kwok, L. F., Phusavat, K., & Yang, H. H. (2021). Shaping the future learning environments with smart elements: Challenges and opportunities. [springer.com]. *International Journal of Educational Technology in Higher Education, 18*, 1–9. PMID: 34778521

DeMink-Carthew, J., & Netcoh, S. (2022). Mixed feelings about choice: Exploring variation in middle school student experiences with making choices in a personalized learning project. In Dialogues in Middle Level Education Research Volume 1 (pp. 73-105). Routledge. tandfonline.com

du Plooy, E., Casteleijn, D., & Franzsen, D. (2024). Personalized adaptive learning in higher education: a scoping review of key characteristics and impact on academic performance and engagement. Heliyon. cell.com

Dumont, H. & Ready, D. D. (2023). On the promise of personalized learning for educational equity. Npj science of learning. nature.com

Ellikkal, A. & Rajamohan, S. (2024). AI-enabled personalized learning: empowering management students for improving engagement and academic performance. Vilakshan-XIMB Journal of Management. emerald.com

Ezzaim, A., Dahbi, A., Aqqal, A., & Haidine, A. (2024). AI-based learning style detection in adaptive learning systems: A systematic literature review. [HTML]. *Journal of Computers in Education*, •••, 1–39.

Gamage, K. A. A., Gamage, A., & Dehideniya, S. C. P. (2022). Online and hybrid teaching and learning: Enhance effective student engagement and experience. Education Sciences. mdpi.com

Garlinska, M., Osial, M., Proniewska, K., & Pregowska, A. (2023). *The influence of emerging technologies on distance education. Electronics.* mdpi.com *Govea, J., Ocampo Edye, E.* Revelo-Tapia.

Gearhart, C. A., Blaydes, M., & McCarthy, C. J. (2022). Barriers to and facilitators for teachers' wellbeing. Frontiers in Psychology. frontiersin.org

Grabner-Hagen, M. M. & Kingsley, T. (2023). From badges to boss challenges: Gamification through need-supporting scaffolded design to instruct and motivate elementary learners. Computers and Education Open. sciencedirect.com

Halkiopoulos, C. & Gkintoni, E. (2024). Leveraging AI in e-learning: Personalized learning and adaptive assessment through cognitive neuropsychology—A systematic analysis. Electronics. mdpi.com

Heilporn, G., Lakhal, S., & Bélisle, M. (2021). An examination of teachers' strategies to foster student engagement in blended learning in higher education. [springer.com]. *International Journal of Educational Technology in Higher Education*, *18*(1), 25. PMID: 34805484

Hellín, C. J., Calles-Esteban, F., Valledor, A., Gómez, J., Otón-Tortosa, S., & Tayebi, A. (2023). Enhancing student motivation and engagement through a gamified learning environment. [mdpi.com]. *Sustainability*, *15*(19), 14119.

Hidayat, L. E., Amalia, S. N., Rohmana, W. I. M., Virdyna, N. K., Ardi, P., & Suryati, N. (2025). EFL Teachers' Understanding and Practices of Classroom-Based Diagnostic Assessment in Differentiated Instruction. In Differentiated Instruction, Equity, and Inclusion in Language Education (pp. 181-218). IGI Global Scientific Publishing. [HTML]

Hooda, M., Rana, C., Dahiya, O., Rizwan, A., & Hossain, M. S. (2022). Artificial intelligence for assessment and feedback to enhance student success in higher education. [wiley.com]. *Mathematical Problems in Engineering*, *2022*(1), 5215722.

Ismail, S. M., Rahul, D. R., Patra, I., & Rezvani, E. (2022). Formative vs. summative assessment: impacts on academic motivation, attitude toward learning, test anxiety, and self-regulation skill. Language Testing in Asia. springer.com

Kayyali, M. (2024). *Global Perspectives on Personalized Learning: Case Studies and Best Practices.* Transforming Education for Personalized Learning. [HTML]

Khamaj, A. & Ali, A. M. (2024). Adapting user experience with reinforcement learning: Personalizing interfaces based on user behavior analysis in real-time. Alexandria Engineering Journal. sciencedirect.com

Komljenovic, J. (2022). The future of value in digitalised higher education: why data privacy should not be our biggest concern. Higher Education. springer.com

Kong, Y. (2021). The role of experiential learning on students' motivation and classroom engagement. Frontiers in psychology. frontiersin.org

Kuhail, M. A., ElSayary, A., Farooq, S., & Alghamdi, A. (2022). Exploring immersive learning experiences: A survey. Informatics. mdpi.com

Lasekan, O. A., Pachava, V., Godoy Pena, M. T., Golla, S. K., & Raje, M. S. (2024). Investigating factors influencing students' engagement in sustainable online education. [mdpi.com]. *Sustainability*, *16*(2), 689.

Lee, D., Huh, Y., Lin, C. Y., Reigeluth, C. M., & Lee, E. (2021). Differences in personalized learning practice and technology use in high-and low-performing learner-centered schools in the United States. [springer.com]. *Educational Technology Research and Development*, *69*, 1221–1245. PMID: 33584077

Lipnevich, A. A. & Panadero, E. (2021). A review of feedback models and theories: Descriptions, definitions, and conclusions. Frontiers in Education. frontiersin.org

Lu, G., Xie, K., & Liu, Q. (2022). What influences student situational engagement in smart classrooms: Perception of the learning environment and students' motivation. [HTML]. *British Journal of Educational Technology*.

Lythreatis, S., Singh, S. K., & El-Kassar, A. N. (2022). The digital divide: A review and future research agenda. [HTML]. *Technological Forecasting and Social Change*, *175*, 121359.

Majeed, A. & Hwang, S. O. (2021). Data-driven analytics leveraging artificial intelligence in the era of COVID-19: an insightful review of recent developments. Symmetry. mdpi.com

Maleki, A. (2024). Towards a more equitable education: A lens into EFL teachers' pedagogical barriers in online assessments. [HTML]. *International Journal of Lifelong Education*.

Malhotra, R., Massoudi, M., & Jindal, R. (2023). Shifting from traditional engineering education towards competency-based approach: The most recommended approach-review. [HTML]. *Education and Information Technologies*, *28*(7), 9081–9111.

Manu, B. D., Ying, F., Oduro, D., & Boateng, S. A. (2021). Student engagement and social media in tertiary education: The perception and experience from the Ghanaian public university. [sciencedirect.com]. *Social Sciences & Humanities Open*, *3*(1), 100100.

Marín, V. I. & Castaneda, L. (2024). Developing digital literacy for teaching and learning. Handbook of open. springer.com

Mienye, I. D. & Swart, T. G. (2025). ChatGPT in Education: A Review of Ethical Challenges and Approaches to Enhancing Transparency and Privacy. Procedia Computer Science. sciencedirect.com

Minn, S. (2022). AI-assisted knowledge assessment techniques for adaptive learning environments. Computers and Education: Artificial Intelligence. sciencedirect.com

Moorhouse, B. L. & Kohnke, L. (2024). The effects of generative AI on initial language teacher education: The perceptions of teacher educators. System. sciencedirect.com

Morris, R., Perry, T., & Wardle, L. (2021). Formative assessment and feedback for learning in higher education: A systematic review. Review of Education. wiley.com Bimpeh, Y. (2024). AI Powered Adaptive Formative Assessment: Validity and Reliability Evaluation. In Artificial Intelligence in Education: The Intersection of Technology and Pedagogy (pp. 127-144). Cham: Springer Nature Switzerland. [HTML]

Nair, V. & Yunus, M. M. (2021). A systematic review of digital storytelling in improving speaking skills. Sustainability. mdpi.com

Nguyen, L. A. T. & Habók, A. (2024). Tools for assessing teacher digital literacy: a review. Journal of Computers in Education. springer.com

Pan, K., & Sen, R. (2024). Navigating the Evolving Landscape of Personalized Learning in AIED: Recent Trends and Innovations. Explainable AI for Education: Recent Trends and Challenges, 169-192. [HTML]

Porath, S., & Hagerman, D. (2021). Becoming connected learners through personalized learning. [HTML]. *Middle School Journal.*

Pratama, M. P., Sampelolo, R., & Lura, H. (2023). Revolutionizing education: harnessing the power of artificial intelligence for personalized learning. Klasikal: Journal of education, language teaching and science, 5(2), 350-357. journalfkipuniversitasbosowa.org

Prinsloo, P., & Kaliisa, R. (2022). Data privacy on the African continent: Opportunities, challenges and implications for learning analytics. [wiley.com]. *British Journal of Educational Technology*, *53*(4), 894–913.

Prinsloo, P., Slade, S., & Khalil, M. (2022). The answer is (not only) technological: Considering student data privacy in learning analytics. [HTML]. *British Journal of Educational Technology*, *53*(4), 876–893.

Qushem, U. B., Christopoulos, A., Oyelere, S. S., Ogata, H., & Laakso, M. J. (2021). Multimodal technologies in precision education: Providing new opportunities or adding more challenges? [mdpi.com]. *Education Sciences*, *11*(7), 338.

Rahimi, R. A. & Oh, G. S. (2024). Rethinking the role of educators in the 21st century: navigating globalization, technology, and pandemics. Journal of Marketing Analytics. [HTML]

Ramírez-Montoya, M. S., Andrade-Vargas, L., Rivera-Rogel, D., & Portuguez-Castro, M. (2021). Trends for the future of education programs for professional development. [mdpi.com]. *Sustainability*, *13*(13), 7244.

Salas-Pilco, S. Z., Yang, Y., & Zhang, Z. (2022). Student engagement in online learning in Latin American higher education during the COVID-19 pandemic: A systematic review. [wiley.com]. *British Journal of Educational Technology*, *53*(3), 593–619. PMID: 35600418

Schmid, R., Pauli, C., Stebler, R., Reusser, K., & Petko, D. (2022). Implementation of technology-supported personalized learning—Its impact on instructional quality. [tandfonline.com]. *The Journal of Educational Research*, *115*(3), 187–198.

Shaheen, N. L. (2022). Technology accessibility: How US K-12 schools are enacting policy and addressing the equity imperative. [HTML]. *Computers & Education*.

Singha, S., Singha, R., Ruben, V. M., Jose, S., Mize, E., & Haokip, A. D. (2024). Navigating the Landscape of Inclusive Education: Bridging the Policy-Practice Divide. In Exploring Educational Equity at the Intersection of Policy and Practice (pp. 176-194). IGI Global. [HTML]

Solari, M., Vizquerra, M. I., & Engel, A. (2023). Students' interests for personalized learning: An analysis guide. [springer.com Gardner]. *European Journal of Psychology of Education*, *38*(3), 1073–1109.

Staller, M. S. & Koerner, S. (2021). Beyond classical definition: The non-definition of gamification. SN Computer Science. springer.com

Susnjak, T., Ramaswami, G. S., & Mathrani, A. (2022). Learning analytics dashboard: A tool for providing actionable insights to learners. [springer.com]. *International Journal of Educational Technology in Higher Education*, *19*(1), 12. PMID: 35194560

Turnbull, D., Chugh, R., & Luck, J. (2021). Transitioning to E-Learning during the COVID-19 pandemic: How have Higher Education Institutions responded to the challenge?. Education and Information Technologies. springer.com

Verde, A. & Valero, J. M. (2021). Teaching and learning modalities in higher education during the pandemic: Responses to coronavirus disease 2019 from Spain. Frontiers in Psychology. frontiersin.org

Whalley, B., France, D., Park, J., Mauchline, A., & Welsh, K. (2021). Towards flexible personalized learning and the future educational system in the fourth industrial revolution in the wake of Covid-19. [tandfonline.com]. *Higher Education Pedagogies*, *6*(1), 79–99.

Yu, Z., Gao, M., & Wang, L. (2021). The effect of educational games on learning outcomes, student motivation, engagement and satisfaction. [HTML]. *Journal of Educational Computing Research*, *59*(3), 522–546.

Zhang, Z. (2022). Promoting student engagement with feedback: Insights from collaborative pedagogy and teacher feedback. [HTML]. *Assessment & Evaluation in Higher Education*.

Zhao, Y., Zhao, M., & Shi, F. (2024). Integrating moral education and educational information technology: A strategic approach to enhance rural teacher training in universities. [HTML]. *Journal of the Knowledge Economy*.

Chapter 7
Advancing Society 5.0 Through AI-Driven Curriculum Innovation:
The Role of AI in Language Assessment of the Common ASEAN Tourism Curriculum (CATC)

Abdul Waris
https://orcid.org/0000-0003-2553-4546
Baku State University, Azerbaijan & Universitas Islam Negeri Raden Fatah Palembang, Indonesia

ABSTRACT

Human Resource Development in the era of society 5.0 is a opportunity and a threat to educational institutions. However, it is important for educational institutions to prepare graduates whose English Proficiency are adjusted to the CEFR. This study aims to explain how the role of Artificial Intelligence (AI) in assisting the implementation of Language Assessment in the Common ASEAN Tourism Curriculum (CATC) at one of the Secondary Vocational Tourism Schools which became a pilot project in Indonesia by conducting in-depth interviews with several parties related to the implementation of CATC. The Language Assessment covers Skill, Attitude, and Knowledge which is adjusted to the ASEAN Competency Standards for Tourism Professional (ACSTP). In addition, AI helps compile the Task Project/role play that will be given to the students of Secondary Tourism Vocational Schools (assessees) as one of the instruments in Language Assessment so that this instrument can be easily understood and done by students (assessees) and teachers (Assessors) easily conduct assessments as summative assessments.

DOI: 10.4018/979-8-3373-1062-6.ch007

Copyright © 2026, IGI Global Scientific Publishing. Copying or distributing in print or electronic forms without written permission of IGI Global Scientific Publishing is prohibited.

INTRODUCTION

Background

Nowadays, English as a global language used in communicating between nations has connected people around the world to increase cooperation between both parties. Indonesia as a developing country also does not want to be left behind to always establish cooperation between nations through English even though Indonesia makes English a foreign language that must be studied. However, Indonesia has implemented English learning at almost every level of education, this shows the importance of English in creating graduates at every level of education. Especially at the Secondary Vocational School level whose graduates are expected not only to have skills in their fields, but also to have English language skills at the operator level and be able to work immediately whose competence is recognised both domestically and abroad. National and regional policies are needed that facilitate the recognition of competence both in certain fields and competence in communicating in English (Bianco, 2013), as a global language that refers to national standards and international standards both British Commonwealth countries that make English a second language, as well as non-British Commonwealth countries that make English a foreign language such as Indonesia. In the era of rapid globalisation, the ability to speak English is one of the main keys in bridging communication between countries. In the context of tourism, where cross-cultural interaction is crucial, English serves as a lingua franca that allows travellers from different backgrounds to communicate effectively. According to a report from the World Tourism Organisation (UNWTO, 2020), more than 80% of international travellers use English as the primary language in their interactions, making it a much-needed skill in the tourism industry.

Since 2000, the Indonesian government has implemented education policies that emphasise the importance of English language acquisition as an integral part of the national curriculum. This focus on English is further reinforced by the 2016 revitalisation policy for Secondary Vocational Tourism Schools, which aims to align educational outcomes with industry demands, particularly in the tourism sector. As part of this policy, curriculum development has been directed toward enhancing students' competencies to meet workforce requirements, including proficiency in English. Moreover, Indonesia's participation in the Association of Southeast Asian Nations (ASEAN) has brought about further alignment through regional agreements, such as the Mutual Recognition Arrangement on Tourism Professionals (MRA-TP), which recognises the importance of English communication skills as a key qualification for tourism professionals across member countries.

Mutual Recognition Arrangements on Tourism Professionals (MRA-TP) is one of the competency recognition agreements between ASEAN member countries for Tourism human resources with reference to the ASEAN Competency Standards for Tourism Professional (ACSTP). The curriculum made from these work competency standards is called the Common ASEAN Tourism Curriculum (CATC) or called the competency-based curriculum. The ASEAN Competency Standards for Tourism Professional (ACSTP) has 242 competency units that are divided into several divisions of labour in the tourism sector (KepMenParEkraf, 2023).

Since mid-2019, Indonesia is committed to improving the competence of tourism human resources by registering the ASEAN Competency Standards for Tourism Professionals to the Indonesian government's ministry of labour as a form of recognition by the Indonesian government of the implementation of CATC in Indonesia. Thus, Indonesia can also conform to international standards in education providers that will produce graduates as human resource providers in the tourism sector. In the same year, at the Secondary Vocational Tourism Schools level, Indonesia has appointed several Secondary Vocational Tourism Schools to implement CATC at the education unit level as a pilot project that will be expanded to all regions in Indonesia. Based on the 242 units of competency available from the CATC reference, English language skills are the focus of this book chapter. The ability to communicate in English is important because this ability is a benchmark in providing the best service to customers, especially those from abroad because English in Indonesia is a foreign language. In addition, it ensures that the language assessment results are recognised and in accordance with CATC standards based on the MRA-TP agreed by ASEAN member countries. The MRA-TP not only recognises professional competence in tourism, but also emphasises the importance of communication skills in English. With 242 units of competency set out in the ASEAN Competency Standards for Tourism Professional (ACSTP), mastery of English is a major focus in curriculum development, particularly in the Common ASEAN Tourism Curriculum (CATC). Because this curriculum is a competency-based curriculum, the English language assessment is also competency-based or called Competency Based Assessment (CBA).

CATC contains English language skills required for students studying in Secondary Vocational Tourism Schools, these graduates are expected to work serving foreign tourists who come from within and outside the country, a good opportunity for educational institutions (Secondary Vocational Tourism Schools) to prepare human resources who have competence in English at the operator level, because it has been determined that Secondary school graduates in Indonesia must be able to communicate with English at level B1 (Intermediate level). However, challenges in CATC implementation in Indonesia still exist, including a lack of training for teachers and limited resources. This is where the role of AI-based curriculum innovation becomes very important. AI technology can provide solutions to improve

English learning and assessment processes, thus enabling more accurate and efficient competency-based English assessment. Previous studies have shown significant impact in utilising AI as an effective language teaching and assessment tool for secondary schools (Angxuan Chen, 2024). In addition, another study also at Van Lang University showed that the use of AI in the creation of English exam questions can improve the efficiency and quality of assessment. AI was used to generate test items tailored to learning objectives and student performance data, enabling more personalised and adaptive assessment (Nykyporets D. N., 2025). Therefore, this research will discuss how AI integration can be a tool in the English assessment process in Secondary Vocational Tourism Schools in Indonesia, as well as how it can be in line with the demands of the tourism industry and international standards.

LITERATURE REVIEW

Curriculum

The curriculum is a fundamental component in producing quality graduate competencies, which serves as a roadmap for educators to achieve learning objectives. The curriculum includes lesson plans, learning approaches, strategies and resources designed to facilitate effective learning ((UIL), 2021). In the context of Society 5.0, where technology and human-centred approaches converge, curriculum must evolve to incorporate innovative teaching methods, including the integration of Artificial Intelligence (AI) to improve learning outcomes.

However, in implementing the curriculum, clear standards are needed as a reference for education providers in order to realise the needs of the industry related to the competencies achieved later and easily placed in the world of work. All education providers must refer to the Regional Work Competency Standards that are adjusted to the needs of the workforce in the industry, as well as skills in the 21st century learning era both locally and internationally

Competency

Competences cover skills, attitudes and knowledge, which are crucial in determining the effectiveness of graduates from a Secondary Vocational Tourism School. These competencies are aligned with qualification frameworks that vary by country and refer to regional and international standards (R. Nikolov, 2014). In the era of Society 5.0, competence is not only about mastery of material, but also the ability to adapt to smart technology and dynamic changes in the world of work (OECD, 2018). Therefore, competency development should include 21st century skills such as critical thinking, collaboration, and digital literacy (World Economic Forum, 2020) (Gardinier, 2021). Competences cover skills, attitudes and knowledge, which are crucial in determining the effectiveness of graduates from a Secondary Vocational Tourism School. These competencies are aligned with qualification frameworks that vary by country and refer to regional and international standards. In the era of Society 5.0, competence is not only about mastery of material, but also the ability to adapt to smart technology and dynamic changes in the world of work (OECD, 2018). Therefore, competency development should include 21st century skills such as critical thinking, collaboration, and digital literacy (WEF, 2020)

Common ASEAN Tourism Curriculum (CATC)

CATC is a curriculum developed based on the ASEAN Common Competency Standards for Tourism Professionals (ACCSPT) to ensure the competency standards of ASEAN tourism human resources (SIREP, 2010) (Secretary, 2021). The curriculum was designed by ASEAN with technical support from the ASEAN Australia Development Cooperation Programme (AADCP) and implemented through the Mutual Recognition Arrangement on Tourism Professionals (MRA-TP) to support labour mobility and improved quality of tourism services ((Secretariat T. A., 2018); (Secretariat T. G., 2022)).

CATC adopts a Competency-Based Curriculum approach that emphasises training and competency assessment (CBT and CBA). The implementation of CATC in Secondary Vocational Tourism Schools in Indonesia has shown positive results, especially in preparing work-ready graduates with operator certificates at the ASEAN Qualification Framework level (KepMenParEkraf, 2023). However, implementation challenges such as limited teacher training and resources must be overcome to maximise the potential of this curriculum.

Competency Based Assessment (CBA)

Competency based assessment (CBA) has become the backbone of measuring the English language proficiency of Secondary Vocational Tourism School graduates ((Crosbie et al., 2012); (Brown, 2004)). Various assessment methods, ranging from assignment observation (role-play scenarios), written quizzes, to portfolios, are used to ensure validity, reliability, and flexibility of assessment.

In the context of Society 5.0, the integration of AI in the CBA process opens up revolutionary opportunities to improve the effectiveness and efficiency of assessment. AI can automate oral and written assessments, provide real-time feedback, and analyse learning data to identify students' individual needs (UNESCO, 2020).

Recent studies show the use of AI in language assessment helps to reduce subjectivity and improve the accuracy of competency evaluation (Smith, J., & Lee, K.AI, 2022).

Implementation of English Curriculum in Indonesian Secondary Tourism Vocational Schools

The English curriculum at Indonesian Secondary Vocational Tourism Schools refers to two main competency standards: Indonesian National Competency Standards (SKKNI) and ASEAN Competency Standards for Tourism Professionals (ACSTP) which have been officially registered with the Ministry of Manpower (Yogi Anggraena, 2022). This curriculum targets English language mastery at the B1 CEFR level which includes the ability to understand general texts, interact in the context of tourism, and produce simple texts related to the tourism field (Aditomo, 2024).

The importance of technology integration, especially AI, in English learning and assessment is very relevant to equip students to be ready to face the challenges of an increasingly competitive and digital-based tourism industry.

Artificial Intelligence (AI) at Indonesian Secondary Tourism Vocational Schools

The transformation of language assessment technology in Secondary Vocational Tourism Schools began in 2015, with the implementation of Computer Based Test (CBT). However, this only applies to the national exam conducted in the final year before students graduate from Secondary Vocational Tourism Schools. The assessment is done by assessing the knowledge aspect only, without looking at the skill and attitude aspects desired in CATC. The use of the latest technology is expected to provide convenience in English assessment. In 2030 Indonesia is predicted to become the largest digital economy player in Southeast Asia (Tim, 2016), of course this affects economic growth, especially in tourism. Several studies have proven the benefits of using AI in vocational education especially in language teaching and language assessment when compared to using conventional approaches, learning outcomes in competency-based curriculum can be achieved well by using AI tools (Nguyen T., 2025) (Nykyporets, Bohdan Kutsyk & Svitlana, 2024). Thus, the use of artificial intelligence (AI) is a must in tourism schools at secondary and tertiary levels. Generative Artificial Intelligence (AI) or also known as AI has various generative forms that can be used in teaching and learning activities and assessments in Tourism Vocational Schools, this is very helpful for Teachers (Trainers) and Teachers (Assessors) in its application as a competency-based curriculum (KBK), thus enabling more interactive and flexible assessment methods, accommodating diverse learning styles.

Artificial Intelligence (AI)-based Approach: The current trend is to utilise AI technology to improve language assessment, provide personalised feedback, and adaptive learning experiences, which is what is needed for the development of English language competence of students graduating from tourism vocational schools.). Its utilisation is adjusted to the expected learning objectives, because AI has different types according to its designation, there are at least five forms of AI that can be used: 1) AI for creating Text content, 2) AI to create voice content, 3) AI to create image content, 4) AI to create Video content, and 5) AI to create presentation content with a combination of outputs (Arie Wibowo Khurniawan, 2024). Among others So that its utilisation makes it easier for teachers to deliver learning Generative artificial intelligence (AI) that can be used in the context of this English language Assessment is Gen AI in the form of text. Gen AI in the form of text means Gen AI that produces output in the form of text, namely role-play scenarios that will be carried out in assignments that adjust commands from the teacher with the keywords that are ordered, The AI that can be used to generate text is as follows:

Table 1. Kind of gen AI

Name of AI	Access	License	URL Address
Gemini	Web, mobile, API	free and fee-based	Gemini - chat to supercharge your ideas
Chat GPT	Web, mobile, API	free and fee-based, specialised education schemes available	ChatGPT
GitHub Copilot	Web, mobile, API	free and fee-based	GitHub · Build and ship software on a single, collaborative platform · GitHub
QuickChat	Web, mobile, API	fee-based	https://www.quickchat.ai
Storylab.Ai	Web	free and fee-based	The Modern Marketers AI Content Creation Toolkit - StoryLab.ai
Writefull	Web, mobile, API	free and fee-based, specialised education schemes available	Writefull X: AI Writing Tools for Students and Researchers

continued on following page

Table 1. Continued

Name of AI	Access	License	URL Address
Microsoft Copilot	Web, mobile, API	free and fee-based, specialised education schemes available	copilot.micros
Dikte.in	Web, mobile, API	free and fee-based, specialised education schemes available	Dikte.in

Source: (Arie Wibowo Khurniawan, 2024).

OPPORTUNITIES AND THREATS OF CATC IMPLEMENTATION

Since the Indonesian government through the Indonesian Ministry of Tourism has tagged 'Wonderful Indonesia', this tagline indirectly contains an invitation for people around the world to come visit Indonesia which is a vast country, consisting of more than 18,000 islands and stretches of coastline, diverse languages, cultures, and has unique flavours and culinary delights that distinguish one another. This is a means of attraction for foreign tourists who will visit Indonesia. However, beautiful scenery, abundant culinary, and a comfortable natural atmosphere are not enough to invite visitors to come to Indonesia. However, the existing human resources must be able to support the implementation of services to foreign tourists who have Hard Skills and Soft Skills in the Tourism Industry. In addition, especially human resources at productive age in Indonesia are predicted to experience a significant increase in 2030. This significant increase will have both positive and negative impacts. It will bring on the positive side when the Indonesian government can create human resources who are actively involved in supporting the tourism industry services so as to generate foreign exchange for the country through learning in tourism Secondary vocational schools for three years. Conversely, if excess human resources are not managed properly, it will have an impact on many criminal acts that occur, especially those that affect the development of the tourism industry in Indonesia and become a threat, not only will it have an impact on the decline in tourists who come and will even drain state revenues.

Human resource management through the Tourism Secondary Vocational School is one of the good efforts in creating tourism human resources to support the services of the Indonesian tourism industry. The application of tourism work competency standards that have been recognised both locally and globally will contribute to the quality of tourism human resources. The implementation of a competency-based curriculum (CBC) is one way of managing tourism human resources in tourism Secondary vocational schools that refer to the competency standards needed by the world labour market. Indonesian tourism Secondary vocational schools implement CBC as a follow-up to the joint policy of several ministries in Indonesia (Ministry of Education and Culture, Ministry of Tourism and Creative Economy, and Ministry of Labour). CBC provides competency-based teaching and learning, and competency-based Assessment, according to the applicable competency standards. Unfortunately, most of the teachers involved in teaching, learning, and assessment at CBC are entering retirement age. On the one hand, they must prepare their activities after retirement, but on the other hand, they must carry out their duties as professional teachers and prepare human resources who will replace them. In implementing CBC, teachers are required to fulfil the following requirements: 1) have a bachelor's degree, 2) certified as a Trainer (Teacher)/Assessor, 3) have English Proficiency level B2 CEFR (Upper Intermediate Level), 4) able to master technology, especially supporting the teaching and learning process, 5) understand the implementation of competency-based curriculum (CBC), 6) expected to have a technical certificate in tourism (Secretariat A., 2018). These six requirements are important in the implementation of the CBC, namely the Common ASEAN Tourism Curriculum (CATC) which is agreed to be recognised by ASEAN member countries, so that the recognition agreement through the Mutual Recognition Arrangement for Tourism Professional (MRA-TP) can be realised properly and cooperation between ASEAN countries is well established, of course these requirements can be met for Secondary Tourism Vocational Schools in Indonesia.

Language Assessment at CATC

Language assessment is the process of identifying the knowledge, skills and attitudes of participants in communicating in English at the operator level against all elements of competence in a unit of competence. English language assessment is a qualification framework (operator) based assessment that refers to the ASEAN Competency Standards for Tourism Professionals (ACSTP) (Brown, 2004).

However, before analysing the language assessment on the Common ASEAN Tourism Curriculum (CATC), this research will focus on the competencies of the Front Office (FO) Certificate II Bellboy which contains English language competencies from 22 units of competency in a total of one certification scheme as a graduate of a Tourism Vocational School with the following competency description:

Table 2. The competency unit

Core and Generic Competencies		
No.	Unit Number	Unit Title
12	D1.LAN.CL1.01	Converse in English at a Basic Operational Level

From a package of competency certification schemes, there is one unit of competency that contains English language competencies that can be taught or conducted language assessments, Converse in English at a basic operational level. thus, this research will only focus on the Converse in English at a basic operational level unit of competency. This unit of competency has a curriculum that refers to the ASEAN Competency Standard Tourism Professional (ACSTP), Converse in English at a Basic operational Level, it can be concluded that there are six topics and seventeen learning objectives using the Development Curriculum (DACUM) method (Boahin, 2018). This will be the scope of the English assessment rubric at the operator level of Tourism Vocational Secondary School graduates who are certified II Front Office and will be analysed for its application with the applicable stages in the Common ASEAN Tourism Curriculum (CATC). In the implementation of Language Assessment there are at least several kinds of assessments used ranging from Peer Assessment, Formative Assessment, and Summative Assessment to ensure the seventeen learning objectives can be achieved. The assessment stages in CATC include Competency Based Assessment (CBA) and Competency Based Trainer (CBT) so it involves the role of Teacher (Trainer) and Assessor in the application of Competency Based Language Assessment (CBLA) starting from Peer Assessment to Summative Assessment. The availability of Teachers (Trainers) and Assessor at one of the Tourism Vocational Secondary School that implement CATC and have been certified as follows:

Table 3. Number of trainer and assessor

School	Qualification for Front Officer (FO)	Number	Type of Standard Competency
X	Trainer	2	ASEAN Competency Standards for Tourism Professional
	Assessor	1	

Language Assessment Methods in CATC

There are several suggested assessment methods for the competency of communicating in English at operator level as this competency covers Skills, Attitude and Knowledge, a number of assessment tools have been identified including:

-Oral Questions
- Project work
- Written/oral Questions
- Third Party Statement

- Observation Checklist.

Meanwhile, if other assessment methods are required other than the methods listed above, the examiner may use other methods by paying attention to and considering the following matters:

a) The nature of the unit
b) The strengths of the participants
c) The number of participants in the class
d) Time required to complete the assessment
e) Time dedicated to the assessment
f) Equipment and resources required.

Alternative assessment methods include:

- Practical demonstration
- Practical demonstration under simulated working conditions
- Problem solving
- Portfolios of evidence
- Critical incident reports
- Journal
- Oral presentation
- Interview
- Video
- Visuals/slides/audio cassettes
- Notebook
- Projects and role play
- Group projects
- Recognition of Prior Learning.

However, the assessment of English language competence carried out at the level of tourism secondary vocational schools must be oriented towards skills, attitude, and knowledge whose graduates have not had previous experience working in this competency in the field of tourism, the assessment methods used are, Oral/written questions and observation checklists that contain role plays that refer to the assignment scenario given by the assessor.

Challenges of Implementing Language Assessment at CATC

The challenge of this implementation is mainly on the teacher who acts as two sides (teacher and assessor), how a teacher integrates AI as a tool used by considering teaching and learning skills in the 21st century and the condition of school facilities and infrastructure, as well as the diversity of student learning styles. Teachers are required to be able to make students able to communicate, collaborate, think critically, and creatively. So, the challenges in teacher training not only affect the quality of teaching, but can also have an impact on students' confidence levels in using English in the work environment. Research shows that lack of training can lead to uncertainty in language acquisition, which in turn affects students' ability to interact with foreign tourists.

Peer Assessment

Peer Assessment conducted in the implementation of the Common ASEAN Tourism Curriculum (CATC) is Diagnostic Assessment, this assessment is carried out during the learning process (ABEYWICKRAMA, 2018), the role of the teacher is important in conducting diagnostic assessment, because CATC consists of two elements of Competency Based Trainer (CBT) which is the role of the Trainer (Teacher), and Competency Based Assessment (CBA) which is the role of the Assessor, because the Comprehensive Learning System (CLS) includes Curriculum, Delivery, and Assessment are elements that each stand-alone but have an influence on each other as a system in the process of achieving language competence Diagnostic Assessment is needed as a consideration in determining the results of Language Assessment (O'Sullivan, 2021). However, before conducting peer assessment in the form of diagnostic assessment, an assessment matrix is needed. The Assessment Matrix indicates three of the most common assessment activities, Assessor may use to assess your understanding of the content of the Students' manual and their performance - Work Projects, Written Questions and Oral Questions. It also indicates where Assessor can find the subject content related to these assessment activities in the Trainee Manual (i.e., under which element or performance criteria). However, the assessors are free to choose which assessment activities are most suitable to best capture evidence of competency as they deem appropriate for individual students.

Table 4.

		Work Projects	Written Questions	Oral Questions
Element 1: Participate in simple conversations on familiar topics with work colleagues				
1.1	Use and respond appropriately to opening comments	1.1	1, 2	1
1.2	Comment on familiar topics	1.2	3, 4	2
1.3	Talk about a past event	1.3	5	3
1.4	Use closing remarks appropriately to end the conversation	1.4	6	4
Element 2: Respond to simple verbal instructions or requests				
2.1	Confirm understanding of supervisor's instructions or requests	2.1	7	5
2.2	Request repetition or clarification of instructions or requests	2.2	8, 9	6
Element 3: Make simple requests				
3.1	Use polite forms to make simple requests	3.1	10	7
3.2	Thank the person responding to your request	3.2	11	8
3.3	Acknowledge the person who cannot respond to your request	3.3	12	9
Element 4: Describe routine procedures				
4.1	Explain a sequence of events in carrying out a routine job	4.1	13	10
4.2	Describe exceptions to routine procedures	4.2	14	11
4.3	Make suggestions on how to improve routine procedures	4.3	15	12
Element 5: Express likes, dislikes and preferences				
5.1	Talk about likes and dislikes of familiar topics and situations	5.1	16	13
5.2	Discuss preferences and give reasons	5.2	17	14
Element 6: Identify different forms of expression in English				
6.1	Construct a formal sentence	6.1	18	15
6.2	Identify indicators of informal expressions in English	6.2	19	16
6.3	Differentiate between 'open-ended' and 'closed' questions	6.3	20	17

Formative Assessment

Formative Assessment is prepared by describing the learning objectives in learning in the Common ASEAN Tourism Curriculum (CATC). The role of the teacher (Trainer) is needed in conducting Formative Assessment because the application of this Assessment is an evaluation of the achievement of learning objectives for the teacher (Trainer) will deliver material on the Converse in English at a basic operational level competency unit at CATC because Formative Assessment at CATC is in the form of Self-Assessment for students by using a form that contains a statement that the assessee (Davison, 2013) competent with the indicators that exist in the seventeen learning objectives in the ASEAN Competency Standards for Tourism Professional (ACSTP) (Abdul Waris & Reza Aprianti, 2023). This statement of competence is filled directly by the student (assessee) to ensure the next assessment process, namely Summative Assessment. Ensure that the student has learnt the unit of competency and declares himself/herself competent and shows readiness for assessment of the student.

Table 5.

SELF-ASSESSMENT GUIDELINE				
Instructions: - Read each question in the left column - Put a tick (√) in the box if you believe you can perform the task described. - Fill in the column on the right by listing the evidence you have to show that you performed these tasks.				
Could I ....?		PC	NYC	Relevant proof
Element 1: Participate in simple conversations on familiar topics with work colleagues				
1.1	Use and respond appropriately to opening comments			
1.2	Comment on familiar topics			
1.3	Talk about a past event			
1.4	Use closing remarks appropriately to end the conversation			
Element 2: Respond to simple verbal instructions or requests				
2.1	Confirm understanding of supervisor's instructions or requests			
2.2	Request repetition or clarification of instructions or requests			
Element 3: Make simple requests				

continued on following page

Table 5. Continued

SELF-ASSESSMENT GUIDELINE				
3.1	Use polite forms to make simple requests			
3.2	Thank the person responding to your request			
3.3	Acknowledge the person who cannot respond to your request			
Element 4: Describe routine procedures				
4.1	Explain a sequence of events in carrying out a routine job			
4.2	Describe exceptions to routine procedures			
4.3	Make suggestions on how to improve routine procedures			
Element 5: Express likes, dislikes and preferences				
5.1	Talk about likes and dislikes of familiar topics and situations			
5.2	Discuss preferences and give reasons			
Element 6: Identify different forms of expression in English				
6.1	Construct a formal sentence			
6.2	Identify indicators of informal expressions in English			
6.3	Differentiate between 'open-ended' and 'closed' questions			
Name of Assesse:	**Date:**		**Signature of Assesse:**	
Reviewed by the assessor:				
Name of Assessor:	Recommendation: *Assessment can be continued/not continued*		Signature and Date:	

Note: PC: Pass Competent, NYC: Not Yet Competent

Summative Assessment

Summative assessment will not be carried out if there is no competent statement on the form carried out in Self-Assessment on Formative Assessment for students because this is the main requirement for competency assessment in the Common ASEAN Tourism Curriculum (CATC). Because Summative is also known as Assessment of learning which is the final determination of learning whether the student (assesse) is competent or not in Conversing in English at the basic operational level competency unit in CATC, at this level of Tourism Vocational School whose graduate profile must be at the Intermediate Level or B1 in the CEFR. Summative Assessment is conducted covering Skills, Attitude, and Knowledge using the following Assessment mapping table:

Table 6. Mapping of language assessment

Competency Unit	**Unit Code:**	**D1.LAN.CL10.01**								
	Unit Title	CONVERSE IN ENGLISH AT A BASIC OPERATIONAL LEVEL								
Performance Criteria	Evidence (Performance, Product, Portfolio, and/or Memorization) are identified based on Performance Criteria and Assessment Approach.	Types of Evidence			Assessment Methods and Tools OCL (Observation Checklist/Check Sheet), SIL (Structured Instruction List), OQL (Oral Question List), WQL (Written Question List), PV (Portfolio Verification), PRC (Product Review Checklist), IQ (Interview Questions)					
		Direct	Indirect	addition	Obsevasi langsung	Structured Activities	Question and answer	Portfolio Verification	Product reviews	Other
Element 1: Participate in simple conversations on familiar topics with work colleagues										
1.1 Use and respond appropriately to opening comments	Results of direct observation Use and respond appropriately to opening comments	√			OCL					
	Results Written/Oral Question and Answer Use and respond appropriately to opening comments			√			OQL/ WQL			
1.2 Comment on familiar topics	Results of direct observation Comment on familiar topics	√			OCL					
	Results of Written/Oral Questions and Answers Comments on familiar topics			√			OQL/ WQL			
1.3 Talk about a past event	Results of direct observation Talk about a past event	√			OCL					
	Results of Written/Oral Questions and Answers Talk about a past event			√			OQL/ WQL			
1.4 Use closing remarks appropriately to end the conversation	Results of direct observation Use closing remarks appropriately to end the conversation	√			OCL					
	Results of Written/Oral Questions and Answers Use closing remarks appropriately to end the conversation			√			OQL/ WQL			

continued on following page

Table 6. Continued

Competency Unit	Unit Code:	D1.LAN.CL10.01								
Element 2: Respond to simple verbal instructions or requests										
2.1 Confirm understanding of supervisor's instructions or requests	Results of direct observation Confirm understanding of supervisor's instructions or requests	√			OCL					
	Results of Written/Oral Questions and Answers Confirm understanding of supervisor's instructions or requests			√			OQL/ WQL			
2.2 Request repetition or clarification of instructions or requests	Results of direct observation Request repetition or clarification of instructions or requests	√			OCL					
	Results of Written/Oral Questions and Answers Request repetition or clarification of instructions or requests			√			OQL/ WQL			
Element 3: Make simple requests										
3.1 Use polite forms to make simple requests	Results of direct observation Use polite forms to make simple requests	√			OCL					
	Results of Written/Oral Questions and Answers Use polite forms to make simple requests			√			OQL/ WQL			
3.2 Thank the person responding to your request	Results of direct observation Thank the person responding to your request	√			OCL					
	Results of Written/Oral Questions and Answers Thank the person responding to your request			√			OQL/ WQL			
3.3 Acknowledge the person who cannot respond to your request	Results of direct observation Acknowledge the person who cannot respond to your request	√			OCL					
	Results of Written/Oral Questions and Answers Acknowledge the person who cannot respond to your request			√			OQL/ WQL			
Element 4: Describe routine procedures										
4.1 Use polite forms to make simple requests	Results of direct observation Use polite forms to make simple requests	√			OCL					
	Results of Written/Oral Questions and Answers Use polite forms to make simple requests			√			OQL/ WQL			
4.2 Describe exceptions to routine procedures	Results of direct observation Describe exceptions to routine procedures	√			OCL					
	Results of Written/Oral Questions and Answers Describe exceptions to routine procedures			√			OQL/ WQL			
4.3 Make suggestions on how to improve routine procedures	Results of direct observation Make suggestions on how to improve routine procedures	√			OCL					
	Results of Written/Oral Questions and Answers Make suggestions on how to improve routine procedures			√			OQL/ WQL			

continued on following page

Table 6. Continued

Competency Unit	Unit Code:	D1.LAN.CL10.01								
Element 5: Express likes, dislikes and preferences										
5.1 Talk about likes and dislikes of familiar topics and situations	Results of direct observation Talk about likes and dislikes of familiar topics and situations	√			OCL					
	Results of Written/Oral Questions and Answers Talk about likes and dislikes of familiar topics and situations			√			OQL/ WQL			
5.2 Discuss preferences and give reasons	Results of direct observation Discuss preferences and give reasons	√			OCL					
	Results of Written/Oral Questions and Answers Discuss preferences and give reasons			√			OQL/ WQL			
Element 6: Identify different forms of expression in English										
6.1 Construct a formal sentence	Results of direct observation Construct a formal sentence	√			OCL					
	Results of Written/Oral Questions and Answers Construct a formal sentence			√			OQL/ WQL			
6.2 Identify indicators of informal expressions in English	Results of direct observation Use polite forms to make simple requests	√			OCL					
	Results of Written/Oral Questions and Answers Identify indicators of informal expressions in English			√			OQL/ WQL			
6.3 Differentiate between 'open-ended' and 'closed' questions	Results of direct observation Differentiate between 'open-ended' and 'closed' questions	√			OCL					
	Results of Written/Oral Questions and Answers Differentiate between 'open-ended' and 'closed' questions			√			OQL/ WQL			

From the Summative Assessment Mapping above, it can be concluded that the methods and tools used in summative assessment are Observation Checklists, oral question lists, and written question lists. In the assessment at the Tourism Secondary Vocational School level because it does not have experience working in the tourism industry that will be attached, the Summative Assessment carried out focuses on the Observation Checklist (OCL) covering Attitude and Skill, to ensure that the Assese (Student) knowledge is predicated on competence, a Written Question List (WQL) and Oral Question List (OQL) are added.

SOLUTIONS AND RECOMMENDATIONS

In this chapter the author will present several solutions and recommendations that can be made in enabling artificial intelligence in language assessment, namely English Language Assessment in the Common ASEAN Tourism Curriculum

(CATC), so that AI occupies its position correctly in achieving learning objectives in Indonesian Tourism Vocational Schools according to the needs of the tourism industry workforce, AI really places its portion as a tool in teaching and learning activities and assessing the abilities of tourism vocational students who have their own peculiarities in meeting labour market demands and policies with ASEAN countries through Mutual Recognition Arrangements for Tourism Professionals (MRA-TP).

As with the opportunities and threats in the previous chapter, to realise the qualifications according to the MRA-TP and produce tourism human resources at the operator level, it is necessary to fulfil six supporting requirements for teachers who teach at Secondary Tourism Vocational School. The first requirement will be easy to achieve because more than 90% of teachers have a bachelor degree, the second requirement is a big challenge for Tourism Vocational Schools, because it requires a large budget, synergy and budget allocation are needed in order to meet the second and fifth requirements at the same time, strategic policies must be formulated to support teacher certification as trainers and assessors so that they have an understanding of applying CATC, the National Professional Tourism Board (NPTB) which is the representative in each country provides master assessors and master trainers in providing understanding and certifying prospective assessors and trainers so that they are eligible to teach and test tourism professional qualifications that are recognised by ASEAN countries. Meanwhile, the third, fifth and sixth requirements are requirements that become one unit in applying hard skills and soft skills competencies in CATC, at the Tourism Vocational Schools studied by the author, most of them have fulfilled the six required criteria, teachers come from English Education undergraduate graduates, and have technical certificates in tourism, and have English proficiency at level B2, because students who will be targeted at level B1 (Intermediate level) in the CEFR. Furthermore, in mastering technology, teachers do not need much time to learn to master the technology used in teaching and learning and English language assessment, teachers can easily use AI in the English language assessment process, especially in the Summative Assessment process, namely The Observation Checklist.

The observation Checklist will be easy to use for assessors in English assessment, students as assessors perform their role-play with their English language skills as Bellboy operators in the tourism industry, by describing the assignment in the form provided allows students to capture the assignment questions and carry it out properly. With the latest technology, namely generative artificial intelligence (AI), because the form of scenarios or assignments carried out in summative assessment is text, it can be used Generative AI which has text content as described in the previous chapter, for example we compare text created manually with text described by generative AI CHATGPT as follows:

Table 7. Manual scenario for Bellboy assignment

Manual Scenario for Bellboy Assignment
In order to qualify as a bellboy, you will be tasked with carrying some of the guest's luggage during check in. Communicate in English formally and politely at the operator level, and use a trolley to deliver guests' luggage after the check in process to the room by following workplace safety and security procedures, promoting hotel events and explaining room facilities. Complete the form used. Work within 20 minutes. To support the achievement of results in accordance with predetermined specifications you are equipped with tools and equipment including: Tools and equipment: Equipment: 1. Trolley 2. Bell 3. Paging System 4. Computer 5. Printer 6. Phone 7. Office stationery Equipment: 1. Suitcase 2. Trunk 3. Cosmetic Case 4. Handbag 5. Luggage Tag 6. Bellboy Errand Card 7. Trolley 8. Stamp in/out

Table 8. Kind of gen AI: ChatGPT

Kind of Gen AI: ChatGPT
Scenario for Bellboy Assignment Objective: To assist a hotel guest by transporting their luggage to their room using a trolley, ensuring adherence to workplace safety and security procedures, promoting hotel events, and explaining the room facilities. Procedure: 1. Initial Interaction with Guest: o Greeting: ■ "Good afternoon, Mr./Ms. [Guest's Last Name]. Welcome to [Hotel Name]. My name is [Your Name], and I will be assisting you with your luggage today." o Confirming Room Details: ■ "I understand you've checked in to room [Room Number]. Is that correct?" 2. Preparing the Trolley: o Inspect the trolley for cleanliness and functionality before use. o Ensure the trolley is equipped with: ■ Anti-slip mat (if applicable). ■ Safety straps to secure luggage. ■ Room for efficient placement of guest belongings. 3. Handling Luggage: o Politely ask for permission: "May I handle your luggage, please?" o Use proper lifting techniques to avoid injury. o Secure the luggage on the trolley with safety straps. 4. Transporting Luggage to the Room: o Follow hotel safety protocols: ■ Avoid blocking corridors or entrances. ■ Ensure the trolley does not collide with walls or furniture. o Engage with the guest: ■ "Allow me to take you to your room. Please follow me." o Inform them about safety measures during transit: "Please watch your step as we proceed." 5. Promoting Hotel Events and Facilities: o While end route to the room, mention ongoing events or special offers: ■ "Mr./Ms. [Last Name], we are hosting a live jazz performance at the lounge this evening starting at 7 PM. It's a wonderful way to unwind." ■ "Additionally, our rooftop bar is offering a happy hour from 5 to 7 PM." 6. Explaining Room Facilities: o Upon arrival at the room, open the door for the guest and wheel the trolley inside. o Unload and place luggage neatly in the designated area. o Provide a brief tour of the room: ■ "Here is the thermostat; you can adjust the room temperature to your preference." ■ "The minibar is stocked with beverages and snacks. The price list is located on top." ■ "This is the safety deposit box for your valuables, and here is the Wi-Fi password." o Check if the guest needs further assistance: "Is there anything else I can assist you with today?" 7. Completing the Task: o Thank the guest politely: "Thank you for staying with us. Please let me know if there's anything else you require. Enjoy your stay." o Return the trolley to its designated area. Form Used: Bellboy Luggage Handling Form Date Time Guest Name Room Number Number of Items Condition of Items (Before) Condition of Items (After) Bellboy Name Guest Signature [DD/MM/YYYY] [HH:MM AM/PM] [Guest's Full Name] [Room Number] [Quantity] [Good/Damaged] [Good/Damaged] [Your Name] This detailed scenario ensures the bellboy maintains professionalism, prioritizes guest satisfaction, and adheres to safety protocols while performing their duties.

From the two scenarios mentioned above, the following table compares the advantages of using AI in language assessment for bellboy duties, with scenarios created manually and using ChatGPT. This table highlights various aspects of both approaches.

Table 9. Comparison of two scenarios

NO	ASPECTS	USING MANUAL SCENARIO	USING CHATGPT SCENARIO
1	Consistency	Variations in means of communication and procedures.	Provide consistent and standardised responses
2	Time Efficiency	Requires time to compile and assess	Can generate scenarios and assessments quickly.
3	Personalisation	Limited to individual experience and knowledge.	Customisable to guest preferences and needs
4	Accuracy	Vulnerable to human error.	Reduce errors with trained algorithms.
5	Training and Feedbackl	Requires ongoing training for staff.	Can provide instant feedback and improvement suggestions.
6	Learning Experience	Depends on hands-on experience.	Provides interactive simulations for learning.
7	Data Analysis	Difficult to collect and analyse data.	Can analyse data in real-time to improve processes.
8	Adaptability	Difficult to adapt to changing needs.	Can be quickly updated to reflect the latest trends.
9	Interaction with Guests	Interaction may lack structure	Provide structured scripts for better interaction.
10	Service Quality Improvement	Depends on individual skills.	Can improve service quality through AI-based recommendations.

This table shows that the use of AI, such as ChatGPT, in language assessment for bellboy tasks can provide many advantages compared to manual approaches. AI not only improves efficiency and consistency, but also provides a better learning experience and more in-depth data analysis. The two role-play scenarios above can be seen that each has advantages and disadvantages, but at a glance we can conclude that the scenario setting with an emphasis on each competency element in accordance with the ASEAN Competency Standards for Tourism Professionals (ACSTP) is illustrated in the second scenario using AI, the role of AI is expected to help teachers who play the role of teachers and assessors. Thus, the qualifications needed for the required CATC implementation are easily fulfilled by teachers, as many teachers who teach in Secondary Tourism Vocational Schools will retire, the qualification of technology mastery by teachers can be easily fulfilled through AI.

FUTURE RESEARCH DIRECTION

There are several recommendations for future research in integrating vocational education oriented towards 21st century learning, AI, and human resource development with applicable competency standards both locally and globally, the recommendations are as follows:

1. Longitudinal Study on the Effectiveness of AI: Conduct a longitudinal study to evaluate the impact of using AI in English assessment on student learning outcomes in Secondary Vocational Tourism School. This study may include analysing student performance data before and after the application of AI in the learning process.
2. Development of AI-based Learning Models: Develop a learning model that integrates AI thoroughly in the curriculum, including in planning, teaching, and assessment. The research could explore how this model can be adapted for different educational contexts in Indonesia and other ASEAN countries.
3. Analysing 21st Century Skills: Examines how the use of AI in English language assessment can help students develop 21st century skills, such as critical thinking, collaboration and digital literacy. This research can provide insights into how AI can support the development of skills relevant to industry needs.
4. Comparison of Assessment Methods: Conduct a comparative study between traditional assessment methods and AI-based assessment in the context of tourism education. This research can explore the advantages and disadvantages of each method and their impact on student motivation and engagement.
5. Stakeholder Engagement: Examine the role of various stakeholders, including the tourism industry, in the development and implementation of AI-based curriculum. This research can help understand how collaboration between education and industry can improve curriculum relevance and graduate job readiness.
6. Technological Innovations in Assessment: Researching the latest technological innovations in language assessment, such as the use of big data analysis and machine learning, to improve the accuracy and efficiency of English language assessment in Secondary Vocational Tourism Schools.

By exploring this research area, it is expected to make a significant contribution to the development of tourism education in Indonesia and improve the quality of human resources who are ready to compete in the global market.

CONCLUSION

The use of artificial intelligence (AI) in English language assessment at Secondary Vocational Tourism Schools in Indonesia shows significant potential to improve the learning and assessment process. AI not only assists teachers in teaching and helps devise more consistent and efficient assessment scenarios, but also provides quick and accurate feedback to students. By integrating AI into the curriculum, particularly in the context of the Common ASEAN Tourism Curriculum (CATC), tourism education in Indonesia can be more responsive to industry needs and international standards. Although there are challenges in implementation, such as teacher training and limited resources, the use of AI can be an innovative solution to improve the quality of employable graduates in the tourism sector.

REFERENCES

Abdul Waris & Reza Aprianti. (2023). Implementation of English Curriculum in Common ASEAN Tourism Curriculum (CATC) in Tourism Vocational Schools in Indonesia. *English Education International Conference (EEIC).* Aceh. Retrieved from https://jurnal.usk.ac.id/EEIC/article/view/36814

ABEYWICKRAMA. H. D. (2018). *LANGUAGE ASSESSMENT PRINCIPLES AND CLASSROOM PRACTICES.* New York: Pearson.

Aditomo, A. (2024). *CAPAIAN PEMBELAJARAN PENDIDIKAN ANAK USIA DINI, JENJANG PENDIDIKAN DASAR, JENJANG PENDIDIKAN MENENGAH, PADA KURIKULUM MERDEKA (LEARNING OUTCOMES IN EARLY CHILDHOOD EDUCATION, PRIMARY EDUCATION, AND SECONDARY EDUCATION, IN THE INDEPENDENT CURRICULUM).* KemenRisTekDikti.

Arie Wibowo Khurniawan, A. P. (2024). *PEMANFAATAN GEN-AI DALAM PEMBELAJARAN KEJURUAN BAGI GURU SMK BIDANG BISNIS DAN PARIWISATA (THE UTILISATION OF GEN-AI IN VOCATIONAL LEARNING FOR SMK TEACHERS IN THE FIELD OF BUSINESS AND TOURISM).* Balai Besar Pengembangan Penjaminan Mutu Pendidikan Vokasi (BBPPMPV) Bisnis Dan Pariwisata Kementerian Pendidikan Dasar dan Menengah, Depok.

Bianco, J. L. (2013). Innovation in Language Policy and Planning: Ties to English Language Education. In Wong, K. H. (Ed.), *INNOVATION AND CHANGE IN ENGLISH LANGUAGE EDUCATION* (pp. 139–154). Routledge.

Boahin, P. (2018). COMPETENCY-BASED CURRICULUM: A FRAMEWORK FOR BRIDGING THE GAP IN TEACHING, ASSESSMENT AND THE WORLD OF WORK. *International Journal of Vocational and Technical Education Research*, 24-37.

Brown, H. D. (2004). *Language assessment: Principle and classroom practices. NewYork: Pearson.* Pearson Education.

Chen, A. Y. Z. (2024). A systematic review and meta-analysis of AI-enabled assessment in language learning: Design, implementation, and effectiveness. *Journal of Computer Assisted Learning (JCAL).* https://doi.org/https://doi.org/10.1111/jcal.13064

Crosbie, W., Hickman, A., Danang, E., & Maguire, A. (2012). *Assesor Manual_Converse in English at a basic operational level.* William Angliss Institute of TAFE.

Davison, C. (2013). INNOVATION IN ASSESSMENT: COMMON MISCONCEPTIONS AND PROBLEMS. In Wong, K. H. (Ed.), *INNOVATION AND CHANGE IN ENGLISH LANGUAGE EDUCATION* (pp. 263–277). Roudletge.

Gardinier, K. A.-L. (2021). Introduction contextualising global flows of competency-based education: Polysemy, hybridity and silences. *Comparative Education*, •••, 1–18.

KepMenParEkraf. (2023, June 20). *BN.2022/No.172,* jdih.kemenparekraf.go.id*: 7 hlm.* Retrieved from jdih.kemenparekraf.go.id/katalog-889-produk-hukum: BN.2022/No.172, jdih.kemenparekraf.go.id: 7 hlm.

Nguyen, D. N. (2025). Artificial intelligence-based assessment in ELT exam creation: a case study of Van Lang University lecturers. *Saudi Journal of Language Studies, Vol. 5 No. 1*(Emerald Publishing Limited), 34-49. https://doi.org/https://doi.org/10.1108/SJLS-06-2024-0030

Nguyen, T. (2025). AI in Language Assessment: Innovations and Challenges. *International Journal of Language Education, 12(1), 22-35, 12*(1), 22-35.

R. Nikolov, E. S. (2014). *COMPETENCE BASED FRAMEWORK FOR CURRICULUM DEVELOPMENT.* Sofia: Za bukvite, O'pismeneh.

Nykyporets, Bohdan Kutsyk & Svitlana. (2024). THE IMPACT OF ARTIFICIAL INTELLIGENCE ON LANGUAGE LEARNING. https://doi.org/DOI: 10.13140/RG.2.2.30485.33767

O'Sullivan, B. (2021). *BRITISH COUNCIL PERSPECTIVES ON ENGLISH LANGUAGE POLICY AND EDUCATION The Comprehensive Learning System.* British Council.

OECD. (2018). The Future of Education and Skills [oecd.org.]. *Education*, •••, 2030.

Secretariat, A. (2018). *Guidelines ASEAN MRA-TP Trainers and Assessors.* ASEAN: A Community of Oppurtunities.

Secretariat, T. A. (2018). Handbook of ASEAN Mutual Recognition Arrangement on Tourism Professionals. Jakarta: ASEAN: A Community of Opportunities.

Secretariat, T. G. (2022, january). https://asean.org. Retrieved 10 22, 2022, from https://asean.org: https://asean.org/wp-content/uploads/2022/08/2022-01-17_Final-draft_RPL-mechanism-for-ATP.pdf

Secretary, A. (2021). *asean.org.* Retrieved from https://asean.org/wp-content/uploads/2021/01/Common-ASEAN-Tourism-Curriculum.pdf

SIREP. (2010). *Teaching Competency Standards in Southeast Asian Countries: ELEVEN COUNTRY AUDIT.* Philippine: SEAMEO INNOTECH.

Smith, J., & Lee, K. A. I. (2022). AI in Language Assessment: Enhancing Validity and Efficiency. *Journal of Educational Technology*, *18*(2), 145–160.

Tim. (2016). *Membangun Pendidikan Menengah Kejuruan Indonesia: Sebuah Peta Jalan Menuju 2030 (Building Indonesian Vocational Secondary Education: A Roadmap to 2030).* The Deutsche Gesellschaft für Internationale Zusammenarbeit (GIZ) GmbH.

(UIL), T. U. (2021). *Curriculum GlobALE Competency Framework for Adults Educators for Adult.* Hamburg: DVV International, German Institute Lifelong Learning, International Council for Adult Education and UNESCO Institute for Lifelong Learning.

UNESCO. (2020). *Education and the COVID-19 pandemic: A global perspective.* https://www.unesco.org/en/covid-19/education-response

WEF. (2020). *he Future of Jobs Report 2020.* World Economic Forum.

Yogi Anggraena, D. G. (2022). *Panduan Pembelajaran dan Asesmen Pendidikan Anak Usia Dini, Pendidikan Dasar, dan Menengah (Guidelines for Learning and Assessment in Early Childhood, Primary and Secondary Education).* Badan Standar, Kurikulum, dan Asesmen Pendidikan, Kementerian Pendidikan, Kebudayaan, Riset, dan Teknologi.

APPENDIX I

Observation Checklist

Table 10. Observation checklist

Student name			
Assessor name			
Location/venue			
Unit of competency	CONVERSE IN ENGLISH AT A BASIC OPERATIONAL LEVEL D1.LAN.CL10.01		
Dates of observation			
Instructions	1. Over a period of time observe the student completing each of the following tasks: a) Participate in simple conversations on familiar topics with work colleagues b) Respond to simple verbal instructions or requests c) Make simple requests d) Express likes, dislikes and preferences		
Did the candidate		Yes	No
Element 1: Participate in simple conversations on familiar topics with work colleagues			
Use and respond appropriately to opening comments			
Comment on familiar topics			
Talk about a past event			
Use closing remarks appropriately to end the conversation			
Element 2: Respond to simple verbal instructions or requests			
Confirm understanding of supervisor's instructions or requests			
Request repetition or clarification of instructions or requests			
Element 3: Make simple requests			
Use polite forms to make simple requests			
Thank the person responding to your request			
Acknowledge the person who cannot respond to your request			
Element 4: Describe routine procedures			
Explain a sequence of events in carrying out a routine job			
Describe exceptions to routine procedures			
Make suggestions on how to improve routine procedures			
Element 5: Express likes, dislikes and preferences			
Talk about likes and dislikes of familiar topics and situations			
Discuss preferences and give reasons			

continued on following page

Table 10. Continued

Student name			
Element 6: Identify different forms of expression in English			
Construct a formal sentence			
Identify indicators of informal expressions in English			
Differentiate between ‘open-ended’ and ‘closed’ questions			
Did the student’s overall performance meet the standard?			
Feedback to student and trainer/assessor			
Strengths:			
Improvements needed:			
General comments:			
Candidate signature		Date	
Assessor signature		Date	

APPENDIX II

Table 11. Oral questions

Student name	
Assessor name	
Location/venue	
Unit of competency	CONVERSE IN ENGLISH AT A BASIC OPERATIONAL LEVEL D1.LAN.CL10.01
Instructions	1. Ask student questions from the attached list to confirm knowledge, as necessary 2. Place tick in boxes to reflect student achievement (Pass Competent 'PC' or Not Yet Competent 'NYC') 3. Write short-form student answer in the space provided for each question.

Questions	Response	
	PC	NYC
1. Give me two examples of an opening comment, statement or question you might use to start a conversation with a work colleague.		
2. Comment on today's weather.		
3. Identify a past event you have experienced and make a comment about that event.		
4. Give me an example of remarks you might use to end a conversation with a work colleague.		
5. How might you confirm understanding of a direction or instruction given to you by a supervisor?		
6. Your supervisor has asked you to perform a workplace task but you did not fully understand the instructions given to you. How will you seek clarification of this direction/request?		
7. Give me an example of how you would politely ask a work colleague to assist you with a task.		
8. A colleague has passed on important workplace information to you. How might you thank him/her for this?		
9. What would you say to a colleague you have asked for assistance but who is unable to help you?		
10. Identify a common workplace task and explain the sequence of events involved in completing that task.		
11. Using the task identified in the previous question give me an example of when there may be a need to make an exception to 'normal routine', and tell me what those differences may be.		
12. You believe you have identified an easier or better way to complete a routine workplace task. How will you pass this suggestion on to management?		
13. Tell me about food you like and dislike. What are those foods and why do you like or dislike them?		
14. What type of job would you like to have and why?		
15. Give me an example of a sentence using the word 'would' and a sentence using the word 'could'.		
16. Identify two informal English expressions and explain what they mean when used in conversation.		
17. What is the difference between an 'open' question and a 'closed' question? Give me an example of each.		

APPENDIX III

Written Questions

CONVERSE IN ENGLISH AT A BASIC OPERATIONAL LEVEL – D1.LAN.CL10.01

Student Name: ____ __________

Answer all the following questions and submit to your Trainer.

1. What are the functions of opening statements?
2. Give two examples of opening statements.
   a)
   b)
3. What is the meaning of the diagrams below?

Figure 1. Diagram

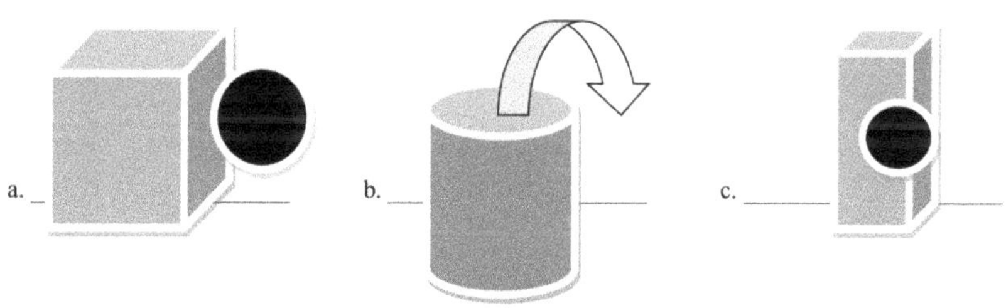

4. What are the three steps to follow when you receive a customer complaint?
   a)
   b)
   c)
5. Conjugate the following verbs into the simple past tense and give example sentences for each.
   a. (see)
   b. (go)
6. Why are closing remarks an important part of a conversation?
7. How can you confirm that you understand your supervisor's instructions?

8. Answer 'True' or 'False' to the following statement: *You should never ask a supervisor to repeat his instructions.*

   True

   False

9. Review the following requests and write down the appropriate method of asking for it.

   a. You want to ask your boss for a day off

   Request:

b. You want to ask your friend for some money

   Request:

10. Answer 'True' or 'False' to the following statement: *There are degrees of politeness in English that are determined by the situation and the type of request.*

    True

    False

11. Write down two different ways to say 'Thank You' in English.

    a)
    b)

12. Answer 'True' or 'False' to the following statement: If a customer doesn't speak my language or English, I should just ignore him/her.

    True

    False

13. Read the following instructions and put the tasks in order.

To make a ham and cheese sandwich:

_____ Then put the slices of ham on the bread.
_____ First, spread mustard or mayonnaise on the bread.
_____ Finally, eat your sandwich.
_____ Next, put the cheese on top.
_____ After that, put the two halves together.

14. Describe your typical day at work using at least three adverbs of frequency.
15. Make formal suggestions to solve the following problems.
    a. (it's very hot in the office)
    b. (the lunch break is too short)
16. Write about three different things you like or dislike using **different expressions**.
17. Answer 'True' or 'False' to the following statement: *When I state my preferences, it's not necessary to give reasons to support them.*

True

False

18. Read the questions below and change them from informal to formal.
    a. (Can I have your name?)
    b. (What do you want to eat?)
19. When is using informal expression appropriate?
20. Write two open-ended and two closed questions.

Open-ended:

a)
b)

Closed:

a)
b)

Chapter 8

Cultural Bias and Linguistic Representation in AI Curriculum Design:
Implications for Society 5.0

Nurhayati Usman
https://orcid.org/0009-0007-9132-2791
IAIN Palooo, Indonesia

Afdhal Kusumanegara
Universitas Islam Negeri Sultan Syarif Kasim Riau, Indonesia

Husnaini Husnaini
IAIN Palopo, Indonesia

Yuyun Ruqiyyat Said
IAIN Palopo, Indonesia

Devi Ismayanti
IAIN Palopo, Indonesia

ABSTRACT

AI curriculum design influences future technologies and society. This study explores cultural bias and linguistic representation in AI curriculum design and its effects on Society 5.0, a human-centered, technologically advanced society. It emphasizes the ethical and practical issues of cultural and language diversity in AI systems and the goals of inclusive and equitable AI education. Cultural bias in AI is linked to biased datasets and developer attitudes, supported by real-world case studies of their social implications. Examining language representation addresses the

DOI: 10.4018/979-8-3373-1062-6.ch008

Copyright © 2026, IGI Global Scientific Publishing. Copying or distributing in print or electronic forms without written permission of IGI Global Scientific Publishing is prohibited.

exclusion of low-resource languages from AI courses and offers remedies. Society 5.0 aligns inclusive AI education with social goals, ethics, and laws. Finally, the report advises curriculum designers, legislators, and academics on culturally and linguistically inclusive AI projects. This paper addresses these difficulties to enable equitable AI education in Society 5.0.

INTRODUCTION

Background and Context

Definition of Society 5.0 and its Vision

Japan's sophisticated, human-centered Society 5.0 integrates internet and physical space to produce a more sustainable, efficient, and egalitarian society (Sony & Karingada, 2024; Reich & Dukes, 2024). It imagines AI, IoT, big data, and robotics collaborating to improve human well-being. This concept uses innovative technology to improve quality of life for all to address global issues like aging populations, environmental issues, and social inequality. Society 5.0 aims to serve its citizens by integrating the digital and physical worlds.

Role of AI in Shaping Societal Evolution

Society 5.0 relies on AI to automate processes, improve decision-making, and improve human lives through predictive analytics, machine learning, and personalized services (Weng et al., 2024; Gao & Feng, 2023). AI can improve healthcare, education, transportation, and urban development to meet social requirements. AI brings ethical, data privacy, and social divide concerns. Addressing these concerns while guaranteeing equitable access and beneficial outcomes for all is essential to integrating AI into Society 5.0. Innovative and inclusive algorithms and systems can impact future social norms and interactions with AI. (Tomašev et al., 2022; Schwartz, 2022).

Problem Statement

Existing cultural biases in AI curriculum design

Due to AI's expanding importance in many areas, an inclusive and fair AI curriculum is needed (Michaeli et al., 2023; Wang & Lester, 2023). Existing AI curriculum seldom overcome cultural bias. These biases result from training materials, databases, and educational frameworks over-representing dominant cultural norms and values (Chinta et al., 2024; Bura & Myakala, 2024). AI coursework often ignores non-Western civilisations. The inaccessibility hinders student learning and perpetuates prejudice un AI systems they design.

AI NLP technologies rely largely on English and a few other dominant languages, under-representing or misrepresenting culturally significant expressions and circumstances from low-resource languages (Wali et al., 2023; Ranathunga, 2023). AI education case studies and datasets can perpetuate stereotypes and overlook minority needs (Chan et al., 2021). This gap between AI curriculum design and cultural variety undermines Society 5.0's human-centered values by making systems unsuited to serve global people fairly.

Impacts of Linguistic Representation on Marginalized Communities

Linguistic representation is another important bias factor that AI curriculum designers miss. Most AI systems prioritise high-resource languages like English, French, and Chinese over low-resource or indigenous languages (Helm et al., 2023). This linguistic gap hinders marginalised people' AI access and worsens digital inequality.

Language diversity is rarely prioritised in AI courses, and students rarely experience the challenges of designing systems for under-represented languages. This omission hinders innovation in AI technologies for multilingual and multicultural cultures (Godwin-Jones, 2024). AI systems may cause marginalised communities to adopt dominant languages, leading to the demise of their native tongues (Godwin-Jones, 2024; Ta & Lee, 2023).

These linked issues highlight the necessity for comprehensive and inclusive AI curriculum design (Wang & Lester, 2023). Addressing cultural prejudices and language under-representation will help educators and policymakers prepare students to design AI systems that support Society 5.0's human-centered aims, creating a more fair and inclusive technological future.

Objectives of the Chapter

Examining the Presence and Implications of Cultural Bias in AI Curricula

Examine AI curriculum cultural biases. Cultural bias occurs when particular cultural norms, values, and viewpoints dominate AI education materials, techniques, and methodologies (Chinta et al., 2024). Western-centric approaches ignore AI systems' societal foundations, causing these biases (Chinta et al., 2024; Ferrara, 2023). The chapter critically examines how these biases affect education using training datasets, case studies, and algorithms. The chapter examines how prejudices affect students and society beyond identification. Culturally biassed curriculum hinders AI students' and practitioners' ethical and practical knowledge of inclusive AI systems. Limits in technology can promote injustice, inequality, and systematic exclusion. Culturally biassed AI systems may worsen inequality in healthcare, education, and law enforcement. The chapter covers these issues to provide balanced and culturally appropriate AI education.

Exploring the Relationship Between Linguistic Diversity and AI Inclusivity

Linguistic diversity and AI inclusion are crucial to the second goal. AI systems' linguistic representation reflects societal inclusion, since language conveys cultural identity and expression (Helm et al., 2023; Ożegalska-Łukasik & Łukasik, 2023). Language diversity is typically overlooked in current AI programs, which prioritize high-resource languages like English and ignore the difficulties of designing systems for low-resource or endangered languages. This chapter examines how AI education omissions marginalize linguistically diverse communities. The chapter discusses how insufficient linguistic representation in AI systems reduces accessibility for underrepresented languages and erodes linguistic diversity. Speech recognition and machine translation techniques often misread indigenous and minority languages, resulting in exclusion.

UNDERSTANDING CULTURAL BIAS IN AI SYSTEMS

Defining Cultural Bias in AI

Explanation of Bias in Machine Learning and AI

Bias in AI and ML systems is caused by pre-existing preconceptions, prejudices, or skewed data, resulting in systematic inaccuracies in output (Mikołajczyk-Bareła & Grochowski, 2023; Ferrara, 2023). In AI, bias occurs when some factors disproportionately impact model predictions or classifications, resulting in unfair or erroneous outcomes (Chen et al., 2023; Mikołajczyk-Bareła & Grochowski, 2023; Ferrara, 2023). Racial, gender, age, and cultural bias might result from the data used to train the model, algorithm design, or lack of diverse representation in the development process.

Machine learning trains AI systems to spot patterns and make judgments on vast datasets. These datasets typically represent societal structures and historical inequalities (Chen, 2023; Nazer et al., 2023; Mihalcea, 2024). The model will reflect imbalances in a training dataset that lacks diversity or is weighted toward a particular population (Arora et al., 2023). For instance, facial recognition algorithms trained on photographs of specific ethnic groups would perform poorly when charged with identifying people from other groups, reinforcing biases against underrepresented communities.

Cultural bias in AI refers to how cultural norms, practices, and values affect AI systems (Ge et al., 2024; Qadri, 2023; Chen, 2023). When AI models are used in various global contexts, inherent cultural biases might have serious effects. An AI system designed in a Western, individualistic society may fail to account for collectivist countries' shared ideals and customs, misinterpreting behaviour or judging decision-making. These culturally biased algorithms can worsen inequities and produce new kinds of exclusion as AI technologies spread worldwide (Chen, 2023; Yam et al., 2023).

Examples of Cultural Bias in AI Systems

A number of high-profile AI system cases have shown the real-world effects of cultural representation neglect (Tao et al., 2024; Peters & Carman, 2024). Racial prejudice in facial recognition is a notable example. Many facial recognition algorithms perform poorly on Black and Asian persons. The National Institute of Standards and Technology (NIST) found in 2019 that commercial facial recognition algorithms misread darker-skinned faces more often than lighter-skinned faces. Training these systems on datasets of lighter-skinned, white people causes this bias, resulting in worse accuracy for people of different ethnicities.

For instance, AI-driven recruiting algorithms are biased. Companies are using AI to streamline recruitment (Nazer et al., 2023). These technologies may promote gender and ethnic biases, according to many investigations. An AI system trained on resumes from a largely male workforce may underrepresent women and ethnic minorities by prioritizing male-dominated industry features and language (Zhou et al., 2024). This biases employment decisions against specific groups based on historical disparities rather than candidate qualifications or potential.

In healthcare, AI cultural prejudices can harm patients. For instance, AI can forecast medical risks and diagnose diseases. AI models trained on data from affluent, largely white populations may miss or misinterpret symptoms in people from diverse ethnic or cultural backgrounds (Abràmoff et al., 2023; Pfohl et al.,

2024). AI systems educated with inadequate data on non-white populations may miss subtle disease symptoms that present differently in various groups, leading to misdiagnosis or delayed treatment.

Language-based AI systems can also exhibit cultural bias in NLP tasks (Pfohl et al., 2024; Abràmoff, 2023). Languages and dialects not included in global datasets can challenge automatic translation techniques and virtual assistants. Idioms, humor, and cultural references prevalent in certain languages or places may be misinterpreted by systems (Godwin-Jones, 2024; Bella et al., 2023). A translation tool may misinterpret a culturally unique term, reducing the AI system's accuracy and usefulness for non-Western users.

These instances demonstrate the need for AI systems that grasp cultural diversity and representation better. To reduce cultural prejudice, AI developers must diversity their training data and guarantee that their development teams are diverse (Mihalcea et al., 2024; Ge, 2024). This method can help design inclusive, accurate, and fair AI systems that serve a worldwide audience without promoting negative cultural preconceptions or exclusions.

Sources of Cultural Bias

Data Collection and Representation Issues

Training and development data for AI systems is a major source of cultural bias. AI models use vast datasets to find trends and predict. However, the accuracy and fairness of these systems depend on the quality and diversity of these datasets (Chen et al., 2023; Hanson, 2023). When data collection techniques ignore cultural diversity or favor specific demographics, the resulting datasets can reinforce cultural prejudices (De Russis et al., 2023; Mittal, 2024).

Labeling and categorizing data can also cause bias. Human annotators labeling data may make subjective classifications due to their cultural viewpoints and assumptions (Ousidhoum et al., 2024; Gross, 2023;). Annotators from different cultures may interpret emotions, behaviors, and actions differently, resulting in inconsistent or biased labels. The AI system learns to recreate labeled data patterns by inheriting these biases (Chen et al., 2023; Ferrara, 2023).

Furthermore, data collection methods often fail to capture all human experiences. Urban, digitally connected populations are often surveyed, online, or sensor data, excluding rural or marginalized communities. This biases AI systems toward the cultural, economic, and social reality of the data's most represented groups, leaving others neglected or misrepresented.

Developer Perspectives and Cultural Blind Spots

The perspectives and cultural backgrounds of AI developers themselves significantly influence the design and functionality of AI systems. Developers, like all humans, are shaped by their own cultural experiences, values, and assumptions (Hulley, 2013; Mihalcea et al., 2024). When development teams lack diversity, the resulting AI systems are more likely to reflect the biases and blind spots of the developers.

For example, AI developers from predominantly Western, individualistic cultures may unconsciously embed cultural norms that prioritize individual autonomy over communal values. This can lead to AI systems that perform well in Western contexts but fail to align with the norms of collectivist cultures, where decision-making and resource-sharing are more community-oriented (Prabhakaran et al., 2022; Wong, 2020). Similarly, developers may overlook the significance of culturally specific elements such as language structure, traditional practices, or local norms when designing AI systems, resulting in tools that fail to resonate with users from different cultural backgrounds (Prabhakaran et al., 2022; hÉigeartaigh et al., 2020).

Cultural blind spots can also manifest in the ethical frameworks adopted by AI developers. Ethical principles such as fairness, accountability, and transparency are often defined within the context of the developers' own cultural understanding (hÉigeartaigh et al., 2020; Prabhakaran et al., 2022; Tidjon & Khomh, 2022). For instance, a fairness metric in one culture might emphasize individual equality, while in another culture, it might focus on equitable outcomes for a community (Anahideh et al., 2021; Garg et al., 2020). Developers who are unaware of these differences risk creating systems that impose culturally inappropriate values on users from other regions.

The lack of representation within AI development teams exacerbates these issues. Women, ethnic minorities, and individuals from the Global South are often underrepresented in the technology sector, particularly in AI research and development (Chan et al., 2021; Roche et al., 2021; Prabhakaran et al., 2022). This homogeneity limits the range of perspectives brought into the design process, reinforcing existing biases and narrowing the system's applicability across diverse cultural contexts (Chan et al., 2021; Matsiko & Nelson, 2023).

LINGUISTIC REPRESENTATION IN AI CURRICULA

AI Curriculum Design: Current Practices

Overview of Prevalent AI Curricula Worldwide

Academic institutions, research groups, and industrial needs shape AI courses (Langley, 2019; Michaeli et al., 2023). AI programs worldwide cover computer science, machine learning, neural networks, data science, and NLP fundamentals (Langley, 2019; Maslej et al., 2024). These programmes teach students AI technology ethics, politics, and societal ramifications while teaching technical skills.

Many top AI programs in North America, Europe, and East Asia stress algorithmic development, data structures, and machine learning models, with a particular concentration on English-language resources. Key courses address supervised and unsupervised learning, deep learning, computer vision, robotics, and NLP. As the global language of technology and science, English dominates these programs' instruction.

Global AI research has led to a shared understanding of AI development best practices, yet English-language materials heavily impact curricula in many countries. Research papers, textbooks, and open-source AI tools—mostly in English—form educational content. AI instructors must often teach these resources without adapting them for linguistic variety (Elstad, 2024; Woo & Choi, 2021).

Some universities, especially in non-English-speaking regions, have introduced AI programs that reflect local linguistic and cultural contexts to solve this issue (Littell et al., 2018; Bella, 2023). Latin America, Africa, and Southeast Asia universities are adding region-specific data and linguistic resources to their AI programs. This includes including local languages in NLP datasets or addressing region-specific AI ethical issues like facial recognition fairness or data privacy issues related to local customs and regulations.

Analysis of Linguistic Inclusivity in the Curriculum

Linguistic variety in AI education is low, although several curricula are recognizing the need for inclusivity. Despite the importance of linguistic variety in NLP, most curricula still emphasize English-centric tools and models (Khanuja, 2022; Godwin-Jones, 2024; Bhatt et al., 2022). Most AI programs use English-language data, from training sets to evaluation benchmarks, overshadowing languages like

Hindi, Swahili, and indigenous languages, which are spoken by large populations but underrepresented in AI research and application.

Lack of linguistic inclusion in AI courses affects AI technology development and societal repercussions (Awino et al., 2022; Wali, 2023). The lack of language diversity in training data is a major issue. This gap biases AI systems, making it harder for them to understand, analyze, and synthesize non-English languages (Bella et al., 2023; Joshi, 2020). AI systems are often ineffective for minority language users, limiting access and opportunity.

Language's sociocultural background is also neglected in curriculum design. Language is intimately rooted in society, identity, and worldview (Shahini et al., 2019; Hub, 2022). Without addressing language, culture, and technology, students cannot create AI systems that are truly inclusive and sensitive to various populations (Prabhakaran et al., 2022; Tena-Meza, 2021). AI education risks creating culturally biased systems that reinforce inequities and the digital divide by ignoring language and cultural diversity.

AI courses' focus on English ignores multilingualism's potential to make AI more global (Prabhakaran et al., 2022; Bella, 2023) The global deployment of AI technology requires multilingual systems (Godwin-Jones, 2024). AI education should be more equitable and accessible with a more inclusive language framework, encouraging students to imagine how AI could help diverse populations. Current AI curriculum emphasises technical capabilities, but linguistic inclusion is difficult. AI education must encompass diverse languages. By including different languages and cultures, AI programs can help students create fair, equitable, and global-responsive technology.

Challenges in Linguistic Representation

Lack of Resources for Low-Resource Languages

The lack of high-quality resources for low-resource languages makes AI linguistic representation difficult (Joshi et al., 2020; Hedderich, 2021). Low-resource languages lack digital and linguistic datasets needed for AI training and are rarely spoken or studied (Ranathunga & Silva, 2022; Hedderich et al., 2021). Many indigenous, regional, and minority languages lack written texts, voice data, and linguistic annotations, unlike English, Chinese, and Spanish. This data gap hinders AI systems' capacity to absorb, understand, and develop these languages.

In natural language processing (NLP), AI models learn linguistic patterns, grammar, and semantics from massive datasets (Ta & Lee, 2023; Godwin-Jones, 2024). Most training data comes from a tiny fraction of the world's languages, leaving thousands of others unrepresented. Low-resource languages frequently have minimal datasets, often based on regional dialects or casual speech, making it challenging to create robust, accurate AI models (Wang, 2024; Wang, 2023). The lack of multilingual resources like language corpora, translation tools, and multilingual language models to accommodate language structures and subtleties exacerbates this issue.

AI models trained on high-resource languages may perform poorly in low-resource languages, resulting in misinterpretations and mistakes (Beukman & Fokam, 2023; Li et al., 2021). The lack of low-resource language support can make it difficult for speakers of these languages to use AI applications to diagnose or translate health information (Helm et al., 2023; Joshi et al., 2019). The digital divide in AI development grows, exacerbating inequities and hurting low-resource language communities.

Impact of Monolingual AI Systems on Multilingual Societies

Monolingual AI systems—those taught and optimized for a single language—have made multilingual societies' issues worse (Bella, 2023; Prabhakaran, 2022). Monolingual AI systems work effectively in environments where users speak the same language as the system, but they fail to account for multilingual societies' complicated linguistic landscapes (Bella et al., 2023; Ta & Lee, 2023). India, South Africa, and Indonesia have many official languages and regional dialects with distinct cultural, linguistic, and syntactic frameworks.

Failure to develop AI systems that understand and generate various languages hinders their efficacy in multilingual cultures (Ta & Lee, 2023; Bella et al., 2023). Even though Hindi, Zulu, and Javanese are widely spoken in their regions, an AI system trained purely on English may not be able to recognize or process user input in these languages. This limitation can lead to bad user experience and exclusion for non-English speakers (Liebling et al., 2020; Esch et al., 2019), worsening the digital divide between monolingual and multilingual populations.

Monolingual AI systems struggle with content creation, real-time translation, and cross-cultural communication (Bella et al., 2023; Nicholas & Bhatia, 2023). Machine translation methods that only support a few major languages often miss linguistic diversity, leading to errors, misunderstandings, and cultural context loss. International business, cross-border education, and diplomatic relations require accurate communication, making AI systems difficult. Monolingual AI reduces digital linguistic diversity. AI systems that favour English marginalise non-English speakers online (Lepp & Sarin, 2024; Ta & Lee, 2023). This trend can erode multilingual cultures' cultural and linguistic identities, causing language dominance and legacy loss.

IMPLICATIONS FOR SOCIETY 5.0

AI Education and Society 5.0 Goals

Connection Between AI Literacy and the Vision of Society 5.0

AI literacy involves comprehending AI technologies, their ramifications, and their real-world applications (Long & Magerko, 2020; Tadimalla & Maher, 2024). As AI becomes more integrated into numerous sectors, AI literacy is crucial for humans to actively shape Society 5.0 (Ben-Ishai et al., 2024). AI literacy in education includes both technical knowledge of AI systems and the ability to critically evaluate their ethical, social, and cultural impacts.

In Society 5.0, people will need a core understanding of AI to make informed decisions, participate in ethical discussions, and responsibly employ AI (Khan et al., 2022; Kelley et al., 2021). As society moves from knowledge-based to AI-driven, people must be able to understand the risks and benefits of AI technologies and how they may affect social structures, economic systems, and cultural dynamics. Society can ensure that its citizens are active participants in AI technology development and governance by including AI literacy into all school curricula.

AI literacy in Society 5.0 can also bridge the digital divide and ensure that various groups are not left behind in the AI. AI education will help people navigate the digital world, promoting social inclusion and lowering inequality. In nations where education and technology have historically been unequal and modern technologies threaten further marginalization, this is crucial.

Role of Culturally and Linguistically Inclusive AI in Societal Transformation

To ensure equal access to AI systems in varied cultural and linguistic contexts, AI curriculum must consider cultural biases and linguistic representations (Prabhakaran et al., 2022; Kazimzade et al., 2019). In Society 5.0, culturally and linguistically inclusive AI must serve various people and contribute to societal transformation (Vinuesa et al., 2020; Palomares, 2021). AI systems that ignore cultural and linguistic distinctions may perpetuate inequalities and biases that hurt underprivileged communities.

For instance, AI systems educated on data sets that largely reflect one culture or language may misread language, perform poorly in non-dominant languages, or fail to represent multiple cultural views. AI curricula must include culturally and linguistically inclusive development and implementation methodologies to combat these biases (Bella et al., 2023; Prabhakaran et al., 2022; Zowghi & Rimini, 2023).

This includes training AI practitioners to identify and correct cultural and language biases in data, making AI models flexible and adaptable to varied cultural contexts, and including multiple perspectives in the development process.

Beyond technology development, culturally and linguistically inclusive AI is crucial. It also affects how society views and interacts with AI (Prabhakaran et al., 2022; Shams, 2023). By emphasizing cultural diversity in AI education, society can foster a more nuanced understanding of AI's capabilities and limitations, promoting a sense of shared responsibility for ensuring that AI serves the collective good fairly and equitably. AI education can assist shape Society 5.0 values, ensuring that technology promotes social cohesiveness and inclusivity.

Finally, AI literacy is essential for Society 5.0's inclusive, sustainable, and socially responsible society. Culturally and linguistically inclusive AI ensures equitable AI transformation that meets the requirements of all groups and promotes a more inclusive global society. As we advance toward this future, AI courses will shape AI's impact on society.

Social Impacts of Bias in AI

Discrimination and Inequality in AI-Powered Systems

AI-powered systems are often regarded objective and impartial, however they can reinforce social biases (Ferrara, 2023; Pessach & Shmueli, 2020). Data used to train AI models, decision-making algorithms, and AI technology implementation across sectors can all introduce biases (Ferrara, 2023; Leavy et al., 2020). When AI systems are trained on historical data, they can learn and replicate the biases in that data, resulting in discriminatory outcomes that disadvantage certain groups.

Biassed data may cause AI hiring algorithms to favor some ethnic or gender groupings over others. AI-driven predictive police technologies and risk assessment algorithms in the criminal justice system target ethnic minorities, perpetuating existing law enforcement inequities (Selbst, 2017; Purves, 2022). Biased data in AI healthcare systems may lead to unequal access to care or misdiagnoses for specific demographic groups (Pesapane et al., 2018; Panch, 2019; Hoffman, 2023). AI systems with these biases reinforce social inequality and develop new types of prejudice that are harder to identify and correct.

AI-driven discrimination is worrisome in Society 5.0. Society 5.0 seeks to establish a harmonious, inclusive society that maximizes the potential of all people (Cheng et al., 2021; Bengio, 2024). AI systems that perpetuate discrimination may worsen power imbalances and social divisions, damaging Society 5.0. To positively impact society (Palomares et al., 2021; Suri, 2024), AI must be designed and used to actively address and eliminate prejudices and distribute its advantages evenly across all populations.

Challenges for Marginalized Groups in Accessing Fair AI Outcomes

Marginalised groups struggle to access fair AI outputs due to AI system biases (Shams et al., 2023; Ferrara, 2023). Racial and ethnic minorities, women, disabled people, and low-income people are commonly included. Marginalised groups may be further disadvantaged by algorithms (Trewin, 2018; Trewin et al., 2019) that ignore their demands and experiences as AI grows more widespread in public and private sector services.

The absence of representation in AI model training data is a serious issue. AI systems may not perform well for certain racial, linguistic, and socioeconomic groups if the data sets used are not varied and representative (Ferrara, 2023; Shams et al., 2023; Arora, 2023). Voice recognition systems trained on native English speakers may misread or exclude non-native accents or speech patterns. Facial recognition technologies trained on primarily white datasets may not distinguish people of various races (Cavazos et al., 2019; Krishnapriya et al., 2019), leading to inaccurate identification and greater surveillance of vulnerable communities.

Marginalised communities may also confront structural impediments to AI-powered healthcare diagnoses, financial services, and education (Panch et al., 2019; Obermeyer, 2019). Due to past discrepancies in financial data, AI algorithms employed in credit scoring or loan approvals may prejudice low-income or racial minority populations (Morse & Pence, 2020; Panch et al., 2019). AI-driven diagnostic systems may miss key health issues that disproportionately afflict particular demographic groups, resulting in lower health outcomes.

These differences make inclusive AI systems that stress fairness and equity necessary. In Society 5.0, where technology is predicted to improve everyone's lives (Silcox et al., 2024; Park et al., 2021), marginalized people must not be left behind. AI systems must be built and implemented with broad community input to reflect a wide range of experiences and demands (Shams et al., 2023; Hossain & Ahmed, 2021). Policies and regulations must also ensure that AI technologies are transparent, accountable, and evaluated to discover and eliminate biases.

Cultural and Linguistic Inclusivity as a Strength

Benefits of Culturally Aware AI for Global Development

Culturally aware AI systems are designed to respect and understand the unique values, practices, and demands of other cultures (Prabhakaran et al., 2022; Ożegalska-Łukasik & Łukasik, 2023). AI technology built with cultural awareness can boost global development in numerous ways. Culturally sensitive AI can improve healthcare, education, and agriculture solutions. In global healthcare systems, AI solutions that account for cultural differences in health attitudes and behaviors can improve diagnosis and treatment outcomes (Guo & Li, 2018; Jha et al., 2023; Silcox, 2024). Local communities are more likely to adopt AI-driven health interventions that consider diet, medicine, and wellness standards, boosting their efficacy.

Culturally aware AI can adjust education to varied student demands and learning styles (Ober et al., 2023; Viberg, 2022). AI can make education more accessible and interesting for diverse students by using culturally relevant materials and approaches. This is crucial in a global setting because educational systems struggle to incorporate diverse cultural perspectives (Ogan & Johnson, 2015; Tsai et al., 2022). These variances can be understood and accommodated by AI-driven educational systems to create inclusive learning environments.

AI technologies that consider local farming practices and environmental conditions can empower small-scale farmers in developing countries by providing personalized advice and predictions based on culturally specific agricultural knowledge. AI systems can boost crop yields, food security, and livelihoods in underprivileged communities.

Role of Diverse Linguistic Representation in Promoting Equality

Language is essential to cultural identity, and linguistic inclusivity ensures that AI systems serve all people, independent of language or dialect (Prabhakaran et al., 2022; Buddemeyer, 2021). In a globalized world, AI systems that support various languages are crucial for equality, especially in locations where language hurdles have limited access to technology and information.

Diverse linguistic representation in AI goes beyond translation and language processing. AI systems that recognize and understand several languages, dialects, and local linguistic idiosyncrasies could improve access to services and opportunities (Ta & Lee, 2023)(Bella et al., 2023; Helm, 2023). In multilingual or indigenous language countries, AI-powered systems that support several languages can ensure that all individuals have equitable access to information, healthcare, legal services, and education.

AI systems that can speak a patient's native language, including dialects, can help doctors diagnose and treat illnesses more correctly (Ciecierski-Holmes et al., 2022; Dave & Patel, 2023). This is crucial in isolated or underserved places, where language challenges hinder patients from receiving care. AI solutions that support many languages can help non-native speakers understand legal procedures, documents, and their rights in legal systems (Shamsi et al., 2020; Luccioni, 2021).

AI-powered multilingual learning platforms can give multilingual pupils a great education (Camacho & Zevallos, 2020). This can help close educational disparities in underdeveloped countries where non-native speakers struggle with insufficient resources in the prevailing language (Kioko et al., 2014; Elosua & Egaña, 2016). AI-driven translation tools, adaptive learning systems, and localised content can democratise learning by allowing multilingual students to use instructional resources.

RECOMMENDATIONS AND CONCLUSION

Recommendations for AI Curriculum Designers

Incorporating Cultural Studies and Ethics in AI Courses

Designing and using AI is shaped by cultural, social, and ethical frameworks. As AI systems make more life-changing judgments, AI education must integrate cultural and ethical lessons. Cultural studies and ethics in AI curricula can assist students comprehend how AI systems affect diverse cultures and develop critical thinking skills to confront prejudices and inequities.

To create adaptive and sensitive AI systems for different populations, AI education should include cultural. AI curriculum designers can prepare students for the challenges of using AI across cultures by teaching cultural theory, global viewpoints, and intercultural communication. Students should investigate how cultural norms, values, and social structures affect AI design and use, as well as how AI affects cultural identities and societal systems. Future AI engineers can use this to construct systems that respect cultural variety rather than reinforce biases.

In addition to cultural studies, AI curricula should include ethics courses on ethical AI development and deployment. Ethical frameworks should prioritize fairness, accountability, and openness in AI design to promote social justice. Students should learn about algorithmic fairness, data privacy, and how AI may worsen inequality. Ethical conversations in AI education can help students understand the social impacts of their work and develop AI systems that value human well-being and dignity.

Ensuring Diverse Linguistic Data in AI Training

Include different language data in AI training, another important advice for curriculum designers. Large datasets are essential for training AI systems, especially those focused on natural language processing (NLP) and machine learning, and their quality and diversity are crucial to making them inclusive and effective for all users. However, many AI systems are trained on data that mostly represents specific cultural and linguistic groups' languages and dialects, biasing and excluding minority languages.

AI curriculum designers should prioritize different linguistic data in training materials to expose students to several languages and dialects. English, Mandarin, and Spanish are widely spoken, but minority, indigenous, and regional languages are generally underrepresented in AI databases. Students should learn to value linguistic diversity and how to acquire, curate, and incorporate different linguistic data into AI models.

AI coursework can include multilingual datasets to help students work with data from multiple languages and cultures. This will assist students comprehend the difficulties of creating inclusive AI systems, such as coping with linguistic variance, dialects, and cultural differences. Curriculum designers should also urge students to consider linguistic data ethics, notably privacy, consent, and cultural appropriation. Language data should be responsibly sourced and handled to avoid increasing AI power disparities.

AI curriculum designers should include case studies and real-world instances of linguistic bias in AI. Case studies could examine AI-powered language translation systems that misrepresented minority languages or speech recognition systems that performed poorly for non-native speakers. Students can better grasp how linguistic biases affect AI system efficacy and fairness by studying these instances.

In conclusion, AI schools should emphasise collaboration with linguistic professionals, cultural consultants, and community members to create AI systems for different languages. Students will learn how to make AI technologies represent the world's language diversity through interdisciplinary collaboration. Addressing cultural bias and linguistic representation will help AI technologies create a more inclusive, equitable, and just Society 5.0. AI curriculum designers must equip future AI professionals on these difficulties. Cultural studies, ethics, and varied linguistic data can help curriculum designers teach students to build AI systems that respect cultural variety and promote social inclusion. These AI education changes will create a future where AI technologies work for everyone, promoting justice and human dignity in a rapidly changing digital world.

CONCLUSION

Summary of Key Findings and their Implications

Cultural bias and linguistic representation in AI curriculum design were examined in the perspective of Society 5.0, a human-centric, inclusive, and sustainable society. The research on AI education revealed numerous critical conclusions that will impact AI technology development and implementation.

First, AI systems often have cultural and linguistic biases because to the prevalence of datasets from high-income, English-speaking countries. These biases can exclude underrepresented communities, increasing inequities and hampering AI's ability to foster inclusivity in Society 5.0. AI can influence results for diverse people in healthcare, education, and governance, making this topic crucial. Biases can hinder efforts to create a more just and equal society if ignored.

Second, the research stressed the relevance of cultural studies, ethics, and linguistic inclusivity in AI curriculum. These components of AI education give students the technical abilities to build AI systems and the ethical frameworks and cultural competencies to make them fair and socially responsible. Inclusive curricula teach pupils about AI's social impacts and promote cultural diversity and social justice.

The study also found that policy-level actions are needed to ensure equity and inclusivity in AI education and system development. To create AI systems that serve all people, standardised educational policies that require cultural and linguistic considerations in AI training and promote international collaboration for equitable AI development are necessary.

Finally, AI advancements that address cultural and language prejudice were essential for diversity. Research into more diverse, representative datasets and AI algorithms that can handle cultural and linguistic diversity will reduce biases and ensure that AI systems are intended for more users.

Call to Action for Educators, Policymakers, and Technologists

This study suggests that educators, legislators, and technologists work together to overcome cultural bias and linguistic exclusion in AI. Every stakeholder group is crucial to establishing a more inclusive AI ecosystem that corresponds with Society 5.0.

AI courses must integrate cultural studies, ethics, and language variety, educators must realize. These issues should be included in undergraduate and graduate courses to encourage students to consider their work's social impact. They should also encourage multidisciplinary learning between AI technologists, linguists, ethicists, and sociologists to develop well-rounded, socially aware AI professionals. Inclusion in AI education can prepare the next generation of developers to construct systems that serve all populations fairly and equitably.

Policymakers should promote standardized AI education regulations that require cultural and linguistic diversity in AI training. Policymakers should also encourage worldwide cooperation to exchange inclusive AI system expertise, resources, and best practices. Policymakers can ensure that AI technologies promote equity, justice, and social cohesiveness in Society 5.0 by developing global frameworks for AI ethics.

Technologists must create AI systems that actively reduce cultural and linguistic prejudices. Improve data collection methods to ensure diverse language and cultural representation, build algorithms that recognize and adapt to cultural situations, and work with interdisciplinary teams to solve these problems. Technologists must consider ethical issues and construct transparent, responsible, and human rights- and dignity-aligned AI systems.

Finally, AI technology must be advanced with diversity, fairness, and cultural awareness. By following these principles in AI education, policy, and development, we can create a future where AI systems reflect Society 5.0's values of improving human well-being, fostering global cooperation, and serving all people regardless of culture or language. We must work together to establish a more inclusive AI ecosystem to realize AI's potential to make society more egalitarian, just, and human-centric.

REFERENCES

Abràmoff, M. D., Tarver, M. E., Loyo-Berríos, N., Trujillo, S., Char, D., Obermeyer, Z., Eydelman, M., & Maisel, W. H. (2023). Considerations for addressing bias in artificial intelligence for health equity [Review of Considerations for addressing bias in artificial intelligence for health equity]. Npj Digital Medicine, 6(1). Nature Portfolio. https://doi.org/DOI: 10.1038/s41746-023-00913-9

Anahideh, H., Nezami, N., & Asudeh, A. (2021). Finding Representative Group Fairness Metrics Using Correlation Estimations. In arXiv (Cornell University). Cornell University. https://doi.org//arxiv.2109.05697DOI: 10.48550

Arora, A., Alderman, J., Palmer, J., Ganapathi, S., Laws, E., McCradden, M. D., Oakden-Rayner, L., Pfohl, S., Ghassemi, M., McKay, F., Treanor, D., Rostamzadeh, N., Mateen, B. A., Gath, J., Adebajo, A. O., Kuku, S., Matin, R., Heller, K., Sapey, E., . . . Liu, X. (2023). The value of standards for health datasets in artificial intelligence-based applications. In Nature Medicine (Vol. 29, Issue 11, p. 2929). Nature Portfolio. https://doi.org/DOI: 10.1038/s41591-023-02608-w

Awino, E., Wanzare, L., Muchemi, L., Wanjawa, B., Ombui, E., Indede, F., McOnyango, O., & Okal, B. O. (2022). Phonemic Representation and Transcription for Speech to Text Applications for Under-resourced Indigenous African Languages: The Case of Kiswahili. In arXiv (Cornell University). Cornell University. https://doi.org/DOI: 10.48550/arXiv.2210

Bella, G. B., Helm, P., & Koch, G. Fausto Giunchiglia. (2023). Towards Bridging the Digital Language Divide. https://arxiv.org/pdf/2307.13405.pdf

Beukman, M., & Fokam, M. (2023). Analysing Cross-Lingual Transfer in Low-Resourced African Named Entity Recognition. In arXiv (Cornell University). Cornell University. https://doi.org/DOI: 10.48550/arXiv.2309

Bura, C., & Myakala, P. K. (2024). Advancing Transformative Education: Generative AI as a Catalyst for Equity and Innovation. In arXiv (Cornell University). Cornell University. https://doi.org//arxiv.2411.15971DOI: 10.48550

Camacho, L., & Zevallos, R. (2020). *Language technology into high schools for revitalization of endangered languages.*, DOI: 10.1109/intercon50315.2020.9220197

Cavazos, J. G., Phillips, P. J., Castillo, C. D., & O'Toole, A. J. (2019). Accuracy comparison across face recognition algorithms: Where are we on measuring race bias? In arXiv (Cornell University). Cornell University. https://doi.org//arxiv.1912.07398DOI: 10.48550

Chen, Y., Clayton, E. W., Novak, L. L., Anders, S., & Malin, B. (2023). Human-Centered Design to Address Biases in Artificial Intelligence. In Journal of Medical Internet Research (Vol. 25). JMIR Publications. https://doi.org/DOI: 10.2196/43251

Chen, Y., Shah, V., & Ritter, A. (2023). Better Low-Resource Entity Recognition Through Translation and Annotation Fusion. In arXiv (Cornell University). Cornell University. https://doi.org/DOI: 10.48550/arXiv.2305

Chen, Z. (2023). Ethics and discrimination in artificial intelligence-enabled recruitment practices. In Humanities and Social Sciences Communications (Vol. 10, Issue 1). Palgrave Macmillan. https://doi.org/DOI: 10.1057/s41599-023-02079-x

Cheng, L., Varshney, K. R., & Liu, H. (2021). Socially Responsible AI Algorithms: Issues, Purposes, and Challenges. In arXiv (Cornell University). Cornell University. https://doi.org//arxiv.2101.02032DOI: 10.48550

Chinta, S. V., Wang, Z., Yin, Z., Hoang, N. N. M., Gonzalez, M., Quy, T. L., & Zhang, W. (2024). FairAIED: Navigating Fairness, Bias, and Ethics in Educational AI Applications. In arXiv (Cornell University). Cornell University. https://doi.org//arxiv.2407.18745DOI: 10.48550

Ciecierski, H. T., Singh, R., Axt, M., Brenner, S., & Barteit, S. (2022). Artificial intelligence for strengthening healthcare systems in low- and middle-income countries: a systematic scoping review [Review of Artificial intelligence for strengthening healthcare systems in low- and middle-income countries: a systematic scoping review]. Npj Digital Medicine, 5(1). Nature Portfolio. https://doi.org/DOI: 10.1038/s41746-022-00700-y

Dave, M., & Patel, N. (2023). Artificial intelligence in healthcare and education. In BDJ (Vol. 234, Issue 10, p. 761). Springer Nature. https://doi.org/DOI: 10.1038/s41415-023-5845-2

De Russis, L., Kumar, N., & Mathur, A. (2023). Data4Good: Designing for Diversity and Development. https://dl.acm.org/doi/10.1145/3399715.3400864

Elosua, P., & Egaña, M. Á. (2016). Socioeconomic patterns and educational performance based on language-of-instruction models in the Basque Autonomous Community. In Journal of Multilingual and Multicultural Development (Vol. 38, Issue 8, p. 686). Taylor & Francis. https://doi.org/DOI: 10.1080/01434632.2016.1224239

Elstad, E. (2024). AI in Education: Rationale, Principles, and Instructional Implications. In arXiv (Cornell University). Cornell University. https://doi.org//arxiv.2412.12116DOI: 10.48550

Ferrara, E. (2023). Fairness And Bias in Artificial Intelligence: A Brief Survey of Sources, Impacts, And Mitigation Strategies. In arXiv (Cornell University). Cornell University. https://doi.org/DOI: 10.48550/arXiv.2304

Gao, X., & Feng, H. (2023). AI-Driven Productivity Gains: Artificial Intelligence and Firm Productivity. In Sustainability (Vol. 15, Issue 11, p. 8934). Multidisciplinary Digital Publishing Institute. https://doi.org/DOI: 10.3390/su15118934

Garg, P., Villasenor, J., & Foggo, V. (2020). Fairness Metrics: A Comparative Analysis. In arXiv (Cornell University). Cornell University. https://doi.org//arxiv.2001.07864DOI: 10.48550

Ge, X., Xu, C., Misaki, D., Markus, H. R., & Tsai, J. L. (2024). *How Culture Shapes What People Want From AI.*, DOI: 10.1145/3613904.3642660

Godwin-Jones, R. (2024). Generative AI, Pragmatics, and Authenticity in Second Language Learning. In arXiv (Cornell University). Cornell University. https://doi.org//arxiv.2410.14395DOI: 10.48550

Gross, N. (2023). What ChatGPT Tells Us about Gender: A Cautionary Tale about Performativity and Gender Biases in AI. In Social Sciences (Vol. 12, Issue 8, p. 435). Multidisciplinary Digital Publishing Institute. https://doi.org/DOI: 10.3390/socsci12080435

Guo, J., & Li, B. (2018). The Application of Medical Artificial Intelligence Technology in Rural Areas of Developing Countries [Review of The Application of Medical Artificial Intelligence Technology in Rural Areas of Developing Countries]. Health Equity, 2(1), 174. Mary Ann Liebert, Inc. https://doi.org/DOI: 10.1089/heq.2018.0037

Hanson, B., Stall, S., Cutcher-Gershenfeld, J., Vrouwenvelder, K., Wirz, C. D., Rao, Y., & Peng, G. (2023). Garbage in, garbage out: mitigating risks and maximizing benefits of AI in research. In Nature (Vol. 623, Issue 7985, p. 28). Nature Portfolio. https://doi.org/DOI: 10.1038/d41586-023-03316-8

Hedderich, M. A., Lange, L., Adel, H., Strötgen, J., & Klakow, D. (2021). A Survey on Recent Approaches for Natural Language Processing in Low-Resource Scenarios. In *Proceedings of the 2022 Conference of the North American Chapter of the Association for Computational Linguistics: Human Language Technologies*. https://doi.org/DOI: 10.18653/v1/2021.naacl-main.201

hÉigeartaigh, S. Ó., Whittlestone, J., Liu, Y., Zeng, Y., & Liu, Z. (2020). Overcoming Barriers to Cross-cultural Cooperation in AI Ethics and Governance. In Philosophy & Technology (Vol. 33, Issue 4, p. 571). Springer Nature (Netherlands). https://doi.org/DOI: 10.1007/s13347-020-00402-x

Helm, P., Bella, G., Koch, G., & Giunchiglia, F. (2023). Diversity and Language Technology: How Techno-Linguistic Bias Can Cause Epistemic Injustice. In arXiv (Cornell University). Cornell University. https://doi.org/DOI: 10.48550/arXiv.2307

Hoffman, S. H. (2023). The Emerging Hazard of AI-Related Health Care Discrimination. https://onlinelibrary.wiley.com/doi/10.1002/hast.1203

Hossain, S., & Ahmed, S. I. (2021). Towards a New Participatory Approach for Designing Artificial Intelligence and Data-Driven Technologies. In arXiv (Cornell University). Cornell University. https://doi.org//arxiv.2104.04072DOI: 10.48550

Hub, E. H. E. (2022). Minoritised languages, education, and technology: Current practices and future directions in low- and middle-income countries. https://doi.org/ DOI: 10.53832/edtechhub.0127

Hulley, S. B. (2013). *Designing Clinical Research* (4th ed.)., http://ci.nii.ac.jp/ncid/ BA7981371X

Jha, D., Rauniyar, A., Srivastava, A., Hagos, D. H., Tomar, N. K., Sharma, V., Keleş, E., Zhang, Z., Demir, U., Topcu, A. E., Yazidi, A., Håakegård, J. E., & Bağcı, U. (2023). Ensuring Trustworthy Medical Artificial Intelligence through Ethical and Philosophical Principles. In arXiv (Cornell University). Cornell University. https:// doi.org/DOI: 10.48550/arXiv.2304

Joshi, P., Barnes, C., Santy, S., Khanuja, S., Shah, S., Srinivasan, A., Bhattamishra, S., Sitaram, S., Choudhury, M., & Bali, K. (2019). Unsung Challenges of Building and Deploying Language Technologies for Low Resource Language Communities. In arXiv (Cornell University). Cornell University. https://doi.org//arxiv.1912 .03457DOI: 10.48550

Joshi, P., Santy, S., Budhiraja, A., Bali, K., & Choudhury, M. (2020). The State and Fate of Linguistic Diversity and Inclusion in the NLP World. In arXiv (Cornell University). Cornell University. https://doi.org//arxiv.2004.09095DOI: 10.48550

Joshi, P., Santy, S., Budhiraja, A., Bali, K., & Choudhury, M. (2020). The state and fate of linguistic diversity and inclusion in the NLP world. arXiv preprint arXiv:2004.09095.

Kelley, P. G., Yang, Y., Heldreth, C., Moessner, C., Sedley, A., Kramm, A., Newman, D. T., & Woodruff, A. (2021). Exciting, Useful, Worrying, Futuristic: Public Perception of Artificial Intelligence in 8 Countries. https://doi.org/DOI: 10.1145/3461702.3462605

Khan, A. A., Akbar, M. A., Fahmideh, M., Peng, L., Waseem, M., Ahmad, A., Niazi, M., & Abrahamsson, P. (2022). AI Ethics: An Empirical Study on the Views of Practitioners and Lawmakers. In arXiv (Cornell University). Cornell University. https://doi.org/DOI: 10.48550/arXiv.2207

Khanuja, S. K. Sebastian Ruder,Partha P. Talukdar. (2022). Evaluating the Diversity, Equity, and Inclusion of NLP Technology: A Case Study for Indian Languages. https://arxiv.org/pdf/2205.12676.pdf

Krishnapriya, K., Vangara, K., King, M. C., Albiero, V., & Bowyer, K. W. (2019). Characterizing the Variability in Face Recognition Accuracy Relative to Race. In arXiv (Cornell University). Cornell University. https://doi.org//arxiv.1904.07325DOI: 10.48550

Langley, P. (2019). An Integrative Framework for Artificial Intelligence Education. In *Proceedings of the AAAI Conference on Artificial Intelligence* (Vol. 33, Issue 1, p. 9670). Association for the Advancement of Artificial Intelligence. https://doi.org/DOI: 10.1609/aaai.v33i01.33019670

Leavy, S., O'Sullivan, B., & Σιαπέρα, E. (2020). Data, Power and Bias in Artificial Intelligence. In arXiv (Cornell University). Cornell University. https://doi.org/DOI: 10.48550/arXiv.2008

Lepp, H., & Sarin, P. (2024). A global AI community requires language-diverse publishing. In arXiv (Cornell University). Cornell University. https://doi.org//arxiv.2408.14772DOI: 10.48550

Li, B., Pang, R., Sainath, T. N., Gulati, A., Zhang, Y., Qin, J., Haghani, P., Huang, W.-C., & Ma, M. (2021). Scaling End-to-End Models for Large-Scale Multilingual ASR. In arXiv (Cornell University). Cornell University. https://doi.org/DOI: 10.48550/arXiv.2104

Liebling, D. J., Lahav, M., Evans, A., Donsbach, A., Holbrook, J., Smus, B., & Boran, L. (2020). *Unmet Needs and Opportunities for Mobile Translation AI.*, DOI: 10.1145/3313831.3376261

Littell, P., Kazantseva, A., Kühn, R., Pine, A., Arppe, A., Cox, C., & Junker, M.-O. (2018). Indigenous language technologies in Canada: Assessment, challenges, and successes. In International Conference on Computational Linguistics (p. 2620). https://aclanthology.org/C18-1222/

Luccioni, A. S., Pham, K. H., Lam, C. S. N., Aylett-Bullock, J., & Luengo-Oroz, M. (2021). Ensuring the Inclusive Use of Natural Language Processing in the Global Response to COVID-19. In arXiv (Cornell University). Cornell University. https://doi.org/DOI: 10.48550/arXiv.2108

Maslej, N., Fattorini, L., Perrault, R., Parli, V., Reuel, A., Brynjolfsson, E., Etchemendy, J., Ligett, K., Lyons, T., Manyika, J., Niebles, J. C., Shoham, Y., Wald, R., & Clark, J. A. (2024). Artificial Intelligence Index Report 2024. In arXiv (Cornell University). Cornell University. https://doi.org//arxiv.2405.19522DOI: 10.48550

Matsiko, A., & Nelson, B. J. (2023). Robotics and AI in the Global South. In Science Robotics (Vol. 8, Issue 85). American Association for the Advancement of Science. https://doi.org/DOI: 10.1126/scirobotics.adm9727

Michaeli, T., Seegerer, S., & Romeike, R. (2023). What Students Can Learn About Artificial Intelligence — Recommendations for K-12 Computing Education. In arXiv (Cornell University). Cornell University. https://doi.org//arxiv.2305.06450DOI: 10.48550

Mihalcea, R., Ignat, O., Bai, L., Borah, A., Chiruzzo, L., Jin, Z., Kwizera, C., Nwatu, J., Poria, S., & Solorio, T. (2024). Why AI Is WEIRD and Should Not Be This Way: Towards AI For Everyone, With Everyone, By Everyone. In arXiv (Cornell University). Cornell University. https://doi.org//arxiv.2410.16315DOI: 10.48550

Mikołajczyk-Bareła, A., & Grochowski, M. (2023). A survey on bias in machine learning research. In arXiv (Cornell University). Cornell University. https://doi.org//arxiv.2308.11254DOI: 10.48550

Mittal, S., Thakral, K., Singh, R., Vatsa, M., Glaser, T., Ferrer, C. C., & Hassner, T. (2024). On responsible machine learning datasets emphasizing fairness, privacy and regulatory norms with examples in biometrics and healthcare. In Nature Machine Intelligence (Vol. 6, Issue 8, p. 936). Nature Portfolio. https://doi.org/DOI: 10.1038/s42256-024-00874-y

Morse, A., & Pence, K. M. (2020). Technological Innovation and Discrimination in Household Finance. https://doi.org/DOI: 10.3386/w26739

Nazer, L., Zatarah, R., Waldrip, S., Ke, J. X. C., Moukheiber, M., Khanna, A. K., Hicklen, R., Moukheiber, L., Moukheiber, D., Ma, H., & Mathur, P. (2023). Bias in artificial intelligence algorithms and recommendations for mitigation [Review of Bias in artificial intelligence algorithms and recommendations for mitigation]. PLOS Digital Health, 2(6). Public Library of Science. https://doi.org/DOI: 10.1371/journal.pdig.0000278

Ober, T. M., Lehman, B., Gooch, R., Oluwalana, O., Solyst, J., Phelps, G., & Hamilton, L. S. (2023). Culturally Responsive Personalized Learning: Recommendations for a Working Definition and Framework. In ETS Research Report Series (Vol. 2023, Issue 1, p. 1). Wiley. https://doi.org/DOI: 10.1002/ets2.12372

Obermeyer, Z., Powers, B. W., Vogeli, C., & Mullainathan, S. (2019). Dissecting racial bias in an algorithm used to manage the health of populations. In Science (Vol. 366, Issue 6464, p. 447). American Association for the Advancement of Science. https://doi.org/DOI: 10.1126/science.aax2342

Ogan, A., & Johnson, W. L. (2015). Preface for the Special Issue on Culturally Aware Educational Technologies. In International Journal of Artificial Intelligence in Education (Vol. 25, Issue 2, p. 173). Springer Science+Business Media. https://doi.org/DOI: 10.1007/s40593-015-0036-1

Ousidhoum, N., Beloucif, M., & Mohammad, S. M. (2024). Building Better: Avoiding Pitfalls in Developing Language Resources when Data is Scarce. In arXiv (Cornell University). Cornell University. https://doi.org//arxiv.2410.12691DOI: 10.48550

Ożegalska-Łukasik, N., & Łukasik, S. (2023). Culturally Responsive Artificial Intelligence — Problems, Challenges and Solutions. In arXiv (Cornell University). Cornell University. https://doi.org//arxiv.2312.08467DOI: 10.48550

Palomares, I., Martínez-Cámara, E., Montes, R., García-Moral, P., Chiachío, M., Chiachío, J., Alonso, S., Melero, F. J., Molina, D., Fernández, B. C., Santaella, C. M., Marchena, R., de Vargas, J. P., & Herrera, F. (2021). A panoramic view and swot analysis of artificial intelligence for achieving the sustainable development goals by 2030: progress and prospects. In Applied Intelligence (Vol. 51, Issue 9, p. 6497). Springer Science+Business Media. https://doi.org/DOI: 10.1007/s10489-021-02264-y

Panch, T., Mattie, H., & Atun, R. (2019). Artificial intelligence and algorithmic bias: implications for health systems [Review of Artificial intelligence and algorithmic bias: implications for health systems]. Journal of Global Health, 9(2). Edinburgh University Global Health Society. https://doi.org/DOI: 10.7189/jogh.09.020318

Park, J.-S., Bragg, D., Kamar, E., & Morris, M. R. (2021). *Designing an Online Infrastructure for Collecting AI Data From People With Disabilities*., DOI: 10.1145/3442188.3445870

Pessach, D., & Shmueli, E. (2020). Algorithmic Fairness. In arXiv (Cornell University). Cornell University. https://doi.org/DOI: 10.48550/arXiv.2001

Peters, U., & Carman, M. (2024). Cultural Bias in Explainable AI Research: A Systematic Analysis. In Journal of Artificial Intelligence Research (Vol. 79, p. 971). AI Access Foundation. https://doi.org/DOI: 10.1613/jair.1.14888

Pfohl, S., Cole-Lewis, H., Sayres, R., Neal, D., Asiedu, M., Dieng, A., Tomašev, N., Rashid, Q. M., Azizi, S., Rostamzadeh, N., McCoy, L. G., Celi, L. A., Liu, Y., Schaekermann, M., Walton, A., Parrish, A., Nagpal, C., Singh, P., Dewitt, A., & Singhal, K. K. (2024). A toolbox for surfacing health equity harms and biases in large language models. In *Nature Medicine*. Nature Portfolio., DOI: 10.1038/s41591-024-03258-2

Prabhakaran, V., Qadri, R., & Hutchinson, B. (2022). Cultural Incongruencies in Artificial Intelligence. In arXiv (Cornell University). Cornell University. https://doi.org/DOI: 10.48550/arXiv.2211

Purves, D. (2022). Fairness in Algorithmic Policing. In Journal of the American Philosophical Association (Vol. 8, Issue 4, p. 741). Cambridge University Press. https://doi.org/DOI: 10.1017/apa.2021.39

Qadri, R., Shelby, R., Bennett, C. L., & Denton, E. (2023). AI's Regimes of Representation: A Community-centered Study of Text-to-Image Models in South Asia. In *2022 ACM Conference on Fairness, Accountability, and Transparency* (p. 506). https://doi.org/DOI: 10.1145/3593013.3594016

Ranathunga, S., & de Silva, N. (2022). Some Languages are More Equal than Others: Probing Deeper into the Linguistic Disparity in the NLP World. In arXiv (Cornell University). Cornell University. https://doi.org//arxiv.2210.08523DOI: 10.48550

Ranathunga, S., & de Silva, N. (2023). Some Languages are More Equal than Others: Probing Deeper into the Linguistic Disparity in the NLP World. https://arxiv.org/pdf/2210.08523.pdf

Reich, J., & Dukes, J. (2024). Toward a New Theory of Arrival Technologies. https://doi.org/DOI: 10.35542/osf.io/x6vn7

Roche, C., Lewis, D., & Wall, P. J. (2021). Artificial Intelligence Ethics: An Inclusive Global Discourse? In arXiv (Cornell University). Cornell University. https://doi.org/DOI: 10.48550/arXiv.2108

Selbst, A. D. (2017). Disparate Impact in Big Data Policing. In SSRN Electronic Journal. RELX Group (Netherlands). https://doi.org/DOI: 10.2139/ssrn.2819182

Shahini, R., Davis, H., & Borthwick, K. (2019). *Design recommendations to address cultural issues in multicultural MOOCs: a systematic literature review.*, DOI: 10.14705/rpnet.2019.36.956

Shams, R. A., Zowghi, D., & Bano, M. (2023). Challenges and Solutions in AI for All. In arXiv (Cornell University). Cornell University. https://doi.org/DOI: 10.48550/arXiv.2307

Shamsi, H. A., Almutairi, A. G., Mashrafi, S. A., & Kalbani, T. A. (2020). Implications of Language Barriers for Healthcare: A Systematic Review [Review of Implications of Language Barriers for Healthcare: A Systematic Review]. Oman Medical Journal, 35(2). Oman Medical Specialty Board. https://doi.org/DOI: 10.5001/omj.2020.40

Silcox, C., Zimlichmann, E., Huber, K., Rowen, N. P., Saunders, R. S., McClellan, M., Kahn, C. N., Salzberg, C., & Bates, D. W. (2024). The potential for artificial intelligence to transform healthcare: perspectives from international health leaders. In npj Digital Medicine (Vol. 7, Issue 1). Nature Portfolio. https://doi.org/DOI: 10.1038/s41746-024-01097-6

Sony, M., & Karingada, K. T. B. (2024). Education 4.0 unravelled: deciphering critical success factors for successful implementation. In Journal of Applied Research in Higher Education. Babe -Bolyai University. https://doi.org/DOI: 10.1108/jarhe-10-2023-0459

Suri, S. (2024). Defining our future with generative AI. In Nature Computational Science (Vol. 4, Issue 9, p. 641). Nature Portfolio. https://doi.org/DOI: 10.1038/s43588-024-00694-5

Ta, R., & Lee, N. (2023). How Language Gaps Constrain Generative AI Development. In International Journal of Comparative Studies in International Relations and Development (Vol. 9, Issue 1, p. 48). https://doi.org/DOI: 10.48028/iiprds/ijcsird.v9.i1.03

Tadimalla, S. Y., & Maher, M. L. (2024). AI Literacy for All: Adjustable Interdisciplinary Socio-technical Curriculum. In arXiv (Cornell University). Cornell University. https://doi.org//arxiv.2409.10552DOI: 10.48550

Tao, Y., Viberg, O., Baker, R. S., & Kizilcec, R. F. (2024). Cultural bias and cultural alignment of large language models. In Nexus, P. N. A. S. (Ed.), *Issue 9). Oxford University Press* (Vol. 3)., DOI: 10.1093/pnasnexus/pgae346

Tidjon, L. N., & Khomh, F. (2022). The Different Faces of AI Ethics Across the World: A Principle-Implementation Gap Analysis. In arXiv (Cornell University). Cornell University. https://doi.org//arxiv.2206.03225DOI: 10.48550

Tomašev, N., Maynard, J. L., & Gabriel, I. (2022). Manifestations of Xenophobia in AI Systems. In arXiv (Cornell University). Cornell University. https://doi.org/DOI: 10.48550/arXiv.2212

Trewin, S. (2018). AI Fairness for People with Disabilities: Point of View. In arXiv (Cornell University). Cornell University. https://doi.org//arxiv.1811.10670DOI: 10.48550

Tsai, C., Ma, Y., Chang, Y., & Lai, Y.-H. (2022). Integrating Multiculturalism Into Artificial Intelligence-Assisted Programming Lessons: Examining Inter-Ethnicity Differences in Learning Expectancy, Motivation, and Effectiveness. In Frontiers in Psychology (Vol. 13). Frontiers Media. https://doi.org/DOI: 10.3389/fpsyg.2022.868698

Viberg, O., Jivet, I., & Scheffel, M. (2022). Designing Culturally Aware Learning Analytics: A Value Sensitive Perspective. In arXiv (Cornell University). Cornell University. https://doi.org//arxiv.2212.09645DOI: 10.48550

Vinuesa, R., Azizpour, H., Leite, I., Balaam, M., Dignum, V., Domisch, S., Felländer, A., Langhans, S. D., Tegmark, M., & Nerini, F. F. (2020). The role of artificial intelligence in achieving the Sustainable Development Goals [Review of The role of artificial intelligence in achieving the Sustainable Development Goals]. Nature Communications, 11(1). Nature Portfolio. https://doi.org/DOI: 10.1038/s41467-019-14108-y

Wali, E., Chen, Y., Mahoney, C., Middleton, T., Babaeianjelodar, M., Njie, M., & Matthews, J. (2023). Is Machine Learning Speaking my Language? A Critical Look at the NLP-Pipeline Across 8 Human Languages. https://arxiv.org/pdf/2007.05872.pdf

Wang, J., Guo, B., & Chen, L. (2022). Human-in-the-loop Machine Learning: A Macro-Micro Perspective. In arXiv (Cornell University). Cornell University. https://doi.org/DOI: 10.48550/arXiv.2202

Wang, N., & Lester, J. C. (2023). K-12 Education in the Age of AI: A Call to Action for K-12 AI Literacy. In International Journal of Artificial Intelligence in Education (Vol. 33, Issue 2, p. 228). Springer Science+Business Media. https://doi.org/DOI: 10.1007/s40593-023-00358-x

Wang, W. X. Z. W. R. S. (2024). Monolingual and Multilingual Misinformation Detection for Low-Resource Languages: A Comprehensive Survey. https://arxiv.org/abs/2410.18390

Wang, X. W. Carnegie Mellon University, xinyiw1@cs. cmu. edu, Sebastian Ruder, Google Research, ruder@google. com, Graham Neubig, Carnegie Mellon University, gneubig@cs. cmu. edu. (2023). Expanding Pretrained Models to Thousands More Languages via Lexicon-based Adaptation. https://arxiv.org/pdf/2203.09435.pdf

Weng, Y., Wu, J., Kelly, T., & Johnson, W. (2024). Comprehensive Overview of Artificial Intelligence Applications in Modern Industries. https://doi.org/DOI: 10.20944/preprints202409.1638.v1

Wong, P. (2020). Cultural Differences as Excuses? Human Rights and Cultural Values in Global Ethics and Governance of AI. In Philosophy & Technology (Vol. 33, Issue 4, p. 705). Springer Nature (Netherlands). https://doi.org/DOI: 10.1007/s13347-020-00413-8

Woo, J. H., & Choi, H. (2021). Systematic Review for AI-based Language Learning Tools. In arXiv (Cornell University). Cornell University. https://doi.org/DOI: 10.48550/arXiv.2111

Yam, K. C., Tan, T. C. Y., Jackson, J. C., Shariff, A., & Gray, K. (2023). Cultural Differences in People's Reactions and Applications of Robots, Algorithms, and Artificial Intelligence. In Management and Organization Review (Vol. 19, Issue 5, p. 859). Cambridge University Press. https://doi.org/DOI: 10.1017/mor.2023.21

Zhou, M., Abhishek, V., Derdenger, T., Kim, J.-H., & Srinivasan, K. (2024). Bias in Generative AI. In arXiv (Cornell University). Cornell University. https://doi.org//arxiv.2403.02726DOI: 10.48550

Zowghi, D., & da Rimini, F. (2023). Diversity and Inclusion in Artificial Intelligence. In arXiv (Cornell University). Cornell University. https://doi.org//arxiv.2305.12728DOI: 10.48550

Chapter 9
Game-Based Learning in the AI Era:
Designing Curricula for Society 5.0

Dewi Furwana
https://orcid.org/0009-0003-4171-0359
IAIN Palopo, Indonesia

Wisran Wisran
https://orcid.org/0009-0007-9265-603X
IAIN Palopo, Indonesia

Husnaini Husnaini
IAIN Palopo, Indonesia

Andi Asrifan
https://orcid.org/0000-0002-9934-6129
Universitas Negeri Makassar, Indonesia

ABSTRACT

Society 5.0 demands educational frameworks that integrate technology with a human-centered approach to promote societal well-being. This chapter explores how game-based learning (GBL) and artificial intelligence (AI) foster creativity, collaboration, and problem-solving. Grounded in constructivist and experiential learning theories, GBL transforms passive education into active engagement, while AI personalizes learning through adaptive content and immersive technologies like virtual and augmented reality. Curriculum design emphasizes digital literacy, global awareness, and ethical considerations, addressing challenges such as the digital divide and data privacy. Emerging trends include gamified lifelong learning and

DOI: 10.4018/979-8-3373-1062-6.ch009

Copyright © 2026, IGI Global Scientific Publishing. Copying or distributing in print or electronic forms without written permission of IGI Global Scientific Publishing is prohibited.

workforce training, supported by strong policies, funding, and research. Case studies demonstrate how AI and GBL create inclusive, adaptive educational environments aligned with Society 5.0's vision.

VISION AND CHARACTERISTICS OF SOCIETY 5.0

Definition and Goals of Society 5.0

Society 5.0 aims to improve human well-being, social equity, and environmental sustainability by integrating technological advances—especially AI, IoT, robotics, and big data—into daily life (Rosenthal, 2009). This Japanese concept builds on Industry 4.0, which stresses automation and cognitive technologies to improve industrial operations. Society 5.0 addresses global concerns like aging populations, environmental degradation, and social inequality beyond industrial optimization. The goal is to balance technology and human values to create an inclusive, sustainable, and empowering society.

Society 5.0's vision is based on three goals:

1. **Inclusivity**: Society 5.0 seeks to eradicate resource, opportunity, and service inequities. This is crucial for addressing social, geographic, and technical gaps. Inclusivity guarantees that everyone, regardless of background, has equitable access to technical advances like better education, healthcare, and social services. (Dijk, 2017)
2. **Sustainability**: Society 5.0 seeks to preserve the earth and improve its residents' social well-being. In this context, technological innovations like AI to improve energy efficiency, reduce waste, and create environmentally friendly solutions in transportation, agriculture, and urban development aim to boost economic growth and promote sustainable development. (Hasan et al., 2023)
3. **Human Empowerment**: Society 5.0 is based on individual empowerment. Instead of replacing human work, technology is used to improve skills, creativity, and decision-making. Artificial intelligence can do regular tasks quickly and help people reach their personal and professional potential. (Wendrich 2020)

Integration of AI and Human-Centered Methods

AI and other advanced technologies are key to Society 5.0, which prioritizes human well-being and community progress. Society 5.0 prioritizes people over industry and economy, unlike previous technological revolutions. Technology should meet humanity's needs, not just advance for its own sake.

AI analyzes large amounts of data from many sources, provides important insights, and automates and improves healthcare, transportation, education, and urban planning (Ciecierski-Holmes et al., 2022). AI can improve education by adapting educational content to fit student needs, enabling tailored learning environments. AI systems can assess students' learning styles, strengths, and weaknesses, and adapt courses to their needs. This customisation ensures that no student is excluded, making education more inclusive and accessible for all, regardless of skill or circumstance.

In addition to its practical advantages in some areas, AI in Society 5.0 raises ethical problems. AI system design and deployment must reflect society ideals including fairness, openness, and responsibility (Abioye et al., 2021). AI systems must protect privacy and avoid biases that could perpetuate inequality. Human-centric collaboration between humans and machines enhances human talents rather than replacing them. This alliance empowers individuals and communities to use technology to improve human capacities and creativity. (Shneiderman, 2020)

CHALLENGES AND OPPORTUNITIES IN EDUCATION

The transition to Society 5.0 presents challenges and opportunities, particularly in education. Guaranteeing equitable access to digital resources for Society 5.0 is a major concern. For those without access to digital technologies, the digital gap remains a major issue. Many populations, especially in impoverished or rural areas, lack reliable internet connections, digital devices, and the ability to use them (Philip et al., 2017). This access disparity may prevent some from taking advantage of AI and other modern technology's educational benefits.

Along with addressing the digital gap, schools must use AI-driven and game-based learning methods (Wang & Lester, 2023).

This requires major changes in pedagogy, curriculum, and educator development. AI-driven platforms, gamification, and data-informed training must be learned by educators. Some educators who use traditional teaching methods may resist this change, requiring ongoing support and training.

Despite these drawbacks, Society 5.0 has unmatched potential to improve education. AI-driven technology can adjust education to each student's requirements and preferences, making learning more efficient and effective. Instant feedback from

AI technology helps students understand their mistakes and improve. Ke Zhang (2021). AI-driven gamified and immersive learning experiences can also boost student engagement and deepen learning.

AI in education improves inclusivity. Technology can give impoverished or rural students access to high-quality instructional materials (U.S. Department of Education, 2023). Virtual learning environments, online courses, and AI-driven coaching can help kids without access to traditional schools.

Society 5.0 views education as a key driver of social and economic progress. Education gives people the skills and knowledge they need to succeed in an AI-driven world, creating an inclusive, sustainable, and human-centric society. By bringing together educators, legislators, and technology developers, curricula can prepare students for future challenges and possibilities, creating a resilient, adaptable, and values-based society (Yue & Ji, 2020).

GAME-BASED LEARNING DEFINITION AND PRINCIPLES

GBL improves learning by using game aspects including mechanics, dynamics, and narratives (Alper et al., 2021). Game-Based Learning (GBL) engages students through challenges, involvement, and prompt feedback, unlike passive learning. Active participation improves comprehension, retention, and critical thinking. GBL turns learning into an engaging experience where students are active participants in their education. GBL fundamentals include:

1. Engagement: Games provide immersive worlds that engage learners and maintain their interest in learning. Interactive elements encourage students to experiment, investigate, and persevere in problem-solving.
2. Challenge: Games employ phases or tasks that increase in complexity, encouraging critical thinking and obstacle-overcoming. This balance between challenge and attainability encourages lifelong learning skills like perseverance and problem-solving.
3. Feedback: Game-Based Learning (GBL) requires prompt feedback. Visual indicators, scores, progress bars, and correction instructions give learners rapid feedback. This rapid feedback helps students identify and correct their mistakes, enabling continuous improvement.
4. Autonomy: Game-Based Learning (GBL) allows learners to choose their engagement techniques, allowing them to explore instructional materials at their own pace. This autonomy gives them ownership over their learning, which may boost motivation and engagement.

5. Collaboration and Competition: Multiplayer games foster teamwork and communication, while competitive elements boost motivation and ambition. The dual technique promotes social and interpersonal skills and a supportive and collaborative learning environment (Costello & Lambert, 2018).

THE HISTORY OF EDUCATIONAL GAMES

Games for learning have a long history, but the tools and methods have evolved.

- Early Foundations: Chess and Monopoly taught strategy, planning, and finance. RPGs encouraged creativity, problem-solving, critical thinking, and complex situational awareness (Palmer & Rodgers, 1983).
- In the 1980s, computers and digital instructional games emerged. The Oregon Trail and Carmen Sandiego combined narrative with problem-solving to make history and geography fun (Martins et al., 2022).
- Internet and Mobile Revolution: The internet made instructional games available worldwide in the 2000s. Kahoot! and Minecraft: Education Edition brought interactive and collaborative learning in schools. These games enabled real-time competition, quizzes, and creative construction projects, making learning more engaging (2017).
- The latest innovations in Game-Based Learning (GBL) incorporate AI, VR, and AR to create immersive and adaptive educational environments. AI-driven educational games adapt information to individual learning speeds and preferences, while VR and AR simulate real-world situations to prepare students for complex issues in healthcare, engineering, and urban planning (Zhai et al., 2021).

BENEFITS OF GAMIFICATION IN EDUCATION

Gamification, which integrates game aspects like points, leaderboards, and prizes into non-gaming environments, offers numerous benefits to education. These components correspond effectively with the interactive and adaptive characteristics of Game-Based Learning, enhancing engagement and impact in the educational process. Several principal advantages of gamification in education encompass:

1. **Enhanced Engagement**: The engaging and enjoyable characteristics of gamified learning attract students' focus, increasing their willingness to engage. Students actively involved in their learning are more likely to remember information and exhibit interest for the subject matter (Yaccob et al., 2022).
2. **Improved Retention**: Engagement in games that necessitate problem-solving and critical thinking markedly enhances knowledge retention. Active involvement is more efficacious than passive techniques, such as rote memorizing, in facilitating long-term knowledge retention.(Chariyev, 2020)
3. **Skill Development**: Games impart essential life skills, like critical thinking, decision-making, cooperation, and time management. These are transferable talents that students can utilize in real-world scenarios, equipping them for the intricacies of contemporary society. (Παπαστεργίου, 2008).
4. **Personalized Learning**: AI-driven games customize to distinct learning styles and speeds, offering personalized assistance for every student. This tailored methodology guarantees that every learner, irrespective of their initial level, may advance and thrive at their own rhythm. (JOYCE & Harris, 2018).
5. **Safe Learning Environment**: Games offer an environment in which learners can experiment, err, and fail without the apprehension of real-world repercussions. This promotes risk-taking and cultivates resilience and a growth mindset, which are vital attributes for lifelong learning. (Li & Pan, 2023).
6. **Inclusivity**: Digital games can be developed to meet various learning requirements, including those of students with impairments. Gamified learning enhances inclusivity in education by offering accessible and adaptable learning environments, so ensuring that all learners, irrespective of their background or aptitude, have equitable access to quality education. (Razali et al., 2020).

ALIGNMENT WITH SOCIETY 5.0

Playful, innovative game-based learning promotes cognitive development, creativity, social connection, and emotional intelligence, aligning with Society 5.0 goals. GBL prepares students for an AI-centric world with a realistic and engaging approach as technology changes our lifestyles and education. Using AI, VR, and AR in gaming, educators may create targeted, immersive experiences that simulate real-world challenges to help students develop the skills needed to navigate Society 5.0 (Zhai et al., 2021).

Game-based learning helps educators foster teamwork, creativity, and adaptability, which are crucial in the fast-changing, tech-driven society of the future (Li & Pan, 2023). Game-Based Learning (GBL) can provide a more interesting, inclusive, and successful educational environment as AI changes education. In future chapters, we will examine how this methodology might be used to create curriculum that meets Society 5.0's goals and prepares students for an AI-driven world.

Intersection of AI and Game-Based Learning

Role of AI in Enhancing Game-Based Learning Experiences

AI has transformed Game-Based Learning (GBL) into more personalized, flexible, and engaging educational experiences. GBL settings can monitor user interactions in real time, predict learners' requirements, and provide individualized feedback using AI technologies, improving engagement and efficacy (Mello et al., 2023).

A major benefit of AI in GBL is its ability to personalize learning. AI allows for more tailored instruction than traditional methods. AI algorithms can adjust the game's complexity, material, and pace based on learners' strengths, weaknesses, and progress. This keeps pupils challenged without overwhelming them, which is frequent in traditional classrooms where students can't move at their own pace.

Key AI Contributions to GBL Improvement:

1) Personalization: Real-time AI evaluation of student performance enables immediate educational environment adjustments. If a student excels at some tasks, the system can provide increasingly tougher scenarios, but struggling students may receive focused help and easier assignments. This ensures that learning experiences are neither too easy nor too difficult, balancing engagement and development.
2) Adaptive Feedback: AI excels in providing quick, context-aware feedback. This feedback helps students correct mistakes and understand complex concepts. This method helps pupils learn from their mistakes and improve by iterating.
3) Intelligent Tutoring Systems: AI can simulate tutoring and mentoring in gaming. AI chatbots or virtual teachers provide students with questions, challenges, and suggestions. These technologies make learning more interactive and personalized, which is beneficial in online and self-directed learning.
4) Immersive Environments: Combining AI with VR/AR technologies creates very immersive educational experiences. These tools help students practice identifying diseases, studying past civilizations, and testing scientific theories in realistic settings. AI-driven game-based learning improves engagement and retention by presenting authentic events in a controlled, virtual environment.
5) Analytics and Insights: AI collects data on student behaviors, actions, and learning patterns to help educators understand individual and collective performance. Using real-time data, instructors can adjust their methods and interventions. It

helps game makers improve educational efficacy by refining learning experiences (Khadri, 2024).

AI improves GBL by personalizing, engaging, and scaling education. Artificial intelligence helps create personalized learning settings that foster critical thinking, problem-solving, and creativity.

Case Studies of AI-Powered Educational Games

Several case studies highlight how AI is improving educational games, demonstrating AI's transformative potential in education.

1. Adaptive Learning Platform: Smart Sparrow uses AI to tailor instructional content based on real-time learner data. Medical simulations demonstrate how instructors can customize instruction. Based on the learner's actions and decisions, the AI adjusts patient scenarios to help build diagnostic and treatment skills in a realistic, dynamic context (Meşe, 2023).
2. Duolingo (Language Acquisition) provides gamified language learning using artificial intelligence. Machine learning algorithms track user performance and customize training. Streak awards, leaderboards, and interactive activities motivate students. Duolingo's AI also identifies common verbal errors and suggests ways to improve (Hacker, n.d.).
3. Minecraft: Education Edition uses AI to improve problem-solving and creativity in fields like computers and environmental science. AI-powered bots help pupils with complex tasks like creating sustainable ecosystems and programming. This popular game uses AI to increase students' critical thinking and teamwork, making it a great resource for multidisciplinary education (AI-Infused Collaborative Inquiry in Upper Elementary School: A Game-Based Learning Approach, 2021).
4. Century Tech (AI-Driven Education Platform): This AI-driven platform offers personalized learning experiences in several fields. The adaptive engine assesses student involvement and comprehension and suggests learning activities. AI-powered curriculum tailored to pupils' needs has improved reading and numeracy (Khadri, 2024).
5. Immersive Learning: Dreamscape Learn teaches STEM fundamentals using AI, VR, and narrative-driven games. Students explore marine ecosystems and physics with AI-driven creatures in realistic virtual environments. AI and VR create an immersive learning experience that helps students understand complex concepts and learn by doing. AI in game-based learning makes education more flexible, customized, immersive, entertaining, and effective. AI-driven

educational games will help prepare students for an AI-oriented future as these technologies evolve, aligning with Society 5.0's goals of a human-centric, technology-enhanced society (Khadri, 2024).

Constructivism and Game-Based Learning

Constructivism holds that learners learn by interacting with their surroundings. This theory states that learners develop knowledge through exploration, experience, and reflection. Games that encourage dynamic, immersive learning are examples of constructivism in GBL.

Constructivist games offer several learning opportunities:

1. Active Learning: Game-Based Learning requires students to actively engage with content, unlike passive learning. Players can explore ancient civilizations, make decisions as historical figures, and follow events in a historical game. This direct link helps students remember and internalize information. Ishak et al., 2020
2. Game-Based Learning (GBL) encourages critical thinking and creativity via problem-solving. In an environmental challenge game, players must analyze factors, consider solutions, and make decisions that affect the outcome, improving their problem-solving skills (Kucher, 2021).
3. Reflection: Constructivist games often feature feedback mechanisms that prompt learners to evaluate their activities. Players can receive immediate feedback after finishing a job or challenge to assess their performance and improve their techniques. This repetitive process improves learning (O'Neil et al., 2010).

By stressing active involvement, investigation, and reflection, constructivist game-based learning immerses students in the learning process, making the knowledge more meaningful and useful in real life.

Constructivism and Game-Based Learning

Constructivism holds that learners learn by interacting with their surroundings. This theory states that learners develop knowledge through exploration, experience, and reflection. Games that encourage dynamic, immersive learning are examples of constructivism in GBL.

Constructivist games offer several learning opportunities:

1. Active Learning: Game-Based Learning requires students to actively engage with content, unlike passive learning. Players can explore ancient civilizations, make decisions as historical figures, and follow events in a historical game. This direct link helps students remember and internalize information. Ishak et al., 2020
2. Game-Based Learning (GBL) encourages critical thinking and creativity via problem-solving. In an environmental challenge game, players must analyze factors, consider solutions, and make decisions that affect the outcome, improving their problem-solving skills (Kucher, 2021).
3. Reflection: Constructivist games often feature feedback mechanisms that prompt learners to evaluate their activities. Players can receive immediate feedback after finishing a job or challenge to assess their performance and improve their techniques. This repetitive process improves learning (O'Neil et al., 2010).

By stressing active involvement, investigation, and reflection, constructivist game-based learning immerses students in the learning process, making the knowledge more meaningful and useful in real life.

Experiential and Game-Based Learning

David Kolb's experiential learning emphasizes immediate experience, followed by action and reflection. Both GBL and this technique stress experience learning and progressive learning. Kolb's experiential learning cycle includes concrete experience, reflective observation, abstract conceptualization, and active inquiry. These phases match gameplay levels, making games ideal for experiential learning.

In GBL,

1. learners engage in gameplay, taking on roles in virtual or real-world simulations. For instance, a financial literacy game may simulate financial decisions and their repercussions (Onele, 2020).
2. Reflective Observation: Players evaluate their performance after playing. They may evaluate their methods, decisions, and results to improve. An environmental conservation game can have players consider how their actions damaged the ecosystem and learn from their mistakes (2020).
3. Abstract Conceptualization: Learners apply gameplay insights to theoretical knowledge. Players can apply their physics knowledge to gaming problems, connecting classroom learning to experience (Baskara, 2024).

4. Active Experimentation: Players employ their ideas from reflections and conceptualization to apply new techniques in future problems or real-world scenarios. This stage supports lifelong learning and adaptability, essential academic and professional abilities (Bui & Khuu, 2020).

Through experiential learning, GBL helps students understand theoretical concepts and apply them in real-world circumstances, developing decision-making, flexibility, and collaborative skills.

Gamification for Teaching

Gamification adds points, levels, prizes, and leaderboards to non-gaming situations to boost engagement and incentive. Gamification makes learning more engaging and enjoyable in education. Gamified learning engages students with content via intrinsic and extrinsic motivators (Winanti et al., 2021).

Gamification makes learning fun and challenging, unlike rote remembering or passive listening. As they progress through levels, earn points, or meet goals, children feel accomplished and more engaged. Purpose, competition, and reward make learning more engaging.

Self-Motivation vs. Extrinsic Rewards

Game-Based Learning (GBL) uses intrinsic and extrinsic rewards to keep students engaged. These motivators help students focus, overcome challenges, and achieve their academic goals.

1. Intrinsic Motivation: The desire to engage in activities for personal gain, such as problem-solving, skill mastery, or intellectual curiosity. Expertly designed games that provide autonomy, mastery, and purpose boost intrinsic motivation in game-based learning. Puzzle games may inspire players to overcome challenges for the sake of discovery and mastery.
2. In contrast, extrinsic motivation involves external rewards like points, badges, or rankings. Extrinsic rewards can encourage students, especially early on, but they should not replace intrinsic motivations. A gamified mathematics platform may initially use badges or points to engage students, but as they progress, intrinsic satisfaction from solving complex problems and gaining new skills should take over (Palacios et al., 2023). A good GBL design balances intrinsic and extrinsic rewards to drive students to study and flourish. This balance promotes long-term engagement, making learning more fun and meaningful.

An efficient GBL design balances intrinsic and extrinsic rewards to motivate students both externally and internally. This equilibrium encourages prolonged engagement, making learning more enjoyable and gratifying.

Cognitive and AI Development

Critical thinking, problem-solving, and metacognition are enhanced by artificial intelligence (AI), which has transformed education. AI helps learners acquire cognitive abilities for success in a dynamic setting by meeting specific learning needs and providing rapid feedback. AI helps cognitive development through personalization, adaptive content alteration, and metacognition.

How AI Learns Differently

Learning is diverse because everyone has different interests, strengths, and obstacles. To accommodate each learner's learning style, AI-driven educational systems customize content.

1. Personalization AI systems use Data Analytics to analyze learner data like as reaction times, error patterns, engagement levels, and performance metrics. This data helps the AI identify learning needs and deliver customized information. To address a student's algebraic equation struggles, the AI may include practice problems, thorough explanations, and interactive simulations to the lesson plan. The AI improves its understanding of the learner's needs over time, offering individualized support for optimal success (Gligorea et al., 2023).
2. Dynamic Content Adjustment AI-driven teaching methods are flexible and responsive, unlike rigid curriculum methods. After a pupil masters a topic, the AI will present more advanced knowledge, keeping them challenged and engaged. To help learners understand a concept, the system can remove content, reword explanations, or present in several ways. This real-time material adaptation ensures that learning is neither too difficult nor too easy, creating an ideal learning environment (Krissilov et al., 2018).
3. Learning modalities AI delivers knowledge in multiple methods to serve visual, auditory, kinesthetic, and reading/writing learners. To accommodate learners' different information processing patterns, an AI-driven language-learning software may feature images, infographics, aural phrases, and interactive activities. AI provides knowledge in multiple formats so students can interact with it in a way that suits them, improving learning accessibility and efficacy (Saputra et al., 2023).

AI's tailored, adjustable features offer an inclusive learning environment where every student can thrive and maximize cognitive development by meeting their demands.

Supporting Metacognition with AI

Metacognition is self-reflection and learning management. It includes self-awareness, reflection, and adaptability to improve learning. Metacognitive skills are developed through artificial intelligence tools and feedback that help learners monitor, reflect, and improve their cognitive approaches.

1. Self-Assessment Tools

AI-driven platforms often incorporate self-assessment features to track student progress. Students can assess their learning progress using dashboards that provide accuracy rates, completion times, and strengths and shortcomings. AI provides real-time data to help students reflect on their successes and challenges, improving self-awareness and goal-setting. If a student's performance drops in a domain, they may set new goals to improve (Zastudil et al., 2023).

2. Guided Reflection

AI systems can help students reflect on their strategies after completing tasks. These reflection prompts help students examine their cognitive processes and act more intentionally. After completing a problem on a game-based learning platform, the AI may ask: "What actions did you take to address this issue?" or "How could you tackle this challenge differently in the future?" Introspective questions help students analyse their reasoning and cognitive processes, improving decision-making and intellectual development (Jones & Hammond, 2022).

3. Real-Time Feedback

AI systems can help students reflect on their strategies after completing tasks. These reflection questions help students examine their cognitive processes and act more intentionally. After overcoming a problem on a game-based learning platform, the AI may ask: "What actions did you take?" or "How could you tackle this challenge in the future?" Reflective inquiries encourage students to examine their reasoning and cognitive processes, improving decision-making and intellectual development (Jones & Hammond, 2022).

4. Scaffolding and Support

AI helps students solve complex problems as a virtual coach. Scaffolding breaks down a complex topic into smaller, digestible parts to help students overcome obstacles. AI can give students insights, methods, and recommendations throughout a project. In a sophisticated coding game, the AI may suggest grammar fixes or code organizing strategies. AI helps learners build problem-solving and self-regulation skills by giving timely assistance. Students learn to manage more complex tasks without constant support (Darvishi et al., 2023).

AI helps learners take charge of their learning through self-assessment, guided reflection, real-time feedback, and scaffolding. Metacognitive skills let students evaluate, appraise, and adjust their strategies, improving learning.

Engagement/Retention Design

AI helps learners take charge of their learning through self-assessment, guided reflection, real-time feedback, and scaffolding. Metacognitive skills let students evaluate, appraise, and adjust their strategies, improving learning. Engaging Game Design Elements

1. Clearly defined objectives and goals

Setting clear goals is essential to game design. Clear objectives in educational games help students understand expectations and how to succeed. These goals inspire and guide education. A historical teaching game may require players to replicate a chronology, with each milestone serving as a learning objective and a challenge. Explicit objectives provide players meaning and integrate gameplay with educational goals (Loo, 2022).

2. Challenge & Progression

Excessively easy or difficult games might cause boredom or frustration. Engaging games balance challenge and accessibility, keeping students engaged without overwhelming them. Progressive difficulty helps players improve by making tasks harder as they go. This keeps students engaged and gives them a sense of accomplishment as they learn new material (Ishaq & Alvi, 2023).

3. Feedback and Rewards

Learning and player behavior depend on constructive feedback. Educational games give students performance feedback via visuals, audio, or pop-ups. Prompt feedback lets students evaluate their progress and correct mistakes immediately. Positive reinforcement like points, badges, and level unlocks encourages learners to keep going. Players feel accomplished and motivated with these benefits (Thampy et al., 2023).

4. Narrative & Storytelling

An effective narrative adds context and emotion to teaching, improving engagement. Narrative games immerse players in the game world, making them more relatable and memorable. A compelling story keeps players engaged and helps them remember the facts. A game set in ancient civilizations may let players play as historical leaders, helping them comprehend the social, political, and economic dynamics of the time and improving the tale (Loo, 2022).

5. Interactivity and Autonomy

Interactivity is key to student engagement. Providing opportunities for decision-making, exploration, and problem-solving helps students take charge of their education. Gamers feel empowered to make decisions that alter the game's trajectory, which boosts motivation. Choosing strategies during simulations or following a story increases learner investment and engagement (Clément et al., 2024).

6. Social Interaction

Social games include multiplayer modes, leaderboards, and collaborative assignments make learning lively. Social connection fosters collaboration, communication, and positive competition, which improves learning. Educational games are more enjoyable and memorable when players work together to solve problems or achieve goals (Franco & DeLuca, 2019).

Psychology of Play-Based Learning

1. Intrinsic Motivation and Fun

Play is enjoyable, making it a great educational tool. Play drives intrinsic motivation, the desire to enjoy and enjoy an activity. Games naturally give enjoyable challenges that engage deeply. Students who appreciate the material are more likely to persevere and stay engaged. Self-determination theory emphasises autonomy, competence, and relatedness as motivation boosters (Baskara, 2024).

2. Repetition and Mastery

Games encourage repetition by making practicing fun. Educational games that require frequent interaction, such as math problems or vocabulary practice, reinforce learning and help students master. Gamifying repetitive tasks motivates students to practice more, improving abilities and fluency. This strategy makes practice less monotonous, encouraging learners to repeat skill-building exercises (2020).

3. Safe Failure and Experimentation

Game-based learning allows for low-risk experimentation and failure. Traditional educational contexts can discourage risk-taking and creativity due to error fear. Failure is acceptable and expected in games. Players can try different methods, make mistakes, and learn from them without facing consequences. This safe environment encourages students to experiment, learn, and improve their skills, developing creativity and problem-solving (Beaulieu & Beno, 2024).

4. Cognitive Flow

Mihaly Csikszentmihalyi defined cognitive flow as intense focus and engagement in an activity. Flow occurs when a learner's skills match the task. Balanced challenges in well-structured games create flow. When learners reach flow, they become entirely immersed in the game, improving engagement and learning (Motevalli et al., 2020).

5. Emotional Connection and Memory

Emotions strongly affect memory. Learners are more likely to remember material when they are excited, happy, or content. Emotions and memory are used to create emotionally engaging educational games. The pleasure of solving complicated puzzles or the satisfaction of completing difficult tasks in games improves learning and retention (Alper et al., 2021).

CURRICULUM-SOCIETY ALIGNMENT 5.0 GOALS

Educational curriculum design must adapt to prepare humans for the challenges and opportunities of Society 5.0, which envisions a human-centric future where advanced technology like AI are seamlessly incorporated into society. This requires technological expertise and human-centric skills like critical thinking, creativity, teamwork, and flexibility. Society 5.0 objectives must be aligned with the curriculum to prepare students for an AI-driven world while protecting human values and societal welfare.

Educational systems must prioritize a balanced approach while creating a Society 5.0 curriculum to provide students with the knowledge and skills needed to flourish in a complex, technology-driven world. Students must learn to think critically, interact well, and create to keep up with rapidly changing technologies.

AI-Era Skills and Competencies

Learners need technical, cognitive, and social skills to succeed in Society 5.0. These skills help human growth and advance social and technological advancements in this new era.

1. Digital Literacy and Tech Proficiency

Digital literacy is vital in a culture when AI and digital technology are everywhere. A Society 5.0 curriculum must give students the knowledge and skills to use new technology. This includes programming, data analysis, and understanding how AI systems are used in recommendation algorithms and autonomous vehicles. Success in almost every field requires the ability to use and exploit digital tools.

Technical competency includes understanding technology's ethical and social impacts. How does AI affect privacy? Automation's impact on employment? The curriculum should include these principles to teach students how to use and create technology responsibly (Tan & Subramonyam, 2023).

2. Problem-solving and adaptability

Current issues are complex, and the future will require critical thinkers and problem-solvers. Society 5.0 requires strong problem-solving skills. This includes solving urgent issues and adapting to new circumstances. A curriculum for the AI era must promote critical thinking and adaptation.

Simulations may demand students to navigate a series of dynamic scenarios, adapting to new knowledge and changing conditions. These experiences teach students to approach problems from multiple angles and adjust their reasoning as new aspects surface (Iwamoto et al., 2023).

3. Global and Cultural Awareness

Technology improves interconnectedness, and Society 5.0 emphasizes global cooperation and cultural diversity. In this situation, understanding other cultures, languages, and perspectives is crucial. Educational systems must teach global and cultural awareness to prepare students for a multicultural world.

Students must have cross-cultural experiences, study global issues like climate change, and work with foreign peers on projects. Students could study the effects of technology on different places or worldwide policy decisions in the digital age. This global perspective helps students become responsible, empathic citizens who can improve a diverse world (Michaeli et al., 2023).

4. Social Responsibility and Ethical Awareness

Ethics become increasingly important in all aspects of decision-making as technology advances. Education for Society 5.0 must emphasize ethical technology use, notably AI, automation, and data protection. Students must understand how their actions affect society and make decisions that benefit everyone.

Ethical issues like AI's impact on privacy and automation's on employment must be discussed and solved in curriculum. These activities instill obligation and accountability, preparing students to make ethical decisions in their personal and professional lives (Baskara, 2024).

5. Lifelong Learning

Rapid technological growth requires constant skill and knowledge acquisition. Education systems should encourage lifelong learning, where students view learning as a continual process beyond formal education. This requires curiosity, growth mindset, and independent learning.

Lifelong learning requires self-directed learning opportunities that allow students to explore personal interests or improve skills (Zhao & Watterston, 2021).

Students may be encouraged to take online courses in emerging fields like data science or digital marketing to ensure their professional agility and flexibility.

Integrating Critical Thinking, Collaboration, and Creativity

In addition to technological talents, Society 5.0 stresses human-centric competencies that robots cannot reproduce. Critical thinking, teamwork, and innovation are needed to solve AI's difficult problems.

1. Critical Thinking

Critical thinking supports problem-solving and decision-making. Encourage students to evaluate information, assess facts, and think critically about complex issues to prepare them for an AI-dominated world. A Society 5.0 curriculum should emphasize analytical reasoning through talks, case studies, and simulations. These exercises force students to consider multiple viewpoints, make evidence-based judgments, and understand their consequences (Schiff et al., 2021).

Students could study the ethical implications of AI in healthcare or how automation may affect employment markets. These debates foster critical thinking and ensure students understand the social impacts of technology.

2. Collaboration

In Society No task is addressed alone in 5.0. Future difficult situations require collaboration and good communication. Curriculum should include group projects, transdisciplinary tasks, and cooperative games that simulate real-world scenarios (Kaur & Aziz, 2020). Students can design a smart city using engineering, environmental science, and social studies skills. These experiences teach students how to work in teams and solve problems.

3. Creativity and Innovation

Innovation and social progress require creativity. 5.0 Students should be encouraged to experiment, design think, and solve problems open-endedly to foster creativity. Project-based learning, maker spaces, and game-based platforms encourage students to find creative solutions to real-world problems (Zhanqiang, 2023).

Students may create a gamified sustainability software or a tech solution to a local social issue. These projects combine art and technology, teaching pupils both. Through innovation, kids can become future change-makers, advancing technology and society.

Game-Based Curriculum Framework

A game-based curriculum must align educational goals with game mechanics and include extensive assessment. An immersive and engaging teaching environment that motivates students and yields quantitative learning results is the goal. By carefully assessing these elements, teachers can create curricula that captivate students while promoting critical learning objectives and skill development as required.

Game Mechanics and Learning Objectives Alignment

Game-based curriculum efficacy depends on how well educational objectives are integrated into game design. Game mechanics should be carefully chosen and arranged to facilitate learning. This alignment is essential to keeping gameplay purposeful, instructive, and exciting for students.

1. Establishing Clear Learning Objectives

A game-based curriculum needs clear learning objectives to guide game creation and student learning. These objectives should focus on the knowledge, skills, and behaviors students should learn from the game. In a science game, learning objectives may include ecological concepts, the scientific method, and environmental sustainability.

The game's objectives should be quantifiable and achievable and aligned with curriculum standards. This alignment ensures the game achieves instructional goals. If the game teaches physics, students may create a virtual roller coaster or launch a space shuttle to understand the laws of motion (Cardinot & Fairfield, 2018).

2. Aligning Game Mechanics with Objectives

Game mechanics are the rules, frameworks, and interactions that drive gameplay. The mechanics must be carefully selected and connected with learning objectives to promote education.

- **Exploration mechanics** in games can encourage curiosity and discovery, making them ideal for subjects like geography, history, and biology. A historical game may allow students to explore numerous eras and make decisions based on historical events, improving their understanding of history (Benton et al., 2021).
- **Puzzle mechanics** foster problem-solving and critical thinking, making them ideal for fields like arithmetic, logic, and computer science. Students must

use math and logic to solve complex equations or logic puzzles in mathematical games (Ghosal et al., 2024).

- **Mechanisms for role-playing**: Empathy, decision-making, and morality are improved by role-playing. Games that simulate historical events or real-world scenarios, such as social studies ethical dilemmas or literary moral dilemmas, help students make reflective decisions.

Students feel developed by advancement, incentives, and challenges, which reinforces educational content and motivates them to learn. These gameplay elements help students meet learning objectives (Alper et al., 2021).

3. Interactive Engagement Maintenance

To maintain heightened engagement levels, games must actively engage learners in decision-making, experimentation, and innovative problem-solving (Yaccob et al., 2022). A physics-based game might let students build and evaluate virtual bridges and buildings while learning about material strength and gravity. Interactive learning experiences help students apply academic knowledge.

Real-time feedback like progress trackers, hints, and remedial suggestions improves game mechanics and educational goals. These feedback methods keep students engaged and motivated, guiding them to mastery and correcting faults.

Game-Based Learning Assessment Integration

GBL assessment should be integrated within the game, not separate or disruptive. Assessment in game mechanics lets learners track their progress and make modifications in real time.

1. Formative Assessment

Formative assessments in games provide constant feedback to help students meet learning goals. A language-learning game may recognize incorrect grammar as pupils go, suggesting improvements. This rapid feedback helps pupils correct mistakes, promoting learning and retention.

Games can have progress indicators like accuracy percentages, completion rates, and level or task completion times. These indicators let students and educators assess a student's knowledge and intervene when needed (Takeuchi & Vaala, 2014).

2. Summative Assessment

Summative assessments in game-based learning occur after a level, challenge, or game. These assessments assess a learner's comprehension of game concepts. A "boss battle" at the end of a history-based game may require pupils to negotiate peace accords or make political decisions based on historical events.

These tests assess knowledge retention and application in complex real-world situations. Summative assessments validate students' understanding and ability to apply game information (Ismail et al., 2022).

3. Performance Metrics and Analytics

AI-driven games can track complex performance indicators to assess student engagement and progress. These measurements may include task time, error rates, completion times, and advancement rates. By analyzing this data, educators may identify each student's strengths, shortcomings, and engagement trends.

If a student takes too long or makes too many mistakes, the teacher may change the curriculum or give extra help. This data-driven approach makes learning more personalized (Ober et al., 2023).

4. Portfolio-Based Assessment

Some games let students create and exhibit digital designs, textual solutions, or finished items to demonstrate their understanding. A digital portfolio can assess originality, comprehension, and skill application using these artifacts.

Portfolio-based assessments let students show their learning path rather than just the final result. This assessment technique emphasises self-reflection and work refinement throughout time (n.d.).

5. Promoting Reflection and Self-Assessment

In-game journals, post-game questionnaires, and self-assessment prompts are used in many game-based courses to develop metacognition. These tools let students reflect on their gaming strategies, decisions, and actions. After completing a level, students may be asked, "Which strategies proved most effective for you?" or "What alterations would you implement in the future?"

These reflective exercises help students understand their learning processes, enabling critical analysis and accountability for their progress. Student self-assessment and reflection help them recognize strengths and weaknesses and develop lifelong learning skills (Pang, 2020).

Models and Case Studies

Game-based curriculum demonstrate potential in improving student engagement, learning outcomes, and essential skills in educational settings globally. Successful game-based learning implementations enable educators and policymakers identify effective tactics and lessons gained. This global perspective can inform future game-based learning programs.

Successful Global Game-based Curriculum Implementations

1. Finland: Basic Education Minecraft

Overview:

Finland, recognized for its advanced education systems, has integrated Minecraft into its basic school curriculum to teach subjects such as math, history, and environmental science (Saricam & Yıldırım, 2021).

Implementation:

- Students utilize Minecraft's building mechanics to make historical landmark models or solve math challenges. They may rebuild old cities or recreate complicated geometric shapes.
- Teachers create in-game tasks that correspond with national curriculum objectives, such as investigating sustainable agricultural techniques or understanding ecological principles in Minecraft's world-building tools.

Impact:

- Improved spatial reasoning and creativity among students by promoting critical thinking about space and design.
- Enhanced student collaboration through group projects, promoting teamwork and communication.
- Minecraft offers a hands-on, interactive learning experience that makes complex subjects more graspable and entertaining for kids.

2. Japan: Game-Based AI Language Learning

Overview:

In Japan, schools use AI-powered games like Duolingo to teach English in an interactive and engaging manner (Auliawan & Ong, 2020).

Implementation:

- Students get points for correct grammar, pronunciation, and vocabulary usage in simulated discussions.
- The AI-powered technology adjusts class intensity based on student success, ensuring ongoing challenge without overwhelming them.

Impact:

- Improved language fluency: Students demonstrate higher pronunciation, grammatical comprehension, and English speaking confidence.
- The AI system's dynamic and adaptable nature engages students by personalizing learning experiences and providing rapid feedback.

Best Practices and Lessons Learned

The successes of these global examples have yielded some key lessons and best practices for game-based curriculum design.

1. Customization, Culture Relevance
   - **Lesson:** Adapt games to local cultural and educational requirements for successful adoption. Local history or language-specific problems make learning more relevant.
   - **Best Practice:** Work with local educators and cultural experts to design game material that takes into account area values, curriculum goals, and cultural differences. This makes games student-friendly and instructional (Benton et al., 2021).
2. Support and Training for Teachers
   - **Lesson:** Effective game-based learning relies on teachers. Without training, teachers may struggle to incorporate games into their lessons.
   - **Best Practice:** Provide ongoing professional development and tools to equip teachers with game mechanics. This includes aligning games with educational goals and facilitating learning in game-based environments (Zhao et al., 2021).
3. Fun and Learning Balance
   - **Lesson:** Games can engage, but educational material should not be swamped by enjoyment and rewards. Learning should always be the focus.
   - **Best Practice:** Create instructional games with clear objectives and compelling challenges for critical thinking. Games should help players learn, and rewards and fun should encourage learning (Pasqualotto et al., 2022).

4. Scalability, Accessibility
   - **Lesson:** Game-based models like BYJU's can scale to millions of learners. In certain communities, especially for impoverished pupils, technology is still unavailable.
   - **Best Practice:** Make game-based curricula accessible on several platforms, including mobile and offline modes, to reduce the digital divide. Consider regional resource availability to maximize game-based learning's reach and efficacy (Su, 2014).
5. Continuous Evaluation and Feedback
   - **Lesson:** Continuous evaluation and feedback are essential for game-based curricula to achieve instructional goals.
   - **Best Practice:** Use adaptive AI technologies for real-time student progress monitoring and feedback. Adjust content dynamically using performance metrics to give learners individualized support and keep them engaged. This feedback loop improves game play and learning (Gligorea et al., 2023).

ETHICS AND CHALLENGES

To employ AI and game-based learning successfully and inclusively, various issues must be addressed as these technologies become more widespread in educational systems. These problems include technological game development and integration, ethical, and societal issues, especially when aligned with Society's aims. 5.0. To benefit from these modern instructional tools, all learners must overcome technological barriers, regardless of socioeconomic background or location.

Tech Barriers

As AI-driven and game-based learning aids are integrated into educational systems, technological hurdles may prevent their general adoption. Addressing these limitations is crucial for inclusive education and utilizing technology for Society 5.0.

Expensive Development and Implementation

1) Developing AI-powered instructional games and applications requires significant expenditure. Include development, testing, deployment, and maintenance costs. Schools with limited funds may not be able to afford advanced VR equipment or AI-powered **analytics.**
2) Challenges:

Affordability: Lower-income schools may have challenges in funding license fees, hardware, and specialized software for game-based learning. Underfunded schools may struggle to afford advanced equipment like VR headsets or AI-based data analytics systems that track student growth.

3) **Solution:** Government subsidies and partnerships between schools and tech companies can make these technologies more inexpensive and accessible (Richey et al., 2020).

Infrastructure Limits

1) In rural or underprivileged areas, educational institutions sometimes lack the essential technology for AI and game-based learning.
2) Challenges:
    - Outdated Equipment: Schools may lack the necessary computers or IT support to successfully use AI-driven educational solutions.
    - Limited internet access is a barrier for delivering cloud-based instructional information and using real-time interactive gaming platforms in many institutions.
3) To overcome these limitations, schools should invest in improving their technical infrastructure to implement innovative courses. Affordable, high-speed internet is essential for schools (OECD, 2020).

Data Security and Privacy Issues

1) Using AI-based learning technologies requires collecting extensive student data, including personal and learning activities. This presents serious privacy, security, and data ethics problems.
2) Challenges:

Data Protection: Concerns about data breaches or exploitation of student information may prevent educators, parents, and legislators from using AI-based learning platforms.

Ethical Issues: Data collection, storage, and sharing raise ethical concerns, particularly with third-party access.

3) **Solution:** Schools and developers must prioritize data protection, openness, and rigorous privacy restrictions. Data collection, storage, and sharing should be regulated to reduce privacy problems (Luan et al., 2020).

Technology Readiness in Developing Regions

1) Many locations, especially rural or economically challenged ones, struggle to implement game-based learning due to inadequate technology access.
2) **Challenges:**

Infrastructure Gaps: Schools in these places may lack resources to implement game-based learning tools. Increased Inequality: Limited technological access worsens the digital gap, marginalizing students in these places.

3) **Solution:**

Afzal et al. (2023) suggest that promoting technology access through initiatives like low-cost devices or community tech hubs can help close the gap.

REFERENCES

Παπαστεργίου, M. (2008). Digital Game-Based Learning in high school Computer Science education: Impact on educational effectiveness and student motivation. In Computers & Education (Vol. 52, Number 1, p. 1). Elsevier BV. https://doi.org/DOI: 10.1016/j.compedu.2008.06.004

Abioye, S., Oyedele, L. O., Akanbi, L., Ajayi, A., Delgado, J. M. D., Bilal, M., Akinadé, O. O., & Ahmed, A. (2021). Artificial intelligence in the construction industry: A review of present status, opportunities and future challenges [Review of Artificial intelligence in the construction industry: A review of present status, opportunities and future challenges]. Journal of Building Engineering, 44, 103299. Elsevier BV. https://doi.org/DOI: 10.1016/j.jobe.2021.103299

Afzal, A., Khan, S., Daud, S., Ahmad, Z., & Butt, A. (2023). Addressing the Digital Divide: Access and Use of Technology in Education. In journal of social sciences review (Vol. 3, Number 2, p. 883). https://doi.org/DOI: 10.54183/jssr.v3i2.326

AI-Infused Collaborative Inquiry in Upper Elementary School. A Game-Based Learning Approach. (2021). https://ojs.aaai.org/index.php/AAAI/article/view/17836

Alper, A., Öztaş, E. Ş., Atun, H., Çınar, D., & Moyenga, M. (2021). A Systematic Literature Review towards the Research of Game-Based Learning with Augmented Reality. In International Journal of Technology in Education and Science (Vol. 5, Number 2, p. 224). https://doi.org/DOI: 10.46328/ijtes.176

Auliawan, A. G., & Ong, S. (2020). *The Usage of AI Robot in English Language Teaching for City Revitalization Case Study*. Toda Daini Elementary School.

Baskara, F. (2024). A Theoretical Analysis of ChatGPT Integration in Flipped Classrooms to Enhance Personal Learning Space.

Beaulieu, É., & Beno, S. (2024). Healthy childhood development through outdoor risky play: Navigating the balance with injury prevention [Review of Healthy childhood development through outdoor risky play: Navigating the balance with injury prevention]. Paediatrics & Child Health, 29(4), 255. Oxford University Press. https://doi.org/DOI: 10.1093/pch/pxae016

Benton, L., Mavrikis, M., Vasalou, A., Joye, N., Sumner, E., Herbert, E., Révész, A., Symvonis, A., & Raftopoulou, C. N. (2021). Designing for "challenge" in a large-scale adaptive literacy game for primary school children. In British Journal of Educational Technology (Vol. 52, Number 5, p. 1862). Wiley. https://doi.org/DOI: 10.1111/bjet.13146

Bui, L. T. N., & Khuu, V. T. (2020). Inquiry-based learning: an effective approach to teaching science aiming to develop students' competencies. In Vietnam Journal of Education (online)/Vietnam Journal of Education/Giáo d c (Vol. 4, Number 1, p. 61). https://doi.org/DOI: 10.52296/vje.2020.9

Cardinot, A., & Fairfield, J. A. (2018). Game-Based Learning to Engage Students With Physics and Astronomy Using a Board Game. In International Journal of Game-Based Learning (Vol. 9, Number 1, p. 42). IGI Global. https://doi.org/DOI: 10.4018/ijgbl.2019010104

Chariyev, T. X. (2020). THE DEVELOPMENT OF INDEPENDENT AND CREATIVE THINKING OF STUDENTS IN THE LEARNING PROCESS. In Theoretical & Applied Science (Vol. 82, Number 2, p. 605). International Academy Of Theoretical & Applied Science. https://doi.org/DOI: 10.15863/tas.2020.02.82.101

Ciecierski-Holmes, T., Singh, R., Axt, M., Brenner, S., & Barteit, S. (2022). Artificial intelligence for strengthening healthcare systems in low- and middle-income countries: a systematic scoping review [Review of Artificial intelligence for strengthening healthcare systems in low- and middle-income countries: a systematic scoping review]. Npj Digital Medicine, 5(1). Nature Portfolio. https://doi.org/DOI: 10.1038/s41746-022-00700-y

Clément, B., Sauzéon, H., Roy, D., & Oudeyer, P.-Y. (2024). Improved Performances and Motivation in Intelligent Tutoring Systems: Combining Machine Learning and Learner Choice. In arXiv (Cornell University). Cornell University. https://doi.org//arxiv.2402.01669DOI: 10.48550

Costello, R., & Lambert, M. (2018). Motivational Influences for Higher Education (HE) Students. In International Journal of Online Pedagogy and Course Design (Vol. 9, Number 1, p. 38). IGI Global. https://doi.org/DOI: 10.4018/ijopcd.2019010103

Darvishi, A., Khosravi, H., Sadiq, S., Gašević, D., & Siemens, G. (2023). Impact of AI assistance on student agency. In *Computers & Education* (Vol. 210, p. 104967). Elsevier BV., DOI: 10.1016/j.compedu.2023.104967

Franco, P. F., & DeLuca, D. A. (2019). Learning Through Action: Creating and Implementing a Strategy Game to Foster Innovative Thinking in Higher Education. In Simulation & Gaming (Vol. 50, Number 1, p. 23). SAGE Publishing. https://doi.org/DOI: 10.1177/1046878118820892

Ghosal, D., Han, V. T. Y., Ken, C. Y., & Poria, S. (2024). Are Language Models Puzzle Prodigies? Algorithmic Puzzles Unveil Serious Challenges in Multimodal Reasoning. In arXiv (Cornell University). Cornell University. https://doi.org//arxiv.2403.03864DOI: 10.48550

Gligorea, I., Cioca, M., Oancea, R., Gorski, A.-T., Gorski, H., & Tudorache, P. (2023). Adaptive Learning Using Artificial Intelligence in e-Learning: A Literature Review [Review of Adaptive Learning Using Artificial Intelligence in e-Learning: A Literature Review]. Education Sciences, 13(12), 1216. Multidisciplinary Digital Publishing Institute. https://doi.org/DOI: 10.3390/educsci13121216

Hacker, S. (n.d.). proposal.docx. Retrieved January 14, 2025, from https://www.cs.cmu.edu/~shacker/thesis/proposal.pdf

Hasan, Md. T., Shamael, M. N., Akter, A., Islam, R., Mukta, Md. S. H., & Islam, S. (2023). An Artificial Intelligence-based Framework to Achieve the Sustainable Development Goals in the Context of Bangladesh. In arXiv (Cornell University). Cornell University. https://doi.org//arxiv.2304.11703DOI: 10.48550

Ishak, S. A., Din, R., & Hasran, U. A. (2020). Defining Digital Game-Based Learning for Science, Technology, Engineering, and Mathematics: A New Perspective on Design and Developmental Research. In Journal of Medical Internet Research (Vol. 23, Number 2). JMIR Publications. https://doi.org/DOI: 10.2196/20537

Ishaq, K., & Alvi, A. (2023). Personalization, Cognition, and Gamification-based Programming Language Learning: A State-of-the-Art Systematic Literature Review. In arXiv (Cornell University). Cornell University. https://doi.org//arxiv.2309.12362DOI: 10.48550

Ismail, S. M., Rahul, D. R., Patra, I., & Rezvani, E. (2022). Formative vs. summative assessment: impacts on academic motivation, attitude toward learning, test anxiety, and self-regulation skill. In Language Testing in Asia (Vol. 12, Number 1). Springer Science+Business Media. https://doi.org/DOI: 10.1186/s40468-022-00191-4

Iwamoto, T., Matsumoto, M., Kuriyama, M., Minami, R., & Murao, K. (2023). Study on Experiences to Enhance Design Thinking Skills. In *2022 Portland International Conference on Management of Engineering and Technology (PICMET)* (p. 1). https://doi.org/DOI: 10.23919/picmet59654.2023.10216862

Jones, H., & Hammond, L. (2022, October 19). The journey not the destination: Liminality and lifelong learning. In Medical Education (Vol. 57, Number 2, p. 115). Wiley. https://doi.org/DOI: 10.1111/medu.14956

JOYCE. J., & Harris, L. A. (2018). Artificial Intelligence (AI) and Education. https://digital.library.unt.edu/ark:/67531/metadc1228526/m2/1/high_res_d/IF10937_2018Aug01.pdf

Kaur, D., & Aziz, A. A. (2020). The Use of Language Game in Enhancing Students' Speaking Skills. In International Journal of Academic Research in Business and Social Sciences (Vol. 10, Number 12). https://doi.org/DOI: 10.6007/ijarbss/v10-i12/8369

Krissilov, V., Huy, V. N., & Zinovatna, S. L. (2018). INFORMATION MODEL OF DISTANCE LEARNING SYSTEM IN TERMS OF DATA COMMUNICATION IN HETEROGENEOUS INTERNET NETWORKS. In Odes'kyi Politechnichnyi Universytet Pratsi (Vol. 1, Number 54, p. 62). Odesa National Polytechnic University. https://doi.org/DOI: 10.15276/opu.1.54.2018.08

Kucher, T. (2021). Principles and Best Practices of Designing Digital Game-Based Learning Environments. In International Journal of Technology in Education and Science (Vol. 5, Number 2, p. 213). https://doi.org/DOI: 10.46328/ijtes.190

Li, X., & Pan, X. (2023). A Review of Gamification Teaching Based on Creative Thinking Development [Review of A Review of Gamification Teaching Based on Creative Thinking Development]. *Journal of Education Humanities and Social Sciences*, *14*, 46. DOI: 10.54097/ehss.v14i.8794

Loo, B. F. W. (2022). Strategy and Defense Policy for Small States: Problems and Prospects.

Martins, A. R. de Q., Pagliarini, E. R., Kalil, F., & Pazinato, A. M. (2022). GAMIFICATION AS AN INSTRUMENT FOR ENHANCING THE ENGAGEMENT ON #TEUFUTURO PROGRAM. In Revista Observatório (Vol. 8, Number 1). Universidade Federal do Tocantins. https://doi.org/DOI: 10.20873/uft.2447-4266.2022v8n1a6pt

Mello, R. F., Freitas, E., Pereira, F. D., Cabral, L., Tedesco, P., & Ramalho, G. (2023). Education in the age of Generative AI: Context and Recent Developments. In arXiv (Cornell University). Cornell University. https://doi.org//arxiv.2309.12332DOI: 10.48550

Meşe, İ. (2023, January 1). The Impact of Artificial Intelligence on Radiology Education in the Wake of Coronavirus Disease 2019. In Korean Journal of Radiology (Vol. 24, Number 5, p. 478). Korean Society of Radiology. https://doi.org/DOI: 10.3348/kjr.2023.0278

Michaeli, T., Romeike, R., & Seegerer, S. (2023). What Students Can Learn About Artificial Intelligence – Recommendations for K-12 Computing Education. In IFIP advances in information and communication technology (p. 196). Springer Science+Business Media. https://doi.org/DOI: 10.1007/978-3-031-43393-1_19

Motevalli, S., Perveen, A., & Michael, M. T. A. (2020). Motivating Students to Learn: An Overview of Literature in Educational Psychology. In International Journal of Academic Research in Progressive Education and Development (Vol. 9, Number 3). https://doi.org/DOI: 10.6007/ijarped/v9-i3/7779

O'Neil, H. F., Chuang, S.-H., & Huang, T. (2010). Instructional System Provided Feedback. In *Elsevier eBooks* (p. 226). Elsevier BV., DOI: 10.1016/b978-0-08-044894-7.00312-2

Ober, T. M., Lehman, B., Gooch, R., Oluwalana, O., Solyst, J., Phelps, G., & Hamilton, L. Culturally responsive personalized learning: Recommendations for a working definition and framework. ETS Research Report Series, 2023(1), 1-14.

OECD. (2020). The impact of COVID-19 on student equity and inclusion: Supporting vulnerable students during school closures and school re-openings. In OECD policy responses to coronavirus (Covid-19). https://doi.org/DOI: 10.1787/d593b5c8-en

Onele, N. O. (2020). Virtual Reality: A Tool for Improving the Teaching and Learning of Technology Education. In IntechOpen eBooks. IntechOpen. https://doi.org/DOI: 10.5772/intechopen.90809

Palacios, H. F. M., Cumbicos, K. M. C., & Peralta, S. R. T. (2023). El impacto de la gamificación en la motivación y el aprendizaje de los estudiantes de matemáticas de educación básica superior. In Ciencia Latina Revista Científica Multidisciplinar (Vol. 7, Number 3, p. 6494). Latin American Association for the Advancement of Sciences. https://doi.org/DOI: 10.37811/cl_rcm.v7i3.6650

Palmer, A. S., & Rodgers, T. S. (1983). Games In Language Teaching. In Language Teaching (Vol. 16, Number 1, p. 2). Cambridge University Press. https://doi.org/DOI: 10.1017/s0261444800009836

Pang, N. S.-K. (2020). Teachers' Reflective Practices in Implementing Assessment for Learning Skills in Classroom Teaching. In ECNU Review of Education (Vol. 5, Number 3, p. 470). SAGE Publishing. https://doi.org/DOI: 10.1177/2096531120936290

Pasqualotto, A., Parong, J., Green, C. S., & Bavelier, D. (2022). Video Game Design for Learning to Learn. In International Journal of Human-Computer Interaction (Vol. 39, Number 11, p. 2211). Taylor & Francis. https://doi.org/DOI: 10.1080/10447318.2022.2110684

Philip, L., Cottrill, C., Farrington, J., Williams, F., & Ashmore, F. (2017). The digital divide: Patterns, policy and scenarios for connecting the 'final few' in rural communities across Great Britain. In *Journal of Rural Studies* (Vol. 54, p. 386). Elsevier BV., DOI: 10.1016/j.jrurstud.2016.12.002

Razali, N., Nasir, N. A., Ismail, M. E., Sari, N., & Salleh, K. M. (2020). Gamification Elements in Quizizz Applications: Evaluating the Impact on Intrinsic and Extrinsic Student's Motivation. In IOP Conference Series Materials Science and Engineering (Vol. 917, Number 1, p. 12024). IOP Publishing. https://doi.org/DOI: 10.1088/1757-899x/917/1/012024

Richey, J. E., Lobczowski, N. G., Carvalho, P. F., & Koedinger, K. R. (2020). Comprehensive Views of Math Learners: A Case for Modeling and Supporting Non-math Factors in Adaptive Math Software. In Lecture notes in computer science (p. 460). Springer Science+Business Media. https://doi.org/DOI: 10.1007/978-3-030-52237-7_37

Rosenthal, G. (2009). Economic and Social Council. In Oxford University Press eBooks (p. 136). Oxford University Press. https://doi.org/DOI: 10.1093/oxfordhb/9780199560103.003.0007

Saputra, I., Astuti, M., Sayuti, M., & Kusumastuti, D. (2023). Integration of Artificial Intelligence in Education: Opportunities, Challenges, Threats and Obstacles. A Literature Review. In Indonesian Journal of Computer Science (Vol. 12, Number 4). https://doi.org/DOI: 10.33022/ijcs.v12i4.3266

Saricam, U., & Yıldırım, M. (2021). The Effects of Digital Game-based STEM Activities on Students' Interests in STEM Fields and Scientific Creativity: Minecraft Case. In International Journal of Technology in Education and Science (Vol. 5, Number 2, p. 166). https://doi.org/DOI: 10.46328/ijtes.136

Schiff, D., Rakova, B., Ayesh, A., Fanti, A., & Lennon, M. (2021). Explaining the Principles to Practices Gap in AI. In IEEE Technology and Society Magazine (Vol. 40, Number 2, p. 81). Institute of Electrical and Electronics Engineers. https://doi.org/DOI: 10.1109/mts.2021.3056286

Shneiderman, B. (2020). Human-Centered Artificial Intelligence: Three Fresh Ideas. In AIS Transactions on Human-Computer Interaction (p. 109). Association for Information Systems. https://doi.org/DOI: 10.17705/1thci.00131

Su, Y. (2014). Development of the Teaching Games System Based on Mobile Learning. In *Applied Mechanics and Materials* (Vol. 685, p. 651). Trans Tech Publications., DOI: 10.4028/www.scientific.net/amm.685.651

Takeuchi, L., & Vaala, S. E. (2014). Level up Learning: A National Survey on Teaching with Digital Games. https://files.eric.ed.gov/fulltext/ED555585.pdf

Tan, M., & Subramonyam, H. (2023). More than Model Documentation: Uncovering Teachers' Bespoke Information Needs for Informed Classroom Integration of ChatGPT. In arXiv (Cornell University). Cornell University. https://doi.org//arxiv.2309.14458DOI: 10.48550

Thampy, H., Walsh, J., & Harris, B. (2023). Playing the game: The educational role of gamified peer-led assessment. In The Clinical Teacher (Vol. 20, Number 4). Wiley. https://doi.org/DOI: 10.1111/tct.13594

Wendrich, R. E. (2020). CREATIVE THINKING: COMPUTATIONAL TOOLS IMBUED WITH AI. In *Proceedings of the Design Society DESIGN Conference* (Vol. 1, p. 481). Cambridge University Press. https://doi.org/DOI: 10.1017/dsd.2020.7

Winanti, W., Abbas, B. S., Suparta, W., Heryadi, Y., & Gaol, F. L. (2021). Gamification Framework for Programming Course in Higher Education. In Journal of Games Game Art and Gamification (Vol. 5, Number 2, p. 54). Bina Nusantara University. https://doi.org/DOI: 10.21512/jggag.v5i2.7479

Yaccob, N. S., & Rahman, S. F. Abd., Mohamad, S. N. A., Rahim, A. A. A., Rashid, K. K. A., Aldaba, A. M. A., Yunus, M. M., & Hashim, H. (2022). Gamifying ESL Classrooms through Gamified Teaching and Learning. In Arab World English Journal (Number 8, p. 177). Arab World English Journal. https://doi.org/DOI: 10.24093/awej/call8.12

Yue, X., & Ji, R. (2020). Teacher Professional Competencies in Education for Sustainable Development. In *IntechOpen eBooks*. IntechOpen., DOI: 10.5772/intechopen.94991

Zastudil, C., Rogalska, M., Kapp, C., Vaughn, J., & MacNeil, S. (2023). Generative AI in Computing Education: Perspectives of Students and Instructors. In arXiv (Cornell University). Cornell University. https://doi.org//arxiv.2308.04309DOI: 10.48550

Zhai, X., Chu, X., Chai, C. S., Jong, M. S., Starčič, A. I., Spector, M., Liu, J., Jing, Y., & Li, Y. (2021). A Review of Artificial Intelligence (AI) in Education from 2010 to 2020 [Review of A Review of Artificial Intelligence (AI) in Education from 2010 to 2020]. Complexity, 2021(1). Hindawi Publishing Corporation. https://doi.org/DOI: 10.1155/2021/8812542

Zhang, K., & Aslan, A. B. (2021). AI technologies for education: Recent research & future directions. Computers and education. *Artificial Intelligence*, *2*, 100025.

Zhanqiang, M. (2023). Strategies for Cultivating Creative Thinking Ability of Students Majoring in Educational Technology. In Frontiers in Educational Research (Vol. 6, Number 19). https://doi.org/DOI: 10.25236/fer.2023.061911

Zhao, D., Playfoot, J., Nicola, C. D., Guarino, G., Bratu, M., Salvadore, F. D., & Muntean, G. (2021). An Innovative Multi-Layer Gamification Framework for Improved STEM Learning Experience. In Access, I. E. E. E. (Ed.), Vol. 10, p. 3879). Institute of Electrical and Electronics Engineers., DOI: 10.1109/access.2021.3139729

Zhao, Y., & Watterston, J. (2021). The changes we need: Education post COVID-19. In Journal of Educational Change (Vol. 22, Number 1, p. 3). Springer Science+Business Media. https://doi.org/DOI: 10.1007/s10833-021-09417-3

Chapter 10
Innovating Curriculum Design with AI and Gamification:
A Roadmap for Society 5.0

I Komang Mertayasa
https://orcid.org/0000-0002-4753-8268
Institut Agama Hindu Negeri Tampung Penyang, Indonesia

Putu Wisnu Saputra
https://orcid.org/0009-0004-6482-1913
Institut Agama Hindu Negeri Tampung Penyang, Indonesia

ABSTRACT

The digital revolution marked by the concept of Society 5.0 drives innovation in curriculum design through the integration of AI and gamification. This aims to create a more adaptive, interactive, and data-driven learning experience to enhance engagement and learning outcomes. AI is used to analyze learning data, provide real-time feedback, and adjust individual learning paths. Gamification applies game elements such as challenges, rewards, and leaderboards to motivate students. This integration offers extraordinary potential in enhancing educational effectiveness by tailoring the learning experience to individual needs. Its implementation requires attention to ethical aspects, algorithm transparency, and data privacy protection. this paper proposes a design framework for an AI-based gamification curriculum that considers personalized learning, data-driven feedback systems, and supporting technological infrastructure. With this approach, education can be more responsive to the challenges of the 21st century and equip students with relevant skills to face a technology-based future.

DOI: 10.4018/979-8-3373-1062-6.ch010

Copyright © 2026, IGI Global Scientific Publishing. Copying or distributing in print or electronic forms without written permission of IGI Global Scientific Publishing is prohibited.

INTRODUCTION

Society 5.0, a vision for a super-smart society, integrates advanced technologies like AI and IoT with human-centred values. It emphasises inclusivity, collaboration, and ethical awareness in addressing social challenges. Inclusive curriculum design becomes essential to ensure marginalised communities also benefit from these innovations.

Curriculum design is crucial in equipping future generations with the skills and knowledge needed to navigate the complexities of Society 5.0. This societal paradigm emphasises the integration of advanced technology, critical thinking, and ethical considerations into the educational framework. By incorporating these elements into the curriculum, educational institutions can prepare students not only to adapt to rapid technological changes but also to engage wisely with the ethical implications of these advancements. Research has shown that a curriculum prioritising critical thinking can enhance students' analytical abilities, enabling them to connect new concepts with existing knowledge and apply this understanding to solve various problems (Devi et al., 2016; Sughra & Usmani, 2022). Strategies to enforce ethical implementation include mandatory AI ethics training for educators, transparency protocols in AI tools, and regular audits for bias in educational datasets.

Interdisciplinary learning is crucial in fostering innovation and creativity among students. By encouraging collaboration across various fields, the curriculum can help students develop a holistic understanding of complex issues. This approach not only enhances their problem-solving skills but also prepares them to contribute positively to society. Students exposed to an integrated curriculum show improved critical thinking skills and a more in-depth approach to learning, which is crucial for tackling challenges from various aspects (Sughra & Usmani, 2022). Additionally, real-world applications and direct experiences embedded in the curriculum can significantly enhance students' practical skills, making them more adept at tackling real-life problems (Allahverdi, 2021).

Encouraging a growth mindset is another important aspect of modern curriculum design. By fostering curiosity and resilience, educators can help students adapt to new challenges and seize emerging opportunities. This is highly relevant in the context of Society 5.0, where the ability to learn continuously and adapt becomes very important. Various studies have highlighted the importance of developing critical thinking skills as a means to foster a growth mindset, which is crucial for lifelong learning and professional success (Pu et al., 2019). Moreover, the integration of ethical considerations into the curriculum ensures that students not only acquire technical knowledge but also develop the moral compass necessary for responsible decision-making in their future careers (Mugisha et al., 2021). A comprehensive educational programme that emphasises technical knowledge and soft skills is crucial for empowering individuals to make meaningful contributions to society and its environment. By prioritising critical thinking, interdisciplinary collaboration, real-world applications, and ethical considerations, curriculum design can effectively prepare students to face the challenges and opportunities of Society 5.0. Strategies to enforce ethical implementation include mandatory AI ethics training for educators, transparency protocols in AI tools, and regular audits for bias in educational datasets.

The integration of artificial intelligence (AI) and gamification in the world of education presents transformative opportunities to enhance the learning experience, making it more engaging and personalised for students. AI technology enables educators to create adaptive learning environments tailored to the needs of each student, thereby overcoming the limitations of traditional educational methods. For example, AI can analyse student performance data in real-time, allowing educators to identify areas where students are struggling and provide targeted interventions. This capability is supported by research showing that AI can facilitate personalised learning experiences that adapt to students' preferences and progress, ultimately improving academic outcomes (Popenici & Kerr, 2017; Abbas et al., 2023; Aparicio-Gómez, 2024). For instance, in Indonesia, some urban schools use AI-based tools like Ruangguru to customise learning paths based on student diagnostics, increasing engagement and performance.

Gamification, which combines elements of game design such as rewards, competition, and collaboration into the educational context, increasingly enhances student engagement. Research has shown that gamification has a positive impact on academic achievement and motivation, as it encourages active participation and fosters a sense of competition among students (Buckley & Doyle, 2014; Rohmah, 2022). By integrating gamification elements, such as leaderboards and achievement badges, educators can create an interactive learning environment that motivates students to strive hard to master challenging subjects. This approach not only makes learning enjoyable but also strengthens the learning process by providing immediate feedback and recognition of achievements (Legaki et al., 2020).

The combination of AI and gamification can create a more dynamic educational experience that prepares students for success in the digital era. AI-driven platforms can adjust the difficulty levels and pace of instruction based on individual student performance, ensuring that students are appropriately challenged without feeling overwhelmed (Dichev & Dicheva, 2017; Tonbuloğlu, 2023). Additionally, gamification can maintain student interest and engagement, making learning a more enjoyable and rewarding experience (Pratama, 2023; Rivera & Garden, 2021). This dual approach empowers educators to accommodate diverse learning styles and paces, ultimately fostering an inclusive educational environment that supports all students in reaching their full potential (Zhang, 2024; Onesi-Ozigagun, 2024).

Society 5.0, a vision for a super-smart society, integrates advanced technologies like AI and IoT with human-centred values. It emphasises inclusivity, collaboration, and ethical awareness in addressing social challenges. Inclusive curriculum design becomes essential to ensure marginalised communities also benefit from these innovations.

THE ROLE OF AI IN CURRICULUM DESIGN

1. The use of AI to analyse student data and personalise the learning experience

The integration of artificial intelligence (AI) in the world of education has fundamentally changed curriculum design, enabling a more personalised and adaptive learning experience for students. By utilising data analysis, AI can identify the strengths and weaknesses of each student, allowing educators to tailor lessons to their learning needs. This personalised approach not only enhances student engagement and motivation but also facilitates the mastery of key concepts at a pace suitable for each student. Research shows that AI-based analytics can provide valuable insights to educators about student progress, enabling timely interventions and adjustments to necessary instructional strategies (Uygun, 2024).

AI's ability to suggest relevant resources and activities based on individual learning styles significantly enhances the effectiveness of the curriculum. Various studies have shown that adaptive learning technology can create a dynamic educational environment that responds to diverse student needs, fostering an inclusive atmosphere where all students can thrive (Eslit, 2023; Walter, 2024). This adaptability is crucial in the current digital era, where traditional teaching methods that are one-size-fits-all are increasingly insufficient to handle the diverse learning preferences and speeds of students (Zhang, 2024).

The shift towards individualised teaching facilitated by AI has been associated with improved academic performance and a deeper understanding of the material among students. By shifting from general teaching methods, educators can provide targeted support to those who may struggle in specific areas, thereby improving overall learning outcomes (Khater et al., 2023; Nagi et al., 2023). The capacity of AI to effectively track student progress allows for a deeper understanding of each student's journey, enabling educators to implement timely and appropriate interventions (Ejaz et al., 2022).

2. AI-supported content creation and evaluation tools

The integration of artificial intelligence (AI) in educational environments has been proven to significantly enhance the efficiency and effectiveness of the teaching and learning process. AI devices can help educators save time and create more engaging and personalised learning materials tailored to the needs and learning styles of each student. For example, AI can generate quizzes, worksheets, and study guides that are tailored to meet the unique needs of each student, thereby promoting a more individualised learning experience (Akavova et al., 2023; Abbas et al., 2023). This capability not only simplifies the preparation of educational resources but also ensures that the materials are relevant and aligned with the students' learning objectives.

AI-supported assessment tools provide immediate feedback to students, allowing them to monitor their progress and identify areas that need improvement. This direct feedback mechanism is crucial for fostering a dynamic and interactive learning environment, as it allows students to engage more deeply with the material and take responsibility for their learning journey (Shah, 2024). The ability of AI to analyse student performance data increasingly empowers educators to make informed decisions regarding instructional strategies, thereby enhancing the overall educational experience (Fazil, 2024).

The personalisation provided by AI technology can enhance student engagement and academic success. By analysing learning patterns and preferences, AI can help create personalised learning plans to motivate students and keep them focused on their academic goals (Abbas et al., 2023). Additionally, the real-time feedback provided by the AI system allows educators to promptly identify students who are struggling and implement timely interventions, thereby optimising support for each student (Fazil, 2024). This adaptability not only enhances the learning experience for students but also helps teachers refine their instructional methods to maximise impact (Nguyen, 2022).

3. Applying AI to track student progress and provide feedback

AI allows educators to access real-time data on student performance and engagement, helping them identify learning difficulties and provide appropriate support or additional resources. The integration of artificial intelligence (AI) in the field of education has shown significant potential to enhance the teaching and learning experience by providing real-time insights into student performance and engagement. AI technology can analyse data on student behaviour and academic performance, allowing educators to identify areas where students may be struggling and offer appropriate assistance. For example, Akavova et al. discuss how AI can create intelligent systems that provide personalised feedback and adapt learning experiences to meet individual student needs, thereby fostering a more engaging learning environment (Akavova et al., 2023). This adaptability is crucial because it allows educators to intervene promptly when students show signs of difficulty, ultimately leading to improved academic outcomes (Fazil, 2024).

AI's ability to generate insights from data enables a deeper understanding of student engagement and motivation levels. Popenici and Kerr highlight that AI can facilitate the monitoring of student focus and engagement through advanced technologies, such as brain-computer interfaces, which can inform instructional strategies (Popenici & Kerr, 2017). By leveraging these insights, teachers can make informed decisions about the best ways to support and motivate their students, thereby creating a dynamic classroom experience that is responsive to students' needs (Kamruzzaman, 2023). This data-driven approach not only enhances the educational experience but also empowers educators to focus more on personalised instruction rather than administrative tasks (Alkan, 2024).

The potential of AI to revolutionise education also extends to the development of personalised learning pathways. Research shows that AI-driven systems can dynamically adjust content delivery and assessments based on the characteristics of each student, in line with the principles of personalised learning. This targeted approach not only enhances student engagement but also improves overall academic performance, as evidenced by research showing a positive correlation between AI integration and student success (Gligorea et al., 2022; Katiyar, 2024). The transformative impact of AI in education is underscored by its ability to create more personalised and effective educational experiences for all stakeholders involved (Harry, 2023).

INTEGRATING GAMIFICATION INTO CURRICULUM DESIGN

1. The principles of gamification and its impact on student engagement

Gamification, defined as the integration of game design elements in a non-game context, has been proven to significantly increase student engagement in educational environments. By integrating elements such as competition, rewards, and progress into curriculum design, educators can create a more interactive and enjoyable learning experience for students. Research shows that gamification encourages higher levels of motivation and participation, which are crucial for effective learning outcomes. For instance, studies like Dirgantoro et al. (2022) and Petrusly (2024), which looked at gamified learning environments and saw big improvements in student engagement and critical thinking skills, show that gamification techniques are a key part of getting students excited about learning and making learning more fun.

Additionally, gamification has been linked to improved information retention and the development of essential skills such as problem-solving and collaboration. The work of Kim & Castelli (2021) supports this statement, showing that gamification strategies can enhance study time and academic achievement. Similarly, Alsadoon (2023) highlights the role of gamification in meeting basic psychological needs, which in turn enhances motivation and engagement. This is in line with the findings of Fuster-Guilló et al. (2019), who reported that gamified learning experiences positively impact student motivation and satisfaction, further reinforcing the idea that gamification can create a more engaging classroom environment.

In addition to increasing engagement and motivation, gamification also empowers students by giving them a sense of control over their learning journey. This empowerment can enhance students' confidence and self-esteem as they navigate through gamified tasks and challenges. Research by Hidayat (2021) emphasises that gamification can significantly enhance student motivation, showing that when students feel in control, they are more likely to engage deeply with the material. Additionally, the incorporation of technology in gamified learning environments helps students develop digital literacy skills, which are crucial in the 21st century. As highlighted by Johnson et al. (2016), the integration of gamification in education not only enhances engagement but also prepares students to face future challenges in a technology-driven world.

2. Incorporating game elements to enhance learning outcomes

The integration of gamification in educational environments has been proven to significantly enhance student motivation and engagement while encouraging collaboration and teamwork among their peers. Research shows that gamified learning environments, which incorporate elements such as leaderboards, badges, and rewards, create interactive and dynamic educational experiences that encourage active participation and the drive to excel among students. For example, Karabıyık highlights that gamified learning not only increases motivation but also improves success in subjects like mathematics by using a reward-based system that aligns with students' competitive nature (Karabıyık, 2024). This is in line with Zainal's (2023) findings, which noted that gamification encourages flexibility and engagement in vocabulary learning, further supporting the idea that gamified environments can effectively replace traditional methods.

The gamification approach not only makes learning more enjoyable but also fosters important skills such as critical thinking, problem-solving, and collaboration. Research by Özhan and Kocadere shows that gamified environments enhance emotional engagement and motivation, which are crucial for success in an educational context (Özhan & Kocadere, 2019). This is also supported by Spanellis, who discusses how gamification can enhance learning on-site by promoting a fun environment conducive to collaboration and identity expression (Spanellis et al., 2021).

The shift toward gamification in the world of education is not just a trend but also a strategic approach to improving learning outcomes. By leveraging technology and gamification, educators can ignite the spirit of learning, preparing students to face future challenges. Evidence shows that when students are rewarded for their efforts, they are more likely to engage deeply with the material and strive to be the best, thereby fostering a culture of motivation and collaboration within the educational environment (Polat, 2023; Rueckert et al., 2020).

FRAMEWORK FOR AI-GAMIFIED CURRICULUM DESIGN

1. Learning Analysis and Personalisation using AI

AI algorithms are pivotal in analysing data related to students' learning patterns, cognitive styles, and performance histories. These analyses enable the development of personalised learning pathways that adapt to the unique needs of each student. For instance, Abbas et al. highlight that AI tools can significantly enhance educational performance by tailoring content delivery to individual learning preferences, thereby improving engagement and knowledge retention (Abbas et al., 2023). Similarly, Liu emphasises the role of AI in learner analysis and performance prediction, which supports personalised and adaptive learning environments (Liu, 2024). This adaptability is further supported by Thimmanna et al., 2024 who discuss how AI-driven curriculum adjustments can enhance educational outcomes by aligning with individual learner characteristics (Thimmanna et al., 2024). For instance, in Indonesia, some urban schools use AI-based tools like Ruangguru to customise learning paths based on student diagnostics, increasing engagement and performance.

The effectiveness of AI in personalising education is also evident in various applications, such as intelligent tutoring systems and adaptive learning platforms. Pendy notes that AI's potential to transform education includes the development of intelligent tutoring systems that cater to personalised learning experiences (Pendy, 2023). Furthermore, Rasheed et al. provide a systematic review indicating that AI technologies can enhance personalised learning, although privacy concerns remain a significant issue that needs addressing (Rasheed et al., 2023). This is echoed by Murtaza et al., who argue that personalised e-learning systems, powered by AI, significantly improve learning outcomes compared to traditional methods (Murtaza et al., 2022).

The integration of AI in educational settings is not limited to content delivery; it also encompasses the use of chatbots and virtual assistants that provide real-time feedback and support. For example, the study by Chang et al. illustrates how mobile chatbots can promote students' learning achievement and self-efficacy, thereby enhancing the learning experience (Chang et al., 2021). This aligns with the findings of Kamruzzaman et al. (2023), who report that AI-powered algorithms can analyse student data to create tailored learning experiences, including personalised assessments and feedback.

2. Design of Gamification Elements

Badges and leaderboards are among the most frequently implemented gamification elements in educational contexts. Balci et al. conducted a comparative study that demonstrated how badges and leaderboards positively influence academic performance and motivation in both fully and partially gamified online courses. The authors define badges as digital credentials awarded for specific achievements, while leaderboards rank students based on their performance, fostering a competitive environment that can enhance motivation (Balci et al., 2022). Similarly, Setyoadi & Patmanthara (2024) emphasise that incorporating game design elements, including points, badges, and leaderboards, can significantly boost student engagement and motivation by making learning more interactive and competitive.

Challenges also play a crucial role in gamification by providing students with goals to strive for, which can enhance their intrinsic motivation. Li and Liu note that gamification involves the application of game mechanics such as challenges and levels to increase learner engagement in non-game environments (Li & Liu, 2022). This perspective is supported by Tyni et al., who highlight that gamification elements, including challenges and rewards, are particularly effective in contexts where motivation is crucial, such as education (Tyni et al., 2022). The incorporation of challenges encourages students to push their limits and achieve mastery, which can lead to a more profound engagement with the material.

The use of reward systems, such as points and feedback, is essential for reinforcing desired behaviours and maintaining motivation. According to Huesca et al., the combination of points, badges, and leaderboards generates commitment and engagement among students, creating positive expectations that facilitate significant learning (Huesca et al., 2023). This aligns with the findings of Antonaci et al., who conducted a systematic literature review and found that gamification elements significantly impact performance, motivation, and engagement in online learning environments (Antonaci et al., 2019). The authors argue that while gamification often serves as an external reward system, its effectiveness in fostering intrinsic motivation should not be overlooked.

3. Adaptive Learning Pathways

Adaptive Learning Pathways (ALPs) represent a significant advancement in educational technology, leveraging artificial intelligence (AI) to tailor learning experiences according to individual student performance. This approach enhances engagement and optimises learning outcomes by dynamically adjusting the difficulty and content of educational materials based on real-time assessments of student understanding and progress.

AI's capability to analyse vast amounts of data allows for the creation of personalised learning experiences that adapt to the unique needs of each student. Zhao et al. emphasise that adaptive learning systems utilise AI to evaluate students' current knowledge levels and predict future learning trajectories, thereby recommending the most effective learning paths tailored to individual capabilities (Zhao et al., 2024). This aligns with findings from Barua et al., who note that AI-assisted tools have demonstrated positive impacts on learning, particularly for students with neurodevelopmental disorders, by facilitating personalised learning goals and enhancing educational outcomes (Barua et al., 2022).

The integration of AI in education is not limited to content delivery; it also encompasses assessment and feedback mechanisms that are crucial for adaptive learning. Chen et al. highlight that AI can customise curricula and content in response to student needs, which fosters higher retention rates and improves the overall learning experience (Chen et al., 2020). This adaptability is further supported by the work of Jayavardhini, who discusses the role of generative AI in creating intelligent tutoring systems that provide real-time feedback and support tailored to each student's learning style (Jayavardhini, 2024).

The importance of teacher training in effectively implementing AI-driven adaptive learning pathways cannot be overstated. Park and Kwon argue that professional development programmes for educators significantly enhance their self-efficacy in teaching AI, which is essential for the successful integration of these technologies into the classroom (Davis, 2024). Furthermore, Alshehri emphasises the need for educators to develop competencies specific to AI to fully leverage its potential in creating personalised learning environments (Alshehri, 2023).

4. Data-Driven Feedback and Assessment

Data-Driven Feedback and Assessment (DDF&A) is an innovative approach in educational technology that utilises artificial intelligence (AI) to process performance data, thereby providing real-time, informative feedback to students. AI's ability to analyse performance data in real-time is crucial for delivering timely and relevant feedback. Ji et al. highlight that AI performance assessment mechanisms in blended learning environments significantly enhance students' motivation for continuous learning by providing immediate feedback that improves their sense of control over learning tasks (Ji et al., 2024). Such feedback mechanisms are vital in creating a supportive learning environment where students feel empowered to reflect on their learning processes.

The integration of AI in educational settings facilitates the development of personalised feedback systems that cater to individual learning needs. Akavova et al. discuss how AI can create intelligent systems that not only provide personalised feedback but also adapt to students' learning styles and preferences, thereby enhancing the overall educational experience (Akavova et al., 2023). This adaptability is echoed by Lim et al., who emphasise the importance of contextualised feedback that is embedded within the learning process, allowing students to recognise and utilise feedback as a continuous part of their learning journey (Lim et al., 2020).

The role of AI in fostering reflective learning experiences is particularly noteworthy. For instance, Kang et al. illustrate how AI tutors can provide substantial feedback that encourages students to reflect on their performance, thus enhancing their learning outcomes in practical contexts like dance education (Kang et al., 2023). This reflective practice is essential for deep learning, as it allows students to critically assess their understanding and identify areas for improvement.

The use of AI in feedback mechanisms can significantly alleviate the workload of educators, allowing them to focus on higher-order teaching tasks. Tubino and Adachi argue that AI-powered feedback tools can enhance students' feedback literacy while reducing the burden on teachers by automating low-level feedback processes (Tubino & Adachi, 2022). This shift enables educators to dedicate more time to fostering critical thinking and deeper learning among students.

5. Technology and Infrastructure Implementation

The implementation of AI-based LMS is a transformative step in education, as highlighted by Pardosi et al. (2024), who discuss how such systems can adapt course materials to fit individual learning paces and styles, thereby providing a personalised learning experience. This adaptability is crucial in addressing diverse learner needs and ensuring that educational content is relevant and engaging. Similarly, Trang & Thư (2024) emphasise the potential of AI-driven technologies to improve student engagement and learning efficiency, while also noting challenges such as the digital divide and the necessity for substantial investment in technology and teacher training.

These insights underscore the importance of a robust technological infrastructure to support effective learning environments.

Machine learning algorithms play a significant role in optimising gamification strategies within educational contexts. López & Tucker (2020) present a machine learning model designed to predict performance in gamified learning environments, which can help educators tailor gamification elements to enhance student engagement and learning outcomes. This predictive capability allows for a more nuanced understanding of how students interact with gamified content, enabling educators to adjust strategies in real-time to maximise effectiveness. Furthermore, Fırat (2023) discusses the broader implications of integrating AI applications into LMS, suggesting that such integration can significantly enhance e-learning experiences by providing actionable insights based on student interactions.

The challenges associated with integrating AI into LMS are also noteworthy. Alenezi (2024) highlights obstacles faced by faculty members in utilising AI applications within established LMS platforms like Blackboard, pointing to the need for ongoing support and training to fully leverage these technologies. This indicates that while the potential benefits are substantial, successful implementation requires careful consideration of faculty readiness and institutional support.

Moreover, the use of analytical techniques in conjunction with machine learning can further enhance the effectiveness of gamification strategies. However, the reference provided for this claim, Agostinelli's work, focuses on predictive maintenance and security management systems rather than educational technologies, making it irrelevant to the context of gamification in education (Agostinelli, 2021). Therefore, this point should be omitted as it lacks appropriate support.

The integration of technology and infrastructure, particularly through AI-based LMS and machine learning algorithms, is essential for optimising educational experiences. These technologies not only facilitate personalised learning but also enhance engagement through gamification strategies. However, addressing the challenges of implementation, including faculty training and institutional support, is crucial for realising the full potential of these innovations in education. The integration of artificial intelligence (AI) and gamification in curriculum design is more simply illustrated in Figure 1.

Figure 1. Framework For Integrating AI And Gamification In The Curriculum

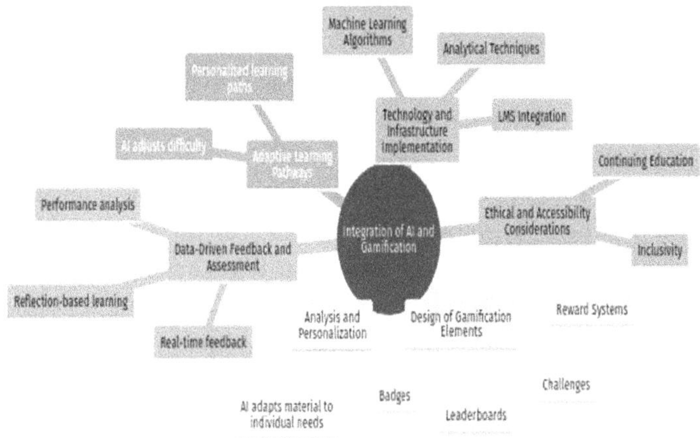

CONSIDERATIONS AND ETHICAL CHALLENGES OF AI-SUPPORTED CURRICULUM DESIGN

1. Ensuring data privacy and security in AI-supported curriculum design

The integration of artificial intelligence (AI) in the education sector is increasingly recognised as crucial for maintaining the trust of students, parents, and educators. Establishing clear guidelines and protocols for the collection, storage, and use of student data is crucial to ensure ethical practices and protect student privacy. Researchers have emphasised the need for an ethical framework to guide the application of AI in educational settings, highlighting that such a framework can mitigate the potential risks associated with AI technology (Nguyen et al., 2022; Limongi, 2024). Moreover, transparency in AI algorithms is crucial to prevent bias and discrimination, as opaque systems can lead to distrust among stakeholders (Larsson & Heintz, 2020). The "black box" nature of many AI systems raises concerns about their decision-making processes, necessitating efforts to enhance algorithmic transparency (Chai, 2024).

Educators must be adequately trained to use AI tools ethically and responsibly, ensuring that these tools support student learning without violating students' rights or autonomy (Nguyen et al., 2022; Harry, 2023). This training is crucial for fostering an environment where AI can be utilised to personalise learning experiences, identify students who are struggling early on, and provide targeted interventions. The potential benefits of AI in education are immense, as it can facilitate personalised learning pathways that adapt to individual student needs, thereby improving educational outcomes. With proper oversight and accountability measures, AI can help bridge the educational gap and create a more inclusive and equitable learning environment (Luan et al., 2020; Familoni, 2024).

Along with the development of technology, prioritising ethical standards in the application of AI is very important. This not only involves the development of strong ethical guidelines but also the active participation of various stakeholders, including educators, policymakers, and technology developers (Limongi, 2024; Pendy, 2023). By fostering a culture of trust, collaboration, and transparency, the education community can harness the power of AI to enhance student success and well-being while addressing the ethical implications associated with its use (Alali, 2024; Nguyen et al., 2022). Ultimately, with careful consideration of these factors, AI has the potential to revolutionise the educational landscape, making learning more personalised and effective for all students.

2. Addressing concerns about the impact of gamification on student motivation

Engagement is an important factor in the successful implementation of artificial intelligence (AI) in educational environments. The integration of gamification has emerged as a powerful strategy to enhance student interest and participation. However, it is important to recognise the potential pitfalls associated with gamification, particularly the risk of students becoming overly focused on rewards and extrinsic competition, which can diminish the true learning objectives. Research shows that, although gamification can significantly enhance engagement, educators must strive to maintain a balance between gamification elements and educational goals to ensure that learning remains the primary focus (Alenezi, 2023).

The literature highlights that gamification, defined as the application of game design elements in non-game contexts, can enhance motivation and engagement among students (Khakpour & Colomo-Palacios, 2020; Julita, 2024). However, it is crucial to continuously monitor and evaluate the effectiveness of these strategies. As Zourmpakis et al. (2023) show, continuous assessment is needed to find out if gamification really improves learning outcomes or if it's just a way to get people interested on the surface. Zourmpakis et al. (2023), for example, stress how important it is to measure learning outcomes and motivational factors in order to fully evaluate how well gamification works in educational settings. This dual focus can help educators refine their approaches and ensure that gamification positively contributes to students' learning experiences.

The integration of AI with gamification offers the potential for personalised learning experiences that meet the individual needs of students. AI can analyse student data to adjust challenges and rewards, thereby fostering a more engaging and effective learning environment (Narayanan, 2024; Erbaşı, 2023). By leveraging AI technology, educators can create adaptive learning pathways that align with the unique strengths and weaknesses of students, ultimately enhancing their motivation and success. This personalised approach not only addresses the diverse learning preferences of students but also encourages active participation in their learning journey (Pendy, 2023).

3. Potential bias in AI algorithms and its implications for curriculum design

When artificial intelligence (AI) is used in schools, it's important to think about the biases that might be built into the algorithms. These biases can have a big impact on the lessons and how they are taught. Educators must be aware that bias in AI can stem from the data used to train these systems, leading to skewed or inappropriate educational materials. Alrayes highlights the critical need for transparency in AI models, noting that bias can inadvertently shape educational experiences if not properly addressed (Alrayes, 2024). Akgün and Greenhow also talk about the ethical problems that AI can cause in K–12 education and call for a close study of the AI technology's assumptions and data sources (Akgün & Greenhow, 2021). This critical examination is crucial to ensure that students receive a balanced and fair education, free from distortions that can be caused by bias.

Effectively integrating AI technology into the classroom also requires a commitment to transparency and accountability in its development and implementation. According to Yazdanpanah et al. (2022), governing bodies should make sure that AI systems are watched so that they don't break the law or societal norms. This is in line with the findings of Jobin and Ienca, who noted that ethical AI principles, including transparency and fairness, are crucial for the responsible implementation of AI (Jobin & Ienca, 2019). Educators should engage in ongoing professional development to stay informed about AI advancements, which will enable them to better understand and address the challenges posed by this technology (Balta, 2023). By developing a culture of transparency and accountability, educators can reduce the risks associated with AI and harness its potential to enrich the educational landscape.

In the end, a proactive approach to addressing bias and ethical challenges in AI is crucial for educators who want to leverage AI's capabilities to enhance student learning. Balta emphasises the need for ethical considerations in educational research involving AI, highlighting the importance of accountability in addressing bias and ensuring data privacy (Balta, 2023). Similarly, D'Souza underscores the need to establish clear roles and responsibilities among stakeholders to promote the ethical use of AI in education (D'Souza, 2024). By prioritising these principles, educators can navigate the complexities of AI integration and create a more equitable and effective learning environment for all students.

DIRECTIONS AND RECOMMENDATIONS FOR FUTURE CURRICULUM DEVELOPMENT

1. Strategies to enhance AI and gamification in curriculum design

To effectively enhance the integration of artificial intelligence (AI) and gamification in curriculum design, educational institutions must prioritise investment in training and resources for teachers. This investment is crucial because it enables educators to adapt to new technologies and methodologies, ensuring they can provide engaging and effective learning experiences for students. Workshops, online courses, and access to experts in the field are essential components of this training. For example, Thimmanna emphasises the need for a structured approach in the curriculum that incorporates AI, highlighting the importance of training educators to meet future healthcare needs in biomedical education (Thimmanna et al., 2024). Similarly, Otero et al. (2023) underscore the need for a curriculum that reflects academic continuity and can adapt to the specific conditions of schools, which can be achieved through professional development for teachers.

Collaboration between educators, technology developers, and researchers is also crucial in identifying best practices and developing innovative solutions. The literature shows that interdisciplinary collaboration can enhance curriculum frameworks and educational programmes, especially in fields such as medicine where AI is becoming increasingly relevant (Tolentino, 2024; Wood et al., 2021). A transdisciplinary approach that aligns curriculum needs with societal demands was proposed by Aliabadi (Aliabadi, 2023) as a way to add AI to the school curriculum. This would require a shift toward more interactive and collaborative learning environments. These collaborative efforts foster a culture of experimentation and continuous improvement, enabling schools to adapt to the ever-evolving landscape of educational technology.

2. Training educators to effectively integrate AI and gamification into teaching practices.

The integration of advanced educational technology, particularly artificial intelligence (AI) and gamification, is crucial for preparing students to face the rapidly evolving digital landscape. Schools that equip teachers with the necessary tools and resources can significantly enhance the educational experience, ensuring that students receive cutting-edge education that meets the future workforce's needs. Research shows that continuous professional development is crucial for teachers to effectively utilise this technology in their teaching practices. For example, Tzafilkou et al. emphasise the importance of continuous training to enhance teachers' digital competencies, which is crucial for effective teaching in the digital era (Tzafilkou et al., 2023). Similarly, Kurniawati et al. (2018) highlight the need for teachers to develop through various stages of digital media use to integrate technology into their classrooms.

Adapting teaching methods to meet the preferences of students from the digital generation is becoming increasingly important. The use of AI and gamification can encourage a more engaging and interactive learning environment. Although specific references to Li's work do not directly support this claim, the general idea of enhancing instructional capabilities through digital literacy is widely recognised in educational research. This is in line with the findings of Gamrat et al., who advocate for personalised professional development programmes that enable teachers to tailor their learning experiences to better meet the needs of their students (Gamrat et al., 2014). Such a personalised approach not only enhances learning practices but also contributes to a more dynamic classroom environment.

3. Policy recommendations to support the adoption of innovative curriculum design practices

To assist educators in incorporating artificial intelligence (AI) and gamification into their instruction, it is essential to offer professional development opportunities aimed at augmenting their skills and expertise. Research indicates that systematic training can markedly improve educators' ability to adopt innovative pedagogical techniques, including the integration of technology in the classroom (Güler & Özkan, 2018). Moreover, educational institutions must commit resources to invest in cutting-edge technology and software. Research indicates that access to contemporary educational tools enhances the learning experience and equips students with necessary skills for professions in a technology-driven economy (Hollands et al., 2019).

Collaborations with industry experts are crucial for aligning the curriculum with the contemporary requirements and expectations of the workforce. Collaboration between the education sector and industry can yield a pertinent curriculum, matching students' competencies with the requirements of the contemporary job market and equipping them for future professions (Cranley et al., 2012). Moreover, authorities ought to emphasise financing for research that assesses the effects of AI and gamification in education. This research is essential for facilitating evidence-based decision-making, guaranteeing that all students have access to superior and innovative educational opportunities (Majdzadeh et al., 2011). Funding for this research allows the education system to discern optimal practices and efficient technologies to enhance student learning results (Bastani et al., 2023).

This policy's implementation can reconcile traditional schooling with the evolving demands of the workforce. It is essential to develop critical thinking, problem-solving, and collaborative skills in students – skills that are vital for success in the digital age (Larsen et al., 2011). Conversely, investment in educational innovation and research improves learning quality and fosters the development of a competitive and adaptable global workforce (Strydom et al., 2010). The education system can proactively adapt to 21st-century issues, equipping students for success in a constantly changing world (Orton et al., 2011).

CONCLUSION

In conclusion, the strategic integration of AI and gamification in curriculum design is a transformative approach to meet the demands of Society 5.0. This requires not only technical innovation but also ethical, contextual, and inclusive implementation strategies.

The integration of artificial intelligence (AI) and gamification in curriculum design offers various significant benefits for students, educators, and the workforce. This technology has the potential to revolutionise education by preparing students to face the ever-evolving challenges of the modern world. AI and gamification can foster critical thinking, problem-solving, collaboration, and adaptation skills while also creating personalised and dynamic learning experiences. With the adoption of this technology, educators can provide more effective, engaging, and relevant learning experiences that meet the needs of 21st-century students. This technology-based approach not only supports the development of 21st-century skills but also inspires creativity and curiosity in students, helping them become lifelong learners ready to contribute to the global economy. Through Society 5.0, with a focus on the integration of technology and human capabilities, education and the workforce can transform towards more advanced innovation and collaboration. With sustained investment in research and development, the integration of AI and gamification promises better learning outcomes, encouraging students to adapt and actively contribute in a technology-based society. The adoption of AI and gamification in education is not just a demand of the times but a strategic step to equip students with relevant skills and knowledge for the future.

REFERENCES

Abbas, N., Imran, A., Manzoor, R., Hussain, T., & Hussain, M. (2023). Role of artificial intelligence tools in enhancing students' educational performance at higher levels. *Journal of Artificial Intelligence Machine Learning and Neural Network*, (35), 36–49. DOI: 10.55529/jaimlnn.35.36.49

Agostinelli, S. (2021). Actionable framework for city digital twin-enabled predictive maintenance and security management systems.. https://doi.org/DOI: 10.2495/bim210191

Akavova, A., Temirkhanova, Z., & Lorsanova, Z. (2023). Adaptive learning and artificial intelligence in the educational space. E3s Web of Conferences, 451, 06011. https://doi.org/DOI: 10.1051/e3sconf/202345106011

Akgün, S., & Greenhow, C. (2021). Artificial intelligence in education: Addressing ethical challenges in k-12 settings. *AI and Ethics*, *2*(3), 431–440. DOI: 10.1007/s43681-021-00096-7 PMID: 34790956

Alali, R. (2024). Opportunities and challenges of integrating generative artificial intelligence in education. *International Journal of Religion*, *5*(7), 784–793. DOI: 10.61707/8y29gv34

Alenezi, A. (2023). Teacher perspectives on ai-driven gamification: Impact on student motivation, engagement, and learning outcomes. *Information Technologies and Learning Tools*, *97*(5), 138–148. DOI: 10.33407/itlt.v97i5.5437

Alenezi, A. (2024). Obstacles to the use of ai applications in blackboard for faculty members at northern border university, saudi arabia. Mier Journal of Educational Studies Trends & Practices, 248-268. https://doi.org/DOI: 10.52634/mier/2024/v14/i2/2581

Aliabadi, R. (2023). Transdisciplinary ai education: the confluence of curricular and community needs in the instruction of artificial intelligence., 137-151. https://doi.org/DOI: 10.1007/978-981-99-7947-9_11

Alkan, A. (2024). Artificial intelligence: its role and potential in education. İnsan Ve Toplum Bilimleri Araştırmaları Dergisi, 13(1), 483-497. https://doi.org/DOI: 10.15869/itobiad.1331201

Allahverdi, A. (2021). Sample senior design projects of industrial engineering program at kuwait university. *Asean Journal of Engineering Education*, *4*(1). Advance online publication. DOI: 10.11113/ajee2020.4n1.14

Alrayes, A. (2024). Chatgpt in education – understanding the bahraini academics perspective. *Electronic Journal of e-Learning*, *22*(2), 112–134. DOI: 10.34190/ejel.22.2.3250

Alsadoon, H. (2023). The impact of gamification on student motivation and engagement: An empirical study. *Dirasat: Educational Sciences*, *50*(2), 386–396. DOI: 10.35516/edu.v50i2.255

Alshehri, B. (2023). Pedagogical paradigms in the ai era: Insights from saudi educators on the long-term implications of ai integration in classroom teaching. *IJESA*, *2*(8), 159–180. DOI: 10.59992/ijesa.2023.v2n8p7

Antonaci, A., Klemke, R., & Specht, M. (2019). The effects of gamification in online learning environments: A systematic literature review. *Informatics (MDPI)*, *6*(3), 32. DOI: 10.3390/informatics6030032

Aparicio-Gómez, O. (2024). Tejiendo conexiones: la simbiosis transformadora entre aprendizaje e inteligencia artificial. Hachetetepé Revista Científica De Educación Y Comunicación, (28). https://doi.org/DOI: 10.25267/hachetetepe.2024.i28.1103

Balci, S., Secaur, J., & Morris, B. (2022). Comparing the effectiveness of badges and leaderboards on academic performance and motivation of students in fully versus partially gamified online physics classes. *Education and Information Technologies*, *27*(6), 8669–8704. DOI: 10.1007/s10639-022-10983-z PMID: 35308640

Balta, N. (2023). Ethical considerations in using ai in educational research., 2(1), 14205. https://doi.org/DOI: 10.51853/jorids/14205

Barua, P., Vicnesh, J., Gururajan, R., Oh, S., Palmer, E., Azizan, M., & Acharya, U. (2022). Artificial intelligence enabled personalised assistive tools to enhance education of children with neurodevelopmental disorders a review. *International Journal of Environmental Research and Public Health*, *19*(3), 1192. DOI: 10.3390/ijerph19031192 PMID: 35162220

Bastani, P., Kavosi, Z., Alipoori, S., & Imani-Nasab, M. (2023). Evidence- based policy and decision-making among health managers: A case of shiraz university of medical sciences. *Galen Medical Journal*, *6*(1). Advance online publication. DOI: 10.31661/gmj.v6i1.729

Buckley, P., & Doyle, E. (2014). Gamification and student motivation. *Interactive Learning Environments*, *24*(6), 1162–1175. DOI: 10.1080/10494820.2014.964263

Chai, F. (2024). Grading by ai makes me feel fairer? how different evaluators affect college students' perception of fairness. *Frontiers in Psychology*, *15*. Advance online publication. DOI: 10.3389/fpsyg.2024.1221177 PMID: 38371704

Chang, C., Hwang, G., & Gau, M. (2021). Promoting students' learning achievement and self-efficacy: A mobile chatbot approach for nursing training. *British Journal of Educational Technology*, *53*(1), 171–188. DOI: 10.1111/bjet.13158

Chen, L., Chen, P., & Lin, Z. (2020). Artificial intelligence in education: A review. *IEEE Access : Practical Innovations, Open Solutions*, *8*, 75264–75278. DOI: 10.1109/access.2020.2988510

Cranley, L., Doran, D., Tourangeau, A., Kushniruk, A., & Nagle, L. (2012). Recognizing and responding to uncertainty: A grounded theory of nurses' uncertainty. *Worldviews on Evidence-Based Nursing*, *9*(3), 149–158. DOI: 10.1111/j.1741-6787.2011.00237.x PMID: 22233501

D'Souza, R. (2024). Twelve tips for addressing ethical concerns in the implementation of artificial intelligence in medical education. *Medical Education Online*, *29*(1). Advance online publication. DOI: 10.1080/10872981.2024.2330250 PMID: 38566608

Davis, R. (2024). Korean in-service teachers' perceptions of implementing artificial intelligence (ai) education for teaching in schools and their ai teacher training programs. *International Journal of Information and Education Technology (IJIET)*, *14*(2), 214–219. DOI: 10.18178/ijiet.2024.14.2.2042

Devi, V., Vashe, A., Rao, R., Abraham, R., Pallath, V., & Torke, S. (2016). Curricular impact on learning approaches and critical thinking skills of medical students. *Education in Medicine Journal*, *8*(4). Advance online publication. DOI: 10.5959/eimj.v8i4.468

Dichev, C., & Dicheva, D. (2017). Gamifying education: what is known, what is believed and what remains uncertain: a critical review. *International Journal of Educational Technology in Higher Education*, *14*(1). Advance online publication. DOI: 10.1186/s41239-017-0042-5

Dirgantoro, K., Bermuli, J., & Soesanto, R. (2022). Is moodle gamification effective in reviewing student's motivation related to interest in learning online? *Educational Journal Journal of Research Results and Literature Review in the Field of Education, Teaching, and Learning*, *8*(1), 114. DOI: 10.33394/jk.v8i1.4790

Ejaz, H., McGrath, H., Wong, B., Guise, A., Vercauteren, T., & Shapey, J. (2022). Artificial intelligence and medical education: A global mixed-methods study of medical students' perspectives. *Digital Health*, *8*, 205520762210890. DOI: 10.1177/20552076221089099 PMID: 35521511

Erbaşı, Z. (2023). The role and potential of artificial intelligence and gamification in education: The example of vakıf participation bank. *Orclever Proceedings of Research and Development*, *3*(1), 243–254. DOI: 10.56038/oprd.v3i1.329

Eslit, E. (2023). Blending boundaries in the new normal: Leveraging technology, ai and global perspectives in modern education. *Journal of Learning and Educational Policy*, (41), 8–18. DOI: 10.55529/jlep.41.8.18

Familoni, B. (2024). Advancements and challenges in ai integration for technical literacy: A systematic review. *Engineering Science & Technology Journal*, *5*(4), 1415–1430. DOI: 10.51594/estj.v5i4.1042

Fazil, A. (2024). Exploring the broad impact of ai technologies on student engagement and academic performance in university settings in afghanistan. *Riggs Journal of Artificial Intelligence and Digital Business*, *2*(2), 56–63. DOI: 10.31004/riggs.v2i2.268

Fırat, M. (2023). Integrating ai applications into learning management systems to enhance e-learning. Öğretim Teknolojisi Ve Hayat Boyu Öğrenme Dergisi - Instructional Technology and Lifelong Learning, 1-14. https://doi.org/DOI: 10.52911/itall.1244453

Fuster-Guilló, A., Pertegal-Felices, M., Jimeno-Morenilla, A., Azorín-López, J., Soliveres, M., & Restrepo-Calle, F. (2019). Evaluating impact on motivation and academic performance of a game-based learning experience using kahoot. *Frontiers in Psychology*, *10*. Advance online publication. DOI: 10.3389/fpsyg.2019.02843 PMID: 31920872

Gamrat, C., Zimmerman, H., Dudek, J., & Peck, K. (2014). Personalized workplace learning: An exploratory study on digital badging within a teacher professional development program. *British Journal of Educational Technology*, *45*(6), 1136–1148. DOI: 10.1111/bjet.12200

Gligorea, I., Yaseen, M., Cioca, M., Gorski, H., & Oancea, R. (2022). An interpretable framework for an efficient analysis of students' academic performance. *Sustainability*, *14*(14), 8885. DOI: 10.3390/su14148885

Güler, S., & Özkan, Y. (2018). Podcast applications in pre-service language teacher education from a constructivist perspective. *World Journal on Educational Technology Current Issues*, *10*(3), 131–141. DOI: 10.18844/wjet.v10i3.3552

Harry, A. (2023). Role of ai in education. *Interdiciplinary Journal and Hummanity (Injurity)*, *2*(3), 260–268. DOI: 10.58631/injurity.v2i3.52

Hidayat, D. (2021). The implementation of gamification system in asian higher education teaching. *Journal of Games Game Art and Gamification*, *2*(1). Advance online publication. DOI: 10.21512/jggag.v2i1.7218

Hollands, F., Pan, Y., & Escueta, M. (2019). What is the potential for applying cost-utility analysis to facilitate evidence-based decision making in schools? *Educational Researcher*, *48*(5), 287–295. DOI: 10.3102/0013189x19852101

Huesca, G., Campos, G., Larre, M., & Pérez-Lezama, C. (2023). Implementation of a mixed strategy of gamification and flipped learning in undergraduate basic programming courses. *Education Sciences*, *13*(5), 474. DOI: 10.3390/educsci13050474

Jayavardhini, P. (2024). Ai study partner: Development of an llm and gen ai-enhanced study assistant tool. *Interantional Journal of Scientific Research in Engineering and Management*, *08*(03), 1–5. DOI: 10.55041/ijsrem29626

Ji, H., Suo, L., & Hua, C. (2024). Ai performance assessment in blended learning: Mechanisms and effects on students' continuous learning motivation. *Frontiers in Psychology*, *15*. Advance online publication. DOI: 10.3389/fpsyg.2024.1447680 PMID: 39737232

Jobin, A., & Ienca, M. (2019). The global landscape of ai ethics guidelines. *Nature Machine Intelligence*, *1*(9), 389–399. DOI: 10.1038/s42256-019-0088-2

Johnson, D., Deterding, S., Kuhn, K., Staneva, A., Stoyanov, S., & Hides, L. (2016). Gamification for health and wellbeing: A systematic review of the literature. *Internet Interventions : the Application of Information Technology in Mental and Behavioural Health*, *6*, 89–106. DOI: 10.1016/j.invent.2016.10.002 PMID: 30135818

Julita, R. (2024). The impact of gamification on efl students' reading comprehension. *JEFLE*, *4*(2), 136. DOI: 10.26418/jefle.v4i2.74901

Kamruzzaman, M. (2023). Ai- and iot-assisted sustainable education systems during pandemics, such as covid-19, for smart cities. *Sustainability*, *15*(10), 8354. DOI: 10.3390/su15108354

Kang, J., Kang, C., Yoon, J., Ji, H., Li, T., Hyunmi, M., & Han, J. (2023). Dancing on the inside: A qualitative study on online dance learning with teacher-ai cooperation. *Education and Information Technologies*, *28*(9), 12111–12141. DOI: 10.1007/s10639-023-11649-0 PMID: 37361738

Karabıyık, Ü. (2024). Investigation of the effect of gamified learning on motivation and success in math class. *Journal of Education and Practice*, *8*(1), 32–52. DOI: 10.47941/jep.1645

Katiyar, P. (2024). Ai-driven personalized learning systems: enhancing educational effectiveness. eatp. https://doi.org/DOI: 10.53555/kuey.v30i5.4961

Khakpour, A., & Colomo-Palacios, R. (2020). Convergence of gamification and machine learning: A systematic literature review. *Technology Knowledge and Learning*, *26*(3), 597–636. DOI: 10.1007/s10758-020-09456-4

Khater, A., Zaaqoq, A., Wahdan, M., & Ashry, S. (2023). Knowledge and attitude of ain shams university medical students towards artificial intelligence and its application in medical education and practice. *Educational Research and Innovation Journal*, *3*(10), 29–42. DOI: 10.21608/erji.2023.306718

Kim, J., & Castelli, D. (2021). Effects of gamification on behavioral change in education: A meta-analysis. *International Journal of Environmental Research and Public Health*, *18*(7), 3550. DOI: 10.3390/ijerph18073550 PMID: 33805530

Kurniawati, N., Maolida, E., & Anjaniputra, A. (2018). The praxis of digital literacy in the efl classroom: Digital-immigrant vs digital-native teacher. *Indonesian Journal of Applied Linguistics*, *8*(1). Advance online publication. DOI: 10.17509/ijal.v8i1.11459

Larsen, M., Gulis, G., & Pedersen, K. (2011). Use of evidence in local public health work in denmark. *International Journal of Public Health*, *57*(3), 477–483. DOI: 10.1007/s00038-011-0324-y PMID: 22116391

Larsson, S., & Heintz, F. (2020). Transparency in artificial intelligence. *Internet Policy Review*, *9*(2). Advance online publication. DOI: 10.14763/2020.2.1469

Legaki, N., Xi, N., Hamari, J., Karpouzis, K., & Assimakopoulos, V. (2020). The effect of challenge-based gamification on learning: An experiment in the context of statistics education. *International Journal of Human-Computer Studies*, *144*, 102496. DOI: 10.1016/j.ijhcs.2020.102496 PMID: 32565668

Li, R. and Liu, J. (2022). Applying gamification in english learning. https://doi.org/DOI: 10.2991/assehr.k.220504.490

Lim, L., Dawson, S., Gašević, D., Joksimovíc, S., Fudge, A., Pardo, A., & Gentili, S. (2020). Students' sense-making of personalised feedback based on learning analytics. *Australasian Journal of Educational Technology*, *36*(6), 15–33. DOI: 10.14742/ajet.6370

Limongi, R. (2024). The use of artificial intelligence in scientific research with integrity and ethics. *Rev. Artif. Intell. Educ*, *5*(00), e0022. DOI: 10.37497/rev.artif.intell.educ.v5i00.22

Liu, L. (2024). Survey and analysis of primary school teachers' use of generative artificial intelligence. *Lecture Notes in Education Psychology and Public Media*, *74*(1), 43–52. DOI: 10.54254/2753-7048/2024.bo17693

López, C., & Tucker, C. (2020). Toward personalized adaptive gamification: A machine learning model for predicting performance. *IEEE Transactions on Games*, *12*(2), 155–168. DOI: 10.1109/tg.2018.2883661

Luan, H., Géczy, P., Lai, H., Gobert, J., Yang, S., Ogata, H., & Tsai, C. (2020). Challenges and future directions of big data and artificial intelligence in education. *Frontiers in Psychology*, *11*. Advance online publication. DOI: 10.3389/fpsyg.2020.580820 PMID: 33192896

Majdzadeh, R., Yazdizadeh, B., Nedjat, S., Gholami, J., & Ahghari, S. (2011). Strengthening evidence-based decision-making: Is it possible without improving health system stewardship? *Health Policy and Planning*, *27*(6), 499–504. DOI: 10.1093/heapol/czr072 PMID: 22027555

Mugisha, M., Uwitonze, A., Chesire, F., Senyonga, R., Oxman, M., Nsangi, A., & Rosenbaum, S. (2021). Teaching critical thinking about health using digital technology in lower secondary schools in rwanda: A qualitative context analysis. *PLoS One*, *16*(3), e0248773. DOI: 10.1371/journal.pone.0248773 PMID: 33750971

Murtaza, M., Ahmed, Y., Shamsi, J., Sherwani, F., & Usman, M. (2022). Ai-based personalized e-learning systems: Issues, challenges, and solutions. *IEEE Access : Practical Innovations, Open Solutions*, *10*, 81323–81342. DOI: 10.1109/access.2022.3193938

Nagi, F., Salih, R., Alzubaidi, M., Shah, H., Alam, T., Shah, Z., … & Househ, M. (2023). Applications of artificial intelligence (AI) in medical education: a scoping review.. https://doi.org/DOI: 10.3233/shti230581

Narayanan, K. (2024). Hybrid gamification and ai tutoring framework using machine learning and adaptive neuro-fuzzy inference system. *Journal of Advanced Research in Applied Sciences and Engineering Technology*, *42*(2), 221–233. DOI: 10.37934/araset.42.2.221233

Nguyen, T. (2022). Artificial intelligent based teaching and learning approaches: A comprehensive review. *International Journal of Evaluation and Research in Education (Ijere)*, *12*(4), 2387. DOI: 10.11591/ijere.v12i4.26623

Onesi-Ozigagun, O. (2024). Revolutionizing education through ai: A comprehensive review of enhancing learning experiences. *International Journal of Applied Research in Social Sciences*, *6*(4), 589–607. DOI: 10.51594/ijarss.v6i4.1011

Orton, L., Lloyd-Williams, F., Taylor-Robinson, D., O'Flaherty, M., & Capewell, S. (2011). The use of research evidence in public health decision making processes: Systematic review. *PLoS One*, *6*(7), e21704. DOI: 10.1371/journal.pone.0021704 PMID: 21818262

Otero, L., Catalá, A., Morante, M., Taboada, M., López, B., & Barro, S. (2023). Ai literacy in k-12: A systematic literature review. *International Journal of STEM Education*, *10*(1). Advance online publication. DOI: 10.1186/s40594-023-00418-7

Özhan, Ş., & Kocadere, S. (2019). The effects of flow, emotional engagement, and motivation on success in a gamified online learning environment. *Journal of Educational Computing Research*, *57*(8), 2006–2031. DOI: 10.1177/0735633118823159

Pardosi, V., Xu, S., Umurohmi, U., Nurdiana, N., & Sabur, F. (2024). Implementation of an artificial intelligence based learning management system for adaptive learning. *Al-Fikrah Jurnal Manajemen Pendidikan*, *12*(1), 149. DOI: 10.31958/jaf.v12i1.12548

Pendy, B. (2023). Artificial intelligence: The future of education. *Jurnal Indonesia Sosial Sains*, *2*(11). Advance online publication. DOI: 10.59141/jiss.v2i11.801

Petrusly, P. (2024). *The effect of gamification using kahoot on students' critical thinking abilities: the role of mediating learning engagement and motivation*. Kuey., DOI: 10.53555/kuey.v30i5.1524

Polat, E. (2023). Gamification implementation for educational purposes: A scoping review (2013-2018). *Educational Technology Quarterly*, *2023*(3), 367–400. DOI: 10.55056/etq.589

Popenici, S., & Kerr, S. (2017). Exploring the impact of artificial intelligence on teaching and learning in higher education. *Research and Practice in Technology Enhanced Learning*, *12*(1). Advance online publication. DOI: 10.1186/s41039-017-0062-8 PMID: 30595727

Pratama, M. (2023). Revolutionizing education: Harnessing the power of artificial intelligence for personalized learning. *Klasikal Journal of Education Language Teaching and Science*, *5*(2), 350–357. DOI: 10.52208/klasikal.v5i2.877

Pu, D., Ni, J., Song, D., Zhang, W., Wang, Y., Wu, L., & Wang, Y. (2019). Influence of critical thinking disposition on the learning efficiency of problem-based learning in undergraduate medical students. *BMC Medical Education*, *19*(1). Advance online publication. DOI: 10.1186/s12909-018-1418-5 PMID: 30606170

Rasheed, Z., Ghwanmeh, S., & Abualkishik, A. (2023). Harnessing artificial intelligence for personalized learning: A systematic review. *Data & Metadata*, *2*, 146. DOI: 10.56294/dm2023146

Rivera, E., & Garden, C. (2021). Gamification for student engagement: A framework. *Journal of Further and Higher Education*, *45*(7), 999–1012. DOI: 10.1080/0309877x.2021.1875201

Rohmah, N. (2022). A vocational school cutting-edge learning strategy: Examining gamification towards student engagement and achievement. *Jurnal Kependidikan Jurnal Hasil Penelitian Dan Kajian Kepustakaan Di Bidang Pendidikan Pengajaran Dan Pembelajaran*, *8*(3), 655. DOI: 10.33394/jk.v8i3.5779

Rueckert, D., Pico, K., Kim, D., & Sánchez, X. (2020). Gamifying the foreign language classroom for brain-friendly learning. *Foreign Language Annals*, *53*(4), 686–703. DOI: 10.1111/flan.12490

Setyoadi, E., & Patmanthara, S. (2024). Students' goal orientation and gamification in learning for academic performance: A systematic literature review. *Research and Development in Education (Raden)*, *4*(1), 390–403. DOI: 10.22219/raden.v4i1.32630

Shah, J. (2024). Rethinking higher education through multidisciplinary studies. jes, 20(4s), 2060-2063. https://doi.org/DOI: 10.52783/jes.2309

Spanellis, A., Pyrko, I., & Dörfler, V. (2021). Gamifying situated learning in organisations. *Management Learning*, *53*(3), 525–546. DOI: 10.1177/13505076211038812

Strydom, W., Funke, N., Nienaber, S., Nortje, K., & Steyn, M. (2010). Evidence-based policymaking: A review. *South African Journal of Science*, *106*(5/6). Advance online publication. DOI: 10.4102/sajs.v106i5/6.249

Sughra, U., & Usmani, A. (2022). Comparison of critical thinking among undergraduate medical students of conventional and integrated curricula in twin cities. *Pakistan Journal of Medical Sciences*, *38*(6). Advance online publication. DOI: 10.12669/pjms.38.6.5409 PMID: 35991275

Thimmanna, A. V. N. S., Naik, M. S., Radhakrishnan, S., & Sharma, A. (2024). Personalized learning paths: Adapting education with AI-driven curriculum. [EEL]. *European Economic Letters*, *14*(1), 31–40.

Tolentino, R. (2024). Curriculum frameworks and educational programs in ai for medical students, residents, and practicing physicians: Scoping review. *JMIR Medical Education*, *10*, e54793. DOI: 10.2196/54793 PMID: 39023999

Tonbuloğlu, B. (2023). An evaluation of the use of artificial intelligence applications in online education. *Journal of Educational Technology and Online Learning*, *6*(4), 866–884. DOI: 10.31681/jetol.1335906

Trang, N., & Thư, P. (2024). The role of ai in improving student learning outcomes: Evidence in vietnam. *International Journal of Multidisciplinary Research and Analysis*, *07*(06). Advance online publication. DOI: 10.47191/ijmra/v7-i06-48

Tubino, L. & Adachi, C. (2022). Developing feedback literacy capabilities through an ai automated feedback tool. Ascilite Publications, e22039. https://doi.org/DOI: 10.14742/apubs.2022.39

Tyni, J., Tarkiainen, A., López-Pernas, S., Saqr, M., Kahila, J., Bednarik, R., & Tedre, M. (2022). Games and rewards: A scientometric study of rewards in educational and serious games. *IEEE Access : Practical Innovations, Open Solutions*, *10*, 31578–31585. DOI: 10.1109/access.2022.3160230

Tzafilkou, K., Perifanou, M., & Economides, A. (2023). Assessing teachers' digital competence in primary and secondary education: Applying a new instrument to integrate pedagogical and professional elements for digital education. *Education and Information Technologies*, *28*(12), 16017–16040. DOI: 10.1007/s10639-023-11848-9 PMID: 37361819

Uygun, D. (2024). Teachers' perspectives on artificial intelligence in education. *Advances in Mobile Learning Educational Research*, *4*(1), 931–939. DOI: 10.25082/amler.2024.01.005

Walter, Y. (2024). Embracing the future of artificial intelligence in the classroom: The relevance of ai literacy, prompt engineering, and critical thinking in modern education. *International Journal of Educational Technology in Higher Education*, *21*(1). Advance online publication. DOI: 10.1186/s41239-024-00448-3

Wood, E., Ange, B., & Miller, D. (2021). Are we ready to integrate artificial intelligence literacy into medical school curriculum: Students and faculty survey. *Journal of Medical Education and Curricular Development*, *8*. Advance online publication. DOI: 10.1177/23821205211024078 PMID: 34250242

Yazdanpanah, V., Gerding, E., Stein, S., Dastani, M., Jonker, C., Norman, T., & Ramchurn, S. (2022). Reasoning about responsibility in autonomous systems: Challenges and opportunities. *AI & Society*, *38*(4), 1453–1464. DOI: 10.1007/s00146-022-01607-8

Zainal, N. (2023). University students' perspectives on gamification in vocabulary learning: A literature review. *Malaysian Journal of Social Sciences and Humanities (Mjssh)*, *8*(5), e002314. DOI: 10.47405/mjssh.v8i5.2314

Zhang, J. (2024). AI in teacher education: Unlocking new dimensions in teaching support, inclusive learning, and digital literacy. *Journal of Computer Assisted Learning*, *40*(4), 1871–1885. DOI: 10.1111/jcal.12988

Zhao, J., Juithong, S., & Nilnopkoon, P. (2024). Effecting an adaptive learning system on academic achievement as regulations for measuring pharmacist qualifications to licensure of pharmaceutical management students. *IJSASR*, *4*(3), 573–582. DOI: 10.60027/ijsasr.2024.4357

Zourmpakis, A., Kalogiannakis, M., & Papadakis, S. (2023). Adaptive gamification in science education: An analysis of the impact of implementation and adapted game elements on students' motivation. *Computers*, *12*(7), 143. DOI: 10.3390/computers12070143

Chapter 11
AI-Powered Lifelong Learning System:
AI-Driven Mobile Learning for a Transformative Educational Landscape

Nofvia De Vega
https://orcid.org/0000-0001-9191-5019
Universitas Borneo Tarakan, Indonesia

ABSTRACT

This chapter examines the function of Artificial Intelligence (AI) and Mobile Assisted Language Learning (MALL) in reshaping education in Society 5.0. Illustrating how AI solutions embedded in MALL via adaptive paths and real-time feedback lead to highly personalized and inclusive learning experiences. The work highlights the importance of cultural sensitivity in AI applications. It provides a framework for designing AI-enabled systems considering the various needs of a diverse, multilingual learning environment. It also explores AI as an agent for digital citizenship, preparing students for a future driven by technology, and offers evidence-based practices to assist educators and policymakers.

INTRODUCTION

The world of education is expanding, and Artificial Intelligence (AI) and Mobile Assisted Language Learning (MALL) are revolutionizing how we perceive, learn, and teach English and other subjects. This chapter discusses the potential future contributions of advanced technologies to enlivening education experiences for

DOI: 10.4018/979-8-3373-1062-6.ch011

opyright © 2026, IGI Global Scientific Publishing. Copying or distributing in print or electronic forms without written permission of IGI Global Scientific Publishing is prohibited.

the vision of Society 5.0, which aims to combine technology and human values in synergy. Thus, the educational ecosystem is inclusive, personalized, and accessible to everyone, bringing well-rounded human development against the loaded-down challenges of a digital world, which is the aim of society 5.0. Traditionally, the educational model was biased toward standard approaches that do not account for most common learner needs. However, advancements in AI now allow for the review of huge data sets to uncover the individual learning pathways that help create adaptive learning pathways at particular speeds and according to personal learning styles. This personalized approach to education better engages students and encourages self-directed learning, a core requirement of contemporary educational demands. AI complements Mobile Assisted Language Learning (MALL), enabling learners to access educational resources from their mobile devices, resulting in increased flexibility and convenience when using AI to learn a language. MALL is an effective medium for supporting interactive and contextualized learning experiences, which can be enhanced with AI, such as real-time feedback and customized learning materials based on each individual's proficiency level. The primary objectives of this chapter are as follows:

1. To analyze the potential of AI and MALL in creating a more personalized, engaging, and inclusive learning environment.
2. To discuss the importance of cultural sensitivity in AI applications within diverse educational contexts.
3. To explore how these technologies can support the development of digital citizenship among learners, equipping them with essential skills for navigating a technology-driven society.
4. To present evidence-based practices and case studies demonstrating the effective integration of AI-enhanced MALL strategies in education.

By the end of this chapter, readers will see how AI and MALL convergence can drive the development of innovative educational methodologies specifically designed to enable its students to succeed in the imminent digital complex scenario. In this chapter, we endeavor to understand how these technologies bring meaning and context to their use in fostering personalized learning relevant to the learner's needs.

BACKGROUND

With the AI and MALL paradigms becoming increasingly prevalent in a fast-evolving education system, emerging teaching and learning methods based on these technologies rapidly transform our current approach. With the Human plus technology approach of Society 5.0, these technologies offer enormous potential to enhance the educational experience. Society 5.0 advocates the alignment between technological progress and human values, seeking to build contexts where learning is a well-being, inclusive, and accessible activity. From this point, AI revolutionizes matters, providing personalized learning solutions tailored to each student's interests. Traditionally, educational models have based curricula on standardized methods, which do not address the range of learning styles, paces, and backgrounds of students. Rane et al. (2023) argue that by analyzing large data groups, AI can detect individual learning patterns and preferences, whereby paths can be applied to each Learner, providing adaptive learning. Beyond that, it improves engagement while allowing students to advance at their own pace, which is a dire need for personalized education in modern times.

Mobile-assisted language learning (MALL) supports AI from mobile devices by assisting with language learning. By leveraging this approach, learners can access educational content anytime and anywhere, which promotes flexibility and convenience. According to Morgana & Kukulska-Hulme's (2021) study, MALL can assist language acquisition through interactive and contextualized learning experiences. With AI on top, MALL can provide real-time feedback and personalized content depending on the Learner's FB level and ensure that he/she is neither bored for being over their head nor flustered by difficulty. This chapter will discuss concrete tools and pedagogical strategies incorporating MALL with AI to show how this can produce engaging and successful learning environments. With the globalization of education, it has become extremely important for AI to be culturally sensitive in its applications since learners are from diverse backgrounds. Legette, Hope, Harris, & Griffin (2021) state that cultivating cultural responsiveness in teaching helps engender student engagement and better learning outcomes because it establishes a feeling of belonging and relevance. Including cultural elements in AI education tools assure educators that the learning experience is diverse and inclusive. This chapter will discuss how AI can incorporate cultural sensitivity by making education more equitable and enjoyable.

In addition, the chapter underscored the need for increasing digital citizenship and lifelong learning aided by AI. Teaching students how to walk responsibly in online environments is crucial in this modern, technology-driven society. Online behavior, privacy awareness, and critical evaluation of digital content are all part of digital citizenship, the competencies they need to take part in the digital world ethically (Richardson & Milovidov, 2019). This initiative can be supported by AI, which provides platforms for teaching these skills in practical scenarios and simulations. Furthermore, it is becoming more and more essential to be always in the process of learning as the job market changes. With continuous skill development through AI-powered mobile learning platforms, learners progress and can adapt to new challenges while staying relevant in an ever-changing world (Strielkowski, Grebennikova, Lisovskiy, Rakhimova, & Vasileva, 2024).

TRANSFORMING LANGUAGE EDUCATION

The educational landscape has witnessed a significant shift recently as advanced technologies like Mobile-Assisted Language Learning (MALL) and Artificial Intelligence (AI) have been integrated. In their quest to improve the learning experience, however, educators have been waiting for AI to become a powerful tool that simulates human intelligence processes such as learning, reasoning, and self-correction. From an educational standpoint, the power of AI can dissect immense amounts of data to identify the strengths and weaknesses of individual students and then deliver a learning experience that is customized to them. According to this research Huang, Lu, & Yang (2023), personalizing this process improves engagement and learning outcomes. On the other hand, MALL takes advantage of mobile devices to help learners learn languages via educational content that can be accessed flexibly and conveniently at any time and anywhere. AI and MALL are converging to form a dynamic synergy that not only improves the use of language learning but also prepares the students to meet success in a rapidly changing technology-based world. This chapter defines AI and MALL individually and describes their interconnections to understand how integrating them can transform educational practices and create inclusive and engaging learning environments.

Defining Artificial Intelligence in Education

Artificial Intelligence is the machine's ability to simulate human intelligence processes such as learning, deduction, and induction. These processes consist of a number of functions, including knowledge, reasoning, problem-solving, and self-correction. In education spaces, the data analytics capabilities of AI are used to handle large amounts of data and cater the learning experience to students' needs. Dimitriadou & Lanitis (2023) claim that AI can follow students' behaviour, performance, and learning preferences and tend to their strengths and weaknesses accordingly. Educators can create personalized learning pathways to engage with students and potentially improve academic outcomes through this capability. An example of this is driven platforms like Intelligent Tutoring Systems (ITS), which constantly adjust the instructional content on the platform by monitoring the student's progress in real-time. These systems continuously assess the Learner's understanding, allowing for changing the difficulty of tasks, offering problem-specific feedback, and recommending supplementary materials to create a situation-anchored learning environment that is changing along with a learner's needs. It is important because, with this adaptability, we can address diverse learning styles and paces of different learners, giving an inclusive learning experience.

Figure 1. AI-driven education outcomes

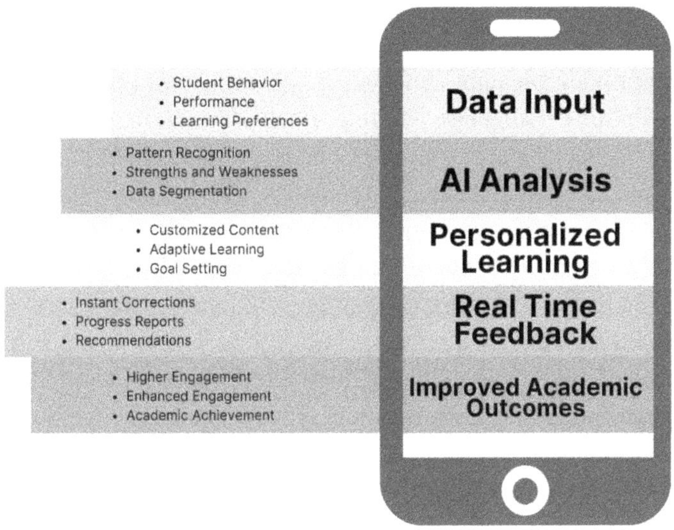

As shown in Figure 1, flowchart components describe how AI-driven personalized learning can be implemented in education, beginning with Data Input. During this initial phase, important student data, including student behavior, is gathered, which captures how s/he uses learning materials (how long s/he spends on tasks and participates in discussions). Performance data is collected via assessment scores, quiz results, and project evaluation. We also need to understand Learning Preferences, especially engaging students and getting a feeling for their feedback and engagement. Are they visual learners, auditory learners, or kinesthetic learners? Then AI Analysis takes over, using advanced algorithms to analyze the collected data and find meaningful insights. Pattern Recognition uncovers trends in student learning behaviors and performance, among other things. In addition, the analysis allows educators to spot each candidate's strengths and weaknesses and pinpoint where each student is thriving and where they could benefit from extra assistance. Lastly, Data Segmentation helps find students with similar learning profiles or needs and targets the intervention accordingly.

Understanding Mobile-Assisted Language Learning (MALL)

Mobile-Assisted Language Learning (MALL) is an innovative way to use mobile devices (smartphones or tablet PCs) to assist language learning. This method enables learners to learn the educational content whenever and wherever they want, thereby improving the flexibility and convenience of the language acquisition process (Kukulska-Hulme, Lee, & Norris, 2017). As a solution that efficiently exploits a combination of applications, podcasts, and social media, MALL utilizes mobile technology to provide engaging, interactive, and contextually appropriate language practice possibilities. Language learning activities supported by MALL include vocabulary building, grammar exercises, and real-time communication with native speakers through language exchange applications. The mobility inherent to MALL allows users to integrate language practice into their daily lives in a manner much less restricted by traditional classroom learning. One of the best features of this flexibility is that it allows for just the perfect solutions for adult learners or people with busy schedules who can learn at specific points without hindering the training demands. Richardson & Milovidov's (2019) research shows that MALL increases learner engagement by providing different types of learners with varying learning styles and improves learners' overall learning experience. To make learning more inclusive, MALL offers resources that appeal to various kinds of people, e.g., gamified applications and podcasts. Although this feedback occurs much more quickly with mobile applications than with print and other forms of learning, it is still brief and immediate, providing a strong sense of motivation and retention among learners (Stockwell, 2008)

Additionally, MALL encourages learner autonomy in which individuals select at what time and how they will use language learning resources. According to Richardson & Milovidov (2019), this self-directed approach enables learners to take responsibility for their educational journey, thus facilitating a greater willingness to study more actively and engage more in learning. Similarly, Vega, Basri, & Nur (2025) states that MALL enables social interaction between learners; thus, learners can communicate with people of different cultural backgrounds. This interaction contributes to language and an appreciation of cultural backgrounds, which is crucial for effective communication. To conclude, MALL enhances language practice options and increases the adaptedness and effectiveness of language learning. MALL achieves all of this by incorporating flexibility, engagement of the Learner, and social interaction, collectively enriching the Learner's language skills.

The Synergy of AI and Mobile-Assisted Language Learning (MALL)

The intermingling of Mobile Assisted Language Learning (MALL) and Artificial Intelligence (AI) marks a significant new phase in the theory and practice of teaching and learning languages. This synergy augments the efficiency and effectiveness of the learning experience and brings together a wide variety of student needs in the fast-changing digital landscape. Probably the most significant advantage of the union of AI with MALL is the possibility to produce personalized learning experiences that adjust according to the individual experience of each Learner with its own pace and skill level. Analysis of the users' interactions with mobile LLA is also possible with AI algorithms – assessing their strengths and weaknesses. For instance, AI-driven analytics are used at Duolingo and Rosetta Stone to customize the exercises according to each Learner's needs so learners are not too challenged or too bored (Vashishth, Sharma, Sharma, & Kumar, 2024). According to Alamri, Lowell, Watson, & Watson's (2020) research, personalized learning pathways significantly improve student engagement and retention, thus creating an enhanced learning environment.

THE MAGIC OF MOBILE-ASSISTED LANGUAGE LEARNING (MALL)

Mobile-Assisted Language Learning (MALL) is a revolutionary method of education that uses mobile technologies to teach languages anytime and anywhere. This breakthrough method transcends the limitations of the traditional, forcing learners to connect with instructional content from various environments while commuting or waiting in line, thus making the learning process more encompassing and applicable. Additionally, MALL is based on constructivist theory, which calls for active participation in the learning process and real-world interaction, consistent with Vygotsky's social development theory that stresses the significance of social interaction in cognitive development. There are several advantages that MALL allows us to provide, such as increased accessibility and more personalized learning opportunities for our students, but providing MALL-based learning also comes with some challenges, such as the digital divide and differences in student motivation. Given these dynamics, this literature review is important for teachers and policymakers who seek to use MALL as an equitable and powerful educational tool.

Benefits, Challenges, and Educational Equity

Mobile Assisted Language Learning (MALL) uses mobile devices, including smartphones and tablets, to facilitate students' learning and interaction with instructional content at any time and location. A compelling foray into this revolutionary method has transformed language instruction by eliminating traditional obstacles. Learners can practice language skills anywhere outside the classroom with MALL, whether waiting for public transport, traveling, or shopping. Learning because of this flexibility becomes more immersive and nurtures students to grasp real-life language skills, which is of utmost significance to effective language learning. MALL's concept is based on constructivist learning theories that assign great importance to learners' active involvement and real-world learning experience. Vygotsky's Social Development Theory states that social interaction is of fundamental importance in cognitive development. Recognition that MALL allows learners to interact with language in a multiplicity of contexts is thus an advantage because it can enhance one's communication ability. Further, mobile learning corresponds to Kolb's experiential learning principles, which state that knowledge is obtained by experiencing and reflecting. Learners can improve their proficiency and confidence by interacting with language in everyday settings. Though providing many benefits, MALL also involves diverse challenges and controversies. The principal source of the problem is the digital gap, the discrepancy concerning the ability to access mobile technology and the internet. Van de Werfhorst, Kessenich, & Geven (2020) found that unequal access to digital resources deepens educational inequalities because students from poorer socio-economic backgrounds have little or no access to these resources. Smartphones and a reliable internet connection are prerequisites for learners to access educational online content, resulting in many learners not accessing relevant educational online content and hence losing out on opportunities for learning and getting practice. The problem is acute, particularly in rural areas or low-income communities, which may not have easy access to technology.

Lastly, MALL is only applicable when learners are self-disciplined and motivated. MALL is not structured in an instructional guidance and direct interaction manner as we see in most traditional classroom settings, so since learners have to take more responsibility for their learning, MALL combines the two. However, for some students, this change is both a challenge and a surprise because it requires them to think for themselves and work independently, concepts that don't fit into a desire for full direct supervision and structure. In the words of Self Determination Theory Deci & Ryan (2000), intrinsic motivation is important for successful learning outcomes. If learners aren't motivated to engage in MALL, they won't reap all its benefits.

The Personalization Revolution in Mobile-Assisted Language Learning

One of the distinguishing elements of Mobile-Assisted Language Learning (MALL) is its capacity to deliver personalized learning experiences tailored to the individual needs of each student. Mobile learning applications facilitate adaptation by analyzing user interactions, preferences, and performance to tailor material and activities. For example, adaptive algorithms used by platforms such as Duolingo change the difficulties of tasks according to a learner's progress and proficiency. It guarantees that students are not under–or over-challenged, and as such, they are motivated and feel achieving. Carroll, Lindsey, Chaparro, & Winslow's (2021) research demonstrates that personalized learning increases student engagement and retention because students maintain motivation as the learning content matches their interests and skill sets.

The principles of differentiated instruction suggest delivering personalized learning experiences that meet the needs of different learning styles and at varying speeds. Tomlinson (2016) argues that students will succeed academically when instruction is individualized to their needs. An example is the MALL platforms, which allow learners to learn about the material they are interested in, such as thematic vocabulary lessons or contextually relevant scenarios. This method extends interaction and matches constructivist learning theories on activity and learning relevance. That said, the data privacy and security challenges of personalization via MALL are real. As mobile apps amass trillions of bytes of personal data to personalize experiences, the dangers of what is done with it, stored with it, shared, or sold are considerable. Consent and transparency issues are particularly critical in the case of younger learners who, depending on their age, may not fully understand the implications of data sharing. For example, in the United States, the Family Educational Rights and Privacy Act (FERPA) focuses on protecting students' educational records and requires educational organizations to guarantee that mobile applications comply with private policies.

Transforming Language Learning

Understanding the impact of MALL is made easier by making such comparisons with traditional methods of language learning. Traditionally, instruction involves much face-to-face instruction in a classroom setting. Though these methods provide learners with structured learning and direct instructor interaction, they may not be flexible or easily accessible. Often, students are expected to work with a standard curriculum schedule that can be limiting for students with busy schedules or varying learning paces. The effects of mobile-assisted language learning (MALL) on the learning process are compared with those of traditional language learning in our research. Access Only in classroom settings Accessible anywhere, anytime One-size-fits-all approach Highly personalization Highly personalized experiences Real-time feedback, or feedback delayed until often. Passive, lecture-based Engagement vs Interactive, gamified experiences. The Learning Environment is persistent and rigid, with Flexible and context-driven approaches. To better understand the impact of MALL, it's helpful to compare it with traditional language learning methods. Traditional approaches often rely heavily on face-to-face instruction in a classroom setting. While these methods provide structured learning and direct instructor interaction, they may lack flexibility and accessibility. Students are typically required to adhere to a fixed schedule and curriculum, which can be a barrier for those with busy lifestyles or varying learning paces.

Table 1. Traditional vs. mobile-assisted language learning

Feature	**Traditional Language Learning**	**Mobile-Assisted Language Learning (MALL)**
Accessibility	Limited to classroom settings	Anytime, anywhere access
Personalization	One-size-fits-all approach	Highly personalized experiences
Feedback	Often delayed	Real-time feedback
Engagement	Passive, lecture-based	Interactive and gamified experiences
Learning Environment	Fixed and structured	Flexible and context-driven
Feature	Traditional Language Learning	Mobile-Assisted Language Learning (MALL)

Table 1 shows that though traditional methods constitute structure and direct support of the learning process, they do not necessarily accommodate individual learning preferences better than MALL. Due to their interactive and gamified nature, MALL tends to engage learners more, as skills gained are immediately and intuitively applied in various situations. To sum up, MALL is a revolutionary asset in language learning, as it opens the door to capabilities that allow learners to access and tailor their experience based on their needs and interests. However, the challenge remains in addressing accompanying challenges, such as the digital divide and sufficient concerns about data privacy. Through these challenges, we have been able to harness the full force of MALL to offer a more equitable, practical language learning experience that is responsive to a diverse student population.

AI MEETS MALL

This part presents a revolutionary way to incorporate artificial intelligence into the design of mobile-assisted language learning (MALL) educational applications responsive to learner needs. The starting point for this process is a fine needs analysis so that AI algorithms can evaluate students' language proficiency level, learning objectives, and preferences. Sharable has allowed platforms like Babbel and Duolingo to leverage this data to create personalized content that adapts to the individual's learning style and keeps them engaged and challenged. Another considerable merit of AI in MALL is the strength of offering dynamic learning activities, classifying student results in real-time, and changing the exercises to suit the individual student. Its adaptability and effective feedback mechanisms make learning easier by providing scope for immediate corrections and Easier To Remember. The potential to develop customized, fascinating, and quality language learning encounters as training establishments more frequently begin to use AI-driven procedures are being opened up, empowering learners to accomplish their language objectives in an exceptionally computerized world.

Designing Distinctive Educational

Mobile-assisted language learning (MALL), integrating artificial intelligence (AI), is a new way of designing educational applications to meet learners' different needs. The process starts with an in-depth needs analysis, taking in all the collected data about the target audience's language proficiency levels, learning goals, and preferences. AI algorithms can analyze this data to identify common characteristics and challenges of the learner population. For example, Babbel uses initial assessments to measure the user's ability to inform the content's design. Following that, the phase is the design of the personalized content. Using AI, instructional materials can then be developed to an individual's learning style. For example, Duolingo modifies its courses using machine learning based on a user's performance, so if a person is having trouble with specific terminology, later exercises focus more on that subject. Research shows that personalized learning pathways significantly improve motivation and retention within language learning as students dig deeper into content relevant to their experiences (as researched by Kupchyk & Litvinchuk (2021).

The third stage uses AI to generate dynamic educational experiences and adaptive learning pathways. One significant advantage of MALL applications is that they can continuously monitor student performance and make the exercises more difficult or change the form of the exercise based on how a student performs. For example, if a user is very good at vocabulary but not so good at listening, the system will emphasize listening work and adjust vocabulary work to ensure it is neither too easy nor easy. This adaptability is incredibly important for maintaining learner engagement and for growing. Then, the design of MALL applications should develop effective feedback mechanisms after. Real-time feedback can then be used to evaluate the Learner's performance so the concepts can be reinforced and any misunderstanding can be appropriately corrected. Take, for instance, Busuu, one platform that utilizes speech recognition to evaluate pronunciations, allowing learners to instantly acquire feedback and fix speaking skills on the move in real-time. Timely feedback studies show that this assists in expanding the learning process in students, as they can rectify while the material is fresh, supporting the data of understanding (Lang, 2021).

Developing Intelligent Context Delivery Systems

Intelligent content delivery systems for language learning are a complex process that combines technologies and methodologies to create a compelling and personalized learning environment. It begins with setting clear learning objectives that match curriculum standards and learner needs and then the content curation process in the content delivery (Lewis, 2021). Following this, user data collection is very critical; an initial assessment of the Learner's skill set will be carried out; this means that the software analyses how long they spend on a given task and indicates buzz words indicating a preference or where improvements can be made. AI algorithms then analyze this data using natural language processing (NLP) to generate curricula tailored to each Learner (Shaik et al., 2022). Content curated by you is assembled into adaptive learning pathways that adjust in real time depending on your students' performance. For instance, a system can allocate exercises based on which areas scholars are good at and which areas trouble him or her, and as such, the scholars will be challenged and supported based on their areas of excellence (Margot & Kettler, 2019). To increase learner engagement, games are used to gamify learning, multimedia content is included to provide rich audio and visual learning, and simulations are integrated to enhance learning with real-world projects. Data is available to prove that interactive and gamified elements increase learner motivation and retention (Saleem, Noori, & Ozdamli, 2022). In addition, AI facilitated real-time feedback mechanisms and gave suggestions so learners could learn and adjust their approaches before misconceptions were formed (Seo, Tang, Roll, Fels, & Yoon, 2021). Finally, the process is one of continuous improvement guided by data-driven insights and user feedback, which helps to guide changes in the content and delivery methods. By conducting regular analyses of engagement data, we can identify trends and areas that need improvement to make an intelligent content delivery system effective and accurate (Al-Ahdal & Alharbi, 2021). Integrating these components, intelligent content delivery systems can weave together personalized, engaging, efficient language learning experiences tailored to each Learner's needs, ultimately boosting the efficiency of language education in the digital age.

Instant Feedback in Learning Technologies

Feedback is instant in MALL, the most important component that affects learner engagement and motivation and impacts language learning outcomes. To be effective, feedback needs to be provided on time, i.e. immediately after learners' actions, so mistakes can be corrected immediately and prevented from becoming misconceptions. Dempsey (1993) states that it is necessary to provide timely feedback to reinforce arriving at the correct response and attend to correct errors before they are 'set' in the instructional unit. For example, language learning apps that automatically provide exercise results allow learners to adapt their understanding and strategic approaches immediately based on those results. Specificity is another aspect; feedback should be clear and detailed, pinpointing what was correct or incorrect in the learning process. Mistakes in feedback are more confusing than they seem since they can guide the learners to frustration and confusion; for example, only telling them that their answer is 'wrong' doesn't lead them to any learning. According to Elford, Smith, & James (2024), feedback should answer three key questions: "Where am I going?" (goals), "How am I going?" (progress), and the prompt (Where to next?). (next steps). Through this specificity, learners can pinpoint the aspects of the subject that need to be improved and take part in a thorough interaction with the material at hand.

An additional role of positivity is related to sustaining learner motivation. Correct answers are rewarded with positive reinforcement, promoting continued practice and building confidence. I've read that affirming feedback helps keep learners engaged in content (Barkley & Major, 2020). For example, taking language learning apps and introducing gamified components like awarding points or badges for accurate answers can increase motivation and create a sense of accomplishment. The feedback should also be actionable, and other than telling you that you 'got it wrong,' the callback should provide learners with concrete steps to correct or improve themselves. Learners will take ownership of their learning process and adopt a growth mindset when you give them actionable feedback. That suggests what needs improvement, for example, additional practice exercises or resources to do with the elements that gave students the most trouble (Baik, Larcombe, & Brooker, 2019).

Table 2. Quality of instant feedback in MALL

Feedback Characteristic	Description	Performance Levels
Timeliness	Immediate feedback after learner responses to enable prompt correction of errors	1. Poor Feedback is delayed (hours or days) 2. Fair Feedback is provided within a few hours but not immediately 3. Good Feedback is provided immediately after the response 4. Excellent Feedback is instant and contextual, allowing for real-time adjustments
Specificity	Feedback must be clear and detailed, providing precise information about correct and incorrect responses	1. Poor Feedback is vague, leaving learners confused 2. Fair Feedback indicates correctness but lacks detail 3. Good Feedback specifies correct/incorrect aspects but may lack depth 4. Excellent Feedback is precise, addressing specific errors with detailed explanations
Positivity	Feedback includes positive reinforcement to encourage learner motivation and confidence	1. Poor Feedback is entirely negative 2. Fair Minimal positive reinforcement is included 3. Good Balances positive and constructive feedback 4. Excellent Predominantly positive, celebrating achievements and encouraging further efforts
Actionability	Feedback offers clear, actionable next steps for improvement	1. Poor No actionable steps were provided 2. Fair General areas for improvement are suggested but lack specifics 3. Good Specific suggestions for practice are included 4. Excellent Detailed, actionable steps tailored to the Learner's needs are provided
Personalization	Feedback is tailored based on individual learner performance and challenges	1. Poor Feedback is generic and not tailored 2. Fair Some individual differences are considered but lack depth 3. Good Mostly personalized, addressing specific challenges 4. Excellent Highly personalized, with targeted resources based on the Learner's unique needs

Classification levels in Table 3 allow an orderly classification of the quality of instant feedback in Mobile-Assisted Language Learning (MALL). Feedback is categorized into four distinct quality levels based on an overall score derived from assessing five critical characteristics: Which trend is timeliness, specificity, positivity, actionability, and personalization. It means low-quality feedback with a score of 5 to 8 represents feedback that is effective in none of the areas but does not meet the needs of learners. Scores between 9 and 12 denote Moderate Quality, where certain useful elements exist and could be progressively implemented. While feedback is sometimes reliable, it may not offer sufficient information or direction for advancement. Feedback of High Quality (13 to 16) appears effective in several (but not necessarily all) of these areas but may also suffer from some minor weaknesses. Finally, a score of 17 – 20 indicates excellent quality feedback, being comprehensive and effective at all characteristics, and helping to improve learning with better engagement, motivation, and language acquisition outcomes. Educators can use this framework to understand better and think critically about their feedback practices to become more effective in language learning.

Table 3. Classification levels

Overall Score	Feedback Quality Level	Description
5-8	Low Quality	Feedback lacks timeliness, specificity, positivity, actionability, and personalization.
9-12	Moderate Quality	Feedback provides some useful elements but is inconsistent in effectiveness across characteristics.
13-16	High Quality	Feedback is mostly effective, with strengths in several areas, but may have minor weaknesses.
17-20	Excellent Quality	Feedback is comprehensive and effective across all characteristics, significantly enhancing learning.

EMPOWERING LEARNERS THROUGH AI IN MALL

Integrating artificial intelligence (AI) into Mobile-Assisted Language Learning (MALL) empowers learners to shape the educational landscape with personalized learning opportunities to meet their needs. And with the current academic environment becoming more diverse by the day, the need to customize learning pathways has never been more urgent, which AI technologies help us achieve. AI can analyze a learner's data to identify what they do well and what they don't, and therefore tailor content in real-time for platforms like Duolingo or Rosetta Stone. This personalization encourages engagement and motivation and helps students understand and improve their language skills. Moreover, the educators are presented as the facilitators of learning who handle students who made their AI-assisted rides and foster collaboration and equity in the learning process among the different kinds of learners. The learning experience evolves as gamification strategies are infused into existing teaching concepts. In the end, adding AI into MALL enhances language education and gives every learner, regardless of ethnicity or capacity, the opportunity to reach their language goal in a supportive and encouraging place.

Personalized Learning Experiences

Recently, personalized learning has become a focal point in the current educational climate, realizing the need for trussed educational experiences that meet the individual's diverse needs. Integrating AI into Mobile Assisted Language Learning (MALL) fundamentally changes how educators deliver the content and become more customized and adapted to individual student learning styles, preferences, and pace. AI technologies are key in personalizing the learning experience through algorithms that adapt educational content based on user performance. For example, Duolingo and Rosetta Stone platforms use data analytics to modify lessons in real-time. For example, the AI will be able to react dynamically to a learner's profile, and knowing that the Learner is good in vocabulary but seems to struggle with grammar, it will ensure the Learner continues to be challenged with appropriate material and relevant material. AI in MALL also enables one of its key features, its ability to analyze learner data, which allows it to ascertain exact strengths and weaknesses and then develop a customized adaptive learning path in accordance with the Learner's requirement. For instance, if a teacher uses an AI tool to assess students' speaking proficiency using voice recognition, the system can identify pronunciation accuracy and fluency and suggest exercises to catch those areas for intensification, such as intonation and speed.

Motivation and Engagement Strategies

Gamification refers to harmonizing game elements into an educational context to make learning more enjoyable and engaging. Incorporating such features as points, badges, leaderboards, and challenges allows us to tap into what motivates learners intrinsically and encourages active participation. AI enhances gamification by turning these elements into personalized, individualized, self-determining processes according to the Learner's preferences and performance. For example, an AI-powered language learning app might analyze students' progression and areas where they are good or bad. This data then allows the app to adapt its challenges such that if it notices a learner is advanced, it will deliver more complex tasks, while if a learner needs additional support, it will provide more gradual supportive challenges. This approach allows students to work independently while covering various difficulty levels. Hellín et al. (2023) showed that gamified learning environments can improve learning outcomes by increasing students' motivation and engagement. Integration with Traditional Methods gamification can provide an enhanced and more dynamic learning platform when integrated with traditional teaching methods.

Supporting Diverse Learner Needs

Diverse learner needs must be supported in any language learning setting that intends to be inclusive. Mobile Assisted Language Learning (MALL) applications driven by AI can indeed contribute to dealing with different learner profiles, such as learners with a disability and learners from other cultures. AI technologies can be designed to offer bespoke support for language learners with disabilities so that they can get better learning experiences and results. For instance, learners with speech impairments can use AI-powered speech recognition tools, which give them instant feedback on their pronunciation and articulation. Furthermore, text-to-speech functionality allows students with visual disabilities or difficulties reading to hear content read out loud (Young, Courtad, Douglas, & Chung, 2019). Additionally, based on learning patterns and challenges, AI can create personalized learning paths for students while engaging them with customized materials needed for them specifically. Furthermore, adaptive learning environments vary the types and difficulty of content they present according to a learner's real-time progress so that students with disabilities are neither hyper-challenged nor under-challenged. Ultimately, AI tools can leverage the added advantage of incorporating multiple sensory learning techniques covering vision, hearing, and experience senses, like kinesthetic learners, to retain learners of all sorts.

INTEGRATING AI INTO MALL CURRICULA

Integrating artificial intelligence (AI) in Mobile Assisted Language Learning (MALL) curricula is a changing design and development approach to language education that tailors learning programs to meet various learner needs. It begins with a learner-centered curriculum that links to recognized academic standards, typically the Common European Framework of Reference for Languages (CEFR), guaranteeing that curriculum objectives are achieved consistently. Using AI tools, we can now analyze student data to build bespoke learning pathways to cater to each student, providing real-time feedback on their progress in speaking and writing. Being able to assess this capability not only promotes overall language development but also allows educators to make data-driven decisions that modify instruction strategies and interventions. Additionally, including AI literacy in the curriculum helps prepare students for critical consumption of the technologies they engage with, and ethical questions around data privacy and algorithmic bias continue to matter. Alongside AI tools, educators can design innovative, collaborative, and experiential learning experiences that help develop students with the appropriate language skills needed for an interconnected world.

Curriculum Design and Development

Language education curriculum design and development is a system process of fashioning education based on set educational standards and formulated programs that serve the different needs of learners. Learning must be a learner-centered approach that draws on and relates to the student's interests and background (Makena, 2020). Moreover, curricula are aligned to set standards, such as the Common European Framework of Reference for Languages (CEFR), to achieve learning objectives (Mohamed, 2023). A well-designed curriculum integrates many language skills (listening, speaking, reading, and writing) to foster language development. Additionally, assessment strategies must comprise a comprehensive range of robust assessment mechanisms, namely formative and summative assessments, to measure student progress and the success of the curriculum (Samin, 2019).

Incorporating AI technologies in current language curricula can improve the benefits and results of language learning. Using student data, AI can analyze and customize learning for students, creating learning paths that are appropriate and challenging for each student. In addition, AI-powered tools offer real-time feedback on speaking and writing tasks, which helps students improve their skills in real-time (Oseremi, Yinka, Nsisong, & Damilola, 2024). For example, chatbots and virtual tutors can supplement instruction in the classroom by providing more practice and support outside of the school. Further, educators can tap into AI analytics to learn about student performance, guiding data-driven decisions for curriculum fine-tuning and targeted interventions (B. George & Wooden, 2023).

While designers of new language courses use AI capability, course developers can develop a more innovative way to make learning intriguing. Also, incorporating AI literacy into the curriculum aids students in understanding what technologies they use and aids them in critically considering the implications of language learning (Walter, 2024). In scenario-based learning, simulated real-life situations can be used in job interviews or cultural exchanges where an AI engine can help enrich the learning. In addition, project-based learning stimulates students to use their language skills creatively (such as by creating their own AI applications for language learning) (Nayak, Satpathy, & Jain, 2024). Another aspect is that the ethical implications of using AI in language education, such as data privacy and algorithmic bias (A. Nguyen, Ngo, Hong, Dang, & Nguyen, 2023), must be considered. Finally, creating new courses can encourage collaborative, experiential learning using AI tools, such as language assistance in foreign language courses where students will work on projects requiring them to use these tools together, sharpening teamwork and communication skills.

Figure 2. A curriculum framework diagram

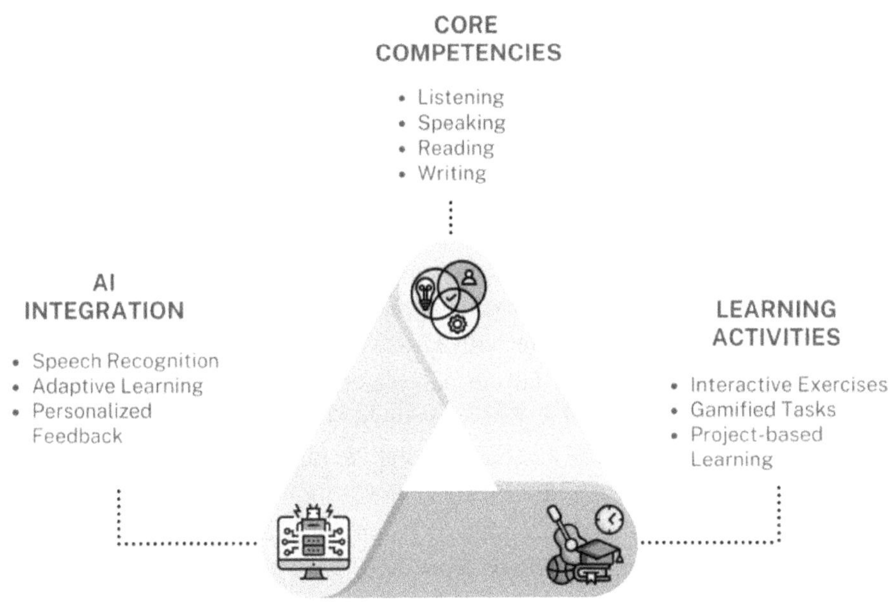

Figure 2 is language curriculum design development in language education necessitates the intelligent use of AI technologies. With its emphasis on personalized learning, real-time feedback, and creative course design, educators can develop compelling and technologically effective language learning experiences that equip students for a dynamic and interdependent world. Core competencies: listening, speaking, reading, and writing function as tools supported by the various AI tools and learning activities, all brought together in a Curriculum Framework Diagram that illustrates how it all works. The Layered Curriculum Model also highlights how each part of the model, starting from foundational competencies to assessment strategies, sits on top of one another to form one well-rounded learning experience. Aligning specific language skills to AI tools for learning. A Matrix of Learning Objectives and AI Tools can guide educators in pairing particular language skills with corresponding AI learning resources that help achieve learning objectives. Last, a flowchart of the curriculum development process visualizes the course of action from needs analysis to implementation and shows how AI can improve each step of the curriculum development process. With these visualizations, educators can aid in communicating and comprehending cross-function processes with stakeholders to create the most suited curriculums tailored to different class levels, today's digital age, and the mixed classes nature.

Professional Development for Educators

Educators need professional development to properly use AI technology for Mobile-Assisted Language Learning (MALL). With the fast and continued advancement of technology, the role of education in this field has started to evolve, and educators must be informed about the skills and knowledge required to use AI tools for language pedagogy. Therefore, training programs should begin with the basics: understanding AI technology, its applications in language education, and more. Teachers should be conversant with AI-driven language applications, chatbots, and adaptive learning platforms that can parse instruction and supply real-time, unprejudiced feedback (Zaghlool & Khasawneh, 2023). In addition, such familiarity builds their technical expertise and enables them to maximize the potency of these tools in their classrooms.

A critical component of this training is its practical application. According to Yannier et al. (2021), while hands-on workshops are only practical to teach educators how to experiment with AI tools in a safe environment, they can also allow these educators to incorporate such technologies into their lesson plans with high confidence levels. For example, educators can participate in simulations on top of speech recognition software to test pronunciation and utilize AI platforms for designing personalized learning paths for their students. These practical experiences are essential for educators to envision AI's impact on student engagement and learning outcomes. In addition, training should include methods for effective assessment of the data produced by AI tools. This data is crucial to understanding how to analyze and inform decisions about instructional adjustments and targeted interventions (Bondie, Dahnke, & Zusho, 2019). For instance, educators need to be able to identify patterns of student performance data and then tailor their teaching strategies according to the needs of their learners. This data-driven approach does a couple of other things, including improving instructional effectiveness and increasing student personalization of learning.

Apart from initial training, creating communities of practice (CoP) is critical to facilitating ongoing support and innovation for educators. MALL educators are part of collaborative networks, CoPs, sharing experiences, resources, and practices that make visiting best practices about AI (De Carvalho-Filho, Tio, & Steinert, 2020). By supporting a community around continuous learning, these communities allow educators to find peers with whom they can discuss different challenges and successes and augment their professional development. Educators can participate in CoPs, where educators can have the opportunity to observe one another's peers, co-teach, and collaborate in lesson planning, giving a fuller understanding of what it means to teach effectively.

Beyond that, CoPs can set up regular workshops, webinars, and discussion forums for educators to be constantly abreast with the latest innovations in AI and MALL. Educators should have continuous professional development in a technology that is changing continually because instructors must be current with innovative practices (Sancar, Atal, & Deryakulu, 2021). For example, a CoP may invite experts to talk about emerging AI tools or organize hands-on sessions on the new applications of AI for educators to get into. In addition to improving their technical skills, it places educators nearby, with a shared purpose and sense of community among them. CoPs also increase the peer support and mentoring aspects of professional development.

Lastly, CoPs help to share resources such as lesson plans, assessment tools, and research to identify the best uses of AI in language learning. The result is collaborative knowledge sharing, which improves the quality of the instruction the community makes available to its educators, as diverse materials and strategies are now available to them (D. Nguyen & Ng, 2022). By collectively combining their expertise, educators can develop entire curricula using the full power of AI technologies that would otherwise not be possible through a single individual. First, as an end note, educators' professional development in the direction of AI and MALL is essential to improve language instruction and to help create innovation. Training educators on applying and using AI tools will enable them to carry out that task effectively in their teaching. Moreover, the communities of practice that can be developed offer ongoing support and collaboration, fostering that their educators can keep their learning going and adapt to the ever-evolving educational landscape. Through directed training and the development of CoPs, such educational institutions can equip educators to use AI technologies, adding to the positive outcomes of student learning in language education.

Evaluating Effectiveness and Outcomes

Understanding AI's impact on student performance and engagement is key and requires evaluating how well the integration of AI improves outcomes in language learning. A variety of metrics can, therefore, be used to assess this impact properly. Standardized language proficiency tests and pre- and post-assessments are available to measure the learner's learning gain, such that educators can evaluate to what extent AI technologies support language acquisition (Pokrivcakova, 2019). Another critically important metric is the engagement level, which can be measured as participation rate, time spent on a task, and the delivery rate of learning modules. AI tools typically utilize gamification to enhance motivation and increase engagement (Bachiri, Mouncif, & Bouikhalene, 2023). Moreover, the quality of the feedback provided by the AI tools is measured as a crucial metric; depending on whether the feedback is given immediately, it relates to the current language task of the user, which then allows the user to make the necessary changes immediately (A. S. George & George, 2023). Surveys and interviews help to shed light on students' satisfaction with tools (Bagash Mansour Ahmed Al-Sofi, 2021) and how students understand these tools affect their learning outcomes.

In the end, longitudinal studies can provide important information about the long-term consequences of AI integration by measuring students' performance and involvement over extended periods (Harju, Koskinen, & Pehkonen, 2019). A key aspect of educational institutions is continuous improvement through learner feedback and data analysis processes to implement improvement. It involves data-driven decision-making; educators look at performance data to understand strengths and weaknesses and to target interventions (Schildkamp, 2019). Feedback loops can create regular input from learners regarding their learning experiences, influencing instructional adjustments (Carless, 2019). Furthermore, AI tools and instructional strategies should iterate based on data analysis to refine technology to meet learners' needs (Lameras & Arnab, 2021). Educators need professional development to analyze data and adapt teaching practices to be effective, as stated by (Popova, Evans, Breeding, & Arancibia, 2022). Lastly, creating communities of practice to actively engage educators in regular exchange along the lines of sharing best practices and learning from each other related to the effective application of AI in language learning can amplify success with AI integration in language learning (Tomkin, Beilstein, Morphew, & Herman, 2019). They utilize these metrics and continuous improvement processes in educational education to make the most of the available AI technologies that help improve language learning outcomes.

Figure 3. Metrics for assessing impact

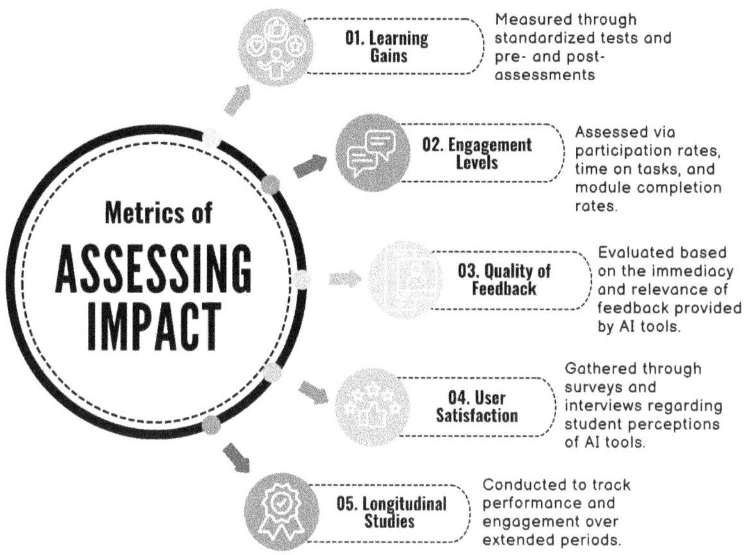

In figure 3 shows an analysis of the impact of AI in language learning and the outcomes its integration produces will aid in determining the real benefits conveyed through it in the most optimum manner and how it aligns with the needs of students. With numerous metrics available, like learning gains, engagement levels, the quality of the feedback, user satisfaction, and longitudinal studies, educators can learn a lot from the role AI tools play in impacting student performance and learning. In addition, incorporating continuous improvement processes built around learner feedback and data analysis permits institutions to update their instructional strategies and adjust technologies to serve learners best. To make the most out of the AI technologies possible as the language education landscape evolves, these technologies will require evaluation and adjustment, increasing language learning outcomes and creating an environment for a more prosperous and interactive learning experience.

SOLUTION AND RECOMMENDATIONS

Mobility-assisted language learning is combined with artificial intelligence to create an innovative way of bringing up language education. With this integration, it is possible to craft personalized learning experiences based on each student's unique measures by analyzing massive amounts of data about individual learners.

This highly customized approach creates highly engaged learners and produces more excellent learning outcomes, as learners can engage with content tailored to their language proficiency and learning preferences. Moreover, it is also important that technology be designed to incorporate real-time feedback, which provides immediate constructive and corrective feedback during language learning activities, thereby preventing learners from making misconceptions and reinforcing the correct learning path. With timely and specific feedback, educators can develop a more motivated and engaged learning environment that persists in motivating learners to take risks. In addition, AI tools for education need to be attuned to cultural settings and variety in learners' backgrounds. In return, this cultural sensitivity helps to ensure all students feel respected and valued and enriches the learning experience by fostering an inclusive atmosphere. Moreover, user accessibility should be improved to ensure maximum benefits from MALL technologies for individuals with disabilities so that the users can use them without obstacles in language education. To benefit from the technology's advanced educational features, providing equitable access to technology in underprivileged communities is paramount to correct the digital divide. Educators ' professional development for this approach is a significant item of integrating flipping. This training allows teachers to toggle on AI-enhanced MALL tools and use them to scale and make the learning experience more personalized. Continuously trained teacher programs on new technologies can empower educators and position them to live and use the changing educational landscape better. Therefore, the integration of AI and MALL can shape the future of language education into a personalized realm, speedy response, culturally inclusive, easily accessible, and educated educators. These are areas in which educational institutions can concentrate their efforts to create a dynamic and engaging learning environment that can respond to the needs of all learners. It is a composite answer from relevant research and summarizes the holistic approach needed for successful language education in today's digital age.

CONCLUSION

The merger of Artificial Intelligence (AI) and Mobile Assisted Language Learning (MALL) facilitates a new language teaching and learning paradigm. With MALL frameworks giving AI capabilities, educational institutions can use the power of personalized learning experiences to engage students and realize the maximum learning results. This synergy also has one of the key benefits: continuous feedback in real-time, which is important for language acquisition. Speech recognition applications are some of the tools that learners can use to improve their speaking and writing skills because they get instant corrections and suggestions as they speak.

Furthermore, the cultural sensitivity of the AI applications is also an important aspect of this transformation. AI's capacity to curate educational content to match students' diverse backgrounds makes learning inclusive: all learners are representative and considered. Being culturally responsive increases motivation, but it also enhances the ability to comprehend language more deeply when we know this is based on the interests and life experiences of the students. While this integration provides opportunities, we must look for the ethical risks that ingrain AI solutions specifically, especially the problems around data privacy and algorithmic bias that can erode trust in these systems. Research is still underway to understand the varied ways AI supports language learning and ensure we are leveraging it well and equitably. Outlining research directions, the continuous scrutiny and adaptation of educational practice to meaningfully integrate such innovations are highlighted. Finally, in this fast-changing technological landscape, AI and MALL will improve the learner experience and prepare the students to navigate the complexities of a networked (virtually) world. This conclusion points to the need for forward-looking strategies in language proficiency education and the need for existing literature and insight to be approached to create innovative teaching and learning methods.

REFERENCES

Al-Ahdal, A. A. M. H., & Alharbi, M. A. (2021). MALL in Collaborative Learning as a Vocabulary-Enhancing Tool for EFL Learners: A Study Across Two Universities in Saudi Arabia. *SAGE Open*, *11*(1). Advance online publication. DOI: 10.1177/2158244021999062

Alamri, H., Lowell, V., Watson, W., & Watson, S. L. (2020). Using personalized learning as an instructional approach to motivate learners in online higher education: Learner self-determination and intrinsic motivation. *Journal of Research on Technology in Education*, *52*(3), 322–352. DOI: 10.1080/15391523.2020.1728449

Bachiri, Y.-A., Mouncif, H., & Bouikhalene, B. (2023). Artificial Intelligence Empowers Gamification: Optimizing Student Engagement and Learning Outcomes in E-learning and MOOCs. [IJEP]. *International Journal of Engineering Pedagogy*, *13*(8), 4–19. DOI: 10.3991/ijep.v13i8.40853

Bagash Mansour Ahmed Al-Sofi, B. (2021). Student satisfaction with e-learning using blackboard LMS during the Covid-19 circumstances: Realities, expectations, and future prospects. *Pegem Journal of Education and Instruction*, *11*(4). Advance online publication. DOI: 10.47750/pegegog.11.04.26

Baik, C., Larcombe, W., & Brooker, A. (2019). How universities can enhance student mental wellbeing: The student perspective. *Higher Education Research & Development*, *38*(4), 674–687. DOI: 10.1080/07294360.2019.1576596

Barkley, E. F., & Major, C. H. (2020). *Student engagement techniques: A handbook for college faculty*. John Wiley & Sons.

Bondie, R. S., Dahnke, C., & Zusho, A. (2019). How Does Changing "One-Size-Fits-All" to Differentiated Instruction Affect Teaching? *Review of Research in Education*, *43*(1), 336–362. DOI: 10.3102/0091732X18821130

Carless, D. (2019). Feedback loops and the longer-term: Towards feedback spirals. *Assessment & Evaluation in Higher Education*, *44*(5), 705–714. DOI: 10.1080/02602938.2018.1531108

Carroll, M., Lindsey, S., Chaparro, M., & Winslow, B. (2021). An applied model of learner engagement and strategies for increasing learner engagement in the modern educational environment. *Interactive Learning Environments*, *29*(5), 757–771. DOI: 10.1080/10494820.2019.1636083

De Carvalho-Filho, M. A., Tio, R. A., & Steinert, Y. (2020). Twelve tips for implementing a community of practice for faculty development. *Medical Teacher*, *42*(2), 143–149. DOI: 10.1080/0142159X.2018.1552782 PMID: 30707855

De Vega, N., Basri, M., & Nur, S. (2025). Exposing tech skills shaping mobile learning in cross-disciplinary English learners. [EduLearn]. *Journal of Education and Learning*, *19*(2), 1117–1124. DOI: 10.11591/edulearn.v19i2.21351

Deci, E. L., & Ryan, R. M. (2000). The "What" and "Why" of Goal Pursuits: Human Needs and the Self-Determination of Behavior. *Psychological Inquiry*, *11*(4), 227–268. DOI: 10.1207/S15327965PLI1104_01

Dempsey, J. V. (1993). Interactive instruction and feedback. *Educational Technology*.

Dimitriadou, E., & Lanitis, A. (2023). A critical evaluation, challenges, and future perspectives of using artificial intelligence and emerging technologies in smart classrooms. *Smart Learning Environments*, *10*(1), 12. DOI: 10.1186/s40561-023-00231-3 PMID: 40478141

Elford, M. D., Smith, H. H., & James, S. (2024). Teaching Feedback in Assessment. In *GET Feedback* (pp. 193–209). Routledge.

George, A. S., & George, A. S. H. (2023). A review of ChatGPT AI's impact on several business sectors. *Partners Universal International Innovation Journal*, *1*(1), 9–23.

George, B., & Wooden, O. (2023). Managing the Strategic Transformation of Higher Education through Artificial Intelligence. *Administrative Sciences*, *13*(9), 196. DOI: 10.3390/admsci13090196

Harju, V., Koskinen, A., & Pehkonen, L. (2019). An exploration of longitudinal studies of digital learning. *Educational Research*, *61*(4), 388–407. DOI: 10.1080/00131881.2019.1660586

Hellín, C. J., Calles-Esteban, F., Valledor, A., Gómez, J., Otón-Tortosa, S., & Tayebi, A. (2023). Enhancing Student Motivation and Engagement through a Gamified Learning Environment. *Sustainability*, *15*(19), 14119. DOI: 10.3390/su151914119

Huang, A. Y. Q., Lu, O. H. T., & Yang, S. J. H. (2023). Effects of artificial Intelligence–Enabled personalized recommendations on learners' learning engagement, motivation, and outcomes in a flipped classroom. *Computers & Education*, *194*, 104684. DOI: 10.1016/j.compedu.2022.104684

Kukulska-Hulme, A., Lee, H., & Norris, L. (2017). The Handbook of Technology and Second Language Teaching and Learning. In Chapelle, C. A., & Sauro, S. (Eds.), *The handbook of technology and second language teaching and learning*. Wiley., DOI: 10.1002/9781118914069

Kupchyk, L., & Litvinchuk, A. (2021). Constructing personal learning environments through ICT-mediated foreign language instruction. *Journal of Physics: Conference Series, 1840*(1), 012045. DOI: 10.1088/1742-6596/1840/1/012045

Lameras, P., & Arnab, S. (2021). Power to the Teachers: An Exploratory Review on Artificial Intelligence in Education. *Information (Basel), 13*(1), 14. DOI: 10.3390/info13010014

Lang, J. M. (2021). *Small teaching: Everyday lessons from the science of learning*. John Wiley & Sons.

Legette, K. B., Hope, E. C., Harris, J., & Griffin, C. B. (2021). *Integrating Culturally Relevant Pedagogy with Teacher Social and Emotional Competencies and Capacities Training to Support Racially Minoritized Students*. https://doi.org/DOI: 10.1108/S0749-742320210000021007

Lewis, E. (2021). Best Practices for Improving the Quality of the Online Course Design and Learners Experience. *The Journal of Continuing Higher Education, 69*(1), 61–70. DOI: 10.1080/07377363.2020.1776558

Makena, B. (2020, July). *Learner-Centered Approaches As a Form of Developing English Proficiency Among Learners From Disadvantaged Background*. 430–437. https://doi.org/DOI: 10.21125/edulearn.2020.0190

Margot, K. C., & Kettler, T. (2019). Teachers' perception of STEM integration and education: A systematic literature review. *International Journal of STEM Education, 6*(1), 2. DOI: 10.1186/s40594-018-0151-2

Mohamed, S. (2023). The development of an Arabic curriculum framework based on a compilation of salient features from CEFR level descriptors. *Language Learning Journal, 51*(1), 33–47. DOI: 10.1080/09571736.2021.1923781

Morgana, V., & Kukulska-Hulme, A. (2021). *Mobile assisted language learning across educational contexts*. Routledge.

Nayak, A., Satpathy, I., & Jain, V. (2024). *The Project-Based Learning Approach*. PBL., DOI: 10.4018/979-8-3693-3041-8.ch010

Nguyen, A., Ngo, H. N., Hong, Y., Dang, B., & Nguyen, B.-P. T. (2023). Ethical principles for artificial intelligence in education. *Education and Information Technologies*, *28*(4), 4221–4241. DOI: 10.1007/s10639-022-11316-w PMID: 36254344

Nguyen, D., & Ng, D. (2022). Teacher collaboration for change: Sharing, improving, and spreading. In *Leadership for Professional Learning* (pp. 178–191). Routledge.

Oseremi, O.-O., Yinka, J. O., Nsisong, L. E.-U., & Damilola, O. O. (2024). Revolutionizing Education Through AI: A Comprehensive Review of Enhancing Learning Experiences. *International Journal of Applied Research in Social Sciences*, *6*(4), 589–607. DOI: 10.51594/ijarss.v6i4.1011

Pokrivcakova, S. (2019). Preparing teachers for the application of AI-powered technologies in foreign language education. *Journal of Language and Cultural Education*, *7*(3), 135–153. DOI: 10.2478/jolace-2019-0025

Popova, A., Evans, D. K., Breeding, M. E., & Arancibia, V. (2022). Teacher Professional Development around the World: The Gap between Evidence and Practice. *The World Bank Research Observer*, *37*(1), 107–136. DOI: 10.1093/wbro/lkab006

Rane, N., Choudhary, S., & Rane, J. (2023). Education 4.0 and 5.0: Integrating Artificial Intelligence (AI) for Personalized and Adaptive Learning. SSRN *Electronic Journal*. https://doi.org/DOI: 10.2139/ssrn.4638365

Richardson, J., & Milovidov, E. (2019). *Digital citizenship education handbook: Being online, well-being online, and rights online*. Council of Europe.

Saleem, A. N., Noori, N. M., & Ozdamli, F. (2022). Gamification Applications in E-learning: A Literature Review. *Technology. Knowledge and Learning*, *27*(1), 139–159. DOI: 10.1007/s10758-020-09487-x

Samin, S. (2019). Mechanisms For Implementing Assessments in The Independent Curriculum: Analytical Study In Educational Institutions. *Jurnal At-Tarbiyat: Jurnal Pendidikan Islam, 6*(2). https://doi.org/DOI: 10.37758/jat.v6i2.671

Sancar, R., Atal, D., & Deryakulu, D. (2021). A new framework for teachers' professional development. *Teaching and Teacher Education, 101*, 103305. DOI: 10.1016/j.tate.2021.103305

Schildkamp, K. (2019). Data-based decision-making for school improvement: Research insights and gaps. *Educational Research*, *61*(3), 257–273.

Seo, K., Tang, J., Roll, I., Fels, S., & Yoon, D. (2021). The impact of artificial intelligence on learner–instructor interaction in online learning. *International Journal of Educational Technology in Higher Education, 18*(1), 54. DOI: 10.1186/s41239-021-00292-9 PMID: 34778540

Shaik, T., Tao, X., Li, Y., Dann, C., McDonald, J., Redmond, P., & Galligan, L. (2022). A Review of the Trends and Challenges in Adopting Natural Language Processing Methods for Education Feedback Analysis. *IEEE Access : Practical Innovations, Open Solutions, 10*, 56720–56739. DOI: 10.1109/ACCESS.2022.3177752

Stockwell, G. (2008). Investigating learner preparedness for and usage patterns of mobile learning. *ReCALL, 20*(3), 253–270. DOI: 10.1017/S0958344008000232

Strielkowski, W., Grebennikova, V., Lisovskiy, A., Rakhimova, G., & Vasileva, T. (2024). AI-driven adaptive learning for sustainable educational transformation. *Sustainable Development.* Advance online publication. DOI: 10.1002/sd.3221

Tomkin, J. H., Beilstein, S. O., Morphew, J. W., & Herman, G. L. (2019). Evidence that communities of practice are associated with active learning in large STEM lectures. *International Journal of STEM Education, 6*(1), 1. DOI: 10.1186/s40594-018-0154-z

Tomlinson, B. (2016). The Importance of Materials Development for Language Learning. *Issues in Materials Development*, (1998), 1–9. https://doi.org/DOI: 10.1007/978-94-6300-432-9_1

van de Werfhorst, H. G., Kessenich, E., & Geven, S. (2020, August 18). *The Digital Divide in Online Education. Inequality in Digital Preparedness of Students and Schools before the Start of the COVID-19 Pandemic.* https://doi.org/DOI: 10.31235/osf.io/58d6p

Vashishth, T. K., Sharma, V., Sharma, K. K., & Kumar, B. (2024). *Enhancing Literacy Education in Higher Institutions With AI Opportunities and Challenges.* https://doi.org/DOI: 10.4018/979-8-3693-2728-9.ch009

Walter, Y. (2024). Embracing the future of Artificial Intelligence in the classroom: The relevance of AI literacy, prompt engineering, and critical thinking in modern education. *International Journal of Educational Technology in Higher Education, 21*(1), 15. DOI: 10.1186/s41239-024-00448-3

Yannier, N., Hudson, S. E., Koedinger, K. R., Hirsh-Pasek, K., Golinkoff, R. M., Munakata, Y., & Brownell, S. E. (2021). Active learning: "Hands-on" meets "minds-on.". *Science, 374*(6563), 26–30. DOI: 10.1126/science.abj9957 PMID: 34591619

Young, M. C., Courtad, C. A., Douglas, K. H., & Chung, Y.-C. (2019). The Effects of Text-to-Speech on Reading Outcomes for Secondary Students With Learning Disabilities. *Journal of Special Education Technology*, *34*(2), 80–91. DOI: 10.1177/0162643418786047

Zaghlool, Z. D., & Khasawneh, M. A. S. (2023). Incorporating the Impacts and Limitations of AI-Driven Feedback, Evaluation, and Real-Time Conversation Tools in Foreign Language Learning. *Migration Letters : An International Journal of Migration Studies*, *20*(7), 1071–1083.

Chapter 12
Developing Digital Citizenship Skills

Satya Subrahmanyam
https://orcid.org/0000-0003-0441-2742
Holy Spirit University of Kaslik, Lebanon

ABSTRACT

In the era of Society 5.0, where technology increasingly shapes society, developing digital citizenship skills has become essential. This chapter explores the integration of artificial intelligence (AI) into curriculum innovation to foster digital citizenship, emphasizing the need for ethical, responsible, and effective participation in the digital realm. It defines digital citizenship as a blend of technical proficiency and ethical responsibility, discussing AI's role in personalized learning and content delivery. The chapter presents a framework for developing core competencies like digital ethics, privacy, and critical thinking, while addressing challenges such as misinformation and unequal access to technology. It advocates for AI-driven approaches, including gamification and simulation, to enhance learning and offers strategies for embedding digital citizenship across educational curricula to prepare individuals for the complexities of Society 5.0.

INTRODUCTION

Everyone, regardless of age, has to work on their digital citizenship in this highly linked world. Being a good digital citizen means using technology and the internet in a responsible, ethical, and knowledgeable way. With the ever-changing digital world, it is crucial for people to equip themselves with the right information, attitudes, and abilities to traverse online settings securely and efficiently. An individual must be able to evaluate digital material critically, know their rights and obligations

DOI: 10.4018/979-8-3373-1062-6.ch012

opyright © 2026, IGI Global Scientific Publishing. Copying or distributing in print or electronic forms without written permission of IGI Global Scientific Publishing is prohibited.

in the digital realm, communicate politely when using the internet, and safeguard personal information. Promoting digital citizenship is essential in preparing people to be engaged, knowledgeable members of the digital society as technology becomes more pervasive in all aspects of life, including education, employment, and everyday activities. Also, it's very helpful in the fight against fake news, cyberbullying, and internet addiction. This chapter explores the core concepts of digital citizenship, why it is important in today's world, and how to actively cultivate these skills in various educational and professional settings.

Defining Digital Citizenship

The term "digital citizenship" describes the standards of acceptable and conscientious usage of the internet and other digital resources. Managing one's digital identity, navigating digital information, and maintaining ethical standards in the digital domain are all part of it (Ribble, 2012). With technology permeating every part of our lives, it's more important than ever to be a good digital citizen. This includes being literate, creating material ethically, communicating respectfully, and protecting our rights and privacy online. To be an upstanding citizen in today's always-on, always-connected world is to be an upstanding citizen in any community.

Relevance of Digital Citizenship in Society 5.0

The Japanese government's Society 5.0 concept envisions a human-centered society that integrates cyberspace and physical space using advanced technologies like AI, big data, and the IoT to balance economic growth and social issues (Cabinet Office, Government of Japan, 2019). In this setting, digital citizenship is crucial. Citizens must learn appropriate digital engagement skills as they interface with intelligent systems in education, healthcare, government, and commerce. This involves recognizing technology's ethical implications, protecting digital rights, and employing digital technologies to benefit society.

Digital citizenship in Society 5.0 empowers individuals to fully engage in a digital society, not only online conduct. People are both consumers and co-creators of technology in this view, and their responsible engagement may greatly impact society's innovation advantages. Thus, the digital citizen needs both technical skills and morality to traverse complicated tech-mediated situations.

The Intersection of AI, Digital Life, and Responsible Behavior

Artificial intelligence is reshaping human interaction with technology by automating decisions, personalizing content, and enabling real-time communication. While these advancements offer numerous benefits, they also raise important questions about bias, misinformation, surveillance, and autonomy. AI-powered algorithms curate content that users see on social media and news platforms, often creating echo chambers that can distort perceptions and influence behaviors (O'Neil, 2016). The rise of generative AI tools, such as deepfakes and automated bots, demands heightened awareness and critical thinking among users to differentiate between authentic and manipulated content.

Therefore, the development of digital citizenship skills in the age of AI must include AI literacy—the ability to understand how AI systems function, how data is used, and the ethical implications of automated decision-making. Responsible behavior in digital environments requires knowledge of one's digital footprint, recognition of algorithmic influence, and a commitment to ethical standards in content creation and information sharing (Floridi et al., 2018). Digital citizenship thus becomes a dynamic competence that evolves with technology and societal needs.

Fostering Digital Responsibility from Early Education to Lifelong Learning

Developing digital citizenship abilities in early school and throughout life is important. Cyberbullying, internet addiction, and unsuitable information are particularly harmful to children and teenagers. Digital citizenship may teach pupils digital empathy, ethics, and critical media literacy in elementary and secondary schools. Teaching students about online privacy, data protection, and digital health may help them utilize technology securely (Subrahmanyam, 2024).

Digital citizenship education in higher education must handle complicated concerns including digital identity management, academic integrity in digital contexts, and AI in research and communication. Universities educate people who can lead society via ethical innovation and digital leadership. A fast-changing digital environment requires lifelong learning. Adults must upgrade their digital skills to adapt to jobs, civic, and personal developments. Government programs, business training, and community education may promote digital stewardship across various communities. Lifelong learning in Society 5.0 involves both skill building and ethical digital involvement.

Society 5.0 relies on digital citizenship, which requires a citizen who is digitally savvy, ethical, and socially responsible. AI and digital life increase the need for crucial technological engagement, understanding, and constructive contribution to a shared digital future. Digital citizenship must be fostered from early school through lifetime learning to guarantee that technological advances correspond with human values and social well-being. In an AI-integrated society, digital citizenship skills will be essential for a balanced and inclusive digital transition.

CONCEPTUAL FRAMEWORK OF DIGITAL CITIZENSHIP

The principles, practices, and abilities that make up digital citizenship are all part of what it means to be a responsible and ethical user of the internet. Being aware of one's digital footprint and one's rights and obligations in the digital realm are essential components of this. Important elements like privacy, digital literacy, and online safety help people interact productively, respect others' rights, and stay secure while using the internet. This structure encourages people to think critically and utilize technology responsibly in different online environments.

Historical Evolution of Digital Citizenship

Digital citizenship has changed due to the fast growth of the internet and associated technologies. Early digital engagement discussions focused on computer skills. The ethical, behavioral, and social effects of digital interaction grew increasingly important as the internet got more complicated and integrated into daily life. In the early 2000s, Mike Ribble created "digital citizenship" to describe ethical internet use. Ribble (2012) identified nine digital citizenship components: availability, commerce, literacy, etiquette, law, rights and duties, health and safety, and security. This paradigm must be followed by educators and policymakers who want all students to utilize technology safely.

Digital citizenship is now seen as a holistic framework that includes ethical, social, political, and cognitive aspects of digital engagement as societies move toward Society 5.0 (Cabinet Office, Government of Japan, 2019). It includes the skills required in a data-driven future with AI, smart gadgets, and complicated digital ecosystems.

Core Principles of Digital Citizenship

Digital citizenship comprises several interrelated principles that guide individuals in navigating the digital world ethically and responsibly.

The term **"digital access"** describes people's level of participation in the digital society, which includes having equal access to digital resources, internet connection, and technology. The term "digital divide" describes how inequalities in participation in the digital realm grow in the absence of universal access (Warschauer, 2004).

The cornerstone of digital citizenship is the promotion of digital inclusion, which guarantees that all individuals in society may reap the benefits of technological advancements and make significant contributions to online discussions.

Having **digital literacy** goes beyond just knowing how to use a computer; it also involves being able to use digital tools to research, analyze, create, and share information. Included in this are skills in media literacy, critical thinking, and recognizing biased or misleading content online (Ng, 2012). One aspect of digital literacy that is relevant to AI-driven information systems and algorithmic content delivery is knowing how data is acquired, processed, and used for decision-making.

Digital Etiquette involves respectful and considerate behavior in digital interactions. It includes understanding the social norms of online communication, recognizing the impact of one's words and actions, and maintaining civility in digital discourse. As communication becomes more digitized, from emails and messaging apps to virtual learning environments, teaching digital etiquette becomes critical in fostering respectful online communities (Ribble, 2012).

Digital Rights and Responsibilities

As digital citizens, individuals are entitled to rights such as freedom of expression, privacy, and access to information. These rights come with corresponding responsibilities, including respecting the rights of others, reporting harmful behavior, and using digital resources ethically. Digital citizenship education must strike a balance between empowering users to assert their rights and emphasizing accountability for online actions (Ohler, 2011).

Digital Law and Security refers to the legal and ethical standards that govern the use of technology, including issues related to copyright, plagiarism, identity theft, cybercrime, and data protection. Understanding digital law is essential for maintaining trust and security in digital environments. Digital security involves practices to protect personal data and devices from unauthorized access, including password management, encryption, and awareness of cybersecurity threats (Livingstone & Haddon, 2009).

Digital Health and Wellness relates to the physical and psychological well-being of individuals in the digital age. Prolonged screen time, social media use, and exposure to digital content can affect mental health, posture, sleep patterns, and emotional regulation. Promoting digital wellness includes educating users on healthy digital habits, screen time balance, and strategies for managing online stress and cyberbullying (Chassiakos et al., 2016).

These principles serve as a multidimensional framework for cultivating digital competence, empathy, and ethical reasoning, enabling individuals to contribute constructively to digital society.

Theoretical Underpinnings of Digital Citizenship

The development of digital citizenship is informed by several educational and philosophical theories, which provide a foundational basis for understanding how individuals learn and behave in digital environments.

Constructivism

Learners build knowledge via active involvement and meaningful connection with their environment, according to constructivist learning theory, which was championed by researchers like Piaget and Vygotsky. Constructivism lends credence to the notion that students acquire digital norms and behaviors by hands-on experience, group work, and reflection in authentic digital settings when it comes to digital citizenship. Students may internalize the ideals of responsible digital engagement via the use of digital tools that facilitate problem-solving, critical inquiry, and social connection (Jonassen, 1999).

Educators using constructivist approaches often emphasize experiential learning, such as project-based digital storytelling, online collaboration, and discussions on digital dilemmas, enabling learners to grapple with the complexities of digital life in a hands-on manner.

Digital Humanism

The ethical and philosophical framework known as "digital humanism" places human values at the core of technological development and implementation. It promotes digital innovation with people in mind, with the goal of making sure that advancements in technology don't undermine individual worth, autonomy, or society's overall health (Floridi, 2016). The field of digital humanism falls under the umbrella of digital citizenship and aims to teach people to be more empathetic, ethical, and responsible online citizens.

This approach is particularly relevant in the age of AI and datafication, where algorithmic decisions can impact individuals' rights and societal structures. Educating citizens to critically engage with these technologies through a humanistic lens ensures that digital systems serve the common good.

Civic Education and Critical Pedagogy

Digital citizenship also draws from traditions of civic education and critical pedagogy, which aim to empower individuals to participate actively and thoughtfully in democratic societies. Paulo Freire's notion of critical pedagogy emphasizes dialogue, reflection, and action as a means to achieve emancipation and social justice (Freire, 1970). Applied to digital contexts, this approach encourages learners to question power structures in the digital world, challenge misinformation, and use technology for civic engagement and social change.

By integrating civic education into digital citizenship, educators can cultivate digital citizens who are not only consumers of technology but also change-makers who advocate for equitable digital policies and ethical technological development.

Digital citizenship now includes duty and empowerment. Digital citizenship is history-based and multidisciplinary, including access, literacy, etiquette, rights, legislation, and welfare. Digital humanism, constructivist learning, and civic education underpin ethical and meaningful digital engagement curriculum and policy. Society 5.0 connects physical and digital areas, making digital citizenship skills important and educational. By grounding digital citizenship in pedagogical theory and practice, teachers and policymakers can help people navigate the AI-driven world with confidence, competence, and conscience.

DIGITAL CITIZENSHIP IN THE AGE OF AI

Digital citizenship must adapt to the challenges and responsibilities of an AI-driven society, from voice assistants and recommendation algorithms to facial recognition and autonomous systems. Digital citizenship in the era of AI includes understanding how AI affects communication, identity, and behavior; using AI technologies responsibly; recognising algorithmic biases; and upholding privacy and autonomy in the face of widespread monitoring. These obligations highlight the critical need to include AI literacy into Society 5.0's digital citizenship framework.

Impact of AI on Communication, Identity, and Behavior

AI technologies are changing how people communicate, express themselves, and interact. Chatbots and virtual assistants replicate human communication in real time using NLP. AI-driven content curation systems, especially on social media, alter information flow and public conversation. These technologies promote and manage communication, shaping users' identities.

Generational AI models can produce hyper-realistic text, pictures, audio, and video, blurring the distinctions between genuine and artificial communication (Floridi et al., 2018). Individuals may create or confront digitally modified identities or deepfakes, threatening online interactions and identity building.

Algorithmic reinforcement of user preferences may create echo chambers, polarize opinions, and limit diversity (Pariser, 2011). AI's nudging or behavioral prediction may restrict user autonomy. Thus, being a digital citizen in an AI setting requires critical thinking on how these technologies affect perceptions, behaviors, and social realities.

Ethical Use of AI Tools and Data

Ethical use of AI technology and the data they utilize is a vital component of AI-driven digital citizenship. Large datasets are often used by AI systems to discover trends and provide predictions. Considerable ethical questions, such as those pertaining to responsibility, justice, and consent, may be brought up by these data-driven systems.

Users must be aware that their online behaviors—searches, clicks, and interactions—are continuously harvested and analyzed by AI systems to train algorithms and personalize experiences. Ethical digital citizenship therefore demands transparency in how data is collected, used, and shared. Users should actively seek to understand privacy policies, give informed consent, and advocate for ethical data governance (Zuboff, 2019).

Responsible usage of artificial intelligence technologies is an issue that digital citizens must address. Included in this is the prevention of abuse of AI-generated material, such as the use of such tools to plagiarize, fabricate deceptive deepfakes, or automate malicious bots. When implementing AI technologies into classrooms, workplaces, and communities, it is important to keep ethical frameworks like beneficence, non-maleficence, autonomy, and justice in mind (Jobin et al., 2019).

Recognizing Misinformation and Algorithmic Biases

The propagation of false information is a major problem in the era of artificial intelligence, and algorithmic content recommendation systems are making matters worse. In their pursuit of user engagement, these systems accentuate divisive or sensational material, which in turn fuels misinformation campaigns and undermines faith in online sources of data.

Digital citizens must develop the skills to recognize misinformation and critically evaluate the credibility of online sources. This involves understanding how algorithms prioritize content and how AI-generated texts or images can be manipulated to deceive. The rise of deep-fake technology and AI-generated news articles necessitates heightened skepticism and verification practices among users (Subrahmanyam, 2024).

Issues related to algorithmic bias are also important. Machine learning algorithms are biased, reflecting and even amplifying the prejudices inherent in the data used to train them. O'Neil (2016) argues that this may cause discrimination in sectors including healthcare, financing, police, and employment. A citizen who is tech-savvy should be able to see potential bias in AI, know what limits these models have, and fight for AI that is open, responsible, and equitable.

Educating citizens about these biases and how to challenge them is essential for promoting equity and justice in AI-augmented societies. This is particularly relevant as AI systems increasingly influence societal decision-making processes.

The Concept of AI Literacy as Part of Digital Citizenship

AI literacy refers to the ability to understand, evaluate, and interact responsibly with AI systems. It includes not only technical knowledge—such as how AI systems are built and function—but also ethical, social, and philosophical dimensions.

Integrating AI literacy into digital citizenship equips individuals with the competencies to make informed decisions, question AI-driven recommendations, and engage meaningfully in discussions about AI governance. According to Long and Magerko (2020), AI literacy should include:

- Understanding what AI is and how it works
- Awareness of AI's limitations and potential biases
- Ability to interpret AI outputs critically
- Knowledge of AI's ethical implications

AI literacy also empowers citizens to participate in shaping policies and technologies that align with societal values. In education, this involves embedding AI concepts into curricula across disciplines, fostering interdisciplinary understanding of AI's societal role.

Lifelong AI learning is essential, as AI systems continue to evolve rapidly. Governments and institutions must support public education initiatives to ensure that AI literacy is accessible to all, thereby preventing further digital divides and ensuring inclusive participation in Society 5.0.

Role of AI in Surveillance and Privacy Concerns

AI technologies play a pivotal role in modern surveillance systems, raising significant concerns about privacy and civil liberties. From facial recognition used in public spaces to predictive policing tools, AI-driven surveillance can lead to invasive monitoring and potential abuses of power (Brayne, 2020).

These systems often operate with limited oversight and transparency, and their deployment can disproportionately affect marginalized communities. Digital citizens must be informed about their digital rights and the implications of surveillance technologies. This includes understanding how data is collected, stored, and used by governments, corporations, and other entities.

Privacy in the age of AI is not just an individual concern but a collective issue. The "networked privacy" model highlights how one person's actions can compromise others' data (Marwick & boyd, 2014). Hence, digital citizenship must incorporate collective awareness and advocacy for data protection laws, ethical surveillance practices, and robust digital rights frameworks.

Participatory governance models, where citizens are involved in setting boundaries and norms for surveillance technologies, are crucial to preserving democratic values in AI-powered societies.

CHALLENGES TO DEVELOPING DIGITAL CITIZENSHIP SKILLS

Digital citizenship—the responsible, ethical, and informed use of digital technologies—is more important in AI-driven Society 5.0. Despite its expanding relevance, digital citizenship skills development and distribution face several obstacles. These difficulties originate from socio-economic, educational, generational, technical, and AI-related imbalances. Addressing these many hurdles is essential to creating an inclusive, egalitarian, and ethical digital society. The digital divide, age disparities, disinformation, cyberbullying, the lack of a uniform digital ethics curriculum, and AI's ethical complexity are discussed in this section.

Digital Divide and Unequal Access to Technology

One of the most persistent challenges to developing digital citizenship is the digital divide—the unequal access to digital devices, internet connectivity, and digital literacy education across different socio-economic and geographic populations. This divide exists both between and within countries, exacerbating existing inequalities in education, employment, and civic participation (van Dijk, 2020).

In low-income or rural communities, students and families often lack basic access to computers, smartphones, and reliable broadband. Consequently, they are excluded from opportunities to develop critical digital skills and understand their rights and responsibilities online. Even within technologically advanced nations, disparities based on income, age, disability, and language proficiency limit equitable participation in the digital realm (UNESCO, 2021).

The digital divide affects not only access but also quality of use. For example, marginalized groups may have access to mobile devices but lack the capacity to engage with complex digital tools or navigate ethical dilemmas in online environments. Thus, addressing the digital divide is a foundational step toward inclusive digital citizenship education.

Generational Gaps in Digital Behavior and Knowledge

Generational disparities further complicate efforts to foster comprehensive digital citizenship. While younger generations, often termed "digital natives," are immersed in digital environments from an early age, this familiarity does not necessarily equate to informed or ethical use (Palfrey & Gasser, 2016). Many young users demonstrate high levels of digital consumption but limited critical thinking about privacy, misinformation, or algorithmic manipulation.

Conversely, older generations may lack digital fluency and confidence, leaving them vulnerable to misinformation or online fraud. These generational gaps in digital behavior and knowledge create challenges in designing inclusive digital literacy programs that meet diverse needs.

Educational institutions may struggle to adapt curricula quickly enough to address the evolving behaviors and needs of different age cohorts. Intergenerational learning initiatives, where younger and older individuals collaborate to exchange digital skills and perspectives, could offer promising strategies to bridge this gap (Livingstone et al., 2019).

Misinformation, Cyberbullying, and Digital Manipulation

AI-generated material and advanced digital platforms have accelerated disinformation, cyberbullying, and digital manipulation—key risks to responsible digital citizenship. Algorithmically amplified misinformation may mislead public opinion, provoke violence, and undermine democratic institutions (Wardle & Derakhshan, 2017). AI technologies like deepfakes and synthetic media make it harder to identify fake information, requiring sophisticated media literacy and critical thinking. Many users are manipulable since traditional schooling seldom teaches such abilities.

Cyberbullying, another widespread problem, affects all ages, especially teens. AI-powered systems seldom moderate or disclose online abuse. Cyberbullying may have long-term psychological impacts, and anonymity might empower it (Kowalski et al., 2014). Attention engineering methods leverage cognitive biases and emotions to increase engagement. This reduces autonomy and may cause addiction or polarization, particularly in youth. Digital citizenship must overcome technological and psychological distortions.

Lack of Standardized Curriculum for Digital Ethics

A major institutional challenge lies in the absence of a standardized, globally accepted curriculum for digital ethics and citizenship. While some educational frameworks have integrated digital literacy, the ethical, legal, and civic dimensions of digital engagement remain inconsistently addressed across schools and regions (Ribble, 2011).

This curricular gap results in fragmented and uneven instruction, where students may learn basic technical skills without gaining a deeper understanding of ethical digital behavior, human rights, or civic responsibilities online. The pace of technological change often outstrips the capacity of curricula to keep up, rendering educational content quickly outdated.

Teachers also face limitations in training and resources. Many educators lack the professional development required to effectively teach digital citizenship, particularly in relation to emerging technologies like AI. As a result, there is an urgent need to develop interdisciplinary, adaptive curricula that embed digital ethics across subject areas and educational levels (Livingstone et al., 2019).

Ethical Dilemmas Posed by AI and Machine Decision-Making

Artificial intelligence complicates digital citizenship with new ethical issues. AI is being used in life-changing decisions including employment algorithms, predictive policing, loan approvals, and educational evaluations. These systems typically function as "black boxes," without transparency and accountability (Pasquale, 2015). Digital citizens must understand machine decision-making's ethical consequences for justice, consent, accountability, and human dignity. How should one react to an opaque algorithm denying a job? Or when public venues utilize face recognition without consent? Traditional ethical paradigms must be rethought in light of machine autonomy.

AI systems may reinforce biases in their training data, resulting in discrimination. Digital citizenship must address social justice and fairness by understanding and fighting algorithmic prejudice (Eubanks, 2018). AI questions authorship, authenticity, and originality. As AI-generated art, music, and literature become more ubiquitous, digital citizens must handle ownership, intellectual property, and originality, which conventional ethical education seldom covers.

CURRICULUM INNOVATION FOR DIGITAL CITIZENSHIP

Society 5.0 envisions a human-centered, super-smart society where digital technology and AI are smoothly interwoven into everyday life, making digital citizenship a crucial educational aim. Digital citizenship includes technological skills, ethical awareness, critical thinking, and civic involvement (Ribble, 2011). Education systems must develop digital citizenship curriculum to educate students for this changing world. This section discusses integrating digital citizenship in K–12 and higher education using AI-driven platforms, project-based learning, gamification, and effective assessment tools.

Embedding Digital Citizenship in K–12 and Higher Education

Introducing lessons on digital citizenship into formal education at every level is a good place to start when designing new curricula. To make sure that students in K-12 have early exposure to digital citizenship ideas, current topics like computer science, language arts, social studies, and online safety may have digital rights, responsible communication, and digital ethics woven into them. The International Society for Technology in Education (ISTE) claims that kids should start learning how to use technology safely, legally, and ethically in elementary school (ISTE, 2016).

In higher education, digital citizenship should not be confined to information technology or media studies departments. Instead, it should be infused across disciplines to address field-specific concerns, such as ethical AI use in engineering, plagiarism in academia, and data privacy in healthcare. Universities can offer standalone courses on digital citizenship, as well as integrate digital responsibility themes into core curricula. A transdisciplinary approach helps students contextualize digital behavior within their professional and civic identities (Belshaw, 2016).

AI-Driven Platforms for Personalized Digital Ethics Learning

Artificial intelligence offers powerful tools for transforming digital citizenship education through personalization. AI-driven platforms can assess students' existing knowledge, behaviors, and attitudes, then deliver tailored content to address gaps and promote ethical reflection. Adaptive learning systems can present scenarios involving online harassment, misinformation, or data privacy, and adjust complexity based on student performance (Chen et al., 2020).

Natural Language Processing (NLP) technologies can also be used to analyze student responses to ethical dilemmas and provide real-time feedback, promoting deeper engagement with moral reasoning. These tools support differentiated instruction by accounting for diverse learning styles, literacy levels, and cultural contexts.

AI-based learning analytics can help educators track students' progress in digital citizenship skills over time, identifying trends and informing curriculum design. These platforms must be designed ethically, ensuring transparency, data privacy, and student autonomy to avoid reinforcing the very issues they aim to address (Holmes et al., 2019).

Project-based and Experiential Learning Models

Project-based and experiential learning approaches are highly effective for cultivating digital citizenship, as they place students in real-world contexts where digital tools and ethical decision-making intersect. In project-based learning (PBL), students collaborate to investigate complex problems, design solutions, and present findings using digital media. Through this process, they encounter and reflect upon digital rights, privacy concerns, teamwork in digital environments, and responsible content creation (Boss & Krauss, 2018).

Students might work on a campaign to combat cyberbullying in their school using social media, or they could develop a digital literacy workshop for community members. Such activities foster civic engagement, empathy, and critical media literacy—key components of digital citizenship.

Experiential learning also includes service-learning projects where students engage with communities to address digital inclusion or provide training in digital skills. These experiences help bridge the gap between theory and practice and foster social responsibility in the digital age.

Gamification and Simulation Tools for Real-World Scenarios

One way to make digital citizenship education more engaging and motivating is to use gamification, which is incorporating game design aspects into educational settings. Teachers may create engaging lessons that mimic real-life moral quandaries by combining interactive narrative, points, badges, and leaderboards. (Referenced in Gee, 2007).

Simulation-based tools are particularly effective for helping students explore the consequences of digital actions in a safe, controlled environment. Students might engage in a role-playing game that involves managing a fictional social media platform, responding to user complaints about hate speech, or navigating data privacy regulations.

These tools not only improve engagement but also develop problem-solving, empathy, and perspective-taking. Virtual reality (VR) and augmented reality (AR) simulations can further deepen learning by placing students in lifelike digital scenarios involving surveillance, misinformation, or AI ethics (Slater & Sanchez-Vives, 2016).

By interacting with these environments, learners can practice decision-making, experience the consequences of unethical digital behavior, and better understand the implications of their actions in the digital world.

Assessment Techniques for Digital Citizenship Competencies

Digital citizenship assessment demands a comprehensive approach beyond testing. Assessments must include knowledge, ethics, and civic duty since digital citizenship entails conduct, attitude, and critical thinking. Performance-based evaluations work well. Digital portfolios, reflective diaries, group projects, peer assessments, and scenario-based evaluations are examples. Students may analyze online controversies, uncover disinformation, and propose ethical digital citizenship answers (Heick, 2020).

Rubrics may evaluate ethical information usage, polite communication, digital cooperation, and responsible content development. These rubrics should follow the ISTE Standards for Students or the Nine Elements of Digital Citizenship (Ribble, 2011). Student self-assessment and peer feedback may promote metacognition and digital behaviour reflection. These tools encourage growth attitude and responsibility, crucial for digital citizenship. New technologies, such as AI-based formative assessment systems, provide real-time digital feedback. Xhatbots and NLP algorithms can evaluate online tone and monitor group project participation.

ROLE OF EDUCATORS AND EDUCATIONAL INSTITUTIONS

In the era of digital transformation and AI's rising effect on education and society, educators and educational institutions must foster digital citizenship. Teachers are role models, ethical advisors, and knowledge facilitators in digital contexts. Educational institutions foster responsible, inclusive, and resilient digital cultures. As Society 5.0 blends physical and digital realities, educators need tools, competences, and institutional frameworks to teach digital citizenship. This section discusses educators' duties, digital pedagogy, modeling behavior, inclusive digital environments, and complete policy systems.

Educator Training and Digital Pedagogy

To properly teach digital citizenship, educators must be technologically savvy and ethical. Digital ethics, media literacy, cyberbullying prevention, AI ramifications, and online privacy must be taught in professional development programs. As new technologies change communication, information availability, and student participation, instructors must use digital pedagogy (Subrahmanyam, 2024).

Digital pedagogy integrates digital technologies with ethical, critical, and collaborative learning practices. LMSs, discussion forums, AI-powered tutoring systems, and digital storytelling tools are used to create meaningful learning experiences. Teachers must be ready to confront disinformation, online conduct, and AI's societal effect to encourage critical thinking in digital spaces.

Digital citizenship modules in teacher education must provide pedagogical frameworks and psychological methods for responsible online communities (Trust, 2020). Continuous professional learning facilitated by digital learning communities and knowledge-sharing networks may help instructors keep up with new technologies and standards.

Role Modeling Responsible Digital Behavior

Educators serve as powerful role models for students, and their digital conduct significantly influences learners' attitudes and behaviors. Modeling responsible digital behavior includes demonstrating respectful online communication, citing digital sources correctly, adhering to data privacy principles, and maintaining a professional digital footprint. By exhibiting transparency, ethical decision-making, and empathy in digital interactions, educators can instill these values in students (Ribble, 2011).

When an educator openly discusses the ethical challenges posed by generative AI or explains the decision-making process behind verifying sources, students witness applied digital ethics in real time. Instructors who engage respectfully in digital forums and promote inclusive discussions reinforce norms of digital civility and engagement.

Faculty members who address instances of cyberbullying, plagiarism, or digital harassment constructively can teach students how to respond appropriately in similar scenarios. Such real-world examples of digital citizenship help students internalize abstract principles and apply them in their personal and academic lives.

Creating Inclusive, Secure Digital Learning Environments

A foundational aspect of fostering digital citizenship is ensuring that learning environments—both physical and digital—are inclusive, safe, and supportive. Educational institutions must recognize and address the digital divide that affects marginalized communities, providing equitable access to devices, internet connectivity, and digital literacy programs (Selwyn, 2020).

Security is equally crucial. Institutions must implement robust cybersecurity measures to protect students' personal data and ensure that digital platforms comply with data protection regulations. Transparent communication about data usage, permissions, and privacy settings is essential in building trust between educators and learners (Livingstone & Third, 2017).

Instructors should foster psychologically safe online spaces where students feel respected and empowered to share their perspectives. Moderating digital discussions to prevent harassment and encouraging diverse viewpoints cultivates an environment where students learn the importance of ethical online engagement.

Policy Recommendations for Institutional Frameworks

Ethical, legal, and pedagogical institutional norms and frameworks are needed to help educators promote digital citizenship. Institutions should create digital citizenship rules that include online conduct, academic integrity, digital material usage, and penalties for violators. To achieve inclusive, context-specific, and technologically updated policies, teachers, students, IT workers, and administrators should co-create them. These standards should address data privacy, algorithmic decision-making, and educational technology biases (Williamson & Piattoeva, 2020).

Institutional initiatives must manage cyberbullying, data breaches, and digital platform abuse with explicit standards. Digital ethics committees or task forces may supervise policy implementation, advise on complicated problems, and promote accountability. Grants, scholarships, and recognition programs should encourage professors to innovate in digital education and promote digital citizenship. Technology, community, and government partnerships may boost institutional capacity for ethical digital involvement. Digital literacy, AI ethics, and online safety training should be required for professional advancement. Mentoring programmes where tech-savvy educators help one another may boost capacity-building and collaborative learning.

CASE STUDIES AND BEST PRACTICES

As the digital world grows more intertwined into everyday life, digital citizenship education is a worldwide issue. Many nations, institutions, and organizations are transforming digital citizenship education. These case studies and best practices show how curricular innovation, AI-powered technologies, and supportive policy frameworks may foster digital citizenship. The legislative frameworks of UNESCO, grassroots efforts like Common Sense Education, AI-integrated learning platforms, and smart classroom models give meaningful insights into raising responsible, ethical, and knowledgeable digital citizens.

Global Initiatives in Digital Citizenship Education

A number of international frameworks and programs are paving the way for standardizing digital citizenship education. Among them, UNESCO has been instrumental in promoting media and information literacy (MIL) and digital competencies as foundational skills in the 21st century. The *UNESCO Global Framework for Digital Literacy* focuses on competencies such as critical thinking, online safety, privacy awareness, and understanding of AI-driven technologies. It provides guidance for governments and educators to build national-level curricula (UNESCO, 2021).

In the United States, *Common Sense Education* has developed one of the most widely used digital citizenship curricula. Covering topics such as digital footprints, cyberbullying, fake news, and data privacy, their curriculum spans from kindergarten through high school. It is grounded in academic research and provides age-appropriate resources, interactive lessons, and family engagement materials (Common Sense Education, 2023).

Similarly, the European Commission's *Digital Education Action Plan* (2021–2027) emphasizes the integration of digital skills—including AI literacy and ethical technology use—into all levels of education. It supports teacher training, cross-country collaboration, and the development of national digital competence frameworks (European Commission, 2021).

In Asia, Singapore's *Digital Readiness Blueprint* and South Korea's emphasis on smart education demonstrate a policy-driven approach to embedding digital literacy and citizenship into national educational goals. These programs combine infrastructure investment with teacher training and AI-based learning solutions to ensure that students not only access but also critically engage with technology (Lim et al., 2020).

Innovative Curriculum Models Using AI

Artificial intelligence is increasingly being used to deliver personalized, scalable, and adaptive learning experiences that support digital citizenship. These AI-integrated curriculum models do more than deliver knowledge—they foster ethical reasoning, reflection, and responsible behavior.

Adaptive Learning Systems

Platforms like *DreamBox* and *Smart Sparrow* use AI algorithms to analyze learner behaviors and adjust content delivery in real time. This model supports differentiated instruction, allowing students to progress at their own pace while receiving customized feedback. Adaptive systems can integrate scenarios related to ethical digital use, such as identifying misinformation or protecting personal data, encouraging learners to apply critical thinking in dynamic settings (Pane et al., 2015).

AI Tutors and Conversational Agents

Virtual AI tutors, such as IBM's Watson Tutor and Carnegie Learning's MATHia, are being utilized to assist in both subject matter instruction and the development of soft skills. These tutors can simulate real-life dilemmas related to digital ethics—such as responding to online harassment or verifying the credibility of a news source—allowing students to explore responses and receive guided feedback (Luckin et al., 2016).

AI-Driven Ethical Simulations

Simulations and serious games powered by AI are particularly effective in teaching digital citizenship. Programs like *The Digital Compass* and *Interland* immerse students in interactive environments where they must make choices about digital behavior. These tools use natural language processing and behavioral tracking to personalize experiences and deepen understanding (Fessakis et al., 2018).

Learning Analytics and Predictive Models

AI-powered analytics can also help educators identify at-risk students, monitor engagement, and assess competencies in digital literacy. The use of dashboards in AI learning platforms can show how often students engage with digital citizenship materials or whether they demonstrate improvement in ethical reasoning over time (Ifenthaler & Yau, 2020).

Success Stories from Smart Classrooms and Digital Literacy Programs

Several educational institutions worldwide have effectively implemented digital citizenship programs using innovative technologies and pedagogical strategies.

Finland: Whole-School Digital Literacy Approach

In Finland, schools have adopted a holistic digital literacy strategy that spans across subjects and grade levels. Digital citizenship is not taught as a separate course but integrated into daily classroom activities. Teachers use AI-supported language tools, media platforms, and collaborative apps to teach students about online safety, information evaluation, and respectful communication. This integrated approach, supported by government policy, has positioned Finland as a global leader in digital education (Arola & Kupiainen, 2020).

United Arab Emirates: AI in Moral Education

The UAE's Moral Education curriculum incorporates digital ethics, focusing on digital wellbeing, respect in online environments, and understanding the societal impact of technology. Using AI chatbots and personalized learning platforms, students explore ethical dilemmas and cultural values in both Arabic and English. The initiative combines traditional values with modern digital competencies, reflecting Society 5.0's vision of harmonizing technology with human wellbeing (Al Suwaidi, 2021).

Canada: School District-Level Initiatives

The Ottawa Catholic School Board has implemented the *Digital Citizenship Education Framework*, which integrates Common Sense Education resources, local community involvement, and teacher-led projects. Students create digital portfolios to demonstrate ethical use of technology, such as crafting multimedia presentations on privacy rights or developing campaigns against cyberbullying. The initiative is backed by AI tools that provide real-time feedback and assessments (Zilka, 2020).

India: Rural Digital Literacy and Citizenship

Through partnerships with non-profits like *Pratham* and *Digital Empowerment Foundation*, rural schools in India are increasingly using mobile-based AI learning platforms to teach digital skills. Programs like *Read to Me* and *AI For Youth* introduce students to both technical and ethical aspects of the digital world, helping bridge the urban-rural divide. These initiatives demonstrate how scalable, low-cost AI interventions can effectively promote digital citizenship even in resource-constrained settings (Bhatia & Lahiri, 2021).

The worldwide movement for digital citizenship recognizes that digital skills, ethics, and accountability are crucial in today's linked society. Through comprehensive frameworks, innovative AI-driven curriculum models, and compelling smart classroom case studies, education institutions are showing the potential of purposeful design and collaborative involvement. These projects demonstrate that digital citizenship involves critical thinking, empathy, and civic duty, not just technological abilities. Thoughtful use of AI technology, supporting institutional practices, and inclusive policies may allow students to become conscious digital citizens in Society 5.0.

STRATEGIC RECOMMENDATIONS FOR ADVANCING DIGITAL CITIZENSHIP

Education, policy, and leadership must change with society's digital development. Digital citizenship—the responsible, ethical, and informed use of digital technologies—is essential for personal empowerment and social cohesiveness. Extensive digital citizenship demands multilevel strategy. It comprises strong policy and leadership frameworks, creative public-private collaborations, alignment with national AI initiatives, and multidisciplinary cooperation. This section offers strategies to integrate digital citizenship into socio-educational systems to promote inclusion, resilience, and responsibility in the digital era.

Policy and Leadership Frameworks for Digital Citizenship

Strong governance and visionary leadership are vital in steering societies toward responsible digital futures. National and institutional policies must integrate digital citizenship not only as a pedagogical imperative but also as a civic responsibility.

National Education Policies

Governments should explicitly include digital citizenship in national education frameworks. The *U.S. Department of Education's National Educational Technology Plan* (2022) emphasizes safe and ethical digital use, advocating for the development of comprehensive digital literacy curricula and teacher training. Similar strategies should be adopted globally, aligning with UNESCO's (2021) Global Framework on Digital Literacy Competencies.

Institutional Leadership

School and university leaders must develop localized policies that embed digital citizenship into curricula, teacher professional development, and school culture. Leadership should prioritize digital ethics, inclusivity, and cybersecurity in institutional strategies. Strategic leadership in Estonia—recognized for its digital-first education system—has enabled national implementation of coding, cybersecurity, and digital citizenship lessons in primary schools (Pangrazio & Selwyn, 2019).

Data Governance and Accountability

Policies must address student data privacy, algorithmic accountability, and platform transparency. Institutional data governance policies should define clear boundaries regarding the use of AI and digital tools, ensuring ethical data practices in learning environments (West, 2019).

Public-Private Partnerships in Advancing Digital Responsibility

The private sector, particularly technology companies, plays an essential role in shaping the digital environment. Collaborative initiatives between governments, educators, NGOs, and corporations can accelerate the reach and effectiveness of digital citizenship education.

EdTech and Platform Providers

Companies like Google, Microsoft, and Apple are key stakeholders. Google's *Be Internet Awesome* and Microsoft's *Digital Civility Index* offer resources and campaigns aimed at young users and educators. Partnerships with these providers can ensure that educational institutions receive technical support, up-to-date content, and capacity-building tools.

NGOs and Civil Society

Organizations such as Common Sense Media, the Family Online Safety Institute (FOSI), and the Internet Society offer resources, training, and policy advocacy in digital responsibility. Governments should collaborate with these entities to co-create curricula, host digital citizenship weeks, and engage parents in the learning process (Livingstone et al., 2020).

Funding and Innovation Incubators

Public-private partnerships can also facilitate funding for digital literacy initiatives in underserved communities. Initiatives like *Digital Promise* in the U.S. bring together philanthropic organizations, government agencies, and educational institutions to promote equitable access to technology and innovation in teaching digital ethics (Digital Promise, 2021).

Integration of Digital Citizenship in National AI Strategies

As AI technologies become integral to governance, business, and education, it is critical that digital citizenship is embedded in national AI strategies. This ensures that citizens are not just passive consumers of AI-driven services but informed participants capable of engaging with, questioning, and co-shaping AI systems.

Ethical AI Education

AI education must include modules on algorithmic bias, data privacy, and the ethical implications of autonomous systems. The European Union's *Ethics Guidelines for Trustworthy AI* emphasize that AI literacy is a foundational aspect of digital citizenship, promoting transparency, accountability, and human oversight (European Commission, 2020).

Citizen Engagement and Transparency

AI strategies should include public engagement programs to build trust and digital literacy among citizens. For example, Canada's *Directive on Automated Decision-Making* requires impact assessments and public disclosures, creating opportunities for citizens to understand and influence the use of AI in government services (Government of Canada, 2020).

Inclusive Policy Design

Digital citizenship must be framed within AI policies to protect marginalized communities from surveillance, discrimination, or digital exclusion. Strategic recommendations include human-rights-based approaches, stakeholder consultations, and inclusive data practices (Jobin, Ienca, & Vayena, 2019).

Promoting Interdisciplinary Collaboration Across Education, Technology, and Ethics

Addressing the multifaceted challenges of digital citizenship requires cross-sectoral and interdisciplinary collaboration. Educators, technologists, ethicists, and policymakers must co-create frameworks, curricula, and innovations that are holistic, future-focused, and socially responsible.

Integrated Curriculum Design

Universities and schools should develop interdisciplinary modules that combine computer science, media studies, philosophy, and civic education. Stanford University's *Ethics, Society, and Technology* initiative brings together engineers and social scientists to explore responsible innovation (Stanford, 2021).

Professional Learning Communities (PLCs)

Educators should engage in PLCs that include technologists and ethicists. These collaborative spaces can facilitate co-development of teaching tools, ethical scenarios, and case-based simulations for classroom use (Wang et al., 2022).

Research and Evidence-Based Practice

Joint research initiatives between academia and industry can help generate evidence on best practices in digital citizenship. Journals and conferences focused on AI ethics, digital literacy, and education technology should be supported and expanded to include interdisciplinary contributions.

Ethical Design and Innovation Labs

Education ministries and technology developers should create 'Ethical AI Labs' or 'Digital Citizenship Innovation Hubs' where students, teachers, and developers can co-create AI tools that align with democratic values and ethical principles. These labs can serve as testbeds for participatory design and civic tech innovations.

Digital citizenship is a changing skill that combines education, ethics, and technology. Multi-stakeholder engagement, strategic policy frameworks, public-private partnerships, and smart integration into national AI initiatives are needed to grow it. Educational institutions must model ethical technology usage, promote data ethics, and prepare students for digital era challenges. Digital citizenship is essential for democratic participation, personal liberty, and global equality in a world mediated by algorithms and digital platforms. A digitally responsible society requires strategic leadership, cooperation, and innovative investments.

FUTURE DIRECTIONS IN DIGITAL CITIZENSHIP

As the digital ecosystem evolves, new technologies like the metaverse, BCIs, and quantum internet are changing how people communicate, learn, and participate in society. These changes need a forward-thinking approach to digital citizenship that trains people to properly use existing technologies and ethically adapt to future ones. The future of digital citizenship includes preparing people for developing technologies, promoting lifelong digital accountability, and encouraging active citizen involvement via AI co-creation in democratic digital environments.

Preparing Citizens for Emerging Technologies

The advent of the **metaverse**, **BCIs**, and the **quantum internet** represents a leap in the immersive and intelligent capabilities of digital environments. These technologies present both opportunities and ethical challenges that require proactive educational strategies.

The Metaverse

The metaverse—a persistent, immersive virtual world enabled by AR, VR, and AI—demands new competencies in identity management, digital etiquette, and socio-emotional intelligence in synthetic environments (Mystakidis, 2022). As avatars become extensions of the self, digital citizenship must encompass norms of respectful communication, intellectual property ethics, and digital consent in 3D spaces.

Brain-Computer Interfaces (BCIs)

BCIs enable direct interaction between the brain and digital systems, raising profound questions about data privacy, mental autonomy, and human augmentation. Preparing citizens for BCI technology involves educating them on the implications of neurodata collection and ethical decision-making in enhanced human-computer interactions (Yuste et al., 2017).

Quantum Internet

With promises of ultra-secure communication and exponentially faster data processing, the quantum internet will revolutionize cybersecurity and data sovereignty. Citizens must be educated on quantum encryption principles and how these technologies affect their digital rights and information access (Gyongyosi & Imre, 2019).

Educational institutions should begin integrating "future literacies" into curricula—developing awareness and ethical reasoning skills around technologies that are still emerging but will likely be ubiquitous within a decade.

Building a Culture of Lifelong Digital Responsibility

In a world of rapid technological change, digital citizenship can no longer be confined to childhood or school-age education. Instead, it must evolve into a **lifelong pursuit**—a continuous process of reflection, learning, and adaptation.

Lifelong Learning Ecosystems

Lifelong digital learning can be supported by public libraries, community learning centers, workplace training programs, and online platforms. These should offer modular, competency-based courses that address evolving digital needs across age groups (Selwyn & Facer, 2014).

Intergenerational Learning

Programs that encourage knowledge exchange between generations—such as older adults learning digital safety from youth and, conversely, youth understanding data ethics from adults—can help bridge generational gaps in digital behavior and awareness (Livingstone & Helsper, 2007).

Social Norms and Responsibility

Promoting digital responsibility as a cultural norm involves more than instruction—it requires reinforcement through policy, media, and community values. Campaigns on digital ethics, respect in online discourse, and the consequences of disinformation can embed civic responsibility into everyday digital life (Floridi, 2015).

A holistic digital citizenship framework must cultivate critical thinking, empathy, and civic engagement as core values that persist across different stages of life and technological shifts.

AI Co-Creation and Citizen Empowerment in Democratic Digital Spaces

The increasing prevalence of artificial intelligence in governance, education, and communication necessitates not just digital literacy but **participatory digital citizenship**. Citizens must be empowered to shape, critique, and collaborate in the development of digital systems that affect their lives.

AI Co-Creation and Civic Tech

Citizen engagement in AI co-design promotes inclusivity and accountability. Participatory design methodologies allow users to contribute to the creation of algorithms and interfaces that align with democratic values and community needs (Costanza-Chock, 2020). Initiatives like *AI4All* and *Public Interest Technology* foster citizen involvement in shaping ethical AI.

Digital Deliberation and E-Participation

Digital citizenship in democratic societies must include the right and capability to participate in online decision-making processes. Tools such as digital forums, online referenda, and AI-moderated deliberative platforms can enhance participatory democracy (Susskind, 2020). Citizens should be trained to assess digital sources, articulate informed opinions, and engage in civil digital discourse.

Transparency and Algorithmic Accountability

Educating citizens to understand how algorithms shape access to information, bias decisions, and influence behavior is critical. Empowered digital citizens can demand transparency, participate in data governance, and advocate for ethical oversight of AI systems (Pasquale, 2015).

Future-forward digital citizenship must evolve from a set of competencies into an **agency-oriented paradigm**, where individuals are not only compliant users but active co-creators and stewards of digital society.

CONCLUSION

Finally, a more accountable, moral, and welcoming online community will be shaped in large part by the ever-changing idea of digital citizenship. The integration of technologies such as blockchain, artificial intelligence (AI), and the metaverse is driving the need for a new breed of ethically aware, tech-savvy people as we approach Society 5.0, defined by the merging of physical and digital realms. Everyone, regardless of age, has to learn proper digital citizenship, which includes having access to the internet, being literate, and being responsible online. In addition to being essential for getting about in the modern digital environment, these abilities are crucial for taking on the challenges of the technological landscape of the future.

The human-centered goal of Society 5.0, which aims to enhance quality of life, promote social inclusion, and support sustainable development via the harnessing of technical breakthroughs, relies heavily on digital citizenship. Fostering people who comprehend the potential benefits and moral quandaries posed by technology may be achieved by incorporating these ideas into educational institutions across the board, from K-12 to lifetime learning. That way, they may interact with emerging innovations like the metaverse and AI in ways that are fair, considerate, and beneficial to society as a whole.

REFERENCES

Al Suwaidi, J. (2021). Teaching moral education in a digital era: A UAE perspective. *International Journal of Educational Development*, *85*, 102453.

Arola, E., & Kupiainen, R. (2020). Digital literacy and citizenship in Finnish education. *Media Education Research Journal*, *11*(2), 15–28.

Belshaw, D. (2016). *The essential elements of digital literacies*. CreateSpace Independent Publishing.

Bhatia, A., & Lahiri, S. (2021). AI for youth: Bridging digital divides in India. *International Review of Education*, *67*(4), 535–552.

Boss, S., & Krauss, J. (2018). *Reinventing project-based learning: Your field guide to real-world projects in the digital age* (3rd ed.). ISTE.

Brayne, S. (2020). *Predict and surveil: Data, discretion, and the future of policing*. Oxford University Press.

Cabinet Office, Government of Japan. (2019). *Society 5.0: A people-centric super-smart society*.

Chassiakos, Y. L., Radesky, J., Christakis, D., Moreno, M. A., & Cross, C. (2016). Children and adolescents and digital media. *Pediatrics*, *138*(5), e20162593. PMID: 27940795

Chen, L., Chen, P., & Lin, Z. (2020). Artificial intelligence in education: A review. *IEEE Access : Practical Innovations, Open Solutions*, *8*, 75264–75278.

Common Sense Education. (2023). *Digital Citizenship Curriculum*.

Costanza-Chock, S. (2020). *Design Justice: Community-Led Practices to Build the Worlds We Need*. MIT Press.

Digital Promise. (2021). *About Digital Promise*.

Eubanks, V. (2018). *Automating inequality: How high-tech tools profile, police, and punish the poor*. St. Martin's Press.

European Commission. (2020). *Ethics Guidelines for Trustworthy AI*.

European Commission. (2021). *Digital Education Action Plan (2021–2027)*.

Fessakis, G., Gouli, E., & Mavroudi, E. (2018). Digital games in education: Teaching ethical thinking. *Journal of Educational Computing Research*, *56*(3), 491–517.

Floridi, L. (2015). *The Onlife Manifesto: Being Human in a Hyperconnected Era*. Springer.

Floridi, L. (2016). *The fourth revolution: How the infosphere is reshaping human reality*. Oxford University Press.

Floridi, L., Cowls, J., Beltrametti, M., Chatila, R., Chazerand, P., Dignum, V., & Schafer, B. (2018). AI4People—An ethical framework for a good AI society: Opportunities, risks, principles, and recommendations. *Minds and Machines*, *28*(4), 689–707. PMID: 30930541

Freire, P. (1970). Pedagogy of the oppressed. *Continuum : an Interdisciplinary Journal on Continuity of Care*.

Gee, J. P. (2007). *What video games have to teach us about learning and literacy* (2nd ed.). Palgrave Macmillan.

Government of Canada. (2020). *Directive on Automated Decision-Making*.

Gyongyosi, L., & Imre, S. (2019). A survey on quantum computing technology. *Computer Science Review*, *31*, 51–71.

Heick, T. (2020). *How to teach digital citizenship in the classroom: Resources for teachers*. TeachThought.

Holmes, W., Bialik, M., & Fadel, C. (2019). *Artificial intelligence in education: Promises and implications for teaching and learning*. Center for Curriculum Redesign.

Ifenthaler, D., & Yau, J. Y. K. (2020). Utilising learning analytics to support study success in higher education. *Technology. Knowledge and Learning*, *25*, 305–320.

International Society for Technology in Education (ISTE). (2016). *ISTE Standards for Students*.

Jobin, A., Ienca, M., & Vayena, E. (2019). The global landscape of AI ethics guidelines. *Nature Machine Intelligence*, *1*(9), 389–399.

Jonassen, D. H. (1999). Designing constructivist learning environments. In Reigeluth, C. M. (Ed.), *Instructional-design theories and models: A new paradigm of instructional theory* (Vol. II, pp. 215–239). Lawrence Erlbaum Associates.

Kowalski, R. M., Giumetti, G. W., Schroeder, A. N., & Lattanner, M. R. (2014). Bullying in the digital age: A critical review and meta-analysis of cyberbullying research among youth. *Psychological Bulletin*, *140*(4), 1073–1137. PMID: 24512111

Lim, C. P., Zhao, Y., Tondeur, J., Chai, C. S., & Tsai, C. C. (2020). Bridging the digital divide in Asia: Perspectives on policies and practices in digital literacy. *Educational Technology Research and Development*, *68*, 1–3.

Livingstone, S., Byrne, J., & Third, A. (2020). *Children's rights in the digital age: A download from children around the world*. UNICEF Office of Research-Innocenti.

Livingstone, S., & Haddon, L. (2009). EU Kids Online: Final report. LSE, London: EU Kids Online.

Livingstone, S., & Helsper, E. (2007). Gradations in digital inclusion: Children, young people and the digital divide. *New Media & Society*, *9*(4), 671–696.

Livingstone, S., Stoilova, M., & Nandagiri, R. (2019). *Children's data and privacy online: Growing up in a digital age*. London School of Economics and Political Science.

Livingstone, S., & Third, A. (2017). Children and young people's rights in the digital age: An emerging agenda. *New Media & Society*, *19*(5), 657–670.

Long, D., & Magerko, B. (2020). What is AI literacy? Competencies and design considerations. *Proceedings of the 2020 CHI Conference on Human Factors in Computing Systems*, 1–16.

Luckin, R., Holmes, W., Griffiths, M., & Forcier, L. B. (2016). *Intelligence unleashed: An argument for AI in education*. Pearson Education.

Marwick, A. E., & boyd, d. (2014). Networked privacy: How teenagers negotiate context in social media. *New Media & Society*, *16*(7), 1051–1067.

Mystakidis, S. (2022). Metaverse. *Encyclopedia*, *2*(1), 486–497.

Ng, W. (2012). Can we teach digital natives digital literacy? *Computers & Education*, *59*(3), 1065–1078.

O'Neil, C. (2016). *Weapons of math destruction: How big data increases inequality and threatens democracy*. Crown Publishing Group.

Ohler, J. (2011). *Digital community, digital citizen*. Corwin Press.

Palfrey, J., & Gasser, U. (2016). *Born digital: How children grow up in a digital age* (2nd ed.). Basic Books.

Pane, J. F., Steiner, E. D., Baird, M. D., & Hamilton, L. S. (2015). *Continued progress: Promising evidence on personalized learning*. RAND Corporation.

Pangrazio, L., & Selwyn, N. (2019). 'Personal data literacies': A critical literacies approach to enhancing understandings of personal digital data. *New Media & Society*, *21*(2), 419–437.

Pariser, E. (2011). *The filter bubble: What the Internet is hiding from you*. Penguin Press.

Pasquale, F. (2015). *The Black Box Society: The Secret Algorithms That Control Money and Information*. Harvard University Press.

Ribble, M. (2011). *Digital citizenship in schools: Nine elements all students should know* (2nd ed.). ISTE.

Ribble, M. (2012). *Digital citizenship in schools: Nine elements all students should know* (2nd ed.). International Society for Technology in Education.

Selwyn, N. (2020). *Should robots replace teachers? AI and the future of education*. Polity Press.

Selwyn, N., & Facer, K. (2014). *The politics of education and technology: Conflicts, controversies, and connections*. Palgrave Macmillan.

Slater, M., & Sanchez-Vives, M. V. (2016). Enhancing our lives with immersive virtual reality. *Frontiers in Robotics and AI*, *3*, 74.

Stanford University. (2021). *Ethics*. Society, and Technology Hub.

Subrahmanyam, S. (2024). Collaboration and collective action: Addressing the deepfake challenge as a community. In Gupta, G., Bohara, S., Kovid, R. K., & Pandla, K. (Eds.), *Deepfakes and their impact on business* (pp. 143–172). IGI Global Scientific Publishing.

Subrahmanyam, S. (2024). Implementing agile talent management practices to adapt to changing higher education landscapes. In Kayyali, M. (Ed.), *Cultivating creativity and navigating talent management in academia* (pp. 187–210). IGI Global Scientific Publishing.

Subrahmanyam, S. (2024). The role of leadership in nurturing innovation and creativity among faculty and staff. In Kayyali, M. (Ed.), *Cultivating creativity and navigating talent management in academia* (pp. 449–468). IGI Global Scientific Publishing.

Susskind, J. (2020). *Future Politics: Living Together in a World Transformed by Tech*. Oxford University Press.

Trust, T. (2020). The 3 Cs of professional development: Creating, collaborating, and coaching. *Educational Technology Research and Development, 68*, 1429–U.S. Department of Education. (2022). *National Educational Technology Plan.*

UNESCO. (2021). *Digital learning and the digital divide: Policies and practices to build digital citizenship*. United Nations Educational, Scientific and Cultural Organization.

UNESCO. (2021). *Media and Information Literacy: A critical approach to literacy in a digital world.*

van Dijk, J. (2020). *The digital divide*. Polity Press.

Wang, Q., Woo, H. L., Quek, C. L., Yang, Y., & Liu, M. (2022). Using the community of inquiry framework to scaffold online learning. *Educational Technology Research and Development*, *70*(3), 841–859.

Wardle, C., & Derakhshan, H. (2017). *Information disorder: Toward an interdisciplinary framework for research and policymaking*. Council of Europe.

Warschauer, M. (2004). *Technology and social inclusion: Rethinking the digital divide*. MIT Press.

West, S. M. (2019). Data capitalism: Redefining the logics of surveillance and privacy. *Business & Society*, *58*(1), 20–41.

Williamson, B., & Piattoeva, N. (2020). Education governance and datafication. *Learning, Media and Technology*, *45*(3), 251–258.

Yuste, R., Goering, S., Arcas, B. A. Y., Bi, G., Carmena, J. M., Carter, A., & Wolpaw, J. (2017). Four ethical priorities for neurotechnologies and AI. *Nature*, *551*(7679), 159–163. PMID: 29120438

Zilka, G. C. (2020). Awareness of digital rights and digital citizenship among youth. *Education and Information Technologies*, *25*(6), 5573–5586.

Zuboff, S. (2019). *The age of surveillance capitalism: The fight for a human future at the new frontier of power*. PublicAffairs.

Compilation of References

Abbas, N., Imran, A., Manzoor, R., Hussain, T., & Hussain, M. (2023). Role of artificial intelligence tools in enhancing students' educational performance at higher levels. *Journal of Artificial Intelligence Machine Learning and Neural Network*, (35), 36–49. DOI: 10.55529/jaimlnn.35.36.49

Abdul Waris & Reza Aprianti. (2023). Implementation of English Curriculum in Common ASEAN Tourism Curriculum (CATC) in Tourism Vocational Schools in Indonesia. *English Education International Conference (EEIC)*. Aceh. Retrieved from https://jurnal.usk.ac.id/EEIC/article/view/36814

Abdullah, K. H., Abd Aziz, F. S., Dani, R., Hammood, W. A., & Setiawan, E. (2023). Urban Pollution: A Bibliometric Review. *ASM Science Journal*, *18*, 1–16. DOI: 10.32802/ASMSCJ.2023.1440

ABEYWICKRAMA. H. D. (2018). *LANGUAGE ASSESSMENT PRINCIPLES AND CLASSROOM PRACTICES*. New York: Pearson.

Abioye, S., Oyedele, L. O., Akanbi, L., Ajayi, A., Delgado, J. M. D., Bilal, M., Akinadé, O. O., & Ahmed, A. (2021). Artificial intelligence in the construction industry: A review of present status, opportunities and future challenges [Review of Artificial intelligence in the construction industry: A review of present status, opportunities and future challenges]. Journal of Building Engineering, 44, 103299. Elsevier BV. https://doi.org/DOI: 10.1016/j.jobe.2021.103299

Abràmoff, M. D., Tarver, M. E., Loyo-Berríos, N., Trujillo, S., Char, D., Obermeyer, Z., Eydelman, M., & Maisel, W. H. (2023). Considerations for addressing bias in artificial intelligence for health equity [Review of Considerations for addressing bias in artificial intelligence for health equity]. Npj Digital Medicine, 6(1). Nature Portfolio. https://doi.org/DOI: 10.1038/s41746-023-00913-9

Adera, N. (2025). Innovative learning spaces and blended learning: Quest for 21st century competency teaching and learning approaches. Creating Dynamic Space in Higher Education: Modern Shifts in Policy, Competencies, and Governance, 139-174. [HTML]

Aditomo, A. (2024). *CAPAIAN PEMBELAJARAN PENDIDIKAN ANAK USIA DINI, JENJANG PENDIDIKAN DASAR, JENJANG PENDIDIKAN MENENGAH, PADA KURIKULUM MERDEKA (LEARNING OUTCOMES IN EARLY CHILDHOOD EDUCATION, PRIMARY EDUCATION, AND SECONDARY EDUCATION, IN THE INDEPENDENT CURRICULUM).* KemenRisTekDikti.

Afzal, A., Khan, S., Daud, S., Ahmad, Z., & Butt, A. (2023). Addressing the Digital Divide: Access and Use of Technology in Education. In journal of social sciences review (Vol. 3, Number 2, p. 883). https://doi.org/DOI: 10.54183/jssr.v3i2.326

Agalianos, A., Whitty, G., & Noss, R. (2006). The Social Shaping of Logo. *Social Studies of Science*, *36*(2), 241–267.

Agarwal, P., & Sharma, S. (2023). Smart Urban Traffic Management System using Energy Efficient Optimized Path Discovery. *Proceedings of the 3rd International Conference on Artificial Intelligence and Smart Energy, ICAIS 2023*, 858 – 863. https://doi.org/DOI: 10.1109/ICAIS56108.2023.10073840

Agostinelli, S. (2021). Actionable framework for city digital twin-enabled predictive maintenance and security management systems.. https://doi.org/DOI: 10.2495/bim210191

Ahmad, I., Sharma, S., Kumar, R., Dhyani, S., & Dumka, A. (2023). Data Analytics of Online Education during Pandemic Health Crisis: A Case Study. *2nd Edition of IEEE Delhi Section Owned Conference, DELCON 2023 - Proceedings*. https://doi.org/DOI: 10.1109/DELCON57910.2023.10127423

AI-Infused Collaborative Inquiry in Upper Elementary School. A Game-Based Learning Approach. (2021). https://ojs.aaai.org/index.php/AAAI/article/view/17836

Ait Baha, T., El Hajji, M., Es-Saady, Y., & Fadili, H. (2024). The impact of an educational chatbot on student learning experience. *Education and Information Technologies*, *29*, 10153–10176.

Akavova, A., Temirkhanova, Z., & Lorsanova, Z. (2023). Adaptive learning and artificial intelligence in the educational space. E3s Web of Conferences, 451, 06011. https://doi.org/DOI: 10.1051/e3sconf/202345106011

Akgün, S., & Greenhow, C. (2021). Artificial intelligence in education: Addressing ethical challenges in k-12 settings. *AI and Ethics*, *2*(3), 431–440. DOI: 10.1007/s43681-021-00096-7 PMID: 34790956

Al Suwaidi, J. (2021). Teaching moral education in a digital era: A UAE perspective. *International Journal of Educational Development*, *85*, 102453.

Al-Ahdal, A. A. M. H., & Alharbi, M. A. (2021). MALL in Collaborative Learning as a Vocabulary-Enhancing Tool for EFL Learners: A Study Across Two Universities in Saudi Arabia. *SAGE Open*, *11*(1). Advance online publication. DOI: 10.1177/2158244021999062

Alali, R. (2024). Opportunities and challenges of integrating generative artificial intelligence in education. *International Journal of Religion*, *5*(7), 784–793. DOI: 10.61707/8y29gv34

Alam, A., & Mohanty, A. (2023). Educational technology: Exploring the convergence of technology and pedagogy through mobility, interactivity, AI, and learning tools. Cogent Engineering. tandfonline.com

Alamri, H., Lowell, V., Watson, W., & Watson, S. L. (2020). Using personalized learning as an instructional approach to motivate learners in online higher education: Learner self-determination and intrinsic motivation. *Journal of Research on Technology in Education*, *52*(3), 322–352. DOI: 10.1080/15391523.2020.1728449

Al-Ansi, A. M., Jaboob, M., Garad, A., & Al-Ansi, A. (2023). Analyzing augmented reality (AR) and virtual reality (VR) recent development in education. [sciencedirect.com]. *Social Sciences & Humanities Open*, *8*(1), 100532.

Albino, V., Berardi, U., & Dangelico, R. M. (2015). Smart Cities: Definitions, Dimensions, Performance, and Initiatives. *Journal of Urban Technology*, *22*(1), 3–21.

Alenezi, A. (2024). Obstacles to the use of ai applications in blackboard for faculty members at northern border university, saudi arabia. Mier Journal of Educational Studies Trends & Practices, 248-268. https://doi.org/DOI: 10.52634/mier/2024/v14/i2/2581

Alenezi, A. (2023). Teacher perspectives on ai-driven gamification: Impact on student motivation, engagement, and learning outcomes. *Information Technologies and Learning Tools*, *97*(5), 138–148. DOI: 10.33407/itlt.v97i5.5437

AlGerafi, M. A. M., Zhou, Y., Oubibi, M., & Wijaya, T. T. (2023). Unlocking the potential: A comprehensive evaluation of augmented reality and virtual reality in education. Electronics. mdpi.com

Aliabadi, R. (2023). Transdisciplinary ai education: the confluence of curricular and community needs in the instruction of artificial intelligence., 137-151. https://doi.org/DOI: 10.1007/978-981-99-7947-9_11

Alkan, A. (2024). Artificial intelligence: its role and potential in education. İnsan Ve Toplum Bilimleri Araştırmaları Dergisi, 13(1), 483-497. https://doi.org/DOI: 10.15869/itobiad.1331201

Allahverdi, A. (2021). Sample senior design projects of industrial engineering program at kuwait university. *Asean Journal of Engineering Education*, *4*(1). Advance online publication. DOI: 10.11113/ajee2020.4n1.14

Allenby, B., & Sarewitz, D. (2011). *The Techno-Human Condition*. MIT Press.

Alper, A., Öztaş, E. Ş., Atun, H., Çınar, D., & Moyenga, M. (2021). A Systematic Literature Review towards the Research of Game-Based Learning with Augmented Reality. In International Journal of Technology in Education and Science (Vol. 5, Number 2, p. 224). https://doi.org/DOI: 10.46328/ijtes.176

Alrayes, A. (2024). Chatgpt in education – understanding the bahraini academics perspective. *Electronic Journal of e-Learning*, *22*(2), 112–134. DOI: 10.34190/ejel.22.2.3250

Alsadoon, H. (2023). The impact of gamification on student motivation and engagement: An empirical study. *Dirasat: Educational Sciences*, *50*(2), 386–396. DOI: 10.35516/edu.v50i2.255

Alshehri, B. (2023). Pedagogical paradigms in the ai era: Insights from saudi educators on the long-term implications of ai integration in classroom teaching. *IJESA*, *2*(8), 159–180. DOI: 10.59992/ijesa.2023.v2n8p7

Amerstorfer, C. M., & Freiin von Münster-Kistner, C. (2021). Student perceptions of academic engagement and student-teacher relationships in problem-based learning. [frontiersin.org]. *Frontiers in Psychology*, *12*, 713057. PMID: 34777094

Angelidou, M. (2015). Smart Cities: A Conjuncture of Four Forces. *Cities (London, England)*, *47*, 95–106.

Angwin, J., Larson, J., Mattu, S., & Kirchner, L. (2016). Machine bias. *ProPublica*. Retrieved from https://www.propublica.org/article/machine-bias-risk-assessments-in-criminal-sentencing

Ansari, M. F., & Afzal, A. (2022). Sensitivity and Performance Analysis of 10 MW Solar Power Plant Using MPPT Technique. *Lecture Notes in Electrical Engineering*, *894 LNEE*, 512–518. https://doi.org/DOI: 10.1007/978-981-19-1677-9_46

An, T., & Li, Y. (2014). On Theoretical Prospect of Educational Technology From the Perspective of Philosophy of Technology. *Educational Research*, *4*, 37–42.

Anthopoulos, L., & Fitsilis, P. (2010). "From Digital to Ubiquitous Cities: Defining a Common Architecture for Urban Development." *Proceedings of the 6th International Conference on Intelligent Environments*, 301-306.

Antonaci, A., Klemke, R., & Specht, M. (2019). The effects of gamification in online learning environments: A systematic literature review. *Informatics (MDPI)*, *6*(3), 32. DOI: 10.3390/informatics6030032

Aparicio-Gómez, O. (2024). Tejiendo conexiones: la simbiosis transformadora entre aprendizaje e inteligencia artificial. Hachetetepé Revista Científica De Educación Y Comunicación, (28). https://doi.org/DOI: 10.25267/hachetetepe.2024.i28.1103

Arendt, H. (1958). *The Human Condition*. University of Chicago Press.

Arie Wibowo Khurniawan, A. P. (2024). *PEMANFAATAN GEN-AI DALAM PEMBELAJARAN KEJURUAN BAGI GURU SMK BIDANG BISNIS DAN PARIWISATA (THE UTILISATION OF GEN-AI IN VOCATIONAL LEARNING FOR SMK TEACHERS IN THE FIELD OF BUSINESS AND TOURISM)*. Balai Besar Pengembangan Penjaminan Mutu Pendidikan Vokasi (BBPPMPV) Bisnis Dan Pariwisata Kementerian Pendidikan Dasar dan Menengah, Depok.

Aristotle. (350 BCE/1999). *Nicomachean Ethics* (T. Irwin, Trans.). Hackett Publishing.

Arola, E., & Kupiainen, R. (2020). Digital literacy and citizenship in Finnish education. *Media Education Research Journal*, *11*(2), 15–28.

Arora, A., Alderman, J., Palmer, J., Ganapathi, S., Laws, E., McCradden, M. D., Oakden-Rayner, L., Pfohl, S., Ghassemi, M., McKay, F., Treanor, D., Rostamzadeh, N., Mateen, B. A., Gath, J., Adebajo, A. O., Kuku, S., Matin, R., Heller, K., Sapey, E., . . . Liu, X. (2023). The value of standards for health datasets in artificial intelligence-based applications. In Nature Medicine (Vol. 29, Issue 11, p. 2929). Nature Portfolio. https://doi.org/DOI: 10.1038/s41591-023-02608-w

Arora, R., Chauhan, A., Singh, A. P., & Sharma, R. (2023). Optimization of a production inventory model of imperfect quality items for three-layer supply chain in fuzzy environment. *Benchmarking*. Advance online publication. DOI: 10.1108/BIJ-11-2021-0678

Arthur, W. B. (2009). *The Nature of Technology: What it is and How it Evolves*. Penguin.

Atiyeh, B., Emsieh, S., Hakim, C., & Chalhoub, R. (2023). A narrative review of artificial intelligence (AI) for objective assessment of aesthetic endpoints in plastic surgery. *Aesthetic Plastic Surgery*, *47*(6), 2862–2873. DOI: 10.1007/s00266-023-03328-9 PMID: 37000298

Auliawan, A. G., & Ong, S. (2020). *The Usage of AI Robot in English Language Teaching for City Revitalization Case Study*. Toda Daini Elementary School.

Awal, G., & Khanna, R. (2019). Determinants of millennial online consumer behavior and prospective purchase decisions. *International Journal of Advanced Science and Technology*, *28*(18), 366–378.

Awino, E., Wanzare, L., Muchemi, L., Wanjawa, B., Ombui, E., Indede, F., McOnyango, O., & Okal, B. O. (2022). Phonemic Representation and Transcription for Speech to Text Applications for Under-resourced Indigenous African Languages: The Case of Kiswahili. In arXiv (Cornell University). Cornell University. https://doi.org/DOI: 10.48550/arXiv.2210

Bachiri, Y.-A., Mouncif, H., & Bouikhalene, B. (2023). Artificial Intelligence Empowers Gamification: Optimizing Student Engagement and Learning Outcomes in E-learning and MOOCs. [IJEP]. *International Journal of Engineering Pedagogy*, *13*(8), 4–19. DOI: 10.3991/ijep.v13i8.40853

Bagash Mansour Ahmed Al-Sofi, B. (2021). Student satisfaction with e-learning using blackboard LMS during the Covid-19 circumstances: Realities, expectations, and future prospects. *Pegem Journal of Education and Instruction*, *11*(4). Advance online publication. DOI: 10.47750/pegegog.11.04.26

Baik, C., Larcombe, W., & Brooker, A. (2019). How universities can enhance student mental wellbeing: The student perspective. *Higher Education Research & Development*, *38*(4), 674–687. DOI: 10.1080/07294360.2019.1576596

Baker, R. S., & Hawn, A. (2022). Algorithmic bias in education. *International Journal of Artificial Intelligence in Education*, •••, 1–41.

Balci, S., Secaur, J., & Morris, B. (2022). Comparing the effectiveness of badges and leaderboards on academic performance and motivation of students in fully versus partially gamified online physics classes. *Education and Information Technologies*, *27*(6), 8669–8704. DOI: 10.1007/s10639-022-10983-z PMID: 35308640

Balta, N. (2023). Ethical considerations in using ai in educational research., 2(1), 14205. https://doi.org/DOI: 10.51853/jorids/14205

Bansal, S., Kumar, V., Kumari, A., & Kuzmin, E. (2023). Understanding the Role of Digital Technologies in Supply Chain Management of SMEs. In K. V., K. G.L., A. V., & K. E. (Eds.), *Lecture Notes in Information Systems and Organisation: Vol. 61 LNISO* (pp. 195 – 205). Springer Science and Business Media Deutschland GmbH. https://doi.org/DOI: 10.1007/978-3-031-30351-7_16

Bansal, N., Bhatnagar, M., & Taneja, S. (2023). Balancing priorities through green optimism: A study elucidating initiatives, approaches, and strategies for sustainable supply chain management. In *Handbook of Research on Designing Sustainable Supply Chains to Achieve a Circular Economy*. IGI Global., DOI: 10.4018/978-1-6684-7664-2.ch004

Barad, K. (2019). After the end of the world: Entangled nuclear colonialisms, matters of force, and the material force of justice. *Theory & Event*, *22*(3), 524–550.

Barkley, E. F., & Major, C. H. (2020). *Student engagement techniques: A handbook for college faculty*. John Wiley & Sons.

Barua, P., Vicnesh, J., Gururajan, R., Oh, S., Palmer, E., Azizan, M., & Acharya, U. (2022). Artificial intelligence enabled personalised assistive tools to enhance education of children with neurodevelopmental disorders a review. *International Journal of Environmental Research and Public Health*, *19*(3), 1192. DOI: 10.3390/ijerph19031192 PMID: 35162220

Baskara, F. (2024). A Theoretical Analysis of ChatGPT Integration in Flipped Classrooms to Enhance Personal Learning Space.

Bastani, P., Kavosi, Z., Alipoori, S., & Imani-Nasab, M. (2023). Evidence- based policy and decision-making among health managers: A case of shiraz university of medical sciences. *Galen Medical Journal*, *6*(1). Advance online publication. DOI: 10.31661/gmj.v6i1.729

Batty, M., Axhausen, K. W., & Giannotti, F.. (2012). Smart Cities of the Future. *The European Physical Journal. Special Topics*, *214*(1), 481–518.

Bayne, S. (2015). What's the Matter with 'Technology-Enhanced Learning'? *Learning, Media and Technology*, *40*(1), 5–20.

Beane, J. A. (1995). Curriculum integration and the disciplines of knowledge. *Phi Delta Kappan*, *76*(8), 616–622.

Beaulieu, É., & Beno, S. (2024). Healthy childhood development through outdoor risky play: Navigating the balance with injury prevention [Review of Healthy childhood development through outdoor risky play: Navigating the balance with injury prevention]. Paediatrics & Child Health, 29(4), 255. Oxford University Press. https://doi.org/DOI: 10.1093/pch/pxae016

Beckera, R., & Birdib, A. (2018). Flipping the Classroom: Old Ideas, New Technologies. *International Review of Economics Education*, *29*, 1–5.

Bella, G. B., Helm, P., & Koch, G. Fausto Giunchiglia. (2023). Towards Bridging the Digital Language Divide. https://arxiv.org/pdf/2307.13405.pdf

Belshaw, D. (2016). *The essential elements of digital literacies*. CreateSpace Independent Publishing.

Belwal, N., Juneja, P., & Sunori, S. K. (2023). Decoupler Control for a MIMO Process Model in an Industrial Process - A Review. *2023 2nd International Conference on Ambient Intelligence in Health Care, ICAIHC 2023*. https://doi.org/DOI: 10.1109/ICAIHC59020.2023.10431463

Benjamin, W. (2001). The Work of Art in the Age of Mechanical Reproduction. In Arendt, H. (Ed.), *Illuminations* (pp. 217–251). Pimlico. (Original work published 1935)

Benko, A., & Lányi, C. S. (2009). History of artificial intelligence. In *Encyclopedia of Information Science and Technology* (2nd ed., pp. 1759–1762). IGI Global.

Benton, L., Mavrikis, M., Vasalou, A., Joye, N., Sumner, E., Herbert, E., Révész, A., Symvonis, A., & Raftopoulou, C. N. (2021). Designing for "challenge" in a large-scale adaptive literacy game for primary school children. In British Journal of Educational Technology (Vol. 52, Number 5, p. 1862). Wiley. https://doi.org/DOI: 10.1111/bjet.13146

Berlin, I. (1958). Two concepts of liberty. In I. Berlin, *Four Essays on Liberty* (pp. 118–172). Oxford University Press.

Beukman, M., & Fokam, M. (2023). Analysing Cross-Lingual Transfer in Low-Resourced African Named Entity Recognition. In arXiv (Cornell University). Cornell University. https://doi.org/DOI: 10.48550/arXiv.2309

Bhatia, A., & Lahiri, S. (2021). AI for youth: Bridging digital divides in India. *International Review of Education*, *67*(4), 535–552.

Bhatnagar, M., Rajaram, R., Taneja, S., & Kumar, P. (2024). Balancing acts: The Yin and Yang of debit and credit on the stage of financial well-being. In *Emerging Perspectives on Financial Well-Being*. IGI Global., DOI: 10.4018/979-8-3693-1750-1.ch002

Bhatnagar, M., & Sehajpal, S. (2024). Leveraging AI for Financial Sustainability in Healthcare. In Ercan, O., Azad, S., Sanjay, T., Rajendra, R., & Paulo, D. J. (Eds.), *Sustainability, Innovation, and Consumer Preference* (pp. 411–426). IGI Global Scientific Publishing., DOI: 10.4018/979-8-3693-9699-5.ch017

Bhatnagar, M., Taneja, S., Kumar, P., & Özen, E. (2024). Does financial education act as a catalyst for SME competitiveness? *International Journal of Education Economics and Development*, *15*(3), 377–393. DOI: 10.1504/IJEED.2024.139306

Bhimdiwala, A., Neri, R. C., & Gomez, L. M. (2022). Advancing the design and implementation of artificial intelligence in education through continuous improvement. *International Journal of Artificial Intelligence in Education*, •••, 1–27.

Bianco, J. L. (2013). Innovation in Language Policy and Planning: Ties to English Language Education. In Wong, K. H. (Ed.), *INNOVATION AND CHANGE IN ENGLISH LANGUAGE EDUCATION* (pp. 139–154). Routledge.

Biesta, G., Heugh, K., Cervinkova, H., Rasinski, L., Osborne, S., Forde, D., Wrench, A., Carter, J., Anders Safstrom, C., Soong, H., O'Keeffe, S., Paige, K., Rigney, I., O'Toole, L., Hattam, R., Peters, M. A., & Tesar, M. (2021). Philosophy of education in a new key: Publicness, Social Justice, and Education; A South-North Conversation. *Educational Philosophy and Theory*. Advance online publication. DOI: 10.1080/00131857.2021.1929172

Boahin, P. (2018). COMPETENCY-BASED CURRICULUM: A FRAMEWORK FOR BRIDGING THE GAP IN TEACHING, ASSESSMENT AND THE WORLD OF WORK. *International Journal of Vocational and Technical Education Research*, 24-37.

Bondie, R. S., Dahnke, C., & Zusho, A. (2019). How Does Changing "One-Size-Fits-All" to Differentiated Instruction Affect Teaching? *Review of Research in Education*, *43*(1), 336–362. DOI: 10.3102/0091732X18821130

Boss, S., & Krauss, J. (2018). *Reinventing project-based learning: Your field guide to real-world projects in the digital age* (3rd ed.). ISTE.

Bostrom, N. (2014). *Superintelligence: Paths, Dangers, Strategies*. Oxford University Press.

Braden, A. (1995). Review of Instructional Technology: The Definition and Domains of the Field. *Educational Technology Research and Development*, *43*(1), 81–83.

Bradley, V. M. (2021). Learning Management System (LMS) use with online instruction.. International Journal of Technology in Education. ed.gov

Braidotti, R. (2019). *Posthuman knowledge*. Polity Press.

Brayne, S. (2020). *Predict and surveil: Data, discretion, and the future of policing*. Oxford University Press.

Brown, H. D. (2004). *Language assessment: Principle and classroom practices. NewYork: Pearson*. Pearson Education.

Buchanan, R. A., Forster, D. J., Douglas, S., Nakar, S., Boon, H. J., Heath, T., Heyward, P., D'Olimpio, L., Ailwood, J., Eacott, S., Smith, S., Peters, M., & Tesar, M. (2021). Philosophy of education in a new key: Exploring new ways of teaching and doing ethics in education in the 21st century. *Educational Philosophy and Theory*. Advance online publication. DOI: 10.1080/00131857.2021.1880387

Buckley, P., & Doyle, E. (2014). Gamification and student motivation. *Interactive Learning Environments*, *24*(6), 1162–1175. DOI: 10.1080/10494820.2014.964263

Bui, L. T. N., & Khuu, V. T. (2020). Inquiry-based learning: an effective approach to teaching science aiming to develop students' competencies. In Vietnam Journal of Education (online)/Vietnam Journal of Education/Giáo d c (Vol. 4, Number 1, p. 61). https://doi.org/DOI: 10.52296/vje.2020.9

Buolamwini, J., & Gebru, T. (2018). Gender shades: Intersectional accuracy disparities in commercial gender classification. *Proceedings of the 1st Conference on Fairness, Accountability and Transparency*, 77–91.

Cabinet Office of Japan. (2017). *Society 5.0: Aiming for a new human-centered society*. Retrieved from https://www8.cao.go.jp/cstp/society5_0/

Cabinet Office, Government of Japan. (2019). *Society 5.0: A people-centric super-smart society*.

Caiado, R. G. G., Scavarda, L. F., Vidal, G., de Mattos Nascimento, D. L., & Garza-Reyes, J. A. (2023). A taxonomy of critical factors towards sustainable operations and supply chain management 4.0 in developing countries. *Operations Management Research*. https://doi.org/DOI: 10.1007/s12063-023-00430-8

Camacho, L., & Zevallos, R. (2020). *Language technology into high schools for revitalization of endangered languages*., DOI: 10.1109/intercon50315.2020.9220197

Caragliu, A., Del Bo, C., & Nijkamp, P. (2011). Smart Cities in Europe. *Journal of Urban Technology*, *18*(2), 65–82.

Cardinot, A., & Fairfield, J. A. (2018). Game-Based Learning to Engage Students With Physics and Astronomy Using a Board Game. In International Journal of Game-Based Learning (Vol. 9, Number 1, p. 42). IGI Global. https://doi.org/DOI: 10.4018/ijgbl.2019010104

Cardona, M. A., Rodríguez, R. J., & Ishmael, K. (2023). *Artificial intelligence and the future of teaching and learning*. Lumina Foundation.

Carless, D. (2019). Feedback loops and the longer-term: Towards feedback spirals. *Assessment & Evaluation in Higher Education*, *44*(5), 705–714. DOI: 10.1080/02602938.2018.1531108

Carroll, M., Lindsey, S., Chaparro, M., & Winslow, B. (2021). An applied model of learner engagement and strategies for increasing learner engagement in the modern educational environment. [HTML]. *Interactive Learning Environments*, *29*(5), 757–771.

Cavaliere, L. P. L., Byloppilly, R., Khan, S. D., Othman, B. A., Muda, I., & Malhotra, R. K. (2024). Acceptance and effectiveness of Industry 4.0 internal and external organisational initiatives in Malaysian firms. *International Journal of Management and Enterprise Development*, *23*(1), 1–25. DOI: 10.1504/IJMED.2024.138422

Cents-Boonstra, M., Lichtwarck-Aschoff, A., Denessen, E., Aelterman, N., & Haerens, L. (2021). Fostering student engagement with motivating teaching: An observation study of teacher and student behaviours. [tandfonline.com]. *Research Papers in Education*, *36*(6), 754–779.

Chahar, A., & Christobel, Y. A. Ritika, Adakane, P. K., Sonal, D., & Tripathi, V. (2022). The Implementation of Big Data With Cloud and Edge Computing in Enhancing the Smart Grid Information Processes Through Sem Model. *2022 2nd International Conference on Advance Computing and Innovative Technologies in Engineering, ICACITE 2022*, 608 – 611. https://doi.org/DOI: 10.1109/ICACITE53722.2022.9823896

Chai, F. (2024). Grading by ai makes me feel fairer? how different evaluators affect college students' perception of fairness. *Frontiers in Psychology*, *15*. Advance online publication. DOI: 10.3389/fpsyg.2024.1221177 PMID: 38371704

Chalmers, D. J. (1995). Facing up to the problem of consciousness. *Journal of Consciousness Studies*, *2*(3), 200–219.

Chan, C. K. Y., & Tsi, L. H. Y. (2023). The AI revolution in education: Will AI replace or assist teachers in higher education? arXiv:2305.01185 [cs.CY]. https://doi.org//arXiv.2305.01185DOI: 10.48550

Chang, C., Hwang, G., & Gau, M. (2021). Promoting students' learning achievement and self-efficacy: A mobile chatbot approach for nursing training. *British Journal of Educational Technology*, *53*(1), 171–188. DOI: 10.1111/bjet.13158

Chariyev, T. X. (2020). THE DEVELOPMENT OF INDEPENDENT AND CREATIVE THINKING OF STUDENTS IN THE LEARNING PROCESS. In Theoretical & Applied Science (Vol. 82, Number 2, p. 605). International Academy Of Theoretical & Applied Science. https://doi.org/DOI: 10.15863/tas.2020.02.82.101

Chassiakos, Y. L., Radesky, J., Christakis, D., Moreno, M. A., & Cross, C. (2016). Children and adolescents and digital media. *Pediatrics*, *138*(5), e20162593. PMID: 27940795

Chen, A. Y. Z. (2024). A systematic review and meta-analysis of AI-enabled assessment in language learning: Design, implementation, and effectiveness. *Journal of Computer Assisted Learning (JCAL).* https://doi.org/https://doi.org/10.1111/jcal.13064

Chen, Y., Clayton, E. W., Novak, L. L., Anders, S., & Malin, B. (2023). Human-Centered Design to Address Biases in Artificial Intelligence. In Journal of Medical Internet Research (Vol. 25). JMIR Publications. https://doi.org/DOI: 10.2196/43251

Chen, Z. (2023). Ethics and discrimination in artificial intelligence-enabled recruitment practices. In Humanities and Social Sciences Communications (Vol. 10, Issue 1). Palgrave Macmillan. https://doi.org/DOI: 10.1057/s41599-023-02079-x

Chen, G., Chen, P., Huang, W., & Zhai, J. (2022). Continuance intention mechanism of middle school student users on online learning platform based on qualitative comparative analysis method. [wiley.com]. *Mathematical Problems in Engineering*, *2022*(1), 3215337.

Chen, J. J., & Perez, C. (2023). Enhancing assessment and personalized learning through artificial intelligence. *Childhood Education*, *99*(6), 72–79. DOI: 10.1080/00094056.2023.2282903

Chen, L., Chen, P., & Lin, Z. (2020). Artificial intelligence in education: A review. *IEEE Access : Practical Innovations, Open Solutions*, *8*, 75264–75278. DOI: 10.1109/access.2020.2988510

Chen, Y., Shah, V., & Ritter, A. (2023). Better Low-Resource Entity Recognition Through Translation and Annotation Fusion. In arXiv (Cornell University). Cornell University. https://doi.org/DOI: 10.48550/arXiv.2305

Cheung, S. K., Kwok, L. F., Phusavat, K., & Yang, H. H. (2021). Shaping the future learning environments with smart elements: Challenges and opportunities. [springer.com]. *International Journal of Educational Technology in Higher Education*, *18*, 1–9. PMID: 34778521

Chiang, F. K., Zhu, G. X., Wang, Q., Cui, Z. F., Cai, S., & Yu, S. Q. (2016). Research and Trends in Mobile Learning from 1976 to 2013: A Content Analysis of Patents in Selected Databases. *British Journal of Educational Technology*, *47*(6), 1006–1019.

Chourabi, H., Nam, T., & Walker, S.. (2012). "Understanding Smart Cities: An Integrative Framework." *45th Hawaii International Conference on System Sciences (HICSS)*, 2289-2297.

Christensen, C., Horn, M., & Johnson, C. (2008). *Disrupting Class: How disruptive innovation will change the way the world learns*. McGraw-Hill.

Churchland, P. M. (1989). *Neurophilosophy: Toward a Unified Science of the Mind-Brain*. MIT Press.

Ciecierski, H. T., Singh, R., Axt, M., Brenner, S., & Barteit, S. (2022). Artificial intelligence for strengthening healthcare systems in low- and middle-income countries: a systematic scoping review [Review of Artificial intelligence for strengthening healthcare systems in low- and middle-income countries: a systematic scoping review]. Npj Digital Medicine, 5(1). Nature Portfolio. https://doi.org/DOI: 10.1038/s41746-022-00700-y

Clegg, S., & Steel, J. (2002). "Flexibility as Myth? New Technologies and Post-Fordism in Higher Education." *Proceedings of the Networked Learning Conference*.

Coeckelbergh, M. (2020). *AI Ethics*. MIT Press.

Common Sense Education. (2023). *Digital Citizenship Curriculum.*

Costanza-Chock, S. (2020). *Design Justice: Community-Led Practices to Build the Worlds We Need*. MIT Press.

Costello, R., & Lambert, M. (2018). Motivational Influences for Higher Education (HE) Students. In International Journal of Online Pedagogy and Course Design (Vol. 9, Number 1, p. 38). IGI Global. https://doi.org/DOI: 10.4018/ijopcd.2019010103

Cranley, L., Doran, D., Tourangeau, A., Kushniruk, A., & Nagle, L. (2012). Recognizing and responding to uncertainty: A grounded theory of nurses' uncertainty. *Worldviews on Evidence-Based Nursing*, *9*(3), 149–158. DOI: 10.1111/j.1741-6787.2011.00237.x PMID: 22233501

Crawford, K., & Paglen, T. (2019). Excavating AI: The politics of images in machine learning training sets. *Excavating AI Project*. https://excavating.ai

Crawford, J., Cowling, M., & Allen, K.-A. (2023). Leadership is needed for ethical ChatGPT: Character, assessment, and learning using artificial intelligence (AI). *Journal of University Teaching & Learning Practice*, *20*(3), 457–476. DOI: 10.53761/1.20.3.02

Crosbie, W., Hickman, A., Danang, E., & Maguire, A. (2012). *Assesor Manual_Converse in English at a basic operational level*. William Angliss Institute of TAFE.

Cuban, L. (2001). *Oversold and Underused: Computers in the Classroom*. Harvard University Press.

Czerniewicz, L. (2010). Educational Technology–Mapping the Terrain with Bernstein as Cartographer. *Journal of Computer Assisted Learning*, *26*(6), 523–534.

D'Errico, F. (2007). The Origin of Humanity and Modern Cultures: Archaeology's View. *Diogenes*, *54*(2), 122–133.

D'Souza, R. (2024). Twelve tips for addressing ethical concerns in the implementation of artificial intelligence in medical education. *Medical Education Online*, *29*(1). Advance online publication. DOI: 10.1080/10872981.2024.2330250 PMID: 38566608

Dameri, R. P., & Cocchia, A. (2013). "Smart City and Digital City: Twenty Years of Terminology Evolution." *ItAIS: The Italian Association for Information Systems*, 1-9.

Dangwal, A., Kaur, S., Taneja, S., & Ozen, E. (2022). A bibliometric analysis of green tourism based on the scopus platform. In *Developing Relationships, Personalization, and Data Herald in Marketing 5.0*. IGI Global., DOI: 10.4018/978-1-6684-4496-2.ch015

Darvishi, A., Khosravi, H., Sadiq, S., Gašević, D., & Siemens, G. (2023). Impact of AI assistance on student agency. In *Computers & Education* (Vol. 210, p. 104967). Elsevier BV., DOI: 10.1016/j.compedu.2023.104967

Dave, M., & Patel, N. (2023). Artificial intelligence in healthcare and education. In BDJ (Vol. 234, Issue 10, p. 761). Springer Nature. https://doi.org/DOI: 10.1038/s41415-023-5845-2

Davis, R. (2024). Korean in-service teachers' perceptions of implementing artificial intelligence (ai) education for teaching in schools and their ai teacher training programs. *International Journal of Information and Education Technology (IJIET)*, *14*(2), 214–219. DOI: 10.18178/ijiet.2024.14.2.2042

Davuluri, S. K., Alvi, S. A. M., Aeri, M., Agarwal, A., Serajuddin, M., & Hasan, Z. (2023). A Security Model for Perceptive 5G-Powered BC IoT Associated Deep Learning. *6th International Conference on Inventive Computation Technologies, ICICT 2023 - Proceedings*, 118 – 125. https://doi.org/DOI: 10.1109/ICICT57646.2023.10134487

De Carvalho-Filho, M. A., Tio, R. A., & Steinert, Y. (2020). Twelve tips for implementing a community of practice for faculty development. *Medical Teacher*, *42*(2), 143–149. DOI: 10.1080/0142159X.2018.1552782 PMID: 30707855

De Russis, L., Kumar, N., & Mathur, A. (2023). Data4Good: Designing for Diversity and Development. https://dl.acm.org/doi/10.1145/3399715.3400864

De Vega, N., Basri, M., & Nur, S. (2025). Exposing tech skills shaping mobile learning in cross-disciplinary English learners. [EduLearn]. *Journal of Education and Learning*, *19*(2), 1117–1124. DOI: 10.11591/edulearn.v19i2.21351

Deakin, M. (2010). A Review of City Portals: The Transformation of Service Provision Under the Democratization of the Fifth Utility. *International Journal of Public Information Systems*, *6*(2), 35–45.

Deci, E. L., & Ryan, R. M. (2000). The "What" and "Why" of Goal Pursuits: Human Needs and the Self-Determination of Behavior. *Psychological Inquiry*, *11*(4), 227–268. DOI: 10.1207/S15327965PLI1104_01

Deleuze, G. (1995). *Negotiations*. Columbia University Press.

DeMink-Carthew, J., & Netcoh, S. (2022). Mixed feelings about choice: Exploring variation in middle school student experiences with making choices in a personalized learning project. In Dialogues in Middle Level Education Research Volume 1 (pp. 73-105). Routledge. tandfonline.com

Dempsey, J. V. (1993). Interactive instruction and feedback. *Educational Technology*.

Deng, L. (2018). Artificial intelligence in the rising wave of deep learning: The historical path and future outlook. *IEEE Signal Processing Magazine*, *35*(1), 180–177. DOI: 10.1109/MSP.2017.2762725

Dépelteau, F. (2008). Relational Thinking: A Critique of co-Deterministic Theories of Structure and Agency. *Sociological Theory*, *26*(1), 51–73.

Descartes, R. (1996). *Meditations on First Philosophy* (Cottingham, J., Trans.). Cambridge University Press. (Original work published 1641)

Devi, V., Vashe, A., Rao, R., Abraham, R., Pallath, V., & Torke, S. (2016). Curricular impact on learning approaches and critical thinking skills of medical students. *Education in Medicine Journal*, *8*(4). Advance online publication. DOI: 10.5959/eimj.v8i4.468

Dewey, J. (1916). Democracy and Education: An Introduction to the Philosophy of Education. New York, *NY: the Free Press.*

Dichev, C., & Dicheva, D. (2017). Gamifying education: what is known, what is believed and what remains uncertain: a critical review. *International Journal of Educational Technology in Higher Education*, *14*(1). Advance online publication. DOI: 10.1186/s41239-017-0042-5

DiGiacomo, D. K., Greenhalgh, S., & Barriage, S. (2022). How students and principals understand ClassDojo: Emerging insights. *TechTrends*, •••, 1–13. PMID: 34345879

Digital Promise. (2021). *About Digital Promise.*

Dimitriadou, E., & Lanitis, A. (2023). A critical evaluation, challenges, and future perspectives of using artificial intelligence and emerging technologies in smart classrooms. *Smart Learning Environments*, *10*(1), 12. DOI: 10.1186/s40561-023-00231-3 PMID: 40478141

Dirgantoro, K., Bermuli, J., & Soesanto, R. (2022). Is moodle gamification effective in reviewing student's motivation related to interest in learning online? *Educational Journal Journal of Research Results and Literature Review in the Field of Education, Teaching, and Learning*, *8*(1), 114. DOI: 10.33394/jk.v8i1.4790

Dirks, S., & Keeling, M. (2009). "A Vision of Smarter Cities: How Cities Can Lead the Way into a Prosperous and Sustainable Future." *IBM Global Services*, 1-19.

Dogan, M. E., Goru Dogan, T., & Bozkurt, A. (2023). The use of artificial intelligence (AI) in online learning and distance education processes: A systematic review of empirical studies. *Applied Sciences (Basel, Switzerland)*, *13*(5), 56–88. DOI: 10.3390/app13053056

Dogra, V., Verma, D., Dalapati, G. K., Sharma, M., & Okhawilai, M. (2022). Special focus on 3D printing of sulfides/selenides for energy conversion and storage. In *Sulfide and Selenide Based Materials for Emerging Applications: Sustainable Energy Harvesting and Storage Technology*. Elsevier., DOI: 10.1016/B978-0-323-99860-4.00012-5

Donnelly, K. (2007). Australia's Adoption of Outcomes Based Education: A Critique. *Issues in Educational Research, 17*(2), 183–206.

du Plooy, E., Casteleijn, D., & Franzsen, D. (2024). Personalized adaptive learning in higher education: a scoping review of key characteristics and impact on academic performance and engagement. Heliyon. cell.com

Dumont, H. & Ready, D. D. (2023). On the promise of personalized learning for educational equity. Npj science of learning. nature.com

Dusek, V. (2006). *Philosophy of Technology: An Introduction.* Blackwell Publishing.

Dutta, S., Ranjan, S., Mishra, S., Sharma, V., Hewage, P., & Iwendi, C. (2024, February). Enhancing educational adaptability: A review and analysis of AI-driven adaptive learning platforms. In *2024 4th International Conference on Innovative Practices in Technology and Management (ICIPTM)* (pp. 1–5). IEEE.

Ejaz, H., McGrath, H., Wong, B., Guise, A., Vercauteren, T., & Shapey, J. (2022). Artificial intelligence and medical education: A global mixed-methods study of medical students' perspectives. *Digital Health, 8,* 205520762210890. DOI: 10.1177/20552076221089099 PMID: 35521511

Elford, M. D., Smith, H. H., & James, S. (2024). Teaching Feedback in Assessment. In *GET Feedback* (pp. 193–209). Routledge.

Ellikkal, A. & Rajamohan, S. (2024). AI-enabled personalized learning: empowering management students for improving engagement and academic performance. Vilakshan-XIMB Journal of Management. emerald.com

Elosua, P., & Egaña, M. Á. (2016). Socioeconomic patterns and educational performance based on language-of-instruction models in the Basque Autonomous Community. In Journal of Multilingual and Multicultural Development (Vol. 38, Issue 8, p. 686). Taylor & Francis. https://doi.org/DOI: 10.1080/01434632.2016.1224239

Erbaşı, Z. (2023). The role and potential of artificial intelligence and gamification in education: The example of vakıf participation bank. *Orclever Proceedings of Research and Development, 3*(1), 243–254. DOI: 10.56038/oprd.v3i1.329

Eslit, E. (2023). Blending boundaries in the new normal: Leveraging technology, ai and global perspectives in modern education. *Journal of Learning and Educational Policy,* (41), 8–18. DOI: 10.55529/jlep.41.8.18

Esposito, A., Sangrà, A., & Maina, M. (2013). "Chronotopes in Learner-Generated Contexts. A Reflection About the Interconnectedness of Temporal and Spatial Dimensions to Provide a Framework for the Exploration of Hybrid Learning Ecologies of Doctoral e-Researchers." *LC Research Paper Series,* 6: 15–28.

Eubanks, V. (2018). *Automating Inequality: How High-Tech Tools Profile, Police, and Punish the Poor.* St. Martin's Press.

Eubanks, V. (2018). *Automating inequality: How high-tech tools profile, police, and punish the poor.* St. Martin's Press.

European Commission. (2020). *Ethics Guidelines for Trustworthy AI.*

European Commission. (2021). *Digital Education Action Plan (2021–2027).*

Evangeline, D., & Parkavi, A. (2022, May). Comparative Study on Online Teaching and Learning Tools. In *ICCCE 2021: Proceedings of the 4th International Conference on Communications and Cyber Physical Engineering* (pp. 49-57). Singapore: Springer Nature Singapore.

Eynon, R. (2015). The Quantified Self for Learning: Critical Questions for Education. *Learning, Media and Technology*, *40*(4), 407–411.

Ezzaim, A., Dahbi, A., Aqqal, A., & Haidine, A. (2024). AI-based learning style detection in adaptive learning systems: A systematic literature review. [HTML]. *Journal of Computers in Education*, •••, 1–39.

Familoni, B. (2024). Advancements and challenges in ai integration for technical literacy: A systematic review. *Engineering Science & Technology Journal*, *5*(4), 1415–1430. DOI: 10.51594/estj.v5i4.1042

Fazil, A. (2024). Exploring the broad impact of ai technologies on student engagement and academic performance in university settings in afghanistan. *Riggs Journal of Artificial Intelligence and Digital Business*, *2*(2), 56–63. DOI: 10.31004/riggs.v2i2.268

Feenberg, A. (2002). *Transforming Technology: A Critical Theory Revisited.* Oxford University Press.

Ferrara, E. (2023). Fairness And Bias in Artificial Intelligence: A Brief Survey of Sources, Impacts, And Mitigation Strategies. In arXiv (Cornell University). Cornell University. https://doi.org/DOI: 10.48550/arXiv.2304

Fessakis, G., Gouli, E., & Mavroudi, E. (2018). Digital games in education: Teaching ethical thinking. *Journal of Educational Computing Research*, *56*(3), 491–517.

Fırat, M. (2023). Integrating ai applications into learning management systems to enhance e-learning. Öğretim Teknolojisi Ve Hayat Boyu Öğrenme Dergisi - Instructional Technology and Lifelong Learning, 1-14. https://doi.org/DOI: 10.52911/itall.1244453

Floridi, L. (2014). *The Fourth Revolution: How the Infosphere is Reshaping Human Reality*. Oxford University Press.

Floridi, L. (2015). *The Onlife Manifesto: Being Human in a Hyperconnected Era*. Springer.

Floridi, L. (2016). *The fourth revolution: How the infosphere is reshaping human reality*. Oxford University Press.

Floridi, L., Cowls, J., Beltrametti, M., Chatila, R., Chazerand, P., Dignum, V., & Schafer, B. (2018). AI4People—An ethical framework for a good AI society: Opportunities, risks, principles, and recommendations. *Minds and Machines*, *28*(4), 689–707. DOI: 10.1007/s11023-018-9482-5 PMID: 30930541

Franco, P. F., & DeLuca, D. A. (2019). Learning Through Action: Creating and Implementing a Strategy Game to Foster Innovative Thinking in Higher Education. In Simulation & Gaming (Vol. 50, Number 1, p. 23). SAGE Publishing. https://doi.org/DOI: 10.1177/1046878118820892

Freire, P. (1970). Pedagogy of the oppressed. *Continuum : an Interdisciplinary Journal on Continuity of Care*.

Freire, P. (2005). *Pedagogy of the Oppressed (30th Anniversary Edition)*. Continuum.

Friesen, N. (2009). *Re-thinking e-Learning Research: Foundations, Methods, and Practices*. Peter Lang.

Fuster-Guilló, A., Pertegal-Felices, M., Jimeno-Morenilla, A., Azorín-López, J., Soliveres, M., & Restrepo-Calle, F. (2019). Evaluating impact on motivation and academic performance of a game-based learning experience using kahoot. *Frontiers in Psychology*, *10*. Advance online publication. DOI: 10.3389/fpsyg.2019.02843 PMID: 31920872

Gamage, K. A. A., Gamage, A., & Dehideniya, S. C. P. (2022). Online and hybrid teaching and learning: Enhance effective student engagement and experience. Education Sciences. mdpi.com

Gamage, K. A. A., Dehideniya, S. C. P., Xu, Z., & Tang, X. (2023). ChatGPT and higher education assessments: More opportunities than concerns? *Journal of Applied Learning and Teaching*, *6*(2), 654–679. DOI: 10.37074/jalt.2023.6.2.32

Gamrat, C., Zimmerman, H., Dudek, J., & Peck, K. (2014). Personalized workplace learning: An exploratory study on digital badging within a teacher professional development program. *British Journal of Educational Technology*, *45*(6), 1136–1148. DOI: 10.1111/bjet.12200

Gao, X., & Feng, H. (2023). AI-Driven Productivity Gains: Artificial Intelligence and Firm Productivity. In Sustainability (Vol. 15, Issue 11, p. 8934). Multidisciplinary Digital Publishing Institute. https://doi.org/DOI: 10.3390/su15118934

Gardinier, K. A.-L. (2021). Introduction contextualising global flows of competency-based education: Polysemy, hybridity and silences. *Comparative Education*, •••, 1–18.

Garlinska, M., Osial, M., Proniewska, K., & Pregowska, A. (2023). *The influence of emerging technologies on distance education. Electronics.* mdpi.com *Govea, J., Ocampo Edye, E.* Revelo-Tapia.

Garroutte, E., & Westcott, K. (2013). The story is a living being: Companionship with stories in Anishinaabe Studies. In Doerfler, J., Sinclair, N. J., & Stark, H. K. (Eds.), *Centering Anishinaabeg studies: Understanding the world through stories* (pp. 61–80).

Gearhart, C. A., Blaydes, M., & McCarthy, C. J. (2022). Barriers to and facilitators for teachers' wellbeing. Frontiers in Psychology. frontiersin.org

Gee, J. P. (2007). *What video games have to teach us about learning and literacy* (2nd ed.). Palgrave Macmillan.

Gehlen, A. (1988). *Man: His Nature and Place in the World.* Columbia University Press.

George, A. S., & George, A. S. H. (2023). A review of ChatGPT AI's impact on several business sectors. *Partners Universal International Innovation Journal*, *1*(1), 9–23.

George, B., & Wooden, O. (2023). Managing the Strategic Transformation of Higher Education through Artificial Intelligence. *Administrative Sciences*, *13*(9), 196. DOI: 10.3390/admsci13090196

Ge, X., Xu, C., Misaki, D., Markus, H. R., & Tsai, J. L. (2024). *How Culture Shapes What People Want From AI.*, DOI: 10.1145/3613904.3642660

Ghosh, O & Kumar, B. (2025). The Impact of Remote Experimentation on Student Engagement. *Revolutionizing Education With Remote Experimentation and Learning Analytics,* 523-544, DOI: DOI: 10.4018/979-8-3693-8593-7.ch031

Giffinger, R., Fertner, C., Kramar, H., ... (2007). "Smart Cities: Ranking of European Medium-Sized Cities." *Vienna University of Technology*, 1-28.

Glaude, E. S.Jr. (2020). *Begin again: James Baldwin's America and its urgent lessons for our own.* Crown.

Gligorea, I., Cioca, M., Oancea, R., Gorski, A.-T., Gorski, H., & Tudorache, P. (2023). Adaptive Learning Using Artificial Intelligence in e-Learning: A Literature Review [Review of Adaptive Learning Using Artificial Intelligence in e-Learning: A Literature Review]. Education Sciences, 13(12), 1216. Multidisciplinary Digital Publishing Institute. https://doi.org/DOI: 10.3390/educsci13121216

Gligorea, I., Yaseen, M., Cioca, M., Gorski, H., & Oancea, R. (2022). An interpretable framework for an efficient analysis of students' academic performance. *Sustainability*, *14*(14), 8885. DOI: 10.3390/su14148885

Godbole, V., Kukrety, S., Gautam, P., Bisht, M., & Pal, M. K. (2023). Bioleaching for Heavy Metal Extraction from E-waste: A Sustainable Approach. In *Microbial Technology for Sustainable E-waste Management.* Springer International Publishing., DOI: 10.1007/978-3-031-25678-3_4

Gonfa, Y. H., Tessema, F. B., Tadesse, M. G., Bachheti, A., & Bachheti, R. K. (2023). Medicinally Important Plant Roots and Their Role in Nanoparticles Synthesis and Applications. In *Secondary Metabolites from Medicinal Plants: Nanoparticles Synthesis and their Applications.* CRC Press., DOI: 10.1201/9781003213727-11

Gopal, S., Gupta, P., & Minocha, A. (2023). Advancements in Fin-Tech and Security Challenges of Banking Industry. *4th International Conference on Intelligent Engineering and Management, ICIEM 2023.* https://doi.org/DOI: 10.1109/ICIEM59379.2023.10165876

Government of Canada. (2020). *Directive on Automated Decision-Making.*

Grabner-Hagen, M. M. & Kingsley, T. (2023). From badges to boss challenges: Gamification through need-supporting scaffolded design to instruct and motivate elementary learners. Computers and Education Open. sciencedirect.com

Grady, J. B. (1994). Interdisciplinary Curriculum Development.

Greco, S., & Cinganotto, L. (2023). Re-thinking education in the age of AI. *Journal of E-Learning and Knowledge Society,* I-IV Pages. https://doi.org/DOI: 10.20368/1971-8829/1135873

Gross, N. (2023). What ChatGPT Tells Us about Gender: A Cautionary Tale about Performativity and Gender Biases in AI. In Social Sciences (Vol. 12, Issue 8, p. 435). Multidisciplinary Digital Publishing Institute. https://doi.org/DOI: 10.3390/socsci12080435

Güler, S., & Özkan, Y. (2018). Podcast applications in pre-service language teacher education from a constructivist perspective. *World Journal on Educational Technology Current Issues*, *10*(3), 131–141. DOI: 10.18844/wjet.v10i3.3552

Guo, J., & Li, B. (2018). The Application of Medical Artificial Intelligence Technology in Rural Areas of Developing Countries [Review of The Application of Medical Artificial Intelligence Technology in Rural Areas of Developing Countries]. Health Equity, 2(1), 174. Mary Ann Liebert, Inc. https://doi.org/DOI: 10.1089/heq.2018.0037

Gupta, C., Jindal, P., & Malhotra, R. K. (2022). A Study of Increasing Adoption Trends of Digital Technologies - An Evidence from Indian Banking. In D. N. & C. A. (Eds.), *AIP Conference Proceedings* (Vol. 2481). American Institute of Physics Inc. https://doi.org/DOI: 10.1063/5.0104572

Gupta, A., Dixit, A. K., Kumar, K. S., Lavanya, C., Chakravarthi, M. K., & Gangodkar, D. (2022). Analyzing Robotics and Computer Integrated Manufacturing of Key Areas Using Cloud Computing. *Proceedings of 5th International Conference on Contemporary Computing and Informatics, IC3I 2022*, 194 – 199. https://doi.org/DOI: 10.1109/IC3I56241.2022.10072581

Gupta, P., Gopal, S., Sharma, M., Joshi, S., Sahani, C., & Ahalawat, K. (2023). Agriculture Informatics and Communication: Paradigm of E-Governance and Drone Technology for Crop Monitoring. *9th International Conference on Smart Computing and Communications: Intelligent Technologies and Applications, ICSCC 2023*, 113 – 118. https://doi.org/DOI: 10.1109/ICSCC59169.2023.10335058

Gyongyosi, L., & Imre, S. (2019). A survey on quantum computing technology. *Computer Science Review*, *31*, 51–71.

Hacker, S. (n.d.). proposal.docx. Retrieved January 14, 2025, from https://www.cs.cmu.edu/~shacker/thesis/proposal.pdf

Hajoary, P. K., Balachandra, P., & Garza-Reyes, J. A. (2023). Industry 4.0 maturity and readiness assessment: An empirical validation using Confirmatory Composite Analysis. *Production Planning and Control*. Advance online publication. DOI: 10.1080/09537287.2023.2210545

Halagatti, M., Gadag, S., Mahantshetti, S., Hiremath, C. V., Tharkude, D., & Banakar, V. (2023). Artificial intelligence: The new tool of disruption in educational performance assessment. In Tyagi, P., Grima, S., Sood, K., Balamurugan, B., Özen, E., & Eleftherios, T. (Eds.), *Smart analytics, artificial intelligence and sustainable performance management in a global digitalised economy (110A)* (pp. 261–287). Emerald Publishing Limited., DOI: 10.1108/S1569-37592023000110A014

Halkiopoulos, C. & Gkintoni, E. (2024). Leveraging AI in e-learning: Personalized learning and adaptive assessment through cognitive neuropsychology—A systematic analysis. Electronics. mdpi.com

Hamilton, J. G., & Klebba, J. M. (2011). Experiential learning: A course design process for critical thinking. *American Journal of Business Education*, *4*(12), 1–12.

Hanson, B., Stall, S., Cutcher-Gershenfeld, J., Vrouwenvelder, K., Wirz, C. D., Rao, Y., & Peng, G. (2023). Garbage in, garbage out: mitigating risks and maximizing benefits of AI in research. In Nature (Vol. 623, Issue 7985, p. 28). Nature Portfolio. https://doi.org/DOI: 10.1038/d41586-023-03316-8

Harari, Y. N. (2014). *Sapiens: A brief history of humankind*. Random House.

Haraway, D. (1985). A manifesto for cyborgs: Science, technology, and socialist feminism in the 1980s. *Socialist Review*, *80*, 65–108.

Haraway, D. (1988). Situated Knowledges: The Science Question in Feminism and the Privilege of Partial Perspective. *Feminist Studies*, *14*(3), 575–599.

Harden, R. M., & Stamper, N. (1999). What is a spiral curriculum? *Medical Teacher*, *21*(2), 141–143. PMID: 21275727

Harju, V., Koskinen, A., & Pehkonen, L. (2019). An exploration of longitudinal studies of digital learning. *Educational Research*, *61*(4), 388–407. DOI: 10.1080/00131881.2019.1660586

Harrer, S. (2023). Attention is not all you need: The complicated case of ethically using large language models in healthcare and medicine. *EBioMedicine*, *90*, 104512. DOI: 10.1016/j.ebiom.2023.104512 PMID: 36924620

Harry, A. (2023). Role of ai in education. *Interdiciplinary Journal and Hummanity (Injurity)*, *2*(3), 260–268. DOI: 10.58631/injurity.v2i3.52

Hayles, N. K. (1999). *How We Became Posthuman: Virtual Bodies in Cybernetics, Literature, and Informatics*. University of Chicago Press.

Hedderich, M. A., Lange, L., Adel, H., Strötgen, J., & Klakow, D. (2021). A Survey on Recent Approaches for Natural Language Processing in Low-Resource Scenarios. In *Proceedings of the 2022 Conference of the North American Chapter of the Association for Computational Linguistics: Human Language Technologies*. https://doi.org/DOI: 10.18653/v1/2021.naacl-main.201

Hegel, G. (1967). *The Phenomenology of the Mind* (Baillie, J. B., Trans.). Harper Torchbooks.

Hegel, G. W. F. (1977). *The Phenomenology of Spirit* (Miller, A. V., Trans.). Oxford University Press. (Original work published 1807)

Heick, T. (2020). *How to teach digital citizenship in the classroom: Resources for teachers*. TeachThought.

Heidegger, M. (1927/1962). *Being and Time* (Macquarrie, J., & Robinson, E., Trans.). Harper & Row.

Heidegger, M. (1959). *An Introduction to Metaphysics* (Manheim, R., Trans.). Yale University Press.

Heidegger, M. (1971). *Poetry, Language, Thought* (Hofstader, A., Trans.). Harper and Row.

Heidegger, M. (1977). *The Question Concerning Technology, and Other Essays*. Harper Torchbooks.

Heidegger, M. (1977). *The Question Concerning Technology*. Harper & Row.

Heidegger, M. (2000). *Elucidations of Holderlin's Poetry* (Hoeller, K., Trans.). Humanity Books.

hÉigeartaigh, S. Ó., Whittlestone, J., Liu, Y., Zeng, Y., & Liu, Z. (2020). Overcoming Barriers to Cross-cultural Cooperation in AI Ethics and Governance. In Philosophy & Technology (Vol. 33, Issue 4, p. 571). Springer Nature (Netherlands). https://doi.org/DOI: 10.1007/s13347-020-00402-x

Heilporn, G., Lakhal, S., & Bélisle, M. (2021). An examination of teachers' strategies to foster student engagement in blended learning in higher education. [springer.com]. *International Journal of Educational Technology in Higher Education*, *18*(1), 25. PMID: 34805484

Hellín, C. J., Calles-Esteban, F., Valledor, A., Gómez, J., Otón-Tortosa, S., & Tayebi, A. (2023). Enhancing student motivation and engagement through a gamified learning environment. [mdpi.com]. *Sustainability*, *15*(19), 14119.

Hellín, C. J., Calles-Esteban, F., Valledor, A., Gómez, J., Otón-Tortosa, S., & Tayebi, A. (2023). Enhancing Student Motivation and Engagement through a Gamified Learning Environment. *Sustainability*, *15*(19), 14119. DOI: 10.3390/su151914119

Helm, P., Bella, G., Koch, G., & Giunchiglia, F. (2023). Diversity and Language Technology: How Techno-Linguistic Bias Can Cause Epistemic Injustice. In arXiv (Cornell University). Cornell University. https://doi.org/DOI: 10.48550/arXiv.2307

Hew, K., & Cheung, W. (2014). Students' and Instructors' Use of Massive Open Online Courses (MOOCs): Motivations and Challenges. *Educational Research Review*, *12*, 45–58.

Hidayat, L. E., Amalia, S. N., Rohmana, W. I. M., Virdyna, N. K., Ardi, P., & Suryati, N. (2025). EFL Teachers' Understanding and Practices of Classroom-Based Diagnostic Assessment in Differentiated Instruction. In Differentiated Instruction, Equity, and Inclusion in Language Education (pp. 181-218). IGI Global Scientific Publishing. [HTML]

Hidayat, D. (2021). The implementation of gamification system in asian higher education teaching. *Journal of Games Game Art and Gamification*, *2*(1). Advance online publication. DOI: 10.21512/jggag.v2i1.7218

Hoffman, S. H. (2023). The Emerging Hazard of AI-Related Health Care Discrimination. https://onlinelibrary.wiley.com/doi/10.1002/hast.1203

Hollands, F., Pan, Y., & Escueta, M. (2019). What is the potential for applying cost-utility analysis to facilitate evidence-based decision making in schools? *Educational Researcher*, *48*(5), 287–295. DOI: 10.3102/0013189x19852101

Holmes, W., Bialik, M., & Fadel, C. (2019). *Artificial intelligence in education: Promises and implications for teaching and learning*. Center for Curriculum Redesign.

Hooda, M., Rana, C., Dahiya, O., Rizwan, A., & Hossain, M. S. (2022). Artificial intelligence for assessment and feedback to enhance student success in higher education. *Mathematical Problems in Engineering*, *2022*, 5215722. Advance online publication. DOI: 10.1155/2022/5215722

Hossain, G. F., Case, D., & Smith, C. (2024). Technologies and Student Feedback Collection and Analysis. *Teaching And Learning In The Digital Era. Issues & Studies*, •••, 327.

Huang, A. Y. Q., Lu, O. H. T., & Yang, S. J. H. (2023). Effects of artificial Intelligence–Enabled personalized recommendations on learners' learning engagement, motivation, and outcomes in a flipped classroom. *Computers & Education*, *194*, 104684. DOI: 10.1016/j.compedu.2022.104684

Huang, L. (2023). Ethics of artificial intelligence in education: Student privacy and data protection. *Science Insights Education Frontiers*, *16*(2), 2577–2587.

Huang, M., & Liu, T. F. (2016). Education Facing to Thinking of Heidegger and Its Theoretical Predicaments. *Educational Research*, *12*, 12–21.

Hub, E. H. E. (2022). Minoritised languages, education, and technology: Current practices and future directions in low- and middle-income countries. https://doi.org/DOI: 10.53832/edtechhub.0127

Huesca, G., Campos, G., Larre, M., & Pérez-Lezama, C. (2023). Implementation of a mixed strategy of gamification and flipped learning in undergraduate basic programming courses. *Education Sciences*, *13*(5), 474. DOI: 10.3390/educsci13050474

Hulley, S. B. (2013). *Designing Clinical Research* (4th ed.)., http://ci.nii.ac.jp/ncid/BA7981371X

Hung, R., Zhengmei, P., Kato, M., Nishihira, T., Okabe, M., Di, X., Kwak, D.-J., Hwang, K., Tschong, Y., Chien, C.-H., Peters, M. A., & Tesar, M. (2020). Philosophy of education in a new key: East Asia. *Educational Philosophy and Theory*. Advance online publication. DOI: 10.1080/00131857.2020.1772028

Ibrahim, H., Asim, R., Zaffar, F., Rahwan, T., & Zaki, Y. (2023). Rethinking homework in the age of artificial intelligence. *IEEE Intelligent Systems*, *38*(2), 24–27. DOI: 10.1109/MIS.2023.3255599

Ifenthaler, D., & Yau, J. Y. K. (2020). Utilising learning analytics to support study success in higher education. *Technology. Knowledge and Learning*, *25*, 305–320.

Ihde, D. (1990). *Technology and the Lifeworld*. Indiana University Press.

Ihde, D. (2003). A Phenomenology of Technics. In Kaplan, D. (Ed.), *Readings in the Philosophy of Technology* (pp. 137–160). Rowman & Littlefield Publisher.

International Society for Technology in Education (ISTE). (2016). *ISTE Standards for Students*.

Ishak, S. A., Din, R., & Hasran, U. A. (2020). Defining Digital Game-Based Learning for Science, Technology, Engineering, and Mathematics: A New Perspective on Design and Developmental Research. In Journal of Medical Internet Research (Vol. 23, Number 2). JMIR Publications. https://doi.org/DOI: 10.2196/20537

Ismail, S. M., Rahul, D. R., Patra, I., & Rezvani, E. (2022). Formative vs. summative assessment: impacts on academic motivation, attitude toward learning, test anxiety, and self-regulation skill. In Language Testing in Asia (Vol. 12, Number 1). Springer Science+Business Media. https://doi.org/DOI: 10.1186/s40468-022-00191-4

Ismail, S. M., Rahul, D. R., Patra, I., & Rezvani, E. (2022). Formative vs. summative assessment: impacts on academic motivation, attitude toward learning, test anxiety, and self-regulation skill. Language Testing in Asia. springer.com

Iwamoto, T., Matsumoto, M., Kuriyama, M., Minami, R., & Murao, K. (2023). Study on Experiences to Enhance Design Thinking Skills. In *2022 Portland International Conference on Management of Engineering and Technology (PICMET)* (p. 1). https://doi.org/DOI: 10.23919/picmet59654.2023.10216862

Jackson, A. Y., & Mazzei, L. A. (2012). *Thinking with theory in qualitative research*. Routledge Press.

Jackson, L., Alston, K., Bialystok, L., Blum, L., Burbules, N. C., Chinnery, A., Hansen, D. T., Hytten, K., Mayo, C., Norris, T., Stitzlein, S. M., Thompson, W. C., Waks, L., Peters, M. A., & Tesar, M. (2020a). Philosophy of education in a new key: Snapshot 2020 from the United States and Canada. *Educational Philosophy and Theory*. Advance online publication. DOI: 10.1080/00131857.2020.1821189

Jandric, P., Jaldemark, J., Hurley, Z., Bartram, B., Matthews, A., Jopling, M., Manero, J., MacKenzie, M., & Irwin, J. ~ Rothmuller, N., Green, B., Ralston, S. J., Pyyhtinen, O., Hayes, S., Wright, J., Peters, M. A., & Tesar, M. (2020). Philosophy of education in a new key: Who remembers Greta Thunberg? Education and environment after the coronavirus. *Educational Philosophy and Theory*. Advance online publication. DOI: 10.1080/00131857.2020.1811678

Januszewski, A., & Persichitte, K. (2008). A History of the AECT's Definitions of Educational Technology. In Januszewski, A., & Molenda, M. (Eds.), *Educational Technology: A Definition with Commentary* (pp. 259–282). Routledge.

Jaswal, N., Kukreja, V., Sharma, R., Chaudhary, P., & Garg, A. (2023). Citrus Leaf Scab Multi-Class Classification: A Hybrid Deep Learning Model for Precision Agriculture. *2023 4th IEEE Global Conference for Advancement in Technology, GCAT 2023*. https://doi.org/DOI: 10.1109/GCAT59970.2023.10353507

Jayavardhini, P. (2024). Ai study partner: Development of an llm and gen ai-enhanced study assistant tool. *Interantional Journal of Scientific Research in Engineering and Management*, *08*(03), 1–5. DOI: 10.55041/ijsrem29626

Ji, H., Suo, L., & Hua, C. (2024). Ai performance assessment in blended learning: Mechanisms and effects on students' continuous learning motivation. *Frontiers in Psychology*, *15*. Advance online publication. DOI: 10.3389/fpsyg.2024.1447680 PMID: 39737232

Jindal, G., Tiwari, V., Mahomad, R., Gehlot, A., Jindal, M., & Bordoloi, D. (2023). Predictive Design for Quality Assessment Employing Cloud Computing And Machine Learning. *2023 3rd International Conference on Advance Computing and Innovative Technologies in Engineering, ICACITE 2023*, 461 – 465. https://doi.org/DOI: 10.1109/ICACITE57410.2023.10182915

Jindal, T., Sheoliha, N., Kishore, K., Uike, D., Khurana, S., & Verma, D. (2022). A Conceptual Analysis on the Impact of Internet of Things (IOT) Towards on Digital Marketing Transformation. *2022 2nd International Conference on Advance Computing and Innovative Technologies in Engineering, ICACITE 2022*, 1943 – 1947. https://doi.org/DOI: 10.1109/ICACITE53722.2022.9823714

Jobin, A., & Ienca, M. (2019). The global landscape of ai ethics guidelines. *Nature Machine Intelligence, 1*(9), 389–399. DOI: 10.1038/s42256-019-0088-2

Jobin, A., Ienca, M., & Vayena, E. (2019). The global landscape of AI ethics guidelines. *Nature Machine Intelligence, 1*(9), 389–399.

Johnson, D., Deterding, S., Kuhn, K., Staneva, A., Stoyanov, S., & Hides, L. (2016). Gamification for health and wellbeing: A systematic review of the literature. *Internet Interventions : the Application of Information Technology in Mental and Behavioural Health, 6*, 89–106. DOI: 10.1016/j.invent.2016.10.002 PMID: 30135818

Jonassen, D. H. (1999). Designing constructivist learning environments. In Reigeluth, C. M. (Ed.), *Instructional-design theories and models: A new paradigm of instructional theory* (Vol. II, pp. 215–239). Lawrence Erlbaum Associates.

Jones, H., & Hammond, L. (2022, October 19). The journey not the destination: Liminality and lifelong learning. In Medical Education (Vol. 57, Number 2, p. 115). Wiley. https://doi.org/DOI: 10.1111/medu.14956

Joshi, P., Santy, S., Budhiraja, A., Bali, K., & Choudhury, M. (2020). The state and fate of linguistic diversity and inclusion in the NLP world. arXiv preprint arXiv:2004.09095.

Joshi, K., Patil, S., Gupta, S., & Khanna, R. (2022). Role of Pranayma in emotional maturity for improving health. *Journal of Medical Pharmaceutical and Allied Sciences, 11*(2), 4569–4573. DOI: 10.55522/jmpas.V11I2.2033

Joshi, K., Sharma, R., Singh, N., & Sharma, B. (2023). Digital World of Cloud Computing and Wireless Networking: Challenges and Risks. In *Applications of Artificial Intelligence in Wireless Communication Systems*. IGI Global., DOI: 10.4018/978-1-6684-7348-1.ch003

Josphineleela, R., Jyothi, M., Natrayan, L., Kaviarasu, A., & Sharma, M. (2023). Development of IoT based Health Monitoring System for Disables using Microcontroller. *Proceedings - 7th International Conference on Computing Methodologies and Communication, ICCMC 2023*, 1380 – 1384. https://doi.org/DOI: 10.1109/ICCMC56507.2023.10084026

JOYCE. J., & Harris, L. A. (2018). Artificial Intelligence (AI) and Education. https://digital.library.unt.edu/ark:/67531/metadc1228526/m2/1/high_res_d/IF10937_2018Aug01.pdf

Julita, R. (2024). The impact of gamification on efl students' reading comprehension. *JEFLE*, *4*(2), 136. DOI: 10.26418/jefle.v4i2.74901

Jumper, J., Evans, R., Pritzel, A., Green, T., Figurnov, M., Ronneberger, O., & Hassabis, D. (2021). Highly accurate protein structure prediction with AlphaFold. *Nature*, *596*(7873), 583–589. DOI: 10.1038/s41586-021-03819-2 PMID: 34265844

Kai, S., Almeda, M. V., Baker, R. S., Heffernan, C., & Heffernan, N. (2018). Decision tree modeling of wheel spinning and productive persistence in skill builders. *Journal of Educational Data Mining*, *10*(1), 789–822. DOI: 10.5281/zenodo.3344810

Kaliappan, S., Natrayan, L., & Garg, N. (2023). Checking and Supervisory System for Calculation of Industrial Constraints using Embedded System. *Proceedings of the 4th International Conference on Smart Electronics and Communication, ICOSEC 2023*, 87 – 90. https://doi.org/DOI: 10.1109/ICOSEC58147.2023.10275952

Kamenskih, A. (2022). The analysis of security and privacy risks in smart education environments. *Journal of Smart Cities and Society*, *1*(1), 17–29.

Kamra, J., Mani, A. P., & Tripathi, V. M. (2023). Decarbonization Trajectory in Cement Industry. In S. P., N. S., R. J.J.P.C., R. J.J.P.C., R. J.J.P.C., L.-I. G.-A. D., P. T., C. L., & P. L. (Eds.), *2023 8th International Conference on Smart and Sustainable Technologies, SpliTech 2023*. Institute of Electrical and Electronics Engineers Inc. https://doi.org/DOI: 10.23919/SpliTech58164.2023.10193682

Kamruzzaman, M. (2023). Ai- and iot-assisted sustainable education systems during pandemics, such as covid-19, for smart cities. *Sustainability*, *15*(10), 8354. DOI: 10.3390/su15108354

Kang, J., Kang, C., Yoon, J., Ji, H., Li, T., Hyunmi, M., & Han, J. (2023). Dancing on the inside: A qualitative study on online dance learning with teacher-ai cooperation. *Education and Information Technologies*, *28*(9), 12111–12141. DOI: 10.1007/s10639-023-11649-0 PMID: 37361738

Kannan, P. R., Periasamy, K., Pravin, P., & Vinod Kumaar, J. R. (2022). An experimental investigation of wire breakage and performance optimisation of WEDM process on machining of recycled aluminium alloy metal matrix composite. *Materials Science Poland*, *40*(3), 12–26. DOI: 10.2478/msp-2022-0030

Kanojia, P., Malhotra, R. K., & Uniyal, A. K. (2022). Organizational Commitment and the Academic Staff in HEI's in North West India. *Proceedings - 2022 International Conference on Recent Trends in Microelectronics, Automation, Computing and Communications Systems, ICMACC 2022*, 365–370. https://doi.org/DOI: 10.1109/ICMACC54824.2022.10093347

Kant, I. (1990). *Kant on Education*. Heath and Co.

Kant, I. (1996). *Groundwork of the Metaphysics of Morals* (Gregor, M., Trans.). Cambridge University Press. (Original work published 1785)

Karabıyık, Ü. (2024). Investigation of the effect of gamified learning on motivation and success in math class. *Journal of Education and Practice*, *8*(1), 32–52. DOI: 10.47941/jep.1645

Katiyar, P. (2024). Ai-driven personalized learning systems: enhancing educational effectiveness. eatp. https://doi.org/DOI: 10.53555/kuey.v30i5.4961

Kato, M., Saito, N., Matsushita, R., Ueno, M., Izawa, S., Maruyama, Y., Sugita, H., Ono, F., Muroi, R., Miyazaki, Y., Yamana, J., Peters, M. A., & Tesar, M. (2020). Philosophy of education in a new key: Voices from Japan. *Educational Philosophy and Theory*. Advance online publication. DOI: 10.1080/00131857.2020.1802819

Kaur, D., & Aziz, A. A. (2020). The Use of Language Game in Enhancing Students' Speaking Skills. In International Journal of Academic Research in Business and Social Sciences (Vol. 10, Number 12). https://doi.org/DOI: 10.6007/ijarbss/v10-i12/8369

Kaur, J., Khanna, R., Kumar, R., & Sunil, G. (2024). Role of Blockchain Technologies in Goods and Services Tax. *Proceedings - 2024 3rd International Conference on Sentiment Analysis and Deep Learning, ICSADL 2024*, 607–612. https://doi.org/DOI: 10.1109/ICSADL61749.2024.00104

Kaushal, D., Kumar, S., Raj, R., & Negi, A. (2022). Understanding the effect of entrepreneurial orientation, innovation capability and differentiation strategy on firm performance: A study on small and medium enterprises. *International Journal of Business and Globalisation*, *30*(1), 57–80. DOI: 10.1504/IJBG.2022.122280

Kayal, A. (2024). Transformative Pedagogy: A Comprehensive Framework for AI Integration in Education. In *Explainable AI for Education: Recent Trends and Challenges* (pp. 247–270). Springer Nature Switzerland.

Kayyali, M. (2024). *Global Perspectives on Personalized Learning: Case Studies and Best Practices*. Transforming Education for Personalized Learning. [HTML]

Kelley, P. G., Yang, Y., Heldreth, C., Moessner, C., Sedley, A., Kramm, A., Newman, D. T., & Woodruff, A. (2021). Exciting, Useful, Worrying, Futuristic: Public Perception of Artificial Intelligence in 8 Countries. https://doi.org/DOI: 10.1145/3461702.3462605

KepMenParEkraf. (2023, June 20). *BN.2022/No.172,* jdih.kemenparekraf.go.id*: 7 hlm.* Retrieved from jdih.kemenparekraf.go.id/katalog-889-produk-hukum: BN.2022/No.172, jdih.kemenparekraf.go.id: 7 hlm.

Khakpour, A., & Colomo-Palacios, R. (2020). Convergence of gamification and machine learning: A systematic literature review. *Technology Knowledge and Learning*, *26*(3), 597–636. DOI: 10.1007/s10758-020-09456-4

Khamaj, A. & Ali, A. M. (2024). Adapting user experience with reinforcement learning: Personalizing interfaces based on user behavior analysis in real-time. Alexandria Engineering Journal. sciencedirect.com

Khan, A. A., Akbar, M. A., Fahmideh, M., Peng, L., Waseem, M., Ahmad, A., Niazi, M., & Abrahamsson, P. (2022). AI Ethics: An Empirical Study on the Views of Practitioners and Lawmakers. In arXiv (Cornell University). Cornell University. https://doi.org/DOI: 10.48550/arXiv.2207

Khanna, L. S., Yadav, P. S., Maurya, S., & Vimal, V. (2023). Integral Role of Data Science in Startup Evolution. *Proceedings - 2023 15th IEEE International Conference on Computational Intelligence and Communication Networks, CICN 2023*, 720 – 726. https://doi.org/DOI: 10.1109/CICN59264.2023.10402129

Khanna, R., Jindal, P., & Noja, G. G. (2023). Blockchain technologies, a catalyst for insurance sector. In *The Application of Emerging Technology and Blockchain in the Insurance Industry*.

Khanuja, S. K. Sebastian Ruder,Partha P. Talukdar. (2022). Evaluating the Diversity, Equity, and Inclusion of NLP Technology: A Case Study for Indian Languages. https://arxiv.org/pdf/2205.12676.pdf

Khater, A., Zaaqoq, A., Wahdan, M., & Ashry, S. (2023). Knowledge and attitude of ain shams university medical students towards artificial intelligence and its application in medical education and practice. *Educational Research and Innovation Journal*, *3*(10), 29–42. DOI: 10.21608/erji.2023.306718

Khosrow-Pour, M. (Ed.). (2015). *STEM education: Concepts, methodologies, tools, and applications* (Vol. 1–3). IGI Global.

Kim, J., & Castelli, D. (2021). Effects of gamification on behavioral change in education: A meta-analysis. *International Journal of Environmental Research and Public Health, 18*(7), 3550. DOI: 10.3390/ijerph18073550 PMID: 33805530

Kirkwood, A., & Price, L. (2014). Technology-Enhanced Learning and Teaching in Higher Education: What is 'Enhanced' and How Do We Know? A Critical Literature Review. *Learning, Media and Technology*, *39*(1), 6–36.

Kizilcec, R. F., & Lee, H. (2022). Algorithmic fairness in education. In *The ethics of artificial intelligence in education* (pp. 174–202). Routledge.

Kizito, I. G., & Hassan, S. (2024). PhET Interactive Simulations as an effective tool for teaching chemistry: A review. *International Journal of STEM Education, 19*(1), 1–12.

Koh, E., & Doroudi, S. (2023). Learning, teaching, and assessment with generative artificial intelligence: Towards a plateau of productivity. *Learning: Research and Practice*, *9*(2), 109–116. DOI: 10.1080/23735082.2023.2264086

Kohli, P., Sharma, S., & Matta, P. (2022). Secured Authentication Schemes of 6G Driven Vehicular Communication Network in Industry 5.0 Internet-of-Everything (IoE) Applications: Challenges and Opportunities. *2022 IEEE 2nd International Conference on Mobile Networks and Wireless Communications, ICMNWC 2022*. https://doi.org/DOI: 10.1109/ICMNWC56175.2022.10031781

Kollipara, V. N. H., Kalakota, S. K., Chamarthi, S., Ramani, S., Malik, P., & Karuppiah, M. (2023). Timestamp Based OTP and Enhanced RSA Key Exchange Scheme with SIT Encryption to Secure IoT Devices. *Journal of Cyber Security and Mobility*, *12*(1), 77–102. DOI: 10.13052/jcsm2245-1439.1214

Komkowski, T., Antony, J., Garza-Reyes, J. A., Tortorella, G. L., & Pongboonchai-Empl, T. (2023a). A systematic review of the integration of Industry 4.0 with quality-related operational excellence methodologies. *The Quality Management Journal*, *30*(1), 3–15. DOI: 10.1080/10686967.2022.2144783

Komkowski, T., Antony, J., Garza-Reyes, J. A., Tortorella, G. L., & Pongboonchai-Empl, T. (2023b). Integrating Lean Management with Industry 4.0: An explorative Dynamic Capabilities theory perspective. *Production Planning and Control*. Advance online publication. DOI: 10.1080/09537287.2023.2294297

Komljenovic, J. (2022). The future of value in digitalised higher education: why data privacy should not be our biggest concern. Higher Education. springer.com

Komninos, N. (2011). Intelligent Cities: Variable Geographies of Smart Urbanism. *Intelligent Buildings International*, *3*(3), 172–188.

Kong, Y. (2021). The role of experiential learning on students' motivation and classroom engagement. Frontiers in psychology. frontiersin.org

Kour, M., Taneja, S., Özen, E., Sood, K., & Grima, S. (2025). *Financial Landscape Transformation Technological Disruptions*.

Kowalski, R. M., Giumetti, G. W., Schroeder, A. N., & Lattanner, M. R. (2014). Bullying in the digital age: A critical review and meta-analysis of cyberbullying research among youth. *Psychological Bulletin, 140*(4), 1073–1137. PMID: 24512111

Kowsalya, K., & Rani, R. P. J. Ritu, Bhiyana, M., Saini, M., & Patil, P. P. (2023). Blockchain-Internet of things-Machine Learning: Development of Traceable System for Multi Purposes. *2023 3rd International Conference on Advance Computing and Innovative Technologies in Engineering, ICACITE 2023*, 1112 – 1115. https://doi .org/DOI: 10.1109/ICACITE57410.2023.10183065

Krishna, A., & Meda, V. (2024). Planning and Requirements Management in Projects. In *AI Integration in Software Development and Operations: Transformation Through AI Infusion in DevOps, Testing, and SRE* (pp. 59–105). Apress.

Krishna, S. H., Upadhyay, A., Tewari, M., Gehlot, A., Girimurugan, B., & Pundir, S. (2022). Empirical investigation of the key machine learning elements promoting e-business using an SEM framework. *Proceedings of 5th International Conference on Contemporary Computing and Informatics, IC3I 2022*, 1960 – 1964. https://doi .org/DOI: 10.1109/IC3I56241.2022.10072712

Krissilov, V., Huy, V. N., & Zinovatna, S. L. (2018). INFORMATION MODEL OF DISTANCE LEARNING SYSTEM IN TERMS OF DATA COMMUNICATION IN HETEROGENEOUS INTERNET NETWORKS. In Odes'kyi Politechnichnyi Universytet Pratsi (Vol. 1, Number 54, p. 62). Odesa National Polytechnic University. https://doi.org/DOI: 10.15276/opu.1.54.2018.08

Kucher, T. (2021). Principles and Best Practices of Designing Digital Game-Based Learning Environments. In International Journal of Technology in Education and Science (Vol. 5, Number 2, p. 213). https://doi.org/DOI: 10.46328/ijtes.190

Kuhail, M. A., ElSayary, A., Farooq, S., & Alghamdi, A. (2022). Exploring immersive learning experiences: A survey. Informatics. mdpi.com

Kukulska-Hulme, A., Lee, H., & Norris, L. (2017). The Handbook of Technology and Second Language Teaching and Learning. In Chapelle, C. A., & Sauro, S. (Eds.), *The handbook of technology and second language teaching and learning*. Wiley., DOI: 10.1002/9781118914069

Kumar, A. S., & Desi, A. B. (2023). Collaborative logistics, tools of machine and supply chain services in the world wide industry 4.0 framework. In *Artificial Intelligence, Blockchain, Computing and Security: Volume 2* (Vol. 2). CRC Press. https://doi.org/DOI: 10.1201/9781032684994-15

Kumar, R., Lande, A., Kumar, D., Malhotra, R. K., & Sharma, A. (2023). Technology Bridging -in Entrepreneurs and Consumers in Product Development. *ISED 2023 - International Conference on Intelligent Systems and Embedded Design*. https://doi.org/DOI: 10.1109/ISED59382.2023.10444599

Kumar, R., Malhotra, R. K., Pandey, S., Gehlot, A., Gautam, I., & Chamola, S. (2023). Role of Artificial Intelligence in Input Tax Credit Reconciliation. *Proceedings - 2023 3rd International Conference on Pervasive Computing and Social Networking, ICPCSN 2023*, 497–501. https://doi.org/DOI: 10.1109/ICPCSN58827.2023.00086

Kumar, V., & Korovin, G. (2023). A Comparision of Digital Transformation of Industry in the Russian Federation with the European Union. In K. V., K. G.L., A. V., & K. E. (Eds.), *Lecture Notes in Information Systems and Organisation: Vol. 61 LNISO* (pp. 45 – 57). Springer Science and Business Media Deutschland GmbH. https://doi.org/DOI: 10.1007/978-3-031-30351-7_5

Kumar, A., Saxena, M., Sastry, R. V. L. S. N., Chaudhari, A., Singh, R., & Malathy, V. (2023). Internet of Things and Blockchain Data Supplier for Intelligent Applications. *Proceedings of International Conference on Contemporary Computing and Informatics, IC3I 2023*, 2218 – 2223. https://doi.org/DOI: 10.1109/IC3I59117.2023.10397630

Kumar, R., Goel, R., Singh, T., Mohanty, S. M., Gupta, D., Alkhayyat, A., & Khanna, R. (2024). Sustainable Finance Factors in Indian Economy: Analysis on Policy of Climate Change and Energy Sector. *Fluctuation and Noise Letters*, *23*(2). Advance online publication. DOI: 10.1142/S0219477524400042

Kumar, R., Kandpal, B., & Ahmad, V. (2023). Industrial IoT (IIOT): Security Threats and Countermeasures. *International Conference on Innovative Data Communication Technologies and Application, ICIDCA 2023 - Proceedings*, 829 – 833. https://doi .org/DOI: 10.1109/ICIDCA56705.2023.10100145

Kumar, R., Kathuria, S., Malholtra, R. K., Kumar, A., Gehlot, A., & Joshi, K. (2023). Role of Cloud Computing in Goods and Services Tax(GST) and Future Application. *2nd International Conference on Sustainable Computing and Data Communication Systems, ICSCDS 2023 - Proceedings*, 1443–1447. https://doi.org/DOI: 10.1109/ICSCDS56580.2023.10104597

Kumar, R., & Khanna, R. (2023a). Role of Artificial Intelligence in Digital Currency and Future Applications. *Proceedings of the 2023 2nd International Conference on Augmented Intelligence and Sustainable Systems, ICAISS 2023*, 42–46. https://doi.org/DOI: 10.1109/ICAISS58487.2023.10250480

Kumar, R., & Khanna, R. (2023b). RPA (Robotic Process Automation) in Finance & Accounting and Future Scope. *Proceedings of the 2023 2nd International Conference on Augmented Intelligence and Sustainable Systems, ICAISS 2023*, 1640–1645. https://doi.org/DOI: 10.1109/ICAISS58487.2023.10250496

Kumar, R., Khannna Malholtra, R., & Grover, C. A. N. (2023). Review on Artificial Intelligence Role in Implementation of Goods and Services Tax(GST) and Future Scope. *2023 International Conference on Artificial Intelligence and Smart Communication, AISC 2023*, 348–351. https://doi.org/DOI: 10.1109/AISC56616.2023.10085030

Kumar, R., Malhotra, R. K., & Grover, N. (2023). Data Mining in Credit Scoring and Future Application. *International Conference on Innovative Data Communication Technologies and Application, ICIDCA 2023 - Proceedings*, 1096–1100. https://doi.org/DOI: 10.1109/ICIDCA56705.2023.10100032

Kumar, R., Saxena, A., & Singh, R. (2023). Robotic Process Automation Bridge -in Banking Institute and Consumers. *2023 International Conference on Disruptive Technologies, ICDT 2023*, 428 – 431. https://doi.org/DOI: 10.1109/ICDT57929.2023.10150500

Kumar, R., Singh, T., Mohanty, S. N., Goel, R., Gupta, D., Alharbi, M., & Khanna, R. (2023). Study on online payments and e-commerce with SOR model. *International Journal of Retail & Distribution Management*. Advance online publication. DOI: 10.1108/IJRDM-03-2023-0137

Kupchyk, L., & Litvinchuk, A. (2021). Constructing personal learning environments through ICT-mediated foreign language instruction. *Journal of Physics: Conference Series*, *1840*(1), 012045. DOI: 10.1088/1742-6596/1840/1/012045

Kurniawati, N., Maolida, E., & Anjaniputra, A. (2018). The praxis of digital literacy in the efl classroom: Digital-immigrant vs digital-native teacher. *Indonesian Journal of Applied Linguistics*, *8*(1). Advance online publication. DOI: 10.17509/ijal.v8i1.11459

Ladson-Billings, G. (2021). I'm here for the hard re-set: Post pandemic pedagogy to preserve our culture. *Equity & Excellence in Education*, *54*(1), 68–78. DOI: 10.1080/10665684.2020.1863883

Ladyman, J. (2007). Ontological, Epistemological, and Methodological Positions. In Kuipers, T. A. F. (Ed.), *General Philosophy of Science* (pp. 303–376). North Holland.

Lameras, P., & Arnab, S. (2021). Power to the Teachers: An Exploratory Review on Artificial Intelligence in Education. *Information (Basel)*, *13*(1), 14. DOI: 10.3390/info13010014

Lang, J. M. (2021). *Small teaching: Everyday lessons from the science of learning*. John Wiley & Sons.

Langley, P. (2019). An Integrative Framework for Artificial Intelligence Education. In *Proceedings of the AAAI Conference on Artificial Intelligence* (Vol. 33, Issue 1, p. 9670). Association for the Advancement of Artificial Intelligence. https://doi.org/DOI: 10.1609/aaai.v33i01.33019670

Larsen, M., Gulis, G., & Pedersen, K. (2011). Use of evidence in local public health work in denmark. *International Journal of Public Health*, *57*(3), 477–483. DOI: 10.1007/s00038-011-0324-y PMID: 22116391

Larsson, S., & Heintz, F. (2020). Transparency in artificial intelligence. *Internet Policy Review*, *9*(2). Advance online publication. DOI: 10.14763/2020.2.1469

Lasekan, O. A., Pachava, V., Godoy Pena, M. T., Golla, S. K., & Raje, M. S. (2024). Investigating factors influencing students' engagement in sustainable online education. [mdpi.com]. *Sustainability*, *16*(2), 689.

Latchem, C. (2014). BJET Editorial: Opening up the Educational Technology Research Agenda. *British Journal of Educational Technology*, *41*(1), 3–11.

Latour, B. (2004). Why Has Critique Run Out of Steam? From Matters of Fact to Matters of Concern. *Critical Inquiry*, *30*(2), 225–248.

Latour, B. (2005). *Reassembling the Social*. Oxford University Press.

Latour, B. (2005). *Reassembling the Social: An Introduction to Actor-Network Theory*. Oxford University Press.

Leavy, S., O'Sullivan, B., & Σιαπέρα, E. (2020). Data, Power and Bias in Artificial Intelligence. In arXiv (Cornell University). Cornell University. https://doi.org/DOI: 10.48550/arXiv.2008

Lee, J., & Soylu, M. Y. (2023). *ChatGPT and assessment in higher education*. Center for 21st Century Universities. https://www.c21u.gatech.edu/sites/default/files/publication/2023/03/C21U%20ChatGPT%20White%20Paper_ Final.pdf

Lee, D., Huh, Y., Lin, C. Y., Reigeluth, C. M., & Lee, E. (2021). Differences in personalized learning practice and technology use in high-and low-performing learner-centered schools in the United States. [springer.com]. *Educational Technology Research and Development*, *69*, 1221–1245. PMID: 33584077

Lee, J. H., Hancock, M. G., & Hu, M. C. (2014). Towards an Effective Framework for Building Smart Cities: Lessons from Seoul and San Francisco. *Technological Forecasting and Social Change*, *89*, 80–99.

Legaki, N., Xi, N., Hamari, J., Karpouzis, K., & Assimakopoulos, V. (2020). The effect of challenge-based gamification on learning: An experiment in the context of statistics education. *International Journal of Human-Computer Studies*, *144*, 102496. DOI: 10.1016/j.ijhcs.2020.102496 PMID: 32565668

Legette, K. B., Hope, E. C., Harris, J., & Griffin, C. B. (2021). *Integrating Culturally Relevant Pedagogy with Teacher Social and Emotional Competencies and Capacities Training to Support Racially Minoritized Students*. https://doi.org/DOI: 10.1108/S0749-742320210000021007

Lewin, D., & Lundie, D. (2016). Philosophies of digital pedagogy. *Studies in Philosophy and Education*, *3*(35), 235–240.

Lewis, E. (2021). Best Practices for Improving the Quality of the Online Course Design and Learners Experience. *The Journal of Continuing Higher Education*, *69*(1), 61–70. DOI: 10.1080/07377363.2020.1776558

Li, R. and Liu, J. (2022). Applying gamification in english learning. https://doi.org/DOI: 10.2991/assehr.k.220504.490

Li, B., Pang, R., Sainath, T. N., Gulati, A., Zhang, Y., Qin, J., Haghani, P., Huang, W.-C., & Ma, M. (2021). Scaling End-to-End Models for Large-Scale Multilingual ASR. In arXiv (Cornell University). Cornell University. https://doi.org/DOI: 10.48550/arXiv.2104

Liebling, D. J., Lahav, M., Evans, A., Donsbach, A., Holbrook, J., Smus, B., & Boran, L. (2020). *Unmet Needs and Opportunities for Mobile Translation AI*., DOI: 10.1145/3313831.3376261

Lim, C. P., Zhao, Y., Tondeur, J., Chai, C. S., & Tsai, C. C. (2020). Bridging the digital divide in Asia: Perspectives on policies and practices in digital literacy. *Educational Technology Research and Development*, *68*, 1–3.

Lim, L., Dawson, S., Gašević, D., Joksimovíc, S., Fudge, A., Pardo, A., & Gentili, S. (2020). Students' sense-making of personalised feedback based on learning analytics. *Australasian Journal of Educational Technology*, *36*(6), 15–33. DOI: 10.14742/ajet.6370

Limongi, R. (2024). The use of artificial intelligence in scientific research with integrity and ethics. *Rev. Artif. Intell. Educ*, *5*(00), e0022. DOI: 10.37497/rev.artif.intell.educ.v5i00.22

Lindgren, R., Tscholl, M., Wang, S., & Johnson, E. (2016). Enhancing Learning and Engagement Through Embodied Interaction Within a Mixed Reality Simulation. *Computers & Education*, *95*, 174–187.

Lin, P. (2016). Why ethics matters for autonomous cars. In Maurer, M., Gerdes, J. C., Lenz, B., & Winner, H. (Eds.), *Autonomes Fahren* (pp. 69–85). Springer., DOI: 10.1007/978-3-662-48847-8_4

Lipnevich, A. A. & Panadero, E. (2021). A review of feedback models and theories: Descriptions, definitions, and conclusions. Frontiers in Education. frontiersin.org

Litjens, G., Kooi, T., Bejnordi, B. E., Setio, A. A. A., Ciompi, F., Ghafoorian, M., & van Ginneken, B. (2017). A survey on deep learning in medical image analysis. *Medical Image Analysis*, *42*, 60–88. PMID: 28778026

Littell, P., Kazantseva, A., Kühn, R., Pine, A., Arppe, A., Cox, C., & Junker, M.-O. (2018). Indigenous language technologies in Canada: Assessment, challenges, and successes. In International Conference on Computational Linguistics (p. 2620). https://aclanthology.org/C18-1222/

Liu, L. (2024). Survey and analysis of primary school teachers' use of generative artificial intelligence. *Lecture Notes in Education Psychology and Public Media*, *74*(1), 43–52. DOI: 10.54254/2753-7048/2024.bo17693

Livingstone, S., & Haddon, L. (2009). EU Kids Online: Final report. LSE, London: EU Kids Online.

Livingstone, S., Byrne, J., & Third, A. (2020). *Children's rights in the digital age: A download from children around the world.* UNICEF Office of Research-Innocenti.

Livingstone, S., & Helsper, E. (2007). Gradations in digital inclusion: Children, young people and the digital divide. *New Media & Society*, *9*(4), 671–696.

Livingstone, S., Stoilova, M., & Nandagiri, R. (2019). *Children's data and privacy online: Growing up in a digital age*. London School of Economics and Political Science.

Livingstone, S., & Third, A. (2017). Children and young people's rights in the digital age: An emerging agenda. *New Media & Society, 19*(5), 657–670.

Li, X., & Pan, X. (2023). A Review of Gamification Teaching Based on Creative Thinking Development [Review of A Review of Gamification Teaching Based on Creative Thinking Development]. *Journal of Education Humanities and Social Sciences, 14*, 46. DOI: 10.54097/ehss.v14i.8794

Long, D., & Magerko, B. (2020). What is AI literacy? Competencies and design considerations. *Proceedings of the 2020 CHI Conference on Human Factors in Computing Systems*, 1–16.

Loo, B. F. W. (2022). Strategy and Defense Policy for Small States: Problems and Prospects.

López, C., & Tucker, C. (2020). Toward personalized adaptive gamification: A machine learning model for predicting performance. *IEEE Transactions on Games, 12*(2), 155–168. DOI: 10.1109/tg.2018.2883661

Luan, H., Géczy, P., Lai, H., Gobert, J., Yang, S., Ogata, H., & Tsai, C. (2020). Challenges and future directions of big data and artificial intelligence in education. *Frontiers in Psychology, 11*. Advance online publication. DOI: 10.3389/fpsyg.2020.580820 PMID: 33192896

Lucas, W. A., Cooper, S. Y., Ward, T., & Cave, F. (2009). Industry placement, authentic experience, and the development of venturing and technology self-efficacy. *Technovation, 29*(11), 738–752.

Luccioni, A. S., Pham, K. H., Lam, C. S. N., Aylett-Bullock, J., & Luengo-Oroz, M. (2021). Ensuring the Inclusive Use of Natural Language Processing in the Global Response to COVID-19. In arXiv (Cornell University). Cornell University. https://doi.org/DOI: 10.48550/arXiv.2108

Luckin, R., Holmes, W., Griffiths, M., & Forcier, L. B. (2016). *Intelligence unleashed: An argument for AI in education*. Pearson Education.

Lu, G., Xie, K., & Liu, Q. (2022). What influences student situational engagement in smart classrooms: Perception of the learning environment and students' motivation. [HTML]. *British Journal of Educational Technology*.

Luthra, S., Sharma, M., Kumar, A., Joshi, S., Collins, E., & Mangla, S. (2022). Overcoming barriers to cross-sector collaboration in circular supply chain management: A multi-method approach. *Transportation Research Part E, Logistics and Transportation Review, 157*. Advance online publication. DOI: 10.1016/j.tre.2021.102582

Lythreatis, S., Singh, S. K., & El-Kassar, A. N. (2022). The digital divide: A review and future research agenda. [HTML]. *Technological Forecasting and Social Change*, *175*, 121359.

Majdzadeh, R., Yazdizadeh, B., Nedjat, S., Gholami, J., & Ahghari, S. (2011). Strengthening evidence-based decision-making: Is it possible without improving health system stewardship? *Health Policy and Planning*, *27*(6), 499–504. DOI: 10.1093/heapol/czr072 PMID: 22027555

Majeed, A. & Hwang, S. O. (2021). Data-driven analytics leveraging artificial intelligence in the era of COVID-19: an insightful review of recent developments. Symmetry. mdpi.com

Makena, B. (2020, July). *Learner-Centered Approaches As a Form of Developing English Proficiency Among Learners From Disadvantaged Background*. 430–437. https://doi.org/DOI: 10.21125/edulearn.2020.0190

Maleki, A. (2024). Towards a more equitable education: A lens into EFL teachers' pedagogical barriers in online assessments. [HTML]. *International Journal of Lifelong Education.*

Malhotra, R. K., & Gupta, S. (2021). Tele health in the digital era during covid -19 a case study of Uttarakhand. *Journal of Medical Pharmaceutical and Allied Sciences*, *10*, 109–112. DOI: 10.22270/jmpas.vic2i1.2016

Malhotra, R., Massoudi, M., & Jindal, R. (2023). Shifting from traditional engineering education towards competency-based approach: The most recommended approach-review. [HTML]. *Education and Information Technologies*, *28*(7), 9081–9111.

Mandalapu, S. R., Sivamuni, K., Chitra Devi, D., Aswal, U. S., Sherly, S. I., & Balaji, N. A. (2023). An Architecture-based Self-Typing Service for Cloud Native Applications. *Proceedings of the 4th International Conference on Smart Electronics and Communication, ICOSEC 2023*, 562 – 566. https://doi.org/DOI: 10.1109/ICOSEC58147.2023.10276313

Manu, B. D., Ying, F., Oduro, D., & Boateng, S. A. (2021). Student engagement and social media in tertiary education: The perception and experience from the Ghanaian public university. [sciencedirect.com]. *Social Sciences & Humanities Open*, *3*(1), 100100.

Margot, K. C., & Kettler, T. (2019). Teachers' perception of STEM integration and education: A systematic literature review. *International Journal of STEM Education*, *6*(1), 2. DOI: 10.1186/s40594-018-0151-2

Marín, V. I. & Castaneda, L. (2024). Developing digital literacy for teaching and learning. Handbook of open. springer.com

Marker, M. (2018). There is no place of nature; there is only the nature of place: Animate landscapes as methodology for inquiry in the Coast Salish territory. *International Journal of Qualitative Studies in Education : QSE*, *31*(6), 453–464. DOI: 10.1080/09518398.2018.1430391

Marsal-Llacuna, M.-L., Colomer-Llinàs, J., & Meléndez-Frigola, J. (2015). Lessons in Urban Monitoring Taken from Sustainable and Livable Cities to Better Address the Smart Cities Initiative. *Technological Forecasting and Social Change*, *90*, 611–622.

Martínez-Comesaña, M., Rigueira-Díaz, X., Larrañaga-Janeiro, A., Martínez-Torres, J., Ocarranza-Prado, I., & Kreibel, D. (2023). Impact of artificial intelligence on assessment methods in primary and secondary education: Systematic literature review. *Revista de Psicodidáctica* (English Ed.), 28(2), 93–103. https://doi.org/DOI: 10.1016/j.psicoe.2023.06.002

Martins, A. R. de Q., Pagliarini, E. R., Kalil, F., & Pazinato, A. M. (2022). GAMIFICATION AS AN INSTRUMENT FOR ENHANCING THE ENGAGEMENT ON #TEUFUTURO PROGRAM. In Revista Observatório (Vol. 8, Number 1). Universidade Federal do Tocantins. https://doi.org/DOI: 10.20873/uft.2447-4266.2022v8n1a6pt

Marwick, A. E., & boyd, d. (2014). Networked privacy: How teenagers negotiate context in social media. *New Media & Society*, *16*(7), 1051–1067.

Marx, K. (1964). *Economic and Philosophic Manuscripts of 1844.* International Publishers.

Marx, K. (1975). *Economic and Philosophical Manuscripts of 1844* (Livingstone, R., & Benton, G., Trans.). Penguin.

Marx, K. (1978). Economic and Philosophic Manuscripts of 1844. In Tucker, R. C. (Ed.), *The Marx-Engels Reader* (pp. 66–125). Norton. (Original work published 1844)

Mary Joshitta, S., & Sunil, M. P. Badriasulaimanalfurhood, Bodhankar, A., Ch.Sreedevi, & Khanna, R. (2023). The Integration of Machine Learning Technique with the Existing System to Predict the Flight Prices. *2023 3rd International Conference on Advance Computing and Innovative Technologies in Engineering, ICACITE 2023*, 398–402. https://doi.org/DOI: 10.1109/ICACITE57410.2023.10182539

Masal, V., Pavithra, P., Tiwari, S. K., Singh, R., Panduro-Ramirez, J., & Gangodkar, D. (2022). Deep Learning Applications for Blockchain in Industrial IoT. *Proceedings of 5th International Conference on Contemporary Computing and Informatics, IC3I 2022*, 276 – 281. https://doi.org/DOI: 10.1109/IC3I56241.2022.10073357

Maslow, A. H. (1943). A theory of human motivation. *Psychological Review*, *50*(4), 370–396. DOI: 10.1037/h0054346

Mason, M. (2008). Complexity Theory and the Philosophy of Education. *Educational Philosophy and Theory*, *40*(1), 4–18.

Matsiko, A., & Nelson, B. J. (2023). Robotics and AI in the Global South. In Science Robotics (Vol. 8, Issue 85). American Association for the Advancement of Science. https://doi.org/DOI: 10.1126/scirobotics.adm9727

Matta, P., & Pant, B. (2020). TCpC: A graphical password scheme ensuring authentication for IoT resources. *International Journal of Information Technology (Singapore)*, *12*(3), 699–709. DOI: 10.1007/s41870-018-0142-z

Mayes, T. (1995). Learning Technology and Groundhog day. In Strang, W., Simpson, V. B., & Slater, D. (Eds.), *Hypermedia at Work: Practice and Theory in Higher Education* (pp. 21–37). University of Kent Press.

Medhi, M. K., Ambust, S., Kumar, R., & Das, A. J. (2023). Characterization and Purification of Biosurfactants. In *Advancements in Biosurfactants Research*. Springer International Publishing., DOI: 10.1007/978-3-031-21682-4_4

Mehershilpa, G., Prasad, D., Sai Kiran, C., Shaikh, A., Jayashree, K., & Socrates, S. (2023). EDM machining of Ti6Al4V alloy using colloidal biosilica. *Materials Today: Proceedings*. Advance online publication. DOI: 10.1016/j.matpr.2023.02.443

Meşe, İ. (2023, January 1). The Impact of Artificial Intelligence on Radiology Education in the Wake of Coronavirus Disease 2019. In Korean Journal of Radiology (Vol. 24, Number 5, p. 478). Korean Society of Radiology. https://doi.org/DOI: 10.3348/kjr.2023.0278

Michaeli, T., Romeike, R., & Seegerer, S. (2023). What Students Can Learn About Artificial Intelligence – Recommendations for K-12 Computing Education. In IFIP advances in information and communication technology (p. 196). Springer Science+Business Media. https://doi.org/DOI: 10.1007/978-3-031-43393-1_19

Mienye, I. D. & Swart, T. G. (2025). ChatGPT in Education: A Review of Ethical Challenges and Approaches to Enhancing Transparency and Privacy. Procedia Computer Science. sciencedirect.com

Mika, C. T. H. (2017). *Indigenous education and the metaphysics of presence: A worlded philosophy*. Routledge.

Mill, J. S. (1998). *Utilitarianism* (Crisp, R., Ed.). Oxford University Press. (Original work published 1863)

Minn, S. (2022). AI-assisted knowledge assessment techniques for adaptive learning environments. Computers and Education: Artificial Intelligence. sciencedirect.com

Minocha, S., & Reeves, A. (2010). Design of Learning Spaces in 3D Virtual Worlds: An Empirical Investigation of Second Life. *Learning, Media and Technology*, *35*(2), 111–137.

Mishra, A. K., & Wazid, M. (2023). Design of a cloud-based security mechanism for Industry 4.0 communication. *ICSCCC 2023 - 3rd International Conference on Secure Cyber Computing and Communications*, 337 – 343. https://doi.org/DOI: 10.1109/ICSCCC58608.2023.10176702

Mitcham, C. (2006). From Phenomenology to Pragmatism: Using Technology as an Instrument. In Selinger, E. (Ed.), *Postphenomenology: A Critical Companion to Ihde* (pp. 21–33). State University of New York Press.

Mittal, S., Thakral, K., Singh, R., Vatsa, M., Glaser, T., Ferrer, C. C., & Hassner, T. (2024). On responsible machine learning datasets emphasizing fairness, privacy and regulatory norms with examples in biometrics and healthcare. In Nature Machine Intelligence (Vol. 6, Issue 8, p. 936). Nature Portfolio. https://doi.org/DOI: 10.1038/s42256-024-00874-y

Mohamed, S. (2023). The development of an Arabic curriculum framework based on a compilation of salient features from CEFR level descriptors. *Language Learning Journal*, *51*(1), 33–47. DOI: 10.1080/09571736.2021.1923781

Mohd, N., Kumar, I., & Khurshid, A. A. (2023). Changing Roles of Intelligent Robotics and Machinery Control Systems as Cyber-Physical Systems (CPS) in the Industry 4.0 Framework. *2023 International Conference on Communication, Security and Artificial Intelligence, ICCSAI 2023*, 647 – 651. https://doi.org/DOI: 10.1109/ICCSAI59793.2023.10421085

Moorhouse, B. L. & Kohnke, L. (2024). The effects of generative AI on initial language teacher education: The perceptions of teacher educators. System. sciencedirect.com

Moorhouse, B. L., Yeo, M. A., & Wan, Y. (2023). Generative AI tools and assessment: Guidelines of the world's topranking universities. *Computers and Education Open*, *5*, 100151. DOI: 10.1016/j.caeo.2023.100151

Moqbel, M. S. S., & Al-Kadi, A. M. T. (2023). Foreign language learning assessment in the age of ChatGPT: A theoretical account. *Journal of English Studies in Arabia Felix*, *2*(1), 76–88. DOI: 10.56540/jesaf.v2i1.62

Mora, L., Bolici, R., & Deakin, M. (2017). The First Two Decades of Smart-City Research: A Bibliometric Analysis. *Journal of Urban Technology*, *24*(1), 3–27.

Morandín-Ahuerma, F. (2023, September 28). Ten UNESCO Recommendations on the Ethics of Artificial Intelligence.

Morgana, V., & Kukulska-Hulme, A. (2021). *Mobile assisted language learning across educational contexts*. Routledge.

Morris, R., Perry, T., & Wardle, L. (2021). Formative assessment and feedback for learning in higher education: A systematic review. Review of Education. wiley.com Bimpeh, Y. (2024). AI Powered Adaptive Formative Assessment: Validity and Reliability Evaluation. In Artificial Intelligence in Education: The Intersection of Technology and Pedagogy (pp. 127-144). Cham: Springer Nature Switzerland. [HTML]

Morse, A., & Pence, K. M. (2020). Technological Innovation and Discrimination in Household Finance. https://doi.org/DOI: 10.3386/w26739

Moten, F. (2018). *Stolen life*. Duke University Press.

Motevalli, S., Perveen, A., & Michael, M. T. A. (2020). Motivating Students to Learn: An Overview of Literature in Educational Psychology. In International Journal of Academic Research in Progressive Education and Development (Vol. 9, Number 3). https://doi.org/DOI: 10.6007/ijarped/v9-i3/7779

Mugisha, M., Uwitonze, A., Chesire, F., Senyonga, R., Oxman, M., Nsangi, A., & Rosenbaum, S. (2021). Teaching critical thinking about health using digital technology in lower secondary schools in rwanda: A qualitative context analysis. *PLoS One*, *16*(3), e0248773. DOI: 10.1371/journal.pone.0248773 PMID: 33750971

Murgatroyd, S. (2023). Rethinking teaching in the age of artificial intelligence. *Revista Paraguaya De Educación A Distancia* (REPED), 4(2), 4–10. https://doi.org/DOI: 10.56152/reped2023-vol4num2-art1

Murray, M. D. (2023). Generative AI art: Copyright infringement and fair use. *SMU Science and Technology Law Review*, *26*(2), 259. DOI: 10.25172/smustlr.26.2.4

Murtaza, M., Ahmed, Y., Shamsi, J., Sherwani, F., & Usman, M. (2022). Ai-based personalized e-learning systems: Issues, challenges, and solutions. *IEEE Access : Practical Innovations, Open Solutions, 10*, 81323–81342. DOI: 10.1109/access.2022.3193938

Mystakidis, S. (2022). Metaverse. *Encyclopedia, 2*(1), 486–497.

Nadeem, S. P., Garza-Reyes, J. A., & Anosike, A. I. (2023). A C-Lean framework for deploying Circular Economy in manufacturing SMEs. *Production Planning and Control.* Advance online publication. DOI: 10.1080/09537287.2023.2294307

Nagi, F., Salih, R., Alzubaidi, M., Shah, H., Alam, T., Shah, Z., … & Househ, M. (2023). Applications of artificial intelligence (AI) in medical education: a scoping review.. https://doi.org/DOI: 10.3233/shti230581

Nair, V. & Yunus, M. M. (2021). A systematic review of digital storytelling in improving speaking skills. Sustainability. mdpi.com

Nam, T., & Pardo, T. A. (2011). "Conceptualizing Smart City with Dimensions of Technology, People, and Institutions." *45th Hawaii International Conference on System Sciences (HICSS)*, 282-292.

Narayanan, K. (2024). Hybrid gamification and ai tutoring framework using machine learning and adaptive neuro-fuzzy inference system. *Journal of Advanced Research in Applied Sciences and Engineering Technology, 42*(2), 221–233. DOI: 10.37934/araset.42.2.221233

Nayak, A., Satpathy, I., & Jain, V. (2024). *The Project-Based Learning Approach.* PBL., DOI: 10.4018/979-8-3693-3041-8.ch010

Nazer, L., Zatarah, R., Waldrip, S., Ke, J. X. C., Moukheiber, M., Khanna, A. K., Hicklen, R., Moukheiber, L., Moukheiber, D., Ma, H., & Mathur, P. (2023). Bias in artificial intelligence algorithms and recommendations for mitigation [Review of Bias in artificial intelligence algorithms and recommendations for mitigation]. PLOS Digital Health, 2(6). Public Library of Science. https://doi.org/DOI: 10.1371/journal.pdig.0000278

Nethravathi, K., Tiwari, A., Uike, D., Jaiswal, R., & Pant, K. (2022). Applications of Artificial Intelligence and Blockchain Technology in Improved Supply Chain Financial Risk Management. *Proceedings of 5th International Conference on Contemporary Computing and Informatics, IC3I 2022*, 242 – 246. https://doi.org/DOI: 10.1109/IC3I56241.2022.10072787

Nguyen, D. N. (2025). Artificial intelligence-based assessment in ELT exam creation: a case study of Van Lang University lecturers. *Saudi Journal of Language Studies, Vol. 5 No. 1*(Emerald Publishing Limited), 34-49. https://doi.org/https://doi.org/10.1108/SJLS-06-2024-0030

Nguyen, L. A. T. & Habók, A. (2024). Tools for assessing teacher digital literacy: a review. Journal of Computers in Education. springer.com

Nguyen, T. (2025). AI in Language Assessment: Innovations and Challenges. *International Journal of Language Education, 12(1), 22-35, 12*(1), 22-35.

Nguyen, A., Ngo, H. N., Hong, Y., Dang, B., & Nguyen, B.-P. T. (2023). Ethical principles for artificial intelligence in education. *Education and Information Technologies*, *28*(4), 4221–4241. DOI: 10.1007/s10639-022-11316-w PMID: 36254344

Nguyen, D., & Ng, D. (2022). Teacher collaboration for change: Sharing, improving, and spreading. In *Leadership for Professional Learning* (pp. 178–191). Routledge.

Nguyen, T. (2022). Artificial intelligent based teaching and learning approaches: A comprehensive review. *International Journal of Evaluation and Research in Education (Ijere)*, *12*(4), 2387. DOI: 10.11591/ijere.v12i4.26623

Ng, W. (2012). Can we teach digital natives digital literacy? *Computers & Education*, *59*(3), 1065–1078.

Nikolopoulou, K. (2024a). Generative artificial intelligence in higher education: Exploring ways of harnessing pedagogical practices with the assistance of ChatGPT. *International Journal of Changes in Education*, *1*(2), 103–111. DOI: 10.47852/bonviewIJCE42022489

Nykyporets, Bohdan Kutsyk & Svitlana. (2024). THE IMPACT OF ARTIFICIAL INTELLIGENCE ON LANGUAGE LEARNING. https://doi.org/DOI: 10.13140/RG.2.2.30485.33767

O'Neil, C. (2016). *Weapons of math destruction: How big data increases inequality and threatens democracy*. Crown Publishing Group.

O'Neil, C. (2016). *Weapons of Math Destruction: How Big Data Increases Inequality and Threatens Democracy*. Crown Publishing Group.

O'Neil, H. F., Chuang, S.-H., & Huang, T. (2010). Instructional System Provided Feedback. In *Elsevier eBooks* (p. 226). Elsevier BV., DOI: 10.1016/b978-0-08-044894-7.00312-2

O'Sullivan, B. (2021). *BRITISH COUNCIL PERSPECTIVES ON ENGLISH LANGUAGE POLICY AND EDUCATION The Comprehensive Learning System*. British Council.

Ober, T. M., Lehman, B., Gooch, R., Oluwalana, O., Solyst, J., Phelps, G., & Hamilton, L. Culturally responsive personalized learning: Recommendations for a working definition and framework. ETS Research Report Series, 2023(1), 1-14.

Ober, T. M., Lehman, B., Gooch, R., Oluwalana, O., Solyst, J., Phelps, G., & Hamilton, L. S. (2023). Culturally Responsive Personalized Learning: Recommendations for a Working Definition and Framework. In ETS Research Report Series (Vol. 2023, Issue 1, p. 1). Wiley. https://doi.org/DOI: 10.1002/ets2.12372

Obermeyer, Z., Powers, B. W., Vogeli, C., & Mullainathan, S. (2019). Dissecting racial bias in an algorithm used to manage the health of populations. In Science (Vol. 366, Issue 6464, p. 447). American Association for the Advancement of Science. https://doi.org/DOI: 10.1126/science.aax2342

OECD. (2018). The Future of Education and Skills [oecd.org.]. *Education*, •••, 2030.

OECD. (2020). The impact of COVID-19 on student equity and inclusion: Supporting vulnerable students during school closures and school re-openings. In OECD policy responses to coronavirus (Covid-19). https://doi.org/DOI: 10.1787/d593b5c8-en

Ogan, A., & Johnson, W. L. (2015). Preface for the Special Issue on Culturally Aware Educational Technologies. In International Journal of Artificial Intelligence in Education (Vol. 25, Issue 2, p. 173). Springer Science+Business Media. https://doi.org/DOI: 10.1007/s40593-015-0036-1

Ohler, J. (2011). *Digital community, digital citizen*. Corwin Press.

Oliver, M. (2011). Technological Determinism in Educational Technology Research: Some Alternative Ways of Thinking about the Relationship Between Learning and Technology. *Journal of Computer Assisted Learning*, *27*(5), 373–384.

Oliver, M. (2013). Learning Technology: Theorising the Tools We Study. *British Journal of Educational Technology*, *44*(1), 31–43.

Oliver, M. (2015). From Openness to Permeability: Reframing Open Education in Terms of Positive Liberty in the Enactment of Academic Practices. *Learning, Media and Technology*, *40*(3), 365–384.

Oliver, M., & Conole, G. (2003). Evidence-Based Practice and e-Learning in Higher Education: Can We and Should We? *Research Papers in Education*, *18*(4), 385–397.

Onele, N. O. (2020). Virtual Reality: A Tool for Improving the Teaching and Learning of Technology Education. In IntechOpen eBooks. IntechOpen. https://doi.org/ DOI: 10.5772/intechopen.90809

Onesi-Ozigagun, O. (2024). Revolutionizing education through ai: A comprehensive review of enhancing learning experiences. *International Journal of Applied Research in Social Sciences*, *6*(4), 589–607. DOI: 10.51594/ijarss.v6i4.1011

Orchard, J., Gaydon, P., Williams, K., Bennett, P., D'Olimpio, L., C¸elik, R., Shah, Q., Neusiedl, C., Suissa, J., Peters, M. A., & Tesar, M. (2020). Philosophy of education in a new key: A 'covid collective' of the philosophy of education society of Great Britain (PESGB). *Educational Philosophy and Theory*. Advance online publication. DOI: 10.1080/00131857.2020.1838274

Orton, L., Lloyd-Williams, F., Taylor-Robinson, D., O'Flaherty, M., & Capewell, S. (2011). The use of research evidence in public health decision making processes: Systematic review. *PLoS One*, *6*(7), e21704. DOI: 10.1371/journal.pone.0021704 PMID: 21818262

Otero, L., Catalá, A., Morante, M., Taboada, M., López, B., & Barro, S. (2023). Ai literacy in k-12: A systematic literature review. *International Journal of STEM Education*, *10*(1). Advance online publication. DOI: 10.1186/s40594-023-00418-7

Ouyang, F., Zheng, L., & Jiao, P. (2022). Artificial intelligence in online higher education: A systematic review of empirical research from 2011 to 2020. *Education and Information Technologies*, *27*(6), 7893–7925. DOI: 10.1007/s10639-022-10925-9

Özen, E., Singh, A., Taneja, S., Rajaram, R., & Davim, J. P. (2024a). *Innovating Sustainability Through Digital Circular Economy*. IGI Global., DOI: 10.4018/979-8-3373-0578-3

Özhan, Ş., & Kocadere, S. (2019). The effects of flow, emotional engagement, and motivation on success in a gamified online learning environment. *Journal of Educational Computing Research*, *57*(8), 2006–2031. DOI: 10.1177/0735633118823159

Pai, H. A., Almuzaini, K. K., Ali, L., Javeed, A., Pant, B., Pareek, P. K., & Akwafo, R. (2022). Delay-Driven Opportunistic Routing with Multichannel Cooperative Neighbor Discovery for Industry 4.0 Wireless Networks Based on Power and Load Awareness. *Wireless Communications and Mobile Computing*, *2022*. Advance online publication. DOI: 10.1155/2022/5256133

Palacios, H. F. M., Cumbicos, K. M. C., & Peralta, S. R. T. (2023). El impacto de la gamificación en la motivación y el aprendizaje de los estudiantes de matemáticas de educación básica superior. In Ciencia Latina Revista Científica Multidisciplinar (Vol. 7, Number 3, p. 6494). Latin American Association for the Advancement of Sciences. https://doi.org/DOI: 10.37811/cl_rcm.v7i3.6650

Palfrey, J., & Gasser, U. (2016). *Born digital: How children grow up in a digital age* (2nd ed.). Basic Books.

Palmer, A. S., & Rodgers, T. S. (1983). Games In Language Teaching. In Language Teaching (Vol. 16, Number 1, p. 2). Cambridge University Press. https://doi.org/DOI: 10.1017/s0261444800009836

Palomares, I., Martínez-Cámara, E., Montes, R., García-Moral, P., Chiachío, M., Chiachío, J., Alonso, S., Melero, F. J., Molina, D., Fernández, B. C., Santaella, C. M., Marchena, R., de Vargas, J. P., & Herrera, F. (2021). A panoramic view and swot analysis of artificial intelligence for achieving the sustainable development goals by 2030: progress and prospects. In Applied Intelligence (Vol. 51, Issue 9, p. 6497). Springer Science+Business Media. https://doi.org/DOI: 10.1007/s10489-021-02264-y

Pan, K., & Sen, R. (2024). Navigating the Evolving Landscape of Personalized Learning in AIED: Recent Trends and Innovations. Explainable AI for Education: Recent Trends and Challenges, 169-192. [HTML]

Panch, T., Mattie, H., & Atun, R. (2019). Artificial intelligence and algorithmic bias: implications for health systems [Review of Artificial intelligence and algorithmic bias: implications for health systems]. Journal of Global Health, 9(2). Edinburgh University Global Health Society. https://doi.org/DOI: 10.7189/jogh.09.020318

Pandey, T., Batra, A., Chaudhary, M., Ranakoti, A., Kumar, A., & Ram, M. (2023). Computation Signature Reliability of Computer Numerical Control System Using Universal Generating Function. *Springer Series in Reliability Engineering*, 149 – 158. https://doi.org/DOI: 10.1007/978-3-031-05347-4_10

Pane, J. F., Steiner, E. D., Baird, M. D., & Hamilton, L. S. (2015). *Continued progress: Promising evidence on personalized learning*. RAND Corporation.

Pang, N. S.-K. (2020). Teachers' Reflective Practices in Implementing Assessment for Learning Skills in Classroom Teaching. In ECNU Review of Education (Vol. 5, Number 3, p. 470). SAGE Publishing. https://doi.org/DOI: 10.1177/2096531120936290

Pangrazio, L., & Selwyn, N. (2019). 'Personal data literacies': A critical literacies approach to enhancing understandings of personal digital data. *New Media & Society*, *21*(2), 419–437.

Pant, R., Gupta, A., Pant, G., Chaubey, K. K., Kumar, G., & Patrick, N. (2022). Second-generation biofuels: Facts and future. In *Relationship between Microbes and the Environment for Sustainable Ecosystem Services: Microbial Tools for Sustainable Ecosystem Services: Volume 3* (Vol. 3). Elsevier. https://doi.org/DOI: 10.1016/B978-0-323-89936-9.00011-4

Papa, R., Gargiulo, C., & Galderisi, A. (2013). "Towards an Urban Planners' Perspective on Smart City." *TeMA - Journal of Land Use. Mobility and Environment*, *6*(1), 5–17.

Papastephanou, M., Zembylas, M., Bostad, I., Benhur Oral, S., Drousioti, K., Kouppanou, A., Strand, T., Wain, K., & Peters, M. A. (Open Reviewer) & Tesar, M. (Open Reviewer) (2020). Philosophy of education in a new key: Education for justice now. *Educational Philosophy and Theory*. Advance online publication. DOI: 10.1080/00131857.2020.1793539

Pardosi, V., Xu, S., Umurohmi, U., Nurdiana, N., & Sabur, F. (2024). Implementation of an artificial intelligence based learning management system for adaptive learning. *Al-Fikrah Jurnal Manajemen Pendidikan*, *12*(1), 149. DOI: 10.31958/jaf.v12i1.12548

Pariser, E. (2011). *The filter bubble: What the Internet is hiding from you*. Penguin Press.

Pariser, E. (2011). *The Filter Bubble: What the Internet Is Hiding from You*. Penguin Press.

Parisi, L., & Dixon-Roman, E. (2020). *Recursive colonialism & cosmo-computation. Social Text Online.* https://social.textjournal.org/periscope_article/recursive-colonialism-and-cosmo-computation/

Park, J.-S., Bragg, D., Kamar, E., & Morris, M. R. (2021). *Designing an Online Infrastructure for Collecting AI Data From People With Disabilities.*, DOI: 10.1145/3442188.3445870

Pasquale, F. (2015). *The Black Box Society: The Secret Algorithms That Control Money and Information*. Harvard University Press.

Pasqualotto, A., Parong, J., Green, C. S., & Bavelier, D. (2022). Video Game Design for Learning to Learn. In International Journal of Human-Computer Interaction (Vol. 39, Number 11, p. 2211). Taylor & Francis. https://doi.org/DOI: 10.1080/10447318.2022.2110684

Pedaste, M., Mäeots, M., Siiman, L., Jong, T., Riesen, S., Kamp, E., Manoli, C., Zacharia, Z., & Tsourlidaki, E. (2015). Phases of Inquiry-Based Learning: Definitions and the Inquiry Cycle. *Educational Research Review*, *14*(2), 47–61.

Pendy, B. (2023). Artificial intelligence: The future of education. *Jurnal Indonesia Sosial Sains*, *2*(11). Advance online publication. DOI: 10.59141/jiss.v2i11.801

Perboli, G., De Marco, A., Perfetti, F., & Marone, M. (2014). A New Taxonomy of Smart City Projects. *Transportation Research Procedia*, *3*, 470–478.

Perkins, M. (2023). Academic integrity considerations of AI large language models in the post-pandemic era: ChatGPT and beyond. *Journal of University Teaching & Learning Practice*, *20*(2), 345–367. DOI: 10.53761/1.20.02.07

Perrotta, C., & Evans, M. A. (2013). Orchestration, Power, and Educational Technology: A Response to Dillenbourg. *Computers & Education*, *69*, 520–522.

Pessach, D., & Shmueli, E. (2020). Algorithmic Fairness. In arXiv (Cornell University). Cornell University. https://doi.org/DOI: 10.48550/arXiv.2001

Peters, U., & Carman, M. (2024). Cultural Bias in Explainable AI Research: A Systematic Analysis. In Journal of Artificial Intelligence Research (Vol. 79, p. 971). AI Access Foundation. https://doi.org/DOI: 10.1613/jair.1.14888

Peters, M. A., Arndt, S., Tesar, M., Jackson, L., Hung, R., Mika, C., Ozolins, J. T., Teschers, C., Orchard, J., Buchanan, R., Madjar, A., Novak, R., Besley, T., & Sturm, S. (open reviewer), Roberts, P. (open reviewer), & Gibbons, A. (open reviewer) (2020). Philosophy of education in a new key. A collective project of the PESA executive. *Educational Philosophy and Theory*. Advance online publication. DOI: 10.1080/00131857.2020.1759194

Petrusly, P. (2024). *The effect of gamification using kahoot on students' critical thinking abilities: the role of mediating learning engagement and motivation*. Kuey., DOI: 10.53555/kuey.v30i5.1524

Pezze, B. D. (2006). Heidegger on Gelassenheit. *Minerva*, *10*, •••. Retrieved March 15, 2020, from https://www.minerva.mic.ul.ie/vol10/Heidegger.html

Pfohl, S., Cole-Lewis, H., Sayres, R., Neal, D., Asiedu, M., Dieng, A., Tomašev, N., Rashid, Q. M., Azizi, S., Rostamzadeh, N., McCoy, L. G., Celi, L. A., Liu, Y., Schaekermann, M., Walton, A., Parrish, A., Nagpal, C., Singh, P., Dewitt, A., & Singhal, K. K. (2024). A toolbox for surfacing health equity harms and biases in large language models. In *Nature Medicine*. Nature Portfolio., DOI: 10.1038/s41591-024-03258-2

Philip, L., Cottrill, C., Farrington, J., Williams, F., & Ashmore, F. (2017). The digital divide: Patterns, policy and scenarios for connecting the 'final few' in rural communities across Great Britain. In *Journal of Rural Studies* (Vol. 54, p. 386). Elsevier BV., DOI: 10.1016/j.jrurstud.2016.12.002

Piro, G., Cianci, I., & Grieco, L. A.. (2014). Information-Centric Services in Smart Cities. *Journal of Systems and Software, 88*, 169–188.

Pokrivcakova, S. (2019). Preparing teachers for the application of AI-powered technologies in foreign language education. *Journal of Language and Cultural Education, 7*(3), 135–153. DOI: 10.2478/jolace-2019-0025

Polat, E. (2023). Gamification implementation for educational purposes: A scoping review (2013-2018). *Educational Technology Quarterly, 2023*(3), 367–400. DOI: 10.55056/etq.589

Popenici, S., & Kerr, S. (2017). Exploring the impact of artificial intelligence on teaching and learning in higher education. *Research and Practice in Technology Enhanced Learning, 12*(1). Advance online publication. DOI: 10.1186/s41039-017-0062-8 PMID: 30595727

Popova, A., Evans, D. K., Breeding, M. E., & Arancibia, V. (2022). Teacher Professional Development around the World: The Gap between Evidence and Practice. *The World Bank Research Observer, 37*(1), 107–136. DOI: 10.1093/wbro/lkab006

Porath, S., & Hagerman, D. (2021). Becoming connected learners through personalized learning. [HTML]. *Middle School Journal.*

Prabhakaran, V., Qadri, R., & Hutchinson, B. (2022). Cultural Incongruencies in Artificial Intelligence. In arXiv (Cornell University). Cornell University. https://doi.org/DOI: 10.48550/arXiv.2211

Pratama, M. P., Sampelolo, R., & Lura, H. (2023). Revolutionizing education: harnessing the power of artificial intelligence for personalized learning. Klasikal: Journal of education, language teaching and science, 5(2), 350-357. journalfkipuniversitasbosowa.org

Pratama, M. (2023). Revolutionizing education: Harnessing the power of artificial intelligence for personalized learning. *Klasikal Journal of Education Language Teaching and Science*, *5*(2), 350–357. DOI: 10.52208/klasikal.v5i2.877

Prinsloo, P., & Kaliisa, R. (2022). Data privacy on the African continent: Opportunities, challenges and implications for learning analytics. [wiley.com]. *British Journal of Educational Technology*, *53*(4), 894–913.

Prinsloo, P., Slade, S., & Khalil, M. (2022). The answer is (not only) technological: Considering student data privacy in learning analytics. [HTML]. *British Journal of Educational Technology*, *53*(4), 876–893.

Pu, D., Ni, J., Song, D., Zhang, W., Wang, Y., Wu, L., & Wang, Y. (2019). Influence of critical thinking disposition on the learning efficiency of problem-based learning in undergraduate medical students. *BMC Medical Education*, *19*(1). Advance online publication. DOI: 10.1186/s12909-018-1418-5 PMID: 30606170

Purves, D. (2022). Fairness in Algorithmic Policing. In Journal of the American Philosophical Association (Vol. 8, Issue 4, p. 741). Cambridge University Press. https://doi.org/DOI: 10.1017/apa.2021.39

Qadri, R., Shelby, R., Bennett, C. L., & Denton, E. (2023). AI's Regimes of Representation: A Community-centered Study of Text-to-Image Models in South Asia. In *2022 ACM Conference on Fairness, Accountability, and Transparency* (p. 506). https://doi.org/DOI: 10.1145/3593013.3594016

Qazi, S., Kadri, M. B., Naveed, M., Khawaja, B. A., Khan, S. Z., Alam, M. M., & Su'ud, M. M. (2024). AI-Driven Learning Management Systems: Modern Developments, Challenges, and Future Trends during the Age of ChatGPT. *Computers, Materials & Continua*, *80*(2).

Qushem, U. B., Christopoulos, A., Oyelere, S. S., Ogata, H., & Laakso, M. J. (2021). Multimodal technologies in precision education: Providing new opportunities or adding more challenges? [mdpi.com]. *Education Sciences*, *11*(7), 338.

R. Nikolov, E. S. (2014). *COMPETENCE BASED FRAMEWORK FOR CURRICULUM DEVELOPMENT.* Sofia: Za bukvite, O'pismeneh.

Rahimi, R. A. & Oh, G. S. (2024). Rethinking the role of educators in the 21st century: navigating globalization, technology, and pandemics. Journal of Marketing Analytics. [HTML]

Raju, K., Balakrishnan, M., Prasad, D. V. S. S. S. V., Nagalakshmi, V., Patil, P. P., Kaliappan, S., Arulmurugan, B., Radhakrishnan, K., Velusamy, B., Paramasivam, P., & El-Denglawey, A. (2022). Optimization of WEDM Process Parameters in Al2024-Li-Si3N4MMC. *Journal of Nanomaterials, 2022*. Advance online publication. DOI: 10.1155/2022/2903385

Raman, R., Kumar, R., Ghai, S., Gehlot, A., Raju, A. M., & Barve, A. (2023). A New Method of Optical Spectrum Analysis for Advanced Wireless Communications. *2023 3rd International Conference on Advance Computing and Innovative Technologies in Engineering, ICACITE 2023*, 1719 – 1723. https://doi.org/DOI: 10.1109/ICACITE57410.2023.10182414

Ramírez-Montoya, M. S., Andrade-Vargas, L., Rivera-Rogel, D., & Portuguez-Castro, M. (2021). Trends for the future of education programs for professional development. [mdpi.com]. *Sustainability*, *13*(13), 7244.

Ram, M., Bisht, D. C. S., Goyal, N., Kazancoglu, Y., & Mathirajan, M. (2022). Newly developed mathematical methodologies and advancements in a variety of engineering and management domains. *Mathematics in Engineering. Science and Aerospace*, *13*(3), 559–562.

Ram, M., Negi, G., Goyal, N., & Kumar, A. (2022). Analysis of a Stochastic Model with Rework System. *Journal of Reliability and Statistical Studies*, *15*(2), 553–582. DOI: 10.13052/jrss0974-8024.1527

Rana, M. S., Cavaliere, L. P. L., Mishra, A. B., Padhye, P., Singh, R. R., & Khanna, R. (2022). Internet of Things (IOT) Based Assessment for Effective Monitoring Data Against Malicious Attacks on Financial Collectors. *2022 2nd International Conference on Advance Computing and Innovative Technologies in Engineering, ICACITE 2022*, 177–181. https://doi.org/DOI: 10.1109/ICACITE53722.2022.9823612

Ranathunga, S., & de Silva, N. (2023). Some Languages are More Equal than Others: Probing Deeper into the Linguistic Disparity in the NLP World. https://arxiv.org/pdf/2210.08523.pdf

Rane, N., Choudhary, S., & Rane, J. (2023). Education 4.0 and 5.0: Integrating Artificial Intelligence (AI) for Personalized and Adaptive Learning. SSRN *Electronic Journal*. https://doi.org/DOI: 10.2139/ssrn.4638365

Rasheed, Z., Ghwanmeh, S., & Abualkishik, A. (2023). Harnessing artificial intelligence for personalized learning: A systematic review. *Data & Metadata*, *2*, 146. DOI: 10.56294/dm2023146

Rawashdeh, A., & Idris, M. (2025). Synchronized curriculum adaptation: A strategy for enhancing skill development in accounting education. *Journal of International Education in Business, 18*(2), 269–288.

Rawat, R., Sharma, S., & Goyal, H. R. (2023). Intelligent Digital Financial Inclusion System Architectures for Industry 5.0 Enabled Digital Society. *Winter Summit on Smart Computing and Networks. WiSSCoN, 2023*. Advance online publication. DOI: 10.1109/WiSSCoN56857.2023.10133858

Rawls, J. (1971). *A Theory of Justice*. Harvard University Press.

Razali, N., Nasir, N. A., Ismail, M. E., Sari, N., & Salleh, K. M. (2020). Gamification Elements in Quizizz Applications: Evaluating the Impact on Intrinsic and Extrinsic Student's Motivation. In IOP Conference Series Materials Science and Engineering (Vol. 917, Number 1, p. 12024). IOP Publishing. https://doi.org/DOI: 10.1088/1757-899x/917/1/012024

Reddy, P. N., Umaeswari, P., Natrayan, L., & Choudhary, A. (2023). Development of Programmed Autonomous Electric Heavy Vehicle: An Application of IoT. *Proceedings of the 2023 2nd International Conference on Electronics and Renewable Systems, ICEARS 2023*, 506 – 510. https://doi.org/DOI: 10.1109/ICEARS56392.2023.10085492

Reepu, R., Taneja, S., Ozen, E., & Singh, A. (2023). A globetrotter to the future of marketing: Metaverse. In *Cultural Marketing and Metaverse for Consumer Engagement*. IGI Global., DOI: 10.4018/978-1-6684-8312-1.ch001

Reich, J., & Dukes, J. (2024). Toward a New Theory of Arrival Technologies. https://doi.org/DOI: 10.35542/osf.io/x6vn7

Reich, K., Garrison, J., & Neubert, S. (2016). Complexity and Reductionism in Educational Philosophy—John Dewey's Critical Approach in 'Democracy and Education' Reconsidered. *Educational Philosophy and Theory, 48*(10), 997–1012.

Reveley, J. (2013). Understanding Social Media Use as Alienation: A Review and Critique. *E-Learning and Digital Media, 1*(10), 83–94.

Ribble, M. (2011). *Digital citizenship in schools: Nine elements all students should know* (2nd ed.). ISTE.

Richardson, J., & Milovidov, E. (2019). *Digital citizenship education handbook: Being online, well-being online, and rights online*. Council of Europe.

Richey, J. E., Lobczowski, N. G., Carvalho, P. F., & Koedinger, K. R. (2020). Comprehensive Views of Math Learners: A Case for Modeling and Supporting Non-math Factors in Adaptive Math Software. In Lecture notes in computer science (p. 460). Springer Science+Business Media. https://doi.org/DOI: 10.1007/978-3-030-52237-7_37

Rivera, E., & Garden, C. (2021). Gamification for student engagement: A framework. *Journal of Further and Higher Education*, *45*(7), 999–1012. DOI: 10.1080/0309877x.2021.1875201

Rohmah, N. (2022). A vocational school cutting-edge learning strategy: Examining gamification towards student engagement and achievement. *Jurnal Kependidikan Jurnal Hasil Penelitian Dan Kajian Kepustakaan Di Bidang Pendidikan Pengajaran Dan Pembelajaran*, *8*(3), 655. DOI: 10.33394/jk.v8i3.5779

Roll, I., Aleven, V., McLaren, B. M., & Koedinger, K. R. (2011). Improving students' help-seeking skills using metacognitive feedback in an intelligent tutoring system. *Learning and Instruction*, *21*(2), 267–280. DOI: 10.1016/j.learninstruc.2010.07.004

Rosenthal, G. (2009). Economic and Social Council. In Oxford University Press eBooks (p. 136). Oxford University Press. https://doi.org/DOI: 10.1093/oxfordhb/9780199560103.003.0007

Rosiek, J. L., Snyder, J., & Pratt, S. L. (2020). The new materialisms and Indigenous theories of non-human agency: Making the case for respectful anti-colonial engagement. *Qualitative Inquiry*, *26*(3–4), 331–346. DOI: 10.1177/1077800419830135

Roth, K., Mollvik, L., Alshoufani, R., Adami, R., Dineen, K., Majlesi, F., Peters, M. A., & Tesar, M. (2020). Philosophy of education in a new key: Constraints and possibilities in present times with regard to dignity. *Educational Philosophy and Theory*. Advance online publication. DOI: 10.1080/00131857.2020.1851189

Roy, A. (2020). The pandemic is a portal. Financial Times. Available at: https://www.ft.com/content/10d8f5e8-74eb-11ea-95fe-fcd274e920ca

Rudolph, J., Ismail, M. F. B. M., & Popenici, S. (2024). Higher education's generative artificial intelligence paradox: The meaning of chatbot mania. *Journal of University Teaching & Learning Practice*, *21*(6), 1–35. DOI: 10.53761/54fs5e77

Rueckert, D., Pico, K., Kim, D., & Sánchez, X. (2020). Gamifying the foreign language classroom for brain-friendly learning. *Foreign Language Annals*, *53*(4), 686–703. DOI: 10.1111/flan.12490

Sable, N. P., Singh, S., Sharma, M. K., Patil, N., & Mishra, A. (2023, December). Machines Thinking Fast: AI-Powered Automating of Information Capture and Retrieval. In *2023 3rd International Conference on Smart Generation Computing, Communication and Networking (SMART GENCON)* (pp. 1–6). IEEE.

Salama, R., Al-Turjman, F., Bordoloi, D., & Yadav, S. P. (2023). Wireless Sensor Networks and Green Networking for 6G communication- An Overview. *2023 International Conference on Computational Intelligence, Communication Technology and Networking, CICTN 2023*, 830 – 834. https://doi.org/DOI: 10.1109/CICTN57981.2023.10141262

Salas-Pilco, S. Z., Yang, Y., & Zhang, Z. (2022). Student engagement in online learning in Latin American higher education during the COVID-19 pandemic: A systematic review. [wiley.com]. *British Journal of Educational Technology*, *53*(3), 593–619. PMID: 35600418

Saleem, A. N., Noori, N. M., & Ozdamli, F. (2022). Gamification Applications in E-learning: A Literature Review. *Technology. Knowledge and Learning*, *27*(1), 139–159. DOI: 10.1007/s10758-020-09487-x

Salinas-Navarro, D. E., Vilalta-Perdomo, E., Michel-Villarreal, R., & Montesinos, L. (2024). Using generative artificial intelligence tools to explain and enhance experiential learning for authentic assessment. *Education Sciences*, *14*(1), 887–900. DOI: 10.3390/educsci14010083

Samin, S. (2019). Mechanisms For Implementing Assessments in The Independent Curriculum: Analytical Study In Educational Institutions. *Jurnal At-Tarbiyat: Jurnal Pendidikan Islam, 6*(2). https://doi.org/DOI: 10.37758/jat.v6i2.671

Sancar, R., Atal, D., & Deryakulu, D. (2021). A new framework for teachers' professional development. *Teaching and Teacher Education*, *101*, 103305. DOI: 10.1016/j.tate.2021.103305

Saputra, I., Astuti, M., Sayuti, M., & Kusumastuti, D. (2023). Integration of Artificial Intelligence in Education: Opportunities, Challenges, Threats and Obstacles. A Literature Review. In Indonesian Journal of Computer Science (Vol. 12, Number 4). https://doi.org/DOI: 10.33022/ijcs.v12i4.3266

Sardoc, M., Coady, C. A. J., Bufacchi, V., Moghaddam, F. M., Cassam, Q., Silva, D., Miscevic, N., Andrejc, G., Kodelja, Z., Vezjak, B., Peters, M. A., & Tesar, M. (2020). Philosophy of education in a new key: On radicalization and violent extremism. *Educational Philosophy and Theory*. Advance online publication. DOI: 10.1080/00131857.2020.1861937

Saricam, U., & Yıldırım, M. (2021). The Effects of Digital Game-based STEM Activities on Students' Interests in STEM Fields and Scientific Creativity: Minecraft Case. In International Journal of Technology in Education and Science (Vol. 5, Number 2, p. 166). https://doi.org/DOI: 10.46328/ijtes.136

Sartre, J.-P. (1992). *Being and Nothingness: An Essay on Phenomenological Ontology*. Washington Square Press.

Sathyapriya, G., Natarajan, U., Sureshkumar, B., Navaneethakrishnan, G., Palanisamy, R., Bajaj, M., & Sharma, N. K., & Kitmo. (2022). Quality and Tool Stability Improvement in Turning Operation Using Plastic Compliant Damper. *Journal of Nanomaterials, 2022*. Advance online publication. DOI: 10.1155/2022/8654603

Sathyaseelan, K., Vyas, T., Madala, R., Chamundeeswari, V., Rai Goyal, H., & Jayaraman, R. (2023). Blockchain Enabled Intelligent Surveillance System Model with AI and IoT. *Proceedings of 8th IEEE International Conference on Science, Technology, Engineering and Mathematics, ICONSTEM 2023*. https://doi.org/DOI: 10.1109/ICONSTEM56934.2023.10142303

Schaffers, H., Komninos, N., Pallot, M., ... (2011). "Smart Cities and the Future Internet: Towards Cooperation Frameworks for Open Innovation." *The Future Internet Assembly*, 431-446.

Schiff, D., Rakova, B., Ayesh, A., Fanti, A., & Lennon, M. (2021). Explaining the Principles to Practices Gap in AI. In IEEE Technology and Society Magazine (Vol. 40, Number 2, p. 81). Institute of Electrical and Electronics Engineers. https://doi.org/DOI: 10.1109/mts.2021.3056286

Schildkamp, K. (2019). Data-based decision-making for school improvement: Research insights and gaps. *Educational Research*, *61*(3), 257–273.

Schmid, R., Pauli, C., Stebler, R., Reusser, K., & Petko, D. (2022). Implementation of technology-supported personalized learning—Its impact on instructional quality. [tandfonline.com]. *The Journal of Educational Research*, *115*(3), 187–198.

Scribes, S. (2024). A discourse on generative AI. *Medium*. https://medium.com/@sundryscribes/a-discourse-on-generative-ai-4ca4a8911e1a

Searle, J. R. (1980). Minds, brains, and programs. *Behavioral and Brain Sciences*, *3*(3), 417–424. DOI: 10.1017/S0140525X00005756

Secretariat, A. (2018). *Guidelines ASEAN MRA-TP Trainers and Assessors*. ASEAN: A Community of Oppurtunities.

Secretariat, T. A. (2018). Handbook of ASEAN Mutual Recognition Arrangement on Tourism Professionals. Jakarta: ASEAN: A Community of Opportunities.

Secretariat, T. G. (2022, january). https://asean.org. Retrieved 10 22, 2022, from https://asean.org: https://asean.org/wp-content/uploads/2022/08/2022-01-17_Final-draft_RPL-mechanism-for-ATP.pdf

Secretary, A. (2021). *asean.org*. Retrieved from https://asean.org/wp-content/uploads/2021/01/Common-ASEAN-Tourism-Curriculum.pdf

Selbst, A. D. (2017). Disparate Impact in Big Data Policing. In SSRN Electronic Journal. RELX Group (Netherlands). https://doi.org/DOI: 10.2139/ssrn.2819182

Selwyn, N. (2010). Looking Beyond Learning: Notes Towards the Critical Study of Educational Technology. *Journal of Computer Assisted Learning*, *26*, 65–73.

Selwyn, N. (2014). Education and 'the Digital'. *British Journal of Sociology of Education*, *35*(1), 155–164.

Selwyn, N. (2020). *Should robots replace teachers? AI and the future of education*. Polity Press.

Selwyn, N. (2022). The future of AI and education: Some cautionary notes. *European Journal of Education*, *57*(4), 620–631. DOI: 10.1111/ejed.12532

Selwyn, N., & Facer, K. (2014). *The politics of education and technology: Conflicts, controversies, and connections*. Palgrave Macmillan.

Seo, K., Tang, J., Roll, I., Fels, S., & Yoon, D. (2021). The impact of artificial intelligence on learner–instructor interaction in online learning. *International Journal of Educational Technology in Higher Education*, *18*(1), 54. DOI: 10.1186/s41239-021-00292-9 PMID: 34778540

Sergio, M., Gabriel, D., Sancristobal, E., Rosario, G., Manuel, C., & Juan, P. (2011). New Technology Trends in Education: Seven Years of Forecasts and Convergence. *Computer Education*, *57*, 1893–1906.

Setyoadi, E., & Patmanthara, S. (2024). Students' goal orientation and gamification in learning for academic performance: A systematic literature review. *Research and Development in Education (Raden)*, *4*(1), 390–403. DOI: 10.22219/raden.v4i1.32630

Shah, J. (2024). Rethinking higher education through multidisciplinary studies. jes, 20(4s), 2060-2063. https://doi.org/DOI: 10.52783/jes.2309

Shah, J. K., Sharma, R., Misra, A., Sharma, M., Joshi, S., Kaushal, D., & Bafila, S. (2023). Industry 4.0 Enabled Smart Manufacturing: Unleashing the Power of Artificial Intelligence and Blockchain. *2023 1st DMIHER International Conference on Artificial Intelligence in Education and Industry 4.0, IDICAIEI 2023*. https://doi .org/DOI: 10.1109/IDICAIEI58380.2023.10406671

Shaheen, N. L. (2022). Technology accessibility: How US K-12 schools are enacting policy and addressing the equity imperative. [HTML]. *Computers & Education.*

Shahini, R., Davis, H., & Borthwick, K. (2019). *Design recommendations to address cultural issues in multicultural MOOCs: a systematic literature review.*, DOI: 10.14705/rpnet.2019.36.956

Shaik, T., Tao, X., Li, Y., Dann, C., McDonald, J., Redmond, P., & Galligan, L. (2022). A Review of the Trends and Challenges in Adopting Natural Language Processing Methods for Education Feedback Analysis. *IEEE Access : Practical Innovations, Open Solutions*, *10*, 56720–56739. DOI: 10.1109/ACCESS.2022.3177752

Shamsi, H. A., Almutairi, A. G., Mashrafi, S. A., & Kalbani, T. A. (2020). Implications of Language Barriers for Healthcare: A Systematic Review [Review of Implications of Language Barriers for Healthcare: A Systematic Review]. Oman Medical Journal, 35(2). Oman Medical Specialty Board. https://doi.org/DOI: 10.5001/omj.2020.40

Shana, Z. A., & Abd Al Baki, S. (2020). Using plickers in formative assessment to augment student learning. [IJMBL]. *International Journal of Mobile and Blended Learning*, *12*(2), 57–76.

Sharma, A. K., Sharma, A., Singh, Y., & Chen, W.-H. (2021). Production of a sustainable fuel from microalgae Chlorella minutissima grown in a 1500 L open raceway ponds. *Biomass and Bioenergy*, *149*. Advance online publication. DOI: 10.1016/j.biombioe.2021.106073

Sharma, K., Pandit, S., Sen Thapa, B., & Pant, M. (2022). Biodegradation of Congo Red Using Co-Culture Anode Inoculum in a Microbial Fuel Cell. *Catalysts*, *12*(10). Advance online publication. DOI: 10.3390/catal12101219

Sharma, S., Kandpal, V., Choudhury, T., Santibanez Gonzalez, E. D. R., & Agarwal, N. (2023). Assessment of the implications of energy-efficient technologies on the environmental sustainability of rail operation. *AIMS Environmental Science*, *10*(5), 709–731. DOI: 10.3934/environsci.2023039

Shashikala, R., Singh, B. P., Azam, M., & Magesh, C. R. Rajat, & Singh, D. P. (2022). IoT Engineering Nanomaterial's Approach To Sustainable Advance Crop Production Management. *2022 2nd International Conference on Advance Computing and Innovative Technologies in Engineering, ICACITE 2022*, 2284 – 2288. https://doi.org/DOI: 10.1109/ICACITE53722.2022.9823573

Shedole, S., & Soni, S. (2017). Predictive analytics to prevent and control chronic diseases. *International Journal of Computer Applications*, *157*(7), 1–5.

Shneiderman, B. (2020). Human-Centered Artificial Intelligence: Three Fresh Ideas. In AIS Transactions on Human-Computer Interaction (p. 109). Association for Information Systems. https://doi.org/DOI: 10.17705/1thci.00131

Siegel, H. (1983). On the obligations of the professional philosopher of education. *Journal of Thought*, *18*(2), 31–37.

Silcox, C., Zimlichmann, E., Huber, K., Rowen, N. P., Saunders, R. S., McClellan, M., Kahn, C. N., Salzberg, C., & Bates, D. W. (2024). The potential for artificial intelligence to transform healthcare: perspectives from international health leaders. In npj Digital Medicine (Vol. 7, Issue 1). Nature Portfolio. https://doi.org/DOI: 10.1038/s41746-024-01097-6

Silva, J., & Gomez, M. (2025). Advancements in Human-Computer Interaction Through Natural Language Processing and Voice Recognition. *Journal of Computing Innovations and Applications*, *3*(1), 8–12.

Singamaneni, K. K., Dhiman, G., Juneja, S., Muhammad, G., AlQahtani, S. A., & Zaki, J. (2022). A Novel QKD Approach to Enhance IIOT Privacy and Computational Knacks. *Sensors (Basel)*, *22*(18). Advance online publication. DOI: 10.3390/s22186741 PMID: 36146089

Singer, P. (1975). *Animal Liberation: A New Ethics for Our Treatment of Animals.* HarperCollins.

Singh, K. D., Singh, P., Chhabra, R., Kaur, G., Bansal, A., & Tripathi, V. (2023). Cyber-Physical Systems for Smart City Applications: A Comparative Study. In K. R., K. R., G. M., G. M., S. R., & S. R. (Eds.), *2023 International Conference on Advancement in Computation and Computer Technologies, InCACCT 2023* (pp. 871 – 876). Institute of Electrical and Electronics Engineers Inc. https://doi.org/DOI: 10.1109/InCACCT57535.2023.10141719

Singha, S., Singha, R., Ruben, V. M., Jose, S., Mize, E., & Haokip, A. D. (2024). Navigating the Landscape of Inclusive Education: Bridging the Policy-Practice Divide. In Exploring Educational Equity at the Intersection of Policy and Practice (pp. 176-194). IGI Global. [HTML]

Singh, A., Kumar, P., & Taneja, S. (2024). Artificial Intelligence and Machine Learning-Powered Smart Finance. In Taneja, P. K. S., & Singh, A. (Eds.), *IGI Global*. IGI Global., DOI: 10.4018/979-8-3693-3264-1

Singh, N. K., Singh, Y., Rahim, E. A., Senthil Siva Subramanian, T., & Sharma, A. (2023). Electric discharge machining of hybrid composite with bio-dielectrics for sustainable developments. *Australian Journal of Mechanical Engineering*. Advance online publication. DOI: 10.1080/14484846.2023.2249577

Singh, R., Chandra, A. S., Bbhagat, B., Panduro-Ramirez, J., Gaikwad, A. P., & Pant, B. (2022). Cloud Computing, Machine Learning, and Secure Data Sharing enabled through Blockchain. *Proceedings of 5th International Conference on Contemporary Computing and Informatics, IC3I 2022*, 282 – 286. https://doi.org/DOI: 10.1109/IC3I56241.2022.10072925

Singh, S. P., Piras, G., Viriyasitavat, W., Kariri, E., Yadav, K., Dhiman, G., Vimal, S., & Khan, S. B. (2023). Cyber Security and 5G-assisted Industrial Internet of Things using Novel Artificial Adaption based Evolutionary Algorithm. *Mobile Networks and Applications*. Advance online publication. DOI: 10.1007/s11036-023-02230-7

Singla, R. K., De, R., Efferth, T., Mezzetti, B., & Sahab Uddin, M., Sanusi, Ntie-Kang, F., Wang, D., Schultz, F., Kharat, K. R., Devkota, H. P., Battino, M., Sur, D., Lordan, R., Patnaik, S. S., Tsagkaris, C., Sai, C. S., Tripathi, S. K., Găman, M.-A., … Shen, B. (2023). The International Natural Product Sciences Taskforce (INPST) and the power of Twitter networking exemplified through #INPST hashtag analysis. *Phytomedicine*, *108*. Advance online publication. DOI: 10.1016/j.phymed.2022.154520 PMID: 36334386

SIREP. (2010). *Teaching Competency Standards in Southeast Asian Countries: ELEVEN COUNTRY AUDIT.* Philippine: SEAMEO INNOTECH.

Slater, M., & Sanchez-Vives, M. V. (2016). Enhancing our lives with immersive virtual reality. *Frontiers in Robotics and AI*, *3*, 74.

Smith, J. (2022). International education trends: Shaping the future of higher education. *International Journal of Open Publication and Exploration*, *10*(1), 1–5.

Smith, J., & Lee, K. A. I. (2022). AI in Language Assessment: Enhancing Validity and Efficiency. *Journal of Educational Technology*, *18*(2), 145–160.

Su, Y. (2014). Development of the Teaching Games System Based on Mobile Learning. In *Applied Mechanics and Materials* (Vol. 685, p. 651). Trans Tech Publications., DOI: 10.4028/www.scientific.net/amm.685.651

Ta, R., & Lee, N. (2023). How Language Gaps Constrain Generative AI Development. In International Journal of Comparative Studies in International Relations and Development (Vol. 9, Issue 1, p. 48). https://doi.org/DOI: 10.48028/iiprds/ijcsird.v9.i1.03

Takeuchi, L., & Vaala, S. E. (2014). Level up Learning: A National Survey on Teaching with Digital Games. https://files.eric.ed.gov/fulltext/ED555585.pdf

Taneja, S., Gupta, S., Singh, A., Bhatnagar, M., & Gaur, A. (2023). Green management - A new paradigm in the world of business. *Green Management - A New Paradigm in the World of Business*, 1–230. https://doi.org/DOI: 10.52305/DLIH6622

Taneja, S., Ozen, E., Kumar, P., & Reepu. (2025). *E-Finance: Transformative Strategies for Sustainable Development in the Digital Era*. Nova Science Publisher Inc. https://doi.org/https://doi.org/10.52305/NZSJ1375

Taneja, S., Bhatnagar, M., Kumar, P., & Grima, S. (2023). A Panel Analysis of the Effectiveness of the Asset Management in Indian Agricultural Companies. *International Journal of Sustainable Development and Planning*, *18*(3), 653–660. DOI: 10.18280/ijsdp.180301

Taneja, S., Bhatnagar, M., Kumar, P., & Rupeika-apoga, R. (2023). India ' s Total Natural Resource Rents (NRR) and GDP : An Augmented Autoregressive Distributed Lag (ARDL) Bound Test. *Journal of Risk and Financial Management*, *16*(2), 91. https://doi.org/doi.org/10.3390/jrfm16020091

Taneja, S., Chahal, B. P. S., Johri, A., Ozen, E., & Kumar, P. (2024). *Neuromarketing's Role in Sustainable Finance*. IGI Global., DOI: 10.4018/979-8-3693-9117-4

Taneja, S., & Sharma, V. (2023). Role of beaconing marketing in improving customer buying experience. In *Enhancing Customer Engagement Through Location-Based Marketing* (pp. 176–184). IGI Global., DOI: 10.4018/978-1-6684-8177-6.ch012

Tao, Y., Viberg, O., Baker, R. S., & Kizilcec, R. F. (2024). Cultural bias and cultural alignment of large language models. In Nexus, P. N. A. S. (Ed.), *Issue 9). Oxford University Press* (Vol. 3)., DOI: 10.1093/pnasnexus/pgae346

Tesar, M. (2021). Philosophy as a method: Tracing the histories of intersections of 'philosophy', 'methodology' and 'education. *Qualitative Inquiry*, *27*(5), 544–553. DOI: 10.1177/1077800420934144

Thampy, H., Walsh, J., & Harris, B. (2023). Playing the game: The educational role of gamified peer-led assessment. In The Clinical Teacher (Vol. 20, Number 4). Wiley. https://doi.org/DOI: 10.1111/tct.13594

Thimmanna, A. V. N. S., Naik, M. S., Radhakrishnan, S., & Sharma, A. (2024). Personalized learning paths: Adapting education with AI-driven curriculum. [EEL]. *European Economic Letters*, *14*(1), 31–40.

Thomson, I. (2004). Heidegger's Perfectionist Philosophy of Education in Being and Time. *Continental Philosophy Review*, *7*(4), 439–467.

Thumlert, K., Castell, S., & Jenson, J. (2015). Short Cuts and Extended Techniques: Rethinking Relations Between Technology and Educational Theory. *Educational Philosophy and Theory*, *47*(8), 786–803.

Tim. (2016). *Membangun Pendidikan Menengah Kejuruan Indonesia: Sebuah Peta Jalan Menuju 2030 (Building Indonesian Vocational Secondary Education: A Roadmap to 2030).* The Deutsche Gesellschaft für Internationale Zusammenarbeit (GIZ) GmbH.

Tolentino, R. (2024). Curriculum frameworks and educational programs in ai for medical students, residents, and practicing physicians: Scoping review. *JMIR Medical Education*, *10*, e54793. DOI: 10.2196/54793 PMID: 39023999

Tomar, S., Sharma, N., & Nehra, N. S. (2023). A sustainable rural entrepreneurship model developed by the organic farmers of India. *Emerald Emerging Markets Case Studies*, *13*(2), 1–17. DOI: 10.1108/EEMCS-09-2022-0329

Tomašev, N., Maynard, J. L., & Gabriel, I. (2022). Manifestations of Xenophobia in AI Systems. In arXiv (Cornell University). Cornell University. https://doi.org/DOI: 10.48550/arXiv.2212

Tomkin, J. H., Beilstein, S. O., Morphew, J. W., & Herman, G. L. (2019). Evidence that communities of practice are associated with active learning in large STEM lectures. *International Journal of STEM Education*, *6*(1), 1. DOI: 10.1186/s40594-018-0154-z

Tomlinson, B. (2016). The Importance of Materials Development for Language Learning. *Issues in Materials Development*, (1998), 1–9. https://doi.org/DOI: 10.1007/978-94-6300-432-9_1

Tonbuloğlu, B. (2023). An evaluation of the use of artificial intelligence applications in online education. *Journal of Educational Technology and Online Learning*, *6*(4), 866–884. DOI: 10.31681/jetol.1335906

Townsend, A. M. (2013). *Smart Cities: Big Data, Civic Hackers, and the Quest for a New Utopia*. W.W. Norton & Company.

Tractenberg, R. E., Gushta, M. M., Mulrooney, T. J., & Weissinger, P. A. (2020). The assessment evaluation rubric: Promoting learning and learner-centered assessments through a comprehensive evaluation of assessments. *International Journal on Teaching and Learning in Higher Education*, *32*(1), 26–37.

Trajtenberg, M. (2018). *AI as the next GPT: A political-economy perspective*. National Bureau of Economic Research., DOI: 10.3386/w24245

Trang, N., & Thư, P. (2024). The role of ai in improving student learning outcomes: Evidence in vietnam. *International Journal of Multidisciplinary Research and Analysis*, *07*(06). Advance online publication. DOI: 10.47191/ijmra/v7-i06-48

Tripathy, S., Verma, D. K., Thakur, M., Patel, A. R., Srivastav, P. P., Singh, S., Chávez-González, M. L., & Aguilar, C. N. (2021). Encapsulated Food Products as a Strategy to Strengthen Immunity Against COVID-19. *Frontiers in Nutrition*, *8*. Advance online publication. DOI: 10.3389/fnut.2021.673174 PMID: 34095193

Trust, T. (2020). The 3 Cs of professional development: Creating, collaborating, and coaching. *Educational Technology Research and Development*, *68*, 1429–U.S. Department of Education. (2022). *National Educational Technology Plan*.

Tsai, C., Ma, Y., Chang, Y., & Lai, Y.-H. (2022). Integrating Multiculturalism Into Artificial Intelligence-Assisted Programming Lessons: Examining Inter-Ethnicity Differences in Learning Expectancy, Motivation, and Effectiveness. In Frontiers in Psychology (Vol. 13). Frontiers Media. https://doi.org/DOI: 10.3389/fpsyg.2022.868698

Tubino, L. & Adachi, C. (2022). Developing feedback literacy capabilities through an ai automated feedback tool. Ascilite Publications, e22039. https://doi.org/DOI: 10.14742/apubs.2022.39

Turkle, S. (2011). *Alone Together: Why We Expect More from Technology and Less from Each Other*. Basic Books.

Turnbull, D., Chugh, R., & Luck, J. (2021). Transitioning to E-Learning during the COVID-19 pandemic: How have Higher Education Institutions responded to the challenge?. Education and Information Technologies. springer.com

Tyni, J., Tarkiainen, A., López-Pernas, S., Saqr, M., Kahila, J., Bednarik, R., & Tedre, M. (2022). Games and rewards: A scientometric study of rewards in educational and serious games. *IEEE Access : Practical Innovations, Open Solutions*, *10*, 31578–31585. DOI: 10.1109/access.2022.3160230

Tzafilkou, K., Perifanou, M., & Economides, A. (2023). Assessing teachers' digital competence in primary and secondary education: Applying a new instrument to integrate pedagogical and professional elements for digital education. *Education and Information Technologies, 28*(12), 16017–16040. DOI: 10.1007/s10639-023-11848-9 PMID: 37361819

UNESCO. (2020). *Education and the COVID-19 pandemic: A global perspective.* https://www.unesco.org/en/covid-19/education-response

UNESCO. (2021). *Digital learning and the digital divide: Policies and practices to build digital citizenship.* United Nations Educational, Scientific and Cultural Organization.

UNESCO. (2021). *Media and Information Literacy: A critical approach to literacy in a digital world.*

Uniyal, A. K., Kanojia, P., Khanna, R., & Dixit, A. K. (2022). Quantitative Analysis of the Impact of Demography and Job Profile on the Organizational Commitment of the Faculty Members in the HEI'S of Uttarakhand. *Communications in Computer and Information Science, 1742 CCIS*, 24–35. https://doi.org/DOI: 10.1007/978-3-031-23647-1_3

Uniyal, S., Mangla, S. K., Sarma, P. R. S., Tseng, M.-L., & Patil, P. (2021). ICT as "Knowledge management" for assessing sustainable consumption and production in supply chains. *Journal of Global Information Management, 29*(1), 164–198. DOI: 10.4018/JGIM.2021010109

Upreti, H., & Malhotra, R. K. (2024). Bridging The Urban-Rural Education Gap In India Through CSR (Corporate Social Responsibility) Initiatives: A Conceptual Study With Special Reference To Sustainable Development Goal 4 (Quality Education). In P. P.K. (Ed.), *E3S Web of Conferences* (Vol. 556). EDP Sciences. https://doi.org/DOI: 10.1051/e3sconf/202455601032

Upreti, H., Uddin, Z., Pandey, A. K., & Joshi, N. (2023). Particle swarm optimization based numerical study for pressure, flow, and heat transfer over a rotating disk with temperature dependent nanofluid properties. *Numerical Heat Transfer Part A, 83*(8), 815–844. DOI: 10.1080/10407782.2022.2156412

Uygun, D. (2024). Teachers' perspectives on artificial intelligence in education. *Advances in Mobile Learning Educational Research, 4*(1), 931–939. DOI: 10.25082/amler.2024.01.005

van de Werfhorst, H. G., Kessenich, E., & Geven, S. (2020, August 18). *The Digital Divide in Online Education. Inequality in Digital Preparedness of Students and Schools before the Start of the COVID-19 Pandemic*. https://doi.org/DOI: 10.31235/osf.io/58d6p

van der Vorst, T., & Jelicic, N. (2019). Artificial intelligence in education: Can AI bring the full potential of personalized learning to education? https://www.econstor.eu/handle/10419/205222

van Dijk, J. (2020). *The digital divide*. Polity Press.

Vanolo, A. (2014). Smartmentality: The Smart City as Disciplinary Strategy. *Urban Studies (Edinburgh, Scotland)*, *51*(5), 883–898.

Varaki, B. S., Sadeqzadeh Qamsari, A., Sefidkhosh, M., Mahdi Sajjadi, S., Mohammadi Chaboki, R., Javidi Kalatehjafarabadi, T., Saffarheidari, H., Mohammadamini, M., Karimzadeh, O., Barkhordari, M., Zarghami-Hamrah, S., Peters, M. A., & Tesar, M. (2021). Philosophy of education in a new key: Reflection on higher education in Iran. *Educational Philosophy and Theory*. Advance online publication. DOI: 10.1080/00131857.2021.1905517

Vashishth, T. K., Sharma, V., Sharma, K. K., & Kumar, B. (2024). *Enhancing Literacy Education in Higher Institutions With AI Opportunities and Challenges*. https://doi.org/DOI: 10.4018/979-8-3693-2728-9.ch009

Verbeek, P. (2008). Cyborg Intentionality: Rethinking the Phenomenology of Human–Technology Relations. *Phenomenology and the Cognitive Sciences*, *7*(3), 387–395.

Verde, A. & Valero, J. M. (2021). Teaching and learning modalities in higher education during the pandemic: Responses to coronavirus disease 2019 from Spain. Frontiers in Psychology. frontiersin.org

Verma, M., Ahmad, W., Park, J.-H., Kumar, V., Vlaskin, M. S., Vaya, D., & Kim, H. (2022). One-step functionalization of chitosan using EDTA: Kinetics and isotherms modeling for multiple heavy metals adsorption and their mechanism. *Journal of Water Process Engineering*, *49*. Advance online publication. DOI: 10.1016/j.jwpe.2022.102989

Vinuesa, R., Azizpour, H., Leite, I., Balaam, M., Dignum, V., Domisch, S., Felländer, A., Langhans, S. D., Tegmark, M., & Nerini, F. F. (2020). The role of artificial intelligence in achieving the Sustainable Development Goals [Review of The role of artificial intelligence in achieving the Sustainable Development Goals]. Nature Communications, 11(1). Nature Portfolio. https://doi.org/DOI: 10.1038/s41467-019-14108-y

Voigt, P., & Von dem Bussche, A. (2017). *The EU General Data Protection Regulation (GDPR): A Practical Guide*. Springer.

Waghid, Y., Davids, N., Mathebula, T., Terblanche, J., Higgs, P., Shawa, L., Herbert Manthalu, C., Waghid, Z., Ngwenya, C., Divala, J., Waghid, F., Peters, M. A., & Tesar, M. (2020). Philosophy of education in a new key: Cultivating a living philosophy of education to overcome coloniality and violence in African Universities. *Educational Philosophy and Theory*. Advance online publication. DOI: 10.1080/00131857.2020.1793714

Wali, E., Chen, Y., Mahoney, C., Middleton, T., Babaeianjelodar, M., Njie, M., & Matthews, J. (2023). Is Machine Learning Speaking my Language? A Critical Look at the NLP-Pipeline Across 8 Human Languages. https://arxiv.org/pdf/2007.05872.pdf

Wallach, W., & Allen, C. (2008). *Moral Machines: Teaching Robots Right from Wrong*. Oxford University Press.

Walter, Y. (2024). Embracing the future of artificial intelligence in the classroom: The relevance of ai literacy, prompt engineering, and critical thinking in modern education. *International Journal of Educational Technology in Higher Education, 21*(1). Advance online publication. DOI: 10.1186/s41239-024-00448-3

Wang, N., & Lester, J. C. (2023). K-12 Education in the Age of AI: A Call to Action for K-12 AI Literacy. In International Journal of Artificial Intelligence in Education (Vol. 33, Issue 2, p. 228). Springer Science+Business Media. https://doi.org/DOI: 10.1007/s40593-023-00358-x

Wang, X. W. Carnegie Mellon University, xinyiw1@cs. cmu. edu, Sebastian Ruder, Google Research, ruder@google. com, Graham Neubig, Carnegie Mellon University, gneubig@cs. cmu. edu. (2023). Expanding Pretrained Models to Thousands More Languages via Lexicon-based Adaptation. https://arxiv.org/pdf/2203.09435.pdf

Wang, J., Guo, B., & Chen, L. (2022). Human-in-the-loop Machine Learning: A Macro-Micro Perspective. In arXiv (Cornell University). Cornell University. https://doi.org/DOI. 10.48550/arXiv.2202

Wang, Q., Woo, H. L., Quek, C. L., Yang, Y., & Liu, M. (2022). Using the community of inquiry framework to scaffold online learning. *Educational Technology Research and Development, 70*(3), 841–859.

Wang, W. X. Z. W. R. S. (2024). Monolingual and Multilingual Misinformation Detection for Low-Resource Languages: A Comprehensive Survey. https://arxiv.org/abs/2410.18390

Wardle, C., & Derakhshan, H. (2017). *Information disorder: Toward an interdisciplinary framework for research and policymaking*. Council of Europe.

Warschauer, M. (2004). *Technology and social inclusion: Rethinking the digital divide*. MIT Press.

Washburn, D., Sindhu, U., Balaouras, S., et al. (2010). "Helping CIOs Understand 'Smart City' Initiatives: Defining the Smart City, Its Drivers, and the Role of the CIO." *Forrester Research Inc.*, 1-17.

WEF. (2020). *he Future of Jobs Report 2020.* World Economic Forum.

Weiss, D. (2008). Human—Technology—World. *Techné: Research in Philosophy and Technology*, *12*(2), 110–119.

Wendrich, R. E. (2020). CREATIVE THINKING: COMPUTATIONAL TOOLS IMBUED WITH AI. In *Proceedings of the Design Society DESIGN Conference* (Vol. 1, p. 481). Cambridge University Press. https://doi.org/DOI: 10.1017/dsd.2020.7

Weng, Y., Wu, J., Kelly, T., & Johnson, W. (2024). Comprehensive Overview of Artificial Intelligence Applications in Modern Industries. https://doi.org/DOI: 10.20944/preprints202409.1638.v1

West, D. M. (2018). *The Future of Work: Robots, AI, and Automation*. Brookings Institution Press.

West, S. M. (2019). Data capitalism: Redefining the logics of surveillance and privacy. *Business & Society*, *58*(1), 20–41.

Whalley, B., France, D., Park, J., Mauchline, A., & Welsh, K. (2021). Towards flexible personalized learning and the future educational system in the fourth industrial revolution in the wake of Covid-19. [tandfonline.com]. *Higher Education Pedagogies*, *6*(1), 79–99.

Whitehead, A. N. (1929). *Process and Reality: An Essay in Cosmology*. Macmillan.

Wiggins, G., & McTighe, J. (2005). *Understanding by design* (Expanded 2nd ed.). Association for Supervision and Curriculum Development (ASCD).

Willet, R. (2018). Learning Through Making in Public Libraries: Theories, Practices, and Tensions. *Learning, Media and Technology*, *43*(3), 250–262.

Williamson, B., & Piattoeva, N. (2020). Education governance and datafication. *Learning, Media and Technology*, *45*(3), 251–258.

Winanti, W., Abbas, B. S., Suparta, W., Heryadi, Y., & Gaol, F. L. (2021). Gamification Framework for Programming Course in Higher Education. In Journal of Games Game Art and Gamification (Vol. 5, Number 2, p. 54). Bina Nusantara University. https://doi.org/DOI: 10.21512/jggag.v5i2.7479

Wineburg, S., & Grossman, P. (2000). Interdisciplinary curriculum: Challenges to implementation. Teachers College Press, 1234 Amsterdam Avenue, New York, NY 10027

Wong, P. (2020). Cultural Differences as Excuses? Human Rights and Cultural Values in Global Ethics and Governance of AI. In Philosophy & Technology (Vol. 33, Issue 4, p. 705). Springer Nature (Netherlands). https://doi.org/DOI: 10.1007/s13347-020-00413-8

Wood, E., Ange, B., & Miller, D. (2021). Are we ready to integrate artificial intelligence literacy into medical school curriculum: Students and faculty survey. *Journal of Medical Education and Curricular Development*, *8*. Advance online publication. DOI: 10.1177/23821205211024078 PMID: 34250242

Woo, J. H., & Choi, H. (2021). Systematic Review for AI-based Language Learning Tools. In arXiv (Cornell University). Cornell University. https://doi.org/DOI: 10.48550/arXiv.2111

Wrathall, A. (2011). We Still Need Education in Thinking: Heidegger's Education in a Technological Age. *Journal of Educational Studies*, *7*(1), 3–14.

Wu, G. S. (2009). *Lectures on the Philosophy of Technology*. China Renmin University Press.

Yaccob, N. S., & Rahman, S. F. Abd., Mohamad, S. N. A., Rahim, A. A. A., Rashid, K. K. A., Aldaba, A. M. A., Yunus, M. M., & Hashim, H. (2022). Gamifying ESL Classrooms through Gamified Teaching and Learning. In Arab World English Journal (Number 8, p. 177). Arab World English Journal. https://doi.org/DOI: 10.24093/awej/call8.12

Yadav, A., Singh, Y., Singh, S., & Negi, P. (2021). Sustainability of vegetable oil based bio-diesel as dielectric fluid during EDM process - A review. In S. Y. (Ed.), *Materials Today: Proceedings* (Vol. 46, pp. 11155 – 11158). Elsevier Ltd. https://doi.org/DOI: 10.1016/j.matpr.2021.01.967

Yam, K. C., Tan, T. C. Y., Jackson, J. C., Shariff, A., & Gray, K. (2023). Cultural Differences in People's Reactions and Applications of Robots, Algorithms, and Artificial Intelligence. In Management and Organization Review (Vol. 19, Issue 5, p. 859). Cambridge University Press. https://doi.org/DOI: 10.1017/mor.2023.21

Yannier, N., Hudson, S. E., Koedinger, K. R., Hirsh-Pasek, K., Golinkoff, R. M., Munakata, Y., & Brownell, S. E. (2021). Active learning: "Hands-on" meets "minds-on.". *Science*, *374*(6563), 26–30. DOI: 10.1126/science.abj9957 PMID: 34591619

Yazdanpanah, V., Gerding, E., Stein, S., Dastani, M., Jonker, C., Norman, T., & Ramchurn, S. (2022). Reasoning about responsibility in autonomous systems: Challenges and opportunities. *AI & Society*, *38*(4), 1453–1464. DOI: 10.1007/s00146-022-01607-8

Yigitcanlar, T., & Kamruzzaman, M. (2018). Does Smart City Policy Lead to Sustainability of Cities? *Land Use Policy*, *73*, 49–58.

Yogi Anggraena, D. G. (2022). *Panduan Pembelajaran dan Asesmen Pendidikan Anak Usia Dini, Pendidikan Dasar, dan Menengah (Guidelines for Learning and Assessment in Early Childhood, Primary and Secondary Education).* Badan Standar, Kurikulum, dan Asesmen Pendidikan, Kementerian Pendidikan, Kebudayaan, Riset, dan Teknologi.

Young, M. C., Courtad, C. A., Douglas, K. H., & Chung, Y.-C. (2019). The Effects of Text-to-Speech on Reading Outcomes for Secondary Students With Learning Disabilities. *Journal of Special Education Technology*, *34*(2), 80–91. DOI: 10.1177/0162643418786047

Yue, X., & Ji, R. (2020). Teacher Professional Competencies in Education for Sustainable Development. In *IntechOpen eBooks*. IntechOpen., DOI: 10.5772/intechopen.94991

Yuste, R., Goering, S., Arcas, B. A. Y., Bi, G., Carmena, J. M., Carter, A., & Wolpaw, J. (2017). Four ethical priorities for neurotechnologies and AI. *Nature*, *551*(7679), 159–163. PMID: 29120438

Yu, Z., Gao, M., & Wang, L. (2021). The effect of educational games on learning outcomes, student motivation, engagement and satisfaction. [HTML]. *Journal of Educational Computing Research*, *59*(3), 522–546.

Zaghlool, Z. D., & Khasawneh, M. A. S. (2023). Incorporating the Impacts and Limitations of AI-Driven Feedback, Evaluation, and Real-Time Conversation Tools in Foreign Language Learning. *Migration Letters : An International Journal of Migration Studies*, *20*(7), 1071–1083.

Zainal, N. (2023). University students' perspectives on gamification in vocabulary learning: A literature review. *Malaysian Journal of Social Sciences and Humanities (Mjssh)*, *8*(5), e002314. DOI: 10.47405/mjssh.v8i5.2314

Zanella, A., Bui, N., & Castellani, A.. (2014). Internet of Things for Smart Cities. *IEEE Internet of Things Journal*, *1*(1), 22–32.

Zhai, X., Chu, X., Chai, C. S., Jong, M. S., Starčič, A. I., Spector, M., Liu, J., Jing, Y., & Li, Y. (2021). A Review of Artificial Intelligence (AI) in Education from 2010 to 2020 [Review of A Review of Artificial Intelligence (AI) in Education from 2010 to 2020]. Complexity, 2021(1). Hindawi Publishing Corporation. https://doi.org/DOI: 10.1155/2021/8812542

Zhai, C., Wibowo, S., & Li, L. D. (2024). The effects of over-reliance on AI dialogue systems on students' cognitive abilities: A systematic review. *Smart Learning Environments*, *11*(1), 28.

Zhang, J. (2024). AI in teacher education: Unlocking new dimensions in teaching support, inclusive learning, and digital literacy. *Journal of Computer Assisted Learning*, *40*(4), 1871–1885. DOI: 10.1111/jcal.12988

Zhang, J., Liu, Y., & Wang, X. (2024). Simulation and virtual reality applications in STEM education: An overview. *International Journal of STEM Education*, *11*(1), 1–15.

Zhang, K., & Aslan, A. B. (2021). AI technologies for education: Recent research & future directions. Computers and education. *Artificial Intelligence*, *2*, 100025.

Zhang, Z. (2022). Promoting student engagement with feedback: Insights from collaborative pedagogy and teacher feedback. [HTML]. *Assessment & Evaluation in Higher Education*.

Zhanqiang, M. (2023). Strategies for Cultivating Creative Thinking Ability of Students Majoring in Educational Technology. In Frontiers in Educational Research (Vol. 6, Number 19). https://doi.org/DOI: 10.25236/fer.2023.061911

Zhao, Y., & Watterston, J. (2021). The changes we need: Education post COVID-19. In Journal of Educational Change (Vol. 22, Number 1, p. 3). Springer Science+Business Media. https://doi.org/DOI: 10.1007/s10833-021-09417-3

Zhao, D., Playfoot, J., Nicola, C. D., Guarino, G., Bratu, M., Salvadore, F. D., & Muntean, G. (2021). An Innovative Multi-Layer Gamification Framework for Improved STEM Learning Experience. In Access, I. E. E. E. (Ed.), Vol. 10, p. 3879). Institute of Electrical and Electronics Engineers., DOI: 10.1109/access.2021.3139729

Zhao, J., Juithong, S., & Nilnopkoon, P. (2024). Effecting an adaptive learning system on academic achievement as regulations for measuring pharmacist qualifications to licensure of pharmaceutical management students. *IJSASR*, *4*(3), 573–582. DOI: 10.60027/ijsasr.2024.4357

Zhao, Y., Pugh, K., Sheldon, S., & Byers, J. (2002). Conditions for Classroom Technology Innovations. *Teachers College Record, 104*(3), 482–515.

Zhao, Y., Zhao, M., & Shi, F. (2024). Integrating moral education and educational information technology: A strategic approach to enhance rural teacher training in universities. [HTML]. *Journal of the Knowledge Economy.*

Zilka, G. C. (2020). Awareness of digital rights and digital citizenship among youth. *Education and Information Technologies, 25*(6), 5573–5586.

Zimmerman, J., Forlizzi, J., & Evenson, S. (2007). "Research Through Design as a Method for Interaction Design Research in HCI." *Proceedings of the SIGCHI Conference on Human Factors in Computing Systems.*

Zootzky, G., & Pfeiffer, A. (2024). Educational transformation through AI: Preparing for a new era of learning. *INTED2024 Proceedings,* 1202–1207. https://doi.org/ DOI: 10.21125/inted.2024.0382

Zourmpakis, A., Kalogiannakis, M., & Papadakis, S. (2023). Adaptive gamification in science education: An analysis of the impact of implementation and adapted game elements on students' motivation. *Computers, 12*(7), 143. DOI: 10.3390/ computers12070143

Zuboff, S. (2019). *The age of surveillance capitalism: The fight for a human future at the new frontier of power.* PublicAffairs.

Zuboff, S. (2019). *The Age of Surveillance Capitalism: The Fight for a Human Future at the New Frontier of Power.* PublicAffairs.

Zygiaris, S. (2013). Smart City Reference Model: Assisting Planners to Conceptualize the Building of Smart City Innovation Ecosystems. *Journal of the Knowledge Economy, 4*(2), 217–231.

Παπαστεργίου, M. (2008). Digital Game-Based Learning in high school Computer Science education: Impact on educational effectiveness and student motivation. In Computers & Education (Vol. 52, Number 1, p. 1). Elsevier BV. https://doi.org/ DOI: 10.1016/j.compedu.2008.06.004

About The Contributors

Andi Asrifan, S.Pd, M.Pd, a distinguished figure in the realm of education, particularly in English Language Education, has made significant contributions through his extensive research, teaching, and leadership roles. As the Head of the Institute for Cooperation and International Affairs at Universitas Muhammadiyah Sidenreng Rappang and now a lecturer in Universitas Negeri Makassar (UNM), Dr. Asrifan's academic journey is marked by a rich tapestry of achievements, including a Doctor of Education in English Language Education. His work spans various facets of education, language, and technology, reflecting the diverse topics covered in his publications and research endeavors. These include, but are not limited to, the impact of the COVID-19 pandemic on educational practices, methodologies in English as a Foreign Language (EFL) classrooms, and the integration of technology in teaching and learning processes. Dr. Asrifan's commitment to advancing educational standards and practices is further evidenced by his active participation in international conferences, webinars, and workshops across countries like India, the Philippines, and Pakistan. These events, organized by various institutions and associations, underscore his role as a global educator and thought leader. His dedication to professional development is also highlighted through his involvement in numerous courses and certifications in personal branding, public speaking, and literacy teaching. Moreover, Dr. Asrifan's leadership extends beyond academia into organizational and educational development, where he has served in various capacities, including as an external examiner for Ph.D. dissertations and a reviewer for scientific journals. His accolades, memberships in professional organizations, and roles as an ambassador for international associations speak volumes of his influence and commitment to fostering educational excellence and sustainable development goals globally.

***

Ria Amelinda, On June 11, 1995, Ria Amelinda was born in Palopo. She teaches political communication at the Department of Communication and Islamic Broadcasting, Institut Agama Islam Negeri (IAIN) Palopo. Her research examines political discourse and Islamic communication practices, highlighting how communication tactics shape public perceptions and civic engagement. She seeks to establish ethical and inclusive political and Islamic communication frameworks.

Nofvia De Vega is an accomplished English lecturer at Universitas Borneo Tarakan. She consistently fosters her professional growth through significant contributions to academic literature, including articles and books, and active participation in various seminars and conferences. Her research primarily focuses on the pedagogical aspects of English language teaching and the effective integration of Information and Communication Technology (ICT) in educational contexts. Within the teaching and learning process, her core competencies are centered on the innovative use of listening and learning media to enhance student engagement and outcomes. Her scholarly work is widely recognized, with numerous articles published in prestigious national and international conference proceedings. Furthermore, she demonstrates a strong commitment to community development by actively leading and participating in various society and social programs throughout Indonesia.

Oindrilla Ghosh is a Research Scholar hailing from the School of Law at Christ (Deemed to be University) Bangalore, India, focuses her research on health of tribal communities. Her work includes 16 total publications on Environmental Disasters that are indexed in SCOPUS and Web of Sciences conference proceedings. She completed her early education at Loreto Day School, Bowbazar and went on to achieve distinction in her undergraduate (B.A/LL.B) and postgraduate (LL.M) studies at Calcutta University. Having served as an Assistant Professor of Law at Kingston Law College,Barasat, Kolkata, Ghosh has actively participated in numerous National Conferences, International Conferences, UN Global Summits, webinars, and seminars organized by prestigious academic institutions. Her expertise lies in health perspectives, environmental studies, human behavior, and related areas. Additionally, she has conducted various workshops, lectures in educational institutions, and is engaged with NGO's to help the needy

Binod Kumar is a graduate student known for his academic excellence, with his 9 total scholarly works indexed in Scopus database. Hailing from Ranchi, Jharkhand in India, Binod is currently pursuing a Master of Laws (LL.M) at the prestigious Radha Govind University. His passion for technology and innovation along with climate changes is evident through his high academic performance and numerous projects. Binod has a keen interest in artificial intelligence, machine learning, neuropsychology, climate changes and disaster management, fields in which he has undertaken several research projects. He is particularly fascinated by the potential of AI to solve real-world problems and is dedicated to learning and applying new techniques in these areas. He volunteers at local NGOs, teaching underprivileged children basic computer skills. With a strong foundation in law and a commitment to making a positive impact, Binod Kumar is poised to become a future leader in the legal industry.

Sooraj Kumar Maurya currently holds the position of Assistant Professor of Philosophy and serves as the Teacher-in-Charge at the Department of Philosophy within Zakir Husain Delhi College (Evening), affiliated with the University of Delhi. He boasts an illustrious academic background, having earned his B.A., M.A., and D. Phil degrees from the esteemed Department of Philosophy at the University of Allahabad. Dr. Maurya exhibits an unwavering commitment to scholarly pursuits and has significantly enriched the field of philosophy. His scholarly achievements include over 35 published research papers featured in esteemed international and national journals and conferences. Dr. Maurya's research interests span a broad spectrum of philosophical themes, with a particular focus on social philosophy, political philosophy, and moral philosophy.

IKomang Mertayasa, an educator at a Hindu university in Central Kalimantan. Komang has an interest in the field of education, particularly in learning models. Some of the research topics Komang has conducted include the Education Revolution with Chat GPT, the implementation of learning models, and the utilization of learning media.

Rosita Rosita is a lecturer at the Faculty of Social Science Education, and a PhD candidate in Curriculum Development at the Faculty of Education, Universitas Pendidikan Indonesia, Indonesia. Her research interests are tourism education, training and development in tourism, curriculum evaluation, and learning assessment. Rosita is now teaching undergraduate students at the Resort & Leisure Management Program and Tourism Education Program. She can be contacted at rosita1019@upi.edu Orcid ID

Putu Wisnu Saputra is an educator at a Hindu college in Central Kalimantan. He has a great interest in education in the fields of Hindu Religion and Technology. Currently, he is actively carrying out the Tri Dharma of Higher Education.

Satya Subrahmanyam is a distinguished academic leader, researcher, and institutional strategist with over 27 years of experience in higher education, leadership, and research management. He holds two PhDs and a Postdoctoral qualification from the Polytechnic Institute of Leiria, Portugal. Currently serving as Professor and Dean (Research) at Holy Spirit University of Kaslik (USEK), Lebanon, he spearheads research initiatives that enhance academic excellence and institutional reputation. He played a pivotal role in the development of the Catholic University in Erbil, Kurdistan, where he established new departments, led research programs, and collaborated on international educational projects. As a founding member and Managing Partner of Vignan Institute of Technology and Management, India, he contributed to its transformation into a premier institution. With expertise in AI-driven business strategies, HR analytics, and leadership in technology adoption, he has published extensively, guided PhD research, and led training programs in corporate and academic settings.

Ahmad Yani is a professor at the Department of Geography Education, Faculty of Social Science Education, Universitas Pendidikan Indonesia. His research interests are in the field of Geography education, particularly Geography curriculum, learning, and technology in learning. He is now teaching undergraduate, master's, and doctoral students at the Faculty of Social Science Education, Universitas Pendidikan Indonesia. He has published books in the curriculum and learning field such as Mindset of Curriculum 2013, Easy Ways to Write HOTS Questions, Developing Geoliteracy, and Political Geography. He can be contacted at ahmadyani@upi.edu Orcid ID

Index

A

B

C

D

E

S

T

V

www.ingramcontent.com/pod-product-compliance
Ingram Content Group UK Ltd.
Pitfield, Milton Keynes, MK11 3LW, UK
UKHW051028041026
15470UKWH00015B/1721

9 798337 310626